FREE ONLINE COURSES –

AVAILABLE IN WEBCT, BLACKBOARD, & COURSECOMPASS!

Are you teaching an online course now? Or would you like to teach a Web-enhanced course? Here's how Prentice Hall can help you to optimize your class!

- **Online Quizzes** with results that automatically feed into the Gradebook.
- **Videos** featuring Jane Reimers.
- **Bulletin Boards** let you and your students post critical messages.
- An **Online Syllabus** keeps students aware of deadlines and updates.
- **Discussion Groups** enable you to hold synchronous or asynchronous meetings with classes, speakers, or groups of students.
- **Link** your students (via the syllabus) to key Internet sites.

Most importantly, you can post any of your own materials—create and post your own lectures, assignment options, and class projects!

PREMIUM COURSECOMPASS WITH E-BOOK

Now you get even more when you team up with CourseCompass to teach your accounting courses! All the quality course content and easy-to-use management tools of CourseCompass—plus a searchable, Web-based e-book:

- **Easy-to-use, anytime, anywhere.** Students can access their textbook from any computer 24 hours a day/7 days a week.
- **One integrated study experience for students.** With one click, students have access to all course materials (text, quizzes, research links), all in one place.
- **Affordable, searchable e-textbook.** Prentice Hall and MetaText have partnered to provide a unique Web-based study experience which, when combined with the online study guide and tools of CourseCompass, provides a value for students.

 MASTERING ACCOUNTING CD-ROM SERIES

Package Mastering Accounting with Reimers (or any other Prentice Hall text) for only $5.00 net.

- **Mastering Accounting**, part of the Mastering Business program, is an **interactive, multimedia CD-ROM** that uses video and interactive exercises to help students link the THEORY they learn in class with **realistic business situations.**
- The episodes and interactive exercises on the CD-ROM are based on CanGo, a fictional e-commerce startup that sells a variety of entertainment products and services online.
- The **dramatic situations** show students how all the **functional areas of business work together** to ensure the growth of the company—as well as how to apply business theories to CanGo's daily operations.
- All of the content—including videos and exercises—was **created and reviewed by university professors** and experts in interactive instructional design.

FINANCIAL
ACCOUNTING

FINANCIAL
ACCOUNTING

A Business Process Approach with Integrated Debits and Credits

Jane L. Reimers

Florida State University
KPMG Professor of Accounting

Upper Saddle River, New Jersey 07458

Library of Congress Cataloging-in-Publication Data

Reimers, Jane L.
    Financial accounting : a business process approach with integrated debits / Jane L. Reimers.
      p. cm.
    Includes index.
    ISBN 0-13-101034-4
    1. Accounting. 2. Financial statements. I. Title.

    HF5635 .R363 2002
    657--dc21

    2002031268

Executive Editor: Deborah Hoffman
Editor-in-Chief: P. J. Boardman
Managing Editor: Alana Bradley
Senior Development Editor: Mike Elia
Senior Editorial Assistant: Jane Avery
Supplements Coordinator: Amy Whitaker
Senior Media Project Manager: Nancy Welcher
Executive Marketing Manager: Beth Toland
Marketing Assistant: Christine Genneken
Managing Editor (Production): Cynthia Regan
Production Editor: Michael Reynolds
Production Assistant: Joe DeProspero
Permissions Supervisor: Suzanne Grappi
Associate Director, Manufacturing: Vinnie Scelta
Production Manager: Dianne M. Peirano
Design Manager: Patricia Smythe
Designer: Blair Brown
Interior Design: Karen Quigley
Cover Design: Blair Brown
Cover Illustration/Photo: Blair Brown
Illustrator (Interior): Electra Graphic
Manager, Print Production: Christy Mahon
Print Production Liaison: Suzanne Duda
Composition: Progressive Information Technologies
Full-Service Project Management: Progressive Publishing Alternatives
Printer/Binder: R. R. Donnelley/Willard
Cover Printer: Lehigh Press

Credits and acknowledgments borrowed from other sources and reproduced, with permission, in this textbook appear on appropriate page within text.

Pearson Education LTD.
Pearson Education Australia PTY, Limited
Pearson Education Singapore, Pte. Ltd
Pearson Education North Asia Ltd
Pearson Education, Canada, Ltd
Pearson Educación de Mexico, S.A. de C.V.
Pearson Education–Japan
Pearson Education Malaysia, Pte. Ltd

10 9 8 7 6 5 4 3
ISBN 0-13-101034-4

For my mom and my son—for always believing in me

I sincerely thank my many friends and colleagues who have helped me during the writing of this book. Greg Gerard and John Salter deserve special mention for their endless patience and unfailing help. I am grateful to Beth Toland for making this version of the book a reality. Debbie Hoffman, my editor and now my friend, has been invaluable in so many ways. And if the book seems to be written for the *student* to find easy to read, the credit goes to Mike Elia, a demanding, topnotch developmental editor. Thanks also to Claire Brantley, my custom editor, who has been extremely helpful and supportive, and to Jane Avery, who has made invaluable contributions to the process. Special thanks to Patti Lopez and Lynn Mazzola for their enormous contributions.

Thanks to all the people who pitched in and helped with encouragement, ideas, problems, solutions, proofing, editing, finding errors in the manuscript, and my colleagues who used early drafts in the classroom: my dad, my brother, Donna Arnold, Tommy Carnes, Tina Carpenter, Cheryl Dunn, Cindy Durtschi, Richard Dusenbury, Elizabeth Erickson, Jerry Ferris, Jayne Gerard, Donna Hall, Linwood Kearney, Nancy LaPorte, Ed McIntyre, Tracy Noakes-Awwad, Jeff Paterson, Pam Perrewé, Ron Pierno, Arianna Pinello, Joan Raley, Amy Ratliff, Ellen Whitehouse, Mercedites Wright, and all the dedicated students who used the book and made excellent suggestions for improving it.

BRIEF CONTENTS

CONTENTS

Try it on for size!

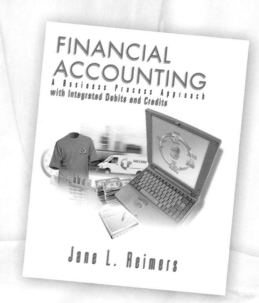

FINANCIAL ACCOUNTING

A BUSINESS PROCESS APPROACH WITH INTEGRATED DEBITS AND CREDITS

A Business Process Approach
to learning financial accounting

Tom's Wear – a running case example

All procedures linked to the Business Process Approach

Coverage of debits and credits
integrated in Chapters 4–10

Excel illustrations and problems
integrated in every chapter

Integration of Cash Flow, Business Risk, and Financial Statements
in every chapter

Study Breaks in every chapter

Online resources available
in Blackboard, CourseCompass, and WebCT

eBook Available

By Jane L. Reimers

(KPMG Professor of Accounting,
Florida State University)
© 2003, 608 pp., Cloth, ISBN: 0-13-101034-4

Meet Jane Reimers

Professor of Accounting at Florida State University

Business majors want to know...

" Why is accounting so important ? "

The fact is, it's no longer enough to simply teach our students how to account for a past transaction. ***Our students need to see how accounting relates to and interacts with business***. They need to know more about the way a business works and how accounting fits into business processes.

In an attempt to bridge the gap between business and accounting, I've written ***Financial Accounting: A Business Process Approach with Integrated Debits and Credits***. I set the stage with a description of what a business is all about. This provides a framework in which students can see how accounting relates to and reports on business activities. The book then emphasizes the basic business processes and how accounting fits into that framework.

There is nothing revolutionary about the accounting in this book. Traditional financial statements and the accounting equation are emphasized, but ***how accounting relates to business processes is at the core***.

This book is for financial statement users and preparers. It's for accounting majors and non-majors and even for non-business majors. It is no longer enough for us to teach students how to record transactions and prepare financial statements or even how to use financial statements. In order for students to understand what accounting is all about, they need to see how it fits into and relates to business processes. ***Financial Accounting: A Business Process Approach with Integrated Debits and Credits*** seeks to do that.

Jane F. Reimers

How is the Business Process Approach applied throughout the text?

Reimers begins with a description of what a business is all about. This provides a framework in which students can see how accounting relates to and reports on business activities. Then, Reimers emphasizes how accounting fits into the framework of basic business processes.

Each chapter offers a quick review of what students have just learned (Here's where we've been...) and a preview of where they're headed (...Here's where we're going) so that they are prepared to tackle new concepts throughout the rest of the text.

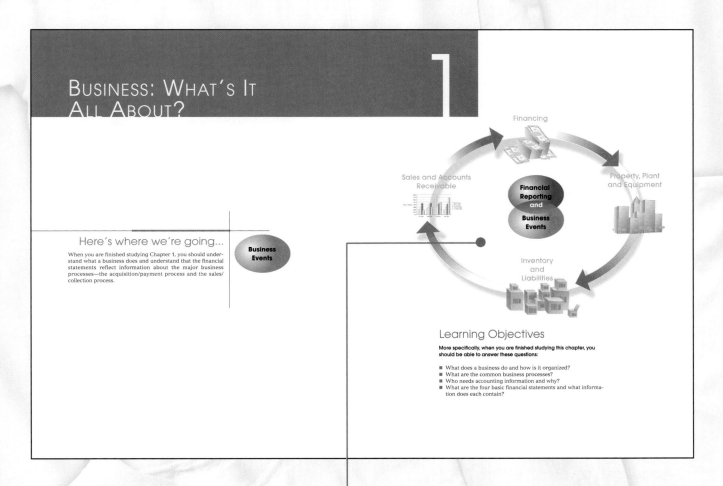

Business Process Model

Every chapter opens with the same image of the business process model. Different parts of the model are highlighted so students can see which part of the model will be discussed in each chapter.

BUSINESS PROCESS

Business Process Icon

This special icon will appear in the margin whenever the text material refers specifically to the Business Process Model.

> *...Finally there is an intro accounting book which is organized around business processes, rather than the various components of financial statements.*

John E. Karayan
California State University,
Pomona

tom's wear

Tom's Wear - A Running Case Example...

Meet Tom...an Entrepreneur

In Chapter One, students are introduced to Tom, an entrepreneur who decides to create a T-shirt business. In subsequent chapters, students will learn financial accounting concepts through Tom's experiences as he grows and expands his business.

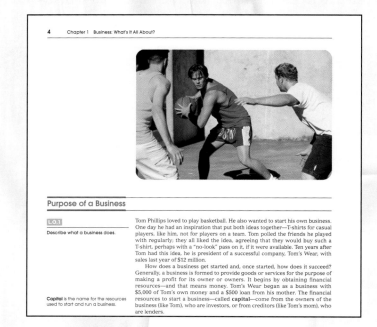

> *The continued use of the Tom's Wear example helps focus students on the connections between this topic and accounting information systems.*
>
> John E. Karayan
> California State University, Pomona

> *I like the idea of Tom's continuing business. I think that this will be effective.*
>
> Cheryl E. Mitchem
> Virginia State University

Optional In-Text Excel Application Problems

These appear in each chapter to enable students to build or enhance their own Excel skills.

Getting Started with Excel for Tom's Wear

This practice set introduces students to the concepts of Excel using the financial information contained in the text.

Tom's Wear with Excel

In every chapter, students can see Tom's Wear's monthly transactions illustrated in Excel—a critical business tool for all students to master.

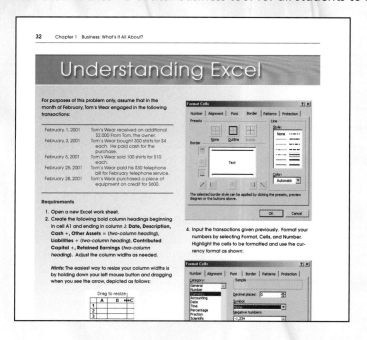

Try Reimers on for size!

Pedagogical Tools for Students...

Study Breaks

Study Breaks appear at least once in every chapter and encourage students to pause from reading and immediately apply what they just learned to solve specific problems.

the residual, indicating that it is the amount left over after the claims of creditors are deducted from a company's assets.

If you constructed a personal income statement, it would cover a period of time. For example, what was your net income total during the year 2002? You'd list all income you received during the year and then subtract all your expenses during the same year. The difference would be your net income for the year. There's no equation to balance. The income statement lists sources of income and subtracts the related expenses, leaving a difference, hopefully positive, called net income. If the subtraction of expenses from revenues results in a negative number, that amount is called a net loss.

1. What is gross profit?
2. What is the difference between a single-step income statement and a multistep income statement?

STUDY BREAK 1-5
SEE HOW YOU'RE DOING

1. What is gross profit?
2. What is the difference between a single-step income statement and a multistep income statement?

STUDY BREAK 1-5
SEE HOW YOU'RE DOING

purposes, we'll look at *monthly* financial statements for Tom's Wear, Inc., throughout this book.

The statement of changes in shareholders' equity for Tom's first month of business is shown in Exhibit 1-15. The statement starts with the shareholders' equity—also called stockholders' or owners' equity—at the beginning of the month. Tom's Wear had no contributed capital, because this is the company's first month. Then capital contributions—owners' contributions to the business—

dividends paid in the life of the company. It is descriptively named—it's the earnings that have been kept (retained) in the company. The amount of retained earnings represents the part of the owners' claims that the company has earned (i.e., *not* contributed). Retained earnings is not the same as cash.

> *I think the study break questions are very good overall.*
>
> Walter Smith
> Marshall University

> *The 'sidebars' are almost too good! They provide a useful 'outline' of the chapter material and a useful place to check back when looking to review a specific topic.*
>
> Pat Doherty
> Boston University

Running Glossary & Margin Notes

Terminology is critical for first-year accounting students. This text uses the margins to include definitions and notes wherever possible to aid in student understanding.

26   Chapter 1 Business: What's It All About?

Exhibit 1-14
Income Statement for Tom's Wear

Tom's Wear, Inc.
Income Statement
For the Month Ended January 31, 2001

Revenue
  Sales
Expenses
  Cost of Goods Sold $36(
  Advertising   5(
  Interest   5
Total Expenses
Net Income

In a corporation, distributions to owners are called **dividends**.

■ Second, the repayment of the loan from Tom's mom is n expense. The only expense related to borrowing money is th to the lender. The repayment of principal is not an expense.

Also notice that **dividends** are excluded from the income could have paid himself a salary for running the business. Th have been an expense, but he decided not to do that. Instead, he cash out of the business as a dividend. Dividends are not a co ings; they are a *distribution* of earnings.

Lands' End's income statement (statement of operations doesn't look like the Tom's Wear income statement. Both hav expenses, but the two companies have presented the data in a Tom's Wear lists revenue first and then groups all the expenses called a **single-step income statement.** Lands' End lists its first and then subtracts the largest expense related to the r goods sold, which gives a subtotal called **gross profit on sales multistep income statement.** If we were to recast Tom's incom a multistep income statement, we would subtract the cost of goods sold of $360 from the sales revenue of $900 to get a subtotal of $540 for Tom's gross profit on sales. Although Lands' End and Tom's Wear have arranged their revenues and expenses differently, net income for each company is still the difference between all revenues and all expenses. That is what net income always is, no matter how the revenues and expenses are grouped on the statement.

In a corporation, distributions to owners are called **dividends**.

A **single-step income statement** groups all revenues together and shows all expenses deducted from total revenue.

A **multistep income statement** starts with sales and subtracts cost of goods sold to get a subtotal called **gross profit on sales,** also known as gross margin. Then, other revenues are added and all other expenses are deducted.

A **single-step income statement** groups all revenues together and shows all expenses deducted from total revenue.

A **multistep income statement** starts with sales and subtracts cost of goods sold to get a subtotal called **gross profit on sales,** also known as gross margin. Then, other revenues are added and all other expenses are deducted.

> *The glossary is a great addition, comprehensive. Good idea [also] to code the exercises to the concepts.*
>
> Jim Makofske
> Fresno City College

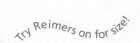 Try Reimers on for size!

> *"The writing style and level are right on target—appropriate and clear for an introductory accounting class… Students should find the text easy to read."*
>
> Patricia Lopez
> Valencia Community College

Tom's Wear
(see page iv for details!)

Students are first introduced to Tom's Wear, the running case example in Chapter 1.

Financial Statements, Business Risks, and Cash Flows

These topics are introduced in Chapter 1 and integrated into every chapter as appropriate.

Debits and Credits, introduced. All transactions discussed and recorded as debits and credits.

> *"I applaud the attention to the area of controls and risks…most texts neglect the area."*
>
> Vaughn S. Radcliffe
> Case Western
> Reserve University

TABLE OF CONTENTS

> *"Excellent beginning chapter. It is much more substantial than the first chapter of most intro books…I like the detail about the firm's purpose and organization. It should aid students to understand why accounting is useful and important to them even if they are not accounting majors."*
>
> Walter Smith
> Marshall University

> *"The sections on revenue recognition and the matching principle are very good and easy to understand…The section on "Putting it all Together…" is great. It gives students one final overview of the usefulness of the financial statements as well as how they are linked together."*
>
> Walter Smith
> Marshall University

> *"What's great about this chapter is that it explains the concept of adjustments—accruals and deferrals—without once getting into debits and credits and journal entries."*
>
> Pat Doherty
> Boston University

> *"Chapter 4 also provides a powerful analysis of the financial statements."*
>
> Vaughn S. Radcliffe
> Case Western Reserve University

II. Business Processes and Accounting Details

In Chapters 5–9, debits/credits in all transactions. Study Break questions designed for solution using debits/credits. Summary Problem for Tom's Wear given in debits/credits. End of chapter includes separate section of problems identified to require completion by recording debits/credits."

CHAPTER 5 ACQUISITIONS: PURCHASES AND USE OF BUSINESS ASSETS

CHAPTER 6 ACQUISITIONS/PAYMENT: INVENTORIES AND LIABILITIES

"The writing style is conversational. You feel like you are in Dr. Reimers' class and she is explaining a concept to you or working through an example."

Cheryl E. Mitchem
Virginia State University

CHAPTER 7 THE SALES AND COLLECTION CYCLE

CHAPTER 8 SPECIAL ACQUISITIONS: FINANCING A BUSINESS WITH DEBT

CHAPTER 9 SPECIAL ACQUISITIONS: FINANCING A BUSINESS WITH EQUITY

"I like the discussion on bonds, as this is a difficult topic and I think that Jane Reimers has done a good job of putting it in simple, easy to understand terms."

Patricia Lopez
Valencia Community College

III. Other Financial Reporting Topics

CHAPTER 10 PREPARING A STATEMENT OF CASH FLOWS

CHAPTER 11 FINANCIAL STATEMENT ANALYSIS

Is Reimers a "User" or "Preparer" book?

It's **BOTH**!

Reimers covers all of the key procedures both accounting majors and non-majors need. But, through her innovative use of Tom's Wear as a running case example, and the framing of each chapter around business activities, all students can see the critical role of accounting.

"[Reimers] strikes a good balance between practitioner and user orientation."

Thomas Conway
Siena College

Business Process Approach

Chs. 6-10 are the heart of the business process approach.

Statement of Cash Flows (Ch. 10)

In addition to the integration of cash flows into each chapter (starting with Chapter 1), there is a "wrap-up" chapter at the end of the book.

The Reimers Teaching and Learning System:

for instructors

Review Copy
(0-13-140543-8)

Instructor's Manual
(0-13-101055-7)

Instructor's Solutions Manual
(0-13-101057-3)

Instructor's Solution Transparencies

(0-13-062265-6)

(0-13-062267-2)

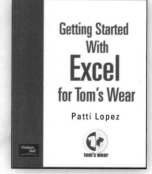

XX   *Try Reimers on for size!*

for students

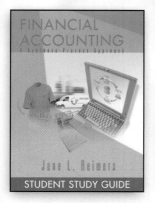

Student Study Guide with Power Notes

Working Papers

Student Resource CD-ROM
Contains the tutorial and general ledger software, spreadsheet templates, Excel tutorial, and data files for the "Getting Started Series"

Technology Resources

PH Re-Enforcer Tutorial Software*

PH General Ledger Software*

Spreadsheet Templates*

Excel Tutorial*

Getting Started Series
(See description on opposite page)

Software Offers
(See description on opposite page)

On Location! Videos
(0-13-035768-5)

Online Resources with Video
(See page x) Available in your choice of Blackboard, WebCT, or CourseCompass

e-Book
Available separately or as part of an online course

Mastering Accounting CD-ROM (See page xi)

The Reimers Companion Website:

3 Online Quizzes for each chapter enable students to test their skills and get immediate scoring and feedback

Bulletin Board enables students and faculty to post messages

Ask the Tutor provides students with an additional resource to provide coaching

Current Events articles help students see the relevance of text topics to today's news

Downloadable Resources include tutorial software, PowerPoints, and much more

*These items are provided free on the Student Resource CD-ROM or can be downloaded from the text's Web site

free Online Resources

Available in Blackboard, WebCT, & CourseCompass!

Are you teaching an online course now? Or would you like to teach a Web-enhanced course? Here's how Prentice Hall can help you to optimize your class!

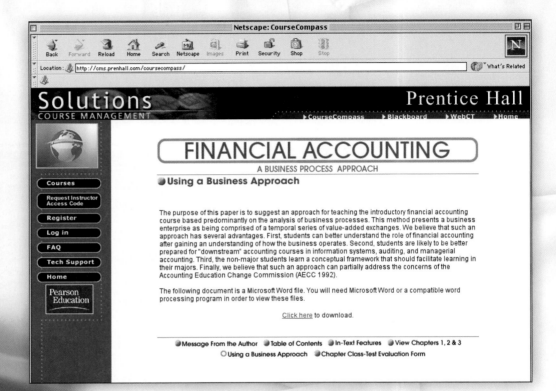

Videos feature Jane Reimers, provide reviews of key concepts, and take students inside real businesses wrestling with accounting challenges.

Online Quizzes and Tests with results that automatically feed into the **Gradebook**

Bulletin Boards that let you hold synchronous or asynchronous meetings with classes, speakers, or groups of students

An **Online Syllabus** keeps students aware of deadlines and updates

Link your students (via the syllabus) to key Internet sites

Most importantly, you can **post your own materials** to our online courses. Create and post your own lectures, assignment options, and class projects!

To see a sample of any of our online courses, please go to:
www.prenhall.com/demo

CourseCompass with eBook

Now you get even more when you team up with CourseCompass to teach your accounting courses! All the quality course content and easy-to-use management tools of CourseCompass—plus a searchable, Web-based e-book:

Easy-to-use, anytime, anywhere. Students can access their textbook from any computer 24 hours a day, 7 days a week.

One integrated study experience for students.
With one click, students have access to all course materials (text, quizzes, research links), all in one place.

Affordable, searchable e-textbook.
Prentice Hall and MetaText have partnered to provide a unique Web-based study experience which, when combined with the online study guide and tools of CourseCompass, provides a value for students.

To visit a CourseCompass with eBook demonstration, please go to
www.coursecompass.com

> " *[Reimers] is well written in a clear and concise style. Explanations of concepts are very clear to readers.* "
>
> Dong-Woo Lee
> California State University,
> Los Angeles

Mastering Accounting
CD-ROM Series

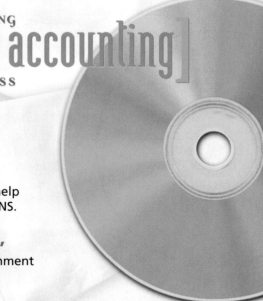

Package Mastering Accounting with Reimers
(or any other Prentice Hall accounting text) for only $5.00 net.

Mastering Accounting, part of the Mastering Business series, is an interactive, multimedia CD-ROM that uses video and interactive exercises to help students link the THEORY they learn in class with realistic BUSINESS SITUATIONS.

The episodes and interactive exercises on the CD are **based on CanGo, a fictional e-commerce startup** that sells a variety of entertainment products and services online.

The dramatic situations show students how all the **functional areas of business work together** to ensure the growth of the company, as well as how to apply business theories to CanGo's daily operations.

All of the content, including videos and exercises, was **created and reviewed by university professors** and experts in interactive instructional design.

Technology Resources

INNOVATION! eBook with CourseCompass

Students receive the benefits of both an online course AND 24/7 online access to their textbook from any computer. Available at a nominal charge.

INNOVATION! Standard Online Courses
in WebCT, CourseCompass, and Blackboard

Teach a complete online course or a Web-enhanced course. Add your own course materials, take advantage of online testing and Gradebook opportunities, and utilize the bulletin board and discussion board functions. Packaged free upon faculty request.

INNOVATION! Getting Started with Excel for Tom's Wear

Getting Started with Excel for Tom's Wear may be packaged with the text upon faculty request at no charge. This manual introduces students to the concepts of Excel using the financial information contained in the text.

INNOVATION! Instructor Course Organizer CD-ROM and Student CD-ROM

The **Instructor CD** contains all print (Instructor's Manual, Solutions Manual, Test Bank) and technology (e.g., software, spreadsheets, videos, data files) supplements on a single CD-ROM. Enjoy the freedom to transport the entire package from office, to home, to classroom. The Instructor CD-ROM enables you to customize any of the ancillaries, print only the chapters or materials you wish to use, or access any item from the package within the classroom! The **Student CD-ROM** is free (upon your request with new text purchase only; it can also be sold stand-alone) and contains the Excel spreadsheets, tutorial and General Ledger software, PowerPoints, and other valuable tools for students.

INNOVATION! Special Offers *Professional Accounting Software Packages*

Package your choice of FREE Getting Started manuals (Peachtree, QuickBooks, Excel, or Simply Accounting) or software (Peachtree, Simply Accounting) featuring the latest releases at $10.00 net with new text purchase.

PH Re-Enforcer and General Ledger Software

The tutorial software enables students to test their understanding of chapter concepts via a variety of problem types. The General Ledger software enables students to complete homework assignments using a general ledger software package. Students may also enter and solve their own problems.

PH Professor: A Classroom Presentation on PowerPoint

PowerPoint presentations created by the author are available for each chapter of the text. Instructors have the flexibility to add slides and/or modify the existing slides to meet the courses needs. FREE upon adoption. Available on the Instructor Course Organizer CD and on the Companion Website.

Companion Website

The Companion Website offers the most expansive internet-based support available.
Our Website provides a wealth of resources for students and faculty resources including:

- Student Study Hall
- Hotlinks to in-text companies
- "Ask the Tutor" Online tutorial assistance
- Study Guide: Practice tests w/immediate grading and feedback
- Faculty lounge

www.coursecompass.com

Instructor Supplements

INNOVATION! Instructor Course Organizer CD-ROM

The Instructor CD contains all print and technology (e.g., spreadsheets, videos) supplements on a single CD-ROM. Enjoy the freedom to transport the entire package from office, to home, or to classroom. The Instructor CD-ROM enables you to customize any of the ancillaries, print only the chapters or materials you wish to use, or access any item from the package within the classroom!

Instructor's Manual

Each chapter of this comprehensive resource consists of a list of the student learning objectives, a narrative overview of main topics, an outline with teaching tips interspersed, a ten-problem multiple choice quiz cross-referenced to the outline and arranged for easy copying (answers are at end of the outline and solutions for all quizzes are on separate pages at the end of the manual), suggested readings, examples of ways to integrate the supplements, and transparency masters.

Test Item File

The printed Test Item File consists of over 1800 questions, including true/false questions, conceptual and quantitative multiple-choice questions, critical thinking problems, and exercises. Each question will identify the difficulty level and the corresponding learning objective. Prentice Hall Test Generator can create exams, and evaluate and track student results. It also provides online testing capabilities. Test Generator items are drawn from the Test Item File.

Instructor's Solutions Manual

In addition to fully worked-out and carefully accuracy checked solutions for every question, exercise, and problem in the text, this manual provides suggestions for alternative chapter sequences, a categorization of assignment material, and check figures.

Solutions Transparencies

Every page of the Solutions Manual has been reproduced in acetate form for use on the overhead projector.

On Location! Videos

These brief videos take students "on location" to real companies where real accounting situations are presented.

Student Resources

INNOVATION! Student CD-ROM

The Student CD-ROM is free (upon faculty request with new text purchase only; it can also be purchased separately) and contains the Excel spreadsheets, PH Re-Enforcer (tutorial) and General Ledger software packages, PowerPoints, Getting Started, data files, and other valuable tools for students.

Student Study Guide/PowerNotes

This chapter-by-chapter learning aid systematically and effectively helps students study financial accounting and get the maximum benefit from their study time. Each chapter provides a chapter overview and a chapter review, a featured exercise that covers in a single exercise all of the most important material included in the chapter, and review questions and exercises with solutions that best test the student's understanding of the material.

Working Papers and eWorking Papers

Working Papers and eWorking Papers are available.

The Reimers Reviewers, Focus Group Attendees, and Class-Testers:

Art Goldman Augustana College (formerly University of Kentucky)

Patricia A. Doherty Boston University

Maureen Crane California State University, Fresno

Robert L. Hurt California State Polytechnic University, Pomona

John E. Karayan California State Polytechnic University, Pomona

Mary Keim California State University, San Marcos

Dong-Woo Lee California State University, Los Angeles

Julie Dawson Carthage College

Vaughan S. Radcliffe Case Western Reserve University

Mary Ann M. Prater Clemson University

Milo Peck Fairfield University

James P. Makofske Fresno City College

Jill Smith Idaho State University

Howard Keller Indiana University, Indianapolis

Walter Smith Marshall University

Clayton A. Hock Miami University of Ohio

Andrea Weickgenannt Northern Kentucky University

E. James Meddaugh Ohio University

T. Sterling Wetzel Oklahoma State University

John W. Hatcher Purdue University

Lynn K. Saubert Radford University

John L. Haverty St. Joseph's University

Linda Whitten San Francisco State University

Thomas Conway Siena College

James B. King II Southern Illinois University

Wilda F. Meixner Southwest Texas State University

John Pendley University of Alabama, Huntsville

Wayne Ingalls University of Maine

Leslie Oakes University of New Mexico

Barbara D. Marino University of North Texas

John H. Salter University of Central Florida

Diane L. Tanner University of North Florida

Jerry Siebel University of South Florida

Gregory C. Yost University of West Florida

Jane Wiese Valencia Community College

Patti Lopez Valencia Community College

Cheryl E. Mitchem Virginia State University

Nancy P. Lynch West Virginia University

Nancy C. Ruhe West Virginia University

> *Jane's explanation of the direct method for preparation of the statement of cash flows is the best I've ever seen.*

Jane Wiese
Valencia Community College

> *I think the writing style is one of the strong points of the text.*

John Pendley
University of Alabama, Huntsville

...and Great Supplementary Texts!

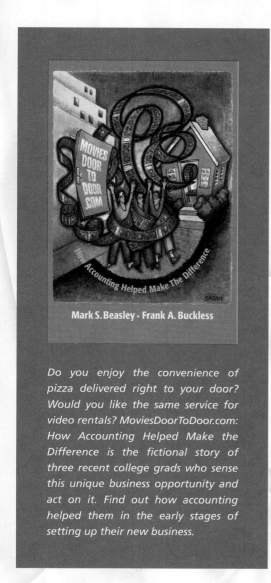

Do you enjoy the convenience of pizza delivered right to your door? Would you like the same service for video rentals? MoviesDoorToDoor.com: How Accounting Helped Make the Difference is the fictional story of three recent college grads who sense this unique business opportunity and act on it. Find out how accounting helped them in the early stages of setting up their new business.

MoviesDoorToDoor.com: How Accounting Helped Make the Difference

Mark S. Beasley (North Carolina State University)
Frank A. Buckless (North Carolina State University)
© 2002, Cloth, 144 pp., ISBN: 0-13-061047-X

What if you had a great idea for your own business? What if you also had the manpower and funds to do it? What if you had no accounting background whatsoever?

Imagine having the tools to build a successful business of your own, but no idea how to use them. You'd likely end up with a lot of headaches, lost revenue, and the nagging thought, "If only I'd known...." Like many unsuccessful entrepreneurs, most students just don't understand the importance of accounting in their future business lives. Fortunately, *MoviesDoorToDoor.com: How Accounting Helped Make the Difference* can help.

This novella presents a situation that any college student can relate too – the desire to be your own boss – while driving home the importance of accounting in starting your own business. An engaging story and an important lesson in one, your students will learn from the ups and downs of three recent college grads starting their own business without a solid background in accounting.

Effective Writing: A Handbook for Accountants, Sixth Edition

Claire B. May and Gordon S. May
© 2002, Paper, 288 pp., ISBN 0-13-093489-5

Suitable for any level accounting course, this text contains assignment material for financial, managerial, tax, auditing, and systems accounting courses. It is designed to help accountants become better communicators.

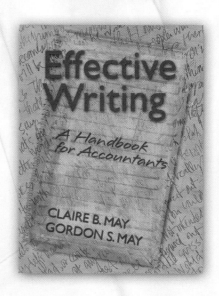

FINANCIAL
ACCOUNTING

BUSINESS: WHAT'S IT ALL ABOUT?

Here's where we're going...

When you are finished studying Chapter 1, you should understand what a business does and understand that the financial statements reflect information about the major business processes—the acquisition/payment process and the sales/collection process.

Business Events

1

Financing

Sales and Accounts Receivable

Financial Reporting and

Business Events

Property, Plant, and Equipment

Inventory and Liabilities

Learning Objectives

More specifically, when you are finished studying this chapter, you should be able to answer these questions:

1. What does a business do and how is it organized?
2. What are the common business processes?
3. Who needs accounting information and why?
4. What are the four basic financial statements and what information does each contain?

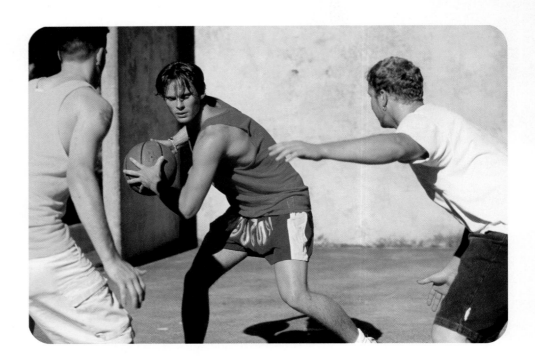

Purpose of a Business

Describe what a business does.

Tom Phillips loved to play basketball. He also wanted to start his own business. One day he had an inspiration that put both ideas together—T-shirts for casual players, like him, not for players on a team. Tom polled the friends he played with regularly; they all liked the idea, agreeing that they would buy such a T-shirt, perhaps with a "no-look" pass on it, if it were available. Ten years after Tom had this idea, he is president of a successful company, Tom's Wear, with sales last year of $12 million.

How does a business get started and, once started, how does it succeed? Generally, a business is formed to provide goods or services for the purpose of making a profit for its owner or owners. It begins by obtaining financial resources—and that means money. Tom's Wear began as a business with $5,000 of Tom's own money and a $500 loan from his mother. The financial resources to start a business—called **capital**—come from the owners of the business (like Tom), who are investors, or from creditors (like Tom's mom), who are lenders.

Capital is the name for the resources used to start and run a business.

Why buy a T-shirt from Tom rather than from the manufacturer of plain T-shirts? For the same reason we order clothes from Lands' End—added value. Lands' End provides a product to its customers with a certain quality and the convenience of mail-order delivery. Its customers find value in this service. What all businesses have in common is that they provide us with something of value. A business may start from scratch and create something of value or it may simply add value to an existing product or service. For some customers, the value that Lands' End adds to the product may be its easy order and delivery procedures. For other customers, the added value may be in the monogram the company will put on shirts or towels to personalize them. Businesses create or add value to earn money for the owners.

A **for-profit firm** is in business to make a profit—that's when revenues exceed expenses. A **not-for-profit organization** exists to provide goods and services to some target group at a reduced cost or no cost.

An enterprise—another name for a business organization—with this goal is called a **for-profit firm.** A business firm that provides goods or services for the sole purpose of helping people instead of making a profit is called a **not-for-profit organization.** A not-for-profit organization is more likely to be called an

Exhibit 1-1
The Firm

organization or agency than a business. Even though it's called *not-for-profit*, this type of organization doesn't mind making a profit. What's different is what a not-for-profit organization does with any profit it makes. Instead of distributing it to owners, a not-for-profit organization uses any profit to provide more goods and services to the people it serves. Both for-profit organizations and not-for-profit organizations provide value. Throughout this book, we will be dealing primarily with for-profit organizations—businesses.

To be a viable business, Tom's Wear needed to provide customers with something of value. Tom purchased T-shirts with his special logo, and then provided them to his customers at a convenient time and place.

What is business all about?

Adding Value → To Make a Profit

A simple model of the firm is shown in Exhibit 1-1. The inputs in a firm include capital, equipment, inventory, supplies, and labor. The business process of acquiring goods and services and paying for them is called the acquisition/payment process. The firm then does something to add value—that's called the conversion process. The process is called conversion because the firm takes inputs and converts them into outputs. The outputs of a firm are its products or services. The business process of selling goods and services and collecting payment for them is called the sales/collection process. As the firm carries out these three business processes—acquiring inputs, converting them to outputs, and providing those outputs to customers—information about these activities is recorded in the company's information system. Both insiders—the owners and the firm's employees—and outsiders—the creditors, governmental agencies, and potential investors—use the information.

A business must successfully plan, control, and evaluate its activities. If it does these activities well, the business will survive. If it does them very well, it will make a profit. Profit is the difference between the revenue—the amount a business earns for the goods it sells or the services it provides—and the expenses of selling those goods or providing those services. The complexity of a company's planning, control, and evaluation processes depends on the type, size, and structure of the business. You'll see this as we look at businesses in two ways: the nature of their operations and who owns them.

The Nature of Business Operations

The operation of a business depends on what the business has been formed to do. From that perspective, there are four types of businesses: service, merchandising, manufacturing, and financial. Although most businesses can be classified as one of these four types, many large businesses are a combination of two or more.

L.O.1

Businesses are classified—by type and by organizational form.

A **service** company *does* something for its customers; a **merchandising** firm *sells a product* to its customers.

> Lands' End is an example of a merchandising business. The company buys the goods from many different companies and then sells those goods to the final consumer. The added value may be visible, like monograms, or it may be invisible, like good service or fast delivery.

A **service** company provides a service—it does something for you, rather than sells something to you. Services range from activities you can't see, such as the advice provided by lawyers or tax consultants, to activities you can see, such as house cleaning or car washing. During the past two decades, our economy has been producing more services than goods.

A **merchandising** business buys goods, adds value to them, and then sells them with the added value. It doesn't *make* the goods, and it doesn't buy them to *use*. Instead, a merchandising business buys the goods for the purpose of adding its own particular value to them and, after adding value, sells them to another company or person.

There are two types of merchandising businesses:

- a wholesale company, which buys goods, adds value, and sells them to other companies; and
- a retail company, which buys goods, adds value, and sells them to customers who consume them—which is why you will see these customers referred to as "final consumers."

Both wholesale and retail merchandising companies add value to the goods they buy. Wholesale companies are not familiar to us because we don't buy things from them. Prentice Hall, the publisher of this text, for example, sells textbooks to your school's bookstore. When you need a book, you go to the bookstore—a retail business—to buy it. You don't go to the wholesale company, Prentice Hall. You don't care what business transactions have to take place to get the book from the factory, where it is printed and the covers are put on, to the bookstore. At the bookstore, the books are provided along with thousands of others, but in a way that you can immediately and conveniently purchase the one or two books you need. The bookstore is an example of a retailer. *Retail store* is widely used to describe the businesses we find in every shopping mall.

A manufacturing business makes the products it sells. Manufacturing companies vary in size and complexity. Making clay pots and vases in a space not larger than a garage is a manufacturing business. Automobile giants like Ford and General Motors, owned by many thousands of people and employing hundreds of thousands of workers at all levels in enormous factories all over the world, are large, complex, manufacturing businesses.

Financial services companies don't make tangible products, and they don't sell products made by another company. They deal in services related to money. One kind of financial services company lends money, for example, banks, which lend money to borrowers to pay for cars and furniture; and mortgage companies, which lend money to pay for a house. Another type of financial services company is an insurance company, which provides some financial protection in the case of loss of life or property.

Ownership Structure of a Business

L.O.1

Describe the various structures a business may have.

No matter what type of product or service it provides, a business must have an owner or owners. The government owns some businesses, but in the United States, an individual or a group of individuals owns most businesses. Business ownership usually takes one of three general forms: a sole proprietorship, a partnership, or a corporation.

Understanding Business

STARTING A NEW BUSINESS: THE BUSINESS PLAN

Starting a new business? The Small Business Administration (SBA) was established by Congress in 1953, to assist small businesses. Among the many contributions SBA makes to ongoing businesses, the SBA provides information and guidance for starting a business. It all starts with a business plan. The SBA describes four sections to be included in the body of the business plan: the business description, the financial management plan, the management plan, and a marketing plan.

The business description **is the foundation for the rest of the business plan. It should give the form of your business enterprise—a sole proprietorship, a partnership, or a corporation. The business description should also describe the nature of your business—manufacturing, merchandising, or service. Then, more specific details should be explained—goals and objectives, operating procedures, location, personnel, marketing, licenses and insurance, and financing plans.**

Once the business description is completed, the focus shifts to specific items for the next three sections.

A financial management plan, **including a start-up budget and an operating budget, must be prepared in** detail. The financial statements are prepared based on the budgets. The financial statements are a significant part of a business plan.

The management plan **addresses the functioning of business operations. Strengths and weaknesses of the personnel and the business as a whole should be assessed. Once identified, potential problems can be addressed and solved. To succeed as a business, management's goal should be to keep the employees and customers happy.**

Finally, the marketing plan **must be created. The marketing plan is designed to attract and keep customers. By identifying and getting to know the sector of the market you want to serve, you can appeal to its wants and needs. Such characteristics as age, sex, income, and educational levels of potential customers can help you prepare a marketing plan to develop a customer base.**

A good business plan is essential for starting a successful company. For more information on the SBA and creating a business plan, visit the SBA web site at **www.sbaonline.sba.gov/.**

Sole Proprietorships

If a single person owns a business, like the clay pot maker in his garage, it is a **sole proprietorship.** A new business often starts as a sole proprietorship. A sole proprietorship accumulates financial information—such as cost of materials, equipment, rent, electricity, and income from sales—but is not required by law to make any of that financial information available to the public. That means the average person is not privy to this information. Naturally, some governmental agencies—like the Department of Revenue—will receive some of this information from the company's sales tax return.

A **sole proprietorship** is a company with a single owner.

A business in the form of a sole proprietorship is not separate from its owner in terms of responsibility and liability—the owner is personally responsible for all the decisions made for the business. For example, the income from the business is included as income on the owner's individual income tax return. The business does not have its own tax return. If you are a sole proprietor, you include your business income with any other income you've earned on your individual tax return, using IRS tax form 1040.

Also, you are responsible for your company's debts. Your company's bills are your bills; if there's not enough money in your company's "pockets" to pay its bills, then you must pay the bills from your pockets. Moreover, you own the company's assets, and your personal assets are the company's assets—even if those personal assets are the only way of paying your company's bills.

Even though the financial records of a business—the company's books—should be kept separately from the owner's personal financial records, there is no separation of the sole proprietorship's books and its owner's books for tax and legal purposes. For example, your business checking account should be separate from your personal checking account, but the income you earn from your business and the income you earn from other sources must both be included on your individual, personal tax return.

Partnerships

A **partnership** is a company owned by two or more individuals.

A business **partnership** is owned by two or more people, although it is similar to a sole proprietorship in the sense that the income both partners earn (or lose) from the business partnership is included on their own personal tax return. When two or more people form a business as partners, they get together with an attorney to define the specific terms of their business relationship. Details like how much work each will do and how they will split up the profits from the business are specified in a document called a partnership agreement. Like a sole proprietorship, the owners—each of the partners—are responsible for everything the company does. For example, if the company is sued for violating an employee's civil rights, then the partners are legally liable. The company's assets are the partners' assets, and the company's debts are the partners' debts. Even so, as with a sole proprietorship, the financial records of a partnership should be kept separate from the partners' personal financial records.

Corporations

A **corporation** is a special legal form for a business in which the business is a legal entity separate from the owners. A corporation may have a single owner or a large number of owners.

Shares of capital stock are the units of ownership in a corporation. The owners of the corporation are called **stockholders** or **shareholders.**

A **corporation** is legally separate and financially separate from its owners. Individual states control the rules for forming corporations within their boundaries. A company must have a corporate charter that describes the business and how the business plans to acquire financing—how many owners it will be allowed to have. Ownership in a corporation is divided into units called **shares of capital stock,** each representing ownership in a fraction of the corporation. An owner of shares of stock in a corporation is called a **stockholder,** or a **shareholder.** In most corporations, many people are owners of the corporation. A corporation whose shares of stock are owned by a very small number of people is called a closely held corporation.

As legal entities, corporations may enter into contracts just like individuals. A corporation pays taxes on its earnings. A corporation's owners do not include the corporation's income in their personal tax returns—unlike the owner of a sole proprietorship or the partners in a partnership. Each individual corporation owner does not have individual legal responsibility for the corporation's actions, as is true for the owners of a sole proprietorship or partnership. For example, a shareholder can't be sued for the illegal actions of the corporation. The managers are held responsible for the actions of the corporation, and only the corporation's assets are at risk.

Lands' End, Inc., is a corporation. Two of the corporation's financial statements are shown in Exhibits 1–2 and 1–3. There are over 40 million shares of Lands' End stock, owned by a large number of people. The company offers new shares of stock to anyone who is able and willing to invest in the company by making them available for sale on a **stock exchange.** A stock exchange is a marketplace for buying and selling shares of a publicly traded corporation.

A **stock exchange** is a marketplace where buyers and sellers of shares of stock exchange their shares. Buying and selling shares of stock is also called **trading.**

After the shares are issued—sold for the first time to the public—investors who want to become owners of a corporation may purchase the shares from people who want to sell the same shares. The buyers and sellers get together,

Exhibit 1-2
Lands' End Income Statements

Lands' End & Subsidiaries		
	Consolidated Statements of Operations for the period ended	
(in thousands, except per share data)	January 26, 2001	January 28, 2000
Revenue:		
Net merchandise sales	$1,354,974	$1,319,823
Shipping and handling revenue	107,309	97,063
Total revenue	1,462,283	1,416,886
Cost of sales:		
Cost of merchandise sales	728,446	727,291
Shipping and handling costs	112,158	99,791
Total cost of sales	840,604	827,082
Gross profit	621,679	589,804
Selling, general and administrative expenses	560,019	512,647
Non-recurring charge (credit)	—	(1,774)
Income from operations	61,660	78,931
Other income (expense):		
Interest expense	(1,512)	(1,890)
Interest income	2,244	882
Other	(7,381)	(1,679)
Total other expense, net	(6,649)	(2,687)
Income before income taxes	55,011	76,244
Income tax provision	20,354	28,210
Net income	$ 34,657	$ 48,034
Basic earnings per share	$ 1.15	$ 1.60
Diluted earnings per share	1.14	1.56
Basic weighted average shares outstanding	30,047	30,085
Diluted weighted average shares outstanding	30,422	30,854

usually through a stockbroker, by using a stock exchange. Stockbrokers represent people who want to buy shares and the people who want to sell shares of a corporation. Stockbrokers work for firms like Merrill Lynch and Charles Schwab. There are several stock exchanges in the United States; the New York Stock Exchange and the American Stock Exchange are two of the largest. If you wanted to be one of the owners of Lands' End, you could purchase shares by contacting a stockbroker.

Another way to buy or sell shares of stock—also known as **trading**—is to use the Internet. Many companies now provide a way for investors to buy and sell stock without a stockbroker. As Internet usage continues to grow at an incredible pace, more and more people are taking advantage of electronic trading in shares of stock.

Regulation. Shareholders usually hire people who are not owners of the corporation to manage the business of the corporation. This separation of ownership and management can create problems. For example, there may be a large number of owners, and they may be far away from the location of the business. How can the owners be sure that the managers are running the corporation the way the owners want it to be run? How do the owners monitor the managers to be sure they are not taking advantage of the power of being a manager of a large company, for example, buying expensive items like country club memberships and luxury cars for the business?

Exhibit 1-3
Lands' End Balance Sheets

Lands' End, Inc. & Subsidiaries		
	Consolidated Balance Sheets at	
(In thousands)	January 26, 2001	January 28, 2000
Assets		
Current assets:		
Cash and cash equivalents	$ 75,351	$ 76,413
Receivables, net	19,808	17,753
Inventory	188,211	162,193
Prepaid advertising	17,627	16,572
Other prepaid expenses	9,715	5,816
Deferred income tax benefits	10,973	10,661
Total current assets	321,685	289,408
Property, plant and equipment, at cost:		
Land and buildings	104,815	102,776
Fixtures and equipment	103,866	102,886
Computer hardware and software	99,979	73,024
Leasehold improvements	4,630	4,453
Construction in progress	4,289	—
Total property, plant and equipment	317,579	283,139
Less-accumulated depreciation and amortization	132,286	117,317
Property, plant and equipment, net	185,293	165,822
Intangibles, net	651	966
Total assets	$507,629	$456,196
Liabilities and shareholders' investment		
Current liabilities:		
Lines of credit	$ 16,940	$ 11,724
Accounts payable	96,168	74,510
Reserve for returns	9,061	7,869
Accrued liabilities	41,135	43,754
Accrued profit sharing	2,357	2,760
Income taxes payable	13,213	10,255
Total current liabilities	178,874	150,872
Deferred income taxes	14,567	9,117
Shareholders' investment:		
Common stock, 40,221 shares issued	402	402
Donated capital	8,400	8,400
Additional paid-in capital	31,908	29,709
Deferred compensation	(121)	(236)
Accumulated other comprehensive income	5,974	2,675
Retained earnings	489,087	454,430
Treasury stock, 10,317 and 9,281 shares at cost, respectively	(221,462)	(199,173)
Total shareholders' investment	314,188	296,207
Total liabilities and shareholders' investment	$507,629	$456,196

The accompanying notes to consolidated financial statements are an integral part of these consolidated balance sheets

The **Securities and Exchange Commission (SEC)** is the governmental agency that monitors the stock market and the financial reporting of the firms that trade in the market.

To protect the owners with respect to issues like these, the government created the **Securities and Exchange Commission (SEC)** to monitor the activities and financial reporting of corporations that sell shares of ownership on the stock exchanges. The SEC sets the rules for stock exchanges and for the financial reporting of publicly traded corporations for the entire United States. The degree of regulation for corporations depends on the size and nature of the business. A business that provides an essential product or service, like electric power generating companies, has more rules to follow than a business that provides something not essential, but discretionary, like toys. Large companies have more rules than smaller companies because large companies provide more opportunities for managers to take advantage of the owners.

Advantages of the corporate structure of a business organization follow:

■ Investors can diversify their financial risk. Being able to buy a small share in a variety of corporations means that persons are able to balance the risks they are taking as business owners. For example, an investor may own shares in a soft drink company and also own shares in a coffee company. If coffee companies have a bad year due to a shortage of coffee beans, people will be likely to buy more soft drinks. By owning a little of each type of company, an investor reduces overall risk.

■ Owners have limited liability. Individual owners risk *only* the amount of money they have invested in the company. That is the amount they paid for the shares of stock. If the corporation is found legally responsible for injury to an employee or customer, or if the business fails, only the corporation's assets are at risk—not the owner's personal property. (In contrast, there is no limit to the legal liability of a sole proprietor or a partner. Both the assets of the business and the personal assets of the owners are at risk.)

> **What is a limited liability partnership (LLP)?**
> In the past 10 years, a new type of organization has been formed that has some characteristics of a partnership and some characteristics of a corporation. It's a business form mostly of interest to partners in professions such as law, medicine, and accounting. An LLP's owners—who are the partners—aren't personally liable for the malpractice of any of the partners. They are personally liable for many types of obligations owed to the LLP's creditors, lenders, and landlords. Owners of an LLP report their share of profit or loss on their personal tax returns. The LLP form of business organization is not available in all states, and it is often limited to a short list of professions. You'll notice that the five largest international accounting firms have all taken this organizational form. The letters LLP will appear after the firm's name.

Disadvantages of the corporate form of ownership include:

■ Separation of management and ownership creates a difference in knowledge about the operations of the business. Suppose you own 100 shares of Lands' End stock. The managers of Lands' End will know many details of the business that you don't know. For example, the managers are aware of all possible investment options for the company's extra cash. They may select the option that minimizes clerical work, whereas an owner might prefer an option that involves more work but would secure a higher return.

There are literally thousands of such details that owners do not know, many of which they don't even want to know. However, the owners want some assurance that managers are acting in the best interests of the shareholders. Owners need information about how well the business is doing to assess how the actions and decisions of the managers are affecting the business. The owners need some assurance that managers are providing complete and accurate information about the business. Both the individual states and the SEC at the federal level set rules for the financial reporting of corporations. A corporation's type of business and its size determine how extensive its reporting requirements are.

■ Corporate income is taxed twice. Here's how: Unlike a sole proprietorship or partnership, a corporation pays income taxes on its net income. After that net income (or at least a part of it) is divided by the number of shareholders of the corporation and distributed among shareholders as **dividends,** the shareholders must include the dividend income on their personal tax

Dividends are the earnings of a corporation distributed to the owners of the corporation. It is a special term for *distributions* that applies only to corporations.

Exhibit 1-4
Examples of Types of Businesses

	Sole proprietorship	Partnership	Corporation
Service	Jane Doe, CPA	Billings, Wren, Childers, and Munns, Attorneys at Law	Head Hunters, Inc.
Merchandising	Charlie's Hot Dog Stand	Bob and Bill's Autoparts Store	Winn Dixie Grocery Stores
Manufacturing	Custom drapery maker	Jane and John's Pottery Place	Ford Motor Corp.
Financial services	Joe Dudd, Stockbroker	Mike and Mark's Loan Service	Citicorp

returns. This amounts to double taxation on the same income. The income of the corporation—which is owned by shareholders—is taxed as corporation income, and what's passed on to owners as dividend income is again taxed, as personal income.

Examples of all types of business are shown in Exhibit 1–4.

**STUDY BREAK 1-1
SEE HOW YOU'RE DOING**

1. **What do all businesses have in common?**
2. **What are the different forms of business ownership?**

Business Activities and the Flow of Goods and Services

L.O. 2

Describe the common business processes.

An Entrepreneur

A person who starts a business is considered an entrepreneur. Let's look at how our entrepreneur, Tom, started his T-shirt business and the sequence of events that followed, analyzing the transactions represented in each event as we go along. Identifying those events is the first step in understanding how a business works. (See Exhibit 1–5.)

We can classify each step in the process of developing a business in terms of exchanges—who gets what and who gives what in return. The get portion and the give portion of the exchange are often considered separate transactions.

An owner's investment in a company is called the owner's **contribution,** because we are looking at the investment from the point of view of the company.

The first exchange starts the business—Tom invests his own $5,000 in the business. From the perspective of the business, this is called a **contribution.** It's often called **contributed capital.** As with all transactions, we look at this from the point of view of the business entity. The event is the exchange of cash for ownership in the business. This is part of the acquisition/payment process.

Exhibit 1-5   How a Business Works

Tom contributes $5,000 of **his own money** to start his business. → Tom's Wear **borrows $500** from Tom's mom to help finance the business → Tom's Wear **purchases** 100 T-shirts from a T-shirt maker → Tom's Wear decides to **advertise** the new business. → Tom's Wear **sells** the shirts to Tom's friends → Tom's Wear **repays** the loan **plus interest** to Tom's mom.

You may have to think about it to see the give part of this exchange—it's the business giving ownership to Tom. Because Tom has chosen to organize his business firm as a corporation, this share of ownership is called stock. For a sole proprietorship or a partnership, the ownership has no special name. Tom has chosen the corporate form of organization because of the limited legal liability of a corporation.

The get part of the exchange is the business getting the $5,000 cash. There is only one agent in this transaction—but Tom actually plays two roles. As an outside agent, Tom, the investor, gives the business cash. As an inside agent of the business, Tom, the manager, gives the outside agent shares of ownership in the business in return. Because Tom is the only shareholder, he owns 100% of the stock.

The second transaction is between Tom's Wear and Tom's mother. The business borrows $500 from her—the second transaction of the new company. Tom's Wear gets an economic resource—cash—and in exchange Tom's Wear gives an I-owe-you (IOU). From the perspective of Tom's Wear, this event is called a **cash receipt.** In any exchange like this one, there is an outside agent—Tom's mom—and an inside agent—Tom. This cash receipt is part of the acquisition/payment process. Borrowing money to finance a business is the get side of the exchange. The give side is the IOU to Mom—well, it's not really the give side until Tom repays the loan with cash. The IOU is useful for describing the *timing difference* between the time of the get and give sides of the exchange. We'll see lots of examples of this type of timing difference in accounting for business events.

> A **cash receipt** is the business event of receiving cash.

The emphasis in financial accounting is on the **acquisition/payment process** and the **sales/collection process.** (The conversion process is the major topic of managerial accounting.) The acquisition/payment process is the group of business activities associated with acquiring and paying for goods and services. The objectives of the acquisition/payment process include purchasing only those goods and services that a company needs and can afford, making sure the goods it orders are received in good condition, properly maintaining them, and providing them to the appropriate people in the company when needed. Although we more often think of companies acquiring and paying for their inventory purchases, companies also acquire human resources, financial resources—that's money—and property, plant, and equipment. When Tom's Wear borrowed the money from Tom's mom, the company was acquiring financial resources.

> The two main business processes we will study in this course are the **acquisition/payment process** and the **sales/collection process.**

To understand what happens in a business transaction, it is helpful to know that every business transaction is made up of three components: **resources, events,** and **agents.**

> **Resources, events,** and **agents** are the three components of all business transactions.

- **Resources** are the things that are exchanged in transactions—both tangible and intangible. Examples of resources—called *economic* resources because of their importance in an economy—are money, goods, and services.

> **Resources** are the things of economic value exchanged.

- **Events** are the actual transactions—the giving or getting of a resource. Paying someone is an event—a cash disbursement. Other examples of events are making a sale and collecting a payment.

> **Events** are the actual giving and getting of the resources.

- **Agents** are the people involved in the transaction. Someone actually gives and gets the resources in the exchange. There are inside agents—employees of the company—and outside agents—people involved in the transactions who are not employed by the company.

> **Agents** are the people who actually make the exchange.

All three components—resources, events, and agents—are easy to identify with a little practice. First, the events are identified. Then, the resources and agents related to each event are identified. Let's look at the transactions in Tom's T-shirt business with these three components in mind.

The next transaction is the company's purchase of 100 T-shirts with a unique logo on them. The get part of the exchange is when Tom's Wear gets the shirts

Exhibit 1–6
**Acquisition and Payment
for T-Shirts**

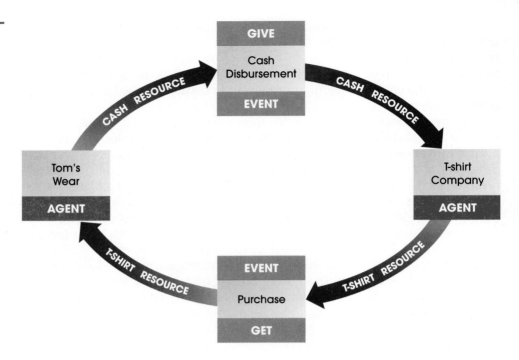

A **purchase** is an event in which the company *gets* goods or services.

A **cash disbursement** is an event in which the company *gives* cash.

A diagram of the **REA model** shows the resources, events, and agents involved in the economic exchange.

for the inventory. The event is a **purchase.** The inside agent is Tom, and the outside agent is the T-shirt manufacturer. The give part of the exchange has the same agents, but the economic resource is cash. The give part of the exchange is when Tom's Wear gives cash to the T-shirt manufacturer, and the event is a **cash disbursement.** All the events are seen through the eyes of Tom's Wear. The transaction would look different if we took the perspective of the T-shirt manufacturer. In business problems, we take one point of view throughout a problem or an analysis. This transaction is part of the acquisition/payment process.

We can represent the giving and getting aspects of an exchange in an **REA model** showing the resources, events, and agents comprising the exchange. The exchange consists of two transactions—one part shows what the business is getting and the other part shows what the business is giving. (See Exhibit 1–6.)

Exhibit 1–7
**Acquisition and Payment
for a Service**

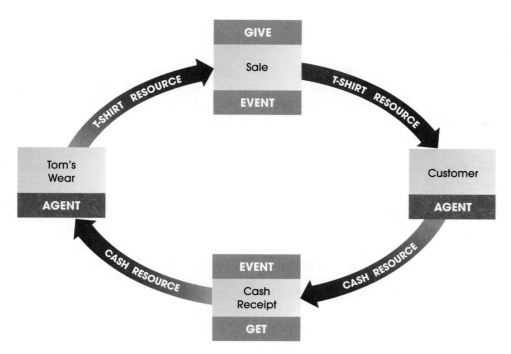

Exhibit 1-8
Sales and Collections

The next transaction, shown in Exhibit 1-7, is the acquisition of a service. The economic resources in this transaction are advertising and cash. The get part is the acquisition or purchase of advertising. The give part is a cash disbursement transaction; the internal agent is Tom; and the external agent is a person at the advertising company.

Tom's Wear now sells the T-shirts. This is an exchange in the sales/collection process. The get transaction is a cash receipt; the resource is cash. The give transaction is the sale, and the resource is the T-shirt. Tom, the inside agent, sells a T-shirt to a customer, the outside agent. The diagram in Exhibit 1-8 shows these transactions.

Tom's Wear repays the $500 loan from Tom's mother. The give part is a cash disbursement. That is, the company gives the economic resource of cash (amount of the loan, called the **principal,** plus **interest,** a cost of borrowing the money) to the outside agent, his mom. Recall that the get part of this exchange occurred near the beginning of our story. The second transaction was when Tom's Wear took the cash, as a loan, from his mom. The IOU was a sort of marker, indicating that there would be a timing difference in the get and give parts of this transaction.

Borrowing money is common in business. The amount of money borrowed is called the **principal** of loan. The cost of borrowing that money—using someone else's money—is called **interest.**

The Acquisition/Payment Process

When a company purchases something, that purchase is classified as part of the acquisition/payment process. When Tom's Wear bought the inventory of T-shirts, the transaction was part of the acquisition/payment process.

There are many steps in the acquisition/payment process. The acquisition—or purchase—part begins when someone in the company identifies the need for something. In many companies, this need is documented on a **purchase requisition**—that's a record of what is requested. Usually, someone at a level of management must approve this request. Then, it is sent to the purchasing department. Modern technology has eliminated the need for paper documents in some businesses. However, whether the request is put on paper or not, the company's information system will record information about this activity.

The purchasing department decides on the **vendor**—a business that provides goods and services—based on factors such as price, quality, and terms of

A **purchase requisition** is a document that is used to request an item or service.

A **vendor** is the company from whom you buy goods or services. The document used to order items from a vendor is called a **purchase order (PO).**

delivery. The items, or services, needed are specified to the vendor in a form called a **purchase order (PO).** This information may be on paper or in a computer file. When filled in with information needed to make the purchase, this purchase order may need approval, usually by someone in the purchasing department, before the order can be placed. Then a copy of the PO goes to the vendor, declaring the intent to purchase. A copy goes to the receiving department, so that the personnel there will know what to expect when the goods are delivered.

The next step in the acquisition/payment process is the receipt of the goods or services ordered. The copy of the purchase order that went to the receiving department when the order was placed is considered an open purchase order, also referred to as an unfilled purchase order. Its purpose in the receiving department is to determine if the delivered goods are actually the ones ordered. Receipt of the goods is recorded on a **receiving report,** which is matched with the PO. Both documents are then forwarded to the accounts payable department. There they wait for the **invoice**—the bill—to arrive from the vendor.

> A **receiving report** is a document on which the company records the items it gets from the vendor when the items arrive.
>
> An **invoice** is a bill for items that have been purchased.

The last step in the acquisition/payment process is making the payment for the goods or services delivered according to the purchase order. On or before the date that the payment is due to the vendor, the purchasing company begins the process of requesting that payment be made to the vendor. After the accounts payable department has verified, via the receiving report and matched PO, that the ordered goods have been received in satisfactory condition, payment will be made by check, debit card, or electronic funds transfer. The procedures and approvals for the payment process may be more complicated, depending on the size of the business and the number and size of the transactions regularly processed by the accounts payable department. No matter how the payment is made, the vendor will end up getting some of the company's cash. So the payment to the vendor is called a cash disbursement.

The steps and paper documents commonly used in this process are shown in Exhibit 1-9. A very small business like Tom's may not formally follow all the steps. As the business grows, the steps will become more formalized to make sure all the transactions are carried out with a minimum of errors.

**STUDY BREAK 1-2
SEE HOW YOU'RE DOING**

1. **What are the three components of every business transaction?**
2. **What is a purchase requisition, and why would a business use one?**

A business may also purchase labor—hire and pay employees—as well as acquire financing—such as a loan from a bank—to help the business expand. Purchasing labor and acquiring financing are special cases of the acquisition/payment process. We will discuss them in detail in later chapters in the book.

Exhibit 1-9   Steps and Documents in the Acquisition/Payment Process

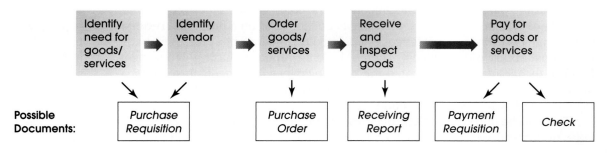

Exhibit 1-10   Steps and Documents in the Sales/Collection Process

| Customer places an order | Customer's credit is approved | Warehouse selects goods for shipment | Goods are shipped | Customer is billed for goods | Payment for goods is received |

Possible Documents:

| Sales Order | Picking Slip | Packing Slip | Shipping Notice | Sales Invoice | Remittance Advice |

The Sales/Collection Process

The sales part of the sales/collection process begins when a customer places an order, called a **sales order** by the company. Triggered by receipt of the sales order, the company examines and approves the customer's credit—if it is a credit sale. A credit sale is a sale for which the customer does not pay cash at the time of the sale but instead agrees to pay later. If the customer's credit is approved, the purchase information is sent to the warehouse, usually on a document called a **picking slip**, or **stock request.** Another document, the **packing slip,** is then sent to the shipping department signaling that the goods are on the way for shipping to the customer. Two copies of the sales order are then sent to the department that prepares the invoices. Remember, if we sell something on credit, we will have to send an invoice to the customer.

At the warehouse, the goods are selected and sent to shipping. When the goods are shipped, a copy of the shipping notice—specifying what goods were shipped to the customer and when they were shipped—is sent to the billing department. The billing department prepares a sales invoice, which is sent to the customer, and records the transaction in the formal accounting records. In this case, an **accounts receivable** is recorded. That is the written record of all customers who have made credit purchases with the amounts that have not yet been collected.

While many businesses have multiple steps in their sales/collection process (Exhibit 1-10), a retail business like Lands' End has a much simpler sales process—the sales portion of the sales/collection process. Usually, a wholesale business has a sales/collection process that is more complicated than that of a retail business. On the other hand, the acquisition/payment process is more complicated for a retail business than it is for a wholesale business. How a business makes decisions about vendors, keeps track of purchases, and makes sure there is sufficient inventory—goods on hand for sale—for the planned sales are topics we will examine in subsequent chapters.

Documents that may be involved in the sales process:

Sales order—document with a list of the items a customer wants to buy (the selling company's side of a purchase order).

Picking slip—a document that tells the inventory clerks what items to get from the inventory.

Packing slip—a document included in the shipped order that describes what is in the order.

Accounts receivable are the amounts that customers owe the business for purchases on credit—buy now, pay later.

Information Needs for Decision Making in Business

To start a new business, Tom had lots of decisions to make. First, how would he finance it? What organizational form should it take? How many T-shirts should he buy? From whom should he buy them? How much should he pay for advertising? How much should he charge for the shirts?

After the first complete operating cycle—that's a period beginning with cash, converting cash to inventory, selling the inventory, and turning inventory sales back into cash—Tom has more decisions to make. Should he buy T-shirts and do the whole thing again? If so, should he buy more T-shirts than he

Describe the information used by a business to make decisions.

bought the first time and from the same vendor? To make decisions like these, Tom must have information. The kind of information usually provided by accountants will provide the basis for getting a good picture of the performance of his business.

Revenue—the amount the company has earned from providing goods or services to customers.

Expenses—the costs incurred to generate revenue.

- What was **revenue** from sales during the accounting period? An accounting period is any length of time that a company uses to evaluate its performance. It can be a month, a quarter, or a year.
- What **expenses** were incurred so those sales could be made? (You've probably heard the expression, "It takes money to make money.")
- What goods does Tom's company have left at the end of the period?
- Should he increase the price of the T-shirts he sells or lower the price?

Besides this kind of financial information, there is other information that can help Tom make decisions about his business. For example, Tom would want information on the reliability of different vendors and quality of their merchandise to decide what vendor to use next time. Before the advances in computer technology that have enabled us to collect, organize, and report huge quantities of information besides financial information, a company had only the basic financial information to help make its business decisions. Today, financial information is just a part of a firm's information system.

A modern supermarket is a great example of a business that collects a tremendous amount of information. With a simple, swift swipe of the grocery item bar code past the checkout scanner, the store information system collects product data, recording and tracking information about vendors, product shelf life, customer preferences and buying habits, and the usual, typical financial information such as price and quantity of each item sold. As we look at business processes and the information needed to run a business, in this book, we will pay attention to the information reflected in the basic financial statements—the income statement, the balance sheet, the statement of changes in owner's equity, and the statement of cash flows. We'll be talking more about each of these statements soon.

STUDY BREAK 1-3
SEE HOW YOU'RE DOING

1. What are revenues and expenses?
2. What are accounts receivable and why would a company have them?

Flow of Information

Who Needs Information About Transactions of the Business?

No part of any business can do what it's supposed to do without information. The functions of the management of a company are to plan, to control, and to evaluate the operation of the business. To perform these functions effectively, management must have information about what the business has done, about what it is currently doing, and about where it looks like it is going or should be going. Traditionally, the accounting information system has provided only very general data about the past of a business firm. A business firm used to keep two sets of records, each for specific purposes: one set for financial reporting and one set for internal decision making. Now, with modern computers and software that can organize information in a variety of ways with a few simple commands, one information system can accumulate and organize all data of a company. The managers of each business area—usually referred to as a department—can obtain and use whatever information is relevant to the decisions they have to make. Accountants, too, can obtain the information they need for preparing the basic financial statements.

In many industries, there are regulatory agencies that require specific information from companies, particularly corporations. For example, the SEC requires corporations that trade on the stock exchanges to file many different kinds of reports about the company's transactions.

For all businesses, payroll taxes and sales taxes must be reported and paid to state revenue agencies. The **Internal Revenue Service (IRS)** requires information from businesses concerning income and expenses, even if the income from the business flows through to the owners as it does for sole proprietorships and partnerships.

To see how many SEC filings a company must make, go to the Web site of any well-known corporation. Under the topic of investor relations, you'll be able to find a copy of all the forms recently filed with the SEC. The SEC also has a huge database of the filings in a system called EDGAR. Most universities have access to EDGAR. Here's a list of the filings made by Aetna, Inc. just during the last 2 months of 2000.

Date Filed	Filing	Description	Company
12-14-00	15-12B	Other	Aetna Inc.
11-30-00	DEFA14A	Other	Aetna Inc.
11-16-00	DEFA14A	Other	Aetna Inc.
11-15-00	DEFA14A	Other	Aetna Inc.
11-15-00	DEFA14A	Other	Aetna Inc.
11-09-00	13F-HR	Other	Aetna Inc.
11-08-00	SC 13G/A	Amended Ownership Statement	Aetna Life and Casualty
11-08-00	DEFA14A	Other	Aetna Inc.
11-08-00	DEFA14A	Other	Aetna Inc.
11-08-00	DEFA14A	Other	Aetna Inc.
11-06-00	8-K	Current Action	Aetna Inc.
11-06-00	DEFA14A	Other	Aetna Inc.
11-02-00	DEFA14A	Other	Aetna Inc.

When a company wants to borrow money, creditors—the people and firms who lend money—require information about the company before they will lend money. Banks want to be sure that the loans they make will be repaid. The creditworthiness—a term indicating that a borrower has in the past made loan payments when due (or failed to make them when due)—of a business must be supported with information about the business. This information is usually very specific and very detailed.

The **Internal Revenue Service (IRS)** is the federal governmental agency responsible for tax collection.

Who else needs information about the business? Potential investors are information consumers. Suppose Tom wanted to find additional owners for his T-shirt business. That means he would be looking for someone who wanted to invest money in his T-shirt business in return for a portion of ownership in the company. A potential owner would want some reliable information about the business before making a financial investment. Publicly traded corporations—whose shares are traded on the stock exchanges—invite anyone willing and financially able to become an owner by offering for sale shares of stock in the corporation. Buying the stock of a corporation is investing in that corporation. Investors want information about a company before they will buy that company's stock. The SEC requires that the information provided by companies whose stock is publicly traded be accurate and reliable. That

The language about what an auditor does is very specific. The auditors want to emphasize that they cannot guarantee that the financial statements are error free. The audit opinion—the report the auditors give about a company's financial statements—says whether or not the financial statements present fairly the financial position of the company for the relevant period of time. For example, the auditors' opinion for Lands' End says,

In our opinion, the financial statements referred to above present fairly, in all material respects, the financial position of Lands' End, Inc. and subsidiaries as of January 28, 2000, and January 29, 1999, and the results of their operations and their cash flows for each of the 3 years in the period ended January 28, 2000, in conformity with generally accepted accounting principles.

An **audit** is an independent examination of a company's financial statements and the accounting system that produced the statements.

A **certified public accountant (CPA)** is someone who has met specific education and exam requirements, set up by the states to make sure only individuals with the appropriate qualifications can perform audits.

means the information in their financial statements must be **audited.** Audited information means it has been examined by professional accountants, called **certified public accountants (CPAs),** who give an opinion on the fairness with which the financial statements have been presented.

Finally, current and potential vendors, customers, and employees also need useful information about the company. They need to evaluate a company's financial condition to make decisions about working for, or doing business with, the company.

What makes information useful? To be useful, information must be:

- timely
- verifiable
- accurate
- relevant

Usefulness depends on who needs the information and for what purpose it is needed. For example, the market price of a share of a company's stock is useful information to a potential investor, if that market price is current, verifiable, and so on. Even if it is timely and verifiable, the market price of a share of stock is not useful to a manager trying to decide on a delivery schedule. We will spend more time discussing what makes financial information useful in the next chapter.

The Financial Accounting Standards Board (FASB) is a group of professional business people, accountants, and accounting scholars who have the responsibility of setting current accounting standards. Accounting standards dictate the way business events are reported, so it makes sense that businesses are very interested in what the FASB does.

Accounting Information: A Part of the Information System

Describe the four basic financial statements and the underlying business processes. Be able to prepare simple financial statements.

The Role of the Information System

Have you ever filed an address change with a company only to find later that one department uses your new address while another department of that same company continues to use your old address? Even with such common data as customer names and addresses, the information is often gathered and maintained in several different places within the same organization. As computers and databases become more common, central data information systems are replacing departmental systems and eliminating their inefficiencies.

Because accountants have traditionally been the recorders and maintainers of financial information, it makes sense that they have expanded their role as the keepers of business information systems to include more than financial information. The cost of obtaining business information has decreased rapidly in the last few years. The financial accounting information a company reports is now just a small part of the total available business information. The accounting information is provided in four basic financial statements and supporting notes.

Overview of the Financial Statements

There are four financial statements a company uses to report its financial condition:

1. balance sheet
2. income statement

3. statement of changes in owner's equity
4. statement of cash flows

We'll look at each briefly. Later chapters will go into each in detail.

Balance Sheet

A **balance sheet** describes the financial situation of a company at a *specific point in time.* It's a snapshot—a freeze frame—that captures the items of value the business possesses at a particular moment and how it has financed them. A balance sheet has three parts:

- assets
- liabilities
- owner's equity

Assets are things of value owned by a business. Cash and equipment are common assets. When a business has an asset, someone has the rights to, that is, a claim to, that asset. There is a claim on every asset in a business. There are two groups who might have claims to a company's assets—creditors and owners.

The claims of creditors are called **liabilities.** Liabilities are amounts the business owes to others outside the business, those who have loaned money to the company and have not yet been fully repaid for their loan. For example, the amount of a loan—like your car loan—is a liability.

The claims of the owner are called **owner's equity.** Stockholders' equity and shareholders' equity are other names for the claims of the owners. Owner's equity is also called net assets because it is the amount left over after the amount of the liabilities is subtracted from the amount of the assets, or liabilities are netted out of assets.

There are two ways for the owners to increase their claims to the assets of the business. One is by making contributions, and the other is by earning it. When the business is successful, the equity that results from doing business and is kept in the company is called **retained earnings.** We'll see the difference between contributed capital and retained earnings more clearly when we go through the first month of business for Tom's Wear.

Together, assets, liabilities, and owner's equity make up the balance sheet, one of the four basic financial statements. The following relationship, called the accounting equation, is the basis for the balance sheet:

$$\text{Assets} = \text{Claims}$$
$$\text{Assets} = \text{Liabilities} + \text{Owner's Equity}$$

Each transaction that takes place in a business can be recorded in the accounting equation, which is actually the balance sheet. In other words, every transaction is changing the balance sheet; but the balance sheet must stay in balance. Let's look at the transactions for Tom's Wear for January and see how each one changes the balance sheet.

Date	Transaction
January 1	Tom contributes $5,000 of his own money to start the business.
January 1	Tom's Wear borrows $500 from Tom's mom for the business.
January 5	Tom's Wear buys 100 T-shirts for $400 cash.
January 10	Tom's Wear pays a company $50 cash for advertising.
January 20	Tom's Wear sells 90 of the T-shirts to Tom's friends for $10 each.
January 30	Tom's Wear repays Tom's mom the $500 plus $5 interest.
January 31	Tom's Wear declares and pays a $100 dividend.

*The **balance sheet** shows the accounting equation in detail. The statement shows:*

Assets—economic resources owned by the business,

Liabilities—obligations of the business to creditors,

*Equity—owners' claims to the assets of the company. There are two types: contributed capital and **retained earnings.***

Before the first transaction, there are no assets, no liabilities, and no equity. So the balance sheet equation is:

Assets	=	Liabilities	+	Shareholders' Equity
0		0		0

Tom starts his company as a corporation. That means the owner's equity will be called shareholders' equity, and his initial contribution will be classified as common stock. We'll discuss the details of owners' equity in Chapter 9. This is how the first transaction affects the accounting equation:

Assets	=	Liabilities	+	Shareholders' Equity
+ $5,000 cash		0	+	$5,000 common stock

Also on January 1, Tom's Wear borrows $500. This is how the second transaction affects the accounting equation:

Assets	=	Liabilities	+	Shareholders' Equity
+ $500 cash		+ $500 notes payable		0

A balance sheet can be prepared at any point in time to show the assets, liabilities, and equity for the company. If Tom's Wear prepared a balance sheet on January 2, these two transactions would be reflected in the amounts on the statement. Exhibit 1-11 shows the balance sheet at that time. With every subsequent transaction the balance sheet will change.

There are several characteristics of the balance sheet that you should look at in Exhibit 1-11. First, the heading on every financial statement specifies three things:

■ the name of the company
■ the name of the financial statement
■ the date

A **fiscal** year is a year in the life of a business. It may or may not coincide with the calendar year.

The date on the balance sheet is one specific date. If the business year for Tom's Wear, also known as its **fiscal** year, is from January 1 to December 31, the balance sheet at the *beginning* of the first year of business is empty. Until there is a transaction, there are no assets, no liabilities, and no equity.

The balance sheet in Exhibit 1-11 for Tom's Wear is dated January 2, 2001. Tom's Wear has been in business for only 1 day. Even though a business would

Exhibit 1-11
Balance Sheet for Tom's Wear

Tom's Wear, Inc.
Balance Sheet
At January 2, 2001

tom's wear

Assets		Liabilities and Shareholders' equity	
Cash	$5,500	Note payable	$ 500
		Common stock	5,000
		Retained earnings	0
		Total liabilities and	
Total assets	$5,500	Shareholders' equity	$5,500

be unlikely to prepare a balance sheet just 1 day after starting the business, this is what the balance sheet for Tom's Wear would look like on January 2. The balance sheet shows the financial condition—assets, liabilities, and owner's equity—at the close of business on January 2. At this time, Tom's Wear had received $5,000 from owner Tom and borrowed $500 from Tom's mom. The total cash—$5,500—is shown as an asset, and the liability of $500 plus the owner's equity of $5,000 together show who has claim to the company's assets.

Because the balance sheet gives the financial position of a company at a specific point in time, a new, updated balance sheet could be produced after every transaction. That would be data overload. When a company presents its income for a period, that's called an income statement. The company must show the balance sheet at the beginning of that period and the balance sheet at the end of that period. Those two balance sheets are called **comparative balance sheets.** For Tom's Wear, the first balance sheet for the fiscal year is empty. That is, on January 1, 2001, the equation was $0 = 0 + 0$. Before we look at the balance sheet at January 31, 2001, we need to see the income statement for the month of January 2001. We need the information on the income statement to see what happened during the time between the two balance sheets.

> **Comparative balance sheets** are the balance sheets from consecutive fiscal periods for a single company.

Look at Lands' End's comparative balance sheets (see Exhibit 1-3). Notice the similarities between the real world of Lands' End and the fictitious world of Tom's Wear—the balance sheets for both actually *balance*. Both companies list assets first, then liabilities and equity. Both companies have used dollars to measure their balance sheet items. There are differences between the balance sheets of the real world and our not-so-real world example, which we'll discuss in later chapters.

---

1. **What are the two parts of shareholders' equity?**
2. **What is a fiscal year?**

STUDY BREAK 1-4
SEE HOW YOU'RE DOING

Before we prepare an income statement for Tom's Wear or a balance sheet at January 31, let's look at each transaction that took place in January and see how each affects the accounting equation worksheet. This analysis is shown in Exhibit 1-12.

When a business is started, it begins with an empty balance sheet. For Tom's Wear, there are no assets, and therefore no claims, on January 1. The first two transactions that started the business, Tom's contribution of $5,000 and the loan from Tom's mom for $500, happened on January 1. First, Tom's contribution increases assets by $5,000 and shareholders' equity by $5,000, because the owner, Tom, has claim to the new asset. The company receives its first asset—cash—and the owner has claim to it. Then, Mom's loan increases assets by $500 and liabilities by $500. The company receives an asset—cash—and a creditor—Tom's mom—has claim to it. Following these two beginning transactions, the operations of the business begin. Each transaction that takes place during the month is shown as it affects the balance sheet. Study each transaction in Exhibit 1-12 as you read the following description of each:

- On January 5, cash is decreased by $400 and inventory is increased by $400. This is called an asset exchange, because the company is simply exchanging one asset—cash—for another asset—inventory. Notice the entire effect of this exchange on the accounting equation is on one side of the equation. That is perfectly acceptable. Also notice an asset exchange has no effect on shareholders' equity. Tom still has claim to the same dollar amount of assets.

- On January 10, Tom pays $50 for advertising. This is a cost Tom's Wear has incurred to generate revenue. Assets are decreased, and retained earnings, a component of shareholders' equity, is decreased. Why is retained earnings decreased? Because when assets are decreased by $50, someone's claim must be reduced. Unless we are paying off a debt, the owner's claims are reduced when assets are decreased. Retained earnings is the part of owners' equity that reflects the amount of equity the business has earned. (Throughout this book, as we study the transactions that take place in a business, we will see that all revenues *increase* retained earnings and all expenses *decrease* retained earnings.)

- On January 20, Tom's Wear sells 90 T-shirts for $10 each. This sale increases assets—cash—by $900. Who has claim to this asset? The owner has this claim. Revenues increase retained earnings. At the time of the sale, something else happens. An asset is reduced. The company no longer has 90 of the original 100 T-shirts in the inventory. Because each shirt cost $4 (and we recorded the T-shirts at their original cost), we now must reduce the asset *inventory* by $360. That reduction in assets is an expense and so the owner's claims—via retained earnings—are reduced by the amount of that expense.

- On January 30, Tom's Wear pays off the $500 loan with $5 interest. The repayment of the $500 principal reduces cash and meets the obligation that had been recorded as a liability. In other words, that liability is settled. The $500 reduction in assets is balanced in the accounting equation with a $500 reduction in the claims of creditors. However, the interest expense represents the cost of borrowing money. For a business, that is called interest expense. Like all expenses, it reduces the owner's claims by reducing retained earnings.

- On January 31, Tom's Wear pays a $100 dividend. That reduction in cash reduces the owner's claims to the assets of the firm, shown by the decrease

Exhibit 1-12   Beginning and Ending Balance Sheets with Transactions for the Month

tom's wear		Assets	=	Liabilities	+	Shareholders' equity	
						Contributed capital	Retained earnings
Balance sheet at 1/1/01 →		0	=	0	+	0	0
Effect of each transaction on the accounting equation:	January 1	$5,000 cash				$5,000 common stock	
	January 1	500 cash		$500 notes payable			
	January 5	(400) cash 400 inventory					
	January 10	(50) cash					(50) advertising expense
	January 20	900 cash (360) inventory					900 sales revenue (360) cost of goods sold (expense)
	January 30	(505) cash		(500) notes payable			(5) interest expense
	January 31	(100) cash					(100) dividends
Balance sheet at 1/31/01 →		$5,345 cash 40 inventory	=	0	+	$5,000 common stock	$385 retained earnings

Exhibit 1-13
The Accounting Equation

in retained earnings. The $100, after it is distributed, is now part of Tom's personal financial assets, which are entirely separate from his business.

Using the accounting equation to track the transactions of a business is a useful way to see how the financial statements are put together. The actual way a company keeps track of its financial transactions and its records—commonly called, its *books*—can vary from a simple manual record-keeping system to a complex computerized system. No matter how a company keeps its records, the financial statements will look the same. The accounting equation is the basis for accumulating accounting information and communicating that information to decision makers. A company starts the year with a balance sheet (only empty at the start of the business firm), engages in business transactions during the year, and ends the year with a new, updated balance sheet. The balance sheet is actually the accounting equation that must be in balance (Exhibit 1-13).

Income Statement

The most well-known financial statement is the **income statement,** also known as the **statement of earnings,** or the **statement of operations,** or the **profit and loss statement (P&L).** The income statement is a summary of all the *revenues* (income from sales or services) a company earns minus all the *expenses* (costs incurred in the earning process) associated with earning that revenue. It describes the performance of a company during a specific period, which is called a fiscal period. Most often, *fiscal period* is used to describe the business year, which may or may not coincide with the calendar year. A fiscal year (*not physical* year) for a company may, for example, begin on July 1. That means the fiscal year of the business runs from July 1 of one year to June 30 of the next calendar year.

Recall, the balance sheet gives the amount of assets, the amount of liabilities, and the amount of shareholders' equity of a business at a specific date. The income statement describes the activity of a company during a period. Look at the income statement for Tom's Wear in Exhibit 1-14. It shows the amount of sales the company made during the month, from January 1, 2001, through January 31, 2001. The expenses shown are also for the same period. The difference between the revenues and expenses is called *net income,* or *net earnings.*

Notice several things about the income statement:

- First, only the cost of the T-shirts that were sold is included as an expense—cost of goods sold, also called cost of sales. The cost of the T-shirts *not sold* is shown as an asset called inventory on the balance sheet.

The **income statement** shows all revenues minus all expenses for an accounting period—a month, a quarter, or a year.

Exhibit 1-14
Income Statement for Tom's Wear

tom's wear

Tom's Wear, Inc.
Income Statement
For the Month Ended January 31, 2001

Revenue		
Sales		$900
Expenses		
Cost of goods sold	$360	
Advertising	50	
Interest	5	
Total expenses		415
Net income		$485

■ Second, the repayment of the loan from Tom's mom is *not shown* as an expense. The only expense related to borrowing money is the interest owed to the lender. The repayment of principal is not an expense.

In a corporation, distributions to owners are called **dividends.**

Also notice that **dividends** are excluded from the income statement. Tom could have paid himself a salary for running the business. That salary would have been an expense, but he decided not to do that. Instead, he decided to take cash out of the business as a dividend. Dividends are not a *component* of earnings; they are a *distribution* of earnings.

Lands' End's income statement (statement of operations in Exhibit 1-2) doesn't look like the Tom's Wear income statement. Both have revenues and expenses, but the two companies have presented the data in a different order. Tom's Wear lists revenue first and then groups all the expenses together. This is called a **single-step income statement.** Lands' End lists its largest revenue first and then subtracts the largest expense related to the revenue, cost of goods sold, which gives a subtotal called **gross profit on sales.** This is called a **multistep income statement.** If we were to recast Tom's income statement into a multistep income statement, we would subtract the cost of goods sold of $360 from the sales revenue of $900 to get a subtotal of $540 for Tom's gross profit on sales. Although Lands' End and Tom's Wear have arranged their revenues and expenses differently, net income for each company is still the difference between all revenues and all expenses. That is what net income always is, no matter how the revenues and expenses are grouped on the statement.

A **single-step income statement** groups all revenues together and shows all expenses deducted from total revenue.

A **multistep income statement** starts with sales and subtracts cost of goods sold to get a subtotal called **gross profit on sales,** also known as gross margin. Then, other revenues are added and all other expenses are deducted.

The Difference Between the Balance Sheet and the Income Statement. You should get a better idea of the difference between the balance sheet and the income statement by thinking about your own personal finances. If you were asked to prepare a personal balance sheet, you would list all your assets, such as your cash on hand (no matter how little) and the cost of your car, clothes, computer, and CD collection. Then you would list all the people to whom you owe money and how much money you owe to each. This might include some credit card companies and perhaps a bank for a car loan. All these assets and liabilities are measured in dollars. The specific point of time associated with a balance sheet must be given. For example, if you were listing your assets and liabilities on the last day of 2002, your balance sheet date would be December 31, 2002. Remember the accounting equation:

$$\text{Assets} = \text{Liabilities} + \text{Owner's Equity}$$

If you subtract the amount of your liabilities—what you owe to others—from your assets, the difference is your equity. Owner's equity is sometimes called the residual, indicating that it is the amount left over after the claims of creditors are deducted from a company's assets.

If you constructed a personal income statement, it would cover a period of time. For example, what was your net income total during the year 2002? You'd list all income you received during the year and then subtract all your expenses during the same year. The difference would be your net income for the year. There's no equation to balance. The income statement lists sources of income and subtracts the related expenses, leaving a difference, hopefully positive, called net income. If the subtraction of expenses from revenues results in a negative number, that amount is called a net loss.

---

1. **What is gross profit?**
2. **What is the difference between a single-step income statement and a multistep income statement?**

Statement of Changes in Owners' Equity

As its name suggests, the statement of changes in owners' equity shows the changes that took place in the amount of owners' equity during a period. For a corporation, the statement is usually called the **statement of changes in shareholders' equity,** because the *owners* are known as *shareholders.* The statement starts with the amount of contributed capital on a given balance sheet date and summarizes the additions and subtractions from that amount during a specific period, usually a year. In this course, we will not see *deductions* from contributed capital. Contributed capital is reduced in only very special circumstances, and those will be studied in more advanced accounting courses. The second part of the statement starts with the beginning balance in **retained earnings** and then shows the additions—net income is the most common—and the deductions—dividends are the most common. Contributed capital and retained earnings are then added to show the total amount of shareholders' equity at the end of the accounting period. For demonstration purposes, we'll look at *monthly* financial statements for Tom's Wear, Inc., throughout this book.

The statement of changes in shareholders' equity for Tom's first month of business is shown in Exhibit 1-15. The statement starts with the shareholders' equity—also called stockholders' or owners' equity—at the beginning of the month. Tom's Wear had no contributed capital, because this is the company's first month. Then capital contributions—owners' contributions to the business—made during the month are listed. Tom contributed $5,000 to the business. In a corporation, contributions take the form of shares of stock. Next is beginning retained earnings, the equity owners have as a result of the business *earning* income, rather than from contributions. The beginning retained earnings balance is zero because January was the company's first month of doing business. Net income for the period—$485—is shown as an increase in retained earnings. The dividends of $100 are shown as a decrease to retained earnings. The amount of retained earnings at the end of the period is then added to contributed capital at the end of the period to give the total shareholders' equity at the end of the period.

After preparing the income statement for the month and the statement of changes in shareholders' equity for the same month, we will be able to prepare the end-of-the-month balance sheet. If we set up the balance sheet horizontally in the accounting equation format, we can view the changes in assets, liabilities, and shareholders' equity from the beginning to the end of the month, with each transaction keeping the accounting equation in balance.

The **statement of changes in shareholders' equity** starts with the beginning amount of contributed capital and shows all changes during the accounting period. Then the statement shows the beginning balance in retained earnings with its changes. The usual changes to retained earnings are the increase from net income and the decrease from dividends paid to shareholders.

Retained earnings is the total of all net income amounts minus all dividends paid in the life of the company. It is descriptively named—it's the earnings that have been kept (retained) in the company. The amount of retained earnings represents the part of the owners' claims that the company has earned (i.e., *not* contributed). Retained earnings is not the same as cash.

Exhibit 1-15
Statement of Changes in Shareholders' Equity for Tom's Wear

Tom's Wear, Inc.
Statement of Changes in Shareholders' Equity
For the Month Ended January 31, 2001

Beginning contributed capital	$ 0	
Stock issued during the month	5,000	
Ending contributed capital		$5,000
Beginning retained earnings	$ 0	
Net income for the month	485	
Dividends	(100)	
Ending retained earnings		385
Total shareholders' equity		*$5,385*

Statement of Cash Flows

The **statement of cash flows** shows all the cash collected and all the cash disbursed during the period. Each cash amount is classified as one of three types:

The **statement of cash flows** is needed to form a complete picture of the financial position of a company. This statement is, perhaps, the easiest to understand. It is simply a list of all the cash that has come into a business—its cash receipts—and all the cash that has gone out of the business—its cash disbursements—during a specific period. In other words, it shows all the cash inflows and all the cash outflows for a fiscal period. Compare the cash inflows and cash outflows for a specific period with the *revenues and expenses* for the same specific period on the income statement. Accountants *measure revenue* as amounts the company has *earned* during the period, even if it is *not* equal to the amount of cash actually *collected*. Accountants *measure expenses* as the costs *incurred* to generate those revenues, even if they are *not* the same as the amounts actually *paid* in cash. Because this way of measuring revenues and expenses may not have an exact correspondence to the amount of cash collected and disbursed, the statement of cash flows is necessary to get a complete picture of the business transactions for the period.

The statement of cash flows is divided into three sections:

Cash from operating activities—cash transactions that relate to the everyday, routine transactions needed to run a business.

Cash from investing activities—transactions involving the sale and purchase of long-term assets used in the business.

Cash from financing activities—transactions related to how a business is financed. Examples: contributions from owners and amounts borrowed as long-term loans.

- **cash from operating activities**
- **cash from investing activities**
- **cash from financing activities**

These represent the three general types of business activities.

Cash inflows and outflows from operating activities pertain to the general activities of the business. For Tom's Wear, purchasing T-shirts is an operating activity. Look at the other cash flows from operations on the statement of cash flows in Exhibit 1-16.

Cash inflows and outflows from investing activities are the cash flows related to the purchase and sale of certain assets in a business. If Tom decided to purchase a piece of equipment to silk screen his own shirts, that purchase would be an investing activity—not an operating activity—because Tom's Wear is not in the business of buying and selling equipment.

Financing activities are related to a company's sources of capital. The two sources of capital, usually cash, for financing a business are contributions from owners and loans from creditors. Both of these transactions are classified as cash inflows from financing activities. Financing outflows include repayment of the principal of loans and distributions to owners. Tom's repayment of the $500 loan is an example of a financing cash outflow.

All four financial statements will be discussed in detail in the chapters to follow. By the time we are finished, you will be able to read and understand what is on most financial statements. You will also be able to analyze business transactions and understand how they affect the financial statements of a business.

Exhibit 1–16
Statement of Cash Flows for Tom's Wear

tom's wear

Tom's Wear, Inc.
Statement of Cash Flows
For the Month Ended January 31, 2001

Cash from operating activities		
Cash collected from customers	$ 900	
Cash paid to vendors for T-shirts	(400)	
Cash paid for advertising	(50)	
Cash paid for interest	(5)	
Total cash from operations		$445
Cash from investing activities		0
Cash from financing activities		
Proceeds from loan	$ 500	
Repayment of loan (principal)	(500)	
Issue of stock	5,000	
Dividends paid	(100)	
Total cash from financing		4,900
Net increase in cash		$5,345

Flow of Information and the Financial Statements

A company records and uses a large amount of information about its transactions. The amount of data and the way the information is collected and stored vary widely from company to company. The information contained in the four financial statements is a specific, well-defined part of the information available from a company's overall information system. The purpose of these four financial statements is to provide the financial information needed to represent and evaluate the transactions of the business. Investors, regulators, vendors, customers, and creditors rely on financial accounting information for decision making.

Business Risks

Starting a business is more than having a good idea about what it should be and obtaining financing to get it going. Both are a good beginning, but they must be followed with sound business planning for acquiring goods and services and selling the company's products or services. Part of that planning is identifying the risks involved. Before we discuss the details of the business activities in the chapters to follow, let's consider the risks of being in business and how we can minimize the negative consequences of those risks.

A **risk** may be generally defined as anything that exposes us to potential injury or loss. In business, risks can

Business Fraud

A recent study by the Association of Certified Fraud Examiners reports that fraud and abuse cost employers an average of $9 a day per employee, which adds up to more than $400 billion annually in the United States. The study defines fraud and abuse as "the use of one's occupation for personal enrichment through the deliberate misuse or misapplication of the employing organization's resources or assets." These statistics make clear that business risks and the need for controls play a significant role in business decisions.

Employees, managers, and even executives indulge in business frauds. In the Association of Certified Fraud Examiners' 2000 Report to the Nation on Occupational Fraud and Abuse, the statistics indicate that the majority of reported frauds were committed by non-managerial employees. The size of the related losses, however, increased with the person's position in the organization. This relationship is shown in the following pair of graphs:

(continued)

Business Fraud (continued)

People and Dollars Involved in Fraud

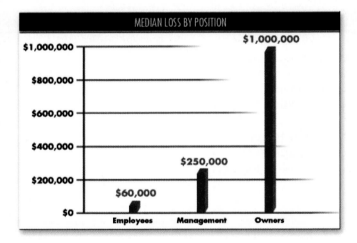

The most prevalent method of perpetrating a business fraud is the misappropriation of a company's assets. Four out of five offenses involve stealing assets — cash, inventory, supplies, equipment, and information. Other offenses include corruption — bribery and conflict of interest — and fraudulent statements — lying.

Source: Association of Certified Fraud Examiners Report to the Nation on Occupational Fraud and Abuse, 2000.

A **risk** is anything that exposes us to potential injury or loss.

A **control** is an activity designed to minimize or eliminate a risk.

turn into significant losses, scandals, or total company failure. There are hundreds of risks that any business faces. Some examples follow:

- the risk of product failure that might result in the death of consumers
- the risk that someone will steal assets from the company
- the risk that poor quality inventory will be purchased and sold

What losses could result? For a serious product failure, like the Firestone tires on the Ford Explorers in the early 2000s, the financial losses to the business could amount to millions of dollars in lawsuit settlements. For employee theft, the potential losses range from significant financial losses to the loss of a company secret that could cause a business to fail. Poor quality inventory could result in the loss of customers and reputation.

Risks relate to all aspects of the business including:

General strategic risks — Should we market our cigarettes to teenagers?
Operating risks — Should we operate without a backup power supply?
Financial risks — Should we borrow the money from the bank or get the money by issuing more stock to our shareholders ?
Information risks — Should we use a manual accounting system?

The potential losses may be the loss of reputation, loss of customers, loss of needed information, or loss of assets. All the losses translate into monetary losses that can put the company at risk for total failure.

Why do people take risks? Every risk brings a *potential* reward. The reward is why we're in business. An entrepreneur like Tom has put his money and his reputation at risk to start a T-shirt business. Why? For the potential of developing a successful business. To deal with the risks and increase the chances to reap the rewards, a firm must establish and maintain control over its operations, assets, and information system. A **control** is an activity performed to minimize or eliminate a risk. As we study the business processes that Tom will be engaged in during his first year in business, we'll look at how he can control the risk involved in each process.

Exhibit 1-17
This Is *Not* Your Father's Accountant

Megan Crampton, whether walking her two dogs or crossing the finish line of a 10-K race, doesn't look like what you might think an accountant would look like. But she is an accountant—even though she certainly doesn't look like the accountant from your parents' or grandparents' days.

Megan has more than 8 years of audit and business advisory experience with one of the world's largest accounting firms, Ernst & Young, working with high-tech and manufacturing clients in Florida. She works with several multinational companies and has been actively involved in taking companies through an initial public offering. Her clients have included: Harris Corporation, Lockheed Martin Corp., Sawtek Inc., Triton Network Systems Inc., Faro Technologies, Florida Digital Network Inc., and LMG Productions. And she still manages to get in quality time for her husband, family, and friends, as well as her dogs.

Megan serves as one of the leaders for the firm's recruiting team at the Florida State University, where she received her bachelor of science degree in accounting and finance. She also serves on the Board of Directors for New Hope's Center for Grieving Children. In addition, Megan is involved with Orlando's Chapter of Women in Technology. And she finds time to train for those 10-K races.

Asked to describe her job, Megan says, "Primarily, I spend my time working with people—solving accounting and business problems. Most people are surprised at how little number-crunching I do!"

No More Mr. Nerd Guy

As technology has made financial statement information a part of all the information available to run a business, the role of the accountant has changed. An accountant was once considered someone who records, classifies, and summarizes the business transactions that affect the information that goes on the financial statements. Keeping the books was an accountant's main job.

Accountants don't spend much time recording transactions anymore. Business transactions are captured by a company's information system, and the information is recorded in enough detail to be useful to many people in the company. Accountants are increasingly called on to analyze financial information and provide ways of improving business transactions. What were once known as *accounting firms* are now known as *professional services firms*. Accounting has become a broad and dynamic field, requiring expertise in all aspects of business. As the business world has changed, so has the role of the accountant. There is a lot of variety in what today's accountant does (Exhibit 1-17). No more Mr. Nerd Guy!

Understanding Excel

For purposes of this problem only, assume that in the month of February, Tom's Wear engaged in the following transactions:

February, 1, 2001	Tom's Wear received an additional $2,000 from Tom, the owner.
February, 3, 2001	Tom's Wear bought 300 shirts for $4 each. He paid cash for the purchase.
February 5, 2001	Tom's Wear sold 100 shirts for $10 each.
February 25, 2001	Tom's Wear paid his $30 telephone bill for February telephone service.
February 28, 2001	Tom's Wear purchased a piece of equipment on credit for $600.

Requirements

1. **Open a new Excel work sheet.**
2. **Create the following bold column headings beginning in cell A1 and ending in column J: Date, Description, Cash +, Other Assets = (*two-column heading*), Liabilities + (*two-column heading*), Contributed Capital +, Retained Earnings (*two-column heading*). Adjust the column widths as needed.**

   Hints: The easiest way to resize your column widths is by holding down your left mouse button and dragging when you see the arrow, depicted as follows:

   Drag to resize

	A	B	C
1			
2			
3			

   You may also resize columns by double-clicking your left mouse button when you see the arrow previously depicted. Double-clicking will automatically resize your column based on the longest line.

   Highlight both cells and click the Merge and Center button to center your two-column headings across both columns. Highlight all your headings and click the Center button to center all column headings.

3. **Underline your heading by selecting Format, Cells, and Border.**

4. Input the transactions given previously. Format your numbers by selecting Format, Cells, and Number. Highlight the cells to be formatted and use the currency format as shown:

5. Print your file and save it to disk by clicking the Save button. Name your file TomsWear1.

Answers to Study Break Questions

1. All businesses have the same goal: to add value or provide value to customers/ clients. Typically, they have three processes: acquiring goods (acquisition/payment), conversion (adding value), and selling the goods or services (sales/collection).
2. The different forms of ownership are (1) sole proprietorships, (2) partnerships, and (3) corporations.

1. Resources, events, and agents are the three components.
2. A purchase requisition is a form on which a request to purchase something is recorded. It is used to document all requests for goods and services.

1. Revenues are the monetary amounts earned by a company by selling goods or providing services. Expenses are the costs incurred to generate revenues.
2. Accounts receivable are the amounts that customers owe a company for goods and services provided but not yet paid for.

1. Contributed capital (also called paid-in capital) and retained earnings are the two parts.
2. It's a *business* year, which may or may not correspond to a calendar year. The word *fiscal* relates to monetary issues (e.g., fiscal policy).

1. *Gross profit* is the difference between *sales* and *cost of goods sold* (i.e., *sales* minus *cost of goods sold*). It's also known as *gross margin*.
2. A single-step income statement presents all revenues first and then deducts all expenses. A multistep income statement starts with *sales* and subtracts the *cost of goods sold*, giving the subtotal, *gross margin*. Then, other revenue and other expenses are itemized.

Questions

1. What is the purpose of a business?
2. Is the goal of all business organizations to make a profit?
3. Name the two main processes that make up most business activities.
4. What are the possible ownership structures for a business?
5. What are the advantages of the corporate form of ownership?
6. What are the disadvantages of the corporate form of ownership?
7. Who are some of the people in need of business information and for what purposes?
8. What is the relationship between the information available to a business and the information provided in financial statements?
9. What are the basic financial statements? Describe the information that each provides.
10. What makes the income statement different from the statement of cash flows?

Short Exercises

SE1-1 For each of the following transactions, identify whether it is better described as part of the acquisition/payment process or the sales/collection process.

L.O. 1-1, 2

a. Merchandise is purchased for resale.
b. Customers buy merchandise on credit.
c. A bank loan is obtained.
d. A check is sent to vendor for previous purchase.
e. Customer sends payment for previous purchase.

L.O. 1-4

SE1-2 Classify the accounts listed below (1 to 7) under the balance sheet headings of:

   a. Assets
   b. Liabilities
   c. Equity

[Use Lands' End's balance sheet to help you with this exercise.]

   1. ____Cash
   2. ____Contributions from owners
   3. ____Inventory
   4. ____Land and buildings
   5. ____Prepaid advertising
   6. ____Accounts payable
   7. ____Retained earnings

L.O. 1-4

SE1-3 Donkey Doughnut Company shows $125,000 worth of assets on its December 31, 2001 balance sheet. If the company's total liabilities are $35,750, what is the amount of owners' equity?

L.O. 1-4

SE1-4 Given the following items and amounts on a company's December 31, 2002 balance sheet, how much cash did the company have on hand on December 31, 2002?

Cash	??
Inventory	$100
Equipment	$500
Liabilities	$450
Owner's equity	$650

L.O. 1-4

SE1-5 Given the following items on a company's December 31, 2003 balance sheet, how much did the company owe its creditors on December 31, 2003?

Cash	$ 1,625	Liabilities	???
Inventory	223		
Equipment	10,647	Contributed capital	$9,300
Other assets	8,235	Retained earnings	5,000
Total	$20,730		

L.O. 1-4

SE1-6 For each of the following, calculate the missing amount:

   a. Revenues $560; Expenses $350; Net Income = _210_
   b. Net Income $500; Expenses $475; Revenues = _975_
   c. Expenses $600; Revenues $940; Net Income = _340_
   d. Revenues $1,240; Net Income $670; Expenses = _570_
   e. Net Income $6,450; Expenses $2,500; Revenues = _8950_

L.O. 1-4

SE1-7 Logan Enterprises has $50,000 in cash, $10,000 in prepaid rent, $20,000 balance due to creditors, and $15,000 balance due from customers. What is the amount of owner's equity?

L.O. 1-4

SE1-8 Given the amounts for the balance sheet on December 31, 2002, how much owner's equity did Greg's Bookstore have on December 31, 2002?

Cash	$200
Inventory	$600
Marketable securities	$300
Accounts payable	$100
Notes payable	$ 50
Salaries payable	$100
Owner's equity	????

SE1-9 After 1 year of business, Mike's Watch Repair, Inc. had $5,000 in assets, $3,000 in liabilities, and $1,500 in contributed capital. What is the amount of retained earnings at the end of the corporation's first year of business?

L.O. 1-4

SE1-10 Rex's Camera Store had a retained earnings balance of $1,000 on Decmber 31, 2001. For year 2002, sales were $10,500 and expenses were $6,500. Cash dividends of $2,500 were distributed on December 31, 2002. What was the amount of retained earnings on December 31, 2002?

L.O. 1-4

Exercises

E1-1 Identify the transactions from the following story. For each, identify the *give* and *get* portion of each. Who would be interested in this information?

L.O. 1-1, 2, 3

Tyrone Smith decided to go into business for himself. As a talented computer programmer, he decided to open a small consulting firm with $10,000 of his own money. The company bought a state-of-the-art desktop computer, complete with the accessories and software needed to get the business off the ground, at a total cost of $6,000. The business required a separate phone line put in his house, which cost $350. Then, Tyrone's company hired an Internet company to design and maintain a Web page for the business at a cost of $250 for the design and $45 per month for maintenance. After placing an advertisement in the business section of the local newspaper, at a cost of $50 per month, Tyrone's business was ready to go.

E1-2 Sue King opened a shoe store called "Sue's Shoes" with $10,000 of personal savings and $5,000 from the bank. The company bought $7,000 of shoes from an Italian manufacturer. The rent expense is $450 monthly. Sue's customers liked the shoes, too, as evidenced by the first month's sales. Sue's Shoes sold shoes that cost $4,000 to customers for $6,000. All the transactions were cash. Identify these get/give transactions and determine if there is an increase or decrease to assets, liabilities, or owner's equity.

L.O. 1-1, 2

Use the following format:

Get	Give	Assets	Liabilities	Owner's equity
e.g., cash	Ownership	+$10,000		+$10,000

E1-3 Use the balance sheet for Doggie Dog Company at December 31, 2000 to answer the following questions:

L.O. 1-3, 4

Assets		Liabilities and Owner's Equity	
Cash	$ 3,000	Accounts payable	$ 1,500
Inventory		Notes payable (van)	12,500
Dog bones	30		
Leashes	465	Capital, Kit T. Kat	6,020
Dog collars	725		
Dog food	500		
Mobile grooming van (net)	15,000		
Prepaid insurance	300		
	$20,020		$20,020

1. What assets did the company have on December 31, 2000? List them.
2. Who had claim to these assets?
3. Is this company a sole proprietorship, a partnership, or a corporation? How can you tell?
4. Who are the potential users of this financial information?

L.O. 1-4

E1-4 Given the following transactions, calculate the (1) amount of assets owned by the Charlie's Hot Dogs at the end of his first month of business, and (2) the amount of net income for the month. All these transactions took place during the first month of business. Charlie had his hot dog stand open for 20 days during the first month of business.

a. Charlie's Hot Dogs was started with a contribution from Charlie of $2,000 and a loan of $1,000 from the bank.
b. Charlie's Hot Dogs purchased $800 worth of hot dogs and buns (his inventory) for cash.
c. Charlie's Hot Dogs hired a friend with a steamer to cook the hot dogs and deliver a portion of them ready to sell to him at noon each day. For this service, Charlie's Hot Dogs paid $20 each day.
d. Charlie's Hot Dogs sold three-fourths of his hot dog and bun inventory for total cash revenues of $1,600.
e. Charlie's Hot Dogs paid the city a $25 fee, due monthly, for his license.
f. Charlie's Hot Dogs repaid $200 of the bank loan along with $10 of interest for the first month.

L.O. 1-2

E1-5 For transactions (b), (c), (d), and (e) in E1-4, what are the resources, events, and agents involved in the give portion of the transaction and what are the resources, events, and agents involved in the get portion of the transaction? Put them in an REA diagram like the one in Exhibit 1–6 that describes the transaction.

L.O. 1-2

E1-6 For each of the transactions in E1-4, tell whether it is best categorized as part of the acquisition/payment process or part of the sales/collection process.

L.O. 1-4

E1-7 For each of the transactions given next, tell whether it (1) increases, (2) decreases, or (3) has no effect on owners' equity. Consider both owners' equity components—contributed capital and retained earnings.

a. Two friends get together, each contributing $5,000 to start the Piglet Corporation.
b. Piglet purchases equipment for $1,000 cash.
c. Piglet purchases $6,000 worth of merchandise inventory for cash.
d. Piglet pays rent of $2,000 in advance for store space in a small shopping mall.
e. Piglet makes cash sales to customers of $4,500.
f. Piglet pays employees $300 for hours worked.
g. Piglet declares and distributes $500 dividends to each of its owners.

L.O. 1-4

E1-8 Assume each transaction below is a cash transaction. Tell how each cash flow would be classified for the statement of cash flows: (1) operating, (2) investing, or (3) financing.

a. Dedee makes a contribution of $100,000 to start the Pony D Riding Stables from her personal funds.
b. The company purchases three horses and various equipment for $35,000 in cash.
c. The company purchases $6,000 worth of advertising time on the local radio for cash.
d. The company pays rent of $10,000 for barn and pasture space as well as use of 50 acres of land for riding trails.
e. The company hires several people to clean stables at a cost of $500 for the month.
f. The first customers pay Pony D Riding Stables $3,000 for 6-months worth of riding lessons.

L.O. 1-2

E1-9 Determine if the following would be classified as part of the acquisition/payment process or the sales/collection process of Dog E. Dog Company.

a. Dog E. Dog purchases stock in Kit E. Kat Company.
b. Dog E. Dog issues checks for the salaries of its employees.
c. Dog E. Dog sells stock holdings of Kit E. Kat for a gain.
d. Land held by Dog E. Dog for investment purposes is sold.
e. Dog E. Dog obtains a trademark for the "Doggie Boomerang," its new product.

E1-10   Identify an increase or decrease to assets, liabilities, owner's equity, revenues, or expenses for the following transactions of Blue Box Corp.:

L.O. 1-4

a. Blue Box earned $10,000 in sales revenues.
b. The firm paid $3,000 cash for supplies.
c. Blue Box paid $2,500 of a $5,000 notes payable to creditors.
d. The company paid $1,500 for rent expense.
e. The company's owner provided $8,000 in additional financing.
f. The firm distributed $2,000 in dividends.
g. Blue Box provided $3,000 of cash loan to another company.

Use the following format:

Item	Assets	Liabilities	Owner's equity	Revenues	Expenses
a	+		+	+	

E1-11   For each of the following transactions, determine if there is an increase, decrease, or no change in net income for Fun Movie Productions, Inc.

L.O. 1-4

a. Fun Movie earned $10,000 in monthly sales.
b. The firm recorded a decrease in inventory of $6,000 due to the monthly sales.
c. Monthly rent of $1,500 was paid.
d. Employees were paid $2,500 for work done.
e. The company purchased land for $7,500.
f. Fun Movie invested $4,000 in another company.
g. The firm paid $1,000 in cash dividends.

E1-12   Complete the following amounts—X, Y, and Z—on the balance sheet (retained earnings on 1/1/01 is 0):

L.O. 1-4

	Dec. 31 2001	Dec. 31 2002
Assets	$1,000	$2,500
Liabilities	X	$1,000
Contributed capital	$ 300	$ 300
Retained earnings	$ 200	Z
Revenue	$ 300	$2,500
Expenses	Y	$1,500

Problems—Set A

P1-1A   Use Lands' End's financial statements in Exhibits 1-2 and 1-3 to answer the following questions. For each, tell where you found the information to answer the question. Use the most recent year given for your answers.

L.O. 1-3, 4

Required:

a. What is Lands' End's form of ownership?
b. What date marks the end of Lands' End's most recent fiscal year?
c. Did Lands' End earn a net income or net loss during the year?
d. Did the owners of Lands' End make any capital contributions during the year?
e. Did Lands' End buy or sell any major equipment during the year?
f. On the last day of the fiscal year, did Lands' End have any debts? If so, what was the total amount?

L.O. 1-4

P1-2A   A set of financial statements for Seminole Company follows.

Seminole Company
Income Statement
For the Year Ended 12/31/02

Sales	$600,000
Cost of goods sold	?
Gross profit on sales	375,000
Administrative expenses	54,000
Operating income	?
Interest expense	6,000
Earnings before income taxes	?
Income taxes (tax rate = 30%)	?
Net income	?

Seminole Company
Balance Sheet
At 12/31/02

Cash	$?	Accounts payable	$ 13,350
Accounts receivable	13,024	Notes payable	9,830
Inventory	43,271		
Equipment	972,684	Contributed capital	605,000
		Retained earnings	?
Total	$1,129,780	Total	?

Required: Fill in the missing amounts (indicated with question marks):

L.O. 1-3, 4

P1-3A   The following transactions apply to Tiger Tire Service Company during May 2002.

1. The owner started the business by depositing $4,000 in a business checking account on May 1.
2. The company provided services to clients and received $3,000 in cash.
3. The company borrowed $1,200 from the bank for the business.
4. The company paid $1,000 of salary expense.
5. A distribution of $1,500 was made to the owner.

Required:

a. What are the total assets of the Tiger Tire at the end of May 2002?
b. Prepare a statement of cash flows for May 2002.
c. What was net income for May?
d. Who might find the information on the Tiger Tire financial statements useful?

L.O. 1-4

P1-4A   The following events are for Wolverine Company for the year 2003, the first year of operations.

1. Mitch contributed $15,000 to start the business.
2. Creditors loaned Wolverine Company $7,000.
3. Wolverine Company provided services to its customers and received $32,000.
4. Wolverine Company paid expenses amounting to $18,000.
5. Wolverine Company purchased land for $9,000.

Required: Show the effects of these preceding transactions on the accounting equation. Then, prepare the four major financial statements for 2003.

L.O. 1-3, 4

P1-5A   What will be the effects (increase, decrease, or no effect) on total assets, total liabilities, and total stockholders' equity in each of the following situations? When stockholders' equity changes, note whether it is *contributed capital* or *retained earnings* that changes.

	Total assets	=	Total liabilities	+	Stockholders' equity	
					Contributed capital	Retained earnings
1. Received cash and issued shares of common stock.	_____		_____		_____	_____
2. Purchased equipment on credit.	_____		_____		_____	_____
3. Received cash from customers for services rendered.	_____		_____		_____	_____
4. Billed customers for services rendered on credit.	_____		_____		_____	_____
5. Received a utility bill but not yet paid.	_____		_____		_____	_____
6. Received cash from the customers in 4.	_____		_____		_____	_____
7. Paid the utility bill received in 5.	_____		_____		_____	_____

P1-6A   You decide to sell T-shirts at a football game during December 2003 at the Citrus Bowl to make some extra money. You engage in the following transactions:

L.O. 1-2, 4

- You (and a couple of family members) invest $3,000 and receive stock in your new company, Citrus Bowl T-Shirts, Inc.
- You pay the rent for space during the 2003 Citrus Bowl, cash of $300.
- You buy 1,000 T-shirts for $6 each, paying $1,500 cash. You'll pay the rest after the football game.
- You sell 1,000 T-shirts for $11 each, all for cash.
- Because you are so successful, you decide to prepay next year's rent (for the 2004 Citrus Bowl), to be sure of getting a good location. The amount you pay is $325.
- You rush to your friend who is taking introductory financial accounting to find out where you stand financially.

Required: Prepare the income statement, the statement of changes in shareholders' equity, and the statement of cash flows for December 2003. Prepare the balance sheet at December 31, 2003.

P1-7A   Given the following information for Pete's Pet Shop:

L.O. 1-4

1. Retained earnings on January 1, 2001 were $100,000.
2. In January, revenues were $50,000 and expenses were $60,000.
3. In February, revenues were $70,000 and expenses were $65,000.
4. In March, revenues were $90,000 and expenses were $55,000.
5. The only dividends paid were in March for $3,000.

Required: Prepare the retained earnings portion of the statement of changes in shareholders' equity for the three months ended March 31, 2001, for Pete's Pet Shop.

P1-8A   Joe is thinking about starting a new fitness club opening on 1/1/2002. Joe estimates he could sell 300 annual memberships for $400 each. He can get gym equipment for $12,000 and would need to hire an employee for $100 per week. Because Joe already

L.O. 1-2, 3, 4

gets free rent for a building where the gym would be, he only has to pay the utilities of $100 per month. He would use his cash savings of $15,000 and obtain a loan from the bank for $50,000. The interest rate would be 10%. Regardless of the amount of net income, he would pay $2,000 of dividends the first year.

Required: Create a projected (*pro forma*) income statement, balance sheet, statement of retained earnings, and statement of cash flows for the first year of Joe's Fitness Club (assume all transactions are cash). Who would be interested in Joe's *pro forma* financial statements?

Problems—Set B

L.O. 1-3, 4

P1-1B Use Lands' End's financial statements (Exhibits 1-2 and 1-3) to answer the following questions. For each, tell where you found the information to answer the question. Use the most recent year given for your answers.

Required:

a. What term does Lands' End use for *owner's equity*?
b. Which financial statement shows revenues and expenses?
c. Which financial statement shows assets and liabilities?
d. Did Lands' End *buy* more or *sell* more inventory during the year?
e. In which of the 2 years shown did Lands' End make the most income?
f. What happened to current liabilities during the year? What does this change mean?
g. What are Lands' End's total liabilities on January 28, 2000?

L.O. 1-4

P1-2B A set of financial statements for Shelby's Music, Inc. follows.

Shelby's Music, Inc.
Income Statement
For the Year Ended December 31, 2005

Sales	$1
Cost of goods sold	375,000
Gross profit on sales	525,000
Administrative expenses	2
Operating income	419,000
Interest expense	3
Earnings before income taxes	407,000
Income taxes (tax rate = 35%)	4
Net income	$5

Shelby's Music, Inc.
Balance Sheet
At December 31, 2005

Cash	$158,592	Accounts payable	$ 14,070
Accounts receivable	18,621	Notes payable	12,520
Inventory	2		
Equipment	895,895	Contributed capital	3
		Retained earnings	425,000
Total	$1	Total	$1,231,000

Required: Fill in the missing amounts.

L.O. 1-3, 4

P1-3B The following transactions apply to Satine's Sewing Service during April 2001.

1. Satine (the owner) started her own business by depositing $6,500 in a business checking account on April 1.

2. Satine and her assistant Nadine sewed choir robes for a local church choir and received $4,000 cash.
3. Satine's Sewing Service paid Nadine $1,500 for April's salary.
4. Satine's Sewing Service borrowed $1,600 from the local bank.
5. Satine's Sewing Service made a distribution of $2,500 to Satine.

Required:

a. What are the total assets of the Satine's Sewing Service at the end of April 2001?
b. Prepare a statement of cash flows for April 2001.
c. What was net income for April?
d. Who might be interested in this information and why?

P1-4B The following events are for Sandra's Sandblasting Company for the year 2006, the first year of operations.

L.O. 1-4

1. Sandra invested $24,000 in the business.
2. Sandra's Sandblasting Company purchased sandblasting equipment for cash of $21,000.
3. Sandra's Sandblasting Company provided sandblasting services to the local community college and received $53,000.
4. Sandra's Sandblasting Company paid expenses amounting to $25,000.
5. Victory National Bank loaned Sandra's Sandblasting Company $18,000.

Required: Show the effects of the preceding transactions on the accounting equation. Then, prepare the four major financial statements for 2006.

P1-5B What will be the effects (increase, decrease, or no effect) on total assets, total liabilities, and total stockholders' equity in each of the following situations? When stockholders' equity changes, note whether it is *contributed capital* or *retained earnings* that changes.

L.O. 1-3, 4

	Total assets	=	Total liabilities	+	Stockholders' equity	
					Contributed capital	Retained earnings
1. Purchased land on credit.	_____		_____		_____	_____
2. Received cash from customers for services performed.	_____		_____		_____	_____
3. Received cash and issued shares of common stock.	_____		_____		_____	_____
4. Received the insurance bill but not yet paid.	_____		_____		_____	_____
5. Billed customers for services performed on credit.	_____		_____		_____	_____
6. Purchased equipment on credit.	_____		_____		_____	_____
7. Received cash from the customers billed in 5.	_____		_____		_____	_____
8. Paid the insurance bill received in 4.	_____		_____		_____	_____
9. Purchased a building with cash.	_____		_____		_____	_____

L.O. 1-2, 4

P1-6B In August 2001, you decide to sell bonsai trees at a kiosk in Rendezvous Mall to make some extra money. You (and a couple of family members) invest cash and receive stock in your new company. You decide to incorporate your new business. The company engages in the following transactions:

- The company receives $4,800 in cash contributions from you and your family.
- The company pays the rent of $750 for the kiosk to sell the bonsai trees at the mall.
- The company buys 1,500 bonsai trees for $7 each, paying $3,000 cash. The company will pay the rest at the beginning of September.
- During August the company sells 1,500 bonsai trees for $20 each, all for cash.
- Because the business is so successful, the company prepays next month's rent, to be sure of keeping the same kiosk in the mall. The amount is $755.
- You rush to your friend who is taking accounting to find out where you stand financially.

Required: Prepare the four basic financial statements based on the preceding six transactions.

L.O. 1-4

P1-7B Given the following information for Pete's Pet Shop:

1. Retained earnings on April 1, 2001 were $127,000.
2. In April, revenues were $85,000 and expenses were $72,000.
3. In May, revenues were $16,582 and expenses were $37,000.
4. In June, revenues were $82,000 and expenses were $18,582.
5. Dividends were paid in April for $8,000 and in June for $19,500.

Required: Prepare the retained earnings portion of the statement of changes in shareholders' equity as of June 30, 2001 for Pete's Pet Shop.

L.O. 1-2, 3, 4

P1-8B Sunny Susan has decided to open a new tanning salon on July 01, 2004. Sunny Susan estimates she could sell 425 memberships (1 year) for $480 each if she had super tanning beds. She gets a special deal on 10 Wolfe Super Tanning Beds for only $5,000 each. She hires her brother Gloomy Glen to wash the towels and clean the beds for $150 per week. Because Sunny Susan's grandmother gave her a free remodeled storefront downtown, her rent is free, and she only has to pay the utilities of $125 per month. She invests her cash savings of $27,500 and obtains a loan from the Grover Hills National Bank for $47,000. Regardless of the amount of net income, she has decided to pay $1,750 in dividends the first year.

Required:

1. Create a projected (*pro forma*) income statement, balance sheet, statement of retained earnings and statement of cash flows for the first year of the Sunny Susan Tanning Salon. Assume all amounts are cash.
2. Who would be interested in these financial statements?

Issues for Discussion

Financial statement analysis

1. Use the annual report from Pier 1 Imports, Inc. to answer these questions:
   a. What type of business is Pier 1 and how is it organized?
   b. Suppose you inherited $10,000 when your great-uncle passed away and you want to invest in a promising company. Would you invest in Pier 1? What information in the annual report would be useful in your decision? Be specific. What information *not* given in the annual report would you want to have?
   c. What is your opinion of the information in the annual report? For example, do you think it is accurate? Useful? Interesting? Informative? Why or why not?

Business risk

2. What kinds of risks does Pier 1 face? Use the information in the annual report and your own experience to answer this question.

Ethics

3. Ken Jones wants to start a small business and has asked his uncle to loan him $10,000. He has prepared a business plan and some financial statements that indicate the business could be very profitable. Ken is afraid his uncle will want some ownership in the company for his investment, but Ken doesn't want to share what he believes will be a hugely successful company. What are the ethical issues Ken must face as he prepares to present his business plan to his uncle? Do you think he should try to emphasize the *risks* of ownership to his uncle to convince him it would be preferable to be a creditor? Why or why not?

Internet Exercise: Disney Corporation

The Walt Disney Company is a diversified worldwide entertainment company with interests in ABC TV, ESPN, film production, theme parks, publishing, a cruise line, Infoseek, and the NHL Mighty Ducks. By using the Disney Web site you can explore vacation options and get Disney's latest financial information.

Please go to the www.prenhall.com/reimers *Web site. Go to Chapter 1 and use the Internet Exercise company link.*

IE1-1 What is the Walt Disney Company key objective?

IE1-2 Go to *Financials* and click on the most recent annual report.

a. What are the *key businesses* of the Walt Disney Company? Identify whether you think the primary business activity is manufacturing, merchandising, or service for each key business segment.
b. Go to *Financial Highlights*. Identify the amount of total revenues, operating income, and stockholders' equity for the most recent year. On which financial statement will you find each amount reported? Is the Walt Disney Company a proprietorship, a partnership, or a corporation? How can you tell?
c. Go to *Financial Review*. What key business segment earns the greatest proportion of revenues? Identify the proportion of revenues earned by each key business segment, listing them in the order of greatest proportion to least proportion. Does this order surprise you? Explain why or why not?

Please note: Internet Web sites are constantly being updated. Therefore, if the information is not found where indicated, please explore the annual report further to find the information.

QUALITIES OF ACCOUNTING INFORMATION

Financial Reporting and Business Events

Here's where you've been...

In Chapter 1, you learned that a business adds value to make a profit. The acquisition/payment process describes how a business gets the resources it needs and pays for them; and the sales/collection process describes how a business sells its service or product and collects the revenue.

The four basic financial statements—the income statement, the statement of changes in shareholder's equity, the balance sheet, and the statement of cash flows—provide information about these business processes.

Here's where you're going...

When you are finished with Chapter 2, you should understand the qualities of the information contained in the financial statements. You should be able to recognize and explain the difference between accrual basis accounting and cash basis accounting.

Financial Reporting and Business Events

2

Financing

Property, Plant, and Equipment

Sales and Accounts Receivable

Inventory and Liabilities

Financial Reporting and Business Events

Learning Objectives

More specifically, when you are finished studying this chapter, you should be able to answer these questions:

1. What are generally accepted accounting principles and why are they necessary?
2. What is the objective of financial reporting? What qualities are necessary to achieve this objective?
3. What are the elements of the financial statements and what are their characteristics?
4. What is accrual accounting and how does it differ from cash basis accounting?

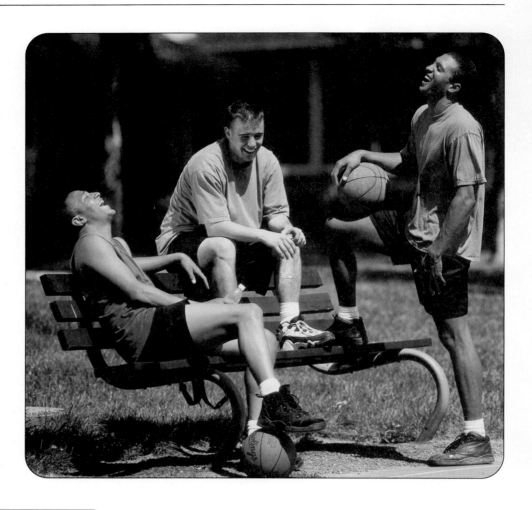

Information for Decision Making

After Tom sold his first batch of T-shirts, he had some decisions to make. The biggest one was whether or not to continue in business. What he needed to know to begin evaluating that decision is—did he make a profit? Profit is the amount left after all expenses of doing business are deducted from all revenues, for a specific period.

For Tom's Wear, this period is his first month of doing business, January 1 through January 31. Information about the month's operations is summarized on the income statement—one of the four basic financial statements. The revenues for the period amounted to $900; that is the total amount the company earned when it sold the 90 shirts. The expenses were the cost of the T-shirts sold, the cost of the advertising, and the interest paid on the loan from Tom's mom. The cost of the 90 T-shirts sold was $360, advertising expense was $50, and the cost of borrowing the money—interest expense—was $5. When those expenses, totaling $415, are deducted from the sales revenue of $900, the remaining $485 is profit. Tom's Wear added value by ordering shirts with the special logo and providing them to Tom's friends at a convenient time and place. And Tom's Wear achieved its goal—to make a profit.

On the income statement in Exhibit 2-1, you will see $485 shown as net income, which is just another name for profit. The term *profit* can be applied to a single sale, a group of sales, or all the transactions for a period of time of business activity, whereas *net income* is a more specific term for describing a company's entire profit for a specific time period. The company made a profit of $540 on the sale, and Tom's Wear's net income for his first month of business activity was $485.

Exhibit 2-1
Income Statement for Tom's Wear

tom's wear

Tom's Wear, Inc.
Income Statement
For the Month Ended January 31, 2001

Revenue		
Sales		$900
Expenses		
Cost of sales	$360	
Advertising expense	50	
Interest expense	5	
Total expenses		415
Net income		$485

Financial reporting provides information for decision making. An income statement, like the one shown for Tom's Wear, is one source of information. When the second month of business activity is complete, Tom will prepare another income statement and will compare the two statements. To make such a comparison meaningful, Tom needs to use the same rules for preparing the two statements. If Tom wanted to compare his company's performance to the performance of another T-shirt company, he would need to be sure that the other company was using the same rules to prepare its income statement. For financial information to be useful for evaluating the performance of a business across time or for comparing two different companies, the same rules must be used consistently.

To enforce this consistency, there is a set of rules called **generally accepted accounting principles (GAAP)** that a company must follow when preparing its financial statements. These rules—usually known as accounting principles—were historically developed through common usage. A principle was acceptable if it was used and acknowledged by most accountants. This is what *generally accepted* means.

As all businesses and their activities became more complex, the need for more consistency became clear. Inconsistent and misleading accounting practices used during the early 1900s were partially responsible for the stock market crash of 1929. In response to the accounting problems uncovered, Congress established the Securities and Exchange Commission (SEC) as the authority for setting accounting rules for publicly traded companies. The SEC, in turn, has allowed accounting professionals to form committees and boards to establish generally accepted accounting principles.

Currently, the **Financial Accounting Standards Board (FASB)** establishes the rules for a company to use in preparing its financial statements. The FASB is a not-for-profit organization made up of professional accountants and business people, as well as a large staff of technical assistants. The terms used to describe the accounting rules include *principles, standards,* and, in the past, even *opinions.* All the different expressions to describe the rules in summation are represented by the words *generally accepted accounting principles (GAAP).*

Generally accepted accounting principles (GAAP) are the rules set by the accounting profession for preparing financial statements.

The **Financial Accounting Standards Board (FASB)** is the current standards-setting body.

Statements of Financial Accounting Concepts

Over the years, as businesses have continued to grow more complex, the number of accounting rules has increased. In the late 1970s, the FASB members decided some specific guidance was needed to help establish new rules. Until

L.O. 1

Define generally accepted accounting principles and understand why they are necessary.

then, there were no written goals or guidelines to help them formulate accounting standards. Although the FASB had been setting accounting principles for years, there was no underlying framework on which to rely when creating and evaluating new principles. There were already hundreds of existing accounting rules in 1978, when the FASB began a series of *statements*—the name the FASB gave to its new guidelines—to provide a framework for establishing accounting principles. The new set of statements, Statements of Financial Accounting Concepts (SFAC) defines and describes the kind of information financial reporting should include.

Objectives of Accounting Information

L.O. 2

Explain the objectives of financial reporting.

The first SFAC defines the objectives of financial reporting. We've already discussed the most general and the most important objective of financial reporting—to provide *useful information* for making decisions. Exactly what constitutes useful information? *How much information* is needed to be useful? As you might suspect, there are limits. SFAC 1 makes four points related to the limits of financial information.

■ The information represented in a financial statement is specific to a business enterprise. Financial reporting does not provide industry-wide or economy-wide information. The information in a financial statement relates to a specific business or company. The owner's personal financial records are not part of the financial records and financial statements of a business. This is called the **separate-entity assumption.**

The **separate-entity assumption** means that a company and its owners keep separate financial records.

■ The information is simplified, summarized, and condensed. There are two reasons for this:
   a. Reporting all transactions in detail would be overwhelming, providing more information than would be useful.
   b. Some of the details of a company's transactions are proprietary—a company wants to keep them secret.

   You should come to realize that many of the measurements in financial statements are approximate. You may see a number and think of it as exact, whereas it is really an estimate of the amount it represents. That's because accountants make many decisions and judgment calls when they are gathering and condensing information for the financial statements.

A **cost-benefit analysis** is an evaluation of a decision or course of action consisting of comparing all the costs of an action with all the benefits. If the benefits of a course of action exceed the costs, then we would select that course of action.

■ There is a cost to providing information. We have to weigh the costs of providing information with the benefits that can be derived from it. **Cost-benefit analysis**—an economic concept that says we must always stack up the *costs* of doing something against its *benefits*—is used to decide what financial information a company should include in its financial statements.

■ The focus of financial reporting is earnings and its components. The income statement gives detailed information about earnings. The other financial statements provide additional information about how the company achieved its earnings.

STUDY BREAK 2-1
SEE HOW YOU'RE DOING

1. What is the purpose of financial statements?
2. Who sets accounting rules?
3. What is the focus of financial reporting?

Qualitative Characteristics of Accounting Information

Accounting information should be useful for evaluating the past and predicting the future. *Usefulness* is the most important characteristic of accounting information. What makes information useful depends, like anything else, on how well it does what it's supposed to do. The Statements of Financial Accounting Concepts define *useful* information as *relevant* and *reliable*. Great! Now we have to determine what relevant and reliable mean. For information to be relevant, it needs to be fresh, not so stale that we can't use it to do what we need to do. We should be able to use the information to evaluate a firm's past performance, to predict where it is going, or both. Reliable means that you can verify the truthfulness of the information. According to the FASB, the information must have "representational faithfulness," meaning it is accurate and truthful.

Two more characteristics of useful information are *comparability* and *consistency*. Users of the basic financial statements often want to compare information in one period with the same sort of information in a financial statement for another period. For example, how does the net income for one year compare to the net income for another year? They may want to compare corresponding financial information between two companies—how one company's net income compares with another company's net income. In putting together the financial statements, we must be sure that they allow meaningful comparisons—comparisons across companies, across financial statements, or between individual items on a single financial statement. How does the amount of cash on hand compare to the amount of money customers still owe the company? Consistency is the characteristic that makes comparability possible. Only if we measure financial concepts, for example, *net income,* the same way from period to period are we able to make meaningful comparisons. For example, if we have decided that distributions to owners are not to be included on the income statement as an expense—a rule in GAAP—then we must be sure to exclude them from every income statement. If we changed the rules in the middle of a basketball game, the score from one half wouldn't mean much when compared with the score from the other half. In accounting, keeping the rules the same from period to period makes the information consistent and thus comparable.

Now we come to **materiality,** a very specific term in accounting, addressing whether or not an item or transaction is large enough to have an influence on decisions. If an item that is generally required to be included in a specific place on the financial statements is so small that it is insignificant compared with the amount of either the rest of the transactions or the amount of the company's assets, it may be considered *not material* (immaterial) and included

L.O. 2

Explain the qualities of accounting information that enable financial reporting to meet its objective of providing useful information to users.

Materiality in accounting refers to the significance of an amount or item on the financial statements. An amount is considered *material* if it would affect someone's interpretation or decision.

Exhibit 2-2 Characteristics of Accounting Information

elsewhere. For example, if a company buys a $5 wastebasket and the rest of the company's assets are pieces of equipment that cost over $1,000 each, the balance sheet may omit the $5 wastebasket from the list of assets. The $5 would be counted as an expense for the period instead. In this example, the benefit of treating the wastebasket as an asset and writing it off (i.e., expensing it) over its useful life is smaller than the bookkeeping costs associated with recording it as an asset. There is a lot of judgment in deciding what is material for the financial statements. Materiality is hard to explain because accountants don't agree on exactly how to apply the idea in practice. It's a controversial issue in accounting. All items that are generally required and are considered *material* must be included in the financial statements as the accounting standards direct.

Elements of the Financial Statements

Define a complete set of financial statements and explain the elements contained in those statements.

A complete set of financial statements includes:

- income statement
- balance sheet (sometimes called the statement of financial position)
- statement of changes in shareholders' equity (also called the statement of changes in *owner's* equity)
- statement of cash flows
- notes to the financial statements

The Statements of Financial Accounting Concepts describe the individual items that are included in the financial statements. To learn what is shown on each financial statement, we'll look at the second month of business for Tom's Wear. We'll take each of the second month's transactions and see how it affects the accounting equation and the financial statements. Then, we'll relate the statements to the items described in the Statements of Financial Accounting Concepts.

As we begin the second month on February 1, 2001, Tom's Wear has a balance sheet that is identical to the balance sheet dated January 31, 2001. Recall that the company's assets, liabilities, and equity balances roll forward when the new period starts.

Transactions for the Second Month of Business

February 1	Tom's Wear purchases 200 T-shirts at $4 each. They are purchased on credit.
February 5	Tom hires a company to advertise his business. The total cost is $150. Tom pays $100 cash at the time of the service and will pay the remaining $50 later.
February 14	Tom decides to get insurance for his business. On February 14, Tom's Wear pays $150 for 3 months of insurance, with coverage beginning on the date of payment.
February 23	Tom's Wear sells 185 T-shirts for $10 each. 170 of these were sold for cash and the remaining 15 were sold on credit.
February 28	Tom's Wear declares and pays a dividend of $100.

The transactions for Tom's second month of business are shown in Exhibit 2-3. The first transaction in February is the purchase of 200 T-shirts, costing $4 each. Last month, Tom's Wear paid cash for the purchase of the T-shirts. This month, the company buys them on credit, also known as **on account.** This means Tom's Wear will pay for them later. The purchase increases the company's assets—$800 worth of T-shirts—and the $800 claim belongs to the vendor. When a company owes a vendor, what is owed is called **accounts payable.** This is the first transaction shown in Exhibit 2-3, where the transactions are presented in a work sheet based on the accounting equation.

Next, Tom hires a company to advertise his business. This cost is $150 for a service. Tom's Wear pays $100 when the service is provided, so the company still owes $50. Like the first transaction, this one also postpones payment. However, in this transaction, Tom's Wear has incurred an expense. In the first transaction—when the inventory was purchased—Tom's Wear gained an asset. The cost of the shirts will become an expense when the shirts are sold. In contrast, the work done related to the advertising is complete, and that signals an expense. (The timing of recognizing expenses can be tricky; the next chapter will discuss timing in detail.) The $150 expense, like all expenses, reduces the owner's claims to the assets of the firm. Assets decrease by $100, the cash paid for the advertising; and the remaining $50 increases creditors' claims—liabilities—because it will be paid later. This is the second transaction shown in Exhibit 2-3.

As his business grows, Tom decides his company needs some insurance. Tom's Wear pays $150 for 3-months worth of coverage, beginning February 14. When a company pays for something in advance, the item purchased is something of future value to the company. Because such an item provides future value, it is classified as an asset. Items purchased in advance may seem like unusual assets, and often have the word *prepaid* with them to provide information about what sort of assets they are. Common prepaid items are insurance, rent, and supplies. In this case, Tom's Wear has purchased an asset called **prepaid insurance.** Cash is decreased by $150, and our new asset—prepaid insurance—is increased

On account means *on credit.* The expression applies to either buying or selling on credit.

Accounts payable are amounts that a company owes its vendors. They are liabilities and are shown on the balance sheet.

Prepaid insurance is the name for insurance a business has purchased but not yet used. It is an asset.

Exhibit 2-3 Effect of Transactions on Accounting Equation

		Assets	=	Liabilities		+	Shareholders' equity	
							Contributed capital	Retained earnings
Balance sheet at February 1, 2001	Cash Inventory	$5,345 40			$ 0		$5,000	$385
1- Purchased 200 shirts on account	Inventory	800		Accounts payable	800			
2- Advertising, cost $150, paid cash for $100, owe $50	Cash	(100)		Other payable	50			Advertising expense (150)
3-Purchased 3-months worth of insurance for $150	Prepaid insurance Cash	150 (150)						
4-Sold 185 shirts for $10 each, $170 for cash, $15 on account	Cash Accounts receivable Inventory	1,700 150 (740)						Sales 1,850 Cost of goods sold (740)
5- Dividend for $100 paid	Cash	(100)						Dividends (100)
Balance sheet at February 28, 2001	Cash Accounts receivable Inventory Prepaid insurance	$6,695 150 100 150		Accounts payable $800 Other payable 50			Common stock 5,000	Retained earnings 1,245

Accounts receivable are amounts customers owe a company for goods or services purchased on credit.

Adjusting the books means to make changes in the accounting records, at the end of the period, just before the financial statements are prepared, to make sure the amounts reflect the financial condition of the company at that date.

by $150. Notice that we have not recorded *insurance expense*. Until some of the insurance is used up—and it can only be used up from one point in time to a subsequent point in time—there is no expense.

The company's success continues with the sale of 185 more T-shirts at $10 each. Although transaction 4 shows these sales as a single transaction, they could have been individual sales. They are grouped together here to make the presentation simple. Of the 185 shirts sold, 170 were sold for cash of $1,700 (= 170 shirts × $10 per shirt) and 15 were sold on credit for $150 (= 15 shirts × $10 per shirt). When a sale is made on credit, the amount owed by customers is called **accounts receivable.** Accounts receivable are assets—things of value to a business. This is the fourth transaction shown in Exhibit 2-3. Notice that the rest of this transaction includes the decrease in inventory of $740 (= 185 shirts × the $4 cost of each) with a corresponding expense—cost of goods sold of $740—which decreases retained earnings by $740.

At the end of the second month of business, Tom's Wear pays a dividend of $100 to its only stockholder, Tom. This transaction reduces assets—cash—by $100, and it reduces retained earnings by $100. This is the fifth transaction shown in Exhibit 2-3.

The financial statements for February can be prepared with the information from these transactions. However, there is still one more step before accurate financial statements can be prepared. This step is called **adjusting the books.** We review the amount that has been recorded for each asset and each claim to make sure every amount correctly reflects the financial situation of the company on the specific date we have chosen for the balance sheet—the last day of the fiscal period (month, quarter, or year). After reviewing the transactions during the month, can you identify any amount that seems incorrect to you? Start at the beginning of the balance sheet work sheet and look at each item that has been recorded. The assets are cash, $6,695; accounts receivable, $150; inventory, $100; and prepaid insurance, $150. Are these amounts accurate at February 28, 2001, the end of Tom's second month of operating his business? Is any asset likely to communicate incorrect information?

Yes—prepaid insurance, as it appears in the company's records will not express what it should. Because the balance sheet will have the date February 28, 2001, we want the amount of prepaid insurance to be accurate at that date. What is the amount of the asset—insurance that is still unused—at the date of the balance sheet? The $150, paid on February 14, applied to 3 months. On February 28, half a month, or 15 days, has passed. So, one-sixth (= 15 days/90 days) of the prepaid insurance has been used. An adjustment must be made to make sure the correct amount of prepaid insurance is shown on the balance sheet. Like routine transactions, adjustments must keep the accounting equation in balance. We subtract $25 (= 1/6 × $150) from the asset column, reducing the amount of prepaid insurance, and we reduce owner's claims by the same $25 amount. This reduction in the owner's claims is an expense—insurance expense—so we show it in the retained earnings column. It will be included on the income statement. The correct amount of the asset—the unused portion—will be shown on the balance sheet at $125.

A review of the other items on the balance sheet doesn't reveal any other problems on this particular balance sheet date. In the next chapter, you will learn there are other situations requiring adjustments before you can prepare the financial statements.

The income statement is prepared first. It lists the revenues and expenses for the period, and you can find those in the retained earnings column in Exhibit 2-3. All revenues increase retained earnings; all expenses decrease retained earnings. The only item that we regularly find in the retained earnings column that is *not* included in the income statement is a distribution to the owners, dividends in a corporation. Generally accepted accounting principles say that distributions are not expenses.

Exhibit 2-4
Income Statement for Tom's Wear

tom's wear

Tom's Wear, Inc.
Income Statement
For the Month Ended February 28, 2001

Revenue		
Sales		$1,850
Expenses		
Cost of sales	740	
Advertising expense	150	
Insurance	25	
Total expenses		915
Net income		$ 935

Revenues and expenses can be found in the retained earnings column of our work sheet. This is all the information we need to prepare the income statement. Simply go down the list of numbers in the retained earnings column, and group the transactions into revenues and expenses to form an income statement.

The sales revenue, often simply called *sales,* is $1,850.

There are three types of expenses listed. One is the cost of goods sold—also known as cost of sales. Recall, this is the expense associated with selling something purchased from someone else. Tom's Wear has cost of goods sold of $740. The other two expenses are $150 for the advertising and $25 for insurance. Be sure you see and understand that the insurance expense is *not* the amount Tom's Wear actually paid to the insurance company. Instead, it is the cost of the insurance that was *used* during the period. The amount that hasn't been used as of February 28 remains on the balance sheet as an asset.

The net income for the period is $935—revenues of $1,850 minus expenses of $915.

The statement of changes in shareholders' equity—also called the statement of shareholders' equity—is prepared next (Exhibit 2-5). This statement provides the details of the changes in shareholders' equity during the year. The information for this statement is found in the two shareholders' equity columns of the work sheet in Exhibit 2-3. Tom's Wear began the month with $5,000 in contributed capital. No new stock was issued during the month. That means owners made no contributions during the month. Retained earnings began the month with a balance of $385. Net income of $935 increases retained earnings, and the dividend of $100 decreases retained earnings. The amount of retained earnings at the end of the period is $1,220 (= $385 + 935 − 100).

Exhibit 2-5
Statement of Shareholders' Equity for Tom's Wear

tom's wear

Tom's Wear, Inc.
Statement of Changes in Shareholders' Equity
For the Month Ended February 28, 2001

Beginning contributed capital	$5,000	
Common stock issued during the month	0	
Ending contributed capital		$5,000
Beginning retained earnings	$ 385	
Net income for the month	935	
Dividends	(100)	
Ending retained earnings		1,220
Total shareholders' equity		$6,220

Exhibit 2-6
Balance Sheet for Tom's Wear

tom's wear

Tom's Wear, Inc.
Balance Sheet
At February 28, 2001

Assets		Liabilities and Shareholders' equity	
Cash	$6,695	Accounts payable	$ 800
Accounts receivable	150	Other payables	50
Inventory	100		
Prepaid insurance	125	Common stock	5,000
		Retained earnings	1,220
		Total liabilities and	
Total assets	$7,070	shareholders' equity	$7,070

Next, Tom's Wear prepares the balance sheet. The balance sheet was really prepared as the transactions were put in the accounting equation work sheet — but not in a way to communicate most effectively. The transactions need to be summarized and organized to communicate their information clearly and effectively, in what is often considered the formal balance sheet presentation. Each asset owned at February 28 is listed, along with the claims to those assets. Notice the similarity between the list of transactions on the work sheet in Exhibit 2-3 and the balance sheet in Exhibit 2-6.

The assets are listed at their amounts on February 28, 2001. There is $6,695 cash. (The details of how this number was calculated will be shown on the statement of cash flows.) Tom's Wear also has accounts receivable of $150 — that's the amount customers still owe the company for T-shirts purchased during the month but haven't been paid for yet. There are 25 shirts left in the inventory, each cost $4, for a total of $100.

The last asset is prepaid insurance, and the amount shown is $125 — the unused portion at February 28. The adjustment reduced prepaid insurance by $25 for the amount used up during the last half of February.

There are two liabilities at February 28, 2001 — accounts payable of $800 and other payables of $50. These amounts are still owed by Tom's Wear to creditors.

The last item is the amount of shareholders' equity. Because we have already prepared the statement of changes in shareholders' equity, we know that $5,000 is the total contributed capital — in the form of stock — and $1,220 is the amount of retained earnings. Together, the liabilities plus shareholders' equity add up to $7,070 — the same $7,070 as the total assets.

The statement of cash flows (Exhibit 2-7) shows every cash collection and every cash disbursement for the month. Each cash transaction is classified as one of three types: operating, investing, or financing. To prepare this statement, we need to pick out the cash items from the transactions in the *asset* column of the work sheet in Exhibit 2-3. For each cash amount, ask yourself if it pertains to operating activities, investing activities, or financing activities.

The first *cash* amount in the asset column of Exhibit 2-3 is the payment of $100 in cash for advertising; that was the second transaction. This $100 is an operating cash flow because it is a cash expense related to routine business activities.

The next cash transaction is the $150 paid to the insurance company. The purchase of insurance is an operating cash flow. Notice the statement of cash flows shows the cash paid — with *no regard for when* the insurance is used.

Transaction 4 involves cash inflows, for a total of $1,700. This transaction was a sale, which is also an operating cash flow. Notice the cash in transaction 4 is $1,700, representing 170 T-shirts sold for cash. Although 185 were actually sold, 15 are not yet paid for. In the statement of cash flows, every item must be *cash* only.

Tom's Wear, Inc.
Statement of Cash Flows
For the Month Ended February 28, 2001

Exhibit 2–7
Statement of Cash Flows for
Tom's Wear

Cash from operating activities		
Cash collected from customers	$1,700	
Cash paid to advertising	(100)	
Cash paid for insurance	(150)	
Total cash from operations		$1,450
Cash from investing activities		0
Cash from financing activities		
Cash paid for dividends	$ (100)	
Total cash from financing		(100)
Net increase in cash		$1,350

The final cash transaction is the distribution of $100 to the owner as dividends. This is classified as a financing cash flow, because it relates to how the business is financed.

Be sure you see that the statement of cash flows includes *every* cash inflow and *every* cash outflow listed in the asset column of the transaction work sheet. Also notice nothing else is included on this financial statement.

The net amount is the change in the amount of cash during the period. If we add this increase of $1,350 to the beginning cash balance of $5,345, we get the ending cash balance of $6,695, shown on the February 28, 2001 balance sheet.

Notes to the financial statements are not included here for Tom's Wear. As we gain an understanding of the complexity of the choices accountants make in preparing financial statements, we will see the need for notes to give the financial statement users information about those choices.

Assets

Looking at the balance sheet at February 28, 2001 for Tom's Wear, Exhibit 2-6, we see on the left the company's assets, also referred to as economic resources. According to SFAC 6, **assets** are those items of value that belong to the company. They are on the balance sheet as a result of past transactions, but they do have value, which they will provide in the future when they will be used to help the business produce revenue.

The first asset on Tom's Wear's balance sheet is cash. The amount has been determined by past transactions, and the money has value because of what it can buy in the future.

Other common assets include accounts receivable (amounts owed to the company by customers) and inventory (items purchased for sale).

The last asset shown is prepaid insurance. This is the *unused* portion of the insurance—it still has value on February 28.

Assets are listed on the balance sheet in order of **liquidity**. Liquidity refers to how easily an asset can be converted into cash. The assets that are expected to be used within a year are called **current assets.** The assets that will not be used within a year are called **noncurrent assets,** or **long-term assets.** So far, Tom's Wear has only current assets. Look at Exhibit 1-3 at the balance sheet of Lands' End. The asset section of the balance sheet shows both current and long-term assets.

Assets are the economic resources of a company, resulting from past transactions.

Liquidity is a measure of how easily an asset can be converted to cash. The more liquid an asset is, the more easily it can be turned into cash.

Current assets are the assets the company plans to turn into cash or use to generate revenue in the next fiscal year.

Noncurrent, or **long-term, assets** are assets that will last for more than a year.

Assets are one of three classifications of items on the balance sheet. The other two types tell *who*—creditors or owners—has claim to these assets. Recall, the balance sheet *is* the accounting equation:

$$\text{Assets} = \text{Liabilities} + \text{Owner's Equity}$$

Liabilities

Liabilities are obligations the company has incurred to obtain the assets it has.

Accounts payable are amounts a company owes to its vendors.

The January 2, 2001 balance sheet, shown in Exhibit 1-11, indicated that Tom's Wear owed $500 to Tom's mom. On February 28, 2001, that is no longer the case. The debt to his mom was paid off in January. On February 28, 2001, the only liabilities Tom's Wear has are accounts payable and other payables. According to SFAC 6, **liabilities** are amounts that the business owes. They are the claims of creditors. Usually, these claims will be paid to creditors in cash. Liabilities, like assets, are the result of past transactions or events. For example, a purchase of inventory items on credit creates a liability called **accounts payable.** The balance sheet on February 28 was prepared after the purchase of the shirts but before Tom paid for them, so the balance sheet shows the cost of the shirts as accounts payable. Once incurred, a liability continues as an obligation of the company until the company pays for it. The accounts payable amount for the T-shirts remains on the balance sheet until Tom pays the bill for the shirts. Often, liabilities involve interest—payment of an additional amount for the right to delay payment. When Tom repaid his mom in 2001, he paid $5 interest for the use of her money.

Current liabilities are liabilities the company will settle—pay off—in the next fiscal year.

Noncurrent, or **long-term, liabilities** are liabilities that will take longer than a year to settle.

A **classified balance sheet** shows a subtotal for many items including current assets and current liabilities.

Liabilities can also be current or noncurrent. If a liability will be settled with a current asset, it's called a **current liability.** For practical purposes, you can think about a current liability as a liability that will be paid off in the next year. **Noncurrent liabilities** will be paid off over a period longer than one year. Most balance sheets show the current assets with a subtotal before showing the noncurrent assets. That format is called a **classified balance sheet.** A classified balance sheet will also show the current liabilities with a subtotal before the long-term liabilities. Look at the balance sheet for Lands' End, shown in Exhibit 1-3. See if you can find the subtotals for current assets and current liabilities. This is a classified balance sheet, because it has two classifications of assets and liabilities—short term and long term.

Equity

Equity is the name for owners' claims to the assets of the firm. It includes both **contributed capital** and capital *earned* by the business. In a corporation, the earned amount of equity is called **retained earnings.**

Equity, sometimes called net assets, is the owners' claims to the assets of the company. There are two ways owners can create equity in a company. The first way is by making capital contributions—**contributed capital.** Usually, the capital is cash, but it could be equipment or other items of value. When Tom started his T-shirt business, he invested $5,000 of his own money. Sometimes this is called the owner's investment in the company. The term *investment* may be confused with investments that the company itself makes with its extra cash. For example, General Motors may invest some of its extra cash in the stock of Lands' End, which General Motors would call an investment. To avoid that confusion, we'll not refer to owners' investments; instead, we'll call these amounts owners' *contributions.*

The second way to create equity in a business is to make a profit. (That's the preferred way.) When Tom's Wear sells a shirt, the profit from that shirt increases Tom's equity in the company.

Contributed capital is sometimes called **paid-in capital.** This is the amount the owners have put into the business.

In corporations, the two types of equity are separated on the balance sheet. The first is **contributed capital,** also known as **paid-in capital;** the second is

retained earnings. In a sole proprietorship or partnership, both types of equity are together called **capital.** Separating these amounts for corporations provides information for potential investors about how much the owners have actually invested in the corporation.

In a sole proprietorship and partnership, the contributed capital and earned capital—**retained earnings**—are shown together in one amount called **capital.**

Measurement and Recognition in Financial Statements

Let's take a closer look at the elements on the balance sheet and income statement. Recall, the balance sheet is simply the accounting equation: Assets = Liabilities + Owner's Equity. The three elements are major categories, each divided into subcategories.

 Recognize how the elements of the financial statements—assets, liabilities, equity, revenue, and expenses—are represented by various items on the financial statements and how they are measured.

Let's start with assets. The most well-known asset is cash. It is listed first on the balance sheet. As we noticed on Lands' End's balance sheet, all other assets are listed in order of their liquidity—how easily they can be converted to cash. A monetary value is computed for each asset. Cash, for example, is the total amount of money in checking and savings accounts. The next asset on the balance sheet is usually accounts receivable—the total amount that customers owe the company for credit sales.

Inventory is another asset, measured at its cost. We saw that Tom's Wear's balance sheet included the cost of the T-shirts still in the inventory on the balance sheet date.

Measuring Assets

So far, we've discussed two characteristics of the way things are measured for the balance sheet.

First, they are measured in monetary units. For us, that means dollars. The actual *number* of T-shirts in the inventory is not shown on the balance sheet. Measuring assets, liabilities, and equity in monetary units is called the **unit-of-measure assumption.** U.S. companies use dollars, Japanese companies use yen, and so on. What all companies have in common is that they use the monetary unit of their country to value the items on the financial statements.

The **unit of measure assumption** refers to the use of monetary units—dollars in the United States—to measure the financial statement items.

Second, the items on the financial statements are recorded at *cost*—that's what we paid for them—sometimes called **historical cost.** They are *not* recorded at the amount we hope they will be sold for. The concept behind this is called the **cost principle** and is closely tied to the **going-concern assumption.** We assume the business is not going to quit operating—that it is going to continue as a going-concern. If you did not assume a business is a going-concern, you could argue that items on the financial statements should be valued at their current value—whatever the company could get for them if it were immediately going out of business. Instead, when a company buys something, it is recorded at the cost at the time of purchase. Some assets continue to be shown at cost on the balance sheet, and others are revalued to a more current amount for each balance sheet. We'll learn the details of which assets *are revalued* and which assets *are not revalued,* in the chapters to come.

The **historical cost principle**—also called the **cost principle**—refers to measuring the financial statement items at their cost at the time of the transaction.

The **going concern assumption** means that we will assume a company will continue to be in business in the future.

Recognizing Revenue and Expenses

When should revenue be included on an income statement? GAAP says when it is *earned,* that's when revenue is **recognized**—meaning that's when revenue is included on the income statement. When Tom delivers a shirt to a customer, Tom's Wear has earned the revenue. This is called the **revenue recognition principle.** When one of Tom's friends says he is going to buy a T-shirt next week, no revenue is recognized. In business you don't count your chickens

To **recognize** revenue means to record it so that it will show up on the income statement.

The **revenue recognition principle** says that revenue should be recognized when it is earned.

before they are hatched. When an exchange actually takes place, or when the earnings process is complete or "virtually complete," that is the time for revenue recognition. When Tom's Wear and a customer exchange the cash and the T-shirt, there is no doubt the transaction is complete. When Tom's Wear delivers the T-shirt and the customer agrees to pay for it later (the sale is on credit), we consider the earnings process virtually complete. Tom's Wear has done its part, so the sale is included on the income statement.

What about expenses? When an expense is recognized depends on when the revenue that results from that expense is recognized. Expenses are recognized—included on the income statement—when the revenue they were incurred to generate is recognized. This is called the **matching principle,** and it is the basis of the income statement. Expenses are matched with the revenue they helped to generate. An example is the cost of goods sold. Only the cost of the T-shirts *sold* is recognized—included as an expense on the income statement. The expense is matched with the revenue from the sale of those shirts. The cost of the unsold T-shirts is not an expense—and will not be an expense—until those shirts are sold. An expense is a cost that has been used to generate revenue. If a cost has been incurred but it hasn't been used up, it is classified as an asset until it is used. Prepaid insurance is an example of a cost that is classified as an asset until it is used; and when it is used, it becomes insurance expense.

The **matching principle** says that expenses should be recognized — shown on the income statement — in the same period as the revenue they helped generate.

Does the customer actually have to pay the company in cash before a sale can be counted as revenue? No. Notice that the sales of all the shirts are included in the sales total, even though 15 of the shirts haven't been paid for yet. When a customer purchases an item on credit, the earnings process is considered virtually complete, even though the cash has not been collected. Similarly, a cost incurred in the generation of revenue does not have to be paid to be included on the income statement. In calculating the revenue and expenses for an income statement, accountants do *not* follow the cash. Instead, they use the time when the "economic substance" of the transaction is complete.

Accountants use the expressions *virtually complete* and *economic substance* to describe the same idea—that a transaction does not have to be technically complete to recognize the resulting revenue. If the transaction is substantially complete, the revenue is recognized. When Tom's Wear sells the T-shirts, delivering them and receiving the customers' promise to pay is considered the economic substance of that transaction. Cash may come before the transaction is complete or it may come afterward. This way of accounting for revenues and expenses—using the economic substance of the transaction to determine when to include it on the income statement instead of using the exchange of cash—is called **accrual accounting.**

Accrual accounting refers to the way we recognize revenues and expenses. We don't rely on the exchange of cash to determine the timing. We recognize revenue when it is earned and expenses when they are incurred — no matter when the cash is received or disbursed.

When to recognize revenue is easy for some businesses and extremely difficult for others. There is a lot of disagreement among accountants about revenue recognition. They agree that revenue should be recognized when the transaction is virtually complete—but they often can't agree exactly when that has happened. This is another topic that you'll learn more about in later chapters.

Exhibit 2–8
Summary of the Foundation for Accounting Principles

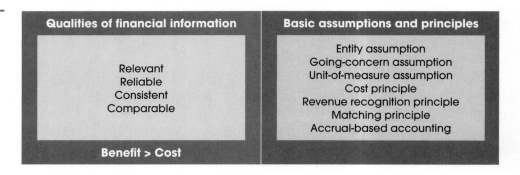

Qualities of financial information	Basic assumptions and principles
Relevant Reliable Consistent Comparable	Entity assumption Going-concern assumption Unit-of-measure assumption Cost principle Revenue recognition principle Matching principle Accrual-based accounting
Benefit > Cost	

Exhibit 2-8 summarizes the characteristics of accounting information, both the qualities and the underlying principles.

Accruals and Deferrals

Accrual Basis Accounting

The term *accrual basis accounting* includes two kinds of transactions in which the exchange of cash does *not* coincide with the economic substance of the transaction. The revenues and expenses are recognized at a time other than the time when the cash is collected or paid.

One kind of accrual basis transaction is an **accrual** and the other is a **deferral.** The meaning of each kind of accrual basis transaction is represented graphically in Exhibit 2-9.

When the action comes before the cash, it is an accrual. When Tom's Wear made a credit sale, it was an accrual transaction. To accrue means to "build up," or "accumulate." In accounting, we are building up our sales or our expenses even though the cash hasn't been exchanged. The sale is completed first—merchandise is delivered to the customer—and the cash payment will come later. Instead of receiving the asset *cash* from the purchaser, the company records an asset called *accounts receivable*—meaning cash due from the purchaser. Accounts receivable is the amount owed to the company by customers. Because GAAP is based on accrual accounting, the necessary part of the transaction for recording the revenue is the actual sale of goods or services, *not* the cash receipt from the customers.

When the dollars come before the action, it is called a *deferral.* When Tom's Wear paid for the insurance, it was an advance purchase—as we all have to pay insurance premiums up front, not after the expiration date of the policy. The amount paid for the insurance was not considered an expense until it was actually used. To defer something, in common language, means to put it off—to delay or postpone it. In the language of accounting, a deferral means that the company will postpone recognizing the expense until it is actually used. When Tom's Wear paid the cash in advance of the period covered by the insurance, the company had to record the cash disbursement. In other words, Tom's Wear recorded it in the business records as cash that had been spent. However, the expense wasn't recognized when the cash was paid. It will be recognized—and remember, that means included on the income statement—when the cost is actually used.

Cash Basis Versus Accrual Basis Accounting

There is another type of accounting called **cash basis accounting**—revenue is only recognized when the cash is collected, and expenses are recorded only when the cash is paid. This is *not* a generally accepted method of accounting according to the FASB and the SEC. Using the exchange of cash as the signal for recognizing revenue and expense doesn't communicate the performance of the business in a way that allows us to evaluate its achievements. The cash flows are important, but alone they do not provide enough information for

L.O. 4

Understand accrual basis accounting and cash basis accounting and the differences between the two. Know that accrual basis accounting is GAAP.

An **accrual** transaction is one in which the revenue is earned or the expense is incurred before the exchange of cash.

A **deferral** transaction is one in which the exchange of cash takes place *before* the revenue is earned or the expense incurred.

Cash basis accounting is a system based on the exchange of cash. In this system, revenue is recognized only when cash is collected, and an expense is recognized only when cash is disbursed. This is not an acceptable method of accounting under GAAP.

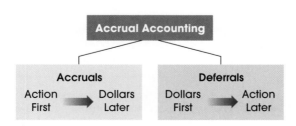

Exhibit 2-9
Accrual Accounting

decision makers. This doesn't stop some businesses from using it as the basis of their own accounting records. Remember, some businesses are not required to follow GAAP. For example, doctors who are sole proprietors may use cash basis accounting in their businesses. This means they recognize only the cash they receive as revenue. If they provide services to someone who has not yet paid for those services at the time an income statement is prepared, they would not include the fee not yet received as revenue for that income statement. That is not GAAP. If the doctors *were* following GAAP, they would count it as revenue and as a receivable (accounts receivable).

Accounting Periods and Cutoff Issues

Why does it matter—for accounting purposes—if there is a difference between the time when the goods or services are exchanged—that's the economic substance of the transaction—and the time when the cash related to that transaction is received or disbursed? If a company makes a sale on credit and the cash is collected later, why does it matter *when* the sale is recognized—included as revenue on the income statement? Tom's Wear will help you see the answers to these questions.

When Tom began his business in 2001, he chose the calendar year as his company's fiscal year. Each of his annual income statements will cover the period from January 1 to December 31 of a specific year. It's important that what appears on the income statement for a specific year is *only* the revenue earned during those 12 months and *only* the expenses incurred to generate that revenue. What is included as a sale during the period? Accountants have decided to use the exchange of goods and services, not the cash exchange, to define when a sale has taken place. Expenses are matched with revenues, also without regard to when the cash is exchanged. This makes the financial statements of all companies that follow GAAP consistent and comparable.

Exhibit 2-10 shows the relationship between the balance sheet and the income statement and the time periods involved.

Recall, the balance sheet is a freeze-frame view of the assets, liabilities, and owner's equity on a specific date. For a company with a fiscal year-end on December 31, that is the date of the balance sheet. Remember, the end-of-the-year balance sheet for one year becomes the beginning-of-the-year balance sheet for the next year. When you are out celebrating New Year's Eve, nothing is happening to the balance sheet. When Tom goes to sleep on December 31, 2001, the cash on the December 31, 2001 balance sheet of Tom's Wear is exactly the amount of cash that the company will have on January 1, 2002. So the final balance sheet for one year simply rolls forward to the next year.

Exhibit 2-10
The Balance Sheet and Income Statement

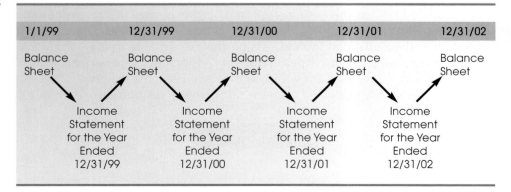

Every balance sheet presents the assets, liabilities, and owners' equity of a business firm at a moment in time. The income statement describes what happened between two balance sheet dates.

Then, transactions start happening—exchanges take place. The revenues and expenses for the period of time are shown on the income statement. The income statement covers a period. A company may construct weekly, monthly, quarterly, or annual financial statements. Many companies prepare monthly and quarterly financial statements; *all* companies prepare annual financial statements. The income statement for a specific year gives the revenues and expenses for that year. It gives information about how the balance sheet has changed between the beginning of the year and the end of the year. The revenues increase owner's claims; expenses reduce owner's claims. If the difference between revenues and expenses is positive—if revenues are greater than expenses—the company has a net income. If the expenses are greater than revenues, the company has a net loss. The net income or net loss is sometimes called the *bottom line*.

1. **What is the difference between cash basis and accrual basis accounting?**
2. **What are the three basic elements of the balance sheet? Define each.**
3. **What is the matching principle?**

STUDY BREAK 2-2
SEE HOW YOU'RE DOING

More About the Financial Statements

Investors—Owners and Creditors

Owners and creditors are both considered investors in a business. Both invest their money to *make* money, and they both take a **risk** in investing their money in the business. *Risk* is the uncertainty associated with *the amount* of future returns and *the timing* of future returns. Some investments are riskier than others are. For example, when a bank makes a loan to a company, the banker evaluates the ability of the company to repay the loan amount—the principal—plus interest—the cost of borrowing the money. If the bank makes a loan to a company that doesn't do well enough to repay the debt, the company may have to sell noncash assets to raise cash to pay off the loan plus interest due. When lending money, the bank must compare the risk with the expected return.

Most often, the risk and return of an investment change value in the same direction—we say they are positively correlated. *Positively correlated* means they move in the same direction—higher risk means higher expected return for taking the higher risk; lower risk means lower expected returns. For higher investment risk, the potential for a higher return is needed to attract investors.

Investing in a company as an owner is riskier than investing as a creditor. A creditor's claim to the assets of a company has priority over an owner's claim. (Creditors have first "dibs" to the assets.) If a company has just enough money either to pay its creditors or to make a distribution to its owner or owners, the creditors *must* be paid, and they *always must be paid,* before anything—if there is anything left—is distributed to the owners. That translates into less risk for a creditor. The owner's risk is that the company will go out of business.

However, the owner, who takes more risk, has the right to share the profit. So the risk for the owner is accompanied by the potential for a higher return. A creditor, on the other hand, will never receive more than the amount of the loan, plus the amount of interest that is agreed on when the loan is made.

Financial information is useful for someone deciding whether or not to invest in a company. Suppose Tom's Wear wanted to borrow money to expand. A bank would want to examine Tom's Wear's income statement, balance sheet,

Financial statements provide information about the **risk** related to investing in a company. Will you get a good return on your investment? How long will it take?

Understanding Business

MANAGING CASH—PLANNING INFLOWS AND OUTFLOWS

In this chapter, you've learned that financial statements are prepared on an accrual basis, but that doesn't mean cash isn't important. As a matter of fact, cash budgeting is one of the most important activities a company performs. The starting point for avoiding a cash crisis is to develop a comprehensive cash flow budget. Smart business owners develop annual or multi-year cash flow projections to make sure they can meet ongoing business needs. Business owners also prepare and use *historical* cash flow statements to gain an understanding about where all the cash came from and where all the cash went.

By estimating your cash inflows and outflows, you can:

■ Make sure you have enough cash to purchase sufficient inventory for planned sales.

■ Take advantage of purchase discounts and special offers.

■ Plan equipment purchases, repairs, and replacements.

■ Be prepared for any financing you may need in periods of cash shortages—short term credit line, small loans, or long-term debt.

■ Increase your chances of success in meeting your obligations.

For a new or growing business, accurate cash flow projections can make the difference between success and failure. For an ongoing business, good cash budgeting can make the difference between moving forward and standing still.

How do you prepare a cash flow projection? According to the Women's Business Center (www.sba.gov/womeninbusiness/index.html), preparing a cash flow projection is like preparing a budget and balancing your checkbook at the same time. First, you estimate your cash inflows. Cash is generated primarily by sales. But in lots of businesses, some of the sales are *on account* (charge accounts, term payments, lay-a-way, trade credit). So you have to estimate when those credit sales will turn into actual cash inflows. Then, you estimate all the cash disbursements you have to make and *when* you have to make them.

How much detail you include in your cash flow projections depends on the complexity of your business. Using a computerized spreadsheet for your cash flow projections can make the process much faster and more accurate. You can enter formulas for the subtotals and totals to eliminate common addition and subtraction errors. You will also be able to easily develop "what-if" scenarios to help you prepare for variation from your estimates.

The goal of cash budgeting is to always have enough cash to keep your business running smoothly. If it turns out that you have more cash than you need, then you will have to figure out how best to use that extra cash—most likely how best to invest it. That's a cash flow problem that you want!

and the statement of cash flows. The reason is to evaluate potential risk—the company's ability to make the required principal and interest payments.

The balance sheet shows a company's assets and who has claim to them. A bank loan officer would use the information on the balance sheet to evaluate Tom's Wear's ability to repay the loan. He would want to be sure that the company didn't have too many debts. The more debt a company has, the more cash it must generate to make the loan payments.

The information on the balance sheet wouldn't be enough to assure the bank loan officer that Tom's Wear would be able to repay the loan. Because a loan is repaid over several months or years, information about the future earning potential of the business is important. Studying the past performance of a business helps predict its future performance. That makes the profit the company earned during the past year relevant to the banker. Details about the sales revenue and expenses incurred to generate that revenue would help the bank evaluate the company's potential to generate enough cash to repay a loan.

Exhibit 2-11
Beginning Balance Sheet for
Clean Sweep and Maids-R-Us

Balance Sheet
At January 1, 2002

Assets	
Cash	$ 900
Supplies	200
Total assets	$1,100
Liabilities	
Notes payable	$ 400
Owner's equity	
Owner, Capital	700
Total liabilities and owner's equity	$1,100

Still, the information on these two financial statements, no matter how relevant to the bank's evaluation, would not be enough. Another piece of the puzzle is the way the company manages its cash. A company may have little debt and lots of earning potential. However, if the company doesn't have enough cash, the loan payments can't be made. Because cash collection is the bank's primary concern, the statement of cash flows provides additional information for the bank.

An Example to Illustrate the Kind of Information Financial Statements Provide

Let's compare two companies, each starting its fiscal year with identical balance sheets. Both use GAAP. Then, during the first month of the year, they have very similar transactions. We'll only look at a few of the transactions and we'll see that their income statements for the month are the same. As you study the example, try to figure out why their income statements are the same. Their ending balance sheets and statements of cash flow are not the same. Where do the differences show up in the financial statements?

The two companies are Clean Sweep and Maids-R-Us. Both are cleaning businesses and both are sole proprietorships. Judy Jones owns Clean Sweep, and Betty Brown owns Maids-R-Us. On January 1, 2002, the two companies have identical balance sheets. Look at each item on the balance sheet in Exhibit 2-11 and be sure you know what it means. Do this before you go on.

Let's take each transaction and look at its effect on the accounting equation. Follow along using Exhibits 2-12 and 2-13.

Transaction 1: Both companies earn $750 worth of revenue. Clean Sweep collects the cash, but Maids-R-Us extends credit to its customers. Clean Sweep records the asset *cash,* while

Both Clean Sweep and Maids-R-Us	Clean Sweep	Maids-R-Us
1. Clean 10 houses for a fee of $75 per house.	Collects the fees in cash at the time the services are rendered.	Agrees to extend credit to the customers. Fees will be collected within 30 days.
2. Make a loan payment plus interest.	Pays off the entire loan plus $40 interest.	Pays only $100 of the loan plus $40 interest.
3. Count the supplies on January 31 and find $25 worth left on hand.	Both will make an adjustment to show $175 worth of supplies used.	

Exhibit 2-13 Effects of Transactions on Accounting Equation

		Clean Sweep Transactions for January:					
		Assets	=	Liabilities	+	Owner's equity	
Balance sheet at January 1, 2002 →	Cash Supplies	$ 900 200	=	Notes payable $400	+	Capital	$ 700
		Effect of each transaction during the year on the accounting equation:					
		Clean Sweep: Transactions for January:					
1-Performs services for $750, collected in cash	Cash	$ 750				Revenue	$ 750
2- Pays off the note plus interest of $40	Cash	$(440)		Notes payable $(400)		Interest expense	$ (40)
3- Adjustment for supplies used during the month	Supplies	$(175)				Supplies expense	$(175)
Balance sheet at January 31, 2002 →	Cash Supplies Total	$1,210 25 $1,235	=	0		Capital	$1,235

Maids-R-Us records the asset *accounts receivable*. Both companies have earned the same amount of revenue, so each will show $750 revenue on its income statement for the month.

Transaction 2: Both companies make a loan payment. Clean Sweep pays the entire amount of the note payable, $400, plus interest of $40. Maids-R-Us pays only $100 of principal on the note payable, plus interest of $40. The only expense in this transaction is the interest expense of $40. Both companies have incurred the same amount of interest expense, so each will show $40 expense on its income statement. The repayment of the principal of a loan does not affect the income statement.

Adjustment: At the end of the period, both companies will record supplies expense of $175, leaving $25 as supplies-on-hand on the January 31 balance sheet. Both income statements will show supplies expense of $175.

We can construct an income statement for each company from the numbers in the owner's equity column in Exhibit 2-13. Because there were no distributions to the owner during the period, all the items in that column will be included in the calculation of net income. Revenues for the month of January amounted to $750; expenses were $215; so net income was $535. This is the case for both companies as shown in Exhibit 2-14. Even though one company extended credit to its customers and the other collected cash for its services, the income statements are identical. The income statement is only concerned with revenues earned and expenses incurred, not with the timing of the related cash flows.

The balance sheet at January 31 for each company can be constructed by simply organizing the details of the ending equation for each company in Exhibit 2-13. For a sole proprietorship, all owner's equity—contributed and earned—is lumped together and called owner's capital. The two balance sheets are shown in Exhibit 2-15. Notice the differences. Assets and liabilities are different for the two companies, but the owner's equity amounts are the same.

It's important to understand why both companies have the same amount of owner's equity. Both had beginning equity of $700 plus net income for the

Exhibit 2-13   *(continued)*

Maids-R-Us Transactions for January:							
	Assets		**=**	**Liabilities**	**+**	**Owner's equity**	
Balance sheet at January 1, 2002 →	Cash	$ 900	=	Notes payable $400	+	Capital	$ 700
	Supplies	200					
Effect of each transaction during the year on the accounting equation:							
Maids-R-Us: Transactions for January:							
1-Performs services for $750 on account	Accounts receivable	$ 750				Revenue	$ 750
2- Pays $100 of the note plus interest of $40	Cash	$ (140)		Notes payable $(100)		Interest expense	$ (40)
3- Adjustment for supplies used during the month	Supplies	$ (175)				Supplies expense	$ (175)
Balance sheet at January 31, 2002 →	Cash	$ 760	=	Notes payable $300	+	Capital	$1,235
	Accounts receivable	750					
	Supplies	25					
	Total	$1,535					

month of $535, for a total of $1,235. That is the number we find on the January 31 balance sheet for owner's equity. The timing of cash receipts and disbursements does not affect owner's equity.

Finally, let's look at the statement of cash flows. As you have seen, the cash receipts and disbursements for the two companies were *not* the same. This shows up clearly on the statement of cash flows. The cash flow statement for each company shows all the cash received and all the cash disbursed for the month. The cash flow statements are shown in Exhibit 2-16.

Putting It All Together—The Objectives of Financial Statements and the Information in Statements of Clean Sweep and Maids-R-Us

Financial information should be useful. What makes it useful is the way the transactions of the business are organized into the four basic financial statements:

1. The income statement
2. The statement of changes in owner's equity
3. The balance sheet
4. The statement of cash flows

Income Statement For the Month Ended January 31, 2002		
Revenue		
Cleaning fees		$750
Expenses		
Supplies	$175	
Interest	40	
Total expenses		215
Net income		$535

Exhibit 2-14
Income Statement for Clean Sweep and Maids-R-Us for January

Exhibit 2-15   Balance Sheet for Clean Sweep and Maids-R-Us at January 31, 2002

Clean Sweep Balance Sheet At January 31, 2002			
Assets		**Liabilities and Owner's equity**	
Cash	$1,210		
Supplies	25	Capital, Jones	$1,235
Total assets	$1,235	Total liabilities and owner's equity	$1,235

Maids-R-Us Balance Sheet At January 31, 2002			
Assets		**Liabilities and Owner's equity**	
Cash	$ 760	Notes payable	$ 300
Accounts receivable	750		
Supplies	25	Capital, Brown	1,235
Total assets	$1,535	Total liabilities and owner's equity	$1,535

The ongoing life of a business is broken into discrete periods so that performance can be evaluated for a specific period. For our cleaning business, the period we use is a month.

■ Income is measured in a way that captures the economic substance of earning revenue and incurring expenses; it is not based on cash collections and cash disbursements. Notice, the net incomes for Maids-R-Us and Clean Sweep for January are exactly the same, in spite of the differences in when the cash is collected and disbursed. Those timing differences are reflected on the balance sheet by the differences in cash and both receivables and payables; and differences are also shown on the statement of cash flows— the statement that provides the details of the timing of cash receipts and disbursements. The four statements have been designed to be relevant, reliable, consistent, and comparable.

In addition to these qualities, accounting information relies on several basic assumptions and principles, as shown in Exhibit 2-8. Let's relate each of the assumptions and principles to the financial statements of Maids-R-Us.

■ The separate entity assumption means that only the business transactions of Maids-R-Us are shown in the financial statements—none of the owner's personal transactions are included.

Exhibit 2-16   Statements of Cash Flows for Clean Sweep and Maids-R-Us

Clean Sweep Statement of Cash Flows For the Month Ended January 31, 2002		
Cash from operating activities		
Cash collected from customers	$750	
Cash paid for interest	(40)	
Total cash from operations		$710
Cash from investing activities		0
Cash from financing activities		
Repayment of loan	(400)	
Total cash from financing		(400)
Net increase in cash		$310

Maids-R-Us Statement of Cash Flows For the Month Ended January 31, 2002		
Cash from operating activities		
Cash paid for interest	$(40)	
Total cash from operations		$ (40)
Cash from investing activities		0
Cash from financing activities		
Repayment of loan	(100)	
Total cash from financing		(100)
Net increase (decrease) in cash		$(140)

- The going concern assumption means we may assume that Maids-R-Us is an ongoing, viable business. According to GAAP, if it were not ongoing, the company would have to have all its assets appraised and listed at liquidation value.
- The unit of measure assumption means everything shown is measured in monetary units, here dollars.
- The cost principle means the items on the financial statements are valued at cost. For example, the supplies on the balance sheet are *not* valued at what they might be worth if resold or at the current cost, which might be higher than the amount that Maids-R-Us paid for them. They are valued at the price Maids-R-Us paid when they were purchased.
- The revenue recognition principle means the revenue on the income statement has been earned. It may not have been collected, but the work of earning it has been completed.
- The matching principle means related revenues and expenses should be on the same income statement. Only the supplies that are used to earn the revenue during the period are counted as *supplies expense*. The unused supplies are reported on the balance sheet until they are actually used.

Accrual accounting is an accounting system in which the measurement of income is *not* based on cash receipts and cash disbursements. Instead, revenue is included in the calculation of income when it is earned, and expenses are included as they are matched to revenue. Timing differences between the economic substance of a transaction and the related cash flows do not affect income. That's why both companies have the same net income even though the timing of the cash flows is different.

Applying Our Knowledge: Ratio Analysis

One activity every business must perform is paying its bills. Investors, bankers, and other interested parties, often want to evaluate a company's ability to meet its current obligations. Simply looking at how much cash a company has does not provide enough information. There is a financial ratio—a comparison of different amounts on the financial statements—that measures the short-term financial health of a company. It's called the **current ratio**, computed by dividing the total amount of current assets by the total amount of current liabilities. You learned earlier in this chapter that current assets are assets that will be used up or converted to cash in the next year, and current liabilities are obligations that will be settled with current assets. So, the current ratio gives information about the company's ability to pay its bills.

The current ratio provides a way to compare the liquidity of one company—that's a measure of how easily a company can turn its current assets into cash to pay its debts as they come due—to other companies of different types and sizes. It also provides information about the liquidity of a single company over time.

Look at the balance sheet for Lucent Technologies for the years ending September 30, 2000, and September 30, 1999, shown in Exhibit 2-17.

The current ratio for the fiscal year ending September 30, 2000, is:

$$\frac{21,490}{10,877} = 1.98$$

The current ratio for the fiscal year ending September 20, 1999, is:

$$\frac{19,240}{9,150} = 2.10$$

BUSINESS PROCESS

The **current ratio** equals *current assets* divided by *current liabilities*, and it measures a company's ability to pay its current bills.

Exhibit 2-17   Consolidated Balance Sheets for Lucent Technologies Inc. and Subsidiaries

(Dollars in Millions, Except per Share Amounts)		
	September 30	
Assets	2000	1999
Cash and cash equivalents	$1,467	$1,686
Receivables less allowances of $501 in 2000 and $318 in 1999	9,558	8,799
Inventories	5,677	4,240
Contracts in process, net of progress billings of $6,744 in 2000 and $5,565 in 1999	1,881	1,102
Deferred income taxes—net	1,165	1,472
Other current assets	1,742	1,941
Total current assets	21,490	19,240
Property, plant and equipment—net	7,084	6,219
Prepaid pension costs	6,440	5,459
Capitalized software development costs	688	436
Goodwill and other acquired intangibles, net of accumulated amortization of $1,072 in 2000 and $502 in 1999	9,945	960
Other assets	3,145	2,151
Net assets of discontinued operations	—	907
Total assets	$48,792	$35,372
Liabilities		
Accounts payable	$2,813	$2,537
Payroll and benefit-related liabilities	1,210	1,788
Debt maturing within one year	3,483	1,705
Other current liabilities	3,371	3,120
Total current liabilities	10,877	9,150
Postretirement and postemployment benefit liabilities	5,548	5,651
Long-term debt	3,076	4,162
Deferred income taxes—net	1,266	870
Other liabilities	1,853	1,603
Total liabilities	22,620	21,436
Commitments and contingencies		
Shareowners' equity		
Preferred stock—par value $1 per share Authorized shares: 250,000,000 Issued and outstanding shares: none	—	—
Common stock—par value $.01 per share Authorized shares: 10,000,000,000 Issued and outstanding shares: 3,384,332,104 at September 30, 2000; 3,142,537,636 at September 30, 1999	34	31
Additional paid-in capital	20,390	7,994
Guaranteed ESOP obligation	(16)	(33)
Retained earnings	6,129	6,188
Accumulated other comprehensive income (loss)	(365)	(244)
Total shareowners' equity	26,172	13,936
Total liabilities and shareowners' equity	$48,792	$35,372

See Notes to Consolidated Financial Statements.

The reduction in the current ratio from 1999 to 2000 indicates a reduction in the company's liquidity. Looking at the current ratio for two consecutive years gives some information about Lucent Technologies, but you would need much more information to reach any conclusions. As you learn more about financial statements, you'll learn additional ratios and several ways to analyze a company's financial statements.

Business Risks

Now that we've discussed the general characteristics of accounting information and the four basic financial statements, let's take a look at how companies make sure the information in those statements is reliable from a user's perspective. The risks associated with financial information are often called information processing risks and, like all risks, companies try to minimize them.

Internal Controls—Definition and Objectives

Internal controls are the policies and procedures the managers of a firm use to protect the firm's assets and to ensure the accuracy and reliability of the firm's accounting records. Internal controls are a company's rules to help it keep its assets safe and to make sure its financial records are accurate. By adhering to those rules, a firm minimizes the risks of being in business. These rules are called *internal* controls because they are put in place and controlled within the company. Controls imposed from outside the firm—laws and regulations, for example—are not internal controls because they aren't rules that originated in the company.

Internal controls are a company's policies and procedures to protect the assets of the firm and to ensure the accuracy and reliability of the accounting records.

Special Internal Control Issues Related to Financial Statements

Accountants are particularly concerned with the financial statements. Whether you are involved in preparing them or using them to make decisions, you must have confidence that the information in them is accurate and reliable. When you see *cash* on a company's balance sheet, you should be confident this is actually the amount of cash the company had on the balance sheet date. The *sales* shown on the income statement should be sales that have been completed—goods delivered to the customers.

Inaccurate information creates enormous problems. The SEC has been especially concerned with the information contained in the financial statements. For example, recently the SEC filed charges against Computron for improperly recording more than $9 million in revenue on its financial statements contained in its reports to the SEC. Improperly recorded revenue was the focus of a recent SEC investigation of the Mexican unit of Xerox Corp. Xerox officials in Mexico failed to set up appropriate allowances for bad debts and improperly classified sales, leases, and rentals, violating GAAP. The causes cited were (1) failure (of the Mexican executives) to adhere to Xerox's corporate policies and procedures, and (2) inadequate internal controls.

Think about a company's accounting information system in terms of inputs, processing, and outputs, as shown in Exhibit 2-18. As you look at this diagram, consider the accounting exercises and problems in this book. An end-of-chapter problem provides the transaction data—that's the input. Your task is to organize and to manipulate—that means to process—the data. You've been using the accounting equation work sheet to help organize and process the data. Then you take the organized information and prepare the four basic financial statements— they are the output of the process. Can you think of any controls to make sure

Exhibit 2-18   An Accounting Information System

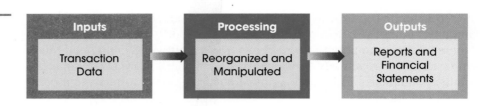

you are processing the information and preparing the output without errors? One control is to check your answer with the answers provided in the back of the book. This would be a detective control—one to help you detect any errors.

Inputs to our information system include data describing the transactions of the business. We want only correct information to get into the system, and we want to be sure it is accurate and complete. Examples of controls to help manage the risk that the information will be fictitious, erroneous, or incomplete are:

1. *Authorization requirements for certain transactions and for certain inputs*— Have you ever waited at the grocery store to have your check approved? Often a supervisor is required to review the information and put initials on the check to indicate approval.
2. *Design and use of adequate documents*—If cashiers have keyed in an incorrect price for an item, they often add it to a correction slip with a list of all the other overpriced or underpriced items erroneously rung up. That corrections slip is one document that helps in keeping accurate information.
3. *Limited access to assets*—To get the cash drawer open, cashiers must enter their personal password, identifying who had access to the cash drawer and when.
4. *Sound personnel policies*—Only certain employees are allowed to run a checkout station. Specific training is necessary.

Processing controls are related to the storage and manipulation of the data. As you can see from the following examples, some controls apply to more than one area. For example, *sound personnel duties* is a control that is necessary to the input, processing, and the output of any information system. Similarly, *limited access* is necessary in all parts of the system. Examples of processing controls are:

1. *Segregation of duties*—Employees who physically control an asset (like cash) should not keep the records related to that same asset.
2. *Documentation controls* (written guidelines and procedures)—Employees need to know exactly what procedures to follow to do their jobs.
3. *Reconciliation and cross-checking*—When the bank sends a monthly statement, it should be compared with the company's cash account and any differences should be investigated.
4. *Restrictions programmed into computerized systems*—Computerized systems have the ability to incorporate controls at many levels. Passwords are access controls. There are also restrictions on the size of an input into a program. For example, a computer may be programmed to accept only sales amounts under $1,000. For larger sales, a supervisor would need to be called to give direct personal approval.

Output controls are related to the accuracy and completeness of the system's output. The output will only be as good as the input and processing. If there is something wrong with either the input or the processing, then the output will be unreliable. However, there are specific controls that apply only to the output:

1. *Periodic review of output*—Each week, a sales manager might ask for a list of the previous week's sales for each member of the sales force. The manager

would review the output to make sure the system is reporting accurate amounts. One way to catch errors of omission would be to have salespersons review their own individual performance from the prior week.

2. *Internal audit*—A large company will often have a staff of accountants whose entire job is to review and evaluate the company's accounting information system. They are called internal auditors. Even though they are company employees, their tasks require them to be independent of the daily operations of the accounting information system.

3. *External audit*—External auditors are accountants hired by the company to verify the fairness of the financial statements. The auditors don't guarantee that there aren't any errors, but they do work hard to make sure that there isn't anything misleading on the financial statements. Auditing firms are often hired for special tasks in addition to auditing the financial statements. They may be hired to review and improve a company's internal control system, analyze its inventory management, review its credit and collection policies, or any number of other business consulting jobs.

To be effective, a system of internal control must rely on the people who perform the duties assigned to them. An internal control system is only as effective as the people who execute it. Human error, collusion, and changing conditions can all weaken a system of internal control.

Summary of Chapters 1 and 2

- A business is started when investors are willing to risk their money to start a business—to provide something of value for customers to make a profit. The investors may be owners or creditors.
- Investors, vendors, customers, and governmental agencies require financial information about businesses. There are four basic financial statements that provide the information: the income statement, the balance sheet, the statement of changes in owner's equity, and the statement of cash flows.
- The financial statements are based on a set of rules called generally accepted accounting principles (GAAP). These rules are not exact. As you learn more about accounting, you'll see that the numbers on the financial statements are not exact.
- To make the financial statements useful, we need to understand the rules and the choices used to construct them.
- The accounting equation,

$$\text{Assets} = \text{Liabilities} + \text{Owner's Equity}$$

is the basis of the balance sheet. It is a freeze-frame picture of the business at a specific point in time.
- The income statement, statement of changes in owner's equity, and statement of cash flows present details about the information on the balance sheet. Each of the other statements covers the period between the dates of two consecutive balance sheets.
- Accounting according to GAAP is accrual based. That means that revenues are recognized when they are earned, not when the cash is collected. Costs are matched to revenues so that they are recognized—put on the income statement as expenses—at the same time as the revenues they helped generate.
- Accrual accounting consists of two types of transactions—accruals and deferrals—in which the exchange of cash takes place at a different time than the exchange of goods or services.

■ With accruals, the action takes place before the exchange of cash. An example is a credit sale. The sale is recorded, but the cash will be collected later. Remember, *accrue* means to "build up." When Tom's Wear makes a sale on account, the company *builds up* sales, even though the cash hasn't been collected yet.

■ With deferrals, the dollars are exchanged before the action occurs. An example is paying for something in advance. When Tom's Wear paid for the insurance in advance, that was a deferral. Remember, *defer* means to "postpone." When Tom's Wear's purchases insurance in advance, prepaid insurance, the company postpones recognition of the expense. The action, in this case, is the passing of the time to which the insurance applies.

■ Adjustments are made before financial statements are prepared. The amounts recorded throughout the year may need to be adjusted to make sure they accurately reflect the assets, liabilities, owner's equity, revenues, and expenses on the date of the statements. How we actually adjust the amounts to correctly reflect the financial position of a company depends on how we keep track of our business transactions.

Understanding Excel

The following is a copy of Tom's Wear statement of changes in shareholders' equity as presented in this chapter.

Tom's Wear, Inc.
Statement of Changes in Shareholders' Equity
For the Month Ended February 28, 2001

Beginning contributed capital	$5,000	
Common stock issued during the month	0	
Ending contributed capital		$5,000
Beginning retained earnings	$ 385	
Net income for the month	935	
Dividends	(100)	
Ending retained earnings		1,220
Total shareholders' equity		$6,220

For purposes of this problem only, assume that in the month of March:

■ Tom's Wear issued additional common stock for a $1,000 contribution.

■ Total revenue for the month was $2,560.

■ Total expenses for the month were $1,150.

■ Tom was paid a dividend of $150.

Requirements

1. Open a new Excel work sheet.

2. By beginning in cell A1, input appropriate heading lines for a statement of changes in shareholders' equity.

Hint: 🖼 Highlight the cells to be centered and click the Merge and Center button to center your heading lines across columns A to C. Each line must be centered separately. (The second line will appear in full after your column widths are increased.)

3. By beginning in cell A5, input the lines of the statement. Adjust the column width of A as needed. (Remember to use the dragging or double-click method from Chapter 1.)

4. Input the appropriate dollar amounts in column B and the appropriate totals in column C. Always use formulas when you calculate totals. For example, ending contributed capital = B5 + B6.

   Hint: Instead of typing your formulas, try the click method. Click on cell C7 and type "=". Click on cell B5, type "+", click on cell B6, and hit enter.

5. Click the Increase Indent button 📇 to indent the words *total shareholders' equity* within the cell.

6. Format the appropriate cells with $ by clicking the cells and the Currency Style button $. Format the other numbers using the Comma Style button , . Highlight all the numbers and click the Decrease Decimal button twice to round the numbers to whole dollars. 📇

7. Underline or double underline the appropriate cells by selecting Format, Cells, and Border.

8. Print your file and save 💾 it to disk. Name your file TomsWear2.

Answers to Study Break Questions

1. The purpose of financial statements is to provide information useful for decision-making.
2. The Financial Accounting Standards Board (FASB) sets the accounting rules. Their authority is delegated from the Securities and Exchange Commission (SEC) as provided to them by Congress.
3. The focus of financial reporting is earnings and its components.

1. The difference between cash basis and accrual basis accounting is the timing of recognizing revenues and expenses. Cash basis accounting recognizes revenue when the cash is collected and expenses when cash is disbursed. In accrual accounting, revenues are recognized in the period in which they are earned (by the completion of the work) and expenses are matched to the revenues they help create.
2. The basic elements of the balance sheet are:

   - Assets—items of future value to a business, used to produce revenue.
   - Liabilities—creditor's claims to the assets of a company; the company's obligations to creditors.
   - Equity—owner's claims to the assets of the firm.

3. The matching principle is an accounting rule that states that expenses should be included on the income statement in the same period as the revenues they helped generate.

Questions

1. What is the difference between *cash basis* accounting and *accrual basis* accounting?
2. What are the four basic financial statements?
3. Who or what has the responsibility for setting accounting standards?
4. What is the FASB? What does it do?
5. Which financial statement pertains to a single moment in time?
6. What is an *asset*? A *liability*?
7. What is the *separate entity assumption*?
8. Explain *materiality* and give an example.
9. What is a *deferral*?
10. What is an *accrual*?
11. What is the *cost of goods sold*?
12. What does *recognize* mean in accounting?
13. Does a company have to collect the money from a sale before the sale can be recognized?
14. Define the *matching principle* and give an example.
15. What does *representational faithfulness* mean?
16. Describe *cost-benefit* analysis.

Short Exercises

SE2-1 Give the accounting principle, assumption, constraint, or information characteristic that is most applicable to each of the following:

L.O. 2-2

- All items purchased (except inventory) for less than $25 are expensed as incurred—even if they will last longer than a year.
- Personal transactions of the owner are kept separately from business transactions.
- The company uses the same inventory method from period to period.

L.O. 2-1

SE2-2 Give the accounting principle, assumption, constraint, or information character-istic that is most applicable to each of the following:

- Equipment is recorded as an asset and expensed over the periods in which it is used.
- The company prepares financial statements regularly.
- When insurance is purchased in advance, it is recorded as an asset.
- Assets like inventory are valued in dollars, not units, for the financial statements.

L.O. 2-1

SE2-3 For each of the following, give the accounting principle that is best described:

a. Buffalo Company reports revenue when it is earned instead of when the cash is col-lected.
b. The land on the Mule Company balance sheet is valued at what it cost, even though it is worth much more.
c. Lion Corp. recognizes depreciation expense for a computer over 5 years, the period in which the computer is used to help generate revenue for the business.
d. The president of Cougar Company thought that it would help the company's balance sheet to include as an asset some land he and his wife personally own. The accoun-tant rejected this idea.

L.O. 2-2

SE2-4 For each of the following numbered items, select, from the given lettered list, the qualitative characteristics described.

a. Relevance
b. Reliability
c. Comparability
d. Consistency
e. Representational faithfulness

1. It is imperative for providing comparisons of a firm from period to period.
2. Two primary qualities make accounting information useful for decision making.
3. Companies in the same industry often use the same accounting methods.
4. A financial statement should not be biased in what is reported.
5. If combining two assets on the balance sheet would be misleading to users, then they should not be combined.

L.O. 2-3

SE2-5 For each item that follows, tell whether it is an asset, a liability, or an equity item.

a. Prepaid insurance
b. Accounts receivable
c. Contributed capital
d. Notes payable
e. Cash
f. Equipment
g. Accounts payable
h. Supplies
i. Inventory

L.O. 2-3

SE2-6 On which financial statement would you be most likely to see each of the following?

a. Sales revenue
b. Salary expense
c. Prepaid insurance
d. Cash from operations
e. Common stock
f. Inventory

L.O. 2-3

SE2-7 Cost as a basis of accounting for assets has been severely criticized. Give several pros and cons for this practice.

L.O. 2-4

SE2-8 Suppose Deer Company performed services for a client on account on March 12, 2002. Deer charged the client $1,500. The client paid for half of the services on March 28, 2002. The remaining balance was paid on April 5, 2002. How did these transactions affect Deer's March 31, 2002 financial statements?

SE2-9 Millie's Moped, Inc. purchased inventory in December 2003 for $60,000 cash. The company sold merchandise that cost $20,000 in December 2003 and the remainder in January 2004. What is the cost of goods sold for December 2003 and for January 2004 if Millie's uses GAAP? What is the cost of goods sold for December 2003 and for January 2004, if Millie's Moped uses cash basis accounting?

L.O. 2-4

SE2-10 Suppose two companies are identical except for their credit policy. Both use GAAP. One company allows cash sales only, whereas the other sells for cash or credit. Suppose the two companies have the same sales revenue and expenses for the year. The only difference between the two is that the first company has no outstanding accounts (receivable), whereas the second has quite a few still outstanding at year-end. Of the four basic financial statements, which one or ones will be different between these two companies? Explain how and why they are different.

L.O. 2-4

Exercises

E2-1 One of your friends started a business in 2004. At the end of the first year, December 31, 2004, he has prepared the following income statement. Give three examples from the statement that indicate the statement is not prepared according to GAAP.

L.O. 2-1

Sales	$3,400
Inventory purchases	(2,000)
Rent for 2004 and 2005	(1,000)
Cash on hand	5,000
Due from customers	500
Net Income	$5,900

E2-2 Your car has broken down, so you have decided to look for a replacement. You find an advertisement on the Internet for a used Miata. When you contact the owner, this is what you find:

L.O. 2-2

1. The car is a 2001 model.
2. The owner said he has used the car only for driving to and from work.
3. The odometer reading is 45,389 miles.
4. The owner says that he has had the oil changed every 3,000 to 4,000 miles since he bought the car new.
5. The owner says this is the best car he has ever owned.
6. The owner will provide a maintenance record prepared by a licensed mechanic.

Evaluate each item from the preceding list in terms of its *relevance* to the decision about whether to buy this car. Then, evaluate each item with respect to its *reliability*. What additional documentation or supporting evidence would you want for your decision?

E2-3 On which financial statement would you be most likely to see each of the following? Tell whether each is an *asset, liability, owner's equity, revenue,* or *expense.*

L.O. 2-3

a. Unearned revenue
b. Salary expense
c. Prepaid insurance
d. Contributed capital
e. Distributions to owners
f. Equipment
g. Sales revenue
h. Cost of goods sold
i. Cash from investing activities
j. Depreciation expense
k. Inventory

L.O. 2-3

E2-4 Ed's Boat Company reported the following information in its records for 2003:

Net income	$ 5,000
Sales	85,000
Beginning balance—retained earnings	26,000
Cost of sales	55,000
Dividends	2,000

a. If the sales revenue given is the only revenue for the year, what were Ed's expenses other than those just listed ?
b. Describe what the beginning balance of $26,000 for retained earnings means? Is this useful information for potential investors?
c. What is the balance of retained earnings at the end of 2003?

L.O. 2-3

E2-5 Listed next are elements of the financial statements discussed in this chapter. Match each element with the descriptions (use each as many times as necessary) that follow.

a. Assets
b. Liabilities
c. Owner's Equity
d. Revenues
e. Expenses

1. _____ Debts of the company
2. _____ Economic resources with future benefit
3. _____ Inflows of assets from delivering or producing goods or services
4. _____ Things of value a company owns
5. _____ The residual interest in the assets of an entity that remains after deducting its liabilities
6. _____ What the company has minus what it owes
7. _____ The owner's interest in the company
8. _____ Probable future sacrifices of economic benefits
9. _____ Outflows or other using up of assets from delivering or producing goods and services
10. _____ Costs that have no future value
11. _____ What the company owes
12. _____ Sales

Problems—Set A

L.O. 2-2, 3

P2-1A The following cash transactions took place during March, the first month of business for Cats and Dogs Company:

1. D. C. Dawg started a business, Cats and Dogs Company, by contributing $6,000.
2. The Cats and Dogs Company borrowed $2,000 from the bank on March 1. The note is a 1-year, 12% note, with both principal and interest to be repaid on February 28 of next year.
3. The company earned $900 in revenue.
4. Expenses amounted to $650.
5. Distributions to owners amounted to $25.

Required:

a. Show how each affects the accounting equation.
b. Give one additional piece of information related to the transaction that could be recorded in an information system for a purpose other than the financial statements.
c. Prepare the four basic financial statements for the month of March.

L.O. 2-3, 4

P2-2A Alligator Company started the year with $1,000 in cash and contributed capital. During 2002, the Alligator Company earned $3,600 of revenue on account. The company collected $2,400 cash from accounts receivable and paid $3,100 cash for operating expenses.

Required:

   a. What happened to total assets (increase or decrease and by how much)?
   b. What is the cash balance on December 31, 2002?
   c. What is the total owner's equity on December 31, 2002?
   d. What is net income for the year?

P2-3A   The Brown Bear Company entered into the following transactions during 2005:

L.O. 2-4

■ Brown Bear was started as a corporation with a $5,000 cash contribution from the owners.
■ Supplies amounting to $400 were purchased on account.
■ Sales on account amounted to $3,200.
■ Cash collections of receivables amounted to $2,500.
■ On November 1, 2005, the company paid $1,200 in advance for an insurance policy.
■ Supplies on hand as of December 31, 2005 amounted to $100.

Required:

   a. How would the adjustment to record the supplies expense affect the accounting equation?
   b. If the insurance policy covered 1 year and the policy began on the date of payment, what is the amount of prepaid insurance that would appear in the asset section of the Brown Bear December 31, 2005 balance sheet?
   c. What is the amount of cash flow from operations for 2005?
   d. What would be the amount of total liabilities appearing on the Brown Bear December 31, 2005 balance sheet?
   e. What is the amount of contributed capital as of December 31, 2005?

P2-4A   Use the following information for Elephant Company *for the year ended December 31, 2004* to answer the following questions. Assume that the shareholders made no new contributions to the company during the year.

L.O. 2-3, 4

Revenues for 2004 = $350
Net income for 2004 = $110
Beginning balance (*December 31, 2003* balance) in retained earnings = $140
Ending balance (*December 31, 2004* balance) in retained earnings = $200
Total liabilities and shareholders' equity at *December 31, 2004* = $600
Total liabilities at *December 31, 2003* = $60
Total liabilities at *December 31, 2004* = $50

Required:

   a. What were the Elephant Company's total expenses during 2004?
   b. What was the amount of the dividends during 2004?
   c. What is the total that owners invested in the Elephant Company as of *December 31, 2004*?
   d. What were total assets on the company's *December 31, 2003* balance sheet?

P2-5A   ABC Company was started a year ago by Terry Lions. Early in 2005, when Terry went to the local bank for a loan, the banker asked for the December 31, 2004 financial statements. Terry had no idea how to prepare the statements, but she had heard of an income statement and a balance sheet. The statements she prepared follow.

L.O. 2-1, 2, 3

ABC Company Income Statement Prepared on April 1, 2005	
Net revenues	$6,757
Cost of goods sold	4,967
Operating expenses	1,397
Prepaid expenses	930
Accounts payable	300
Salaries payable	100
Sales on account	2,345
Net earnings	$ 393

ABC Company
Balance Sheet
Prepared on April 1, 2005

Accounts payable	$ 300	Accounts receivable	$ 235
Cash	21,500	Other revenue	1,406
Short-term investments	165	Salary expense	600
Inventories	15,270	Other current assets	990
Other current liabilities	145	Long-term liabilities	1,000
Long-term assets	416		

Required:

a. For each statement, give four examples that indicate Terry has not followed GAAP in the preparation of the statement.

b. What characteristics of financial statements described in the chapter do you think are missing in Terry's statements? If you were the banker, what would you tell Terry?

Problems—Set B

L.O. 2-2, 3

P2-1B   Given the following transactions:

1. Megan Moore's Aunt Myrtle May willed her an old bakery shop. Megan decided to open a pastry shop, Sugar & Spice by contributing $7,500 on May 1, 2002.
2. The Sugar & Spice Pastry Shop borrowed $6,000 from the bank on May 1. The note is a one-year, 10% note, with both principal and interest to be repaid on April 30, 2003.
3. Megan paid $2,000 to rent equipment for the shop for the month.
4. The electricity and water bills for the month were $850, paid in cash.
5. The Sugar & Spice pastry shop was a hit and earned $5,500 in revenue the first month, all cash.
6. Since the Sunny Susan Tanning Salon closed, Megan hired her friend to be the customer service specialist for the pastry shop. The salary expense was $425, paid for one month.
7. Learning little from her friend Sunny Susan's business failure, Megan withdrew $560 for a shopping spree to celebrate her business's early success.

Required:

a. Show how each transaction affects the accounting equation.
b. Give one additional piece of information related to the transaction that could be recorded in an information system for a purpose other than the financial statements.
c. Prepare the four basic financial statements for the month of May.

L.O. 2-3, 4

P2-2B   Candy Confection Company had $2,500 in cash and contributed capital when it began its fiscal year on July 1, 2005. During the 2005–2006 fiscal year, the Candy Confection Company earned $6,200 of revenue on account. The company collected $3,700 cash from accounts receivable and paid $2,800 cash for operating expenses. At the end of the year, the company bought a new delivery van for cash of $2,100.

Required:

a. What happened to total assets (increase or decrease and by how much) during the fiscal year?
b. What is the cash balance on June 30, 2006?
c. What is the total owner's equity on June 30, 2006?
d. What is net income for the year ended June 30, 2000?

L.O. 2-4

P2-3B   The Green Emerald Magazine Co. entered into the following transactions during 2008.

■ Green Emerald Magazine Co. was started with a $6,100 cash contribution from the owner.
■ There were $750 of supplies purchased on account.

■ Magazine sales, all on account, amounted to $7,200.
■ Cash collections of receivables amounted to $3,900.
■ On March 1, 2008 the company paid $3,600 in advance for an insurance policy.
■ Supplies on hand as of December 31, 2008 amounted to $325.
■ The owner withdrew $400.

Required:

a. How would the adjustment to record the supplies expense affect the accounting equation?
b. If the insurance policy covered two years and the policy began on the date of payment, what is the amount of prepaid insurance that would appear in the asset section of Green Emerald Magazine on the December 31, 2008 balance sheet; what amount of insurance expense would appear on the income statement for the year ended December 31, 2008?
c. What is the total cash flow from financing activities for 2008?
d. What would be the amount of total liabilities appearing on Green Emerald Magazine's December 31, 2008 balance sheet?
e. What is the amount of capital on December 31, 2008?
f. What would be the amount of total assets appearing on Green Emerald Magazine's December 31, 2008 balance sheet?

P2-4B Use the following information for Monster Mania for the year ended June 30, 2006 to answer the questions below. Assume that the shareholders made no new contributions to the company during the year.   L.O. 2-3, 4

Revenues for the year ended *June 30, 2006* = $850
Net income for the year ended *June 30, 2006* = $370
Beginning balance (*June 30, 2005* balance) in retained earnings = $280
Ending balance (*June 30, 2006* balance) in retained earnings = $360
Total liabilities and shareholders' equity at *June 30 2006* = $725
Total liabilities at *June 30, 2005* = $80
Total liabilities at *June 30, 2006* = $40

Required:

a. What were Monster Mania's total expenses during the year ended June 30, 2006?
b. What was paid to shareholders during the year ended June 30, 2006?
c. What is the total that owners invested in the Monster Mania as of June 30, 2006?
d. What were total assets on Monster Mania's June 30, 2005 balance sheet?

P2-5B Yakity Yak Company hired a new, inexperienced accountant to prepare its annual income statement. Use the following income statements for the questions below: L.O. 2-1, 2, 3

Yakity Yak Company
Income Statement
At December 31

	2004	2003
Sales	$9,723,334	$9,346,911
Cost of goods sold	(6,365,857)	(6,375,651)
Gross margin	3,357,477	2,971,260
General and administrative expenses	(2,460,338)	(2,286,917)
Property, plant, and equipment	23,501	1,740,030
Operating income	920,640	2,424,373
Interest expense	(78,297)	(68,528)
Other income, net	51,037	59,265
Accounts payable	(72,623)	(63,616)
Accounts receivable	11,002	—
Income before income taxes	831,759	2,351,494
Income taxes payable	(371,000)	(305,000)
Net income	$ 460,759	$ 2,046,494

Required:

    a. Give four examples that show the statements were not prepared according to GAAP.

    b. What characteristics of financial statements described in the chapter do you think are missing in these statements?

Issues for Discussion

Financial statement analysis

1. Use the annual report from Pier 1 Imports to answer these questions:
   a. Does Pier 1 have a single or a multistep income statement? How can you tell?
   b. Does Pier 1 have a classified balance sheet? How can you tell?
   c. Calculate the current ratio for the two most recent fiscal years. What information does this provide?
   d. Is there any evidence that the information in these financial statements is reliable and verifiable?

Business risk

2. In the Pier 1 annual report, find at least two references to the risks that Pier 1 faces.
3. What evidence can you find in the annual report that Pier 1 has controls in place to minimize information processing risks?

Ethics

4. R&R Equipment Company is preparing its annual financial statements in anticipation of applying for a loan. During the last week of the year, R&R received a shipment of inventory but has not paid for it. The invoice indicates R&R owes $5,000 for the purchase. The owner of R&R, Randy Ray, has decided to omit this asset and the related liability from the year-end balance sheet, reasoning that it is okay because he is omitting both of them, which means there is no difference in the equity.

   What is your opinion of Randy's reasoning? Discuss circumstances under which Randy's decision would be acceptable under GAAP and circumstances under which it would definitely be unacceptable.

Internet Exercise: Hoover's and Pfizer

Hoover's Online, The Business Network offers information about companies, industries, people, and related news items. For researching a company, this Web site is a good place to start gathering basic information.

    Please go to the www.prenhall.com/reimers *Web site. Go to Chapter 2 and use the Internet Exercise company link.*

IE2-1 Use the "search" scroll bar to select *Company* and then search for Pfizer. For Pfizer Inc. click on *Capsule.*

    a. What type of company is Pfizer?
    b. List three products manufactured by Pfizer.
    c. List three of Pfizer's top competitors.

IE2-2 Click on the *Financials* tab. Under "Free Financial Information" click on *Annual Financials.*

    a. For the most recent year list the amounts reported for revenue, cost of goods sold, and total net income. Does the amount reported for revenue represent cash received from customers during the year? If not, what does it represent? What does the amount reported for cost of goods sold represent? Is Pfizer a profitable company? How can you tell?

b. For the most recent year list the amount reported for inventories. Does this amount represent cost or market value? This complies with which generally accepted accounting principle (GAAP)?

c. For the most recent year list the amounts reported for total assets, total liabilities, and total (owner's) equity. Does the accounting equation hold true? Are assets primarily financed with liabilities or equities?

d. Does Pfizer use accrual based or cost based accounting? How can you tell?

Please note: Internet Web sites are constantly being updated. Therefore, if the information is not found where indicated, please explore the Web site further to find the information.

ACCRUALS AND DEFERRALS: TIMING IS EVERYTHING IN ACCOUNTING

Here's where you've been...

In Chapter 2, you studied the qualities of the information contained in the financial statements. This information should be *useful*. You also found that GAAP requires *accrual basis accounting*—revenues are recognized when earned and expenses are matched to those revenues.

Here's where you're going...

From Chapter 3, you should be able to understand how the financial statements show transactions in which the exchange of the cash and the exchange of goods and services happen at different times. These are *accruals* and *deferrals*.

3

Financing

Sales and Accounts
Receivable

Property, Plant,
and Equipment

**Financial
Reporting
and**

**Business
Events**

Inventory
and
Liabilities

Learning Objectives

More specifically, when you are finished studying this chapter, you should be able to answer these questions:

1. What are accruals and how do they affect the financial statements?
2. What are deferrals and how do they affect the financial statements?
3. What are adjustments, when are they made, and why are they necessary?
4. How do you construct the basic financial statements from a given set of transactions that include accruals and deferrals?

Measuring Income

Understand how income is measured, especially how accruals and deferrals affect the measurement of income.

Net income equals all revenues minus all expenses.

After its first month, Tom's Wear prepared a set of financial statements: to measure and report the company's activity during that first month; and to measure and report its financial position at the end of that month. Tom did both again for the second month.

At different points of time in the life of a company, owners, investors, creditors, and other interested parties want to know the company's financial position and accomplishments—to make all kinds of evaluations and decisions, including whether or not the company is meeting its goals. The main goal is usually to make a profit—so measuring the profit the company has made during a specified period plays a big role in evaluating how successfully a company has been doing its business.

Net income, net profit, or net earnings all mean the same—a company's profit. Net income, the most commonly used term, summarizes revenues and expenses for a period of time, usually a year. It can also be measured for a week, a month, or a quarter. For example, many companies provide quarterly financial information to their shareholders. That information would include net income for the *quarter*.

We can consider the continuous life of a business as being composed of discrete periods of time—months, quarters, or years. The way we divide the revenues and expenses among those time periods is a crucial part of accounting. That's why timing is everything in accounting. If revenue is earned in a certain time period, you must be sure that it is included on the income statement for that period—not the one before and not the one after. If you have used some supplies during a period, then you need to include the cost of those supplies as part of the expenses on the income statement for that same period.

Sometimes you will see the income statement referred to as the *statement of operations* and other times as the *profit and loss statement*. However it is referred to, it will usually appear as the first statement in a company's annual report. Exhibit 3-1 shows the income statements for Finish Line, Inc. When

Exhibit 3–1
Revenue and Earnings

From the Statements of Income for Finish Line, Inc.

(In thousands, except per share amounts)	February 26, 2000	February 27, 1999
Net sales	$585,963	$522,623
Cost of sales	423,505	373,170
Gross profit	162,458	149,453
Selling, general and administrative expenses	139,273	117,507
Operating income	23,185	31,946
Interest income—Net	826	1,421
Income before income taxes	24,011	33,367
Income taxes	8,404	12,680
Net income	$ 15,607	$ 20,687

you see sales of $585,963,000 for the year ended February 26, 2000, you know that *all* the sales made in that fiscal year—a year of business for the company—are included in that amount, even if some of the cash hasn't been collected from the customers by February 26, 2000. Similarly, the expenses listed are only the expenses incurred in that fiscal year, whether or not the company has paid for those expenses by February 26, 2000. Finish Line has worked hard to get the amounts right.

The problems created by the differences between

- the time when a company earns revenue by providing a product or service to customers and the time when the cash is collected from the customers

and

- the time when the company incurs an expense and the time when the company pays for the expense

are referred to as **timing differences.** You will see in this chapter how to identify timing differences and present them on the financial statements.

As discussed in the previous chapter, you can think of the timing problems in accounting in two simple ways:

- action before dollars
- dollars before action

An example of action before dollars is when a sale is made *on account.* A customer buys on credit and agrees to pay later. The action of making the sale—the economic substance of the transaction—takes place before dollars are exchanged in payment. This type of transaction—action first, dollars later—is called an **accrual.**

An example of dollars before action is when a firm buys insurance. By its nature, insurance must be purchased in advance of the time period to which it applies. Payment—when the dollars are exchanged—is made first, and the use of the insurance—the action provided by insurance protection—comes later. Dollars first, action later is called a **deferral.**

For timing differences, whether accruals or deferrals, we must look at the accounting information on each side of the difference, and adjust it before it can be presented on the financial statements.

Timing differences refer to the difference between the time a transaction occurs and the time the cash is exchanged.

An **accrual** is a transaction in which the action comes before the exchange of cash.

A **deferral** is a transaction in which the exchange of dollars comes before the action.

Accruals

Understand accruals, how the related adjustments are made, and how they affect the financial statements.

When the substance of a business transaction takes place before any cash changes hands, you include that transaction in the measurement of income. That is, if you have earned it, you must include it as revenue on the income statement. If you incurred an expense to earn that revenue, you must also include that expense on the income statement. Accruals can pertain to both revenues and expenses. There are two types of accruals that need a closer look:

- interest revenue and interest expense
- other revenue and expense

Accruals for Interest Expense and Interest Revenue

The most common timing difference has to do with interest related to borrowing or lending money. When you borrow money, you pay for the use of that money. What you pay is called interest. If you borrowed $500 from a bank on January 1, 2002, and agreed to repay it with 8% interest on January 1, 2003, you would have to pay back a total of $540. On January 1, 2002, when you borrow the money, you get the $500 cash, an asset, and you increase your liabilities. The accounting equation is increased on both sides by $500.

Assets	=	Liabilities	+	Shareholders' equity	
				Contributed capital	Retained earnings
+$500 Cash		+$500 Notes payable			

When you get ready to prepare the financial statements for the year ending December 31, 2002, you see that this liability—notes payable—is still on the books and will be listed on the balance sheet. The reason why is because on December 31, 2002, you still owe the bank the full amount of the loan. What about the $500 cash you received? You may still have it, but it is more likely you spent it during the year to keep your business running. That's why you borrowed it.

What about the cost of borrowing the money—the interest expense? On December 31, 2002 one full year has passed since you borrowed the money. The passing of time has caused interest expense to be incurred.

- Interest expense is the cost of using someone else's money.
- Time passing is the action related to interest expense.

Although the action of using someone else's money during the year has taken place, the dollars have not been exchanged—the interest for using that money. To make the December 31, 2002 financial statements correct, you must show the interest expense of $40 (= $500 × 8%, or $500 × 0.08) on the income statement. Also, you must show—on the balance sheet—the obligation called interest payable. It is a liability, indicating the bank's claim to the $40 as of December 31, 2002. The liability section of the balance sheet will show both the $500 loan and the $40 interest.

Assets	=	Liabilities	+	Shareholders' equity	
				Contributed capital	Retained earnings
		+$40 Interest payable			$(40) Interest expense

The adjustment increases liabilities and decreases retained earnings in the accounting equation. *Making* this adjustment is called **accruing** interest expense; the expense itself is called an accrual. Sometimes a company will label the amount of interest expense accrued as accrued liabilities or accrued expenses instead of interest payable. Each expression means the same thing—interest expense that will be paid in the future.

Suppose you borrowed the $500 on July 1, 2002 (instead of January 1). In this case, you would have use of the money for only half of the year and therefore would have incurred only half a year of interest expense as of December 31, 2002. Remember the formula for interest:

$$\text{Interest} = \text{Principal} \times \text{Rate} \times \text{Time}$$

Making an adjustment for a transaction in which the action has occurred but the cash has not yet changed hands is called **accruing** *the revenue or expense.*

Interest = Principal × Rate × Time

Interest rates, like the 8% annual interest, always pertain to 1 year. As of December 31, 2002, the interest payable on the note would be $500 × 0.08 × 6/12 or $20. The last part of the formula gives the time as a percentage of a year, or the number of months out of 12. Whenever you have to accrue interest, you must be careful to count the months that apply. That will help you make sure you put the right amount of interest expense on the income statement for exactly the period of time you had use of the borrowed money.

If you borrowed the $500 on January 1, 2002, for one full year, what would happen when you pay the bank on January 1, 2003? On one side of the accounting equation, you will reduce cash by $540. The equation will be balanced by a reduction of $500 in notes payable plus the reduction of $40 in interest payable. *There will be* **no** *expense recorded when you actually pay the cash.* Remember, the action has already taken place and the action resulted in interest expense in 2002. There is no interest expense in 2003 because you paid off the loan on January 1, 2003.

This is how timing differences work. The expense is recorded in one period, but the cash is paid in another period.

Assets	=	Liabilities	+	Shareholders' equity	
				Contributed capital	Retained earnings
$(540) Cash		$(500) Notes payable $(40) Interest payable			

Receivables with Interest

In most of our examples, a company will be borrowing money; however, sometimes a company lends money to another company or to an employee. A company that lends money accrues interest *revenue* during the time the loan is outstanding. The amount of interest revenue accrued at the time an income statement is prepared is calculated with the same formula used to calculate interest *expense,* $I = P \times R \times T$. The amount of interest revenue will increase assets—interest receivable—and will increase shareholders' equity—via interest revenue.

Suppose a company loaned $200 to an employee on October 1 at 10% interest, to be repaid on January 1 of the following year. The transaction on October 1 decreases assets—cash—and also increases assets—receivables. Because we use the term *accounts receivable* to describe amounts *customers* owe the company, we call the amounts owed by others—meaning anyone who is not a customer—*other receivables.*

Assets	=	Liabilities	+	Shareholders' equity	
				Contributed capital	Retained earnings
$(200) Cash +$200 Other receivables					

On December 31, the company will accrue interest revenue. Why? Because some time has passed and interest revenue has been earned during that period. With interest, the action is the passage of time, so the action has taken place, but the cash won't change hands until the following January 1. You would record interest revenue of $5 (= $200 × 0.10 × 3/12). You would also record interest receivable of $5. By doing all this, then the financial statements would accurately reflect the following situation on December 31:

■ The company has earned $5 of interest revenue as of December 31.
■ It has not been received at December 31.

Because all revenues increase retained earnings, the interest revenue will be recorded under retained earnings in the accounting equation:

Assets	=	Liabilities	+	Shareholders' equity	
				Contributed capital	Retained earnings
+$5 Interest receivable					+$5 Interest revenue

When the company actually receives the cash for the interest on January 1, along with repayment of the $200 principal, it will not be recorded as interest revenue. Instead, the total $205 cash is recorded as an increase in cash and a decrease in the asset other receivables by $200 and the asset interest receivable by $5. The timing difference resulted in recording the interest revenue in one period and the cash collection in another.

Assets	=	Liabilities	+	Shareholders' equity	
				Contributed capital	Retained earnings
+$205 Cash $(200) Other receivables $(5) Interest receivable					

**STUDY BREAK 3-1
SEE HOW YOU'RE DOING**

1. If you borrowed $1,000 at 7% (interest rates are always assumed to be *per year*), how much interest would you pay for having that money for only 6 months?
2. If you have an outstanding loan and you record interest expense before you actually make the cash payment for the interest, is this an accrual or a deferral? Why?
3. Why would a company record interest expense or interest revenue before any cash is exchanged?

Accruals for Other Revenues and Expenses

There are other types of revenues and expenses that must be accrued at the end of the period so that the financial statements will accurately reflect the business transactions for the period. For example, if you have provided services for a customer during 2003 but have not recorded those services (perhaps because you have not billed the customers yet), you want to be sure to record the revenue on the 2003 income statement. Why record this on the 2003 income statement? Because the action was completed in 2003. You cannot record any cash received for this action in 2003—because you haven't received payment in 2003 as a result of your action in 2003. This is a timing difference, recorded as an accounts receivable.

Accrued revenue and receivables are often paired together in accruals. An increase in assets—accounts receivable—and an increase in shareholders' equity—revenue—both in the same amount, balance the accounting equation. Then when the cash is actually collected, it is not recognized as revenue because it was already recognized in a previous period. That is, receipt of the cash in the following year is not recognized as revenue because the revenue was already recognized in the prior year.

Look at the current asset section of the Starbucks Coffee Company balance sheet at October 1, 2000—in Exhibit 3-2. It shows accounts receivable amounting to $76,385,000. This is a significant amount of money! When you see receivables on a company's balance sheet, it means the related revenues have been earned and included on the income statement for that period even though the cash hasn't been collected yet.

Expenses may also need to be accrued. When you get to the end of an accounting period—that's when you want to prepare financial statements—you examine your records and business transactions to find any expenses that might have been incurred but not recorded. These are the expenses you haven't paid for yet. (If you paid for them, you would have recorded them when you gave the cash to pay for them.) When you receive a bill for some expenses like utilities, you likely will record the expense and the related accounts payable. If you've done that, you won't have to accrue it at the end of the period.

However, there are some typical expenses that companies do not record until the end of the period. These expenses have to be accrued. The most common is salary expense. Typically, you record salary expense when you pay your employees. (In the accounting equation, this transaction would reduce assets—cash—and reduce retained earnings via salary expense.) What do you do if the end of an accounting period does not coincide with payday? What you need to do is record the salary expense for the work that your employees have done since the last time you paid them. *You want to be sure to get the correct amount*

From the Balance Sheet of Starbucks Coffee Company at October 1, 2000	
Assets	
Current assets	
Cash and cash equivalents	$ 70,817,000
Short-term investments	61,336,000
Accounts receivable (Net of allowance of $2,941,000)	*76,385,000*
Inventories	201,656,000
Prepaid expenses and other current assets	20,321,000
Deferred income taxes, net	29,304,000
Total current assets	$459,819,000

Exhibit 3-2
Accounts Receivable for Starbucks

of salary expense on the income statement for the period. This accrual will increase liabilities—salaries payable—and decrease retained earnings via salaries expense. The action—the employees performing the work—has already taken place; but the cash will not be exchanged until the next payday, which will be in the next accounting period.

Suppose you are preparing the financial statements for the accounting period ending on December 31, 2003. That date is Wednesday. If you pay your employees every Friday, the last payday of the year is December 26, 2003. As of December 31, 2003, you will owe them for their work done on Monday, Tuesday, and Wednesday, December 29, 2003, through December 31, 2003. You will need to record the salary expense for those 3 days, even though you won't pay the employees until Friday, January 2, 2004. Recording this salary expense so it is recognized on the correct income statement is called *accruing salary expense.* This adjustment will increase liabilities—salaries payable—and decrease shareholders' equity—by increasing salary expense.

What happens when January 2, 2004 arrives and you actually pay the employees? You will pay them for the week from December 29, 2003, through January 2, 2004. The expense for three of those days—December 29 through December 31—was recorded on December 31, 2003 so that it would be on the income statement for the fiscal year ending December 31, 2003. The expense for the other 2 days—January 1, 2004 and January 2, 2004—has not been recorded yet. The expense for those 2 days belongs on the income statement for the fiscal year ending December 31, 2004. When you pay the employees on January 2, 2004, you will reduce liabilities—the amount of the salaries payable you recorded on December 31, 2003 will be taken out of your accounting records—and you will reduce shareholders' equity—by recording salary expense for those 2 days in 2004.

Putting numbers in an example should help make this clear. Suppose the total amount you owe your employees for a 5-day workweek is $3,500. Look at the calendar in Exhibit 3-3—we're interested in the week beginning December 29.

On December 31, you need to accrue 3 days worth of salary expense. The $3,500 applies to 5 days, but you need to look at it as $700 per day. To accrue the salary expense for 3 days, you increase the liability salaries payable and decrease retained earnings via salary expense by $2,100. Why are you recording the salary expense and salaries payable even though you are not paying your employees until January 2? Because you want to have the expense for those 3 days on the income statement for the year ending *December 31, 2003.* How does this adjustment affect the accounting equation? Both the income statement and the balance sheet are affected by this accrual.

Assets	=	Liabilities	+	Shareholders' equity	
				Contributed capital	Retained earnings
		+$2,100 Salaries payable			$(2,100) Salary expense

On January 2, when you actually pay the employees for an entire week, you will give them cash of $3,500. How much of that amount is expense for work

---

Exhibit 3-3
Calendar for Accruing Salaries

Monday	Tuesday	Wednesday	Thursday	Friday
December 22	December 23	December 24	December 25	December 26
December 29	December 30	December 31	January 1	January 2
January 5	January 6	January 7	January 8	January 9

done in the year 2003 and how much is expense for work done in 2004? We already know that $2,100 is expense for 2003. The other 2 days worth of work done and salary earned—$1,400—applies to 2004. Here's how the transaction on January 2—paying the employees for a full week of work—affects the accounting equation:

Assets	=	Liabilities	+	Shareholders' equity	
				Contributed capital	Retained earnings
$(3,500) Cash		$(2,100) Salaries payable			$(1,400) Salary expense

Cash is reduced; salaries payable is reduced; and retained earnings is reduced via salary expense.

Review the example and make sure you know why the adjustment on December 31 was necessary and how the amount was calculated.

Suppose ABC Company pays its employees a total of $56,000 on the 15th of each month for work done the previous month. ABC generally records salary expense when the employees are paid. If the ABC fiscal year-end is June 30, 2003, does any salary expense need to be accrued at year-end? If so, how much?

Deferrals

The word *defer* means "to put off or to postpone." In accounting, a **deferral** refers to a transaction in which the dollars have been exchanged before the economic substance of the transaction—the action—has taken place. It can refer to both revenues and expenses. As you read and study the examples that follow, remember that you are taking the point of view of the business.

Deferrals Related to Revenue

Suppose a company decides to sell items on the Internet. The man who owns the company is a conservative fellow who isn't too sure about this new way of doing business, so he decides that he will not ship the products until he has received a customer's check and it has cleared the bank. When the company receives a check for $80 for an order, the owner must defer recognition of the revenue until the items are shipped. However, he immediately deposits the check. Technically, he does not have claim to the cash until he ships the items he sold. In fact, the claim to the cash belongs to the customer at the time the company receives and deposits the check. Here's how this cash receipt affects the accounting equation:

Assets	=	Liabilities	+	Shareholders' equity	
				Contributed capital	Retained earnings
+$80 Cash		+$80 Unearned revenue			

L.O. 2

Understand deferrals, how the related adjustments are made, and how they affect the financial statements.

A **deferral** is a transaction in which the cash is received before the action takes place. The cash has to be recorded, but the related revenue or expense is deferred. When we adjust that deferral to recognize any portion that may no longer need to be deferred, we are really *undoing* a deferral.

Unearned revenue is a liability. It represents the amount of goods or services that a company owes its customers. The cash has been collected, but the action of earning the revenue has not taken place.

Unearned revenue is a balance sheet account—a liability. It represents amounts a company owes to others—customers. This is called a deferral because the company is putting off the recognition of the revenue, that is, not showing it on the income statement, until the revenue is actually earned. Please notice that the name of this liability is a bit unusual. It has the word *revenue* in it, but it is *not* an income statement account.

When the items sold are actually shipped, the company will recognize the revenue. This will be done by decreasing unearned revenue and increasing shareholders' equity via revenue. Here's how the accounting equation will be affected:

Assets	=	Liabilities	+	Shareholders' equity	
				Contributed capital	Retained earnings
		$(80) Unearned revenue			+$80 Revenue

Notice that the claim has changed hands—the claim no longer belongs to the customer. Now that the items have been shipped, the owner has claim to the assets.

Another common example of deferred revenue is magazine subscriptions. Customers pay the company in advance, so the dollars are exchanged before the action—delivery of the magazine—takes place. When the customers pay, the cash must be deposited, but the revenue is not recognized. If the magazine company prepares a balance sheet after receiving the cash but before the magazines are actually delivered (so the revenue has not been earned), the balance sheet will show the cash and the obligation to the customers—the liability called *unearned revenue*. That obligation will be removed from the balance sheet when the magazines are delivered.

In a balance sheet prior to its merger with AOL, Time Warner, the owner of a number of magazines, had a large amount of unearned revenue, over $600 million. AOL called it *unearned portion of paid subscriptions*. The Tribune Company, a large corporation that owns newspapers, calls its unearned revenue *deferred income*. Their current liabilities are shown in. Exhibit 3-4.

STUDY BREAK 3-3
SEE HOW YOU'RE DOING

Living Time Magazine collected $300,000 for 12-month subscriptions before it published its first issue in June 2004. How much revenue should the magazine company recognize for the fiscal year ending December 31, 2004? Explain what it means to *recognize revenue* in this situation.

Exhibit 3-4
Unearned Revenue

From the current liabilities section of Tribune Company's balance sheet at December 31, 2000

Long-term debt due within 1 year	$ 141,404,000
Accounts payable	298,175,000
Employee compensation and benefits	231,684,000
Contracts payable for broadcast rights	271,510,000
Deferred income	90,421,000
Income taxes	129,954,000
Other	286,076,000
Total current liabilities	$1,449,224,000

Deferrals Related to Expenses

Four kinds of expenses are commonly paid in advance. We will first discuss expenses for insurance, rent, and supplies. The other is an advance payment for equipment used by a company for more than one fiscal period. All four expenses have in common that the timing of the cash disbursement precedes the actual use of the product or service purchased.

Insurance. Like any of us when we buy insurance, a company pays for insurance in advance of the service provided by the insurance company. In accounting, the advance payment for a service or good to be received in the future is considered the purchase of an asset. For insurance, accountants call the asset **prepaid insurance.** Remember, assets are items of value that the company will use up to produce revenue. Until it is actually used, prepaid insurance is shown in the current asset section of the balance sheet. Suppose Risky Company paid $2,400 for 1 year of insurance coverage, beginning on October 1, the date of Risky's payment to the insurance company. Here's how the payment will affect the accounting equation:

Prepaid insurance is an asset representing insurance that has been purchased but not used. The insurance expense has been deferred until the insurance is actually used (expires).

Assets	=	Liabilities	+	Shareholders' equity	
				Contributed capital	Retained earnings
+$2,400 Prepaid insurance					
$(2,400) Cash					

Purchasing the insurance policy is an asset exchange: cash is exchanged for prepaid insurance. No expense is recorded when the payment is made because the benefit of the cost has not been used. The expense will be recognized when Risky Company actually *uses* the insurance. The signal that the insurance is being used is the passing of time. As time passes, the insurance protection expires and the amount paid for that insurance during that time becomes an expense. You make the adjustment when you prepare the financial statements.

Suppose you want to prepare the financial statements on December 31. How much of the insurance is still *unused*? That's the amount you must show as an asset on the December 31 balance sheet.

How much have you *used* up? That's the amount you must show as an expense on the income statement.

Here's the adjustment Risky Company makes before preparing the December 31 financial statements:

Assets	=	Liabilities	+	Shareholders' equity	
				Contributed capital	Retained earnings
($600) Prepaid insurance					$(600) Insurance expense

The company has used up 3 month of the 12-month insurance policy already paid for. Risky paid $2,400 for the 12-month policy, so the monthly cost of insurance is $200. That means the total insurance expense for 3 months is $600, and the Prepaid Insurance remaining—insurance not yet used up—will be on the December 31 balance sheet in the amount of $1,800.

Exhibit 3-5
Deferred Expenses—Insurance

$500 cash paid for insurance policy at the beginning of 2001 for coverage over two years, 2001 and 2002:

$500

Insurance expense on the income statement for 2001 and for 2002:

Insurance expense $250 for coverage during 2001

Insurance expense $250 for coverage during 2002

*This is an example of a deferral—dollars paid first, action later. The cash payment for insurance coverage does not happen at the same time the insurance is used and becomes insurance expense. In this example, the cash for a two-year insurance policy is paid at the beginning of 2001. The $500 **cash disbursement** will be on the statement of cash flows for 2001, and the prepaid insurance will be an asset on the balance sheet at December 31, 2001. The **expense** will be shown on two different income statements—because the insurance expense applies to two different years. As the cost of the insurance becomes an expense, the amount of prepaid insurance on the balance sheet decreases.*

Prepaid rent is an asset. It represents amounts paid for rent not yet used. The rent expense is deferred until the rented asset has actually been used—when the time related to the rent has passed.

Rent. Rent is also usually paid in advance. In the accounting records, prepaid rent is treated exactly the same way as prepaid insurance. When the company pays the cash for rent in advance, an asset called **prepaid rent** is recorded. The disbursement of cash for prepaid rent is an asset exchange. Suppose Risky paid $9,000 to rent a warehouse for 3 months, beginning on November 1, the date of the payment. The way it would affect the accounting equation follows:

Assets	=	Liabilities	+	Shareholders' equity	
				Contributed capital	Retained earnings
+$9,000 Prepaid rent $(9,000) Cash					

The asset prepaid rent is increased, and cash is decreased.

Notice, no expense is recognized when Risky makes the payment for the rent. Until it is actually used, prepaid rent is an asset.

When would the rent expense be recognized, that is, when would it be put on the income statement? When Risky Company prepares financial statements, the company wants to be sure that the rent expense is shown correctly on the income statement. The amount paid was $9,000, for a period of 3 months, which is $3,000 per month. When Risky prepares the financial statements on December 31, 2 months of rent has been used—that's $6,000. To make sure the income statement reflects the expense for the period ending December 31, the company makes the following adjustment:

Assets	=	Liabilities	+	Shareholders' equity	
				Contributed capital	Retained earnings
$(6,000) Prepaid rent					$(6,000) Rent expense

Notice, rent expense is shown as a reduction in retained earnings, like all expenses.

That leaves 1 month of rent, $3,000, on the balance sheet as prepaid rent. The rent expense for November and December—$6,000—will be shown on the income statement for the year ending December 31.

Advantage Company paid the annual rent on its office space on March 1. The total for a year of rent was $3,600. How much rent expense would be shown on the Advantage December 31 income statement?

Supplies. Supplies are commonly purchased in advance. A company buying supplies is exchanging one asset for another.

The cost of the supplies is not recognized as an expense until the supplies are actually *used*. Suppose Risky Company started March with no supplies on hand and purchased $500 worth of supplies during the month. Here's how the purchase affects the accounting equation:

Be sure you see **supplies** are *not* called inventory. Supplies are miscellaneous items used in the business. When purchased, supplies are recorded as an asset. Supplies expense is recognized after the supplies are used. Inventory is a term reserved for the items a company purchases to resell.

Assets	=	Liabilities	+	Shareholders' equity	
				Contributed capital	Retained earnings
+$ 500 Supplies $(500) Cash					

If Risky prepares monthly financial statements, the company will count the amount of *unused* supplies on March 31 to get the amount that will be shown as an asset on the March 31 balance sheet. Only the amount of unused supplies will be an asset on that date. The difference between the amount *available* to use during March and the amount *remaining* on March 31 is the amount of supplies that must have been used. This amount, representing supplies used, will be an expense on the income statement.

Suppose Risky Company counts the supplies on March 31 and finds that there is $150 worth of supplies left in the supply closet. How many dollars worth of supplies must have been used? $500 minus $150 = $350. After supplies have been counted, Risky must make an adjustment to get the correct amounts for the financial statements. Here's the adjustment that must be made:

Assets	=	Liabilities	+	Shareholders' equity	
				Contributed capital	Retained earnings
$(350) Supplies					$(350) Supplies expense

That will leave $150 for the amount of supplies to be shown on the March 31 balance sheet. The income statement for the month of March will show $350 in supplies expense.

Suppose, during April Risky purchases an additional $500 worth of supplies. Then on April 30 as Risky is preparing financial statements for April, the supplies left on hand are counted. If $200 worth of supplies is on hand on April 30, what adjustment should be made? Recall that at the end of March, Risky had $150 worth of supplies on hand. That means that April started with those

Exhibit 3–6   Deferred Expenses—Supplies

March — $50 worth of supplies used — Cost of supplies **used** in March will be on the income statement as **supplies expense of $50** for the month of March.

April — $30 worth of supplies used — Supplies expense for April will be $30.

May — $40 worth of supplies used — Supplies expense for May will be $40.

June — $20 worth of supplies used — Supplies expense for June will be $20.

July — $30 worth of supplies used — Supplies expense for July will be $30.

February 1: Company buys $240 worth of supplies and pays cash. This will be on the **statement of cash flows.**

Company puts the supplies in the supply closet. The cost of the supplies is recorded as an asset on the **balance sheet.** The company has something of value. Dollars have been exchanged before the action of using the supplies has taken place. This is a deferral: dollars first, action later.

As supplies are used, the cost of those used becomes supplies expense and will be on the **income statement** as an expense in the period the supplies are used.

There are $70 worth of supplies in the supply closet at the end of July. That amount will remain on the balance sheet as an asset until the supplies are used.

supplies. Then $500 worth of supplies was purchased. That means that the company had $650 of supplies available to use during April. What dollar amount of supplies were actually used? Because $200 worth of supplies is left, Risky must have used $450 worth of supplies during April. The adjustment at the end of April would reduce the asset supplies by $450 and would reduce retained earnings by $450 via supplies expense.

**STUDY BREAK 3-5
SEE HOW YOU'RE DOING**

Konny Company started April with $500 worth of supplies. During the month, Konny purchased $650 worth of supplies. At the end of April, supplies on hand were counted, and $250 worth of supplies was left.

■ What amount of supplies would Konny put on its balance sheet at April 30?
■ What amount of supplies expense would appear on its income statement for the month of April?

Equipment.   When a company purchases an asset that will be used for more than one accounting period, the cost of the asset is *not* recognized as an expense when the asset is purchased. The expense of using the asset is recognized during the periods in which the asset is used to generate revenue. When you buy an asset—like a computer or office furniture—you record the purchase. It's an asset exchange because you are exchanging one asset—cash—for another asset—equipment. Then you will recognize a portion of that equipment cost each accounting period in which the equipment is used, hopefully to generate revenue.

The matching principle is the reason the cost of equipment is spread over several periods. Expenses and the revenues they help generate need to be on the same income statement—that's the heart of the matching principle. When it's hard to make that precise match, the next best match is to put an expense on the income statement in the *period* in which it is used. That's what you do with equipment—allocate the cost of the equipment to the periods the equipment is used.

Suppose Risky Company purchases a computer for $5,000. When the purchase is made, the company will record the acquisition of the new asset and the cash payment.

Assets	=	Liabilities	+	Shareholders' equity	
				Contributed capital	Retained earnings
+$ 5,000 Computer $(5,000) Cash					

If you were to classify the purchase as an expense at this point, you would be doing a very poor job of matching revenues and expenses. In this example, you want to recognize the expense of the computer during the years in which you use the computer. Suppose you expect the computer to last for 5 years. If the computer has an estimated **residual value** of zero, you need to recognize $1,000 worth of the computer's cost as an expense in each of the 5 years.

> **Residual value** is the estimated value of an asset at the end of its useful life. It is deducted before the calculation of depreciation expense.

The terminology accountants use with equipment is different than the terminology used with other deferrals. Instead of calling the expense related to using the computer something logical like "computer expense," it is called **depreciation expense**. Don't confuse *depreciation* in this accounting context with *depreciation* commonly used to mean *decline in market value*.

As the asset is used and you want to reduce its amount in your records, you *don't* subtract the amount of the expense directly from the asset's purchase price. Instead, you show the subtractions separately on the balance sheet. Exhibit 3-7 shows how a real company, Finish Line, Inc., presents this information.

> *Depreciating* an asset means to recognize the cost of the asset as an expense over more than one period. Each period's expense is called **depreciation expense.**

Using real financial information to learn an accounting concept can be difficult. An example with our fictitious company will help explain the accounting treatment of the cost of equipment and its depreciation expense over time. Suppose Risky Company purchased the computer for $5,000 on January 1, 1999 and recorded the asset exchange shown in the preceding accounting equation. Then when the company prepares its year-end financial statements, depreciation expense must be recognized. In the accounting records, the net amount shown for the computer needs to be reduced from the purchase price of $5,000 to $4,000 to reflect its use for 1 year. The shareholders' claims to the company assets are reduced via depreciation expense.

The total reduction in the dollar amount of equipment is called **accumulated depreciation.** Each year, accumulated depreciation gets larger. Accumulated depreciation is not the same as depreciation expense. Accumulated depreciation is the total depreciation taken over the entire life of the asset, and depreciation expense is the amount of depreciation for a single year.

> The reduction to the cost of the asset is called **accumulated depreciation.** Accumulated depreciation is a contra-asset, deducted from the cost of the asset on the balance sheet.

On the balance sheet, the original cost of the equipment is shown along with the deduction for accumulated depreciation—the total amount of depreciation

Exhibit 3-7
Property, Plant, and Equipment

From the balance sheet of Finish Line, Inc. at February 26, 2000	
Property and equipment	
Land	$ 315,000
Building	10,391,000
Leasehold improvements	89,909,000
Furniture, fixtures, and equipment	40,737,000
Construction in progress	2,087,000
	143,439,000
Less accumulated depreciation	41,820,000
	$101,619,000

The **book value** of an asset is defined as the cost minus the accumulated depreciation related to the asset. **Carrying value** is another expression for the same amount.

A **contra-asset** is an amount that is deducted from an asset.

that has been recorded during the time the asset has been owned. The resulting amount is called the **book value,** or **carrying value** of the equipment. The book value is the net amount that is included when the total assets are added up on the balance sheet.

Accumulated depreciation is called a **contra-asset** because it is the opposite of an asset. It's a deduction from assets. Accumulated depreciation is always shown separately on the balance sheet so that the original cost of the equipment is kept in tact.

Here's the year-end adjustment to record depreciation of the asset after its first year of use:

Assets	=	Liabilities	+	Shareholders' equity	
				Contributed capital	Retained earnings
$(1,000) Accumulated depreciation					$(1,000) Depreciation expense

The accumulated depreciation is shown on the balance sheet as a deduction from the cost of the equipment. The depreciation expense is shown on the income statement. The book value of the asset is $4,000 (cost minus accumulated depreciation) at the end of the first year.

Exhibit 3-8
Deferred Expenses—Depreciation

Truck purchased on January 1, 2001. The truck will last for seven years. Cost is $49,000. No residual value.

Cost of the truck will be spread over the income statements of the seven years the truck is used as depreciation expense. The expense is being **deferred**, that is *put off*, until the truck is actually used.

The cost of the asset is spread—as an expense—evenly (in this example) over the life of the asset.

Year ended December 31	2001	2002	2003	2004	2005	2006	2007
Depreciation expense	$7,000	$ 7,000	$ 7,000	$ 7,000	$ 7,000	$ 7,000	$ 7,000
Accumulated depreciation	$7,000	$14,000	$21,000	$28,000	$35,000	$42,000	$49,000

Understanding Business

RECOGNIZING REVENUE: WHEN IS IT THE RIGHT TIME?

When to recognize revenue is one of the most difficult judgments a company makes when it is getting ready to prepare its financial statements. Earnings—the net income of a company—receive a lot of attention from the financial press, from stock analysts, and from investors. A company will make every effort to meet the earnings forecasts that have been announced by analysts or expected by investors. Why? Because in the stock market the price of a company's stock often goes down when a company does not meet its earnings forecasts. The timing of revenue recognition is a big factor in the attempt to meet earnings forecasts.

During the last decade, the Securities and Exchange Commission (SEC) has warned companies to give close attention to accounts receivables and other items that result in revenue recognition. According to the SEC, *revenue recognition* remains the "recipe of choice for cooking the books." That means that companies are stretching the revenue recognition rules—or blatantly violating the rules—to increase earnings. In a speech to accounting professionals in 1999, the Director of the SEC Enforcement Division, Richard Walker, emphasized, "It should come as no surprise to anyone that many of

today's frauds are driven by efforts to engage in improper earnings management."

Approximately one-third of the actions brought by the SEC in 1999—32 of the 90—involved improper revenue recognition. Sales were booked and revenue recognized when the sales were not actually complete. Companies recorded sales in cases in which the customers had extremely liberal rights related to returning the product, in cases involving consignment sales, and even in cases where goods were shipped before they were finished. This effort to recognize earnings before generally accepted accounting principles (GAAP) permit their recognition has been shown to be closely linked to a company's efforts to achieve a predicted level of earnings.

There are many examples of how important accounting numbers are to a business. The sales and collection process and how the transactions from that process are reported are closely linked. Customers, investors, owners, and the SEC are all watching to see that the timing of revenue recognition follows the rules and that the income statement reflects the revenue that has really been earned during the period.

After the second year of use, you would again record the same thing—$1,000 more recorded as accumulated depreciation and $1,000 as depreciation expense. The amount of accumulated depreciation will then be $2,000. The amount of depreciation expense is only $1,000 because it represents only a single year—the second year—of depreciation expense. The accumulated depreciation refers to all the depreciation expense for the life of the asset through the year of the financial statement. (See Exhibit 3-8 for another example.)

The book value of the computer at the end of the second year is $3,000—that's the $5,000 cost minus its $2,000 accumulated depreciation.

Tango Company purchased a computer on July 1, 2004, for $6,500. It is expected to last for 5 years and have a residual value of $500 at the end of the fifth year. How much depreciation expense would appear on the Tango December 31, 2004 income statement? What is the book value of the machine at the end of 2005?

STUDY BREAK 3-6
SEE HOW YOU'RE DOING

Summing Up

Accountants want the income statement to reflect the revenues and expenses for the period covered by the statement—none from the period before or the period after. Accountants also want the balance sheet to show the correct amount of assets and liabilities on the date of the statement. To do that, accountants must allocate revenues and expenses to the correct periods. This is done by making adjustments at the end of the accounting period.

Sometimes a company purchases something and pays for it later. Sometimes a company earns revenue but collects the cash for that revenue later.

Accountants do not base the recognition of revenues and expenses on the income statement on the collection of cash or on the disbursement of cash. Revenue and expenses are recognized—that's when they show up on the income statement—when the economic substance of the transaction has taken place. The economic substance of a transaction is the action of providing or receiving goods and services.

When the action has been completed but the dollars have not yet changed hands, it is called an **accrual**. Action comes first, and payment for that action comes later. You accrue—build up, or accumulate—revenue you've earned or expenses you've incurred, even though the cash has not been exchanged.

In some situations, the payment comes first and the action for that payment comes later. Sometimes you pay *in advance* for goods or services; or sometimes your customers pay *you* in advance for those goods or services you will provide in a later period. These situations are called deferrals. Dollars are exchanged, but you *defer* recognition of the revenue or expense until the action of the transaction is complete.

Exhibit 3-9 provides a quick view of accruals and deferrals and what comes first, dollars or action.

Exhibit 3-9
Accruals and Deferrals

	Revenue	Expenses
Action First	**Accrued revenue:** Revenue must be on the income statement even though we haven't received payment. Example: interest on an investment may need to be accrued.	**Accrued expenses:** Expenses must be on the income statement even though we haven't paid for them yet. Example: salaries may need to be accrued.
Dollars First	**Deferred revenue:** Cash has been received from customers, but we haven't done our part to earn it. Example: customers pay in advance for items we will provide later. This results in *unearned revenue*, a liability on the balance sheet.	**Deferred expenses:** Cash has been paid for services or goods we have not used yet, but we have them. Example: supplies purchased but not used must be shown on the balance sheet. The expense is deferred until we use them.

Applying Our Knowledge: Ratio Analysis

Working capital equals *current assets* minus *current liabilities*.

In Chapter 2, you learned about the current ratio and how it helps a company by providing information about the company's ability to meet its short-term obligations. Another measure that helps a company evaluate liquidity is the amount of **working capital** a company has at a particular time. Working capital is defined as current assets minus current liabilities. The current ratio gives a *relative* measure, and the amount of working capital gives an *absolute* measure of a company's ability to finance its operations. Look at the information from the balance sheet of La-Z-Boy, Inc. in Exhibit 3-10.

The working capital for the year ended April 24, 1999 was *$293,160,000* (= $425,588,000 − $132,428,000).
The working capital for the year ended April 29, 2000 was *$455,363,000* (= $692,369,000 − $237,006,000).

Exhibit 3-10   Finding Current Assets and Current Liabilities on the Balance Sheet

From the consolidated balance sheet of La-Z-Boy, Inc.		
(Amounts in thousands, except par value)	As of April 29, 2000	April 24, 1999
Assets		
Current assets		
Cash and equivalents	$ 14,353	$ 33,550
Receivables, less allowance of $25,474 in		
2000 and $19,550 in 1999	394,453	265,157
Inventories	245,803	96,511
Deferred income taxes	22,374	20,028
Other current assets	15,386	10,342
Total current assets	692,369	425,588
Property, plant, and equipment		
Total Property, plant, and equipment	451,371	322,667
Less: accumulated depreciation	223,488	196,678
Property, plant, and equipment—net	227,883	125,989
Goodwill, less accumulated amortization of		
$17,360 in 2000 and $13,583 in 1999	116,668	46,985
Trade names, less accumulated amortization of $1,052 in 2000	135,340	—
Other long-term assets, less allowance of		
$6,747 in 2000 and $6,077 in 1999	46,037	31,230
Total assets	$1,218,297	$629,792
Liabilities and shareholders' equity		
Current liabilities		
Current portion of long-term debt	$13,119	$ 2,001
Current portion of capital leases	457	784
Accounts payable	90,392	45,419
Payroll/other compensation	74,724	53,697
Income taxes	5,002	4,103
Other current liabilities	53,312	26,424
Total current liabilities	237,006	132,428
Long-term debt	233,938	62,469
Capital leases	2,156	219
Deferred income taxes	50,280	5,697
Other long-term liabilities	31,825	14,064
Total liabilities	555,205	214,877
Shareholders' equity		
Preferred shares—5,000 authorized; none issued	—	—
Common shares, $1 par value—150,000 authorized;		
61,328 issued in 2000 and 52,340 issued in 1999	61,328	52,340
Capital in excess of par value	211,450	31,582
Retained earnings	392,458	332,934
Currency translation adjustments	(2,144)	(1,941)
Total shareholders' equity	663,092	414,915
Total liabilities and shareholders' equity	$1,218,297	$629,792

This increase is consistent with the overall increase in the assets and liabilities of La-Z-Boy during this year. Any company considering doing business with La-Z-Boy might compute working capital for several years to identify any increases or decreases. This increase would be a positive indication of the company's ability to finance its operations.

Business Risks

In Chapters 1 and 2, we discussed the risks a business faces, particularly those risks associated with financial information. As Tom starts his business operations, he needs to analyze his risks and devise a plan to minimize these risks.

The size of a company has a direct relationship to risk: the larger the company, the more risk it has to deal with. More risk means more controls. A small company like Tom's Wear may not have the risks that General Motors has, but Tom still has to think about the risks in his business and how to deal with them. Small businesses experience a great deal of fraud due to lack of controls, particularly segregation of duties. Let's look at the five components of an internal control system introduced in Chapter 2 and see how Tom might deal with them.

1. *Control environment.* As Tom establishes his business and his business relationships, he must plan to do business with honesty and integrity. Tom must have no tolerance for dishonesty with his vendors, creditors, customers, and employees. When he hires a new employee, for example, Tom's personnel policies need to reflect this commitment. He must be sure to communicate this to his employees, and then he must be a role model. Tom must set the tone at the top.

2. *Risk assessment.* Tom needs to evaluate his business and information risks. For example, he must assess the risk involved in selling his shirts on credit—the risk that his customers won't pay. He needs to evaluate every aspect of his business—when and where he buys the shirts, where they are stored, how he keeps records of his inventory and sales, how he controls his cash, etc. Even a small operation like Tom's Wear has its share of risks.

3. *Control activities.* How will Tom minimize the risks he has identified? For example, selling on credit presents a risk. One control to help minimize that risk would be extending credit to only those customers who have income above a certain level and a good credit rating. That's a common control for companies that sell on credit. There are dozens of other risks that Tom's Wear faces, and Tom will need to put many controls in place. He'll have a locked warehouse in which to store his inventory, and he'll have a bank account where he keeps most of his cash.

4. *Information system.* Tom's Wear won't need a very complicated information system, but it is still crucial for Tom to keep good records of all business transactions. For example, without them, he wouldn't be able to get the loans he needs to stay in business. As we've discussed, Tom needs more information than what is on his financial statements. He needs a system for keeping track of vendors, customers, and employees. The more complicated the system is, the more controls a company will need to make sure the system is operating correctly.

5. *Monitoring.* Making sure that the controls are working is the final item that makes up a company's internal control system. The best controls won't do any good if they are not operating. It's like having rules that no one follows.

Tom needs to monitor the controls he puts in place. For example, if one of Tom's controls is a lock on the warehouse, he needs to check the building periodically to make sure it is locked. If one of Tom's controls is a prenumbered sales document that has a space for the date, the quantity purchased, the customer name and address, and the sales price of each item sold, then Tom needs to be sure he and his sales people are using the prenumbered documents and recording all that information. Just having such a form is not enough. That's why monitoring is so important. The controls must exist *and* they must be working.

Every part of the business process—sales, collections, purchases, and obtaining financing—needs to have controls to manage the risks associated with the process. As you learn more about these business processes in the chapters to come, think about the risks and the controls needed to make sure that the risks are minimized.

Summary Problem: Tom's Wear in the Third Month of Business

In Chapters 1 and 2, Tom's Wear completed its first 2 months of operations. Exhibit 3-11 shows the company's balance sheet at the end of the second month, which we prepared in Chapter 2.

These are the amounts that are carried over to the next month, so this is the March 1, 2001 balance sheet, too. Let's take Tom's Wear through the third month of business, with the transactions shown in Exhibit 3-12.

At the end of his third month, Tom wants to prepare his financial statements to see how his business is progressing. Let's see how each transaction affects the accounting equation. Then prepare the four financial statements for the month of March.

Construct a basic set of financial statements with both accruals and deferrals.

Transaction 1: Purchase of a long-term asset

Tom's Wear purchases a fixed asset that will last longer than 1 year; therefore, it will be classified as a *long-term* asset. Remember, *current* assets will be used up or converted to cash within 1 year. If the cost of an asset needs to be spread over more than 1 year, it is considered long term. The actual purchase of the asset is recorded as an asset exchange, not as an expense. Here's how the purchase of

Tom's Wear Inc.
Balance Sheet
At February 28, 2001

Assets		Liabilities and Shareholders' equity	
Cash	$6,695	Accounts payable	$ 800
Accounts receivable	150	Other payables	50
Inventory	100		
Prepaid insurance	125	Common stock	5,000
		Retained earnings	1,220
		Total liabilities and	
Total assets	$7,070	shareholders' equity	$7,070

Exhibit 3-11
Tom's Wear Balance Sheet at February 28, 2001

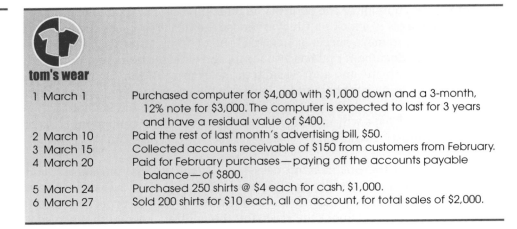

1	March 1	Purchased computer for $4,000 with $1,000 down and a 3-month, 12% note for $3,000. The computer is expected to last for 3 years and have a residual value of $400.
2	March 10	Paid the rest of last month's advertising bill, $50.
3	March 15	Collected accounts receivable of $150 from customers from February.
4	March 20	Paid for February purchases—paying off the accounts payable balance—of $800.
5	March 24	Purchased 250 shirts @ $4 each for cash, $1,000.
6	March 27	Sold 200 shirts for $10 each, all on account, for total sales of $2,000.

the $4,000 computer with $1,000 down and a note payable of $3,000 with an annual interest rate of 12%, due in 3 months, affects the accounting equation:

Assets	=	Liabilities	+	Shareholders' equity	
				Contributed capital	Retained earnings
+$ 4,000 Computer $(1,000) Cash		+$3,000 Notes payable			

The recognition of the expense related to the cost of the computer will be deferred—put off—until Tom's Wear has used the asset and is ready to prepare financial statements.

Transaction 2: Cash disbursement to settle a liability

Last month, Tom hired a company to do some advertising for his business. On February 28, 2001, Tom's Wear had not paid the full amount. Because the work was done in February, the expense was shown on the income statement for the month of February. In March, Tom's Wear pays cash of $50 to settle—eliminate—the liability. Here's how the cash disbursement affects the accounting equation:

Assets	=	Liabilities	+	Shareholders' equity	
				Contributed capital	Retained earnings
$(50) Cash		$(50) Other payables			

The action took place during February, so the expense was shown on that month's income statement. The cash was paid in March, but no expense was recognized in March because that would be double counting the expense. An expense is only recognized *once*.

Transaction 3: Collection of cash to settle a receivable

At the end of last month, Tom's Wear had not received all the cash it was owed by customers. Because the sales were made during February, the revenue from those sales was shown on the income statement for the month of February. Because the cash for the sales was not collected at the time the sales were made, Tom's Wear recorded accounts receivable. Accounts receivable is an asset that will be converted to cash within the next year. When customers pay their bills, Tom's Wear records the receipt of cash and removes the receivable from its records. Here's how the collection of the cash affects the accounting equation:

Assets	=	Liabilities	+	Shareholders' equity	
				Contributed capital	Retained earnings
+$ 150 Cash $(150) Accounts receivable					

Revenue is not recorded when the cash is collected because the revenue was already recorded at the time of the sale. To count it now would be double counting.

Transaction 4: Payment to vendor

At the end of last month, the balance sheet for Tom's Wear showed accounts payable of $800. This is the amount still owed to vendors for February purchases. Tom's Wear pays this debt, bringing the accounts payable balance to zero.

Assets	=	Liabilities	+	Shareholders' equity	
				Contributed capital	Retained earnings
$(800) Cash		$(800) Accounts payable			

Transaction 5: Purchase of inventory

Tom's Wear purchases 250 shirts @ $4 each, for a total of $1,000 and pays cash for the purchase.

Assets	=	Liabilities	+	Shareholders' equity	
				Contributed capital	Retained earnings
$(1,000) Cash +$ 1,000 Inventory					

Transaction 6: Sales

Tom's Wear sells 200 shirts at $10 each, all on account. That means the company extended credit to its customers, and they will pay later.

Assets	=	Liabilities	+	Shareholders' equity	
				Contributed capital	Retained earnings
+$2,000 Accounts receivable					+$2,000 Sales revenue

At the same time sales revenue is recorded, Tom's Wear records the reduction in inventory. The reduction in inventory is an expense called *cost of goods sold*.

Assets	=	Liabilities	+	Shareholders' equity	
				Contributed capital	Retained earnings
$(800) Inventory					$(800) Cost of goods sold

Notice, the sale is recorded at the amount Tom's Wear will collect from the customer. At the same time, the reduction in the inventory is recorded at the cost of the inventory—200 shirts at a cost of $4 per shirt. This is a terrific example of the matching principle.

Notice, there is no explicit recording of profit in the company records. Instead, profit is a derived amount; it is calculated by subtracting cost of goods sold from the amount of sales. For this sale, the profit is $1,200. It is called the *gross profit*—also called *gross margin*—on sales. Other expenses must be subtracted from the gross margin to get to *net profit*, also called *net income*.

Exhibit 3-13 shows a summary of the routine transactions during the month ending March 31, 2001. At the end of the month, Tom will adjust the company records for any accruals and deferrals needed for the financial statements. Look back over the transactions and see if you can identify the adjustments needed.

Required

Make the adjustments needed and then prepare the four financial statements for the month of March 2001.

Solution

Adjustments needed at the end of March 2001	
Depreciation expense for computer	$100
Insurance expense for the month	$ 50
Interest expense on the note payable	$ 30

Exhibit 3-13   Work Sheet for March 2001

		Assets	=	Liabilities	+	Shareholders' equity		
						Contributed capital	Retained earnings	
Balance sheet at March 1, 2001 →	Cash	$ 6,695	=	Accounts payable	$ 800	+	Common	Retained
	Accounts receivable	150		Other payables	50		stock **$5,000**	earnings **$1,220**
	Inventory	100			**$850**			
	Prepaid insurance	125						
		$ 7,070						
March 1	Computer	+$4,000		Notes payable	+3,000			
	Cash	(1,000)						
March 10	Cash	(50)		Other payables	(50)			
March 15	Cash	+150						
	Accounts rec.	(150)						
March 20	Cash	(800)		Accounts payable	(800)			
March 24	Cash	(1,000)						
	Inventory	+1,000						
March 27	Accounts rec.	+2,000					Sales	+2,000
	Inventory	(800)					Cost of goods sold	(800)
Balance Sheet at March 31 →	Cash	$ 3,995	=	Notes payable	**$3,000**	+	Common	Retained
before adjustments	Accounts receivable	2,000					stock **$5,000**	earnings **$2,420**
	Inventory	300						
	Prepaid insurance	125						
	Computer	4,000		*Total liabilities and shareholders' equity*				
	Total assets	**$10,420**		**$10,420**				

Adjustment 1: Depreciation

The computer purchased on March 1 must be depreciated—that is, part of the cost must be recognized as depreciation expense during March. To figure out the depreciation expense, the residual value is subtracted from the cost of the asset, and then the difference is divided by the estimated useful life of the asset. In this case, the residual value is $400, so that amount is subtracted from the cost of $4,000. The remaining $3,600 is divided by 3 years, resulting in a depreciation expense of *$1,200 per year.* Because Tom is doing a monthly statement, he divides the annual amount by 12 months, giving $100 depreciation per month. The adjustment is a reduction to assets and an expense.

L.O. 4

Notice, the residual value is deducted only in the calculation of the amount of depreciation expense. It is not deducted from the cost of the asset in the company's formal records.

Assets	=	Liabilities	+	Shareholders' equity	
				Contributed capital	Retained earnings
$(100) Accumulated depreciation					$(100) Depreciation expense

The reduction to the cost of the computer accumulates each month, so that the carrying value of the asset in the accounting records goes down by $100 each month. Tom doesn't just subtract $100 each month from the computer's cost on the left side of the equation, because generally accepted accounting principles (GAAP) require the cost of a specific asset and the total accumulated depreciation related to that asset to be shown separately.

The subtracted amount is called accumulated depreciation. After the first month, accumulated depreciation related to this particular asset is $100. After the second month, the accumulated depreciation will be $200. That amount—representing how much of the asset cost we count as used—is a *contra-asset,* because it reduces the recorded value of an asset.

The cost of an asset minus its accumulated depreciation is called the *book value* or *carrying value* of the asset. Each time depreciation expense is recorded, the accumulated depreciation increases, and the book value of the asset decreases.

Depreciation expense represents a single period's expense and is shown on the income statement.

Adjustment 2: Insurance Expense

In mid-February, Tom's Wear purchased 3 months worth of insurance for $150, which is $50 per month. On the March 1 balance sheet, there is a current asset called prepaid insurance in the amount of $125. A full month of insurance expense needs to be recorded for the month of March. That amount will be deducted from prepaid insurance.

Assets	=	Liabilities	+	Shareholders' equity	
				Contributed capital	Retained earnings
$(50) Prepaid insurance					$(50) Insurance expense

Adjustment 3: Accruing Interest Expense

On March 1, Tom's Wear signed a 3-month note for $3,000. The note carries an interest rate of 12%. Interest rates are typically given as an **annual rate.** Because Tom is preparing a monthly income statement, he needs to accrue 1 month of interest expense. Using the interest rate formula—Interest = Principal × Rate × Time—produces the following interest computation:

$$\text{Interest} = \$3,000 \times 0.12 \times 1/12\,(1\,\text{Month out of } 12) = \underline{\underline{\$30}}$$

Notice, the calculation of the interest expense does *not* take into consideration the length of the note. The interest expense would be the same if this were a 6-month note or a 2-year note, or a note of any other length of time. Interest expense is calculated based on the time that has passed *as a fraction of a year* because the interest rate used is an **annual rate.**

Assets	=	Liabilities	+	Shareholders' equity	
				Contributed capital	**Retained earnings**
		$30 Interest payable			$(30) Interest expense

These are the needed adjustments at March 31, 2001, for Tom's Wear to produce accurate financial statements according to GAAP.

First, Tom prepares the income statement. Revenues and expenses are found in the retained earnings column of the accounting equation work sheet. Organized and summarized, they produce the income statement for Tom's Wear for March. The income statement covers a period of time—in this case, it covers 1 month of business activity.

Tom's Wear, Inc.
Income Statement
For the Month Ended March 31, 2001

Sales revenue		$2,000
Expenses		
Cost of goods sold	$800	
Depreciation expense	100	
Insurance expense	50	
Interest expense	30	980
Net Income		$1,020

Second, Tom prepares the statement of changes in shareholders' equity—a summary of what has happened to equity during the period. Like the income statement, the statement of changes in shareholders' equity covers a period of time—here, 1 month.

Tom's Wear, Inc.
Statement of Changes in Shareholders' Equity
For the Month Ended March 30, 2001

Beginning contributed capital	$ 5,000	
Contributions during the month	0	
Ending contributed capital		$5,000
Beginning retained earnings	$ 1,220	
Net income for the month	1,020	
Dividends	0	
Ending retained earnings		2,240
Total shareholders' equity		$7,240

Third, Tom prepares the balance sheet—composed of three sections: assets, liabilities, and shareholders' equity, with the amount of each on the last day of the period. The assets are arranged in order of liquidity—that's how easily the asset can be converted to cash. Current assets will be used or converted to cash sometime during the next fiscal year. Long-term assets will last longer than 1 year.

Current liabilities are obligations that will be satisfied using current assets. Long-term liabilities are obligations that will *not* be repaid in the next fiscal year.

Shareholders' equity is shown in two parts—contributed capital and retained earnings.

Because the balance sheet is a sumsmary of all the transactions in the accounting equation, it will balance—assets = liabilities + shareholders' equity.

Tom's Wear, Inc.
Balance Sheet
At March 31, 2001

Assets		Liabilities and Shareholders' equity	
Cash	$ 3,995	Accounts payable	$ 0
Accounts Receivable	2,000	Other payables	0
		Interest payable	30
		Notes payable	3,000
Inventory	300	Total liabilities	3,030
Prepaid insurance	75		
Computer (net of $100	3,900	Common stock	$ 5,000
accumulated		Retained earnings	2,240
depreciation)			
Total assets	$10,270	Total liabilities and	$10,270
		shareholders' equity	

Fourth, Tom prepares the statement of cash flows. Because the first three financial statements—income statement, statement of changes in shareholders' equity, and the balance sheet—are *accrual based* instead of *cash based,* these three financial statements do not provide detailed information about a company's cash—where it came from and how it was spent. The balance sheet gives only the total amount of cash on hand at the close of business on the last day of the fiscal period, and the income statement—the focus of financial reporting— gives no information about cash. This is why the statement of cash flows is needed. Even though accrual accounting does not base the measurement of income on cash, there is no debate about the importance of the sources and uses of cash to a business. The statement of cash flows gives the details of how the cash balance has changed from the first day of the period to the last day.

Tom's Wear, Inc.
Statement of Cash Flows
For the Month Ended March 31, 2001

Cash from operating activities		
Cash collected from customers	$ 150	
Cash paid to vendors	(1,800)	
Cash paid for operating expense	(50)	
Total cash from operations		$(1,700)
Cash from investing activities		
Purchase of asset[a]	$(1,000)	(1,000)
Cash from financing activities		0
Net increase (decrease) in cash		$(2,700)

[a]Computer was purchased for $4,000. A note was signed for $3,000 and cash paid was $1,000.

Check it out. Did the cash balance decrease by $2,700 during March? Yes, cash started at $6,695 on March 1 and ended at $3,995 on March 31, a difference of $2,700.

Understanding Excel

The following is a list of accounts for Tom's Wear at March 31, after adjustments:

Cash	$3,995
Accounts receivable	2,000
Prepaid insurance	75
Inventory	300
Computer, net of depreciation	3,900
Notes payable	3,000
Interest payable	30
Contributed capital	5,000
Retained earnings, March 1	1,220
Sales	2,000
Cost of goods sold	800
Depreciation expense	100
Insurance expense	50
Interest expense	30

For purposes of this exercise only, assume that the following, additional transactions for Tom's Wear during the month of March:

a. On March 31, Tom paid $150 in cash for 2 months of advertising in a college newspaper. The ad will appear in the newspaper in the months of April and May.

b. Tom hired a part-time employee who started work on March 26. Tom owes him $80 for wages in March. The wages will be paid on April 2. (Ignore payroll taxes.)

c. On March 31, a customer ordered some special logo T-shirts and gave Tom a deposit of $200. The T-shirts will be delivered to the customer in April.

d. Tom estimates that he will owe $50 in income taxes for the month of March.

Requirements

1. Open a new Excel work sheet.
2. Create the following bold column headings beginning in column A and ending in column E: **Account, Current Balance, Balance Increases, Balance Decreases, and Ending Balance.**

Hint: To minimize the column width of columns that have multi-word headings, select Format, Cells, and Alignment; then check the "Wrap Text" box.)

3. Enter the previous account information in the **Account** and **Current Balance** columns.
4. Complete the process by:
   a. entering the adjustment amounts indicated in items a to d
   b. computing the adjusted balances

Hint: Compute the balance for the first account by adding the amount in column B to column C and subtracting column D. For example " = B3 + C3 − D3." Either type in your formulas or use the click method. Use the fill handle to copy the formulas to the remaining accounts. Select the cell you want to copy and point to the fill handle. When the arrow changes to a thin crosshair, click your left mouse button and drag the handle over the range that you want copied. Release the mouse button to finish.

5. Prepare an income statement and balance sheet for the month ended March 31. Use appropriate headings, formats, and borders. Adjust the column widths as needed. Use the Increase Indent button to indent the totals.

Hint: Instead of retyping the account names and dollar amounts, input them by referencing cells. For example, "= A4" for the account name or "= E4" for the dollar amount. Remember to use formulas when you add columns of numbers.

6. Print your work sheet and save it to disk. Name your file TomsWear3.

Answers to Study Break Questions

Study Break 3-1

1. You would pay $1,000 × 0.07 × 1/2 = $35 in interest.
2. This is an accrual—the action of incurring the expense via the passage of time precedes the cash payment.
3. At the end of the accounting period, the books need to be adjusted to get the expense in the correct period (to be shown on the income statement in the right time period).

Study Break 3-2

Yes, salary expense needs to be accrued. The expense for June would routinely be recorded on July 15 when the payment is made. To get the June salary expense on the income statement for the year ending June 30, ABC Company needs to accrue the expense. A month of salary expense for June is recorded as *salary expense* and *salaries payable* in the amount of $56,000.

Study Break 3-3

Out of 12 months of magazines, 7 months have been delivered at December 31. That means 7/12 of the $300,000 collected in advance has actually been earned by December 31. When the cash was collected, the recognition of the revenue was *deferred*—put off or postponed—because it hadn't been earned. At December 31, the company recognizes $175,000 worth of revenue. That means it will put $175,000 worth of revenue on the income statement and reduce the liability *unearned revenue* on the balance sheet.

Study Break 3-4

When Advantage Company made the rent payment on March 1, the company recorded a decrease in cash and an increase in the asset *prepaid rent*. Now, it is 10 months later, and 10 months worth of rent has been used. That means it should be recorded as *rent expense*. The March 1 payment was $3,600 for 1 year, which means $300 per month. Now, 10 months × $300 per month = $3,000 must be deducted from *prepaid rent* and added to *rent expense*. Then $3,000 of rent expense will be shown on the income statement.

Study Break 3-5

Konny started with $500 worth of supplies and then purchased an additional $650 worth, which makes a total of $1,150 supplies available for the company to use during the month. At the end of the month, there are $250 worth of supplies remaining. That means that the company must have used $900 worth (= $1,150 − $250). Of the supplies remaining, $250 will be on the balance sheet as a current asset, *supplies;* and, *supplies expense* of $900 will be shown on the income statement for April.

Study Break 3-6

1. The depreciable amount is the cost minus the residual (salvage) value, $6,500 − $500 = $6,000.
2. The estimated life is 5 years.
3. Thus, the depreciation expense per year is $6,000/5 = $1,200 per year.
4. Because the computer was purchased on July 1, 2004, only half a year of depreciation expense, $600, will be shown on the income statement for the year ending December 31, 2004.
5. The book value = cost less accumulated depreciation (that's all the depreciation that has been recorded on the asset during its life) = $6,500 − $600 (for 2004) − $1,200 (for 2005) = $4,700 at December 31, 2005.

Questions

1. How does *accrual accounting* differ from *cash basis accounting*?
2. What is *deferred revenue*?
3. What is *accrued revenue*?
4. What are *deferred expenses*?
5. What are *accrued expenses*?
6. What is *interest*?
7. Explain the difference between *liabilities* and *expenses*.
8. Name two common deferred expenses.
9. What does it mean to *recognize* revenue?

10. How does matching relate to accruals and deferrals?
11. What is *depreciation*?
12. Why is depreciation necessary?

Short Exercises

L.O. 3-1

SE3-1 Eve Company pays all salaried employees biweekly. Overtime pay, however, is paid in the next biweekly period. Eve accrues salary expense only at its December 31 year-end. Information about salaries earned in December 2003 is as follows:

- Last payroll was paid on December 26, 2003, for the 2-week period ended December 26, 2003.
- Overtime pay earned in the 2-week period ended December 26, 2003 was $5,000.
- Remaining workdays in 2003 were December 29, 30, 31, and there was no overtime on those 3 days.
- The regular biweekly salaries total $90,000.

Using a 5-day workweek, what will Eve Company's balance sheet show as a liability—salaries payable—on Decmber 31, 2003?

L.O. 3-1

SE3-2 Lucky Luke Company purchased equipment on November 1, 2005 and gave a 3-month, 9% note with a face value of $20,000. How much interest expense will be recognized on the income statement for the year ending December 31, 2005? What effect does this adjustment have on the statement of cash flows for 2005?

L.O. 3-2

SE3-3 The correct amount of prepaid insurance shown on a company's December 31, 2003 balance sheet was $800. On July 1, 2004, the company paid an additional insurance premium of $400. On the December 31, 2004 balance sheet, the amount of prepaid insurance was correctly shown as $500. What amount of *insurance expense* should appear on the company's 2004 income statement?

L.O. 3-2

SE3-4 The New Start Company collects all service revenue in advance. The company showed an $11,500 liability on its December 31, 2002 balance sheet for service revenue received in advance. During 2003, customers paid $60,000 for future services and the 2003 income statement reported service revenue of $60,700. What amount for the liability *service revenue received in advance* will appear on the 2003 balance sheet?

L.O. 3-2

SE3-5 Silas Company purchased equipment on November 1, 2001, and gave a 3-month, 9% note with a face value of $20,000. On maturity, the note plus interest will be paid to the bank. Fill in the blanks in the following chart:

	Interest expense	Cash paid for interest
November 30, 2001	_____	_____
December 31, 2001	_____	_____
January 31, 2002	_____	_____

L.O. 3-2

SE3-6 Able Company received $4,800 from a tenant on April 1 for 1 year of rent in advance. *In the Able information system, these cash receipts are coded as revenue.* What adjustment will Able have to make when preparing the December 31 financial statements? Show how the adjustment affects the accounting equation.

L.O. 3-2

SE3-7 Cain Company paid $3,600 on June 1, 2001, for a 2-year insurance policy. *In the Cain information system, these cash disbursements are coded as expenses.* What adjustment will Cain have to make when preparing the December 31 financial statements? Show how the adjustment affects the accounting equation.

L.O. 3-2

SE3-8 Peter's Pizza started the month with $500 worth of cleaning supplies. During the month, Peter's Pizza purchased an additional $300 worth of supplies. At the end of the month, $175 worth of supplies remained. Give the amounts that would appear on the financial statements for the month for supplies expense and supplies-on-hand.

SE3-9 Mary rented office space for her new business on March 1, 2002. To get a discount she paid $3,600 for 12 months rent in advance. How will this appear on the financial statements at December 31? Use the following chart for your answers:

L.O. 3-2

	Rent expense	Prepaid rent at December 31
2002	_____	_____
2003	_____	_____

SE3-10 In November and December 2004, Paul Company, a newly organized magazine publisher, received $60,000 for 1,000 subscriptions (3 year) to a new monthly magazine at $20 per year, starting with the first issue in March 2005.

L.O. 3-2

Fill in the following chart related to the amount of revenue to be recognized in each of the given years (with fiscal year-end December 31):

	Revenue recognized	Unearned revenue at December 31
2004	_____	_____
2005	_____	_____
2006	_____	_____
2007	_____	_____

SE3-11 Timothy & Company paid $3,600 on June 1, 2003 for a 2-year insurance policy beginning on that date. The company recorded the entire amount as prepaid insurance. By using the following chart, calculate how much expense and prepaid insurance will be shown on the year-end financial statements. The company's year-end is December 31.

L.O. 3-2

	Cash paid	Insurance expense	Prepaid insurance at December 31
2003	$3,600	_____	_____
2004	0	_____	_____
2005	0	_____	_____

Exercises

E3-1 Thomas Toy Company purchased a new delivery truck on January 1, 2001 for $25,000. The truck is estimated to last for 6 years and will then be sold, at which time it should be worth approximately $1,000. The company uses straight-line depreciation and has a fiscal year-end of December 31.

L.O. 3-2

- How much depreciation expense will be shown on the income statement for the year ending December 31, 2003?
- What is the net book value (also called carrying value) of the truck on the balance sheet for each of the 6 years beginning with December 31, 2001?

E3-2 On March 1, 2005, Kangaroo Company was formed when the owners invested $35,000 cash in the business. On April 1, 2005, the company paid $24,000 cash in advance to rent office space for the coming year. The office space was used as a place to consult with clients. The consulting activity generated $62,000 of cash revenue during 2005. Based on this information alone, prepare an income statement, statement of changes in shareholders' equity, balance sheet, and statement of cash flows as of December 31, 2005.

L.O. 3-3, 4

E3-3 On January 1, 2001, the law firm of Lions, Tigers, and Bears was formed. On February 1, 2001, the company was paid $18,000 in advance for services to be performed monthly during the coming year. Assuming that this was the only transaction completed in 2001, prepare an income statement, statement of changes in shareholders' equity, balance sheet, and statement of cash flows as of December 31, 2001.

L.O. 3-3, 4

L.O. 3-3, 4

E3-4 Best Pest Control was started when its owners invested $20,000 in the business on January 1, 2003. The cash received by the company was immediately used to purchase a $20,000 depreciable asset, which had a $5,000 residual value and an expected useful life of 5 years. The company earned $13,000 of cash revenue during 2003. Based on this information alone, prepare an income statement, statement of changes in owners' equity, balance sheet, and statement of cash flows for 2003.

L.O. 3-4

E3-5 Tell whether each of the following items would appear on the income statement, statement of changes in shareholders' equity, balance sheet, or statement of cash flows. Some items may appear on more than one statement (include all of them in your answer). If an item does not appear on any financial statement, indicate that with *none*.

Interest receivable	Accounts payable
Salary expense	Contributed capital
Notes receivable	Distributions
Unearned revenue	Total assets
Cash flow from investing activities	Interest revenue
Insurance expense	Consulting revenue
Retained earnings	Depreciation expense
Prepaid insurance	Supplies expense
Cash	Salaries payable
Accumulated depreciation	Supplies
Working capital	Cash flow from financing activities
Accounts receivable	Land
Debt-to-equity ratio	Service revenue
Operating expenses	Cash flow from operating activities
Total liabilities	Current ratio
Salaries expense	Interest payable
Net income	Office equipment
Interest expense	Notes payable

Problems—Set A

L.O. 3-1, 2, 3, 4

P3-1A Selected amounts (at December 31, 2003) from The Hay and Barnabas Company's information system appear as follows:

1. Cash paid employees for salaries and wages	$ 300,000
2. Cash collected from sales customers	1,850,000
3. Bonds payable	500,000
4. Cash	150,000
5. Common stock	60,000
6. Equipment	840,000
7. Prepaid insurance	30,000
8. Inventory	250,000
9. Prepaid rent	140,000
10. Retained earnings	130,000
11. Salaries and wages expense	328,000
12. Sales	2,000,000

Required:

Part A.

There are five adjustments that need to be made before the financial statements can be prepared at year end. Show the effect of each of the following (a to e) on the accounting equation.

a. The equipment (purchased on January 1, 2003) has a useful life of 12 years with no salvage value. (Straight-line method is used.)

b. Interest accrued on the bonds payable is $20,000 as of December 31, 2003.

c. Unexpired insurance at December 31, 2003 is $7,000.
d. The rent payment of $140,000 covered the 4 months from December 1, 2003 through March 31, 2004.
e. Salaries and wages of $28,000 were earned but unpaid at December 31, 2003.

Part B.

Indicate the proper balance sheet classification of each of the preceding 12 financial statement items on the December 31, 2003 balance sheet. If the account title would not appear on the balance sheet, indicate the financial statement on which it would be found.

a. Current assets
b. Property, plant, and equipment
c. Current liabilities
d. Long-term liabilities
e. Stockholders' equity

P3-2A The records of Adam's Apple Company revealed the following recorded amounts at December 31, 2004 before adjustments:

L.O. 3-1, 2, 3, 4

Prepaid insurance	$ 1,800
Cleaning supplies	2,800
Unearned service fees	3,000
Notes payable	5,000
Service fees	96,000
Wages expense	75,000
Truck rent expense	3,900
Truck fuel expense	1,100
Insurance expense	0
Supplies expense	0
Interest expense	0
Interest payable	0
Wages payable	0
Prepaid rent—truck	0

Before Adam prepares the financial statements for his business, adjustments must be made for the following items:

a. The prepaid insurance represents an 18-month policy purchased early in January for cash.
b. A count of cleaning supplies on December 31 revealed $500 worth still on hand.
c. One customer paid for 3 months of service in advance on December 1.
d. The truck rent is $300 per month in advance. January 2005 rent was paid late in December.
e. The bank loan was taken out October 1. The interest rate is 12% (1% per month) for 1 year.
f. On Wednesday, December 31, the company owed its employees for working 3 days. The normal workweek is 5 days with wages of $1,500 paid at the end of the week.

Required:

1. Calculate the correct amount for the preceding financial statement items.
2. Compute *net income before taxes* for the year.

P3-3A John's Art Shop purchased a machine on January 1, 2002, for $10,000. John expects to use the machine for 4 years and thinks it will be worth $2,000 at the end of the 4-year period. John uses the straight-line method for computing depreciation.

L.O. 3-1, 2, 3, 4

Required:

1. Show how the machine will be presented in the asset section of the balance sheet at December 31, 2002 and December 31, 2003 after appropriate adjustments.

2. What amount of depreciation expense will be shown on the income statement for 2002? 2003?

L.O. 3-1, 2, 3, 4

P3-4A   The following is a partial list of financial statement items from the records of Twister Company at December 31, 2002.

Prepaid insurance	$10,000
Prepaid rent	18,000
Interest receivable	0
Salaries payable	0
Unearned fee income	30,000
Interest income	10,000

Additional information includes the following:

a. The insurance policy indicates that on December 31, 2002, only 5 months remain on the 24-month policy that originally cost $18,000.
b. Twister has a note receivable with $2,500 of interest due from a customer on January 1, 2003.
c. The accounting records show that one-third of the fees paid in advance by a customer on July 1 has now been earned.
d. The company purchased $18,000 of prepaid rent for 9 months on August 1.
e. At year-end, Twister owed $7,000 worth of salaries to employees for work done in December. The next payday is January 5, 2003.

Required: Describe the needed adjustments, and give the account balances that would be shown on Twister's financial statements for the year ended December 31, 2002.

L.O. 3-1, 2, 3, 4

P3-5A   The following is a list of financial statement items from Chocolate Company as of December 31, 2003.

Prepaid insurance	$ 6,000
Prepaid rent ~~expense~~	10,000
Wages expense	25,000
Unearned subscription income	70,000
Interest expense	38,000

Additional information:

a. The company paid a $7,200 premium on a 3-year business insurance policy on July 1, 2002.
b. Reese borrowed $200,000 on January 2, 2003 and must pay 11% interest on January 2, 2004, for the entire year of 2003.
c. The books show that $60,000 of subscriptions have now been earned.
d. The company paid 10 months of rent in advance on November 1, 2003.
e. Wages for December 31 of $2,000 will be paid to employees on January 3, 2004.

Required: What adjustments must be made prior to the preparation of the financial statements for the year ended December 31, 2003? Give the relevant accounts and the balances that would appear on the financial statements.

L.O. 3-1, 2, 3, 4

P3-6A   The Pickers Packing Company has the following account balances at the end of the year:

Prepaid insurance	$8,000
Rental income	4,200
Wages expense	6,790
Taxes payable	4,168
Interest income	2,475

The company also has the following information available at the end of the year:

1. Of the prepaid insurance, $3,000 has now expired.
2. Of the rental income, $2,200 has not yet been earned.
3. The company must accrue an additional $1,500 of wages expense.
4. The company has earned an additional $500 of interest income, not yet received.

Required: Give the adjustments and show the income statement and balance sheet account balances after the adjustments.

P3-7A   The accounting records for Panda Company contained the following balances as of December 31, 2001:

L.O. 3-1, 2, 3, 4

Assets		Liabilities and equity	
Cash	$40,000	Accounts payable	$17,000
Accounts receivable	16,500	Contributed capital	45,000
Land	20,000	Retained earnings	14,500
Totals	*$76,500*		*$76,500*

The following accounting events apply to Panda's 2002 fiscal year:

Jan.1	The company acquired an additional $20,000 cash from the owners.
1	Panda purchased a computer that cost $17,000 for cash. The computer had an estimated $2,000 salvage value and estimated 3-year useful life.
Mar. 1	The company borrowed $10,000 by issuing a 1-year note at 12%.
May 1	The company paid $2,400 cash in advance for a 1-year lease for office space.
June 1	The company made a $5,000 cash distribution to the owners.
July 1	The company purchased land that cost $10,000 cash.
Aug. 1	Cash payments on accounts payable amounted to $6,000.
1	Panda received $9,600 cash in advance for 12 months of service to be performed monthly for the next year, beginning on receipt of payment.
Sept. 1	Panda sold land for $13,000 cash. The land originally cost $16,000.
Oct. 1	Panda purchased $1,300 of supplies on account.
Nov. 1	Panda purchased a 1-year, $20,000 certificate of deposit at 6%.
Dec. 31	The company earned service revenue on account during the year that amounted to $40,000.
31	Cash collections from accounts receivable amounted to $44,000.
31	The company incurred other operating expenses on account during the year that amounted to $6,000.
31	Salaries that had been earned by the sales staff but not yet paid amounted to $2,300.
31	Supplies worth $200 were on hand at the end of the period.
31	Based on the preceding transaction data, there are five additional adjustments that need to be made before the financial statements can be prepared.

Required: Show each transaction and each necessary adjustment in a work sheet with the accounting equation. Then answer the following questions (all questions pertain to the 2002 financial statements):

a. What is the amount of interest expense that would be shown on the income statement?
b. What is the amount of rent expense that would be shown on the income statement?
c. What is the amount of supplies expense that would be shown on the income statement?
d. What is the total amount of total revenues appearing on the income statement?
e. What is the amount of total expenses that would appear on the income statement?
f. What is the amount of the loss from the sale of land that would be shown on the income statement?
g What is the amount of net income that would be shown on the income statement?
h. What is the amount of total liabilities that would be shown on the balance sheet?
i. What is the amount of unearned revenue that would be shown on the balance sheet?
j. What is the amount of interest payable that would appear on the balance sheet?

k. What is the amount of retained earnings that would appear on the balance sheet?

l. What is the amount of cash flow from financing activities that would be shown on the statement of cash flows?

m. What is the amount of net cash flow from investing activities that would be shown on the statement of cash flows?

n. What is the amount of net cash flow from operations that would be shown on the statement of cash flows?

L.O. 3-1, 2, 3, 4

P3-8A Given the following transactions for Zebra Company for 2002:

- The owners started the business as a corporation by contributing $30,000 cash.
- The company purchased office equipment for $8,000 cash and land for $15,000 cash.
- The company earned a total of $22,000 of revenue of which $16,000 was collected in cash.
- The company purchased $550 worth of supplies for cash.
- The company paid $6,000 in cash for other operating expenses.
- At the end of the year, the company owed employees $3,600 for work that the employees had done in 2002. The next payday, however, is not until January 4, 2003.
- Only $175 worth of supplies was left at the end of the year.

The office equipment was purchased on January 1 and is expected to last for 5 years (straight-line depreciation, no salvage value).

Required: Prepare the income statement for the year ended December 31, 2002 and the balance sheet at December 31, 2002.

Problems—Set B

P3-1B Selected amounts (at December 31, 2004) from Ortega Company's accounting records are shown next. No adjustments have been made.

1.	Notes payable	$500,000
2.	Cash	150,000
3.	Common stock	60,000
4.	Equipment	840,000
5.	Prepaid rent	120,000
6.	Inventory	250,000
7.	Prepaid insurance	140,000
8.	Retained earnings	130,000
9.	Salaries expense during 2004	328,000

Required:

Part A.

There are five adjustments that need to be made before the financial statements for the year ended December 31, 2004 can be prepared. Show the effect of each of the following (a to e) on the accounting equation.

a. The equipment (purchased on January 1, 2004) has a useful life of 12 years with no salvage value (straight-line method is used).

b. Interest on the notes payable needs to be accrued for the year in the amount of $40,000.

c. Unexpired insurance at December 31, 2004 is $40,000.

d. The rent payment of $120,000 was made on June 1. The rent payment is for 12 months beginning on the date of payment.

e. Salaries of $58,000 were earned but unpaid at December 31, 2004.

Part B.

For each item listed next, give the financial statement on which it would be shown and its amount on the annual financial statements for December 31, 2004.

a. Insurance expense

b. Property, plant and equipment (net of accumulated depreciation)

c. Salaries expense
d. Rent expense
e. Interest payable

P3-2B The records of Cabrone Company showed the following amounts at December 31, 2002, before adjustments:

L.O. 3-1, 2, 3, 4

Prepaid insurance	$ 1,500
Supplies	3,500
Unearned service fees	4,000
Notes payable	30,000
Service fees	106,000
Salary expense	65,000
Prepaid rent	3,900
Insurance expense	0
Supplies expense	0
Rent expense	0
Interest expense	0
Interest payable	0
Wages payable	0

Before Ms. Cabrone prepares the financial statements for her business, adjustments must be made for the following items:

a. The prepaid insurance is for a 12-month policy purchased on March 1 for cash. The policy is effective from March 1, 2002 to February 28, 2003.
b. A count of the supplies on December 31 revealed $400 worth still on hand.
c. One customer paid for 4 months of service in advance on December 1. By December 31, 1 month of the service had been performed.
d. The prepaid rent was for 10-months of rent for the company office building, beginning June 1.
e. The bank loan was taken out November 1. The interest rate is 12% (1% per month) for 1 year.
f. As of December 31, the company owed its employees $5,000 for work done in 2002. The next payday is not until January 2003.

Required: Calculate the correct amount for the preceding financial statement items. Compute *net income before taxes* for the year.

P3-3B Night's PJ Shop purchased a new piece of office equipment on January 1, 2004 for $20,000. The company expects to use the equipment for 3 years and thinks it will be worth $2,000 at the end of the 3-year period. The company uses the straight-line method for computing depreciation.

L.O. 3-1, 2, 3, 4

Required:

1. Prepare the asset section of the balance sheet at December 31, 2004 and December 31, 2005 after appropriate adjustments.
2. What amount of depreciation expense will be shown on the income statements for 2004 and for 2005?

P3-4B The following is a partial list of financial statement items from the records of Starnes Company at December 31, 2001.

L.O. 3-1, 2, 3, 4

Prepaid rent	$20,000
Prepaid insurance	12,000
Interest payable	0
Wages payable	0
Unearned service revenue	18,000
Interest expense	5,000

Additional information includes the following:

a. The insurance policy indicates that on December 31, 2001, only 5 months remain on the 12-month policy that originally cost $12,000.
b. Starnes has a note payable with $2,500 of interest that must be paid on January 1, 2002.
c. The accounting records show that two-thirds of the service revenue paid in advance by a customer on March 1 has now been earned.
d. The company purchased $20,000 of prepaid rent for 10 months on August 1.
e. At year-end, Starnes Company owed $5,000 worth of salaries to employees for work done in December. The next payday is January 3, 2002.

Required: Describe the needed adjustments, and give the account balances that would be shown on the Starnes financial statements for 2001.

L.O. 3-1, 2, 3, 4

P3-5B The following is a list of financial statement items from Chewy Candy Company as of June 30, 2003. Chewy's fiscal year is from July 1 to June 30.

Prepaid insurance	$ 3,600
Prepaid rent	5,000
Wages expense	12,000
Unearned subscription revenue	30,000
Interest expense	0

Additional information:

a. The company paid a $3,600 premium on a 3-year insurance policy on January 1, 2003.
b. Chewy borrowed $100,000 on July 1, 2002 with an interest rate of 11%. No interest has been paid as of June 30, 2003.
c. The books show that $10,000 of subscriptions have now been earned.
d. The company paid 10 months of rent in advance on March 1, 2003.
e. Wages for June 30 of $2,000 will be paid to employees on July 3.

Required: What adjustments must be made prior to the preparation of the financial statements for the fiscal year ending June 30, 2003? For the preceding items, give the balances that would appear on the financial statements.

L.O. 3-1, 2, 3, 4

P3-6B The Delphi Desk Company has the following amounts in its records at the end of the fiscal year:

Prepaid insurance	$5,000
Rental income	4,200
Wages expense	6,790
Accounts payable	4,168
Interest income	2,475

The company also has the following information available at the end of the year:

1. Of the prepaid insurance, $1,000 has now expired.
2. Of the rental income, $3,200 has not yet been earned.
3. The company must accrue an additional $1,250 of wages expense.
4. A bill for $300 from the company that provides the desks that Delphi Desk Company sells arrived on the last day of the year. Nothing has been recorded or paid, related to this invoice.
5. The company has earned an additional $300 of interest revenue, not yet received.

Required: Give the adjustments and show the amounts for the preceding items, as they would appear on the income statement and balance sheet for the year.

P3-7B The accounting records for Bebe Company contained the following balances as of December 31, 2003:

Assets		Liabilities and shareholders' equity	
Cash	$50,000	Accounts payable	$17,500
Accounts receivable	26,500		
Prepaid rent	3,600	Contributed capital	48,600
Land	10,500	Retained earnings	24,500
Totals	$90,600		$90,600

The following accounting events apply to Bebe's 2004 fiscal year:

Jan. 1	Bebe purchased a computer that cost $20,000 for cash. The computer had a $2,000 salvage value and a 3-year useful life.
Mar. 1	The company borrowed $20,000 by issuing a 2-year note at 12%.
May 1	The company paid $6,000 cash in advance for a 6-month lease starting on July 1 for office space.
June 1	The company paid cash dividends of $2,000 to the owners.
July 1	The company purchased land that cost $15,000 cash.
Aug. 1	Cash payments on accounts payable amounted to $6,000.
1	Bebe received $6,000 cash in advance for 12 months of service to be performed monthly for the next year, beginning on receipt of payment.
Sept. 1	Bebe sold land for $13,000 cash. The land originally cost $15,000.
Oct. 1	Bebe purchased $1,300 of supplies on account.
Nov. 1	Bebe purchased a 1-year, $10,000 certificate of deposit at 5%.
Dec. 31	The company earned service revenue on account during the year that amounted to $50,000.
31	Cash collections from accounts receivable amounted to $46,000.
31	The company incurred other operating expenses on account during the year that amounted to $6,000.
31	Salaries that had been earned by the sales staff but not yet paid amounted to $2,300.
31	Supplies on hand at the end of the period totaled $200.
31	Based on the preceding transaction data, some additional adjustments that need to be made before the financial statements can be prepared. You should make them now.

Required: Based on the preceding information, show each transaction and each necessary adjustment in a work sheet with the accounting equation. Then answer the following questions (all questions pertain to the 2004 financial statements):

a. What is the amount of interest expense that would be shown on the income statement?
b. What is the amount of rent expense that would be shown on the income statement? (Prepaid rent at Dec. 31 was for Jan.–June of 2004.)
c. What is the amount of supplies expense that would be shown on the income statement?
d. What is the total amount of total revenues appearing on the income statement?
e. What is the amount of total expenses that would appear on the income statement?
f. What is the amount of the loss from the sale of land that would be shown on the income statement?
g. What is the amount of net income that would be shown on the income statement?
h. What is the amount of total liabilities that would be shown on the balance sheet?
i. What is the amount of unearned revenue that would be shown on the balance sheet?
j. What is the amount of interest payable that would appear on the balance sheet?
k. What is the amount of retained earnings that would appear on the balance sheet?
l. What is the amount of cash flow from financing activities that would be shown on the statement of cash flows?

m. What is the amount of net cash flow from investing activities that would be shown on the statement of cash flows?

n. What is the amount of net cash flow from operations that would be shown on the statement of cash flows?

L.O. 3-1, 2, 3, 4   **P3-8B**   Given the following transactions for Quackers Company for 2003:

- The owners started the business as a corporation by contributing $50,000 cash.
- Quackers purchased office equipment for $5,000 cash and land for $15,000 cash.
- Quackers earned a total of $32,000 of revenue of which $20,000 was collected in cash.
- Quackers purchased $550 worth of supplies for cash.
- Quackers paid $6,000 in cash for other operating expenses.
- At the end of the year, Quackers owed employees $3,600 for work that the employees had done in 2003. The next payday, however, is not until January 4, 2004.
- Only $120 worth of supplies was left at the end of the year.

The office equipment was purchased on January 1 and is expected to last for 5 years (straight-line depreciation, no salvage value).

Required: Prepare the income statement for the year ended December 31, 2003 and the balance sheet at December 31, 2003.

Issues for Discussion

Financial statement analysis

1. Use the annual report from Pier 1 Imports, Inc. to answer these questions:
   a. Does Pier 1 have any deferred expenses? What are they, and where are they shown?
   b. Does Pier 1 have accrued expenses? What are they, and where are they shown?
   c. What is the difference between a deferred expense and an accrued expense?
   d. Calculate the amount of working capital for the two most recent fiscal years. What information does this provide?

Business risk

2. What characteristics of Pier 1's business create risks for the company that would not be experienced by most retailers (i.e., unique risks of its particular business)? Use the entire annual report to answer this question.

Ethics

3. DVD-Online, Inc. is in its second year of business. The company is totally Web-based, offering DVD rental to online customers for a fixed monthly fee. For $30 per month, a customer receives 3 DVDs each month, one at a time as the previous one is returned. No matter how many DVDs a customer uses (up to 3), the fee is fixed at $30 per month. Customers sign a contract for a year, so DVD-Online recognizes $360 sales revenue each time a customer signs up for the service. The owner of DVD-Online, John Richards, has heard about GAAP, but he doesn't see any reason to follow these accounting principles. Although DVD-Online is not publicly traded, John does put the company's financial statements on the Web page for customers to see.
   a. Explain how DVD-Online would account for its revenue if it did follow GAAP.
   b. Explain to John Richards why he should use GAAP, and describe why his financial statements may now be misleading.
   c. Do you see this as an ethical issue? Explain.

Internet Exercise: Darden

Please go to the http://www.prenhall.com/reimers *Web site. Go to Chapter 3 and use the Internet Exercise company link.*

IE3-1 If you were at a Darden property, what might you be doing? List two of the Darden chains.

IE3-2 Click on *The Numbers* followed by *Annual Report and Financials* and then select the HTML version of the most recent annual report. Find the *Balance Sheets* by clicking *next* or using the "contents" scroll bar. Does Darden use a calendar year for its fiscal year? How can you tell?

IE3-3 Refer to the asset section.

a. List the title of one asset account that includes accrued revenue—amounts earned but not yet received in cash.
b. List the title of one asset account that includes amounts that have been paid for in cash but have not yet been expensed.
c. List the title of one asset account that includes amounts that will be depreciated.
d. For each account listed in a. through c., identify the amount reported for the most recent year. Do these amounts still need adjusting? Explain why or why not.

IE3-4 List the amounts reported for total current assets and total current liabilities for the most recent year. Compute working capital. For Darden, what does the amount of working capital indicate?

IE3-5 For the two most recent years list the amounts reported for total assets, total liabilities, and total stockholders' equity. For each type of account, identify what the trend indicates. Does the accounting equation hold true both years?

Please note: Internet Web sites are constantly being updated. Therefore, if the information is not found where indicated, please explore the annual report further to find the information.

KEEPING THE BOOKS: THE MECHANICS OF AN ACCOUNTING SYSTEM

Here's where you've been...

Financial Reporting and

Business Events

In Chapter 3, you learned:

- *Accruals* are transactions in which the exchange of cash comes after the exchange of the related goods and services.
- *Deferrals* are transactions in which the exchange of cash comes before the exchange of the related goods and services.

Both are part of accrual basis accounting.

Here's where you're going...

From Chapter 4, you should understand the basic accounting cycle—that's how the traditional general ledger system keeps track of a company's transactions from the beginning of the transaction to the preparation of the financial statements. You'll learn about *debits* and *credits* in this chapter.

Financial Reporting

4

Financing

Sales and Accounts
Receivable

Property, Plant,
and Equipment

**Financial
Reporting
and
Business
Events**

Inventory
and
Liabilities

Learning Objectives

**More specifically, when you are finished studying this chapter, you
should be able to answer these questions:**

1. What is the general ledger system and how does it work?
2. What are the steps in the accounting cycle?
3. What adjustments are needed before preparing financial statements and how do you make those adjustments?
4. What is closing and why is it necessary?
5. What is an ERP? How does that relate to accounting records?

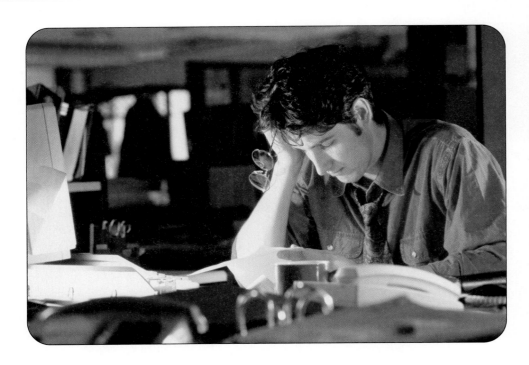

The **general ledger system** is the accountant's traditional way of keeping track of a company's financial transactions and then using those records to prepare the basic financial statements. The debits and credits used in this system are simply a mechanical way to keep track of financial transactions.

An **ERP** is a sophisticated, company-wide information system of which accounting information is only a small part. The accounting part of an ERP may eventually replace the general ledger system, as we know it.

We've been keeping track of Tom's Wear transactions using an accounting equation work sheet. We can do that in a simple world with a small number of transactions. In the real world, that wouldn't work very well. A company in the real world needs a better system to keep track of the large number of transactions represented in the four basic financial statements. A company may have an accounting system that gathers *only* accounting information—just recording the information that applies to the financial statements—and other information systems gathering information for marketing, production, and other parts of the company. Alternatively, a company may have a single, integrated information system in which all company information is recorded—data about suppliers, employees, operations; and the accounting information is simply a small part.

For years, the accountants have had their own separate record-keeping system—called the **general ledger system;** and the other functional areas of the business—marketing, production, sales, etc.—each have had their own system for keeping track of the information they need. Since the development of computers and software programs that can manage large amounts of information, more and more companies are using a single, integrated information system. Thus, instead of keeping their data separately, accountants may get their information from the company's overall information system—often referred to as an **enterprise-wide resource planning system (ERP).**

The accountants' traditional general ledger accounting system has been used for such a long time that it has become entrenched in the format and organization of the basic financial statements of every business. That's one reason we'll discuss the general ledger system in detail in this chapter, even though in many companies it is being absorbed into company-wide information systems. Another reason is that you must be able to understand the output of the general ledger accounting system because the new integrated information systems are designed to produce the financial records in the same format as the general ledger system. The same financial statements are produced with both the general ledger and the integrated types of information systems. We will use the general ledger system, which was designed as a manual system, to demonstrate how transactions are recorded, classified, and summarized for the financial statements.

The General Ledger Accounting System

Keeping track of financial information with a traditional record-keeping system is often called *bookkeeping*. As transactions occur, they are recorded chronologically by a bookkeeper in a book called a **journal**. When we prepare an accounting equation work sheet—showing the effect of each transaction on the accounting equation—we are doing something similar to what we would record in a journal. The resources exchanged are shown with their dollar amounts. The journal contains a record of each transaction as it occurs. An example is shown in Exhibit 4-1. Most companies use more than one journal; each department may have its own journal. Common journals are the (1) sales journal, (2) cash receipts journal, and (3) cash disbursements journal. For simplicity, we'll use a single, general journal for all our transactions.

Because a company may have thousands of transactions during an accounting period, it would be difficult, probably impossible, to try to gather and use the information from a chronological record such as the journal. To be useful, the information needs to be reorganized, grouping together transactions that involve the same resource. For example, when all the transactions that involve cash are grouped together, then the company's cash balance can be easily determined. As you can see from that example, it is useful for similar transactions to be grouped together. The transactions from the journal or journals are transferred to another book called the **general ledger**—a process called **posting** the transactions to the general ledger. Posting is done periodically; it could be daily, weekly, or monthly, depending on the size of the company.

The general ledger is the primary record of the financial information of the business. It is organized by what we have called up to this point, a financial statement *item*. From here on, we will refer to the financial statement items as accounts. Like a financial statement item, an account is the basic classification unit of accounting information. Now we can think of each financial statement item as an account, and each account as a page in the general ledger. On the page for a particular account, we record all the additions to, and deductions from, that account.

For example, one account in the general ledger is Cash. On the Cash page in the general ledger, we find every cash collection and every cash disbursement made by the company. If there are more disbursements or collections than can fit on one page, they will be recorded on as many following pages as needed, all comprising the Cash account. To make it easy to find the amount of cash on hand, the Cash account has a running balance. That means a new balance is calculated after every entry. Think about your own checkbook—that's the

Business transactions are first recorded in a **journal.** Then they are transferred to accounts in the **general ledger** through a process called **posting.**

Page 4: General Journal				
Ref.	Date	Journal entry	Debits	Credits
J-1	June 1	Cash	$65,000	
		Sales		$65,000
		To record the collection of cash for sales.		
J-2	June 4	Equipment	$20,600	
		Cash		$20,600
		To record the purchase of equipment for sales.		

Exhibit 4-1
An Example of the Journal

The journal entries are recorded chronologically. Then, the individual items will be "regrouped" by account as they are posted to the General Ledger. Trace the cash amounts in the journal entries above to the General Ledger Cash account shown in Exhibit 4–2. The amounts for Sales and Equipment will be posted to their own general ledger accounts.

record you keep of each check you write—a subtraction; each deposit you make—an addition; and the resulting total remaining in your checking account—that's your running balance. If you keep a running balance, it is much faster to find out how much cash you have in your account. (Have you discovered what happens when you fail to keep your checkbook balance current?)

Accounts in the general ledger include Cash, Accounts Receivable, Inventory, Prepaid Insurance, Equipment, Accumulated Depreciation, Accounts Payable, Notes Payable, Contributed Capital, and Retained Earnings. (Notice, these are given in the order they appear on the balance sheet.) How many accounts does a company have? Every company is different, and the number of accounts depends on the detail the company wants in its financial records. For example, one company could have an account called Utilities Expenses in which many different utility-related expenses could be accumulated. Another company might prefer to have a separate account for each type of utility expense—a separate page in the general ledger for electricity expense, gas expense, water expense, etc. The number of accounts is determined by the amount of detail a company wants to be able to retrieve from its records. If a company uses very little gas or water, it would be a waste of time and space to keep a separate account for those expenses. A company that uses water in its production process, on the other hand, would definitely want to keep a separate account for water purchases.

Companies also have subsidiary ledgers. These are detailed records that support the balances in the general ledger. For example, the *accounts receivable subsidiary ledger* will have details about the customers—purchases, payments, and account balances for every customer. The total dollar amount in the accounts receivable subsidiary ledger will be the total in the general ledger.

Most companies have a large number of accounts, and they combine the similar ones for the financial statements. When we look at the financial statements, we can't really tell how many individual accounts a company has in its general ledger. Many smaller accounts may be combined for financial statement presentation.

Anyone who wants to know the balance in any account at any time can find it by looking in the general ledger. A list of the balances in all the accounts of a company is called a **trial balance.**

A **trial balance** is a list of all the accounts of a company with the related debit or credit balance.

Before the financial statements can be prepared, adjustments to the records must be made. We discussed those adjustments and how to make them in Chapter 3. Adjustments are needed because of the nature of accrual accounting. On the financial statements, we need to include revenues that have been earned and expenses that have been incurred, even if we have not yet received the cash earned or paid the cash for the expenses incurred during the accounting period. These adjustments are called accruals. The action has taken place, but the dollars have not been exchanged.

We also need to be sure to include on the income statement for the period any revenue we've earned or expenses we've incurred for which the dollars were exchanged at a previous time. These are called deferrals. The dollars were already exchanged, and we recorded the receipt of the cash when we received the cash. However, we did not recognize any revenue or expense at that time. At the end of the accounting period, we have to recognize any revenue we have earned and any expenses that we've incurred.

No matter what kind of accounting system a company uses, the information produced by that system must be adjusted before the financial statements can be prepared. After the adjustments are made, the financial statements are prepared. We have actually done all this—recording the transactions, making the adjustments, and preparing the financial statements—using the accounting equation work sheet. The general ledger system is simply a more feasible way to do it in an actual business.

To use the general ledger system and to understand the information it makes available, we must learn a bit more accounting language. Don't panic over the terms **debit** and **credit.** You will find them easy to understand, but only if first you get rid of any notions of what you already think debit and credit mean. In accounting, each term has a very specific meaning that should not be confused with its more general meaning.

Debit means left side of an account. **Credit** means right side of an account.

Debits and Credits

In accounting, when we say *debit,* we mean the left side; when we say *credit,* we mean the right side. (This should be easy to remember.) Left is the only thing we can say about what *debit* means and right, about what *credit* means—unless we apply the terms to specific accounts.

A general ledger has been traditionally composed of a multi-column page, similar to the one shown in Exhibit 4-2. The debit column on the right shows the running balance in the cash account. Notice there is never a credit balance in this account. Now it is often computerized in a similar format.

In the balance columns, the column on the left is called the debit (DR) column, and the column on the right is called the credit (CR) column. As a shortcut to using formal preprinted two-column paper, accountants often draw a T-account to represent a page in the general ledger. T-accounts shown in Exhibit 4-3 are our representation of the general ledger shown in Exhibit 4-2.

One T-account such as cash, shown next, represents a single page in the general ledger. The left side of a T-account is the debit side, and the right side of a T-account is the credit side.

Cash

Debit	Credit

Numbers we put on the left side of the account are called debits, and *putting* a number in the left column is called *debiting* an account. Debit is a wonderful word that can be an adjective, a noun, or a verb. The same goes for the word credit. The right side of the account is called the credit side; the numbers we put on the right side are called credits; and putting a number in the right column is called *crediting* an account.

In the fifteenth century, a monk named Fra Luca Paccioli wrote about a system that uses debits and credits with the accounting equation. In his system, the accounting equation stays in balance with each transaction *and* the monetary amounts of debits and credits are equal for each transaction. Here's how it works:

1. For the balance sheet equation, the balance in the accounts on the left side of the equation (*assets*) will increase with debits; and the balance in the accounts

Account: **Cash**					Account No. 1002	
					Balance	
Date	Item	Jrnl. ref.	Debit	Credit	Debit	Credit
2003						
June 1		J–1, p. 4	65,000		**65,000**	
June 4		J–2, p. 4		20,600	**44,400**	

This is the **Cash** account. The cash amounts from all the journal entries are posted here. Trace these amounts back to the journal entries shown in Exhibit 4–1.

Exhibit 4–2
The General Ledger

Exhibit 4-3   Debits and Credits in T-Accounts

Asset		Liability		Equity	
Debit increases (normal balance)	Credit decreases	Debit decreases	Credit increases (normal balance)	Debit decreases	Credit increases (normal balance)

Revenue		Expense	
Debit decreases	Credit increases (normal balance)	Debit increases (normal balance)	Credit decreases

on the right side of the equation (*liabilities* and *equity*) will increase with credits. It follows that the balance in an asset account will decrease with credits. Liability and equity account balances decrease with debits. Putting that together,

■ Asset accounts are increased with debits and decreased with credits.
■ Liability and shareholders' equity accounts are increased with credits and decreased with debits.

This means that when we want to add an amount to our cash balance, we put the number of that amount on the left (in the left column of the two columns in the general ledger account for cash)—so that's a debit. When we disburse cash and want to subtract the amount disbursed from the cash account, we put the number of that amount on the right side—so that's a credit. The amount in the *increase* side of an account is called its "normal" balance. Cash has a normal debit balance. Because we put the cash we receive on the debit side and the cash we disburse on the credit side, it makes sense that our Cash account will normally have a debit balance. (It's not normal to disburse more cash than you have—it's pretty unusual.)

In accounting, we do not literally *add* and *subtract* from an account balance—we debit and credit an account to accomplish the same thing. If we make an error, we do not erase the mistake and replace it with the correct answer. Instead, we debit or credit the account to correct the error and make the account balance correct. When accounting records are kept by hand, all entries are made in ink so that no entries can be erased or changed. This has been traditional in accounting to keep the records from being altered. Recording every increase to, and decrease from, an account balance gives a complete record of every change made to the account.

2. Because owner's equity is increased with credits, all accounts that increase owner's equity will increase with credits. Revenue accounts increase with credits and decrease with debits. When we make a sale, we *credit* the Sales account.

3. Because owner's equity is *decreased* with debits, all accounts that decrease owner's equity work in the opposite way as revenue accounts work. For example, expense accounts—where a list of our expenses is kept—increase with debits. As we incur expenses, we put the amounts on the left side of expense accounts.

Indicate whether each of the following accounts normally has a debit (DR) or credit (CR) balance and what type of account it is.

Account title	Expense	Revenue	Asset	Liability	Owner's equity
Accounts payable				CR	
Accounts receivable					
Advertising expense					
Cash					
Depreciation expense					
Furniture and fixtures					
Accumulated depreciation					
Unearned fees					
Salary expense					
Common stock					
Rent expense					
Dividends					
Retained earnings					
(Earned) fees					
Land					
Building					

A summary of the use of debits and credits is shown in Exhibit 4-3. Remember, it's just a clever system to be sure that, when we record a transaction, the accounting equation is kept in balance and, at the same time, debits = credits with every transaction. This system is called double-entry bookkeeping.

The Accounting Cycle

The process that starts with recording individual transactions, produces the four basic financial statements, and gets our general ledger ready for the next accounting period is called the **accounting cycle.** Some of the steps in the accounting cycle won't make any sense to you yet, but this chapter examines each in detail. By the end of this chapter, you should be able to explain and perform each step. The steps in the accounting cycle follow:

1. Record transactions in the journal, the chronological record of all transactions. These are called journal entries.
2. Post the journal entries to the general ledger.
3. At the end of the accounting period, prepare an unadjusted trial balance.
4. Prepare adjusting journal entries and post them to the general ledger.
5. Prepare an adjusted trial balance.
6. Prepare the financial statements.
7. Close the temporary accounts.
8. Prepare a postclosing trial balance.

Let's look at each of these steps in detail.

The **accounting cycle** begins with the transactions of a new accounting period. It includes recording and posting the transactions, adjusting the books, preparing financial statements, and closing the temporary accounts to get ready for the next accounting period.

Identify and perform the steps in the accounting cycle.

Step 1: Recording Journal Entries

In the normal course of business, there are dozens of transactions that must be recorded in the accounting system. Let's look at how the transactions for a company's first year of business would be recorded in a journal. The transactions for the first year of Clint's Consulting Company, Inc. are shown in Exhibit 4-4.

The first transaction in Clint's first year of business is his own contribution of $2,000 to the business. What a journal entry looks like on a journal page follows:

Date	Transaction	Debit	Credit
1/2/01	Cash	$2,000	
	Contributed capital		$2,000
To record owner's contribution			1-1[a]

[a]This is a number we'll use to help us trace journal entries to the general ledger.

The Cash account is increased by $2,000, so Clint would debit the Cash account for $2,000. Owner's equity is increased, so Clint would credit Contributed Capital for $2,000. Notice, in this case two accounts are increased—one with a debit and one with a credit. In some transactions, both accounts are increased; in others, one account can be increased and one account can be decreased; or two accounts can be decreased. The only requirement for a journal entry is that the dollar amount of debits must equal the dollar amount of credits.

In the second transaction, Clint's Consulting Company borrows $4,000 from a local bank. Again, two different accounts are increased—one with a debit and one with a credit—in this transaction. Notice, debits ($4,000) = credits ($4,000).

Date	Transaction	Debit	Credit
1/10/01	Cash	$4,000	
	Notes payable		$4,000
To record the loan from the bank			1-2

Debits are always listed first; credits are listed after all the debits—sometimes there is more than one account to debit or credit—and the accounts being credited are indented like the first sentence of a paragraph. Each page of the journal has a page number that is used to trace journal entries to the

Exhibit 4-4
Transactions for Clint's Consulting Company, Inc. during 2001

Date	Transaction
Jan. 2	Clint contributes $2,000 of his own money to the business
Jan. 10	Clint's Consulting, Inc. borrows $4,000 from a local bank to begin the business
Feb. 4	Clint's buys supplies for $400 cash
Apr. 10	Clint's hires a company to prepare a brochure for the company for $500 cash
July 12	Clint's provides consulting services and earns revenue of $9,000 cash
Aug. 15	Clint's pays someone to do some typing, which costs $350 cash
Oct. 21	Clint's repays the $4,000 note along with $150 interest
Dec. 10	Clint's Consulting, Inc. makes a distribution to Clint, the owner, for $600

general ledger. We'll see this number again when we post the journal entries to the general ledger.

The third transaction is the purchase of supplies for $400 cash. This is recorded with a debit to Supplies and a credit to Cash.

Date	Transaction	Debit	Credit
2/4/01	Supplies	$400	
	Cash		$400
To record the purchase of supplies			1-3

Notice, this transaction increases one asset account—Supplies—and decreases another asset account—Cash. Because Supplies is an asset, it is increased with a debit.

The fourth transaction is Clint's hiring a company to prepare a brochure for his new consulting business. He pays $500 for this service.

Date	Transaction	Debit	Credit
4/10/01	Advertising expense	$500	
	Cash		$500
To record the cost of the brochures			1-4

In this transaction, an expense account, Advertising Expense, is increased by $500. Because expense accounts are eventually deducted from owner's equity, they increase with debits, the opposite of owner's equity accounts. Cash, an asset account, is decreased with a credit of $500.

Next, the company provides consulting services for $9,000 cash.

Date	Transaction	Debit	Credit
7/12/01	Cash	$9,000	
	Consulting fees		$9,000
To record consulting revenue			1-5

In this transaction, Cash is increased with a $9,000 debit. Consulting Fees, a revenue account that will eventually be added to owner's equity, is increased with a $9,000 credit.

Clint's Consulting Company has one employee who types for him occasionally, and he pays this person $350 for typing during his first year of business. This is an expense, which Clint categorizes as Salary Expense. Cash is reduced with a credit for $350, and Salary Expense is increased with a $350 debit.

Date	Transaction	Debit	Credit
8/15/01	Salary expense	$350	
	Cash		$350
To record the cost of an employee to type			1-6

Next, the company repays the loan to the bank, with interest. The principal of the loan—the amount borrowed—was $4,000; the interest—the cost of using someone else's money—was $150. The journal entry for this transaction is an example of an entry with more than one debit.

Date	Transaction	Debit	Credit
10/21/01	Notes payable	$4,000	
	Interest expense	150	
	Cash		$4,150
To record the repayment of a note plus interest			1-7

The debit to Notes Payable reduces the balance in that account. Before this transaction, it had a balance of $4,000. Now, when this debit is posted, the account will have a zero balance. The Interest Expense account will increase by $150 because expense accounts increase with debits. Cash is reduced by $4,150.

The final transaction of Clint's Consulting Company's first year of business is a $600 distribution to Clint, the owner. In a sole proprietorship, a distribution is also called a **withdrawal**. Because Clint's Consulting Company is a corporation, the distribution is called a **dividend**. The Dividends account has a debit balance and will eventually reduce Retained Earnings. Paying a dividend reduces the Cash balance. Remember, a dividend payment is not an expense.

> A distribution to the owner of a sole proprietorship is called a **withdrawal**; in a corporation, distributions to the owners are called **dividends**.

Date	Transaction	Debit	Credit
12/10/01	Dividends	$600	
	Cash		$600
To record a dividend payment			1-8

Step 2: Posting Journal Entries to the General Ledger

Each of the journal entries a company makes must be posted to the general ledger. How often this is done depends on the number of journal entries a company normally makes. Some computerized systems post every journal entry automatically when it is entered into the system. Other companies post transactions to the general ledger daily or weekly.

The accounts for Clint's Consulting Company, Inc. all begin with a zero balance, because this is Clint's first year of business. Each journal entry has the page number from the journal with it when the entry is posted in the general ledger. This provides a way to trace every entry in the general ledger back to the original record of the transaction in the journal. After all the journal entries are posted, it is easy to calculate the balance in any account. The accounts, shown in Exhibit 4-5 are listed in the following order: assets, liabilities, owner's equity, revenues, and expenses.

Step 3: Prepare an Unadjusted Trial Balance

A trial balance is a list of all the accounts in the general ledger, each with its debit or credit balance. The reasons for preparing a trial balance are to confirm that debits equal credits and to have a way to quickly review the accounts for needed adjustments. Exhibit 4-6 shows the unadjusted trial balance for Clint's Consulting at December 31, 2001.

> **L.O. 3**
>
> Know why adjustments need to be made and how to make them before the financial statements are prepared.

Step 4: Adjusting Journal Entries

Recording journal entries as transactions occur and posting them to the general ledger are routine accounting tasks. When a company gets ready to prepare financial statements at the end of the accounting period, there are more

Exhibit 4-5   Clint's Consulting Company, Inc. T-Accounts

Cash (asset)		
1-1 $2,000	$ 400	1-3
1-2 4,000	500	1-4
1-5 9,000	350	1-6
	4,150	1-7
	600	1-8

Supplies (asset)
1-3 $400

Notes payable (liability)
1-7 $4,000 | $4,000 1-2

Contributed capital (cc) (owner's equity)
$2,000 1-1

Consulting fees (revenue)
$9,000 1-5

Advertising expense (expense)
1-4 $500

Dividends (owner's equity temporary account)
1-8 $600

Interest expense (expense)
1-7 $150

Salary expense (expense)
1-6 $350

journal entries needed. These are not routine journal entries; they are called adjusting journal entries. As we discussed in Chapter 3, there are four situations that require adjustments before the financial statements are prepared. We need to adjust our records for *accrued revenues, accrued expenses, deferred revenues,* and *deferred expenses.* Let's look at an example of each of those adjustments in a general ledger system.

Accruals. Accrued Revenue. Suppose Clint's Consulting Company did some consulting for a fee of $3,000, but the company has not been paid yet so the revenue has not been recognized—when it is recognized, it is put on the income statement. At December 31, Clint will adjust the company's records to recognize this revenue, even though he has not collected the cash. First, notice the effect of the adjustment on the accounting equation.

Account	DR	CR
Cash	$ 9,000	
Supplies	400	
Notes payable		$ 0
Contributed capital		2,000
Consulting fees		9,000
Advertising expense	500	
Interest expense	150	
Salary expense	350	
Dividends	600	
	$11,000	$11,000

Exhibit 4-6
Clint's Consulting Company, Inc.
Unadjusted Trial Balance at December 31, 2001

Assets	=	Liabilities	+	CC	+	Retained earnings
+3,000 Accounts receivable						+3,000 Consulting fees

The transaction increases assets—Accounts Receivable (AR). That means Clint would debit AR, because assets are increased with debits. Clint has also increased a revenue account, Consulting Fees. (The $3,000 is recorded in a revenue account, not directly into the retained earnings account. However, the revenue will end up increasing retained earnings on our balance sheet.) Revenue accounts increase with credits, so we would credit the revenue account Consulting Fees for $3,000. The accounting equation is in balance *and* debits = credits for our transaction. Here's what the journal entry would look like:

Date	Transaction	Debit	Credit
12/31/01	Accounts receivable	$3,000	
	Consulting fees		$3,000
To accrue revenue earned in 2001			A-1

Accrued Expenses Another situation that requires an adjustment is accrued expenses. If we have incurred an expense (the dollar amount that *will* be paid for an item or a service that has already been used to produce revenue), the matching principle requires us to put it on the same income statement as the revenue it helped generate.

Sometimes matching an expense with a specific revenue is impossible to do. In that case, we match the expense with the time period when the expense item was used. For example, it is often impossible to match an employee's work with specific revenue the company earns. So the cost of the work done by an employee is put on the income statement as an expense in the accounting period when the work was done.

Let's look at an example of matching salary expense with the period in which the work was done. When companies pay their employees—on normal paydays during the year—they debit the account Salary Expense and credit the account Cash. The Salary Expense account may have a significant balance at year-end because the company has been recording salary expense as the employees have been paid throughout the year. To make sure we've included *all* the salary expense for the year, we must examine the time our employees have worked near the end of the year. The purpose is to be sure to include the cost of *all* work done during a year in the salary expense on that year's income statement.

If we owe employees for work done in December 2001 but we will not pay them until January 2002, we have to accrue salary expense when we are adjusting our accounts at Decemer 31, 2001. Suppose Clint's owes its employee $50 for work done in 2001, but the next payday is in 2002. To get this salary expense on the income statement for the year, Clint must debit Salary Expense for $50 and credit Salaries Payable for $50. The salary expense on the income statement for the year ended December 31, 2001 will now include this $50. Salaries Payable on the balance sheet will show the $50 obligation. Look at the adjustment in the accounting equation, and then look at the journal entry. Notice that in the adjusting entry, just like in a routine journal entry, debits = credits. The accounting equation remains in balance.

Assets	=	Liabilities	+	CC	+	Retained earnings
		+$50 Salaries payable				$(50) Salary expense

Date	Transaction	Debit	Credit
12/31/01	Salary expense	$50	
	Salaries payable		$50
To accrue salary expense at year-end			A-2

STUDY BREAK 4-2
SEE HOW YOU'RE DOING

Suppose a company owes employees $300 on December 31, 2003, the date of the financial statements; and the next payday is January 3, 2004. Give the adjusting journal entry necessary on December 31. How much salary expense will the company recognize when it actually pays the $300 to the employees on January 3, 2004? Give the journal entry for the payment on January 3.

Deferrals. Deferred Revenue Deferred revenue is revenue that hasn't been earned yet, so it is recorded as a liability in a company's records—an obligation—when the cash is collected. Because cash has been collected, it must be recorded; but the goods or services have not yet been provided. The company must defer—put off—recognizing the revenue. When the cash is received, the company increases Cash and increases a liability called Unearned Revenue. In a general ledger system, the amount of cash received is recorded in the Cash account, where it is shown as a debit—that's an increase because assets are increased with debits. The journal entry is balanced with a credit to Unearned Revenue—that's an increase because liabilities are increased with credits.

Suppose Clint had received $4,000 on May 1 for consulting services to be provided over the next 12 months. This is how the receipt of the $4,000 cash for services to be provided in the future affects the accounting equation, followed by the journal entry for the receipt of the $4,000 cash.

Assets	=	Liabilities	+	CC	+	Retained earnings
+$4,000 cash		+$4,000 Unearned consulting fees				

Date	Transaction	Debit	Credit
5/1/01	Cash	$4,000	
	Unearned consulting fees		$4,000
To record the receipt of cash for services to be provided			1-9

Notice that this is *not* an adjusting entry; it's a regular journal entry—made when it occurs during the year—to record the receipt of cash. When we look at the T-accounts again, we'll see it posted with the transactions we posted previously.

Whenever a company has recorded unearned revenue during the year, an adjustment will be necessary at year-end to recognize the portion of the revenue that has been earned during the time between when the cash was received and year-end. If, on that basis, any of the unearned revenue becomes earned revenue by year-end, the Unearned Revenue account will be decreased and the Revenue account will be increased with an adjustment. In terms of debits and credits, the Unearned Revenue account, which is a liability, will be decreased with a debit. In Clint's case, the credit corresponding to that debit will go to Consulting Fees, which means that the earned revenue will now show up on the income statement with the other consulting fees Clint has earned during the year. This adjustment is necessary to be sure all the earned revenue for the year is recognized—meaning, put on the income statement. Suppose Clint had earned half of the revenue at year-end. The adjustment in the accounting equation and the corresponding journal entry for this adjustment follow:

Assets	=	Liabilities	+	CC	+	Retained earnings
		$(2,000) Unearned consulting fees				+$2,000 Consulting fees

Date	Transaction	Debit	Credit
12/31/01	Unearned consulting fees	$2,000	
	Consulting fees		$2,000
To record earned revenue at year-end			A-3

Deferred Expenses. Deferred expenses may need to be adjusted before the financial statements are prepared. Recall, a deferred expense is something the company paid for in advance. One example is Supplies, discussed in Chapter 3. Clint paid $400 for supplies during the year, and he recorded them as an asset. At the end of the year, he must determine how many supplies are left and how many he used. He counts the supplies on hand and then subtracts that amount from the amount he purchased. Suppose Clint finds that there is $75 worth of supplies left in the supply closet on December 31. Since he purchased $400 worth, that means he must have used $325 worth of supplies during the year. He wants to show supplies expense of $325 on the year's income statement; and he wants the asset Supplies to show $75 on the balance sheet at year end. This is the adjustment to get the accounts to their correct year-end balances, first in the accounting equation and then as a journal entry:

Assets	=	Liabilities	+	CC	+	Retained earnings
$(325) Supplies						$(325) Supplies expense

Date	Transaction	Debit	Credit
12/31/01	Supplies Expense	$325	
	Supplies		$325
To record supplies expense for the year			A-4

The T-accounts with the adjusting entries posted to them are shown in Exhibit 4-7.

Exhibit 4-7   Adjusted T-Accounts for Clint's Consulting Co., Inc.

Steps 5 and 6: Preparing the Adjusted Trial Balance and the Financial Statements

After all the adjusting entries have been posted to the general ledger accounts and new balances have been computed in the general ledger, an **adjusted trial balance** is prepared. An adjusted trial balance is simply a list of all the general ledger accounts and their balances, to verify that debits = credits for all the company's accounts after all the adjustments have been made. Preparing an adjusted trial balance—and making sure it actually balances—helps ensure the accuracy of the recording process. If the adjusted trial balance *is* in balance—debits = credits—it can be used to prepare the financial statements.

A trial balance is a list of all the accounts, each with its debit balance or its credit balance. An unadjusted trial balance is prepared before any adjustments have been made. An **adjusted trial balance** is prepared after adjustments have been made, and it can be used to prepare the financial statements.

Exhibit 4-8
Adjusted Trial Balance for Clint's Consulting Company, Inc. for the Year 2001

Account	DR	CR
Cash	$13,000	
Accounts receivable	3,000	
Supplies	75	
Notes payable		$ 0
Salaries payable		50
Unearned consulting fees		2,000
Contributed capital		2,000
Consulting fees		14,000
Advertising expense	500	
Interest expense	150	
Salary expenses	400	
Supplies expense	325	
Dividends	600	
	$18,050	$18,050

The adjusted trial balance is shown in Exhibit 4-8, and the financial statements are shown in Exhibit 4-9.

After the financial statements are prepared, we are *almost* ready to begin another accounting cycle. First, we must get our general ledger ready for a new fiscal year.

L.O. 4

Describe the closing process and explain why it is necessary.

Temporary accounts are the revenue, expense, and dividends accounts. Their balances are brought to zero at the end of the accounting period, called **closing** the accounts.

Step 7: Close the Revenue and Expense Accounts

Revenue accounts and expense accounts are **temporary accounts.** The balances in those accounts will be transferred to retained earnings at the end of each period; therefore, they will start each new period with a zero balance.

Think about the accounting equation and the work sheet we've been using to record transactions. We've been listing the revenues and expenses in the retained earnings column, because they increase and decrease the owner's claims to the assets of the business. The balance sheet will balance only when the revenue and expense amounts are incorporated into the retained earnings balance. The net amount of revenues minus expenses—net income—is incorporated into retained earnings when we prepare the statement of changes in owner's equity.

From a bookkeeping perspective, the revenue and expense accounts are **closed**—meaning their balances are brought to zero—with journal entries. Each account receives a debit or a credit to close it. For example, if a revenue account has a balance of $300—which would be a credit balance—the account is closed with a debit for $300. The corresponding credit in that closing journal entry is to Retained Earnings. Thus, closing the revenue account increases Retained Earnings. On the other hand, closing an expense account will decrease Retained Earnings. For example, if an expense account has a balance of $100—which would be a debit balance—the account is closed with a credit for $100. The corresponding debit for that closing journal entry is to Retained Earnings. Closing the expense account decreases Retained Earnings.

Keep in mind the reason for having revenue accounts and expense accounts. For a single accounting period, usually a year, the revenues and expenses are recorded separately from Retained Earnings so that we can report them on the year's income statement. Then we want those amounts included in retained earnings, and we want the revenue and expense accounts to be "empty" so they can start over, ready for amounts that will come during the coming year. Remember, the income statement covers a single accounting period. We don't want to mix up last year's revenue with this year's revenue in our revenue accounts or last year's expenses with this year's expenses in our expense accounts. The process of bringing these accounts to a zero balance is called closing the accounts, and the journal entries are called closing entries. We cannot close the revenue accounts and expense accounts until we have prepared the financial statements.

Permanent accounts or **real accounts** are accounts that are never closed. They are the asset, liability, and equity accounts.

Asset accounts, liability accounts, and shareholders' equity accounts are **permanent accounts,** or **real accounts.** A balance in any of these accounts is carried over from one period to the next. For example, the amount of cash shown in the cash account will never be zero (unless we spend our last cent). The same is true about all balance sheet accounts. Think about your own personal records. If you keep track of your cash (like your checking account), you will have a continuous record of your cash balance. On the date of a personal balance sheet, you would see how much cash you have on that particular date. As the next year begins, you still have that cash. It doesn't go away because a new year begins.

To get a better idea of what we mean by the continuous record in a permanent account, let's consider a simple example of a *temporary* account. Suppose you were keeping a list of your grocery expenses for the year. At the end of the year, after you have reported the amount of those expenses on your annual

Exhibit 4–9
Financial Statements for Clint's
Consulting Company, Inc. for 2001

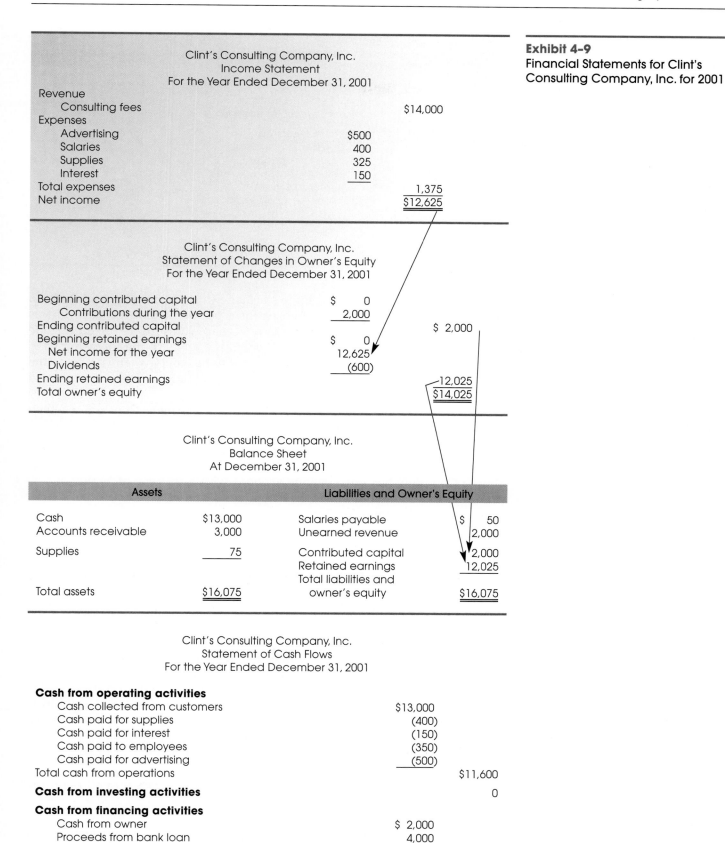

Clint's Consulting Company, Inc.
Income Statement
For the Year Ended December 31, 2001

Revenue		
Consulting fees		$14,000
Expenses		
Advertising	$500	
Salaries	400	
Supplies	325	
Interest	150	
Total expenses		1,375
Net income		$12,625

Clint's Consulting Company, Inc.
Statement of Changes in Owner's Equity
For the Year Ended December 31, 2001

Beginning contributed capital	$ 0	
Contributions during the year	2,000	
Ending contributed capital		$ 2,000
Beginning retained earnings	$ 0	
Net income for the year	12,625	
Dividends	(600)	
Ending retained earnings		12,025
Total owner's equity		$14,025

Clint's Consulting Company, Inc.
Balance Sheet
At December 31, 2001

Assets		Liabilities and Owner's Equity	
Cash	$13,000	Salaries payable	$ 50
Accounts receivable	3,000	Unearned revenue	2,000
Supplies	75	Contributed capital	2,000
		Retained earnings	12,025
		Total liabilities and	
Total assets	$16,075	owner's equity	$16,075

Clint's Consulting Company, Inc.
Statement of Cash Flows
For the Year Ended December 31, 2001

Cash from operating activities		
Cash collected from customers	$13,000	
Cash paid for supplies	(400)	
Cash paid for interest	(150)	
Cash paid to employees	(350)	
Cash paid for advertising	(500)	
Total cash from operations		$11,600
Cash from investing activities		0
Cash from financing activities		
Cash from owner	$ 2,000	
Proceeds from bank loan	4,000	
Repayment of bank loan	(4,000)	
Cash dividends paid	(600)	
Total cash from financing		1,400
Net increase in cash		$13,000

Exhibit 4-10
Closing Entries

Ref.	Date	Journal entry	DR	CR
C-1	12/31	Consulting fees	$14,000	
		Retained earnings		$14,000
		To close revenue account		
C-2	12/31	Retained earnings	1,375	
		Advertising expense		500
		Salary expense		400
		Supplies expense		325
		Interest expense		150
		To close the expense accounts		
C-3	12/31	Retained earnings	$ 600	
		Dividends		$ 600
		To close dividends		

income statement, you would want to start a new list for the next year. Because an income statement reports expenses for a period of time—a year, in this example—your grocery expenses for one year would be reported on *one* income statement, but those expenses would not apply to the following year. You would want the grocery expense account to be empty when you begin the next year. Expense amounts must apply to a specific time period for them to make sense.

Exhibit 4-10 shows the closing journal entries for Clint's Consulting, which are recorded after the financial statements are prepared.

STUDY BREAK 4-3
SEE HOW YOU'RE DOING

Simple Company has one revenue account with a balance of $5,000 at year-end and one expense account with a balance of $3,000. Prepare the closing journal entries for Simple Company.

More About Closing Entries and the Relationship Between the Income Statement and the Balance Sheet. The formal way of making the balances zero in the revenue and expense accounts is called closing the accounts. Why do we bother with closing entries? They set the stage for the next accounting period by zeroing out the balances of all the temporary accounts. This is necessary because these accounts keep track of amounts that go to the income statement, which gives us the net income figure for *one specific period*. Without zeroing out the accounts, net income would include revenues or expenses for more than one period. Closing entries transfer the period's net income (or loss) to the retained earnings account (or to the owner's capital account in a sole proprietorship), so closing entries are the means by which net income flows downstream from the income statement through the statement of changes in owner's equity to the balance sheet.

Here's how the revenue amounts and expense amounts flow through the financial statements:

- *Income statement.* We present the details of net income—the revenues and expenses—on the income statement. The bottom line is net income.
- *Statement of changes in owner's equity.* We show net income as an addition to owner's equity on the statement of changes in owner's equity.
- *Balance sheet.* We present the total amount of owner's equity—which includes net income—on the balance sheet.

After we've used the revenue account balances and the expense account balances to prepare the income statement and after that information has flowed through to the balance sheet, we are ready to close the revenue accounts and expense accounts. That's the formal way of getting the correct balance in Retained Earnings. Here are the steps in detail to record closing entries:

1. Transfer all credit balances from the revenue accounts to Retained Earnings. This is done with a closing entry. The closing journal entry will have a debit to each of the revenue accounts for the entire balance of each—to bring them to a zero balance. The corresponding credit will be to Retained Earnings for the total amount of the period's revenue.

2. Transfer all debit balances from the expense accounts to Retained Earnings. This is done with a closing entry. The closing journal entry will have a debit to Retained Earnings and credits to all the expense accounts for their entire balances to bring them to a zero balance. The debit to Retained Earnings will be for the total amount of the period's expenses.

Exhibit 4-11   T-Accounts with Closing Entries for Clint's Consulting Company, Inc.

Cash (asset)

1-1	$2,000	$ 400	1-3
1-2	4,000	500	1-4
1-5	9,000	4,150	1-7
1-9	4,000	350	1-6
		600	1-8

Contributed capital (CC) (owner's equity)

| | | $2,000 | 1-1 |

Retained earnings

| C-2 | $1,375 | $14,000 | C-1 |
| C-3 | 600 | | |

Dividends

| 1-8 | $600 | **$600** | **C-3** |

Supplies expense (expense)

| A-4 | $325 | **$325** | **C-2** |

Supplies (asset)

| 1-3 | $400 | $325 | A-4 |

Accounts receivable (asset)

| A-1 | $3,000 | | |

Consulting fees (revenue)

		$9,000	1-5
		3,000	A-1
		2,000	A-3
C-1	**$14,000**		

Interest expense (expense)

| 1-7 | $150 | **$150** | **C-2** |

Notes payable (liability)

| 1-7 | $4,000 | $4,000 | 1-2 |

Salaries payable (liability)

| | | $50 | A-2 |

Unearned consulting fees (liability)

| A-3 | $2,000 | $4,000 | 1-9 |

Advertising expense (expense)

| 1-4 | $500 | **$500** | **C-2** |

Salary expense (expense)

| 1-6 | $350 | **$400** | **C-2** |
| A-2 | 50 | | |

Exhibit 4-12
Postclosing Trial Balance for
Clint's Consulting Company,
Inc. at December 31, 2001

Account	DR	CR
Cash	$13,000	
Accounts receivable	3,000	
Supplies	75	
Notes payable		$ 0
Salaries payable		50
Unearned consulting fees		2,000
Contributed capital		2,000
Retained earnings		12,025
Totals	$16,075	$16,075

3. Transfer the Dividends account balance to Retained Earnings. When a distribution is made to the shareholders of a corporation, a special account—Dividends—is often used. This account is a temporary account that carries a debit balance. (When the dividends are paid, Dividends is debited and Cash is credited.) The Dividends account is closed directly to Retained Earnings. The amount of the dividends is not included on the income statement, but it is shown on the statement of changes in shareholders' equity. The journal entry to close this account will have a credit to Dividends and a debit to Retained Earnings.

Look at the closing entries posted to Clint's T-accounts, shown in bold print in Exhibit 4-11. Notice how the revenue and expense accounts have a zero balance.

When closing is done, there is one step left to completing our record keeping for the year: That step is preparing a postclosing trial balance.

Step 8: Preparing a Postclosing Trial Balance

A **postclosing trial balance** is a list of all the accounts and their debit balances or credit balances, prepared after the temporary accounts have been closed. Only balance sheet accounts will appear on the postclosing trial balance.

The final step in the accounting cycle is to prepare a **postclosing trial balance.** Remember, *post* means *after* (like *pre* means *before*). After the temporary accounts are closed, preparing a trial balance—a list of all the accounts with their debit or credit balances—accomplishes two things:

- It is a final check of the equality of debits and credits in the general ledger.
- It confirms that we are ready to start our next period with only real (permanent) accounts.

The postclosing trial balance for Clint's Consulting is shown in Exhibit 4-12.

Review and Summary of the Accounting Cycle

To summarize, there are several steps in the process of preparing financial statements using a traditional general ledger system. Together, they are called the *accounting cycle*.

1. Record the transactions in the journal.
2. Post the journal entries to the ledger.
3. Prepare an unadjusted trial balance.
4. Adjust the accounts at the end of the period—record the adjusting journal entries and post them to the general ledger.
5. Prepare an adjusted trial balance.
6. Prepare the financial statements.

7. Close the temporary accounts to get ready for the next accounting period.

8. Prepare a postclosing trial balance.

What's Next? The General Ledger System Versus Integrated Information Systems

The general ledger system, with debits and credits, has been in existence for nearly 500 years. It is based on a **chart of accounts**—a list of all the accounts that a company wants in its general ledger. Often, accounts are combined for the financial statements, so the level of detail in a company's records corresponds to the number of accounts the company includes in its chart of accounts, *not* by what we see on the financial statements. For example, in Clint's Consulting Company, Inc.'s first year of business, discussed earlier in this chapter, the company may combine Advertising Expense and Supplies Expense on its income statement and list the total as Operating Expenses. When Clint designed the company's general ledger, he decided that he wanted to keep track of advertising costs and supplies separately. That's why he made an account for each.

In the general ledger, each account can be increased or decreased. Debits and credits are combined with the accounting equation to create a system called the double-entry accounting or bookkeeping system. This is a clever system, with checks and balances that help an accountant to minimize errors and to analyze the effects of transactions on the financial statements. Information is stored and organized in a way that provides the information for the four basic financial statements.

However, there is a significant drawback to this traditional system. The problem is that it is dedicated solely to gathering information from business transactions for the financial statements.

In the past 30 years, advancements in technology have made available *computerized* general ledger software, such as Peachtree and Quickbooks. These programs are computerized versions of the traditional manual general ledger accounting system we have been studying in this chapter. The biggest advantage of computerized general ledger systems is a reduction in errors in posting journal entries to the general ledger and the ability to program the preparation of the financial statements. Built-in controls will force the system to stay in balance (debits = credits). Computerized software packages are programmed to produce the financial statements automatically with only journal entries as input.

As terrific as these computerized general ledger packages are, they do not solve the basic problem of the general ledger system—the limited amount of information the general ledger system records about the transactions of the business. The functional areas of the company—like the sales department or the marketing department—must each have its own information system. The sales department has a list of customers, their credit histories, and a record of their purchases. The sales department may have additional sales information by product or by division. None of this information is recorded as part of a general ledger accounting system. If another department needs any of this information, that department has to keep it in its own information system.

Only in the past 5 to 10 years has progress been made in solving the problems associated with multiple information systems. The newest technology allows a company to have one information system that is able to capture enormous amounts of information about every transaction, so that the sales department, the marketing department, the payroll department, the advertising department, the production department—any functional area in the company—and the accountants can all use the same database of information.

L.O. 5

Define an ERP and describe its purpose.

A **chart of accounts** is a list of all the accounts in a company's general ledger.

Understanding Business

ENTERPRISE RESOURCE PLANNING SYSTEMS

Enterprise Resource Planning systems are changing the way businesses manage, process, and use information. ERP systems are computer-based software programs designed to process an organization's transactions and integrate information for planning, production, financial reporting, and customer service. These systems are designed for companies that have computer systems with enormous capabilities. It is estimated that the majority of companies with annual revenues exceeding $1 billion have implemented ERP systems.

Exactly how ERP systems operate varies from company to company, depending on the company's needs.

■ ERP systems are packaged software designed for business environments, both traditional and Web based. *Packaged software* means that the software is commercially available—for purchase or lease—from a software vendor, as opposed to being developed in-house. ERP software packages incorporate what the vendors call "best practices." These are supposed to be the best way of doing certain business activities, such as the best practice for inventory management or production management.

■ An ERP system is composed of modules relating to specific functions. There are modules for: *accounting,* including financial, managerial, and international accounting; *logistics,* including materials requirement planning, production, distribution, sales management, and customer management; and *human resources,* including payroll, benefits, and compensation management.

■ All the modules work together with a common database. This creates an enterprise-wide system instead of separate, independent systems for each function of the business.

■ ERP systems are integrated in terms of software, but not hardware. So, even though two companies may buy ERP packages from the same vendor, the way the system is used will likely be very different. A company may implement modules from more than one vendor in an attempt to customize its ERP system.

■ Because of their popularity and growth, the large ERP vendors are familiar to many of us—SAP, Oracle,

PeopleSoft, J.D. Edwards, and BAAN. Together these vendors hold a major share of the ERP market and provide their system packages along with training to their clients around the world.

■ Because the ERP vendors have already sold their systems to most of the large international companies, the vendors are trying to expand their market to slightly smaller (i.e., middle-market) companies.

Companies implement ERP systems to:

■ consolidate their systems and eliminate redundant data entry and data storage
■ decrease their computer operating costs
■ better manage their business processes
■ accommodate international currencies and international languages
■ standardize policies and procedures
■ enhance and speed up financial reporting
■ improve decision making
■ improve productivity
■ improve profitability

In spite of all the potential benefits of ERP systems, there are drawbacks. ERP systems are costly to implement, with total implementation costs running into the millions of dollars. The use of best practices embedded in the software usually requires companies to change the way they conduct their business processes to match the software. This is not always beneficial—especially when companies have business processes that may give them a competitive advantage. Finally, switching to a new system requires extensive and costly training for those who will use the system.

Given the widespread adoption of ERP systems, it is apparent that the market perceives the ERP system benefits to outweigh the costs. Therefore, whether you choose to go into accounting, information technology, finance, marketing, or management, it is likely that you will encounter an ERP system. However, given the speed with which technology changes, the ERP systems that you will encounter will be even more complex with greater capacities than the ones in existence today.

These information systems are called **enterprise resource planning systems (ERPs)**; they are integrated information systems that capture all of a company's information in a single database. Technically, an ERP is a packaged software system that allows a company to:

- automate and integrate many of its business processes, such as purchasing and production;
- share common data across the entire organization, such as customer information or sales data;
- produce and access information instantaneously.

All the information is recorded without regard for any particular use of the data. Then when someone needs information, it can be retrieved from the database in a variety of ways. For example, sales can be retrieved by date, by customer, by item purchased, just to name a few possibilities.

What are some of the benefits of such a system?

- reduction in inventory and related costs
- faster delivery times
- production problems more easily identified and solved
- improved communication among departments
- decisions can be made faster due to data availability

Because this is a textbook for learning introductory accounting, we are most interested in the data needed for the financial statements. You should be aware that financial data retrieved from an integrated information system like an ERP must be adjusted before the financial statements can be prepared. Most often, the system will produce an unadjusted trial balance; and the accountant goes to work from there to finish the work needed to prepare the financial statements.

How does using an ERP instead of a general ledger system change the information shown on the financial statements?

STUDY BREAK 4-4
SEE HOW YOU'RE DOING

Business Risks

Record keeping presents a significant risk to a business. This risk—information processing risk—is the risk that a company will not properly record the financial information related to its transactions. As we discussed in Chapter 2, we can think of this risk in three parts: inputs, processing, and outputs. In a general ledger system, the input is a journal entry. An accounting system must have controls in place to see that the information in the journal entries is complete and accurate.

Then the input is processed. Journal entries are posted to the general ledger, adjustments are made, and financial statements are prepared. These processing activities need to be monitored for accuracy and completeness. The general ledger system has some built in controls that help minimize errors. The double-entry nature of the debit and credit system is a control for some mathematical errors, and preparing a trial balance at various times is a check to see how that control is working. Many errors in a general ledger accounting system are found and corrected when a trial balance is prepared.

The output of an accounting system is a set of financial statements. The relationship between those statements—net income increases owner's equity and owner's equity is needed to make the balance sheet balance—provides a control for information processing errors. A thorough review of the statements before they are made available to the public or the Securities and Exchange Commission (SEC) is also a necessary control.

Whether the accounting information is processed with a manual general ledger system, a computerized general ledger system, or an enterprise-wide resource planning system, controls should be in place to make sure the input is complete and accurate, the processing is done without errors, and the output is complete and accurate.

Summary Problem: Tom's Wear Transactions for March 2001 in a General Ledger System

We've already analyzed the transactions for Tom's Wear for the third month of business, and prepared the financial statements for March in Chapter 3. Let's repeat the accounting cycle for the same month, this time using debits and credits. The transactions for March are shown in Exhibit 4-13. Each transaction is recorded as an entry in the general journal, chronologically as it occurs during the company's business activity. Exhibit 4-14 shows the transactions in the accounting equation worksheet. Then each transaction is posted to the general ledger (we'll use T-accounts). At March 31, we'll post the adjusting entries needed to prepare the four financial statements. After following along through the adjusted T-accounts, you will prepare the financial statements.

To use a general ledger system, we need to set up the accounts with their balances on March 1, 2001. Exhibit 4-15 shows all the accounts with their beginning balances (indicated with BB). Those accounts, in the Tom's Wear general ledger, will remain with the beginning balances until we post journal entries from the month's transactions.

The first step in the accounting cycle is to record each transaction in chronological order in the journal—as each occurs in the business. Look at each transaction and its journal entry. Notice, for each journal entry there is:

- the date of the transaction
- the account names
- equality between the debits and credits—in every journal entry
- a brief explanation of the transaction

Study each journal entry to make sure you understand how the transaction was recorded.

Exhibit 4-13
Transactions for March 2001 for Tom's Wear, Inc.

tom's wear

March 1	Purchased computer for $4,000 with $1,000 down and a 3-month, 12% note for $3,000. The computer is expected to last for 3 years and have a residual value of $400.
March 10	Paid the rest of last month's advertising bill, $50.
March 15	Collected accounts receivable of $150 from customers from February.
March 20	Paid for February purchases—paying off the accounts payable balance—of $800.
March 24	Purchased 250 shirts @ $4 each for cash, $1,000.
March 27	Sold 200 shirts for $10 each, all on account, for total sales of $2,000.

Journal Entries for March 2001

Ref.	Date	Journal entry	DR	CR
3-1	3/01/01	Equipment	$4,000	
		Cash		$1,000
		Notes payable		3,000
		To record the purchase of a computer with a cash down payment of $1,000 and a note payable of $3,000		
3-2	3/10/01	Other payables	50	
		Cash		50
		To record the payment of a liability for last year's advertising expense		
3-3	3/15/01	Cash	150	
		Accounts receivable		150
		To record the collection of accounts receivable		
3-4	3/20/01	Accounts payable	800	
		Cash		800
		To record payment to vendor for last month's purchase		
3-5	3/24/01	Inventory	1,000	
		Cash		1,000
		To record the purchase of 250 T-shirts at $4 each, paid for in cash		
3-6a	3/27/01	Accounts receivable	2,000	
		Sales		2,000
		To record the sale of 200 T-shirts, on account		
3-6b	3/27/01	Cost of goods sold	800	
		Inventory		800
		To record the expense *cost of goods sold* and reduce the inventory by 200 × $4		

Required

1. Post the journal entries for March using the T-accounts shown in Exhibit 4-15.
2. Then prepare an unadjusted trial balance at March 31.
3. Make the necessary adjusting journal entries at March 31 and post them to the T-accounts. For Tom's Wear, three adjustments need to be made before the financial statements can be prepared. The adjustments are:
   a. Depreciation expense for the computer
   b. Insurance expense for the month
   c. Interest payable on the note
4. Prepare an *adjusted* trial balance at March 31, 2001.
5. Use the adjusted trial balance to prepare the four basic financial statements.

Exhibit 4-14   Work Sheet for March for Tom's Wear

		Assets		=	Liabilities		+	Shareholders' equity	
								Contributed capital	Retained earnings
Balance sheet at March 1, 2001 →	Cash	$ 6,695		=	Accounts payable	$ 800	+	Common stock	Retained earnings
	Accounts				Other payables	50			
	receivable	150				**$850**		**$5,000**	**$1,220**
	Inventory	100							
	Prepaid insurance	125							
		$7,070							
March 1	Equipment	+$4,000			Notes payable	+3,000			
	Cash	(1,000)							
March 10	Cash	(50)			Other payables	(50)			
March 15	Cash	+150							
	Accounts								
	receivable	(150)							
March 20	Cash	(800)			Accounts payable	(800)			
March 24	Cash	(1,000)							
	Inventory	+1,000							
March 27	Accounts								Sales +2,000
	receivable	+2,000							
	Inventory	(800)							Cost of goods sold (800)
Balance sheet at March 31 → *before adjustments*	Cash	$ 3,995		=	Notes payable	**$3,000**	+	**$5,000** Common stock	**$2,420** Retained earnings
	Accounts								
	receivable	2,000							
	Inventory	300							
	Prepaid insurance	125			Total liabilities and shareholders'				
	Equipment	4,000			equity **$10,420**				
	Total assets	**$10,420**							

Solution

1. T-accounts are shown in the answer to part 3.

2.

Tom's Wear, Inc. Unadjusted Trial Balance March 31, 2001		
Cash	$3,995	
Accounts receivable	2,000	
Inventory	300	
Prepaid insurance	125	
Equipment	4,000	
Accumulated depreciation		
Accounts payable		
Other payables		
Interest payable		
Notes payable		$ 3,000
Common stock		5,000
Retained earnings		1,220
Sales		2,000
Cost of goods sold	800	
Insurance expense		
Depreciation expense		
Interest expense		
Totals	*$11,220*	*$11,220*

Exhibit 4-15   T-Accounts for Tom's Wear at the Beginning of March

	Accounts receivable	Inventory	Prepaid insurance
tom's wear	**BB**150	**BB**100	**BB**125

Cash			
BB 6,695	Prepaid rent	Equipment	Accumulated depreciation

Other payables	Accounts payable	Interest payable	Salaries payable
50 **BB**	800 **BB**		

Notes payable	Common stock	Retained earnings	
	5,000 **BB**	1,220 **BB**	

Sales (revenue)	Cost of goods sold	Salary expense

Insurance expense	Depreciation expense	Interest expense

Note: BB = beginning balance

3. Adjusting journal entries and explanations:

a. The computer has been used for one full month, so you must record depreciation expense. The cost was $4,000, an estimated residual value of $400, and a 3-year useful life. Each year the equipment will be depreciated by $1,200 (= (4,000 − 400)/3 years). That makes the depreciation expense $100 per month.

Date	Transaction	Debit	Credit
3/31/01	Depreciation expense	$100	
	Accumulated depreciation		$100
To record the depreciation expense for March			

b. Tom's Wear signed a $3,000 note on March 1 to purchase the computer. A month has passed, and Tom's Wear needs to accrue the interest expense on that note in the amount of $30 (= $3,000 × 0.12 × 1/12).

Date	Transaction	Debit	Credit
3/31/01	Interest expense	$30	
	Interest payable		$30
To record the interest expense for March			

c. In mid-February, Tom's Wear purchased 3 months of insurance for $150, which is $50 per month. On the March 1 balance sheet, there is a current asset called prepaid insurance in the amount of $125. A full month's worth of insurance expense needs to be recorded for the month of March. That amount will be deducted from prepaid insurance.

Date	Transaction	Debit	Credit
3/31/01	Insurance expense	$50	
	Prepaid insurance		$50
To record the insurance expense for the year			

T-Accounts with Adjustments for March 2001 Posted
(Balances Shown at the End of Each Account)

Cash				Accounts receivable			Inventory			Prepaid insurance		
BB $6,695	$1,000	1		BB $ 150	150 3		BB $ 100			BB $125	$50 **Adj-3**	
	50	2		6 2,000			5 1,000	800 7		75		
3 150	800	4					300					
	1,000	5		2,000								
3,995												

Equipment		Accumulated depreciation	
1 $4,000			$100 **Adj-1**
4,000			100

Other payables		Accounts payables		Interest payable		Notes payable	
2 $50	$50 BB	4 $800	$800 BB		$30 Adj-2		$3,000 1
					30		3,000

Common stock		Retained earnings	
	$5,000 BB		$1,220 BB
	5,000		1,220

Sales (revenue)		Cost of goods sold	
	$2,000 6	7 $800	
	2,000	800	

Insurance expense		Depreciation expense		Interest expense	
Adj-3 $50		Adj-1 $100		Adj-2 $30	
50		100		30	

4.

tom's wear

Tom's Wear, Inc.
Adjusted Trial Balance
March 31, 2001

Cash	$ 3,995	
Accounts receivable	2,000	
Inventory	300	
Prepaid insurance	75	
Equipment	4,000	
Accumulated depreciation		$ 100
Accounts payable		
Other payables		
Interest payable		30
Notes payable		3,000
Common stock		5,000
Retained earnings		1,220
Sales		2,000
Cost of goods sold	800	
Insurance expense	50	
Depreciation expense	100	
Interest expense	30	
Totals	$11,350	$11,350

5. The financial statements:

tom's wear

Tom's Wear, Inc.
Income Statement
For the Month Ended March 31, 2001

Sales revenue	$2,000	
Expenses		
Cost of goods sold	$800	
Insurance expense	50	
Depreciation expense	100	
Interest expense	30	(980)
Net income		$1,020

Tom's Wear, Inc.
Statement of Changes in Shareholders' Equity
For the Month Ended March 31, 2001

Beginning contributed capital	$ 5,000	
Contributions during the month	0	
Ending contributed capital		$5,000
Beginning retained earnings	$1,220	
Net income for the month	1,020	
Dividends	0	
Ending retained earnings		2,240
Total shareholders' equity		$7,240

Tom's Wear, Inc.
Balance Sheet
March 31, 2001

Assets		Liabilities and shareholders' equity	
Cash	$ 3,995	Interest payable	$ 30
Accounts receivable	2,000	Notes payable	3,000
Inventory	300	Total liabilities	3,030
Prepaid insurance	75		
		Common stock	5,000
Machine (net of $100	3,900	Retained earnings	2,240
accumulated depreciation)			
		Total liabilities and	
Total assets	$10,270	shareholders' equity	$10,270

Tom's Wear, Inc.
Statement of Cash Flows
For the Month Ended March 31, 2001

Cash from operating activities		
Cash collected from customers	$ 150	
Cash paid to vendors	(1,800)	
Cash paid for operating expenses	(50)	
Total cash from operations		$(1,700)
Cash from investing activities		
Purchase of asset[a]	$(1,000)	(1,000)
Cash from financing activities		0
Net increase (decrease) in cash		$(2,700)

[a]Computer was purchased for $4,000. A note was signed for $3,000 and cash paid was $1,000.

We've seen these exact financial statements before. When we used the accounting equation to keep track of the transactions in Chapter 3, the results were the same as using the general ledger system here. No matter how we do the record keeping, the financial statements are the same. The mechanics of any accounting system—stand-alone or integrated with an enterprise resource planning system—must be designed to produce the information needed for the basic financial statements according to GAAP.

Understanding Excel

The following is Tom's Wear, Inc. adjusted trial balance at March 31, 2001.

Tom's Wear, Inc.
Adjusted Trial Balance
March 31, 2001

	Debit	Credit
Cash	$ 3,995	
Accounts receivable	2,000	
Inventory	300	
Prepaid insurance	75	
Computer	4,000	
Accumulated depreciation		$ 100
Interest payable		30
Notes payable		3,000
Common stock		5,000
Retained earnings		1,220
Sales		2,000
Cost of goods sold	800	
Insurance expense	50	
Depreciation expense	100	
Interest expense	30	
Totals	$11,350	$11,350

For purposes of this exercise only, assume that Tom's Wear, Inc. is closing the books for the month of March.

Requirements

1. Open a new Excel work sheet.
2. Create the following bold column headings beginning in column A and ending in column E: **Ref., Date, Journal Entry, DR,** and **CR.**
3. Enter the required closing journal entries. Adjust your column widths as needed.
4. Prepare a postclosing trial balance for Tom's Wear, Inc. Use appropriate headings and formatting.

   Hint: To sum the total debits and credits select the appropriate cell and click the Auto Sum Σ button.

5. Print your file and save it to disk. Name your file TomsWear4.

Answers to Study Break Questions

Account title	Expense	Revenue	Asset	Liability	Owner's equity
Accounts payable				CR (Credit)	
Accounts receivable			DR		
Advertising	DR				
Cash			DR		
Depreciation expense	DR				
Furniture and fixtures			DR		
Accumulated depreciation			(Contra) CR		
Unearned fees				CR	
Salary expense	DR				
Common stock					CR
Rent expense	DR				
Dividends					DR
Retained earnings					CR
(Earned) Fees		CR			
Land			DR		
Building			DR		

Study Break 4-1

Study Break 4-2

Date	Transaction	Debit	Credit
12/31/03	Salary expense	$300	
	Salaries payable		$300
To accrue salary expense for December 2003			

No expense will be recognized in January 2004. It was recognized in December 2003, but will be paid in January 2004.

Date	Transaction	Debit	Credit
1/3/04	Salaries payable	$300	
	Cash		$300
To record the cash payment of salaries payable			

Study Break 4-3

Date	Transaction	Debit	Credit
12/31/03	Revenue account	$5,000	
	Retained earnings		$5,000
To close the revenue account to retained earnings			

Date	Transaction	Debit	Credit
12/31/03	Retained earnings	$3,000	
	Expense account		$3,000
To close the expense account to retained earnings			

Study Break 4-4   Using an ERP instead of a general ledger system will not change the information shown on the financial statements. The two systems are just ways of keeping track of business information. It doesn't change the information or the reporting of it.

Questions

1. What is the general ledger system and what are its advantages?
2. What is an account?
3. What is the trial balance?
4. Which accounts are permanent and which are temporary?
5. What is the normal balance in each of these accounts?

Accounts receivable	Cash
Accounts payable	Supplies expense
Common stock	Distributions (dividends)
Retained earnings	Inventory
Sales revenue	Bonds payable
Salary expense	Cost of goods sold

6. What are the basic steps in the accounting cycle?
7. Can accounting transactions be recorded directly into the general ledger accounts? What is the advantage of using a journal first?
8. Is a *credit* a good thing or a bad thing? Explain.
9. What are adjusting entries and why are they necessary?
10. What is an ERP?
11. What are the advantages of an ERP system?
12. What are the disadvantages of an ERP system?

13. The REA model is a conceptual model, whereas ERPs are operational models. What's the difference?

14. Compare the focus of a general ledger system with the focus of an ERP system.

15. What are some of the specific control issues with an ERP system?

16. Why do accountants care about ERP systems?

17. How does using an ERP change the company's financial statements (compared with those produced in a general ledger (G/L) system)?

Short Exercises

SE4-1   Given the following accounts, tell whether the normal balance of each account is a debit (DR) or credit (CR).

L.O. 4-1

1. _____ Accounts receivable
2. _____ Notes payable
3. _____ Tom Phillips, Capital account
4. _____ Sales
5. _____ Prepaid insurance
6. _____ Supplies inventory
7. _____ Rent expense
8. _____ Income tax expense
9. _____ Salaries payable
10. _____ Retained earnings

SE4-2   Indicate which of the following events would result in recognizing revenue for the year in which the event takes place; indicate the amount and the account. Give the journal entry that would be made in each case. (Take the selling company's point of view.)

L.O. 4-1, 2, 3

a. A used car salesman sells a car for $12,000; the customer financed the purchase because she didn't have any cash.

b. Steel USA is producing 3 tons of steel for American Cans. It costs $3,600 per ton to produce, but American Cans has promised to pay $5,000 per ton when it receives the steel. Steel USA will probably ship it in the near future.

c. Florida State Boosters has received $50,000 in advanced ticket sales for next year's basketball games.

d. Reader's Digest collected several accounts that were outstanding from last year. Usually accounts are collected in advance; but in this case, the customer received the magazine last year but didn't pay until this year.

e. Customers paid over $5,000 in advance for services to be rendered next year.

SE4-3   Indicate which of the following events would result in recognizing expenses for the year in which the event takes place; indicate the amount and the account. (Take the T-shirt company's point of view.)

L.O. 4-1, 2, 3

a. T-Shirt Inc. paid employees $5,000 for work performed.

b. T-Shirt Inc. purchased 20,000 T-shirts for their inventory for $60,000 on account.

c. T-Shirt Inc. paid the factory cash for the 20,000 shirts purchased.

d. T-Shirt Inc. sold 2,000 T-shirts to the FSU Bookstore for $10,000 cash.

e. T-Shirt Inc. received a utility bill for the last month of the year but won't actually pay it until next year.

f. T-Shirt Inc. paid $5,000 for a 2-year insurance policy—for the current year and for next year.

SE4-4   Selected transactions for Red Company that occurred during the month of December follow. For each transaction, tell how it affects the accounting equation. Then

L.O. 4-1

tell which accounts will be affected and how. (Ignore adjustments that may be needed on December 31.)

e.g., *Red purchased a new computer for $5,000 for cash. It is expected to last for 5 years.* Solution: Assets are increased by $5,000 (equipment) and also reduced by $5,000 (cash): debit (increase) equipment, credit (decrease) cash.

   a. The company issued common stock to investors for $10,000 cash.
   b. The company rented a warehouse for $1,000 per month, and paid for 3 months rent on December 1.
   c. The company purchased inventory for $3,000 on account.

L.O. 4-1

SE4-5   The following selected transactions for Blues Company occurred during the month of March. Give the journal entry for each.

   a. The firm sold items to customers for $5,000: Half was for cash, and half was on account.
   b. Blues paid $2,000 to vendor for part of the purchase in SE4-4.c.
   c. The company incurred general expenses for $300 cash.
   d. Blues purchased supplies for $200 cash.

L.O. 4-1

SE4-6   How do the following transactions affect Babyland's cash account? (Tell if it would be a debit or a credit.)

   a. Babyland purchased $5,000 of baby cribs on account.
   b. The company sold one of their buildings for $25,000 cash.
   c. The employees were paid $2,000 in sales commissions.
   d. The firm gave customers $1,000 for returned merchandise.
   e. Babyland issued stock to investors for $5,000 cash.

L.O. 4-1

SE4-7   How do the following transactions affect the liability and owner's equity accounts for Fast Signs, Inc. during 2001?

   a. Fast Signs paid the remainder of a $3,000 loan.
   b. The company obtained a loan for $10,000.
   c. Fast Signs earned $12,000 in sales for the year.
   d. An estimated $2,500 will be due for yearly income taxes, payable in 2002.

L.O. 4-1

SE4-8   Determine how the accounts would be affected (increase or decrease and debit or credit) for the following transactions occurring in December 2001 for Networking Solutions, Inc.

   a. Networking Solutions received $20,000 investment from the owner.
   b. The company purchased $8,000 of new office computers on account.
   c. The company sold $2,000 of inventory for cash.
   d. Networking Solutions paid $3,000 for next year's rent.
   e. The company paid $4,000 of the amount owed for the computers.
   f. The company declared and distributed $1,000 of dividends.

L.O. 4-4

SE4-9   For each of the following accounts, tell whether it is a permanent account or a temporary account.

   1. _____ Cash
   2. _____ Accounts payable
   3. _____ Jane Smith, Capital account
   4. _____ Revenues
   5. _____ Prepaid insurance
   6. _____ Merchandise inventory
   7. _____ Rent expense
   8. _____ Income tax expense
   9. _____ Income taxes payable
   10. _____ Common stock

Exercises

E4-1 Record the following transactions for JG Company in T-accounts and tell how each affects assets, liabilities, or owner's equity. The year-end for JG Company is December 31.

L.O. 4-1, 2, 3

a. On April 1, JG Company issued a $5,000 note at 8%, both interest and principal due in 1 year.

b. On June 1, JG Company rented a copy machine and paid 1-year of rent in advance at a rate of $250 per month.

c. On June 30, JG Company purchased an insurance policy for a term of 1 year, beginning immediately. The cost was $960.

d. On July 1, JG Company replenished the supply closet with the purchase of $600 worth of supplies for cash. The company started the year with $100 worth of supplies on hand.

e. Over the course of the year, JG Company earned $35,000 of service revenue, collected in cash.

E4-2 Use the information from E4-1, including your answers to a through e to make the necessary adjustments to JG's accounts in preparation for the year-end financial statements. You may need to use the additional information that follows:
  On hand at year-end was $200 worth of supplies.

L.O. 4-1, 2, 3

E4-3 Matt opened his Read A-Lot Bookstore, a sole proprietorship, on April 1, 2002, selling new and used books. The gross profit earned on new book sales is 40%. Matt used $4,000 of his own money to start the business.

L.O. 4-1, 2

a. On April 1, the business buys $3,000 of new books from his supplier with cash.

b. On April 30, customers bring in used books and the business buys them for $750.

c. On June 30, new books are sold for $3,000. Half of these sales are on account.

d. On June 30, the business sells all the used books for $1,500 cash.

Record the transactions into T-accounts for Matt.

E4-4 The trial balance of Clevenger's Computer Center, Inc. on April 1, 2002, lists the company's assets, liabilities, and shareholders' equity on that date.

L.O. 4-1, 2

Account title	Balance Debit	Balance Credit
Cash	$16,000	
Accounts receivable	4,700	
Accounts payable		$ 2,200
Common stock		10,000
Retained earnings		8,500
Total	$20,700	$20,700

During April, Clevenger's completed the following transactions:

a. The company borrowed $5,000 from the bank with a short-term note payable.

b. Clevenger paid cash of $10,000 to acquire land.

c. The company performed service for a customer and collected the cash of $2,500.

d. Clevenger purchased supplies on credit, $175.

e. The company performed service for a customer on account, $1,600.

Required: Set up T-accounts for the accounts given in the April 1 trial balance. Then post the preceding transactions to the accounts. Calculate the account balances and prepare an unadjusted trial balance at April 30.

L.O. 4-3, 4

E4-5 By using the information from E4-4, which accounts will likely need to be adjusted before the monthly financial statements are prepared? In each case, explain why or why not. What additional information would you need in each case to make the appropriate adjustment? Which accounts will need to be closed at the end of the accounting period and why?

L.O. 4-4

E4-6 Given the following adjusted trial balance, record the appropriate closing entries. What is net income for the year?

Climbers Rock Company
Adjusted Trial Balance
December 31, 2005

	Debit	Credit
Cash	$ 13,000	
Accounts receivable	20,000	
Supplies	21,500	
Equipment	20,000	
Accumulated depreciation		$ 9,000
Property	64,000	
Prepaid rent	28,000	
Accounts payable		23,000
Notes payable		25,000
Interest payable		2,000
Paid-in capital		51,000
Retained earnings		29,500[a]
Dividends	4,000	
Sales		94,000
Cost of goods sold	45,000	
Depreciation expense	3,000	
Salaries expense	15,000	
Totals	$233,500	$233,500

[a]Retained earnings at January 1, 2005. (No accounts have been closed.)

L.O. 4-1, 2, 3, 4

E4-7 The Brain Trust Consulting Company began business in 2001. The following transactions took place during January:

Jan.
- 2 Owners invested $50,000 in exchange for stock.
- 2 The company borrowed $10,000 from a local bank with a 12% note and a 6-month term. Both the principal and interest will be repaid in 6 months.
- 6 Supplies were purchased on account for $500.
- 8 Office rent of $800 for January was paid in cash.
- 8 The company purchased computer equipment for $16,000. It should last 4 years, with no residual value.
- 20 The company received $2,200 from a customer for services to be performed in February.
- 5-31 Consulting services performed during January on account totaled $12,000.
- 31 The company paid salaries of $7,000 to employees.
- 31 $400 was paid to the supplies vendor as part of the $500 owed to the vendor from the Jan. 6 purchase. The company only paid part of the invoice because it only used $400 worth of the supplies in January.

Required: Give the journal entry for each transaction. Then make the necessary adjusting entries at January 31, 2001. What else should be done to finish the accounting cycle for the month?

E4-8 Suppose Brain Trust Consulting Company (in E4-7) used an ERP system instead of a general ledger system to record its accounting information. What information about the transactions given in E4-7 would be recorded in the information system that would *not* be recorded in the general ledger?

L.O. 4-5

Problems—Set A

P4-1A The following is account information for Susie's Pottery Barn as of December 31, 2002.

L.O. 4-1, 2, 3, 4

Revenues	$20,000	Equipment	$10,000
Prepaid rent	2,000	Accumulated depreciation, equipment	3,000
Capital, Susie	5,000	Accounts receivable	5,000
Accounts payable	2,000	Salaries expense	2,000
Depreciation expense	1,000	Cash	1,000
Inventory	8,000	Withdrawal	1,000

Required: Prepare a trial balance, income statement, statement of owner's equity, and balance sheet as of December 31, 2002.

P4-2A Fast Feet Shoe Store has the following account information on its adjusted trial balance.

L.O. 4-3, 4

Fast Feet Shoe Store
Adjusted Trial Balance
December 31, 2003

	Debit	Credit
Cash	$ 18,000	
Accounts receivable	22,000	
Supplies	31,000	
Equipment	15,000	
Accumulated depreciation		$ 6,000
Property	34,000	
Prepaid rent	8,000	
Accounts payable		25,000
Notes payable		15,000
Interest payable		2,000
Paid-in capital		21,000
Retained earnings		26,000[a]
Dividends	4,000	
Sales		100,000
Gain on sale of equipment		5,000
Cost of goods sold	50,000	
Depreciation expense	3,000	
Salaries expense	15,000	
Totals	$200,000	$200,000

[a]Balance at January 1, 2003. (No closing entries have been made.)

Required: Prepare the necessary closing entries and a balance sheet as of December 31, 2003.

P4-3A The Hope Meadows Rental Company has the following account balances at the end of the year:

L.O. 4-1, 2, 3, 4, 5

Insurance expense	$ 4,000
Rental income	15,670
Unearned rental income	3,800
Accumulated depreciation	7,625
Wages payable	5,550
Taxes expense	4,398
Depreciation expense	7,625
Wages expense	10,400

The following information is available at the end of the year:

1. Of the insurance expense $1,000 has not yet expired.
2. Of the unearned rental income $1,500 has now been earned.
3. The company currently owes employees $1,200 of wages.
4. The company owes an additional $4,900 in real estate taxes.
5. Depreciation expense has been recalculated, and it should be a total of $8,743 for the year.

Required:

a. Prepare the journal entries necessary to ad   accounts.
b. Use T-accounts to compute and presep   ome statement and balance
   sheet account balances after the adjust   pared.
c. Prepare the closing entries.
d. What information in addition to th   he general ledger
   would Hope Meadows want as part   ystem?

L.O. 4-3, 4

P4-4A Marcie opened a children's comp   ea-n-Pod.com,
selling only via the Internet. During 2003,   g transactions:

a. It started the online business with $
b. The company borrowed $10,000   12 months on
   January 1, 2003.
c. It purchased $9,000 in inventory for
d. The company paid $2,000 to a Webr   ees.
e. It had cash sales of $5,000 for 2003
f. The company paid $1,000 in adverti

Required: From the given information,   December 31,
2003 and prepare the income statement,   balance sheet.
Then prepare the closing entries.

L.O. 4-3, 4

P4-5A A partial list of transactions fr   p, Inc. during
2003 follows:

a. On February 1, 2003, the shop paid   e.
b. The shop purchased $10,000 of supp
c. On March 15, 2003, the shop obtair   00 cash. They
   should last for 5 years. The compan   on in 2003.
d. On April 1, 2003, the shop paid an ar   ), for coverage
   beginning April 1.
e. On June 1, 2003, to increase sales, the   tising for $900.
f. On November 1, 2003, the compan   30,000 at 12%
   from Three Rivers Bank payable on
g. As of December 31, 2003, cash rever
h. At the close of business on Decemb   contract with
   a local company to do all their auto r   in four installments (beginning on March 1, 2004)
i. On December 31, the company paid

[Note: at the end of the year, remaining s

Required: Give the journal entries for the t   ng entries and
post-closing trial balance for Randy's Rad   er 31, 2003.

P4-6A   On June 1, Seth _____ er business as a sole proprietorship. Seth opened a bank account _____ iting $25,000. He paid 2 months of rent in advance totaling $500. O _____ supplies for $600 and two computers at a total cost of $6,500. Set _____ to last for 3 years with no residual value. Seth hired an office ass _____ e assistant $1,000 per month of which he paid $500 on June 15 ar _____ th paid $200 for an Internet advertisement to announce the openi _____ arned $4,200 in June of which he collected $2,800 in cash. At the e _____ d only $100 worth of supplies on hand.

Required: Show Seth _____ unting equation. Make the needed adjust-ments at June 30, an _____ sic financial statements for this company for the month of Jun _____ g entries.

L.O. 4-1, 2, 3, 4

P4-7A   This is an e _____ Chapter 3. In this problem use the general ledger system to k _____ s.

The accounting re _____ Inc. contained the following balances as of December 31, 20 _____

L.O. 4-1, 2, 3

		Liabilities and equity	
Cash		Accounts payable	$17,000
Accounts rece		Contributed capital	45,000
Land		Retained earnings	14,500
Totals			$76,500

The following a _____ da's 2002 fiscal year:

Jan.	1	The _____ al $20,000 cash from the owners.
	1	Pan _____ cost $17,000 for cash. The computer had a _____ ear useful life.
Mar.	1	The _____ y issuing a 1-year note at 12%.
May	1	The _____ advance for a 1-year lease for office space.
June	1	The _____ distribution to the owners.
July	1	The _____ t cost $10,000 cash.
Aug.	1	Ca _____ le amounted to $6,000.
	1	Pa _____ vance for 12 months of service to be _____ t year, beginning on receipt of payment.
Sept.	1	Pa _____ . The land originally cost $16,000.
Oct.	1	Pa _____ ies on account.
Nov.	1	Pa _____ 00 certificate of deposit at 6%.
Dec.	31	Th _____ enue on account during the year that
	31	C _____ receivable amounted to $44,000.
	31	T _____ erating expenses on account during the year
Also:		S _____ y the sales staff but not yet paid amounted
		T _____ es on hand at the end of the period.
		I _____ tion data, there are five additional adjustments _____ he financial statements can be prepared.

Required: _____ ounts, prepare an unadjusted trial balance, make the approp _____ the financial statements (all four) for 2002.

Proble _____

P4-1B   T _____ tion is for Janie's Jewelry Shop as of December 31, 2003.

L.O. 4-1, 2, 3, 4

Sales	$22,000	Other revenue	$13,000
Prepaid advertising	2,000	Equipment	10,000
Capital, Janie	14,000	Accounts receivable	5,000
Accounts payable	4,000	Cost of goods sold	11,000
Operating expense	3,000	Cash	2,000
Inventory	18,000	Distribution to Janie	2,000

Required: Prepare a trial balance, income statement, statement of owner's equity, and balance sheet as of December 31, 2003.

L.O. 4-3, 4

P4-2B Here is an adjusted trial balance from Phillip's Photo Shop.

Phillip's Photo Shop, Inc.
Adjusted Trial Balance
December 31, 2003

	Debit	Credit
Cash	$ 28,000	
Accounts receivable	2,000	
Prepaid rent	1,000	
Equipment	35,000	
Accumulated depreciation		$ 7,000
Land	15,000	
Prepaid insurance	7,000	
Salaries payable		5,000
Notes payable		15,000
Interest payable		2,000
Paid-in capital		20,000
Retained earnings		34,000[a]
Dividends	2,000	
Sales		97,000
Cost of goods sold	52,000	
Rent expense	12,000	
Insurance expense	8,000	
Depreciation expense	3,500	
Salaries expense	14,500	
Totals	$180,000	$180,000

[a]Retained earnings balance on January 1, 2003. (No closing entries have been made.)

Required: Prepare the necessary closing entries and a balance sheet at December 31, 2003.

L.O. 4-1, 2, 3, 4, 5

P4-3B The Hoffman Body Spa, Inc. has the following account balances at the end of the year:

Service revenue	$34,320
Unearned service revenue	3,250
Wages payable	2,550
Accumulated depreciation	2,000
Taxes expense	3,298
Depreciation expense	1,625
Insurance expense	1,850
Wages expense	10,400

The following information is also available:

1. The company accountant forgot to depreciate a hot tub that was purchased at the beginning of the year. The hot tub cost $10,400, has a useful life of 5 years, and has no expected residual value.
2. The Unearned Service Revenue consists of gift certificates sold during the year. Hoffman's has failed to account for the $1,200 worth of certificates that have been used by customers.

3. The company cu⋯⋯wages in addition to those given here.
4. The company ov⋯⋯state taxes.

Required:

a. Prepare the adj⋯⋯y at year-end.
b. Use T-accounts⋯⋯balances in these accounts after the adjustments ha⋯⋯
c. Prepare the clo⋯⋯
d. What informat⋯⋯d in the general ledger would Hoffman Body Spa wan⋯⋯rmation system?

P4-4B GiGi open⋯⋯les as a sole proprietorship to sell her applesauce.   L.O. 4-3, 4

a. GiGi started th⋯⋯ly 1, 2002.
b. On October 1⋯⋯ $10,000 from Local Bank at 12%. The loan was for 1⋯⋯
c. The company⋯⋯ples for cash during the fiscal year, and had $1,000 w⋯⋯
d. The company⋯⋯of jars, lids, and labels for cash. None were left on J⋯⋯
e. The compan⋯⋯shop for 18 months, beginning July 1, 2002. The sh⋯⋯, and electricity costs were included with the rent.
f. Just Apples⋯⋯ce for cash during the first fiscal year.
g. Just Apples⋯⋯

Required: From⋯⋯are the income statement, statement of owner's equity, a⋯⋯ear ending June 30, 2003. Then prepare the closing entries.

P4-5B The fol⋯⋯al list of transactions from Mills Hobby Shop.   L.O. 4-3, 4

a. On March⋯⋯paid $6,000 cash for a 2-year insurance policy.
b. On March⋯⋯0,000 of supplies on account.
c. On April⋯⋯some new display shelves for $2,000. They shou⋯⋯sidual value. Mills will take a full year of depreciati⋯⋯
d. On May 1,⋯⋯of advertising in a local magazine.
e. On Septe⋯⋯nonth loan for $10,000 at 12% from City National v⋯⋯incipal payable on March 1, 2003.
f. For the ye⋯⋯had cash revenues of $34,000.
g. Mills paid⋯⋯ine 29, 2003.

Note: at the e⋯⋯supplies totaled $2,000.

Required: Fr⋯⋯pare the income statement for the fiscal year ending June 3⋯⋯ng entries.

P4-6B On S⋯⋯arted a DVD business on the Internet as a sole proprietorsh⋯⋯unt for the business by depositing $37,000. The new cor⋯⋯n advance totaling $1,200, for rent beginning on Septemb⋯⋯company purchased supplies for $800 and $6,500 worth⋯⋯ired a sales person to help her and agreed to pay the assi⋯⋯le on the last day of the month. Irene's company paid $⋯⋯ent to announce the opening of the business. The compar⋯⋯of which Irene collected $2,800 in cash. At the end of the r⋯⋯rth of supplies on hand, and the inventory on hand on Se⋯⋯   L.O. 4-1, 2, 3, 4

Required: Show the company transactions in the accounting equation. Make the needed adjustments, and then prepare the four basic financial statements for this company for the month of September. Then prepare the closing entries.

L.O. 4-1, 2, 3

P4-7B   (This is the same as P3-7B, but here you will use the general ledger model to keep track of the transactions.) The accounting records for Bebe Company contained the following balances as of December 31, 2003:

Assets		Liabilities and shareholders' equity	
Cash	$50,000	Accounts payable	$17,500
Accounts receivable	26,500	Capital stock	35,000
Prepaid rent	3,600	Additional paid-in capital	13,600
Land	10,500	Retained earnings	24,500
Totals	$90,600		$90,600

The following accounting events apply to Bebe's 2004 fiscal year:

Jan.   1   Bebe purchased a computer that cost $20,000 for cash. The computer had a $2,000 salvage value and a 3-year useful life.

Mar.   1   The company borrowed $20,000 by issuing a 2-year note at 12%.

May   1   The company paid $6,000 cash in advance for a 6-month lease for office space. The lease started immediately.

June   1   The company paid cash dividends of $2,000 to the owners.

July   1   The company purchased land that cost $15,000 cash.

Aug.   1   Cash payments on accounts payable amounted to $6,000.

   1   Bebe received $6,000 cash in advance for 12 months of service to be performed monthly for the next year, beginning on receipt of payment.

Sept.   1   Bebe sold land for $13,000 cash. The land originally cost $15,000.

Oct.   1   Bebe purchased $1,300 of supplies on account.

Nov.   1   Bebe purchased a 1-year, $10,000 certificate of deposit at 5%.

Dec.   31   The company earned service revenue on account during the year that amounted to $50,000.

   31   Cash collections from accounts receivable amounted to $46,000.

   31   The company incurred other operating expenses on account during the year that amounted to $6,000.

Also: Salaries that had been earned by the sales staff but not yet paid amounted to $2,300.

There was $200 of supplies on hand at the end of the period.

Based on the preceding transaction data, there are some additional adjustments that need to be made before the financial statements can be prepared.

Required: Post the journal entries to T-accounts, prepare an unadjusted trial balance, and prepare the financial statements (all four) for the year ended December 31, 2004.

Issues for Discussion

Financial statement analysis

1. Use the annual report from Pier 1 Imports, Inc. to answer these questions:
   a. When you look at the financial statements for Pier 1, can you tell if the company uses a general ledger accounting system? Explain.
   b. Find at least four pieces of quantitative information contained in the Pier 1 annual report that would *not* be found in a general ledger system.

Business risk

2. Who are the au
3. How does havi   ?
4. Compare the r   nent information to the information in
   other parts of   opinion.

Ethics

5. Companies oft   recognizing revenue before it is actually
   earned accor   xpenses that have been incurred. For
   example, to m   a specific period, a company may capi-
   talize a cost t   the following scenario and then decide
   how you wou   anage earnings.

   > You   ge public company. Your bonus is calcu-
   > lated on   ets that you must meet. This year that tar-
   > get is $1   to sign off on any decision made within
   > your div   lowing situation:
   > On   the company ordered $150,000 worth of
   > supplies   l rush. Most of them will be used by year-
   > end. The   the evening of December 27. If you record
   > this sup   net income will be $1.45 million and you
   > will not   ore not receive your bonus of $25,000 that
   > you ha   npany generally expenses supplies when
   > purcha   nse this year for the year ended December
   > 31, 200   upport employees will not receive a bonus.

   What woul

Internet E

The accounting   may be simplified with the aid of a computerized general   ader in e-finance and develops and supports
Quicken®, the   are; TurboTax®, the best-selling tax preparation software;   pular small business accounting software.

*Please go t   ers Web site. Go to Chapter 4 and use the
Internet E*

IE4-1

a. Briefly s   ay's News.
b. In the "C   on type INTU, the stock symbol of Intuit Inc.,
   and ther   mation provided and comment on one item of
   interest.

IE4-2 In th   inancial Statements. For the most recent year
list the amo   on stock, total revenues, and interest expense.
Note that th   ousands.

a. Which   h of these amounts?
b. What v   each of these accounts?
c. Which   ount?
d. Which   the end of the accounting period?
e. Which   l debit balance?
f. Which   ffected by an adjusting journal entry? Explain
   why tl   ljusted.

IE4-3 W   computerized general ledger system such as
QuickBoo   important to understand the accounting cycle
even thou   r systems are available? Explain why or why not.

*Please not   ly being updated. Therefore, if the information is not
found whe   eb site further to find the information.*

ACQUISITIONS: PURCHASE AND USE OF BUSINESS ASSETS

Financial Reporting

Here's where you've been...

In Chapter 4, you learned about the basic accounting cycle—how the traditional general ledger system is used to keep track of a company's transactions and aids in the preparation of the financial statements. You learned how to use *debits* and *credits,* a tool for organizing and tracking accounting information.

Here's where you're going...

From Chapter 5, you should understand how the financial statements show the purchase, use, and sale of assets that last for longer than 1 year.

Property, Plant, and Equipment

Financing

Property, Plant,
and Equipment

Sales and
Receiv...

Financial
Reporting
and
Business
Events

Inventory
and
Liabilities

Learnin... bjectiv...

More specifica... ...dying this chapter, you should be able to answer these questions:

1. What are lo... ...hey
   defined, cla... ...chase?
2. How is the... ...lected in
   the financia... ...ds are used
   to write off... ...useful life?
3. How are (a... ...oductive
   capacity, a... ...concerning
   useful life a... ...reflected in
   the financi...
4. What are c... ...and to what
   assets are t...

5. How is the disposal of an asset reflected in the
   financial statements?
6. How does depreciation for financial statements
   differ from depreciation for taxes?
7. What information about long-term assets is disclosed on the financial statements and how can
   we use it to help us evaluate the business?
8. What business risks are associated with long-
   term assets, and what controls can minimize
   those risks?

To start his business, Tom used some of his own money.

Then his business, Tom's Wear, borrowed some money from Tom's mom. After the business idea is ready for implementation, a business is always started by acquiring financing. The details related to financing a business—getting capital from owners and creditors—are often more complicated than financing for Tom's Wear. We'll discuss those details in later chapters.

In this chapter, we'll continue our discussion of the business cycle with the acquisition of property, plant, and equipment. Setting up the infrastructure for a company is often the next big step in starting a business. As we look at the purchase, the use, and the disposal of business assets that will last for more than 1 year, keep in mind the business processes that result in the accounting information shown on the four basic financial statements. The relationship between the business processes and the accounting information is one of cause and effect in *both* directions. The business activities cause the financial statement effects and the financial statement information, in turn, influences the business activities.

The underlying business process of acquiring **long-term assets**—also known as **fixed assets**—requires input and analysis beyond that required in the acquisition of short-term assets. The acquisition of long-term assets requires more than documenting the need for the purchase, selecting the vendor, placing the order, receiving and inspecting the goods, and paying for the goods or services. The investment in long-term assets is typically much greater than the investment in short-term assets.

One of the considerations in the purchase of a typical long-term asset, like a new piece of equipment, is the asset's revenue-generating potential—the primary benefit of purchasing the asset. In the business decision, the cost of a long-term asset must include all the costs incurred to get the asset ready for its use. Long-term assets often require extensive setup and preparation before they become operational, and employees need to be trained to use them. All these costs must be considered in the process of acquiring a long-term asset. As we work through this chapter, you will see that the way we account for the purchases of long-term assets under generally accepted accounting principles (GAAP) reflects the underlying business process.

BUSINESS PROCESS

Long-term assets = fixed assets:
These terms are used to mean the same thing—assets that will be used for more than one accounting period.

Acquisition of Long-Term Assets: The Business Process

Factories and m_____ are c_____ __ng-term assets because they are expected to be u__ ____ th__ _. A firm purchases long-term assets because those as____ __ ____ce__ __ e revenue in the normal course of business; a firm c____ ___ ____chas__ in_____ resale. (Assets purchased for resale are called invent____ ___. We__ p_____d its first long-term asset—a computer—in its thi__ ____ of bus_____. __ommon for a company to purchase long-term assets __ ____ the ___ __ _ establishing its business.

A company ____ _____ purcha__ ____m assets that *won't* be used in the business. Those _____ such as ___ __ stock in another firm, artwork, and property expect__ ____ ____ase i__ __l__ ld be investments that the company plans to keep fc___ _ ____un __ ___ ___ever, our focus will be on long-term assets that the c_____ _ will ___ __ ___ e revenue.

What assets ___ __nd ho__ to ____r them are important business decisions. The acqu___ __ _____ ___nt for them affect the financial statements. If we bu___ __ __e fo___ ___ ve exchanged one asset—cash—for another—a m_____ __e giv___ ___ we get a machine. That's a simple exchange. If ins___ ____ __n __ __ sign a note payable for the purchase, the exchange i_ __ __ ___plic__ ___ ___ the machine, but the *give* portion of the transactio__ ___ ____rmin__ __ p_____ ___re's a timing difference between the actual get port___ __ ___ exch___ ___ng the machine—and the actual give portion of the _____ ___ ____in__ ___ ney to the lender. By now, you know that these timi___ _____ces __ __ ____ortant in business decisions. The cost of this type of ___ __ _____ __ __ expense. The business decision about how to pay fo__ __ _____ ___ ____nting related to that business decision are closely link___

These dec_____ ___ what __ ____ __y and how to pay for them—do not affect the in___ ____emen__ __ __ __me of the purchase. As you saw in Chapter 3, a_____ __ defe__ ___ ng the expense of a long-term asset until the asse__ __ _ly us___ __ _ siness. When the asset is used and the expense is re_____ __ __ __ ___ciation expense. This is another example of a timi__ ____ence. __ ___ ___hased a machine at one point in time, and we'll us__ __ ___und_ __ ___sequent period of time. The period of time over wh____ __ ___un to ___ __ _chine is a very important input in the business dec____ __ ____acquir__ th__ ___. The way we subsequently depreciate the asset re____ __ __ _ch ____ __ _ e'll discuss the details of depreciation later in this ___.

There ar_ _ _ __ategori__ __ ___m, or fixed, assets: **tangible assets** and **intangible a____**

Tangible __ ___ _ __ass____ __ _ computer—you can see and touch them.

Tangibl_ ___ __ __ _nclud_____

- land, suc_ __ ___ __oper_ ___ __ is built on;
- a plant, s___ __ __ ___ctor___ ___;
- equipme___ ___ __ _ _ m_____;
- natural r___ ___ __ ___ch __ ___ or timber.

Intang_____ ___ ___ ____e __value to the firm, although they are not visible or t_____ __ __ea__ ___ give the owner specific rights. Intangible assets incl___

- copyrig___ ___ ___rest__ __ ___he written content of this book;
- patents___ ___ ___ ___ s___ ___ntel Pentium IV computer chip;
- tradem___ ___ ___ ___ __ C___ ___

BUSINESS PROCESS

L.O. 1

Be able to define and identify different types of long-term assets.

Tangible assets are assets that can be seen and touched. The most common are property, plant, and equipment.

Intangible assets are assets whose true value resides in the rights and privileges given to the owners of the asset. They are often represented by contracts, such as franchises and copyrights.

■ franchises, such as the rights to run and own a McDonalds restaurant; and

■ goodwill, the amount a company pays for another business firm *in excess* of the fair market value of the net assets of that business firm.

Allocating the Cost of Long-Term Assets

 L.O. 2

Be able to explain how the cost of an asset is allocated to the periods in which the asset is used and how that information is reflected in the financial statements.

Capitalizing a cost means to report it on the balance sheet as an asset.

Depreciation is a systematic, rational allocation process to recognize the expense of long-term assets over the periods in which the assets are used.

Writing off = expensing: This means that a cost is put on the income statement as an expense.

Depreciation, depletion, and **amortization**—they all mean to *write off* a cost over more than one accounting period.

The cost of an asset is recorded as an asset at the time of purchase—that's called **capitalizing** the cost. That cost will be recognized as an expense during the periods in which the asset is used. When Tom's Wear bought the computer for $4,000, the transaction was recorded as the acquisition of an asset. Then as the computer is used, Tom's Wear records a portion of the computer cost as an expense on the income statement. Depreciation expense is recorded as part of the process of adjusting the accounting records before the financial statements are prepared. The adjustment decreases the value of the asset in the accounting records—via accumulated depreciation—and decreases owner's equity—via depreciation expense. Allocating the cost of a tangible asset, other than a natural resource, to the accounting periods in which it is used in the operation of the business is called **depreciation.** Each year, for the 3 years the asset is used, Tom's Wear recognizes $1,200 depreciation expense on the income statement. That's $100 per month for the monthly financial statements. The cost of the computer is being divided among the periods in which the asset is being used.

There are several expressions used by accountants to communicate the idea of recognizing a cost on the income statement as an expense. In general, doing this is known as **writing off** the cost. It's not unlike the sense of the expression "writing someone off"—it means getting rid of or disregarding someone. In accounting, we get rid of a cost by reporting it on the income statement as an expense. All that actually means is that the cost has been used up. A used-up cost is an expense. (*Not* getting rid of it means keeping it on the balance sheet as an asset.) Taking a portion of the cost of an asset from the balance sheet to the income statement as an expense for the periods in which the asset is used—by making adjustments to the accounting records—is an example of writing off the cost of the asset.

Sometimes accountants use the term **expensing** to communicate the same idea—recognizing a cost on the income statement as an expense. Expensing most often refers to costs that are written off in one period. For example, when Tom's Wear puts the cost of the shirts he has sold on the income statement as the expense cost of goods sold, it is expensing the cost of those shirts.

When a long-term asset is purchased, the cost is put on the balance sheet as an asset—called *capitalizing* the cost. Expensing and capitalizing a cost are opposites. When a company uses a long-term asset, the capitalized cost is written off over time. The most general expression for writing off the cost of a long-term asset is **amortization. Depreciation** is the specific word that describes the amortization of certain kinds of property, plant, or equipment. **Depletion** is the specific word that describes the amortization of a natural resource. There is no specific word for writing off intangible assets, so accountants use the word *amortization* to describe the writing off of the cost of intangible assets.

The most general word for writing off a long-term asset is amortization. When we refer to writing off an intangible asset, the general term is used—we amortize a franchise.

When we refer to writing off a piece of equipment, the word *depreciation* is used—we *depreciate* a machine.

When specifically referring to a natural resource, the word *depletion* is used—we *deplete* an oil well. All the terms refer to allocating the cost of an asset to more than one accounting period.

For each of the f   kind of   rm assets, give the term for
writing off the a

1. equipment
2. franchise
3. oil well
4. building

Acquisition

Consider the pu   et. The **historical cost principle**—
part of GAAP d   quires a company to record an asset
at the amount p   t for property, plant, and equipment
includes all exp   ble and necessary to get an asset in
place and ready

1. purchase c
2. freight-in–   t delivered
3. insurance
4. installation

The acquis   include:

1. architects'
2. constructi
3. cost of rer   airing it

This is an   between the business process of the
acquisition of   g for that acquisition. The accounting
treatment of i   ures in the acquisition cost of an asset,
shown on the   tion of the need to consider all these
expenditures   ial purchase of an asset. This relationship is an exa   tween the acquisition process and the
underlying ac

When a   two possible accounting treatments.
Either the co   eferring recognition of the expense, or
the cost is ir   an expense. Remember, reporting the
purchase of   heet and deferring recognition of the
expense is c   and recognizing the expense of a purchase immed   e cost of the asset.

When yo   ation and freight in the *acquisition cost*
of an asset, y   osts. They become part of the depreciable amount   g the asset; the total acquisition cost is
expensed as   iation expense.

In the ca   d for use as the location of a building or
factory, the   ause land typically retains its usefulness
and is not   e, accountants have decided it should
remain on   This accounting treatment reflects the
underlying   e purchase of land. Only if land is purchased to u   g, is it written off over the time it is used
by the busi   be considered a natural resource, and it
would be c   st of land may include (1) price paid for
the land, (2   (3) attorneys' fees, (4) costs of preparing

L.O. 1 & 2

Understand the costs involved in the
acquisition of a long-term asset and
how they are reflected on the
financial statements.

Cost is the amount paid for an asset.
The underlying accounting principle
is called the **historical cost principle**.

BUSINESS PROCESS

the land for use, such as clearing or draining, and (5) costs (less residual value) of tearing down existing structures.

STUDY BREAK 5-2
SEE HOW YOU'RE DOING

BUSINESS PROCESS

L.O. 1 & 2

Understand the costs involved in the acquisition of long-term assets and how they are reflected on the financial statements.

The **relative fair market value method** is a way to assign the joint cost of several assets to each of the individual assets purchased together. It is based on the individual values of the assets in the market.

For each of the following expenditures, tell whether it should be capitalized or expensed:

1. payment for employee salaries
2. purchase of a new delivery truck
3. rent paid in advance
4. rent paid in arrears (after the use of the building)

Basket Purchase Allocation

Figuring out the acquisition cost of certain assets can be difficult. Buying a building with the land it occupies is an example of acquiring two assets for a single price. For our accounting records, we need to calculate a separate cost for each asset. Why? The company will need to depreciate the building but will not depreciate the land. This is another example of an accounting problem that reflects the importance of the underlying factors that should be considered in the related business process. When land and a building are purchased together, the company should consider the individual value of each asset and how their joint purchase should affect those values. The accounting treatment requires that information.

For accounting, the purchase price must be divided between the building and land. The most common method for doing this is called the **relative fair market value method.** Suppose a company purchased a building and its land, together for one price, $100,000. The buyer would obtain a market price, usually in the form of an appraisal, for each item separately. Then those appraisals would be used to form a ratio to divide the purchase price of $100,000 between the two assets. Suppose the building appraised at $90,000 and the land appraised at $30,000. The ratio you need is the appraisal of each asset as a fraction of the total appraisal amount. The total is $120,000 (= $90,000 + $30,000). The rest is simple ratio math:

For the Building: $90,000 is to $120,000 as x is to $100,000
$$x = (\$90/\$120) \times \$100,000 = \$75,000$$

Thus, building is recorded at a cost of $75,000. By subtraction, that leaves $25,000 as the cost of the land. If you want to calculate it,

$$\text{Cost of Land} = (\$30/\$120) \times \$100,000 = \$25,000$$

This same method—using a simple ratio—can be used for any number of assets purchased together for a single price.

Recording Acquisition Costs

When your company buys a long-term asset, the company increases its asset account (e.g., Equipment, Machinery, or Furniture). This means you will debit that asset.

- If you pay cash ... ll be to Cash.
- If you sign a no ... will credit Notes payable (a liability).
- All costs incur ... running will be debited to the asset account.

Suppose you pur ... t with a $30,000 note and paid $250 in cash for deliv ... record the purchase of equipment would be:

Date	Debit	Credit
	$30,250	
		$30,000
		250

Nebo Compan ... ding and the land on which it is located. Indep ... he building at $400,000 and the land at $100,0 ... try to record the purchase of the building and l

STUDY BREAK 5-3
SEE HOW YOU'RE DOING

Deprecia

Depreciation, ... is "the systematic, rational allocation of the cost (m ... fixed asset to the periods benefited by the asset." Th ... guage for dividing the cost of an asset among the ac ... it provides benefits. Depreciation does *not* refer to a ... ion, and does not refer to a decrease in its market va ... ss of allocating the cost of an asset cost to the accou ...

If you he ... th $10,000 on our books," that does not mean the ass ... nt if it were to be sold. To say, "An asset is worth $10 ... s that $10,000 is the carrying value or book value ... —it is the undepreciated amount. It's called the *ca* ... the amount we add to our assets on the balance she ... *ook value*, because it is the value of the asset on our ... nonly referred to as our books.

To unde ... preciating assets is all about, you should become fan ... ms—the vocabulary of depreciation:

1. **Cost** o ... mount paid for the asset, including all amoun ... t up and running.
2. **Estima** ... g the company plans to use the asset; it may b ... nits that the asset will produce. For example, th ... ay be 5 years or it may be the production of 100 ... seful life of an asset to the company may be les ... ife of an asset. For example, a company may b ... use it for 3 years. The computer may still have ... er the company is done with it.
3. **Resid** ... e is the estimated value the asset will have when ... —it's the market value on the disposal date.
4. **Depr** ... residual value.
5. **Book** ... of the asset is *cost* less *total depreciation* taken ...

L.O. 2

Understand how the cost of a long-term asset is allocated to the periods in which the asset is used and how that process is reflected on the financial statements.

Terminology for Depreciation:
Cost is what we pay for an asset.

Estimated useful life is how long we plan to use the asset.

Residual value = Salvage value is an estimate of what the asset will be worth when we are done with it.

Depreciable base is cost minus estimated residual value.

Book value = carrying value, which is cost minus accumulated depreciation.

Depreciation and the Financial Statements

L.O. 2

Understand how the cost of a long-term asset is allocated to the periods in which the asset is used and how its use is reflected on the financial statements.

Three common methods of depreciation are used for preparing the financial statements and several others are used for tax returns. Remember, accounting for the financial statements and accounting for tax returns are two different tasks. The financial statements are prepared for shareholders and must follow GAAP; the income tax return is prepared for the IRS and must follow the tax code. Our concern here is how to report depreciation on the financial statements, although we will also talk briefly about depreciation for taxes.

Straight-Line Depreciation

Straight-line depreciation is the method of depreciation in which equal amounts of the cost of an asset are written off each year. Depreciation expense is the same each year.

Straight-line depreciation is the simplest way to allocate the cost of an asset to the periods in which the asset is used. Several steps are needed to calculate the appropriate amount of depreciation expense for each accounting period.

First, you must determine the useful life of the asset—an estimate of how long the asset will be useful to the company. This should be considered in the purchase of an asset, and the estimate is subsequently needed to properly account for the cost of that asset.

Second, you estimate the residual value—the amount you believe the asset will be worth when the company is finished using it. It's the amount you think someone will pay you for the used asset. The estimate of residual value is made by someone who knows a lot about the asset and the relationship between the use of the asset and its market value. This is part of the underlying business process that requires judgment; there is no right answer. Residual value is an estimate, and it's an estimate that may need to be revised more than once during the life of the asset. The useful life and the residual value are related, and these estimates are evaluated during the purchase decision.

BUSINESS PROCESS

Third, to calculate the amount of depreciation expense for each accounting period, usually 1 year, the residual value is deducted from the acquisition cost of the asset. This gives the depreciable base.

Fourth, the depreciable base—the difference between the asset's cost and its estimated residual value—is divided by the estimate of the number of years of the asset's useful life.

Let's look at a simple example.

Suppose Holiday Hotel purchases a new squeeze-your-own orange juice machine for its self-service breakfast bar. Such a machine is expensive and requires large supplies of fresh oranges. After considering the implications—risks and rewards—of purchasing the machine and evaluating the effect such a purchase would have on the financial statements, Holiday Hotel decides to purchase an $11,500 machine with an estimated useful life of 6 years. In addition to the invoice price of $11,500, delivery and installation costs amount to $1,000. Recall that these costs must be capitalized as part of the acquisition cost of the asset. Holiday estimates that the machine will have a residual value of $500 when the hotel is done with it. Do you see how both of these estimates are important inputs into the business decision to purchase the asset in the first place? After the judgments about useful life and residual value are made, Holiday will calculate the yearly depreciation expense. First, Holiday calculates the depreciable base by subtracting the residual value from the cost.

$$
\begin{aligned}
\text{Cost} = \$11,500 + \$1,000 &= \$\,12,500 \\
\text{Residual Value} &= \$\qquad 500 \\
\text{Depreciable Base} = \$12,500 - \$500 &= \$\,12,000
\end{aligned}
$$

Then Holiday ⋯ ⋯se by the number of years of useful life:

Annual de⋯ ⋯00 / 6 years = $2,000 per year

Each year th⋯ ⋯he income statement will be $2,000;
and each year tl⋯ ⋯set will be reduced by $2,000. This
reduction in car⋯ ⋯over the life of the asset, so that the
carrying value c⋯ ⋯quisition cost of the asset is always
preserved in a c⋯ ⋯t be presented on the balance sheet,
so Holiday will ⋯ ⋯depreciation as a separate amount
and subtract it f⋯ ⋯the asset on the balance sheet.

If Holiday ⋯ ⋯e beginning of the year 2001 and
the company's ⋯ ⋯er 31, then the income statement for
the year endin⋯ ⋯uld show depreciation expense of
$2,000. The ba⋯ ⋯e acquisition cost, $12,500, and the
accumulated d⋯ ⋯31, 2001—$2,000—as a reduction.
Here's what it ⋯ ⋯ce sheet at December 31, 2001:

	$12,500
⋯ciation	(2,000)
	$10,500

The follo⋯ ⋯e statement for the year would again
show $2,000 d⋯ ⋯raight-line method gets its name from
the fact that tł⋯ ⋯ted each year, so the book value of the
asset could b⋯ ⋯e. The balance sheet at December 31,
2002 would s⋯ ⋯e of the asset is declining because on
that date Holi⋯

	$12,500
⋯reciation	(4,000)
	$ 8,500

Exhibit 5⋯ ⋯depreciation expense and accumulated
depreciation⋯ ⋯financial statements during the entire
life of the as⋯

At the e⋯ ⋯sset, the carrying value should equal the
residual valı⋯ ⋯e exactly right—the useful life and the
residual valı⋯ ⋯vhat you had estimated when you began
depreciating⋯ ⋯the asset at the end of its useful life for
a price equa⋯

Year		Accumulated depreciation on year-end balance sheet	Carrying or book value on the year-end balance sheet
2001		$ 2,000	$10,500
2002		4,000	8,500
2003		6,000	6,500
2004		8,000	4,500
2005		10,000	2,500
2006		12,000	500

Exhibit 5–1
Straight-Line Depreciation

Recording Straight-Line Method Depreciation Expense

Holiday Hotel purchased the orange juice machine for $12,500. Its estimated useful life is 6 years, and expected residual value is $500. The journal entry to record one year's depreciation expense on the equipment would be:

Date	Transaction	Debit	Credit
	Depreciation expense	$2,000	
	Accumulated depreciation, equipment		$2,000

Each year, the depreciation expense account is closed to Retained earnings, but the accumulated depreciation account, a contra-asset account, is an account that will never be closed. Each year, the balance in the accumulated depreciation account will increase by the amount of the annual depreciation expense.

For example, after the machine has been used and depreciated for 2 years, here is what the general ledger accounts (we'll represent them with T-accounts) look like before closing the revenue and expense accounts for year 2:

	Depreciation expense			Accumulated depreciation, equipment	
Year 1	$2,000	$2,000	(closed to retained earnings)	$2,000	Year 1
Year 2	$2,000			$2,000	Year 2

Do you see that the depreciation expense account has a balance of $2,000 and that the accumulated depreciation account has a balance of $4,000? Each year, at the end of the year, the depreciation expense account will have only 1 year's depreciation expense, while the accumulated depreciation account will have all the expense recorded for the asset since it was purchased.

STUDY BREAK 5-4
SEE HOW YOU'RE DOING

On January 1, 2001, Access Company purchased a new computer system for $15,000. When purchased, the estimated useful life was 5 years, and the estimate of the residual value was $3,000. Using straight-line depreciation, prepare the journal entry to record the depreciation expense for the year ending December 31, 2003.

Activity (units of production) Depreciation

Another way to determine depreciation expense is by estimating the productivity of the asset. How many units will the asset produce or how much work will the asset do during its useful life? This is called the activity method—also known as the units of production method—of determining depreciation expense. Examples of activities are *miles driven* or *units produced*. If your company buys a car, you may decide to drive it for 100,000 miles before you trade it in. The activity method is similar to the straight-line method. The difference is that an estimate of the number of *units of activity* during the asset's useful life is used as the allocation base instead of an estimate of the *number of years* of useful life.

Consider the Holiday Hotel machine and how it was depreciated using the straight-line method, but now let's depreciate it using the activity method. To use this method, you need to estimate how many units the machine will be able to produce during its useful life. Suppose Holiday estimates the machine will be

able to produce ... ring its useful life. The depreciable
base is calculated ... hen using activity depreciation as it
is when using str ... s the cost minus the expected residual value. In this ... base is $12,000 (= $12,500 − $500).
You divide that d ... number of units you expect to produce with the m...

The activity ... an be applied to Holiday's orange
juice machine by ... ase, $12,000, by the estimated num-
ber of glasses of ... will produce. That gives the depreciation *rate*:

= $0.05 per glass

This is the ... which Holiday will depreciate the
machine for ea... . Let's say the machine has a counter
on it, and supp ... lasses of juice were squeezed during
the first year. 1 ... shown on the income statement, for
that year woul... multiplied by $0.05 per glass.

$0.05/glass = $1,800

That is the ... the year, and the book value of the
asset would de ... e year. It's important to keep a cumulative record ... hine produces, so that Holiday Hotel
doesn't depre... 0 estimated residual value. The residual value will ... vhen the asset has produced 240,000
glasses of juic...

Recording ... preciation Expense

No matter wh ... rnal entry to record the annual depreciation expen ...

- a debit to ...
- a credit to ... for the calculated amount of depreciation expen...

Each asset h ... reciation account, which keeps track of
how much th ... ted since it was put into operation. The
journal entry ... expense (activity method) for the year
would be:

Date		Debit	Credit
		$1,800	
	ion, equipment		$1,800

Hopper Co ... nent on January 1, 2005, for $44,000.
The expect ... or 100,000 units of activity, and its
estimated ... n 2005, the firm produced 3,000
units. In 2 ... ,000 units. Using activity depreciation, prep ... record the depreciation expense for
2005 and

STUDY BREAK 5-5
SEE HOW YOU'RE DOING

Understand how the cost of a long-term asset is allocated to the periods in which the asset is used and how the use is reflected on the financial statements.

Accelerated depreciation methods are ones in which larger amounts of the cost of an asset are written off early in the life of an asset and smaller amounts are written off later in the life of the asset.

Declining Balance Method

A third way to depreciate an asset is the declining balance method, which is an **accelerated depreciation** method. Accelerated methods allow more depreciation in the early years of an asset's life and less in the later years. How can this be justified? The matching principle supports the use of such a method. The higher depreciation charges will occur in the early, more productive years, when the equipment is generating more revenue. Depreciating more of the asset in the first few years also helps even out the total expenses related to an asset. In later years, the depreciation expense is lower but repair expenses are likely to be increasing.

To use the declining balance method, a company selects either 150% or 200% as the percentage of the straight-line rate to use as the annual depreciation rate. For example, if the useful life of an asset were 5 years, the straight-line rate would be 1/5, or 20%. That's because 20% of the asset would be depreciated each year for 5 years using straight-line depreciation. The rate used for declining balance would be either 30%, which is 150% of the straight-line rate, or 40%, which is 200%, or twice, the straight-line rate. The most commonly used declining balance rate is 200%, and the method is called the *double-declining balance method*.

Here's how it works, and why it is called double-declining balance.

Every year, the carrying value, or book value, of the asset is depreciated by an amount equal to *2 divided by the useful life in years*. An example will demonstrate that this is an easy way to calculate twice the straight-line rate. Suppose the useful life of an asset is 4 years. Then the double-declining rate would be 2/4 or 1/2. Alternatively, you could calculate the straight-line rate as:

$$100\%/4 \text{ years } = 25\% \text{ per year}$$

That is, using a straight-line rate, you would depreciate the asset 25% each year for 4 years. Then double that depreciation rate to get the double-declining balance depreciation rate, 50%. Thus, 50% = 1/2.

Using this depreciation method for the Holiday Hotel orange juice machine, the book value at the beginning of the first year is $12,500—its acquisition cost. Notice, any residual value is ignored at this time because book value equals cost minus accumulated depreciation. Recall, the useful life of the juice machine is 6 years. So the depreciation rate is 2/6 years = 1/3, and the depreciation expense for the first year is 1/3 × $12,500 = $4,167. The book value of the machine on the balance sheet at December 31, 2001 will be $8,333 (= $12,500 − $4,167).

For the second year, the amount of depreciation is again calculated as 1/3 × book value. Thus, for the second year, the depreciation expense is 1/3 × $8,333 = $2,778. The accumulated depreciation at the end of the second year is $4,167 + $2,778 = $6,945. The book value of the machine on the December 31, 2002 balance sheet would be $12,500 − $6,945 = $5,555.

The declining balance depreciation method is quite different from the straight-line and activity depreciation methods. Although residual value is ignored in the calculation of each year's expense, you must always keep the residual value in mind so that the book value of the asset is never less than its residual value.

Recording Declining Balance Method Depreciation Expense

No matter which method of depreciation is used, the journal entry looks the same: a debit to depreciation expense and a credit to the accumulated depreciation account that goes with the asset. Using double-declining balance depreciation for the orange juice machine, the depreciation expense for the first year is $4,167. The journal entry to record the depreciation expense (double-declining balance method) for the year would be:

Date		Debit	Credit
Depr		$4,167	
	equipment		$4,167

Specific De

Let's look at the [...] epreciating an asset more carefully.
Remember, you [...] es of useful life, and residual value
before you do a [...] ates are part of the business process
of acquiring the [...]

1. Straight lir

Dep [...] tion cost – residual value
[...] ated useful life in years

Suppose a [...] ews, costs $50,000. Its estimated use-
ful life is 4 [...] sidual value is $2,000. Using straight-
line depre [...] a single year's depreciation as:

$$\frac{[...]00}{[...]rs} = \$12,000 \text{ per year}$$

Each yea [...] ion expense on the income statement
will be $1 [...] ng value of the asset will decrease by
$12,000. [...] hibit 5-2.

2. Activity (

[...] al value
[...] useful life $\times$ actual activity

For the [...] is $50,000; useful life is 4 years; and
residual [...] he machine will produce 100,000 units
during i [...]
Sup [...] ed 30,000 units during the first year;
25,000 u [...] 0 units, the third year; and 20,000 units,
during [...] iation schedule is shown in Exhibit 5-3.
See if y [...] number in the table was calculated.

3. Double

[...] = existing book value
[...] seful life in years)

Year of the asset's life		Accumulated depreciation (balance sheet at the end of the year)	Book value of the asset (balance sheet at the end of the year)
1		$12,000	$38,000
2		24,000	26,000
3		36,000	14,000
4		48,000	2,000

Exhibit 5–2
Straight-Line Depreciation

Exhibit 5–3
Activity Depreciation

Year of the asset's life	Depreciation rate × screws produced: rate: ($\frac{\$50,000 - 2,000}{100,000} =$ $0.48 per screw)	Depreciation expense (income statement)	Accumulated depreciation (balance sheet at the end of the year)	Book value of the asset (balance sheet at the end of the year)
1	$0.48 × 30,000	$14,400	$14,400	$35,600
2	0.48 × 25,000	12,000	26,400	23,600
3	0.48 × 25,000	12,000	38,400	11,600
4	0.48 × 20,000	9,600	48,000	2,000

The declining balance method has the following features:

a. Residual value is not subtracted from cost.
b. Book value must be recalculated annually.
c. An asset may not be depreciated below its residual value (true for all methods).

Using the same asset, let's depreciate it using the double-declining balance method.

Using the formula for double-declining balance, you start by multiplying the book value—which is the acquisition cost on the first depreciation date—by 2/4. That means the asset will be depreciated using a rate of 1/2, or 50%.

Each year, depreciate the asset at the rate of 50% of its book value. (Remember, each year the book value changes.) In the last year of the life of the asset, the depreciation expense will be a "plug" figure. That is, plug in for the year's depreciation expense whatever number is necessary for the accumulated depreciation to equal the total amount of depreciation you estimated you would recognize over the life of the asset. In this case (Exhibit 5-4), the last year's depreciation needs to be $4,250 to leave the residual value you estimated—$2,000—at the end of the fourth year. Sometimes depreciation expense for the last year is more than the amount calculated by multiplying the book value by the double-declining rate; sometimes it is less. When the asset has a large residual value, the depreciation expense in the last year is less than the amount calculated using the double-declining depreciation rate and the carrying value. When the asset has no residual value, the depreciation expense in the last year will be more than the calculated amount.

Exhibit 5–4
Double-Declining Balance Depreciation

Year of the asset's life	Depreciation rate = 50%	Book value before depreciating the asset for the year	Depreciation expense for the year	Accumulated depreciation (at the end of the year)
1	0.5	$50,000	$25,000	$25,000
2	0.5	25,000	12,500	37,500
3	0.5	12,500	6,250	43,750
4	0.5	6,250	4,250[a]	48,000

[a]The calculation of (0.5 × $6,250) indicates depreciation expense of $3,125. Because this is the last year of its useful life and the book value after this year's depreciation should be $2,000, the depreciation expense must be $4,250.

An asset costs [obscured] value of $5,000, and has a useful life of 5 years. [obscured] to record the depreciation expense for the [obscured] ouble-declining balance method.

Capital Ex[obscured] Revenue Expenditures

LO. 3

Be able to distinguish between a capital and a revenue expenditure.

A **capital expenditure** is one that will be recorded as an asset, not an expense at the time of purchase. This is capitalizing a cost.

A **revenue expenditure** is one that will be recorded as an expense in the accounting period in which it is incurred. It's an expense.

Any expenditu[obscured] the current accounting period but also several m[obscured] ods is called a **capital expenditure**. A capital expe[obscured] asset when it is purchased and it is depreciated ov[obscured] which it is used.

Any exper[obscured]ly the current accounting period is called a **reven**[obscured]ds like we're saying "an expenditure called a revenu[obscured] an expenditure in the current period may be called [obscured]ning it's an expenditure related to the current period[obscured] is deducted from revenue in the current period—[obscured]ized as an expense—in the current period. We dis[obscured] he chapter when we talked about capitalizing a cost[obscured]

To review, [obscured]lizing or expensing a cost is applied to long-term ass[obscured] contrast between the two ways a cost can be handle[obscured]s:

- We refer to [obscured]ce sheet as an asset as a capital expenditure—ca[obscured]
- We refer t[obscured]ome statement as a revenue expenditure—exp[obscured]

Many cor[obscured] ften based on dollar amounts, that categorize purc[obscured]enditures or revenue expenditures. (What accou[obscured]? Materiality.) The main rules concerning capital ar[obscured]

1. Remode[obscured] system to increase the efficiency of the electrica[obscured]mprovements, such as a more energy-efficient[obscured] are capital expenditures. Because they will offe[obscured] of years, they are classified as assets. Capital [obscured] the useful life of the asset or increase the effic[obscured] asset. They are sometimes referred to as *bette*[obscured]

2. Ordina[obscured]g, tune-ups for vehicles, cleaning and lubrica[obscured], are expenditures that are necessary to mainta[obscured]ng condition. Because these repairs are routine[obscured]useful life of the asset or its efficiency, they a[obscured]itures and are recognized as current expens[obscured]

Suppose T[obscured]ded monthly maintenance and cleaning. The cost of [obscured] a revenue expenditure—recognized as an expense in [obscured]ne. Let's say Tom's Wear had a new piece of hardwar[obscured] expand its capability or its useful life. This cost would [obscured]penditure and capitalized—recorded as part of the [obscured] depreciated along with the asset over its remaining [obscured]

Exhibit 5-5 Comparison of Straight-Line Depreciation and Double-Declining Balance Depreciation

For an asset with a cost of $25,000, estimated residual value of $2,000, and an estimated useful life of 5 years.

Depreciation method	Cost	Residual value	Useful Life		Year 1	Year 2	Year 3	Year 4	Year 5
Double Declining Balance	$25,000	$2,000	5	Depreciation Expense	$10,000	$6,000	$3,600	$2,160	$1,240
				End-of-the-year Book Value	$15,000	$9,000	$5,400	$3,240	$2,000
Straight Line	$25,000	$2,000	5	Depreciation Expense	$4,600	$4,600	$4,600	$4,600	$4,600
				End-of-the-year Book Value	$20,400	$15,800	$11,200	$6,600	$2,000

Annual Depreciation Expense

Book Value of the Asset

Double-declining balance depreciation method will show more depreciation expense in the early years of an asset's life and less in the later years.
Straight-line depreciation will show an equal amount of depreciation expense every year.

Double-declining balance depreciation method shows a rapid decrease in the book value of the asset in the early years of an asset's life and a smaller decrease in the later years.
Straight-line depreciation shows a constant decline in the book value of the asset every year—as represented by a straight-line on the graph.

Notice that the graph for **Annual Depreciation Expense** shows the depreciation expense for 5 years, while the graph of the **Book Value of the Asset** shows 6 amounts. Remember that depreciation expense is shown on the *income statement*, which covers a period of time; and the book value of the asset is shown on the *balance sheet*, which shows amounts at a specific point in time. When the asset is purchased at the end of year 0 (= beginning of year 1), there is no depreciation expense.

Recording Capital Expenditures

When a company remodels or repairs a long-term asset, the costs to do so are capitalized. There are two different ways to record the remodel or repair costs as an asset so that the related expense(s) can be allocated to more than one accounting period.

If the asset gains efficiency or effectiveness but the estimated useful life has not changed, the asset account is increased. This means you would record a debit to the asset account (and a corresponding credit to cash or a payable account). This debit to the asset account increases the book value of the improved asset, so the depreciation expense for the subsequent period requires a new calculation. If the improvement has increased the asset's quality—that is, the asset does something better or more efficiently than it did before the

improvement— ... to account for the improvement
requires a debit ... se that the cost of upgrading equipment amounts t ... ulted in faster output by the equipment. The journ ... tal expenditure to improve the efficiency of the eq ...

Date		Debit	Credit
		$600	
			$600

If the asset ... a useful life of 8 years with no residual value, and ... ng straight-line depreciation for 5
years, the accu ... unt would have a balance of $10,000
($2,000 per yea ... ord the $600 expenditure to upgrade
the equipment, ... 6,600 ($16,600 − $10,000). Now, from
this point in ti ... e to depreciate the remaining $6,600
over the rema ... . So our new depreciation expense
would be $2,20 ... rs.

If the usefu ... d, the cost of the upgrade will reduce
the accumulat ... uppose the $600 expenditure did not
increase the ef ... tead, extended the life from 8 years to
10 years. In o ... e bought 2 additional years of useful
life. Because v ... of 8 years and have depreciated the
asset for 5 ye ... t will be increased by the 2 years we
just "bought" ... e journal entry to record the capital
expenditure o ... ife of the equipment would be:

Date			Debit	Credit
		equipment	$600	
				$600

The book val ... $9,400). That's the same book value as
we calculated ... ample. However, we will calculate our
new depreci ... ining useful life of 5 years. This is the
important p ... increases the efficiency of an asset or
extends the ... capitalized, resulting in a larger book
value to depi ... useful life of the asset.

Revising ... l Life and Residual Value

Sometimes t ... e—the useful life and the residual value of
an asset—n ... ple, experience with an asset may provide
additional in ... re accurate the estimates of its useful life
or residual v ... elated to fixed assets is an ongoing part of
the business ... those assets. In accounting for long-term
assets, revis ... d as an error—you don't go back and correct any pre ... atements. Those amounts were correct at
the time th ... ering that the best estimates at that time
were used ... depreciated balance less the revised estimated resid ... new estimated (remaining) useful life. This
approach is ... preciated balance like the cost at the time
of the new ... estimates of useful life and residual value
to calculate ... r the remaining years of the asset's life.

L.O. 3

Understand how changes in estimates of useful life and residual value are treated and reflected on the financial statements.

Let's return to the machine that cost $50,000, and see what happens when we change the estimates. Its estimated useful life was 4 years, and the estimated residual value was $2,000. Using straight-line depreciation, a single year's depreciation was:

$$\frac{\$50,000 - \$2,000}{4 \text{ years}} = \frac{\$48,000}{4 \text{ years}} = \$12,000 \text{ per year}$$

Suppose that we have depreciated the machine for 2 years. That would make the book value $26,000 (= $50,000 cost − $12,000 depreciation, year one − $12,000 depreciation, year two). As we begin the third year of the asset's life, we realize that we will be able to use it for three *more* years—instead of two more years as we originally estimated—but we now believe the residual value at the end of that time will be $1,000—not $2,000 as originally estimated.

The depreciation expense for the first 2 years will not be changed. The motto is: the past is past. For the next 3 years, however, the depreciation expense will be different than it was for the first 2 years. The undepreciated balance of $26,000 (acquisition cost was $50,000 less $24,000 of accumulated depreciation) is treated as if it were now the cost of the asset. The estimated residual value is $1,000, and the estimated remaining useful life is 3 years. The calculation follows:

$$\frac{\$26,000 - \$1,000}{3 \text{ years}} = \frac{25,000}{3 \text{ years}} = \$8,333 \text{ per year}$$

The asset will now be depreciated for 3 years at $8,333 per year. At the end of that time, the book value of the asset will be $1,000 (= $26,000 − ($8,333 per year × 3 years)).

STUDY BREAK 5-7
SEE HOW YOU'RE DOING

At the beginning of 2005, White Company hired a mechanic at a cost of $2,400 to perform a major overhaul on equipment. The equipment originally cost $10,000 at the beginning of 2001, and the book value of the equipment on the December 31, 2004, balance sheet was $6,000. At the time of the purchase, White Company estimated that the equipment would have a useful life of 10 years and no residual value. The overhaul at the beginning of 2005 extended the useful life of the equipment. White Company's new estimate is that the equipment will now last until the end of 2012—8 years beyond the date of the overhaul. White uses straight-line depreciation for all its assets. Prepare the journal entries to record the capital expenditure and depreciation expense for 2006.

Depletion and Amortization

Know how to account for natural resources and intangible assets.

Depletion

When a company acquires natural resources to use in its business, those resources are assets that are written off in a way that is very similar to the way costs are written off using depreciation. When we refer to the process of writing off a natural resource, we say we are depleting that resource.

Depletion is computed in a way similar to the activity depreciation calculations, but it applies only to writing off the cost of natural resources. Examples of

such natural res⋯ ⋯ for farming, oil wells, and mines. A
depletion cost p⋯ ⋯ling the cost of the natural resource
less any residual ⋯ ⋯s of activity or output available from
that natural reso⋯ ⋯r unit is then multiplied by the units
pumped, mined, ⋯ ⋯ine the total depletion related to the
activity during t⋯

Suppose a ⋯ ⋯ rights to an oil well in Texas for
$100,000 on Jar⋯ ⋯he well will produce 200,000 barrels
of oil during its ⋯ ⋯barrel is ($100,000/200,000 barrels) =
$0.50 per barrel ⋯ ⋯ced in the year 2005, then the deple-
tion related to t⋯ ⋯ in 2005 will be $25,000 (= $0.50 per
barrel × 50,00⋯ ⋯. The⋯ ⋯e of the oil rights will be $75,000
(= $100,000 − ⋯ ⋯1, 2005 balance sheet.

Amortizatio⋯

Writing off an ⋯ ⋯mortizing the asset. The only way of
writing off an ⋯ ⋯ght-line method—the cost is divided
equally among ⋯ ⋯e of the asset. An intangible asset is
recorded at co⋯ ⋯useful life. When the useful life of an
intangible asse⋯ ⋯for the length of its amortization may
be provided b⋯ ⋯sset has a specific life (e.g., often the
legal life of a ⋯ ⋯ asset is amortized over that period of
time unless th⋯ ⋯or a shorter period of time. According
to GAAP, inta⋯ ⋯rtized over more than 40 years.

In genera⋯ ⋯nt (R&D) costs are expensed and are
not capitalize⋯ ⋯sset. This is because it is not clear that
these costs re⋯ ⋯. Software development costs are considered resea⋯ ⋯a product that is technologically feasible; so these ⋯ ⋯d as they are incurred. However, once
the software ⋯ ⋯ally feasible, the subsequent costs are
capitalized as ⋯ ⋯ftware. Deciding when a piece of software is techn⋯ ⋯er example of the judgment required in
making acco⋯

Selling ⋯

L.O. 5

We've boug⋯ ⋯–depreciating, depleting, or amortizing
them over ⋯ ⋯et's deal with getting rid of an asset.
Disposing ⋯ ⋯trade it in, or simply toss it out with the
trash. Whe⋯ ⋯an asset? Sometimes an asset is sold
because it i⋯ ⋯mpany. Other times an asset is replaced
with a new⋯ ⋯e is remaining productive capacity in the
current ass⋯ ⋯is must be made before an asset is sold.
These deci⋯ ⋯nts that are part of long-term budgeting
(called *cap*⋯ ⋯nined in detail in managerial accounting.
For now, le⋯ ⋯how⋯ ⋯alculate whether we would have a gain or
loss if the ⋯

The ga⋯ ⋯f an asset is calculated by comparing the
cash recei⋯ ⋯own as **proceeds**—and the asset's book
value at th⋯ ⋯hree situations will exist:

■ Cash p⋯ ⋯e book value of the asset. If cash proceeds
  are gre⋯ ⋯ere is a **gain**.

Calculate the gain or loss on the
disposal of an asset and understand
how that is reflected on the financial
statements.

Proceeds refer to the cash collected
from the sale of an asset.

Gain refers to a certain kind of
addition to income that is earned
outside the normal course of
business.

Loss refers to a certain kind of reduction to income that is incurred outside the normal course of business.

- Cash proceeds are less than the book value of the asset. If cash proceeds are less than the book value, there is a **loss.**
- Cash proceeds are equal to the book value of the asset. If cash proceeds equal book value, there is no gain or loss.

Suppose you decide to sell an asset that was purchased 7 years ago. At the time of the purchase, you estimated it would last 10 years. It cost $25,000, and you used straight-line depreciation with an estimated residual value of zero. So the depreciation expense each year was $2,500.

After 7 years, you sell the asset for $8,000. Is there a gain or loss on the sale? To determine which, first calculate the book value at the date you sold the asset. Total accumulated depreciation is $2,500/year $\times$ 7 years = $17,500.

$$\text{Book Value} = \$25,000 - \$17,500 = \$7,500 \text{ at the date of sale}$$

Then subtract the book value from the cash proceeds.

$$\$8,000 - \$7,500 = \$500$$

Because the proceeds are larger than the book value, there is a gain on the sale. A gain is a special kind of revenue, shown on the income statement. It is special because it is not a normal part of business operations. You are not in business to buy and sell the equipment you use in your business. Thus, the income from such a transaction is given the special name *gain*.

The transaction affects the accounting equation as follows:

Assets	=	Liabilities	+	Owners' equity
(25,000) Asset				+500 Gain on sale
+17,500 Accumulated depreciation				
+8,000 Cash				

To record the journal entries related to the sale, you need to remove the equipment and its accumulated depreciation from your accounting records. First, you must calculate the amount of accumulated depreciation you have recorded for the equipment. In this case, the depreciation expense has been $2,500 per year, and you have depreciated the asset for 7 years. That means the balance in the accumulated depreciation account for this asset is $17,500. To remove the equipment from your records,

1. remove the equipment with a credit to the equipment account;
2. remove the accumulated depreciation with a debit to the accumulated depreciation—equipment account;
3. record the cash received for the sale; and
4. record the gain or loss to balance the journal entry.

The journal entry to record the sale of equipment for a gain of $500 and to accomplish these four things is:

Date	Transaction	Debit	Credit
	Cash	$ 8,000	
	Accumulated depreciation—equipment	$17,500	
	Equipment		$25,000
	Gain on sale of equipment		$ 500

Suppose instead ‍‍‌‌‌‍‌ ars for $5,000. Is there a gain or loss
on the sale? You ‍‍‌‌‌‍‌ lue is $7,500 at the date of the sale.
Subtract the boc ‍‍‌‌‌‍‌ eeds.

$$= (\$2,500)$$

Because the ‍‍‌‌‌‍‌ e book value, there is a loss on the
sale. A loss is a ‍‍‌‌‌‍‌ nown on the income statement. For
the same reaso ‍‍‌‌‌‍‌ ale of equipment, the reduction in
income from th ‍‍‌‌‌‍‌ pecial name, *loss*.

Suppose yo ‍‍‌‌‌‍‌ the book value, $7,500. There would
be no gain or l ‍‍‌‌‌‍‌ transaction in the accounting equation to see the e ‍‍‌‌‌‍‌ its book value.

Assets		ties	+	Owners' equity
(25,000) Asset				
+17,500 Accum				
depreciation				
+7,500 Cash				

The journal en ‍‍‌‌‌‍‌ quipment for its book value of $7,500
would then ha

Date			Debit	Credit
	Ca		$ 7,500	
	Ac	equipment	$17,500	
				$25,000

There is r ‍‍‌‌‌‍‌ tion only involves assets. As you have
learned, whe ‍‍‌‌‌‍‌ ction is an increase and a decrease to
assets, it is ca

Perry Plants ‍‍‌‌‌‍‌ t that originally cost $24,000. The
company so ‍‍‌‌‌‍‌ 2003, for $8,000 cash. Accumulated
depreciation ‍‍‌‌‌‍‌ ted to $18,000. Prepare the journal
entry to rec

STUDY BREAK 5-8
SEE HOW YOU'RE DOING

Depreci

The accoun ‍‍‌‌‌‍‌ o depreciation needed to prepare the
financial sta ‍‍‌‌‌‍‌ ormation needed for federal income tax
determinati ‍‍‌‌‌‍‌ financial statements is prepared according to GAA ‍‍‌‌‌‍‌ pany's shareholders—the owners of the
company. T ‍‍‌‌‌‍‌ taxes is determined by the legal rules of
the Interna ‍‍‌‌‌‍‌ cases, GAAP and the Internal Revenue
Code requi ‍‍‌‌‌‍‌ on to be reported, so managers need an
informatio ‍‍‌‌‌‍‌ oth sets of data.

Most ‍‍‌‌‌‍‌ d called the modified accelerated cost
recovery s ‍‍‌‌‌‍‌ ting the depreciation deduction for their
tax returns ‍‍‌‌‌‍‌ hod that has been designed to provide an

L.O. 6

Distinguish between depreciation for
accounting records and
depreciation for tax purposes.

MACRS is a common depreciation
method used for taxes. It is very
accelerated.

incentive for managers to invest in new property, plant, and equipment, allowed only for tax purposes. If an asset can be written off quickly—large depreciation deductions over a small number of years—the tax benefit from the higher depreciation deduction leaves the business more cash to invest in new assets in the early years of an asset's life.

How does more depreciation expense result in fewer taxes? Suppose a company's income before depreciation and before taxes is $10,000. If depreciation expense for taxes is $2,000, then the company has taxable income of $8,000. Suppose the company's tax rate is 25%. Then the company must pay $2,000 (= $8,000 × 0.25) in taxes and will have net income after taxes of $6,000.

Suppose the company can depreciate the assets using a more accelerated depreciation method that results in $4,000 worth of depreciation expense. Income before depreciation and taxes is $10,000, so income before taxes will be $6,000 (= $10,000 − $4,000). With a tax rate of 25%, the company will have to pay $1,500 (= $6,000 × 0.25) in taxes, leaving a net income of $4,500.

When depreciation expense is larger, the amount of taxes a company must pay is smaller. A smaller tax bill means less cash has to be paid to the IRS, so the company's net cash flow for the year will be greater.

However, as we have seen from comparing straight-line depreciation and double-declining balance depreciation, *over the life of an asset,* the total depreciation expense is the same no matter what method is used. The difference between the methods is reflected in the way the total depreciation is allocated to the years the asset is used. The reason a company wants to use an accelerated method like MARCS for tax purposes is so that the largest deductions are taken as soon as possible. Saving tax dollars *this* year is preferred to saving them *next* year—because it is cash the company can use in the business to make money now.

Finding and Using Depreciation Information

BUSINESS PROCESS

The investment that a company has in long-term assets is useful information and must be disclosed in some detail in the financial statements and the accompanying notes, according to GAAP. Look at the information from Lands' End's balance sheet in Exhibit 5-6. The amounts shown for land and buildings, fixtures and equipment, and so on are the original cost of those assets. The accumulated depreciation is the total depreciation that has been taken on all these assets since their purchase. What other information about the operational

Exhibit 5-6
From the Balance Sheet of Lands' End

(in thousands)	At January 28, 2000	At January 29, 1999
Property, plant, and equipment, at cost		
Land and buildings	$102,776	$102,018
Fixtures and equipment	175,910	154,663
Leasehold improvements	4,453	5,475
Construction in progress	—	—
Total property, plant and equipment	283,139	262,156
Less-accumulated depreciation and amortization	117,317	101,570
Property, plant, and equipment, net	165,822	160,586
Intangibles, net	966	1,030

Depreciation exp[...]ght-line method over the estimated useful lives of the asse[...]uildings and land improvements and 5
to 10 years for lea[...]re, fixtures, equipment, and software.

Exhibit 5-7
From Notes to the Financial
Statements of Lands' End

assets would be[...]he assets have been written off may
be of interest to[...] In one of the notes to the financial
statements, you[...]ion methods used, as well as information about th[...]Read the information in the notes in
Lands' End 199[...]n in Exhibit 5-7.

Identify the disclosure requirements
related to long-term assets and use
them to analyze the performance of
a company's long-term assets.

Un[...]nding Business

LEASE OR [...]

Generally ac[...](GAAP) try to
make sure th[...]he *substance* of
a company'[...]*m* of the transaction. Beca[...]ements are so
important to[...]e who wants to
evaluate a c[...]a transaction is
reflected on[...]rtant to the
company. S[...]ion based on its
substance r[...]classic example
is buying or[...]ny *buys* an
asset, it is sh[...]d any amount
that the cor[...]f the asset must
be shown a[...]ity.

Suppose[...]ut any addi-
tional liabil[...]would a
company l[...]g it? Could the
company s[...]easing the asset
as the leas[...]orm of the transaction is a[...]re like a purchase, the[...]e, and GAAP says
the transa[...]purchase. In
other word[...]uture financial
commitm[...]s by calling the
transactio[...]ing the expense
when the[...]ans the company
must recc[...]eet and also
record th[...]of the future lease
payment[...]depreciated, just
like any c[...]l by the company.

The accounting standards have very specific rules
about how to account for long-term leases. The criteria for
deciding if a lease qualifies as a capital lease are very
technical, numerous, and highly debated and discussed
by standards-setting boards like the Financial Accounting
Standards Board (FASB) and the Securities and Exchange
Commission (SEC). An accountant comes in handy when
this issue comes up.

In the long-term assets section of a company's balance sheet, you will often see items called *capitalized
leases* or *leasehold improvements.* Capitalized leases
represent assets a company has, in substance, bought
but the *form* of the purchase is a lease. Leasehold
improvements are long-term assets in the form of additions and improvements to leased property. For example,
if a company remodels the interior of a leased office
building, the cost of the remodeling will be called *leasehold improvements.*

A company decides whether to lease an asset or to
purchase an asset based on business factors such as
(1) the type of asset and the risk of obsolescence, (2) the
interest rate of the lease payments compared with the
interest rate of a purchase, (3) the lease's renewal and
purchase options, (4) the acceptable alterations to leased
assets, and (5) the estimated useful life of the leased asset
to the business. However, the accounting treatment should
not influence the economic decision. It goes the other
way—the economic decision influences the accounting
treatment.

Applying Our Knowledge: Ratio Analysis

BUSINESS PROCESS

A company purchases assets to help generate future revenue. Remember the definition of an asset—something of value used by a business to generate revenue. A ratio that measures how well a company is using its assets to generate revenue is *return on assets* (ROA). Like much of the terminology in accounting, the name of this ratio is descriptive. A company's return is what the company is getting back. We want to measure that return as a percentage of assets. So return on assets is literally return—net income—divided by assets.

$$\text{Return on Assets} = \frac{\text{Net income}}{\text{Average Total Assets}}$$

This ratio measures a company's success in using its assets to earn income for the persons who are financing the business. Because interest is part of what has been earned to pay creditors, it is added often back to the numerator. Net income is the return to the owners and interest expense is the return to the creditors. Thus, the numerator is often calculated by adding interest expense back to net income. The denominator is always average total assets.

Using a ratio like ROA gives financial statement users a way to standardize net income across companies. For example, in 2000, Ethan Allen Interiors Inc. had a net income of $90,570,000. La-Z-Boy Inc. had a net income of $87,614,000. It is useful to compare the dollar amounts, and we can see that Ethan Allen had about $3 million more net income than La-Z-Boy. One piece of information that would be useful is how well each company is using its assets to make that net income. If we divide net income by average total assets, we'll get the return on assets for the year.

	Ethan Allen	La-Z-Boy
Net income for fiscal 2000	$ 90,570,000	$ 87,614,000
Beginning assets	480,622,000	629,792,000
Ending assets	543,571,000	1,218,297,000
Return on assets	17.69%	9.48%

It is clear in this comparison that Ethan Allen is earning a better return with its total assets than La-Z-Boy is earning with its assets.

Sometimes a return on assets ratio is computed for a single asset. That's often hard to do because the return or net income for that asset has to be measured apart from all other net income. If a company can measure the incremental revenue, net of expenses, provided by a certain asset, that amount can be divided by the investment in that asset. Can you see how this type of calculation might help a company make a decision about purchasing an asset?

Remember, all ratios have this in common: they mean more when they are compared with the ratios from other years for the same company or with other companies. Industry standards are often available for common ratios to help investors and analysts evaluate a company's performance using ratio analysis.

Business Risks

Identify risks and controls associated with long-term assets.

The most significant risk related to long-term assets is that someone will steal one of those assets. It is not a problem with some large assets, such as a factory, but it is a very serious problem with smaller, mobile fixed assets, such as cars, computers, furniture and fixtures, and inventory. Safeguarding all assets, one

of the major fun... ...l system, is necessary in companies
of all sizes and t... ...ry to protect the company's assets
from theft, as we... ...ntional or unintentional.

Controls to ... ...simple as a lock or a security guard.
Physical contro... ...otect assets. Even when assets are
protected in a...
guards, fences, ...
must be sure th...
people have acc...

Complete a...
ing for the asse...
guarding asset...
control is sepa...
tioned in an...
means that the...
sible for the re...
the assets shou...
people who ha...
the assets. Thi...
cash, inventory...

Beyond th...
tion related t...
safeguarding i...
necessary part...
trol. The pote...
the destructio...
mous. The 20...
disaster brou...
problems res... ...ormation. Hundreds of thousands of
documents ar... ...troyed. For a business to survive the
loss of inform... ...ction like fire or flood, the information
should be bac... ...Many times this task is outsourced—
a firm hires a... ...n data backup and recovery.

Monitori... ...eguard assets. That means that someone needs to... ...rols—physical controls, separation of
duties, and a... ...ures related to protecting assets—are
operating pr...

> **From Yahoo News: Business—Reuters**
> Wednesday September 12, 2001 2:45 PM ET
> Key Data Lost in Attack but Seen Regained
> **NEW YORK (Reuters)**—Tuesday's terror attack on New York's financial district destroyed a wealth of important data and documents, but many companies expect to be up and running soon thanks to back-up files in other locations.
> Top financial companies such as Morgan Stanley, Deutsche Bank AG, and Cantor Fitzgerald are among those now scrambling to reassure investors and retrieve lost data affecting the flow of hundreds of millions of dollars. . .
> Makers of back-up and recovery software booked $2.7 billion in revenues last year, and that figure is expected to grow to $4.7 billion in 2005, according to research firm IDC.
> "My anticipation is that after yesterday's events that figure may increase," said Bill North, an analyst at IDC.
> *(Complete article is not reproduced here.)*

Summar... ...ear Expands in April 2001

Since beginn... ...Wear Inc. has now finished 3 months of
business. Re... ...ewing Tom's March 31 balance sheet in
Exhibit 5-8 ... ...e month of April. Tom's Wear has been
struggling a... ...he can make a big profit breakthrough
if he can ex... ...arch indicates a large demand for his T-
shirts, so he... ...April.

Required

Tom's Wear... ...e shown in Exhibit 5-9. Go through the
transaction... ...he accounting equation work sheet to
make sure y...

1. Make t... ...sing the accounting equation work sheet.
2. Prepar... ...atements for April.

Exhibit 5-8
Balance Sheet for Tom's Wear at the Beginning of April

Tom's Wear, Inc.
Balance Sheet
At April 1, 2001

Assets		Liabilities and Shareholders' equity	
Cash	$ 3,995	Interest payable	$ 30
Accounts receivable	2,000	Notes payable	3,000
Inventory	300	Total liabilities	3,030
Prepaid insurance	75		
		Common stock	5,000
Equipment (net of $100 accumulated depreciation)	3,900	Retained earnings	2,240
		Total liabilities and shareholders' equity	
Total assets	$10,270		$10,270

Transaction 1

Tom's Wear decided to buy a delivery van for the company. In April, he purchased a van for $25,000. He paid an additional $5,000 to have it equipped with the racks for his T-shirts. Tom's Wear financed the $30,000 at 10% per year for 5 years with a local bank. On March 31 of each year beginning in 2002, Tom's Wear will pay the bank the interest it owes for the year plus $6,000 of the $30,000 principal. Tom's Wear expects the van to be driven for approximately 200,000 miles and have a residual value of $1,000 at the end of its useful life. The company decides to depreciate the van using the activity method, based on miles.

Assets	=	Liabilities	+	CC	+	Retained earnings
+30,000 Van		+30,000 Notes payable				

Date	Transaction	Debit	Credit
4/1/2001	Equipment—van	$30,000	
	Long-term notes payable		$30,000
	To record the purchase of a delivery van		

Exhibit 5-9
Transactions for April 2001 for Tom's Wear, Inc.

1	April 1	Purchased a delivery van for $25,000 and paid $5,000 for changes to the van's interior to accommodate his T-shirts, and signed a 5-year, 10% note payable with the following terms: interest is due each March 31 and $6,000 of principal is repaid each March 31.
2	April 10	Hired an employee, Sam Cubby, for 20 hours per week, to fold, sort, and deliver the shirts. Sam will earn $1,000 per month, payable on the 5th of the following month. Sam won't begin work until May.
3	April 1–15	Collected accounts receivable of $2,000 from customers from March.
4	April 1–15	Purchased 1,000 T-shirts at $4 each, on account.
5	April 15	Rented a warehouse for $1,200 per month, beginning on April 15. Paid a total of $2,400 rent for 2 months.
6	April 15	Contracted with several sporting goods stores to stock Tom's Wear shirts and sold 800 shirts for $10 each, all on account, for total sales of $8,000.
7	April 1–30	Paid $300 for other operating expenses.

Transaction 2

Hiring an emplo[...] [...]ormal journal entry. The company
information sys[...] [...]ly record information about Sam
Cubby for the pa[...]

[...]Entry

Transaction 3

Tom's Wear[...] [...]month of sales on account, settling
the $2,000 acco[...] [...]1, 2001 balance sheet.

Assets		+	CC	+	Retained earnings
+$2,000 Cash					
$(2,000) Accou[...]					
receivable					

Date		Debit	Credit
4/1–4/15/200[...]		$2,000	
	[...]ivable		$2,000
To record the	[...]ivable		

Transaction 4

Tom has four[...] [...]stores to buy his shirts, so he must
dramatically i[...] [...]m's Wear purchases 1,000 T-shirts at
$4 each on ac[...]

Assets		+	CC	+	Retained earnings
+$4,000 Inver[...]	[...]nts				

Date		n	Debit	Credit
4/1–4/15/20[...]			$4,000	
	[...]ayable			$4,000
To record th[...]	[...]s at $4 on account			

Transaction[...]

Tom's Wear[...] [...]ch to store its inventory. On April 15, the
company pa[...] [...]ent.

Asse[...]		s	+	CC	+	Retained earnings
+$2,400 Pre[...]						
rent						
$(2,400) Ca[...]						

Date	Transaction	Debit	Credit
4/15/2001	Prepaid rent	$2,400	
	Cash		$2,400
To record prepayment of 2 months' rent at $1,200 per month			

Transaction 6

Tom has arranged the sales of his shirts to a number of sporting good stores in the area. Each month Tom's Wear will deliver 800 shirts for $10 each several different shops. The delivery will be made on the 15th of each month, and the customer will pay by the 10th of the subsequent month. The first deliveries are on April 15.

Assets	=	Liabilities	+	CC	+	Retained earnings
+$8,000 Accounts receivable						+$ 8,000 Sales
$(3,200) Inventory						$(3,200) Cost of goods sold

Date	Transaction	Debit	Credit
4/15/2001	Accounts receivable	$8,000	
	Sales		$8,000
To record the sale of 800 T-shirts, on account			
4/15/2001	Cost of goods sold	$3,200	
	Inventory		$3,200
To record the expense cost of goods sold and reduce the inventory by 800 × $4			

Transaction 7

Tom's Wear paid cash for $300 worth of operating expenses.

Assets	=	Liabilities	+	CC	+	Retained earnings
$(300) Cash						$(300) Operating expenses

Date	Transaction	Debit	Credit
4/1–4/30/2001	Other operating expenses	$300	
	Cash		$300
To record the payment of operating expenses			

Prepare the adjusting journal entries, post to T-accounts, and prepare an adjusted trial balance. Then, prepare the four financial statements. (Check your answer near the end of the chapter.)

U   standing Excel

In this chapter,   van for
$30,000. The pu   epare a
depreciation s   methods of
depreciation   urposes of
this exercise o   0-mile estimated useful   ation to be
taken in the y   o have no
salvage value

Requirements

1. Open a
2. Create th   dings begin-
   ning in c   E: **Year,**
   Beginnir   eciation
   Expense   , and **Ending**
   Book Va   Cells,
   Alignme   e the column
   width of   headings.)
   Click th   all the col-
   umn he

3. Prepare depreciation schedules for straight-line, units of production and double-declining balance methods of depreciation. Use formulas to calculate current depreciation expense, accumulated depreciation, and ending book value.

   Hint: Many of the formulas needed may be input once and copied. For example, beginning book value − current depreciation expense = ending book value. Input the formula one time for each schedule and then copy it to the other years either by using the fill handle or by clicking the Copy and Paste buttons.

4. For units of production, assume the following mileage breakdown: year 1: 5,000 miles; year 2: 15,000 miles; year 3: 12,000 miles; year 4: 10,000 miles, and year 5: 8,000 miles. For double-declining balance, assume that the full undepreciated book value at the end of year 4 will be taken as depreciation expense in year 5.

5. Print your file and save it to disk. Name your file TomsWear5.

Answers   estions

1. Equipmen
2. Franchise
3. Oil well—
4. Building—

1. Payment   sed
2. Purchase   talized
3. Rent paid
4. Rent paid

Study Break 5-1

Study Break 5-2

The total app   land together = $500,000. The percentage of each indiv   calculated. The building was appraised at $400,000. Tha   0,000/500,000 = 4/5). The land was appraised at $100,000. T   100,000/500,000 = 1/5).

After the   ey are applied to the cost of the assets, with 4/5 of $480,0   o the Building and 1/5 of $480,000 = $96,000 to be allocate

The buil   the land will not be depreciated. That is why the amounts

Study Break 5-3

Date		Debit	Credit
		$384,000	
		96,000	
	ole		$480,000
To record	ing		

Study Break 5-4

Using straight-line depreciation, the same amount is expensed every year. That amount is calculated as (Cost minus Estimated Salvage Value) divided by the total number of years of useful life: $(15,000 - 3,000)/5 = \$2,400$. *Thus, $2,400 is the annual depreciation expense.* Each year, that amount is depreciated—added to Accumulated Depreciation (a contra-asset) to reduce the value of the asset on the company's books. Depreciation of 3 years means that $7,200 (= 3 × $2,400) has been added to Accumulated Depreciation. The cost of the asset, $15,000, minus the total Accumulated Depreciation, $7,200, equals the book value at December 31, 2003, $7,800.

Date	Transaction	Debit	Credit
12/31/2003	Depreciation expense	$2,400	
	Accumulated depreciation		$2,400
To record straight-line depreciation expense for 2003			

Study Break 5-5

The depreciable base is cost minus salvage value; it is $44,000 - $4,000 = $40,000. The activity over its life is estimated to be 100,000 units. Thus, the rate is $40,000 divided by 100,000 units = $0.40 per unit. In 2005, depreciation expense is 3,000 units × $0.40 per unit = $1,200. In 2006, depreciation expense is 14,000 units × $0.40 per unit = $5,600.

Date	Transaction	Debit	Credit
12/31/2005	Depreciation expense	$1,200	
	Accumulated depreciation		$1,200
To record activity-based depreciation expense for 2005			
12/31/2006	Depreciation expense	$5,600	
	Accumulated depreciation		$5,600
To record activity-based depreciation expense for 2006			

Study Break 5-6

For double-declining balance, we start with 2 divided by the useful life of 5 years. We use that fraction, 2/5, and multiply it each year by the book value. For the first year, the depreciation expense is $50,000 × 2/5 = $20,000. For the second year, the depreciation expense is ($50,000 - 20,000) × 2/5 = $30,000 × 2/5 = $12,000.

Date	Transaction	Debit	Credit
	Depreciation expense	$12,000	
	Accumulated depreciation		$12,000
To record double-declining balance depreciation expense for year 2			

Study Break 5-7

Book value at overhaul date (2005)	$ 6,000
Add overhaul cost	+2,400
Total to be depreciated over	8,400
remaining useful life	
Divide by remaining useful life	$8,400/8 years
Depreciation per year	**$1,050**

Date	Transaction	Debit	Credit
1/2005	Accumulated depreciation—equipment	$2,400	
	Cash		$2,400
To record the cost of overhauling equipment			
12/31/2006	Depreciation expense	$1,050	
	Accumulated depreciation		$1,050
To record straight-line depreciation expense for 2006			

Date		Debit	Credit
1/1/2003		$ 8,000	
		18,000	
			$24,000
			2,000
To record the as			

Solution to [...]

1. These are th[...] should make before preparing the financial stateme[...] nade in any order.)

Adjustment 1
Tom's Wear nee[...]. On April 1, there was $75 worth of pre-
paid insurance [...]om's Wear purchased 3 months of insurance on Februa[...]hich is $50 per month.

Assets		CC	+	Retained earnings
$(50) Prepaid insurance				$(50) Insurance expense

Date		Debit	Credit
4/30/2001		$50	
	e		$50
To record ins			

Adjustment 2
Another item [...] Prepaid rent. Tom's Wear paid $2,400 for 2
months of ren[...]ril 30, half a months rent should be expensed.

Assets		+	CC	+	Retained earnings
$(600) Prepa					$(600) Rent expense

Date		Debit	Credit
4/30/2001		$600	
			$600
To record r			

Adjustment [...]
Depreciatio[...]eds to be recorded. Recall, it's being depreciated at $100[...]

Ass[...]		s	+	CC	+	Retained earnings
$(100) Acc depreci[...]						$(100) Depreciation expense

Date	Transaction	Debit	Credit
4/30/2001	Depreciation expense	$100	
	Accumulated depreciation—computer		$100
To record April depreciation expense on the computer			

Adjustment 4

Depreciation expense for the new van needs to be recorded. It cost $30,000 and an estimated residual value of $1,000. It is being depreciated using the activity method based on an estimated 200,000 miles. During April, the van was driven 5,000 miles. The rate is $0.145 per mile (= $29,000 depreciable base divided by 200,000 miles). The depreciation expense for the April is $0.145 per mile × 5,000 miles = $725.

Assets	=	Liabilities	+	CC	+	Retained earnings
$(725) Accumulated depreciation						$(725) Depreciation expense

Date	Transaction	Debit	Credit
4/30/2001	Depreciation expense	$725	
	Accumulated depreciation—van		$725
To record April depreciation expense on the van			

Adjustment 5

Interest expense on the note for the computer needs to be accrued. The 3-month, $3,000, note at 12% was signed on March 1. Interest for April will be $30 (= $3,000 × 0.12 × 1/12).

Assets	=	Liabilities	+	CC	+	Retained earnings
		$30 Interest payable				$(30) Interest expense

Date	Transaction	Debit	Credit
4/30/2001	Interest expense	$30	
	Interest payable		$30
To record the interest expense on the computer for April			

Adjustment 6

Interest expense on the note for the van needs to be accrued. The $30,000, note at 10% was signed on April 1. Interest for April will be $250 (= $30,000 × 0.10 = 1/12).

Assets	=	Liabilities	+	CC	+	Retained earnings
		$250 Interest payable				$(250) Interest expense

Date	Transaction	Debit	Credit
4/30/2001	Interest expense	$250	
	Interest payable		$250
To record the interest expense on the van for April			

2. First, the T-accounts are given, with both transactions and adjustments. Then, the adjusted trial balance is presented, followed by the financial statements.

T-Accounts for Tom's Wear with April Journal Entries and Adjustments

Cash

BB	$3,995	$2,400	5
$4,000			

Accounts receivable

BB	$2,000	$2,000	3
			200

Inventory

BB	$300		6b
4	4,000		

Prepaid insurance

6b BB	$75	$50	Adj-1

Prepaid rent

5	$2,400	$600	Adj-2
	1,800		

Interest payable

	$30	BB
	30	Adj-4
	250	Adj-6
	310	

Short-term notes payable

$3,000	BB
3,000	

Long-term notes payable

$30,000	1
30,000	

Common stock

$5,000	BB
5,000	

Retained earnings

$2,240	BB
2,240	

Sales

$8,000	6a
8,000	

Cost of goods sold

6b	$3,200
	3,200

Depreciation expense

Adj-3	$100
Adj-4	725
	825

Other operating expenses

7	$300
	300

Rent expense

Adj-2	$600
	600

Interest expense

Adj-5	$30
Adj-6	250
	280

Insurance expense

Adj-1	$50
	50

Tom's Wear, Inc.
Adjusted Trial Balance
April 30, 2001

	Debits	Credits
Cash	$ 3,295	
Accounts receivable	8,000	
Inventory	1,100	
Prepaid insurance	25	
Prepaid rent	1,800	
Equipment: computer	4,000	
Accumulated depreciation: computer		$ 200
Equipment: van	30,000	
Accumulated depreciation: van		725
Accounts payable		4,000
Interest payable		310
Short-term notes payable		3,000
Long-term notes payable		30,000
Common stock		5,000
Retained earnings		2,240
Sales		8,000
Cost of goods sold	3,200	
Depreciation expense	825	
Other operating expense	300	
Insurance expense	50	
Rent expense	600	
Interest expense	280	
Totals	*$53,475*	*$53,475*

The financial

Inc.
ment
April 30, 2001

Sales revenue		$8,000
Expenses		
Cost of goo	$3,200	
Insurance e:	50	
Rent expens	600	
Depreciatio	825	
Other opera	300	
Interest exp	280	(5,255)
Net income		$2,745

, Inc.
Shareholders' Equity
April 30, 2001

Beginning cont	$5,000	
Contributic	0	
Ending contrib		$5,000
Beginning reta	$2,240	
Net income	2,745	
Dividends	0	
Ending retaine		4,985
Total sharehol		$9,985

r, Inc.
Sheet
0, 2001

	Liabilities and Shareholders' equity	
Cash	Accounts payable	$ 4,000
Accounts rece	Interest payable	310
Inventory	Short-term notes payable	3,000
Prepaid insura	Total current liabilities	7,310
Prepaid rent	Notes payable	30,000
Total current ;	Total liabilities	37,310
Equipment (n	Common stock	5,000
accumulate	Retained earnings	4,985
depreciatio		
Van (net of $7		
accumulate		
depreciatio		
	Total liabilities and	
Total assets	shareholders' equity	$47,295

Tom's Wear, Inc.
Statement of Cash Flows
For the Month Ended April 30, 2001

Cash from operating activities		
Cash collected from customers	$2,000	
Cash paid for operating expenses	(2,700)	
Total cash from operations		*$(700)*
Cash from investing activities		0
Cash from financing activities		0
Net increase (decrease) in cash		$(700)

Note: Additional information: Van was purchased for $30,000. A note was signed for the full amount.

Questions

1. What is included in the cost of property, plant, and equipment?
2. What is the purpose of depreciation?
3. Does GAAP provide a choice of depreciation methods?
4. What is meant by *accelerated depreciation*?
5. What is *residual value* (or *salvage* value)?
6. Describe an *intangible* asset.
7. What is the difference between a *capital expenditure* and a *revenue expenditure*?
8. What is a *basket purchase*? What measurement problem does it create?
9. What does *amortization* mean?
10. What is the difference between *depreciation* and *depletion*?
11. What is the difference between *depreciation expense* and *accumulated depreciation*?
12. What is meant by the *carrying value* of an asset? How does it relate to the market value of the asset?
13. How is a gain or loss on the disposal of an asset calculated?
14. On which financial statement would we see a gain or a loss on the disposal of an asset?
15. What is the difference between depreciation for financial statements and depreciation for taxes? What is the common method used for taxes?
16. Define the ratio *return on assets*. Describe its usefulness.

Short Exercises

L.O. 5-1

SE5-1 Gruber Window Fashions bought a new wood cutting machine as a part of its venture into manufacturing interior shutters. The invoice price of the machine was $90,000. Gruber also had the following expenses associated with purchasing this machine.

Delivery charge	$2,850
Installation	2,500
Power to run the machine for the first year	450

What amount should Gruber record on the books for this equipment?

SE5-2 Settler Co... ...ited office space fast. The firm decided
that it could raise ... ...l build a new office building. The building was completed ... ...he following costs incurred for the new
building:

Building materia...	$110,000
Labor costs (inc...	205,000
Rental of equipr...	9,000
Maintenance or... 15 to December 31	14,000

L.O. 5-1

What amount sh... ...n the books for the new building?

SE5-3 Tylo Cor... ...rounding land, and a delivery truck in a
lump sum purch... ...l set the value of land at $80,000 with the
building, at $145... At what amount should Tylo record each
new asset on its...

L.O. 5-1

SE5-4 Villa Co... ...at a total cost of $960,000. The appraised
values of the in... ...ws:

$600,000
400,000
200,000

L.O. 5-1

What amounts ... ...t for each of the buildings in the Villa Corp.
records?

SE5-5 Calcu... ...depreciation expense for an asset that cost
$12,000, has a... ...an estimated salvage value of $2,000.

L.O. 5-2

SE5-6 If an... ...being depreciated at a rate of $1,000 per year
using the stra... ...life of 10 years, how much did the asset cost?

L.O. 5-2

SE5-7 A m... ...y 2, 2003, for $20,000 and it has an expected
life of 4 years... ...ue. If the machine is still in use 5 years later,
what amoun... ...be reported for the fifth year? (No revision of
the estimate... ...et's life.)

L.O. 5-2

SE5-8 Sup... ...d has an estimated salvage value of $2,000. At
the end of 3... ...e asset is $11,000. What is the useful life of the
asset? Assu...

L.O. 5-2

SE5-9 For... ...nether it should be classified as (1) a revenue
expenditure... ...diture (capitalized), or (3) neither.

L.O. 5-3

a. For rot...
b. Cash d... ...lders.
c. For re... ...s useful life, $6,000 was paid.
d. A pate... ...sed.
e. A mac... ...d and the firm signed a 2-year note for it.
f. For ar... ...0 was paid.
g. For rc... ...ne, $1,000 was paid.

SE5-10 ... ...ng as a capital expenditure or a revenue expenditure for... ...y.

L.O. 5-3

a. In ac... ...aintenance plan, Dalton & Sons paid for a newly
shing...
b. The ... ...building for the executive offices.
c. Dalt... ...tem to increase energy efficiency in the building.
d. The ... ...jor equipment as needed.

L.O. 5-3

SE5-11 On January 1, 2003, the Lance Corp. purchased a machine at a cost of $55,000. The machine was expected to have a useful life of 10 years and no residual value. The straight-line depreciation method was used. In 2005, the estimate of residual value was revised from 0 to $6,000. How much depreciation expense should Lance Corp. record for 2005?

L.O. 5-4

SE5-12 CNA Enterprises newly acquired an oil field that is expected to produce 1,000,000 barrels of oil. The oil field, acquired in January 2001, cost CNA $1.5 million. In 2001, a total of 280,000 barrels were produced. In 2002, production increased to 350,000 barrels. How much depletion should be recorded for each of these years?

L.O. 5-4

SE5-13 Coppery Mining acquired a copper mine at a total of $3,000,000. The mine is expected to produce 6,000,000 tons of copper over its 5-year useful life. During the first year of operations, 850,000 tons of copper were extracted. How much depletion should Coppery record for the first year?

L.O. 5-5

SE5-14 A machine is purchased on January 2, 2005 for $50,000. It has an expected useful life of 10 years and no residual value. After 11 years, it sold for $3,000 cash. Will there be a gain or loss on the sale? How much?

L.O. 5-5

SE5-15 The Crunch Company sold equipment for $35,000. The equipment originally cost $100,000, had an estimated useful life of 10 years, and had no estimated residual value. It was depreciated for 5 years using the straight-line method. In the year of the sale, should Crunch report a gain or a loss on its income statement and in what amount?

L.O. 5-6

SE5-16 A company often selects one method of depreciation for its financial statements and a different method for its tax return. Explain why and give an example of the types of methods that would likely be chosen.

L.O. 5-7

SE5-17 Financial ratios are often used to evaluate company performance. What ratio would give information about how efficiently a company is using its assets? Calculate that ratio for Pier 1 Imports and explain what information it provides.

L.O. 5-8

SE5-18 Write a paragraph describing a specific risk associated with long-term assets and some possible controls that might minimize the risk.

Exercises

L.O. 5-1, 2

E5-1 Coca-Cola purchased a building and land for a total cash price of $180,000. An independent appraiser provided the following market values: building—$150,000; land—$50,000.

a. How much of the purchase price should be allocated to each of the assets?
b. If the building has a useful life of 10 years and an estimated residual value of $35,000, how much depreciation expense should Coca-Cola record each year using the straight-line method?
c. By using the double-declining balance method, what would the book value of the building be at the end of 3 years?

L.O. 5-2

E5-2 Best-Goods Company purchased a delivery truck for $35,000 on January 1, 2002. It had an estimated useful life of 7 years or 210,000 miles. Best-Goods estimated the truck salvage value to be $5,000. The truck was driven 16,000 miles in 2002 and 32,000 miles in 2003.

a. Compute the depreciation expense for each of these years, first using the straight-line method and then the activity method.
b. In your opinion, which method portrays more accurately the actual use of this asset? Why?

E5-3 On January   rchased equipment for $42,000. Norris   L.O. 5-2
was also charged $ tion. The equipment is expected to have
a useful life of 10 y   ,200.

   a. Compute the   e years 2000 through 2002, using the
   straight-line r
   b. Compute the   e years 2000 through 2002, using the
   double-declin
   c. What is the   t on December 31, 2002 under each
   method?

E5-4 Yester Ma   a piece of equipment for 6 years. At the   L.O. 5-3
beginning of the   ng as well as it should have been. First,
Yester relubricate   150. Then, it tried replacing some worn-
out parts—this c   beginning of the seventh year, the company completed   nent that not only fixed the machine but
also added new f   the useful life by 3 years (to a total of 10
years) with no s   st $10,000. (Originally, the machine cost
$60,000, had a s   d an estimated useful life of 7 years.) The
straight-line met

   a. Which of th   res?
   b. Which are r
   c. What amou   statements of years 6 and 7?

E5-5 Zellwige $44,000. The van is expected to have a   L.O. 5-5
10-year useful li   ).

   a. If Zellwiger   30,000, would the company have a gain or
   loss? How   epreciation.)
   b. What woul   sold the van for $30,000 after 6 years?

E5-6 Troy Wi   d a packaging machine 4 years ago for   L.O. 5-5
$18,000. The m   e a salvage value of $2,000 after an 8-year
useful life. Assu   n is used, what would be the gain or loss if
after 4 years th   00; for $7,800?

Problems

P5-1A Pirate   rinting press in 2004. The invoice price was   L.O. 5-1, 2
$158,500, but   gave Pirate a 3% discount for paying cash
for the machi   mounted to $2,500, and Pirate paid $900 for
a special insu   while in transit. Installation cost $2,800; and
Pirate spent   to use the new press. Additionally, Pirate
hired a new s   of $75,000 to be responsible for keeping the
press online

Required:

   a. What am   this new asset?
   b. To calcul   r 2004, what other information do you need?
   Do you   be gathered before the asset is purchased?
   Why or

P5-2A On   o Manufacturing Company purchased equip-   L.O. 5-2
ment for $13   of the equipment is 4 years and the estimated
residual valu   expected to produce 480,000 units during its
service life.

Year	Units
2000	100,000
2001	130,000
2002	140,000
2003	105,000

Required: Calculate the depreciation expense for each year of the 4-year life of the equipment using

  a. the straight-line method
  b. the double-declining balance method
  c. the activity method

L.O. 5-2

P5-3A Balls and Bats, Inc. purchased equipment on January 1, 2005, at a cost of $100,000. The estimated useful life is 4 years with a salvage value of $10,000.

Required:

  a. Prepare two different depreciation schedules for the equipment—one using the double-declining balance method, and the other using the straight-line method. (Round to the nearest dollar.)
  b. Determine which method would result in the greatest net income for the year ending December 31, 2005.
  c. How would taxes affect management's choice between these two methods for the financial statements?

L.O. 5-2

P5-4A Peps Company purchased a new machine at the beginning of 2002 for $6,400. It is expected to last for 5 years and have a salvage value of $400. The estimated productive life of the machine is 100,000 units. Yearly production follows: in 2002—28,000 units; in 2003—22,000 units; in 2004—16,000 units; in 2005—14,000 units; and in 2006—20,000 units.

Required: Calculate the depreciation expense for each year using each of these depreciation methods:

  a. straight-line
  b. activity based on units
  c. double-declining balance

L.O. 5-3

P5-5A

Required: Calculate the gain or loss on the disposal of the following assets:

  a. A truck that cost $25,000 had an estimated useful life of 5 years with no salvage value and was depreciated using the straight-line method. After 4 years, the company sold it for $8,000.
  b. A machine that cost $50,000 had an estimated useful life of 12 years and a salvage value of $2,000, and was depreciated using the straight-line method. After 10 years, the machine was completely worn out and sold for $500 as scrap.
  c. An asset that cost $40,000 had a salvage value of $2,000 and an estimated useful life of 4 years, and was depreciated using the double-declining balance method. After 3 years, it was sold for $10,000.
  d. A machine that cost $15,000, with an estimated useful life of 6 years and no salvage value, was depreciated using the straight-line method. After 5 years, it was deemed to be worthless and hauled to the dump.

L.O. 5-1, 2, 3, 4

P5-6A During 2004, Umpire's Empire, Inc. had some trouble with its information processing due to an umpire strike, so several errors were made.

Required: For each situation, describe the effect any error would have on the Umpire 2004 financial statements if it were not corrected. Then give the adjustment that would need to be made to correct the company accounting records and make the 2004 financial statements accurate. If there is no error, write N/A next to the problem.

a. At the beginni d were purchased together for $100,000. Even though t 0% of the price should be allocated to the building, Ump tire purchase price to the building. The building is bei ith an estimated salvage value of $10,000.

b. During the ye a new gadget to keep track of balls and strikes. The R capitalized it. The firm intends to write it off over 5 yea

P5-7A   The Se new machine on January 2, 2000 for $48,000. The mac ful life of 5 years and a residual value of $3,000. The comp ber 31.

L.O. 5-2, 5

Required:

a. What is the scal years 2000 and 2001 using each of the following m

  1. straigh
  2. double

b. Assume tha use the straight-line method and that the sewing ma December 2001 for $27,000. What was the gain or los ancial statement would the gain or loss appear?

P5-8A   In Jan op Company purchased a computer system that cost $37,0 e system would last for 5 years and would have a salvage 002, and the company uses the straight-line method of dep is independent of the others.

L.O. 5-3

a. Before the rded for the year 2000, Harvey is told by his computer e used until the end of 2002 as planned but that it wil

Required: Ho se related to the computer system should Harvey's Ho its income statement for the year ended December 31

b. Suppose ense is recorded for the year 2000, Harvey's decides only last until the end of 2001. The company anticipa hat time will still be $2,000.

Required: H nse related to the computer system should Harvey's H n its income statement for the year ended December 3

c. Suppos pense is recorded for the year 2000, Harvey's decides ll last until the end of 2003, but that it will be worth

Required: dep ense related to the computer system should Harvey's F on its income statement for the year ended December

d. Befor is recorded for the year 2000, Harvey's exper e used until the end of 2004 if the firm spends $4,00 estimated salvage value at that time would be ze

Required: oney on the upgrades, how much depreciation expense r would Harvey's Hoola Hoop Company show on its incom December 31, 2000?

L.O. 5-2, 5

P5-9A The Cubbie Company purchased a truck 3 years ago for $50,000. It had an expected useful life of 5 years with no salvage value. Cubbie has taken 3 full years of depreciation expense.

Required:

a. Assume that Cubbie uses straight-line depreciation. If the truck is sold for $25,000, will there be a gain or loss on the sale? If so, how much? How will it affect the Cubbie financial statements for the year?

b. Assume that Cubbie uses double-declining balance depreciation. If the truck is sold for $15,000, will there be a gain or loss on the sale? If so, how much? How will it affect the Cubbie financial statements for the year?

c. Assume Cubbie uses straight-line depreciation and sells the truck for $20,000. Would there be a gain or loss on the sale? How would that change if Cubbie had been using double-declining balance depreciation? Compare the total effect on income of using and selling the truck during the past 3 years under the two different methods of depreciation.

L.O. 5-7

P5-10A Use the following information from the Home Depot annual report to answer the questions that follow:

(Numbers are in millions)	January 30, 2000	January 31, 1999
Property and equipment, at cost		
Land	$ 3,248	$2,739
Building	4,834	3,757
Furniture, fixtures, and equipment	2,279	1,761
Leasehold improvements	493	419
Construction in progress	791	540
Capital leases	245	206
	$11,890	$9,422
Less accumulated depreciation and amortization	1,663	1,262
Net property and equipment	$10,227	$8,160

Note on depreciation and amortization

The company's buildings, furniture, fixtures, and equipment are depreciated using the straight-line method over the estimated useful lives of the assets.
Improvements to leased premises are amortized using the straight-line method over the life of the lease or the useful life of the improvement, whichever is shorter.
The company's property and equipment is depreciated using the following estimated useful lives:

	Life
Buildings	10–45 Years
Furniture, fixtures, and equipment	5–20 Years
Leasehold improvements	5–30 Years
Computer software	3–5 Years

Required:

a. Can you tell how much Home Depot paid for the buildings it owns? If so, how do you know?

b. Can you tell how much the buildings are worth (i.e., the market value)?

c. What are Leasehold Improvements? (*Hint:* Read the note on depreciation and amortization and see if you can figure out what they are.)

d. What are Capital Leases? (*Hint:* Read "Understanding Business" in the chapter.)

Problems—

P5-1B Bikini Be [...] ome additional land for its resort. The resort decided to [...] erty, which was for sale. Unfortunately, the land came wit [...] cost of the land with the old motel was $1,500,000. Real e [...] ncluding the title search were $317,850. Bikini Bettie's Bea [...] ,000 to review the contract and complete the purchase of th [...] sort paid $25,750 for the old motel to be demolished and a [...] white sand to be hauled in to make the land beautiful for [...] $80,000 for some palm trees to make its new sun bathing [...] hired three new lifeguards at a salary of $35,000 a year ea [...] crowds.

Required:

a. What amoun [...] new asset?

b. Would there [...] for land at the end of 2008? Explain your answer.

P5-2B Basebal [...] itching machine at a cost of $18,000 at the beginning of Jan [...] stimated to have a salvage value of $2,000 at the end of its [...] ne like this is supposed to deliver 160,000 hours of pitchin [...] of hours that the machine was used per year was 2003– [...] hours; 2005—35,000 hours; and 2006—25,000 hours.

Required: Prepa [...] ng the

a. straight-lin

b. activity met

c. double-dec

For each, make [...] iation expense for each year, as well as the book value of th

P5-3B Carla's [...] hop purchased an automated display rack on January 1, 2 [...] stimated useful life is 5 years with a salvage value of $5,000

Required:

a. Prepare tw [...] edules for the equipment—one using the double-de [...] the other using the straight-line method. (Round to

b. Determine [...] the greatest net income for the year 2010.

c. How wou [...] choice between these two methods for the financial s

P5-4B Clean [...] new water filter machine at the beginning of 2010 for $ [...] t for 8 years and have a salvage value of $32,000. The e [...] machine is 200,000 units. Yearly production was in 2010– [...] 00 units; in 2012—42,000 units; in 2013—21,000 units; i [...] —14,000 units; in 2016—17,000 units; and in 2017—6,000 u

Required: Cal [...] e for each year using each of these deprecia-tion methods

a. straight l

b. activity b

c. double-d [...] he nearest dollar)

L.O. 5-3

P5-5B Calculate the gain or loss on the disposal of the following assets:

a. A company van cost $32,000, had an estimated useful life of 8 years with no residual value, and was being depreciated using the straight-line method. After 6 years, the company sold it for $10,000.

b. A copy machine that cost $35,000 had a residual value of $5,000 and an estimated useful life of 5 years, and was depreciated using the double-declining balance method. After 2 years, it was sold for $15,000.

c. A company truck that cost $48,000 had an estimated useful life of 7 years and a residual value of $6,000, and was depreciated using the straight-line method. After 5 years of many miles of driving on tough terrain, the truck was completely worn out and sold for $1,050 for spare parts.

d. A state-of-the-art computer that cost $29,000 had a salvage value of $2,000, an estimated useful life of 4 years, and was depreciated using the double-declining balance method. After 3 years, it was sold for $5,000.

L.O. 5-1, 2, 3, 4

P5-6B During 2004, Umpire's Empire, Inc. had some trouble with its information processing due to an umpire strike, so several errors were made.

Required: For each situation, describe the effect any error would have on the Umpire 2004 financial statements if it were not corrected. Then give the adjustment that would need to be made to correct the company accounting records and make the 2004 financial statements accurate. If there is no error, simply write N/A next to the problem.

a. The plumber spent a great deal of time repairing broken toilets in the Umpire building this year. Total cost, which Umpire capitalized, was $5,000. Umpire decided it was best to leave it on the books as an asset and not write it off, because the toilets will be used for quite a few more years.

b. Umpire purchased a new van. It cost $20,000 and is expected to last 3 years. It has a salvage value of $2,000. To properly equip it for all the Umpire gear, the inside was customized at a cost of $6,000. The cost of the van was capitalized, and the cost of the customization was expensed.

L.O. 5-2, 5

P5-7B The House of Root Beer bought new brewery equipment on January 1, 2008 for $56,000. The machine is expected to have a useful life of 7 years and a residual value of $7,000. The company fiscal year ends on December 31.

Required:

a. What is the depreciation expense for the fiscal years 2008 and 2009 using each of the following methods?

1. straight line
2. double-declining balance (round to nearest whole dollar)

b. Assume that House of Root Beer decided to use the double-declining method and that the brewery equipment was sold at the end of December 2009 for $42,000. What was the gain or loss on the sale? On which financial statement would the gain or loss appear?

L.O. 5-3

P5-8B In July 2001, Henry's Hat Company purchased a computer system that cost $7,000. The company estimated that the system would last for 5 years and would have a salvage value of $2,000 at the end of June 2006. The company uses the straight-line method of depreciation. Henry's Hat Company has a June 30 fiscal year-end. Each problem that follows is independent of the other.

Required:

a. Suppose that before depreciation expense is recorded for the year ending June 30, 2003, Henry's decides that the computer system will last until the end of July 2007, but that it will be worth only $500 at that time. How much depreciation expense related to the computer system should Henry's Hat Company show on its income statement for the year ended June 30, 2003?

b. Before the dep___ ___d for the fiscal year ending June 30, 2004, the comp___ ___nry that the system can be used until the end of Jur___ ___n upgrades. However, the estimated salvage value ___ ___f the company spends the money on the upgrades, ___ ___ense related to the computer system would Henry' ___ ___income statement for the year ended June 30, 2004?

P5-9B The Quee___ ___ed a van 3 years ago for $62,000. It had an expected usefu___ ___residual value. Queen Grande View has taken three full ye___

L.O. 5-2, 5

Required:

a. Assume that ___ ___ight-line depreciation. If the van is sold for $20,000, ___ ___ the sale? If so, how much? How will it affect the Qu___ ___tements for the year?

b. Assume tha___ ___double-declining balance depreciation. If the van ___ ___e be a gain or loss on the sale? If so, how much? ___ ___ Grande View financial statements for the year?

c. Assume Qu___ ___-declining depreciation and sells the truck for $23,000 ___ ___ss on the sale? How would that change if Queen Gra___ ___ight-line balance depreciation? Compare the total ef___ ___lling the van during the past 3 years under the two dif___ ___.

P5-10B Use ___ ___Sony Annual Report to answer the following questions.

L.O. 5-7

	Dollars in millions March 31, 2000
Property, p___ ___0 and 17)	
Land	$ 1,752
Buildin___	7,306
Machin___	18,444
Constr___	875
	$28,377
Less—	16,532
	11,845
Other Ass___	
Intang___	2,061
Good___	2,772

Property___ ___epreciation

Property, ___ ___ at cost. Depreciation of property, plant, and equipmer___ ___g-balance method for Sony Corp. and Japanese ___ ___ht-line method for foreign subsidiary companies at ra___ ___lives of the assets according to general class, type of c___ ___nt renewals and additions are capitalized at cost. Ma___ ___nor renewals and betterments are charged to income ___

Intangi___

Intangi___ ___rtist contracts, music catalogs, and trademarks, are bei___ ___ basis principally over 16 years, 21 years, and 20 year___

G___ ___ns accounted for as purchases is being amortized o___ ___lly over a 40-year period.

Required:

a. What is Sony's primary method for depreciating its assets?
b. How much did Sony pay for the machinery and equipment it owns?
c. Are any of the assets listed as Property, Plant, and Equipment not being depreciated?
d. Can you tell how much depreciation expense Sony had for the fiscal year ending March 31, 2000?
e. Explain what the $16,532 million of accumulated depreciation represents.
f. Can you find a sentence in the notes that summarizes the accounting treatment for major overhaul or additions to assets discussed in Chapter 5?
g. Why would intangible assets be amortized over 16 years, 21 years, and 20 years?

Recording Transactions

R5-1 (SE5-5) Give the journal entry to record the purchase of equipment that cost $12,000 and has a useful life of 5 years and an estimated salvage value of $2,000. After calculating the annual straight-line depreciation expense for the equipment, give the journal entry that would need to be recorded at the end of each of the next 5 years.

Date	Account	Debit	Credit

R5-2 (SE5-9) For each of the following, give the journal entry to record the transaction. No explanations are required.

a. Paid $2,000 for routine repairs.
b. Paid cash dividends of $500 to shareholders.
c. Paid $6,000 for repairs that will extend the asset's useful life.
d. Purchased a patent for $5,000 cash.
e. Purchased a machine for $10,000 and gave a 2-year note.
f. Paid $50,000 for an addition to a building that increases its usefulness.
g. Paid $1,000 for routine maintenance on a machine.

Transaction	Account	Debit	Credit

R5-3 (SE5-14) A machine is purchased on January 2, 2005, for $50,000. It has an expected useful life of 10 years and no residual value. After 11 years, it was sold for $3,000 cash. Give the journal entry needed to record the sale of the asset.

Date	Account	Debit	Credit

R5-4 (E5-2) Best-Goods Company purchased a delivery truck for $35,000 on January 1, 2002. It had an estimated useful life of 7 years or 210,000 miles. Best-Goods estimated the truck's salvage value to be $5,000. The truck was driven 16,000 miles in 2002 and 32,000 miles in 2003. Using journal entries, first record the purchase of the asset. Then give the

journal entries to r   e for both 2002 and 2003 using the (1)
straight-line metho   iethod of depreciation.

Date				Debit	Credit

R5-5   (E5-5) Zell   for $44,000. The van is expected to have
a 10-year useful li   ).

   a. Suppose Zell   rs for $30,000. Give the journal entry to
     record the sa   ised straight-line depreciation.)
   b. Suppose the   6 years. Give the journal entry to record
     the sale.

Date				Debit	Credit

R5-6   (P5-1A) F   new printing press in 2004. The invoice
price was $158,5   e press gave Pirate a 3% discount for pay-
ing cash on deli   costs amounted to $2,500, and Pirate paid
$900 for a spec   he press while in transit. Installation cost
$2,800, and Pira   ployees to use the new press. Additionally,
Pirate hired a n   lary of $75,000 to be responsible for keep-
ing the press o   Give the journal entry to record the purchase of the ass

Date				Debit	Credit

R5-7   (P5-5A)   ries for the disposal of the following assets:

   a. A truck th   imated useful life of 5 years with no salvage
     value was   traight-line method. After 4 years, the com-
     pany sold
   b. A machir   timated useful life of 12 years and a salvage
     value of   d using the straight-line method. After 10
     years, the   n out and sold for $500 as scrap.
   c. An asset   je value of $2,000 and an estimated useful life
     of 4 year   the double-declining balance method. After
     3 years, i
   d. A machi   stimated useful life of 6 years and no salvage
     value, w   e straight-line method. After 5 years, it was
     deemed   the dump.

Transact			nt	Debit	Credit

R5-8   (P5-6   oire, Inc. had some trouble with its information
processing   o several errors were made.

Required: For each situation, give the journal entry that would need to be made to correct the company's accounting records and to make the 2004 financial statements accurate. (Use two entries if you prefer.) If there is no error, write N/A next to the problem.

a. At the beginning of 2004, a building and land were purchased together for $100,000. Even though the appraisers determined that 90% of the price should be allocated to the building, Umpire's decided to allocate the entire purchase price to the building. The building is being depreciated over 40 years, with an estimated salvage value of $10,000.

b. During the year, Umpire's did some research and development on a new gadget to keep track of balls and strikes. The R&D cost $20,000, and Umpire's capitalized it. The company intends to write it off over 5 years.

Transaction	Account	Debit	Credit

R5-9 (P5-8A) In January 1998, Harvey's Hoola Hoop Company purchased a computer system that cost $37,000. Harvey's estimated that the system would last for 5 years and would have a salvage value of $2,000 at the end of 2002, and the company uses the straight-line method of depreciation. Each problem below is independent of the others.

Required: For each problem, give the journal entry to record the depreciation expense for the year ended December 31, 2000.

a. Before the depreciation expense is recorded for the year 2000, Harvey is told by his computer experts that the system can be used until the end of 2002 as planned but that it will be worth only $500.

b. Suppose that, before depreciation expense is recorded for the year 2000, Harvey's decides that the computer system will only last until the end of 2001. The company anticipates the value of the system at that time will still be $2,000.

c. Suppose that, before depreciation expense is recorded for the year 2000, Harvey's decides that the computer system will last until the end of 2003 but that it will be worth only $1,000 at that time.

d. Before the depreciation expense is recorded for the year 2000, Harvey spends $4,000 on upgrades that extend the useful life of the system until the end of 2004. However, the estimated salvage value at that time will be zero.

Transaction	Account	Debit	Credit

R5-10 (P5-9A) The Cubbie Company purchased a truck 3 years ago for $50,000. It had an expected useful life of 5 years with no salvage value. After 3 full years of use, the truck is sold.

Required: For each independent case below, give the journal entry needed to record the sale of the truck.

a. Assume that Cubbie Company uses straight-line depreciation. The truck is sold for $25,000.

b. Assume that Cubbie Company uses double-declining balance depreciation. The truck is sold for $15,000.

c. Assume that Cubbie Company uses straight-line depreciation and sells the truck for $20,000.

Transaction	Account	Debit	Credit

R5-Comprehensiv

Chapter 5: ̇ancial Statement Preparation Problem

This is the post- ̇ality Printing Company, prepared on
December 31, 200

	DR	CR
Cash	$290,000	
Acco	136,000	
Print	106,350	
Prep	6,000	
Prep ̇nt	18,000	
Acc		$ 13,500
Sala		3,500
Lon		200,000
Cor		200,000
Ret		139,350
	$556,350	$556,350

Transactions d

1. The comp ̇ press at the beginning of 2004. The invoice
   price was ̇er of the press gave Quality a 3% discount
   for payin ̇very. Delivery costs amounted to $2,500, and
   Quality P ̇insurance policy to cover the press while in
   transit. I ̇Quality Printing spent $5,000 training the
   employe ̇onally, Quality Printing hired a new supervisor at ar ̇be responsible for keeping the press on-line
   during b ̇vere made in cash.
2. Collecte ̇ receivable.
3. Purchas ̇ng supplies during the year. Paid cash of
   $100,00 ̇ed on account.
4. Paid an ̇2,000, due every June 30 for insurance coverage fro ̇osts were the same for the previous year.
5. Paid ac ̇nce of $13,500.
6. Paid er ̇ of $72,250. (This includes the amount owed at
   the be
7. Perfor ̇ers: $354,570. Collected $200,000 in cash, with
   the re
8. On De ̇duce principal of the long-term note and paid
   intere ̇riginal balance).

Other inf

a. Ther ̇50 left on hand at year-end.
b. All p ̇used up during the year, and the equipment was
   retur ̇year-end.
c. Sala ̇ployees at year-end (earned but not paid).
d. The ̇w printing press will last for 20 years and have a
   resi ̇of its useful life.

Require ̇company for the year ending December 31, 2004.
Then, p ̇d the transactions for the year. Prepare an unadjusted ̇, 2004, make adjusting entries, and prepare the
income ̇es in owner's equity, balance sheet, and statement
of cash

Issues for Discussion

L.O. 5-6, 7

Financial statement analysis

1. Use the annual report from Pier 1 Imports to answer these questions:
   a. What type of depreciable assets does Pier 1 have? What methods does the company use to depreciate these assets?
   b. What can you tell about the age or condition of the Pier 1's long-term assets? Is the company continuing to invest in property, plant, and equipment?
   c. Is the company making good use of its assets? How can you evaluate this?

Business risk

2. What kinds of risks does Pier 1 face with respect to safeguarding its assets? What types of controls do you think it has to minimize these risks? Are any specific controls mentioned in the annual report?

Ethics

3. Rachel works in a real estate office that is equipped with up-to-date copiers, scanners, and printers. She is frequently the only employee working in the office in the evenings and often has spare time to do personal work. She has begun to use the office equipment for her children's school reports and for her husband's business. Do you think Rachel's use of the office equipment is harmless or is she behaving unethically? Why? If you believe her behavior is unethical, what controls could be in place to prevent it? Have you ever used office resources for personal tasks? Under what conditions could such use be justified?

Internet Exercise: Best Buy

Best Buy Company, Inc. is the number one specialty retailer of consumer electronics, personal computers, entertainment software, and appliances. Ahead of rival Circuit City in sales but not store count, Best Buy has about 420 stores in 41 states, with heavy concentrations in the Midwest, Texas, California, and Florida. Its Musicland Stores subsidiary operates 1,300 music and video retail stores under the Sam Goody, Suncoast, On Cue, and Media Play names.

Please go to the www.prenhall.com/myphlip *Web site, register, and add this textbook to your myphlip page (if you haven't done so already). Go to Chapter 5 and use the Internet Exercise company link. In the left-hand column, click on* Investor Relations *and then on* Financials.

IE5-1   Select the most recent *annual report* in the HTML format. Use the *consolidated balance sheets* to answer the following questions. At the most recent year-end examine "Property and Equipment."

   a. What is the acquisition cost of these assets?
   b. What is the book value (carrying value)?
   c. What amount of the acquisition cost has already been expensed?
   d. Are any of the assets listed not being depreciated?

IE5-2   Use the *notes to financial statements* to answer the following questions (usually the information can be found in note 1):

   a. Find the heading "Property and Equipment." What depreciation method does Best Buy use for property and equipment? What is the range of useful lives for buildings and for fixtures and equipment? Do these useful lives make sense?

b. Find the headi[...] asset is goodwill? How does Best Buy expense this as[...]

c. Close the *Annu*[...]

IE5-3 Under "Ex[...]-*Year Summary.*

a. Identify the a[...]s at the four most recent year-ends. In which year d[...]d? How can you tell? Comment on the change in ass[...]Musicland acquisition and the previous year.

b. Identify the a[...]s and *net earnings* (net income) for the three most re[...]

c. Compute the [...] for the three most recent fiscal years. In which fiscal [...]st use of its assets? How can you tell?

Please note: Intern[...] updated. Therefore, if the information is not found where indica[...]rt further to find the information.

ACQUISITION AND PAYMENT: INVENTORY AND LIABILITIES

Property, Plant, and Equipment

Here's where you've been...

In Chapter 5, you learned about how a company accounts for long-term assets—property, plant, and equipment. You learned how assets are depreciated and how the information relevant to depreciation is presented on the financial statements.

Here's where you're going...

From Chapter 6, you should understand how a company acquires inventory and accounts for payables. You'll learn about LIFO and FIFO, two popular ways of keeping track of inventory purchases and sales.

Inventory and Liabilities

Financing

Property, Plant, and Equipment

Financial
Reporting
and
Business
Events

Sales a...
Re...

Inventory
and
Liabilities

Learn... Ob... es

More specif... studying this chapter, you should be able to answer these questions:

1. What is ...orded at purchase?
2. What a... cost flow
   assump... ...easure and
   report ... ...ng inventory?
3. What a... ...ning of updating inv...
4. What i... ...ors on the
   financi...
5. How is ... the gross profit
   metho...

6. What is the lower-of-cost-or-market rule?
7. What information about inventory is disclosed
   on the financial statements and how can we use
   it to help us evaluate the business?
8. How are liabilities classified, recorded, and
   reported?
9. How is payroll calculated and reported?
10. What risks are associated with the acquisition/
    payment process, and what controls help mini-
    mize those risks?

BUSINESS PROCESS

The acquisition of inventory is one of the major business processes, particularly for merchandising companies. The payment for these purchases is also of primary importance. This is reflected in the operations of most large corporations. They have large departments dedicated to acquiring inventory—the purchasing department—and large departments dedicated to paying the bills—the accounts payable department. Firms, large and small, keep meticulous track of their purchases and payments. The information system—the way these purchase and payment transactions are recorded and reported—provides input for management's planning, control, and evaluation of the acquisition/payment process.

Acquiring Merchandise for Sale

Be able to define inventory and calculate the cost of the inventory.

BUSINESS PROCESS

A merchandising firm exists to earn revenue by selling products, but it can't earn revenue until it purchases the items it plans to sell. The items a merchandising firm acquires to sell, or really to resell, are called inventory; and the acquisition and payment of inventory together form one of the three major business processes—the acquisition/payment process. (The other two are the conversion process and the sales/collection process.)

The acquisition/payment process includes buying, storing, maintaining, and paying for goods and services. This includes acquiring raw materials, utilities, supplies, insurance, repairs, professional services (such as accounting), and inventory. We'll focus on inventory in this chapter.

The objectives of the acquisition/payment process are

- to purchase from reliable vendors items that meet the firm's standards
- to have resources available when needed
- to receive only those items ordered
- to pay vendors in a timely manner for the items received

Un   ...ding Business

INVENTORY   ...S AND TAXES

Generally acce... ...(GAAP) allow
firms quite a bit... ...od of
accounting for... ...ut (LIFO) provides a tax ber... ...First-out
(FIFO)—in a pe... ...al economic
benefit that res... ...e. In the past
century, costs l... ...ake sense for
a company to... ...ings by
choosing LIFO... ...e most
recent survey... ...ted in
Accounting Tr... ...rts that only
about 53% of 1... ...of their
inventories. Wl... ...noice of
inventory meth... ...pose *not* to
use LIFO?

Lower earnin...

If a firm uses l... ...o use LIFO for
financial repc... ...he general
rule that a firr... ...ethod for
financial stat... ...d for taxes.
With respect... ...sistency means
that choosing... ...ver reported
profits for bot... ...nts. Why is that
a problem?

■ Managers... ...s will have a
  negative...

■ Managers may have a compensation contract that is
  tied to earnings; so lower earnings may mean a smaller
  bonus.

Record-keeping costs

Inventory records associated with LIFO are more complicated to keep than inventory records associated with
FIFO. If the tax benefit of using LIFO is small, it might not be
worth the trouble. What would cause the tax benefit to be
small or even nonexistent?

■ A firm may not be paying much in taxes—due to
  losses in prior years that reduce taxes or special tax
  breaks, such as investment tax credits.
■ The inventory levels may fluctuate a lot, so that old lay-
  ers of LIFO inventory would have to be sold, causing a
  reversal of any tax benefit.
■ The firm may turn over the inventory very rapidly, so
  that the inventory method would not have much effect
  on taxes.
■ Costs in some industries are decreasing, so FIFO has
  the tax advantage in those cases.

Most of the time, the choice of an accounting method
is difficult to trace to specific economic consequences.
With inventory, however, the choice of accounting method
can make a significant economic difference to a firm—
real dollars. That makes selecting an inventory cost flow
method an important business decision.

Procedure... ...Goods

The acquisitic... ...when someone in a company requests
goods or serv... ...ly. The person requesting the goods or
services send... ...rchase requisition, to the company's
purchasing a... ...t selects the vendor based on the vendor's prices,... ...vices needed, and the ability to deliver
them in a ti... ...asing agent specifies in a **purchase
order**—the... ...ere information is recorded—what is
needed, pric... ...py of the purchase order is sent to the
vendor, and... ...copies for internal records.

One cop... ...epartment for notification that a shipment of goo... ...dor. This copy is slightly different than
the one sent... ...*blind* purchase order because it does not

A **purchase requisition** is a
company's internal record of the
request for goods or services.

A **purchase order** is the record of the
company's request to a vendor for
goods or services.

indicate the specific quantity of goods that were ordered. The individuals in the receiving department must count the items when they are received. If the quantity were specified on their copy of the purchase order, the employees in the receiving department might be tempted to use that amount instead of actually counting the goods. Counting the goods helps to ensure that all goods requested and ordered were actually received.

Another copy of the purchase order is sent to the accounts payable department where it is considered an *open* purchase order until the goods or services have been received.

On arrival of the vendor's truck at the receiving dock, the receiving department accepts the goods delivered based on the authorization implicit in, and information specified in, the blind purchase order sent earlier from the purchasing department. The items are counted and inspected, and the condition and quantity of goods received are recorded in a **receiving report**.

A copy of the receiving report is also sent to the purchasing department as notification that the goods ordered have been received. Another copy of the receiving report is sent to the accounts payable department to be included in its documentation needed to pay for the goods.

Finally, a copy of the receiving report is sent to the inventory manager, who uses it to update the formal accounting records. After the records are updated for the purchase, the goods may then be transferred to a warehouse or site where they will be stored until they are sold.

A **receiving report** is the record made by the purchasing company of the details of the goods received.

Understand how inventory is related to cost of goods sold.

Merchandise inventory is a current asset composed of goods owned and held for sale in the regular course of business.

BUSINESS PROCESS

Merchandise Inventory

All goods owned and held for sale in the regular course of business are considered **merchandise inventory**. Typically, merchandise inventory is simply called *inventory*. Inventory is a current asset. According to the matching principle, inventory should be expensed in the period in which it is sold.

Why does the value of inventory matter? A merchandising firm records the inventory as an asset until it is sold. When it is sold, inventory becomes an expense—cost of goods sold. So the value of the inventory affects both the balance sheet and the income statement.

Purchases

Like property, plant, and equipment, the costs associated with acquiring inventory and the accounting for those costs are closely related. Gathering all the information to make good decisions is a necessary part of the business process. This information is reflected in the financial statements.

The cost of a purchase is not always the amount quoted by the vendor. Often, a company receives a discount for purchasing a large quantity of items or for paying for them early or both. When buying inventory, a company should take advantage of any discounts available. Purchase discounts are commonly given for prompt payment. For example, a vendor offering a purchase discount would describe it in terms like this:

2/10, n/30

2/10, n/30 describes the terms of a purchase discount. This example means the company would receive a 2% discount if it paid the invoice within 10 days.

read as "two-ten, net-thirty." That means the vendor will give a 2% discount if the buyer pays for the entire purchase within 10 days of the invoice date. If not, the full amount is due within 30 days. A vendor may set any discount terms. What would it mean if the terms were 3/15, n/45? The vendor will give a 3% discount if payment is made within 15 days. Otherwise, full payment must be made within 45 days.

Taking advantage of such discounts can amount to significant savings. When a vendor offers a sales discount, you should take advantage of it. If you

are offered the ter[...]actually charging you almost 36%
annual interest to [...] [...] [...]ay within the discount period and
wait until the last [...] [...] ou are actually paying 36% annual
interest for not p[...] [...] e discount period expires and you
haven't paid unti[...] [...]ice date, you are "borrowing" the
money from the [...] [...] days. By your failure to pay within
the discount per[...] [...] 2% in 20 days. Additionally, 2%
interest on a "loa[...] [...] e as a 36% annual rate, determined
with the help of [...]

$$\frac{x}{360}$$

Solve for x and [...] [...]erest, if you consider a year as having 360 days. S[...] [...]e money from the bank (at 10% or
12% annual inte[...] [...]urchase discounts.

Some good[...] [...] to the vendor because the company
ordered too m[...] [...] e wrong items, or found the goods
slightly damag[...] [...]s is classified as **purchase returns.**
Goods damage[...] [...] by the purchaser with a cost reduction—called a [...] [...]hase discounts and purchase returns
and allowance[...] [...]rchandising firm's *gross purchases* to
get *net purcha*[...]

Any freigh[...] [...]ing company to get the goods to the
company is al[...] [...]e goods. When a merchandising firm
pays for trans[...] [...]rchased, that cost is called **freight-in**
and is conside[...] [...]nventory.

If the term[...] [...]oard **(FOB) shipping point,** then title
to the goods[...] [...] e shipping point (the vendor's warehouse), and t[...] [...]he cost of the transportation from that
point on. If t[...] **tion,** the vendor—the supplier of the
goods—pays[...] [...]ts until the goods reach their destination, when ti[...] [...] when you're the buyer:

- FOB ship[...] [...]mount is called *freight-in* and is included
  in the cos[...] [...]discounts don't apply to freight charges.)
- FOB dest[...] [...]u have no freight-in cost to account for.

When y[...] [...]ay for goods to be delivered to your customers, the[...] [...]e statement as **freight-out,** or **delivery
expense.** F[...] [...]xpense; freight-in is a part of the cost of
the invento[...] [...]elationships between FOB selling point,
FOB destin[...] [...]ller.

The de[...] [...]ses—available discounts and shipping
terms—ca[...] [...]st of the inventory. A company must pay
attention t[...] [...] costs make a difference in the acquisition proce[...] [...]ected in the financial statements.

Purchase returns and **purchase allowances** are amounts that reduce the total cost of purchases of inventory due to returns or reductions related to unsatisfactory merchandise.

Freight-in is part of the cost of the purchased merchandise.

FOB shipping point and **FOB destination** are purchase terms that describe whether the buyer or seller pays the freight related to a purchase. See Exhibit 6-1 for details.

Freight-out, also called **delivery expense** is an operating expense.

**Exhibit 6-1
Shipping Terms**

		FOB destination
Buyer	[...] the cost [...] account	Buyer **does not** pay the shipping cost
Seller	[...]ing cost	Seller pays the shipping cost, which is recorded as a **selling** expense

For each problem, calculate the cost of the inventory purchased.

1. A Company purchased merchandise FOB destination for $10,000. Terms were 2/10, n/30 and payment was made in 8 days. Freight cost was $90.
2. B Company purchased merchandise FOB destination for $10,000. Terms were 2/10, n/30 and payment was made in 29 days. Freight cost was $90.
3. C Company purchased merchandise FOB shipping point for $10,000. Terms were 2/10, n/30 and payment was made in 29 days. Freight cost was $90.
4. D Company purchased merchandise FOB shipping point for $10,000. Terms were 2/10, n/30 and payment was made in 8 days. Freight cost was $90.

Selecting and Accounting for Goods Sold: Inventory Cost Flow

L.O. 2

Be able to use various cost flow assumptions—FIFO, LIFO, and average cost—to calculate inventory and cost of goods sold.

Suppose a grocery store buys a truckload of canned corn—1,000 cans—on the first of February for $0.75 per can. Then suppose the store suddenly expects a huge demand for canned corn, so 1,000 more cans are ordered. The second truckload arrives a few days later. For this second purchase, the unit cost is $0.77 per can. The cans costing $0.77 are indistinguishable from the cans costing $0.75 in the first purchase. Two thousand cans are available to sell during February. There was no beginning inventory at the start of the month because the company had no cans of corn on that date. Suppose the store sells 1,600 cans during February. What is the *cost of goods sold*—also known as *cost of sales*—for the month?

We could figure that out easily if we knew exactly which cans were sold—how many costing $0.75 each and how many costing $0.77 each were sold? The store has no idea. The store simply knows 1,600 cans were sold for $0.79 per can, and 400 cans are left in the inventory (i.e., not sold). There were 2,000 cans available for sale at a total cost of:

$$\$1,520 = (1,000 \text{ cans @ \$0.75 per can}) + (1,000 \text{ cans @ \$0.77 per can})$$

How should the store allocate that amount between the 1,600 cans sold (cost of goods sold) and the 400 cans not sold (ending inventory for February)?

The store will have to make an assumption about which cans flowed out of inventory to customers and which cans remain in inventory. That is, the store assumes an order in which the cans were sold, and that assumption makes it possible to calculate the cost of goods sold to go on the income statement and the cost of ending inventory to go on the balance sheet. The actual physical flow of the goods does *not* have to be consistent with the cost flow assumption. The grocery store could know that all the $0.75 cans could not have been sold because of the way shipments are stored in the warehouse, yet the store is still allowed to use the assumption that the $0.75 cans were sold first in calculating cost of goods sold. *Inventory flow* refers to the physical passage of goods through a business. In accounting, we are generally concerned with *cost flow*—that is, the flow of the costs associated with the goods that pass through a company—instead of *goods* flow, which refers to the actual physical movement of goods.

Keeping Track of the Inventory: Four Cost Flow Assumptions

GAAP allows a company to select one of several inventory cost flow assumptions. Studying several of these methods will help you understand how accounting choices can affect the amounts on the financial statements, even when the transactions are identical. There are four basic inventory cost flow assumptions used to calculate the cost of goods sold and the cost of ending inventory:

 L.O. 2

Define and explain the four inventory cost flow assumptions: Specific identification, FIFO, LIFO, and average cost.

1. **Specific identification** method. With this method, each item sold must be identified as coming from a specific purchase, at a specific unit cost. Specific identification can be used for determining the cost of each item of a small quantity of large, luxury items such as yachts or works of art, but it is almost impossible to use for determining the cost of each item of a large number of identical items. It would take a great deal of time and money to keep track of a large inventory with similar items using specific identification.

   Specific identification requires keeping track of the specific items sold to calculate cost of goods sold.

   Suppose you first bought two units at $3 each and later bought one unit at $4, and then you sold two units during the accounting period. What is cost of goods sold? To answer that question using the specific identification method, you would need to know exactly which two units were sold. That is, you have to specifically identify the units sold. If you sold both of the $3 units, then cost of goods sold would be $6 and ending inventory would be $4. However, if you sold one of the $3 units and the $4 unit, then cost of goods sold would be $7 and ending inventory would be $3.

2. **Weighted-average** method. A weighted-average unit cost is calculated by dividing the total cost of all the goods a company has available for sale by the total number of units available for sale, resulting in an average cost per unit. This average unit cost is *weighted* because the number of units at each different price is used to weight the unit costs. The calculated weighted-average unit cost is applied to all units sold to get cost of goods sold and applied to all units remaining to get a value for ending inventory.

   Weighted-average uses the average cost of all the goods on hand to calculate cost of goods sold.

   In the example of three units purchased, two @ $3 and one @ $4, the weighted-average cost per unit is $10 (total cost of purchases) divided by three (total number of units purchased). Cost of goods sold is two units × $10/3 = $6.67. Ending inventory would be one unit × $10/3 = $3.33.

3. **First-in, First-out method (FIFO)**. The cost of the first goods purchased is assigned to the first goods sold. The cost of the goods on hand at the end of a period is determined from the most recent purchases.

   FIFO uses the cost of the oldest goods on hand to calculate cost of goods sold. This will result in a more current inventory value on the balance sheet and a less current value for cost of goods sold on the income statement.

   By using the same example, two units purchased @ $3 and one unit @ $4, cost of goods sold under FIFO assumes that the two oldest units were sold first. FIFO means the first items purchased are the first *out* of inventory to go to the income statement as cost of goods sold. So cost of goods sold is $6 and ending inventory is $4.

4. **Last-in, First-out method (LIFO)**. The cost of the last goods purchased is assigned to the cost of goods sold, so the cost of the goods on hand at the end of a period is assumed to be the cost of goods purchased earliest.

   LIFO uses the cost of the most recently purchased goods to calculate cost of goods sold. This will result in a more current value for cost of goods sold on the income statement and a less current value for inventory on the balance sheet.

   Again, using the same example, two units @ $3 and one unit @ $4, cost of goods sold is $7. (The last unit in was the $4 unit, so it has to be sold first under LIFO. Then the next most recent unit purchased is one of the $3 units.) Ending inventory is $3.

Notice that the same set of facts and economic transactions can result in different numbers on the financial statements, depending on the choice of cost flow methods. It is important to remember this when using and interpreting financial information.

Record Keeping for the Inventory

Define and use the two choices for inventory record keeping—perpetual and periodic.

Perpetual inventory is a method of record keeping that involves updating the accounting records at the time of every sale.

Periodic inventory is a method of record keeping that involves updating the accounting records only at the end of the accounting period.

In addition to selecting a cost flow assumption, a company must decide *when* to update inventory records and actually calculate cost of goods sold. There are two options. After every sale, the inventory records can be updated. This is called a **perpetual inventory** system because it requires a continuous updating.

Alternatively, the inventory records can be updated at the end of each accounting period. This is called a **periodic inventory** system because the record keeping is done only at the end of each period.

No matter how the record keeping is done, the relationships between beginning inventory, purchases, ending inventory, and cost of goods sold are:

$$
\left.\begin{array}{l}\text{Beginning Inventory}\\ +\ \text{Purchases}\\ -\ \text{Ending Inventory}\end{array}\right\} \quad \text{Goods Available for Sale}
$$
$$
\underline{\text{Cost of Goods Sold}}
$$

The higher the cost of ending inventory, the lower the cost of goods sold will be, the higher the gross margin will be, and the higher net income will be. From that sequence you should be able to see that the value of the ending inventory has a direct effect on net income.

Let's look at an example to see how these choices—one of the four inventory cost flow methods and one of the two record-keeping methods—affect the values for inventory and cost of goods sold.

Recording Inventory Purchases and Freight Costs

Purchases and Purchase Discounts

When a company takes advantage of a *purchase discount,* it reduces the cost of its inventory.

■ If you are using a *perpetual inventory system,* the credit for purchase discounts is made to the inventory account.
■ If you are using a *periodic inventory system,* the credit is made to a purchase discounts account.

Assume that you purchase $10,000 worth of inventory on January 5, 2001, with credit terms 2/10, n/30. The purchase is paid for on January 12. The journal entry to record the purchase of inventory, terms 2/10, n/30, would be:

Date	Transaction	Debit	Credit
1/5/2001	Inventory* or purchases	$10,000	
	Accounts payable		$10,000

*The inventory account is debited when using a perpetual record-keeping system, and an account called *purchases* is debited when using a periodic record-keeping system.

The journal entry to record the payment of the 1/5/2001 $10,000 purchase less the discount of $200 ($10,000 × 2%) would be:

Date	Transaction	Debit	Credit
1/12/2001	Accounts payable	$10,000	
	Inventory** or purchase discounts		$ 200
	Cash		9,800

**Inventory is used in a perpetual system, and purchase discounts is used in a periodic system.

Purchase Returns and Purchase Allowances

Purchase returns and *purchase allowances* are accounted for much like discounts—the account used for recording the return or the allowance depends on whether you are using a perpetual inventory system or periodic inventory system. With a perpetual system, inventory is credited. With a periodic system, the credit is to Purchase returns and allowances. To illustrate: you return $150 of defective merchandise that you have not paid for yet. The journal entry to record the return of $150 of defective merchandise would be:

Date	Transaction	Debit	Credit
	Accounts payable	$150	
	Inventory or purchase returns and allowances		$150

Freight-In

When goods are shipped **(FOB) shipping point,** the freight cost increases the total inventory cost. With a perpetual inventory system, the freight cost will increase inventory. With a periodic inventory system, a separate freight-in account will be maintained. To illustrate: you receive a bill for $85 to cover the shipping cost of merchandise purchased FOB shipping point. The journal entry to record the shipping cost of inventory would be:

Date	Transaction	Debit	Credit
	Inventory or freight-in	$85	
	Accounts payable or cash		$85

Example of Cost Flow Assumptions and Timing of Record Keeping

Phil's Photo Shop started the year 2001 with eight cameras in the inventory. Each had a cost of $10. Phil's Photo Shop sells only one kind of camera—a self-focusing, self-forward winding, easy-to-use model. Exhibit 6-2 shows the record of quantities purchased and at what cost and quantities sold and at what selling price during January 2001.

Be able to use the two record-keeping choices with several of the cost flow assumptions.

Perpetual Inventory

Suppose Phil's Photo Shop uses a *perpetual* inventory system. That means each time a sale is made, the cost of goods sold is calculated. Think about what that means in this example. When Phil's sells the three cameras on January 8, the company calculates the cost of goods sold right then—at the time of the sale, based on exactly which goods are owned at that date. The only items in the inventory on January 8 are the eight cameras in the beginning inventory at $10 each. The cost of goods sold for the January 8 sale is $30 (= 3 cameras × $10/camera).

Exhibit 6-2
Inventory Records for
January 2001

January 1	Beginning inventory	8 Cameras	@ $10 Each
January 8	**Sales**	**3 Cameras**	**@ $20 Each**
January 16	Purchase	5 Cameras	@ $12 Each
January 20	**Sales**	**8 Cameras**	**@ $22 Each**
January 30	Purchase	7 Cameras	@ $14 Each

When a company uses a perpetual inventory system, all inventory purchases are debited to the inventory account. When a sale is made, two journal entries are required, one to record the sale and the other to reduce the inventory and record the cost of goods sold. For example, the January 8 sale for Phil's Photo Shop using a perpetual inventory system would require the following two journal entries to record the sale of three cameras—sales price $20 each, cost $10 each:

Date	Transaction	Debit	Credit
1/8/2001	Cash or accounts receivable	$60	
	Sales		$60
	Cost of goods sold	$30	
	Inventory		$30

What about the sale on January 20? On that date, Phil's sells eight cameras. Which ones? Using a perpetual system, Phil's needs to calculate the cost of goods sold at the time of the sale. But there is a problem. Before the company can figure out the cost of goods sold, Phil's has to make a cost flow assumption. If Phil's decides to use FIFO, then the assumption is that the five cameras left from the beginning inventory and three cameras from the January 16 purchase have been sold. If Phil's decides to use LIFO, then the assumption is that the five cameras from the January 16 purchase are sold first and then the other three cameras (to get the total sold of eight) come from the beginning inventory.

Periodic Inventory

Suppose Phil's uses a *periodic* inventory system. *Cost of good sold is not* calculated or recorded until the company is ready to prepare financial statements at the end of the period. At that time, Phil would count the cameras in the ending inventory and deduct the number still on hand from the number of cameras available to sell during the period—beginning inventory plus purchases made—to get the number of cameras sold during the period (11 cameras in this example). Then the company would make a cost flow assumption. Which cameras will Phil's assume were sold? If the company uses FIFO, Phil's assumes the earliest purchased cameras were sold first. If the company uses LIFO, Phil's assumes the most recent cameras purchased were sold first. If the company uses weighted average, Phil's would calculate the weighted-average cost of a camera and multiply that average unit cost by 11 to get the total cost of goods sold.

If a company does not use specific identification, it must select one of the three remaining inventory cost flow methods. Then when the company selects FIFO, LIFO, or weighted-average cost, a record-keeping method of either perpetual or periodic must be chosen. That produces six possible inventory systems that a company may use, shown in Exhibit 6-3.

When a company uses a periodic inventory system, all inventory purchases are debited to the purchases account. The purchases account is a temporary account used to accumulate the cost of inventory purchased during the period. When a sale is made, only one journal entry is required to record the sale. Cost of goods sold is calculated at the end of the period. The January 8 sale for Phil's

Exhibit 6-3
Inventory Cost Flow and Record-Keeping Assumptions

Cost flow assumption			
Record keeping	FIFO	LIFO	Average cost
Periodic	1	3	5
Perpetual	2	4	6

1. Cost of the first goods purchased are the first to be included in cost of goods sold, and the record keeping is done at the end of the accounting period
2. Cost of the first goods purchased are the first to be included in cost of goods sold, and the record keeping is done every time a sale is made
3. Cost of the last goods purchased are the first to be included in cost of goods sold, and the record keeping is done at the end of the accounting period
4. Cost of the last goods purchased are the first to be included in cost of goods sold, and the record keeping is done every time a sale is made
5. Cost of all the goods available for sale for the entire accounting period are used to calculate a weighted-average cost; this cost is multiplied by the number of units sold to get cost of goods sold; this is done at the end of the accounting period
6. Cost of all the goods available for sale at the time of the sale are used to calculate an average cost; this cost is multiplied by the number of units sold to get cost of goods sold; a new average cost is calculated and the related record keeping is done every time a sale is made

Photo Shop to record the sale of three cameras at $20 each using a periodic inventory system would be:

Date	Transaction	Debit	Credit
1/8/2001	Cash or accounts receivable	$60	
	Sales		$60

The January 16th purchases to record the purchase of five cameras at $12 each using a periodic inventory system would be:

Date	Transaction	Debit	Credit
1/16/2001	Purchases	$60	
	Cash or accounts payable		$60

Using the information from Phil's Photo Shop, let's use a sample of these methods to calculate the cost of goods sold and ending inventory for the month of January.

No matter which of the six combinations a company selects, the **cost of goods available for sale**—beginning inventory plus purchases—is the same.

Cost of goods available for sale is determined by:

Beginning Inventory + Net Purchases = Cost of Goods Available for Sale

For Phil's Photo Shop for January, the cost of goods available for sale is $238. The calculation follows:

$$[(8 \text{ cameras} \times \$10 \text{ each}) + (5 \text{ cameras} \times \$12 \text{ each}) +$$
$$(7 \text{ cameras} \times \$14 \text{ each})] = \$80 + \$60 + \$98 = \$238$$

The inventory cost flow assumption and record-keeping method determine how that dollar amount of *cost of goods available for sale* is divided between *cost of goods sold* and the cost of the *ending inventory*.

Let's start with FIFO.

Cost of goods available for sale is the beginning inventory plus all purchases during an accounting period.

FIFO periodic means (1) the cost flow assumption is that the oldest goods in the inventory are sold first, and (2) inventory records and cost of goods sold are updated only once, at the end of the accounting period.

FIFO Periodic

Phil's Photo Shop calculates the cost of good sold at the end of the month. At that time the company knows the total number of cameras sold in January was 11. Using FIFO, Phil's counts the oldest cameras in the inventory as *sold*. So Phil's counts the beginning inventory of eight cameras @ $10 each as the first part of cost of goods sold. On January 16, five cameras were purchased, so the company will include three of those as part of cost of goods sold, too. That makes 11 cameras Phil's sold during the month.

$$
\begin{aligned}
&\text{8 cameras @ \$10 per camera} = \$\ 80\\
&\text{3 cameras @ \$12 per camera} = \$\ 36\\
&\text{Cost of Goods Sold} = \underline{\underline{\$116}}
\end{aligned}
$$

What's left in the inventory?

$$
\begin{aligned}
&\text{2 cameras @ \$12 per camera} = \$\ 24\\
&\text{7 cameras @ \$14 per camera} = \$\ 98\\
&\text{Ending Inventory} = \underline{\underline{\$122}}
\end{aligned}
$$

Notice that the cost of goods sold plus the ending inventory equals $238—the cost of the goods available for sale during January.

FIFO perpetual means (1) the cost flow assumption is that the oldest goods in the inventory are sold first, and (2) inventory records and cost of goods sold are updated at the time of every sale.

FIFO Perpetual

When a perpetual record-keeping system is used, the cost of goods sold for each sale must be calculated and recorded *at the time of the sale*; and only the cameras from the purchases as of the date of a sale—meaning prior and up to the date of a sale—are available to become part of the cost of goods sold. Perpetual record keeping requires you to pay attention to the dates goods are purchased and sold. Phil's first sale is on January 8. Only cameras from the beginning inventory are available to use to calculate the cost of goods sold for the January 8 sale. (The other purchases are in the future, and nothing is known about them on January 8.) The cost of goods sold for the January 8 sale is three cameras × $10/camera = $30.

Next, eight cameras were sold on January 20. Because the cost flow assumption is FIFO, Phil's uses the cameras left in the beginning inventory as part of the cost of goods sold. So the cost of goods sold for the January 20 sale has to start with the five cameras remaining in the beginning inventory—that will be 5 × $10 each = $50. To get the other three needed to make the total of eight sold, Phil's will count three from the January 16 purchase. That's three @ $12 = $36. So the total cost of goods sold for the January 20 sale is $86 (= $50 + $36).

To summarize the cost of goods sold:

$$
\begin{aligned}
&\text{3 cameras @ \$10 each} = \$\ 30 \text{ — Sale on January 8}\\
&\left.\begin{aligned}
&\text{5 cameras @ \$10 each} = \$\ 50\\
&\text{3 cameras @ \$12 each} = \$\ 36
\end{aligned}\right\} \text{— Sale on January 20}\\
&\textit{Total} \qquad\qquad\qquad\qquad \underline{\underline{\$116}}
\end{aligned}
$$

What's left in the ending inventory?

$$
\begin{aligned}
&\text{2 cameras @ \$12 each} = \$\ 24\\
&\text{7 cameras @ \$14 each} = \$\ 98\\
&\textit{Total} \qquad\qquad\qquad \underline{\underline{\$122}}
\end{aligned}
$$

Notice, all the work to figure out the cost of goods sold using FIFO *perpetual* gives the same amount as using FIFO *periodic,* which is much easier to calculate.

Is this coincidence, or is there a predictable pattern here? Look at the particular cameras that were assumed to be sold under the two methods. You'll see that it's more than coincidence. No matter how the company does the actual record keeping, either FIFO method—perpetual or periodic—will give the same dollar amount of cost of goods sold and the same dollar amount of ending inventory for the period.

LIFO Periodic

When you use periodic record keeping, you start by calculating the total number of cameras sold during the month. In January, Phil's Photo sold 11 cameras. Using LIFO, Phil's counts cameras from the latest purchase as those sold first. For LIFO, start at the bottom of the list of purchases in the sequence in which the cameras were purchased.

The purchase on January 30 was seven cameras, so Phil's counts those as part of cost of goods sold first. (Notice that those specific cameras don't have to be sold to treat them "as if" they were sold. In this case, Phil's *couldn't* have sold them. A cost flow assumption does not have to mimic the actual physical flow of the goods.) The purchase on January 16 was 5 cameras, so the company will count 4 of them in the cost of goods sold to get the total of 11 cameras sold. The total cost of goods sold will be:

> 7 cameras @ $14 per camera = $ 98
> 4 cameras @ $12 per camera = $ 48
> Cost of Goods Sold = $146

What's left in the inventory?

> 1 camera @ $12 per camera = $ 12
> 8 cameras @ $10 per camera = $ 80
> Ending Inventory = $ 92

Notice that the cost of goods sold plus the ending inventory equals $238—the total goods available for sale.

Accounting Choices Make a Difference

Compare the cost of goods sold for LIFO periodic with FIFO. Using FIFO, Phil's cost of goods sold is $116. With LIFO, Phil's cost of goods sold is $146. The numbers in this example are small, but the example demonstrates the point that the choice of inventory cost flow assumption makes a difference in the amounts reported on the financial statements—even when the underlying business process and related transactions are identical.

Average Cost: Periodic Weighted Average

Let's calculate the cost of goods sold and ending inventory for Phil's Photo Shop using the average cost method to demonstrate the third major cost flow assumption. The computations for this method of keeping track of inventory

LIFO periodic means (1) the cost flow assumption is that the newest goods in the inventory are sold first, and (2) inventory records and cost of goods sold are updated only once, at the end of the accounting period.

Periodic weighted-average means (1) the cost of all the goods available for sale for the entire accounting period is used to calculate an average cost, and (2) the cost of goods sold is calculated at the end of the accounting period.

are the simplest of all methods. Phil adds up beginning inventory and all purchases to get the value of the goods available for sale. Phil previously calculated that amount to be $238. Then he divides $238 by the total number of cameras available for sale—that's the number of cameras that comprised the $238—to get an average cost per camera. Phil's Photo Shop had a total of 20 (= 8 + 5 + 7) cameras available for sale. Dividing $238 by 20 cameras gives $11.90 per camera. That average unit cost is used to compute cost of goods sold and ending inventory.

Cost of good sold is the number sold—11 cameras—multiplied by $11.90 per camera, which is $130.90.
Ending inventory is the number in the ending inventory—nine cameras—multiplied by $11.90 per camera, which is $107.10.
These add up to $238 (= $130.90 + $107.10).

Exhibit 6-4   Two Examples of Cost of Goods Sold Using FIFO versus LIFO

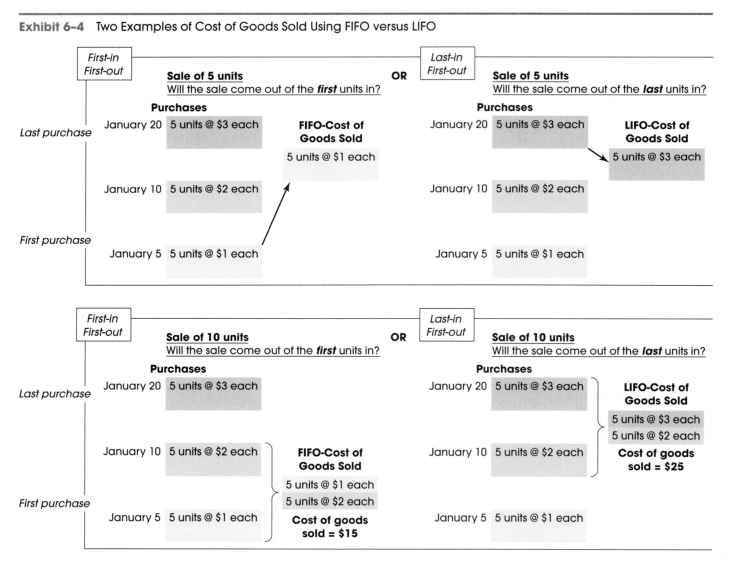

All units are the same inventory item, and the cost is rising sharply during the month of January. Notice that the purchases are listed with the most recent purchase at the top of the list. To calculate FIFO cost of goods sold, the first items purchased are assumed to be sold first. To calculate LIFO cost of goods sold, the last items purchased are assumed to be sold first.

Conclusions About Inventory Cost Flow Assumptions

All the combinations of inventory cost flow assumptions and record-keeping methods, shown in Exhibit 6-3, are used in practice. Actually, there are even more methods, derived from these six, in use. The methods are ones that have been modified slightly to meet the needs of specific industries. For now, we've studied enough of these methods to know that the accounting method a company selects to account for inventory can make a difference in the reported cost of goods sold and inventory amounts. A detailed example is shown in Exhibit 6-4.

STUDY BREAK 6-2
SEE HOW YOU'RE DOING

Jones Saddle Company had the following transactions during August 2002:

- **purchased 30 units @ $20 per unit on August 10, 2002**
- **purchased 20 units @ $21 per unit on August 15, 2002**
- **purchased 20 units @ $23 per unit on August 21, 2002**
- **sold 35 units @ $30 per unit on August 30, 2002**

Prepare journal entries to record the purchases, assuming that Jones Saddle Company uses a perpetual inventory system. Prepare the journal entries to record the sale using (1) FIFO, (2) LIFO, and (3) weighted average.

Because the inventory cost flow assumption affects the financial statements and because the effect can be quite large, generally accepted accounting principles (GAAP) require a company to include details about inventory cost flow assumptions and related costs in the notes to the financial statements.

Inventory and Cost of Goods Sold in Merchandising Operations

After cost of goods sold is calculated, that amount is reported on the income statement as an expense. The income statement for a merchandising firm often takes the format shown next. It is called a multistep income statement because it takes an extra step to subtract cost of goods sold and give the subtotal *gross margin from sales.*

Revenues from sales (net sales)
−Cost of goods sold
Gross margin from sales (also known as gross profit)
−Operating expenses
Income before income taxes
−Income taxes
Net income

Cost of goods sold is the largest expense in most merchandising companies.

Operating expenses are all the other expenses, except interest and taxes.

Income before interest and taxes is also called **operating income,** *earnings before interest and taxes (EBIT),* or *income, from operations.*

Operating income is income before gains, losses, interest, and taxes. Often, in our examples, we don't include non-operating items, which means that operating income is the same as net income.

At the end of 2003, the following amounts were shown in the records of Kenny's Sporting Goods, Inc. Place the amount of each account in the proper column to show where it should appear in the income statement.

Account	Amount	Revenue	Cost of Goods Sold	Other expenses
Administrative expenses	$ 57,000			
Income tax expense	9,000			
Sales	617,000			
Purchases	367,000			
Delivery fees (freight-out)	10,900			
Transportation-in	13,000			
Depreciation expense	6,000			
Sales salaries	74,000			
Purchase discounts	3,300			
Utilities expense	2,100			

Note: In addition, beginning inventory was $60,000 and a physical count of merchandise showed inventory on hand at December 31, 2003, in the amount of $70,000.

Calculate the following:

Cost of goods available for sale.

Cost of goods sold.

Gross profit.

Recording Inventory and Cost of Goods Sold Transactions

Adjustments and Closing under a Perpetual Inventory System

When a company maintains a perpetual inventory system, the current inventory balance and cost of goods sold are maintained at all times. A physical inventory count at the end of the year is needed to verify the inventory balance and identify shrinkage. Using a perpetual system, the following is what a typical inventory account and a cost of goods sold account would look like before the adjustment and closing process:

Inventory				Cost of goods sold		
BB	$7,500	$372	Purchase discounts	BB	$0	
Purchases	26,580	265	Purchase returns and allowances	12/1– 12/31	27,435	
Freight-in	2,395	27,435	Cost of goods sold			
12/31 unadjusted balance	$8,403					

A physical count of inventory calculates an ending inventory value of $8,255, indicating shrinkage of $148.

The inventory account and the cost of goods sold account must be adjusted for the shrinkage, and the cost of goods sold account must be closed to income summary, just like all other expense accounts are closed to income summary. To record inventory shrinkage:

Date	Transaction	Debit	Credit
12/31	Cost of goods sold	$148	
	Inventory		$148

To close costs of goods sold ($27,435 sales + $148 shrinkage):

Date	Transaction	Debit	Credit
12/31	Retained earnings (or income summary)	$27,583	
	Cost of goods sold		$27,583

After these two entries are posted, the inventory account will have the correct ending balance of $8,255 (= $8,403 − $148) and the cost of goods sold account will be reset to $0.

Adjustments and Closing under a Periodic Inventory System

Under a periodic system, the same company would have the following T-accounts and balances before adjustments and closing:

Inventory		Purchases		Freight-in	
BB $7,500		BB $0		BB $0	
		12/1–		12/1–	
		12/31 26,580		12/31 2,395	

Purchase discounts		Purchase returns and allowances	
$0	BB	$0	BB
	12/1–		12/1–
372	12/31	265	12/31

Remember that, under a periodic system, no cost of goods sold account is maintained.

Using a periodic system, because cost of goods sold is not recorded at each sale, it must be calculated at the end of each year as follows:

    Beginning inventory
  + Purchases
  + Freight-in
  − Purchase discounts
  − Purchase returns and allowances
  = Goods available for sale
  − Ending inventory (from physical count)
  = Cost of goods sold

In a periodic system, shrinkage is automatically absorbed into cost of goods sold because the cost of any items lost or stolen cannot be identified separately from the total of the cost of the goods sold. Closing the temporary accounts and updating the inventory balance transfers the cost of goods sold to retained earnings (or an income summary account). These are the closing entries using a periodic system to close temporary accounts and establish the ending inventory balance:

Date	Transaction	Debit	Credit
12/31	Inventory (ending, per physical count)	$8,255	
	Purchase discounts	372	
	Purchase returns and allowances	265	
	Retained earnings (or income summary)		$8,892

To close temporary accounts and the beginning inventory balance:

Date	Transaction	Debit	Credit
12/31	Retained earnings (or income summary)	$36,475	
	Inventory (beginning balance)		$ 7,500
	Purchases		26,580
	Freight-in		2,395

Notice, the difference between the debit made to retained earnings (or income summary) in the second entry ($36,475) and the credit made to retained earnings (or income summary) in the first entry ($8,255) is $27,583, the amount of cost of goods sold.

Inventory Errors

Calculate and explain the effects of inventory errors on cost of goods sold and net income.

Inventory errors affect the balance sheet—inventory—and the income statement—cost of goods sold.

Because inventory indirectly affects cost of goods sold, a major expense, *errors in the calculation of beginning inventory or ending inventory will affect net income.* Tracing the effects of errors requires slow, focused deliberation. To show how inventory errors can affect income, a simple numerical example is given. Read each description that follows and study the related examples.

Ending Inventory Errors

If *ending inventory* is *overstated*, cost of goods sold must be *understated*. Why? It's because ending inventory and cost of goods sold are the two parts of goods available for sale. Cost of goods sold is an expense. If the expense deducted from sales is too small, the result is that net income will be too large. Suppose you have correctly calculated the cost of goods available for sale (beginning inventory + purchases) to be $10. Those goods will either be sold—and become part of cost of goods sold—or they will *not* be sold—and will still be part of the cost of the inventory.

So goods available for sale consists of two parts—cost of goods sold and ending inventory. Suppose the correct ending inventory is $2 but you erroneously give it a value of $3. If ending inventory is incorrectly valued at $3, then cost of goods sold will be valued at $7. Remember, the ending inventory and cost of goods sold must add up to $10 in this example. What is wrong with cost of goods sold? If ending inventory is actually $2, then cost of goods sold *should* be $8. See what happens? You understate cost of goods sold when you overstate the ending inventory. Anytime you understate an expense, you will overstate net income.

If ending inventory is too small—understated, cost of goods sold must be too large—overstated. The result—net income will be understated. Let's use the same example, in which the cost of goods available for sale was correctly computed at $10. If ending inventory is actually $2 but you erroneously under-state it as $1, then cost of goods sold will be valued as $9. It should be $8. Thus, an understatement in ending inventory has caused an overstatement of cost of goods sold. If you overstate an expense, then you will understate net income.

Beginning Inventory Errors

If ending inventory is overstated in 2001, then *beginning inventory* in 2002 will be overstated. After all, it's the same number. So errors in the ending inventory will affect two consecutive years—ending inventory one year and beginning inventory the following year.

If beginning inventory is overstated, then cost of goods available for sale is overstated. If ending inventory is then counted correctly, then cost of goods sold will be overstated. So net income will be understated. Let's continue the previous example. If you value beginning inventory at $3 (and the correct value is $2) and you *correctly* add the purchases for the second year—say, $15 worth—then the cost of goods available for sale will be $18. (Keep in mind, the correct amount is $17.) At year-end, you count the ending inventory correctly at $6. The calculated cost of goods sold would be $12 (ending inventory and cost of goods sold must total $18). However, we know that the true value of goods available for sale is $17. If the correct ending inventory is $6, then the correct cost of goods sold is $11. The calculated cost of goods sold was overstated by $1. When an expense is overstated, then net income will be understated.

If beginning inventory is understated, then goods available for sale is understated. If ending inventory is counted correctly, then cost of goods sold will be understated. So net income will be overstated. Try thinking about the example in the format given in Exhibit 6-5.

As you can see, when you understate the beginning inventory, you end up with cost of goods sold understated. This understated expense will result in an overstatement of net income.

Note, over a period of 2 years, the errors will counterbalance—they will cancel each other out. However, it is important that the financial statements be correct each year, so a company will correct **inventory errors** if they are discovered, instead of waiting for the errors to cancel each other out.

Inventory errors affect net income because they cause cost of goods sold to be wrong. If net income is wrong, then owner's equity will be wrong on the balance sheet and on the statement of changes in shareholders' equity.

STUDY BREAK 6-4
SEE HOW YOU'RE DOING

Berry Corp. miscounted the ending inventory for the year ended December 31, 2003. The balance sheet reported inventory of $3,600,000, but $25,000 worth of items were omitted from that amount. Berry reported net income of $742,640 for the year. What effect did this inventory error have on Berry's cost of goods sold for the year? What is the correct net income for the year ended December 31, 2003?

Exhibit 6–5
Error in the Beginning Inventory

	Calculated amounts	Correct amounts
Beginning inventory	$ 1 (Understated from prior year error)	$ 2
+ Purchases	+15	+15
Goods available for sale	$ 16	$ 17
− Ending inventory	− 6	− 6
Cost of goods sold	$ 10	$ 11

Gross Profit Method of Estimating Ending Inventory

Estimate ending inventory using the gross profit method.

Gross profit percentage is gross margin as a percentage of sales.

There are times when a company might want to *estimate* the cost of the ending inventory instead of counting the units to calculate the exact cost. For example, if a company prepares monthly or quarterly financial statements, GAAP allows ending inventory to be estimated for reporting on those financial statements. This saves a company the trouble of counting the inventory every quarter. Also, if the inventory is destroyed or stolen, a reliable estimate of the cost of the destroyed inventory will be needed for the insurance claim.

First, you must know the usual **gross profit percentage** for the company. That's gross profit divided by sales. You can calculate the gross profit percentage using prior year's sales and cost data. Then you multiply that percentage by the sales for the period, which gives the estimated gross profit. You then subtract the estimated gross profit from sales to get the estimated cost of goods sold. Because you know (1) beginning inventory (from the last period's financial statements); (2) purchases (from your records); and (3) estimated cost of goods sold, you can estimate ending inventory.

For example, Super Soap Company lost its entire inventory in a flood on April 16. Super Soap had prepared a set of financial statements on March 30, when the inventory on hand was valued at $2,500. During the first part of April, purchases amounted to $3,500; the usual gross margin percentage in this business is 40%. If Super Soap had sales of $8,200 during the first 16 days of April, how much inventory was lost?

- If sales were $8,200 and the usual gross profit percentage is 40%, then the gross profit would be $3,280.
- If sales were $8,200 and gross profit is $3,280, then cost of goods sold would be $4,920. (Another way to look at that is: If the gross profit percentage is 40%, then the other 60% must be the cost of goods sold. So 60% of $8,200 = cost of goods sold = $4,920.)
- Beginning inventory + purchases – cost of goods sold = ending inventory, or $2,500 + $3,500 – $4,920 = $1,080. This is our best estimate of the lost inventory.

Valuing Inventory: Lower-of-Cost-or-Market

Define and use the lower-of-cost-or-market rule for valuing inventory.

Lower-of-cost-or-market describes how inventory must be valued on the balance sheet according to GAAP. Inventory is shown either at **cost**—as calculated using a cost flow assumption like FIFO or LIFO—or at **market**—its replacement cost—whichever is lower.

Inventory is an asset on the balance sheet, recorded at cost. Usually, it is a significant amount. To make sure that inventory is not overstated, GAAP requires companies to compare the **cost** of their inventory at the end of the period with the **market** value of that inventory. The company must use the *lower* of either the cost or the market value for the financial statements.

Estimating the market value is the difficult part of this procedure. The market value used is *replacement* cost. That's the cost to buy similar inventory items from the supplier. A company compares the cost of the inventory—as it is recorded in the accounting records—to the replacement cost at the date of the financial statements and uses the lower of the two values for the balance sheet. If the inventory value has to be reduced, the adjustment to reduce the inventory will also reduce net income.

Comparing the cost of inventory to its current replacement cost is more than simply an accounting requirement. Information about the current replacement cost of inventory is important for formulating sales strategies related to various items in inventory and for inventory purchasing decisions.

Let's look at an example. Suppose a company's ending inventory cost is $150,000 and the market (replacement) cost of that inventory is $145,000. Because the company's records show the cost of $150,000 for inventory and GAAP requires the inventory to be valued at the lower of the cost or market value for the year-end balance sheet, the inventory value must be reduced. Accountants call this *writing down* the inventory. Like all adjustments, the adjustment to write down the inventory must keep the accounting equation in balance. Assets are reduced, and there is a corresponding reduction in owner's equity. It will be a loss and will be included as a deduction on the income statement. The adjustment would affect the accounting equation as follows:

BUSINESS PROCESS

Assets	=	Liabilities	+	Owner's equity
$(5,000) Inventory				$(5,000) Loss on inventory write-down

The journal entry to record the inventory write-down of the LCM valuation would be:

Date	Transaction	Debit	Credit
	Loss on inventory write-down	$5,000	
	Inventory		$5,000

Thus, the value of the inventory on the year-end balance sheet will be $145,000, and $145,000 is considered the new cost of the inventory.

If the market value—replacement cost—of the inventory later increases, the recorded value of the inventory is not affected. The value of the inventory on the balance sheet is never increased. Continuing the example, suppose the cost of the inventory at the end of the next year is $125,000 and market value is $128,000. It appears that the market value has rebounded from the previous drop. Still, the value of the inventory for the second year's balance sheet would be the lower of the two. No adjustment would be recorded; the inventory would be valued at its cost of $125,000. The bottom line is that inventory is written *down* to the lower of cost or market at every balance sheet date, but it is not written *up*. This is an example of *conservatism*—the idea that accounts are very careful not to overstate assets or income.

At the end of the year, Milner Company had inventory of $345,000. If the replacement cost of the inventory is $350,000, what amount will Milner show on the year-end balance sheet? Suppose the replacement cost were $339,000. In that case, what amount would Milner show on the year-end balance sheet?

STUDY BREAK 6-5
SEE HOW YOU'RE DOING

Finding and Using Inventory Information

It's easy to see how important inventory is to a retail company. Inventory is a major asset on the balance sheet, and cost of goods sold is a retail company's largest expense. The method of accounting for inventory must be disclosed. For example, for the fiscal year ended on January 30, 2000, Home Depot had sales of $38.4 billion. The cost of goods sold related to those sales was $27 billion. All the other expenses together were less than $8 billion. Merchan-

L.O. 7

Identify the disclosure requirements related to inventory and use inventory information to analyze a company's performance.

dise inventory, shown in the current assets section of the Home Depot balance sheet, amounts to $5,489 million. That is almost one-third of the company's assets. The notes to the financial statements give this additional information: *Inventories are stated at the lower of cost (FIFO) or market*. Notice how this single sentence about inventory tells us that the company uses a FIFO cost flow assumption and has applied the lower-of-cost-or-market rule to the cost of the ending inventory.

Applying Our Knowledge: Ratio Analysis

BUSINESS PROCESS

Inventory turnover ratio is cost of goods sold divided by average inventory.

The way merchandising companies make a profit is to sell their inventory. The faster they sell their inventory, the more profit they make. Buying inventory and then selling it makes the inventory turn over. That is, after inventory is sold, it must be replaced with new purchases of inventory. The more often that happens, the more profit a company is making. Because turning over the inventory is desirable, financial analysts and investors are interested in how quickly a company is turning over its inventory. This varies a great deal from industry to industry.

The **inventory turnover ratio** is defined as *cost of goods sold* divided by the *average inventory* on hand during the year. Let's calculate the inventory turnover ratio for Home Depot for the fiscal year ended on January 30, 2000. The cost of goods sold for the year, found on the income statement, is $27,023 million. The average inventory can be calculated from the beginning and ending inventory amounts shown on the balance sheet. For Home Depot, the average inventory is $4,293 million + $5,489 million divided by 2. The ratio calculation is:

$$\text{Inventory Turnover Ratio} = \frac{\text{Cost of Goods Sold of \$27,023 million}}{\text{Average Inventory of \$4,891 million}} = 5.5 \text{ (rounded)}$$

This means that Home Depot turns over its inventory—sells it and replaces it—about five and a half times each year.

Gross margin on sales ratio is gross margin divided by sales. It is the same as *gross profit percentage*.

Another ratio often computed by both external users—like financial analysts—and internal users—like marketing and sales managers—is **gross margin on sales ratio**. We have already discussed the calculation of the gross margin and its importance to a retail company. The ratio is defined as gross margin divided by sales, and it is one of the most carefully watched ratios by management. It describes the percentage of sales price that is gross profit. A small shift usually indicates a big change in the profitability of the company's sales.

Let's calculate the gross margin on sales ratio for two consecutive years for Home Depot. That comparison will give us some information about the ongoing performance of the company. Any significant change to this ratio would be a signal to management to investigate the cause of the change. In this case, the ratio has increased, which Home Depot would be likely to interpret as good news. A larger percentage of the sale price was profit during the fiscal year ended January 30, 2000, compared with the fiscal year ended January 31, 1999.

For year ended (in millions)	January 30, 2000	January 31, 1999
Sales	$38,434	$30,219
Cost of goods sold	27,023	21,614
Gross margin	11,411	8,605
Gross margin on sales ratio	29.7%	28.5%

Paying for Acquisitions: Liabilities

Inventory is the major acquisition of a merchandising company. After the acquisition, the resulting payment will complete the acquisition/payment process. Although a company may pay cash for its purchases, it is much more common for such purchases to be made on account. We've already discussed shipping terms and purchase discounts; these are important components of the amount of the liability that results from the purchase of inventory. Let's review the steps involved in the acquisition and see how the acquisition portion of the process leads to the payment portion of the process.

When a company buys inventory items on account—on *credit*—an obligation results. Such obligations—*liabilities*—require either future payments of assets or future performance of services. An exchange is not complete until payment to the vendor has been made. However, the company must first receive a bill from the vendor, called a vendor's invoice. When the invoice is received, the accounts payable department reviews the documents it has collected from the various departments involved in the transaction. These documents are the purchase order, the receiving report, and the invoice:

- Reviewing the purchase order confirms that a purchase was actually requested.
- The receiving report is documentation that the goods received are the goods ordered.
- The vendor's invoice helps to confirm the correct amount owed to the vendor. If there is a difference in the quantity or type of items received, the vendor is contacted to resolve the problem. Otherwise, the accounts payable clerk, who also records a liability on the books, marks the invoice for payment.

Many companies keep invoices filed in order of the date payments are due. This is called a *tickler file*—the name indicates something that will get your attention, like being tickled. If the goods are purchased under the terms 2/10, n/30, the vendor is offering a 2% discount on the total amount due if payment is made within 10 days from the date of purchase. The *net* amount, or the total amount is due within 30 days of the date of purchase. A clerk reviews the file every day to locate invoices near their due date and prepares a request for a cash disbursement document, such as a check requisition. When payment is made, the invoices will be marked as paid.

There are three issues with respect to liabilities:

- recognition
- valuation
- classification

A liability is recognized—recorded in the accounting records so that it will appear on the balance sheet—when an obligation is incurred. Liabilities are based on past transactions and are generally recognized when incurred. As we have seen with certain liabilities like *interest payable* or *unearned revenue*, end-of-period adjustments may be necessary to make sure the amounts are correct for the financial statements. Liabilities are valued at the amount due or at the fair market value of the goods or services that must be delivered.

On the balance sheet, liabilities are divided into two classifications based on *when* the company must fulfill the obligation. Current liabilities are liabilities that will be satisfied within 1 year. For example, accounts payable are current liabilities. Vendors typically expect payment within 30 days of receipt of the invoice.

Define the major classifications of liabilities.

BUSINESS PROCESS

Noncurrent, or long term, liabilities are liabilities that will be satisfied sometime beyond the next year. Notes payable usually represent an amount borrowed for a period of time longer than a year. If the note were a 2-year note, for example, it would be considered a noncurrent liability.

Certain types of noncurrent liabilities—such as mortgage debt—may have a current component and a noncurrent component. The section for current liabilities would include the portion of the debt that will be paid in the next year, and the section for noncurrent liabilities would include the remainder.

Common Types of Liabilities

All liabilities—current or long term—can be classified as:

- definitely determinable
- estimated
- contingent

Definitely determinable liabilities are liabilities that can be measured exactly. Examples are accounts payable, bank loans or lines of credit, or notes payable. Some accrued liabilities, such as dividends payable and unearned revenues, are definitely determinable because we know the amount of the obligation.

Estimated liabilities are obligations whose amount is not certain. Warranty liability is an example. Warranty liability is the estimated future costs for repair and replacement to honor a product's warranty. It's recorded at the time of the sale, so it has to be estimated. (We'll discuss this in the next chapter.) Other estimated liabilities include income taxes, property taxes payable, and vacation pay owed. These are all items that need to be recorded as expenses *before* the company knows the exact amounts.

Contingent liabilities are liabilities that are not currently recorded, but they are looming on the horizon. Past events have led to their potential existence, but a company won't know if they really do exist until *future* events, arising out of *past* transactions, reveal the facts. Lawsuits and tax disputes are two sources of contingent liabilities. For contingencies to be included on the balance sheet, they must meet two criteria:

1. The liability must be probable.
2. The amount must be reasonably estimable.

Talk about judgment. Interpreting the meaning of words like *probable* and *reasonably estimable* as they relate to different circumstances requires professional judgment and expertise. Accountants and attorneys help companies decide when liabilities meet these criteria.

Definitely determinable liabilities are obligations that can be measured exactly, like the amount of a note payable.

Estimated liabilities are obligations with some uncertainty in the amount owed, like the cost involved in honoring a warranty.

Contingent liabilities are obligations that have not been recognized at the date of the financial statements, but a *potential* liability exists. Disclosure is the important issue.

BUSINESS PROCESS

L.O. 9

Understand how payroll is calculated and reported.

Acquisition of Human Resources and Payroll Liabilities

Acquiring human resources—that's hiring employees—is similar to acquiring any resource for the company. All companies have employees, so payroll is a common business expense. Due to government requirements for information (as well as Social Security, Medicare, and income taxes) companies have always had to record a great deal more information about payroll than what is needed for accurate and timely financial statements. Hiring and paying employees is a business process that is well suited to the new integrated information systems, and many companies have implemented the part of an enterprise resource planning system that handles payroll.

Some of the steps in establishing an effective payroll system include:

- When an employee is hired, information concerning an employee's marital status and number of dependents is recorded for payroll deduction purposes.
- A company may require an employee to use *time cards* to record the amount of time worked each day.
- The payroll department reviews the time cards, verifies the pay rates, and calculates deductions for Social Security taxes (Federal Insurance Contributions Act [FICA]), federal and state income taxes, and net pay. These totals are recorded in a payroll register that is used by the accounts payable department to make a transfer of cash to the payroll checking account.

Many companies use a separate bank account from which paychecks are prepared and paid. A single check for the entire payroll is transferred to a separate account, and all employee paychecks are written from that account.

Let's look at the details of recording payroll information. We'll do it with the accounting equation, but keep in mind that the actual record keeping will be done quite differently. The results on the financial statements will be the same no matter how the record keeping is done.

Suppose Risky Company hired an employee to guard the company's building, and that employee is paid $500 per week. That amount is the employee's *gross pay*. As you may know from your work experience, this is not the amount the employee takes home.

From the gross pay amount, several deductions are made. First, income taxes are withheld. To withhold taxes means that the employer, Risky Company, deducts amounts from the employee's pay, withholds those specific amounts in the employee's name, and pays them as income taxes in the employee's name. The U.S. government *requires* employers to do this. In doing so, Risky Company is acting as an *agent* for the government. The company simply holds the money back from employees' checks, and then forwards the payment to the government. The amount forwarded for each employee depends on the specific employee's tax situation (e.g., single or married, children, level of income).

Second, the company is also required to deduct Social Security taxes at the current legal rate (6.2% at the time of this writing) and Medicare taxes at the current legal rate (1.45% at the time of this writing). These two amounts must be "matched" by the employer. That means in addition to being an agent for the government, the company must also make its own payment. The company's payment is classified as payroll tax expense, often grouped with *other expenses* on the income statement.

With that background, let's continue with the example. First, let's calculate the various amounts that must be withheld from the $500 gross pay of the employee. Assuming 20% is withheld for income taxes, Risky Company would deduct $100. We'll use Social Security taxes at 6.2%, which amounts to $31.00, and Medicare taxes at 1.45% amount to $7.25. So the amount Risky Company will pay to the employee is $361.75 (= $500 − $100 − $31.00 − $7.25). That amount is called net pay or net wages. The disbursement would affect the accounting equation as follows:

Assets	=	Liabilities	+ Contributed + Capital	Retained Earnings
$(361.75) Cash		+ $100 Income taxes payable (withheld) + $31.00 Social Security payable (withheld) + $7.25 Medicare payable (withheld)		$(500) Salary expense

The journal entry to record salary expense and payroll deductions would be:

Date	Transaction	Debit	Credit
	Salary expense	$500.00	
	Income taxes payable		$100.00
	Social Security taxes payable		31.00
	Medicare taxes payable		7.25
	Cash		361.75

When Risky Company makes payment to the government for Social Security and Medicare, the company will match those amounts. Often, these payments are made by the bank. A company "deposits" its payroll taxes, which actually means the bank makes the payment to the government for the company. The payment to the government, including the company's portion, affects the accounting equation, as shown next:

Assets	=	Liabilities	+	Contributed + Capital	Retained Earnings
$(176.50)ᵃ Cash		$(100) Income taxes payable (withheld) $(31.00) Social Security payable (withheld) $(7.25) Medicare payable (withheld)			$(38.25) Employer's payroll tax expense

ᵃ This includes the employers' portion in addition to that withheld from the employee—(31.00 + 7.25) × 2.

The journal entry to record payroll tax expense and the payment of the taxes is:

Date	Transaction	Debit	Credit
	Payroll tax expense	$ 38.25	
	Income taxes payable	100.00	
	Social Security taxes payable	31.00	
	Medicare taxes payable	7.25	
	Cash		$176.50

STUDY BREAK 6-6
SEE HOW YOU'RE DOING

Sandy earned $1,500 at her job at Paula's Bookstore during February. Sandy has 20% of her gross pay withheld for income taxes, 6.2% withheld for Social Security (FICA) taxes, and 1.45% withheld for Medicare taxes. Prepare the required payroll journal entries assuming that Paula's Bookstore will not submit the taxes to the government until the end of March.

Business Risks

L.O. 10

Understand the risks and controls associated with the purchase/acquisition process.

Two topics discussed in this chapter present special risks to business: (1) inventory, and (2) payroll. Let's look at each area—both at the risks and at the controls to help minimize those risks.

Inventory: Risks and Controls

Like any of a company's assets, the inventory must be protected from damage and theft. The risks associated with the actual purchase of the inventory—selecting a reliable vendor and making sure the items received are the ones ordered—are minimized by policies and procedures we've discussed in previous chapters. The physical safeguarding of the inventory is accomplished with controls like locked storage rooms and limited access. The policies and procedures for ordering inventory and for providing the inventory to the customer when it is purchased are important and should be designed with risk control in mind.

Separation of duties is a control that is needed to minimize the risk of losing inventory to error or theft. The person who keeps the records related to the inventory should be someone different than the person who has physical control of the inventory. This separation of record keeping and physical control of assets makes it impossible for a single individual to steal the inventory and cover it up with false record keeping. When this control is in place and functioning properly, it would take collusion—that's two or more people getting together to plan the fraud—to lose inventory in this way.

Liabilities: Risks and Controls

All areas of a company's record keeping are at risk for errors—both intentional and unintentional. We've discussed this information processing risk in earlier chapters. In the acquisition/payment process, one particular area that faces significant risk is payroll. The payroll policies and procedures need to ensure that only legitimate employees, who have performed the relevant work, are paid. Generally, the person who prepares the payroll checks should not be the person who distributes the checks. Controls need to exist to keep a payroll record-keeping clerk from making out checks to fictitious employees and routing the money to the clerk's own account. Again, separation of duties is a crucial and mandatory control for risk in the payroll area.

In the acquisition/payment process, just as in all business processes, the controls need to be in place, and then those controls need to be tested. When a company is audited by independent auditors, this is one of the jobs the auditors perform. They review the company's internal control system and verify that the existing controls are functioning properly.

Summary Problem: Tom's Wear Faces New Challenges in May

Tom's Wear began in January 2001, and has now completed 4 months of operating as a business. The April 30, 2001 balance sheet becomes the May 1, 2001 balance sheet as Tom's Wear begins May. Review the balance sheet, shown in Exhibit 6-6, before you work your way through the May transactions. The transactions for May are shown in Exhibit 6-7.

Required

1. Make the journal entries for the transactions and the adjusting entries needed for preparation of the financial statements. Post them to T-accounts, and prepare an adjusted trial balance.
2. Prepare the four basic financial statements for the month of May.

(To complete the problem, you'll need to use information from previous chapters.) [Solution is provided near the end of the chapter.]

Exhibit 6-6

Tom's Wear, Inc.
Balance Sheet
At May 1, 2001

Assets		Liabilities and shareholders' equity	
Cash	$ 3,295	Accounts payable	$ 4,000
Accounts receivable	8,000	Interest payable	310
Inventory	1,100	Short-term notes payable	3,000
Prepaid insurance	25	*Total current liabilities*	7,310
Prepaid rent	1,800		
Total current assets	*14,220*	Long-term notes payable	30,000
		Total liabilities	*37,310*
Computer (net of $200 accumulated depreciation)	3,800		
		Common stock	5,000
Van (net of $725 accumulated depreciation)	29,275	Retained earnings	4,985
		Total liabilities and shareholders' equity	
Total Assets	*$47,295*		*$47,295*

Exhibit 6-7
Transactions for May 2001 for Tom's Wear, Inc.

1	May 1	Pays cash for insurance premium, $300 for 3 months; coverage starts May 15.
2	May 10	Collects $7,900 on accounts receivable.
3	May 12	Pays accounts payable of $4,000.
4	May 14	Purchases 1,100 shirts @ $4 each for inventory for cash.
5	May 15	Agrees to sell school system 900 shirts @ $11 each; collects cash of $9,900 in advance of delivery. Half the shirts will be delivered by May 30, and the other half will be delivered in June.
6	May 20	Sells 800 shirts @ $11 each to sporting goods stores on account.
7	May 21	Hires Web designers to start a Web page; $200 for design and $50 per month maintenance fee, 6 months paid in advance. A full month of fee will be charged for May due to start-up costs.
8	May 30	Purchases 1,000 shirts @ $4.20 each, on account.
9	May 31	Note issued on March 1 for 3 months is repaid, with interest.

Note: Other information for May: The van was driven 6,000 miles in May.

Understanding Excel

For purposes of this problem only, assume that in the month of May, Tom's Wear engaged in the following transactions:

May 1, 2001	Beginning inventory was 500 shirts @ $4.00 each.
May 3, 2001	Tom purchased 300 shirts for $4.10 each.
May 5, 2001	Tom sold 600 shirts for $10.50 each.
May 15, 2001	Tom purchased 400 shirts for $4.20 each.
May 18, 2001	Tom sold 400 shirts for $10.50 each.
May 28, 2001	Tom purchased 200 shirts for $4.25 each.
May 30, 2001	Tom sold 100 shirts for $10.50 each.

Tom uses a periodic inventory system.

Requirements

1. Open a new Excel work sheet.
2. By beginning in cell A1, input the following chart based on the information presented previously. Input or calculate the values for the cells highlighted in blue.

   Hints: To sum the total goods available for sale, click on the appropriate cell C7 or E7 and select the Auto Sum ∑ button. Select Format, Cells, Number, and Date to format column A.

	A	B	C	D	E
1	Date	Activity	Units	Unit Cost	Total Cost
2					
3	1-May-01	Beginning balance			
4	3-May-01	Purchase			
5	15-May-01	Purchase			
6	28-May-01	Purchase			
7		Total goods available for sale			
8		Shirts sold			
9		Shirts in ending inventory			
10					

3. Calculate cost of goods sold and ending inventory under the FIFO, LIFO, and weighted-average methods. Remember to use formulas and information entered in cells A1 through E8 to calculate the amounts.

	A	B	C	D
11				
12		FIFO	LIFO	Weighted Average
13	Cost of goods sold			
14	Ending inventory			
15				

4. Calculate the net income under each of the three methods, by inputting the following schedule. The tax rate is 30%. Remember to use formulas where applicable and to copy cost of goods sold from row 13:

	A	B	C	D
16				
17	Income Statements	FIFO	LIFO	Weighted Average
18				
19	Sales			
20	Cost of goods sold			
21	Gross profit			
22	Operating expenses			
23	Income before taxes			
24	Income taxes			
25	Income after tax			

5. Print your file and save it to disk. Name your file TomsWear6.

Answers to Study Break Questions

Study Break 6-1

1. **A** Company took advantage of the discount. (**A** Company did not have to pay the freight): <u>**$9,800**</u>.
2. **B** Company did not take advantage of the discount and did not have to pay the freight: <u>**$10,000**</u>.
3. **C** Company did not take advantage of the discount. **C** did have to pay the freight: <u>**$10,090**</u>.
4. **D** Company took advantage of the discount, and **D** had to pay the freight: <u>**$9,890**</u>.

Study Break 6-2

1. **FIFO:** units sold were 30 @ $20 and 5 @ $21 for a total cost of goods sold of **$705.**
2. **LIFO:** units sold were 20 @ $23 and 15 @ $21 for a total cost of goods sold of **$775.**
3. **Weighted Average:** average cost is $1,480/70 units = $21.14 (rounded); cost of goods sold is $21.14 × 35 units = **$740** (rounded).

Date	Transaction	Debit	Credit
8/10/2001	Inventory	$600	
	Cash or accounts payable		$600
To record the purchase of 30 units @ $20 each			
8/15/2001	Inventory	$420	
	Cash or accounts payable		$420
To record the purchase of 20 units @ $21 each			
8/21/2001	Inventory	$460	
	Cash or accounts payable		$460
To record the purchase of 20 units @ $23 each			
8/30/2001	Cash or accounts receivable	$1,050	
	Sales		$1,050
	Cost of goods sold	705	
	Inventory		705
To record the sale of 35 units @ $30 each, using FIFO			
8/30/2001	Cash or accounts receivable	$1,050	
	Sales		$1,050
	Cost of goods sold	775	
	Inventory		775
To record the sale of 35 units @ $30 each, using LIFO			
8/30/2001	Cash or accounts receivable	$1,050	
	Sales		$1,050
	Cost of goods sold	740	
	Inventory		740
To record the sale of 35 units @ $30 each, using weighted average			

Study Break 6-3

Account	Amount	Revenue	Cost of goods sold	Other expenses
Administrative expenses	$ 57,000			$(57,000)
Income tax expense	9,000			Taxes appear below operating expenses on the income statement
Sales	617,000	$617,000		
Purchases	367,000		$(367,000)	
Delivery fees (freight-out)	10,900			(10,900)
Transportation-in	13,000		(13,000)	
Depreciation expense	6,000			(6,000)
Sales salaries	74,000			(74,000)
Purchase discounts	3,300		3,300	
Utilities expense	2,100			(2,100)

Beginning inventory	$ 60,000
+ Purchases	367,000
+ Transportation-in	13,000
− Purchase discounts	(3,300)
Goods available for sale	$ 436,700
− Ending inventory	(70,000)
Cost of goods sold	**$366,700**
Sales	$ 617,000
− Cost of goods sold	(366,700)
Gross profit	**$250,300**

If ending inventory is too low, then cost of goods sold is too high (overstated). In this case, cost of goods sold is overstated by $25,000. That means that net income is too low, because expenses were too high. Thus, net income should have been $767,640 (= $742,640 + 25,000).

Study Break 6-4

The inventory will be shown on the balance sheet at the *lower* of cost or market.

Study Break 6-5

Cost	Market	Balance sheet
$345,000	$350,000	$345,000
345,000	339,000	339,000

		Study Break 6-6
$1,500.00	Gross pay	
(300.00)	Income taxes	
(93.00)	FICA	
(21.75)	Medicare	
$1,085.25	**Net pay**	

The $414.75 withheld from Sandy's paycheck will be recorded as a liability by Paula's Bookstore. Paula's Bookstore owes that amount to the government. Actually, Paula's Bookstore is acting on Sandy's behalf—it's Sandy's money being paid to the government.

Date	Transaction	Debit	Credit
	Salary expense	$1,500.00	
	Income taxes payable		$300.00
	Social security taxes payable		93.00
	Medicare taxes payable		21.75
	Cash		1,085.25
	To record salary expense and payroll deductions		
	Payroll tax expense	$114.75	
	Social security taxes payable		93.00
	Medicare taxes payable		21.75
	To record employer payroll tax expense		

Solution to Summary Problem

Transaction 1

Pays $300 cash for an insurance premium. Coverage starts May 15.

Date	Transaction	Debit	Credit
5/1/2001	Prepaid insurance	$300	
	Cash		$300
	To record the purchase of insurance		

Transaction 2
Collects $7,900 on accounts receivable.

Date	Transaction	Debit	Credit
5/10/2001	Cash	$7,900	
	Accounts receivable		$7,900
To record the collection of accounts receivable			

Transaction 3
Pays accounts payable $4,000.

Date	Transaction	Debit	Credit
5/12/2001	Accounts payable	$4,000	
	Cash		$4,000
To record payment on account			

Transaction 4
Purchased 1,100 T-shirts at $4.00 each for cash.

Date	Transaction	Debit	Credit
5/14/2001	Inventory	$4,400	
	Cash		$4,400
To record the purchase of 1,100 T-shirts at $4 for cash			

Transaction 5
Agrees to sell school system 900 shirts @ $11 each. Collects cash of $9,900 in advance. Half the shirts will be delivered by May 30 and the other half in June.

Date	Transaction	Debit	Credit
5/15/2001	Cash	$9,900	
	Unearned revenue		$9,900
To record the collection of sales revenue in advance			

Transaction 6
Sells 800 shirts for $11 each on account.

Date	Transaction	Debit	Credit
5/20/2001	Accounts receivable	$8,800	
	Sales		$8,800
To record the sale of 800 T-shirts, on account			
5/20/2001	Cost of goods sold	$3,200	
	Inventory		$3,200
To record the expense cost of goods sold and reduce the inventory by 800 × $4			

Transaction 7
Hires web designers to start a web page—$200 for design and $50 per month maintenance, 6 months paid in advance. A full month's fee is being charged in May.

Date	Transaction	Debit	Credit
5/21/2001	Prepaid web services	$300	
	Miscellaneous operating expenses	200	
	Cash		$500
To record payment for web page setup and maintenance			

Transaction 8

Purchases 1,000 shirts at $4.20 each on account.

Date	Transaction	Debit	Credit
5/30/2001	Inventory	$4,200	
	Accounts payable		$4,200
To record the purchase of 1,000 shirts on account			

Transaction 9

Repays the 3-month note issued on March 1, with interest.

Date	Transaction	Debit	Credit
5/31/2001	Short-term notes payable	$3,000	
	Interest payable	60	
	Interest expense	30	
	Cash		$3,090
To record the repayment of the March 1 note, with interest			

Adjustment 1

Record insurance expense for May—$25 for the first half of the month (beginning prepaid insurance) and $50 for the second half of the month ($100 month beginning May 15).

Date	Transaction	Debit	Credit
5/31/2001	Insurance expense	$75	
	Prepaid insurance		$75
To record insurance expense for May			

Adjustment 2

Record rent expense of $1,200 for the month of May.

Date	Transaction	Debit	Credit
5/31/2001	Rent expense	$1,200	
	Prepaid rent		$1,200
To record rent expense for May			

Adjustment 3

Record web services expense for May.

Date	Transaction	Debit	Credit
5/31/2001	Miscellaneous operating expenses	$50	
	Prepaid web service		$50
To record web maintenance services for May			

Adjustment 4

Record depreciation expense for the van: 6,000 miles × $0.145.

Date	Transaction	Debit	Credit
5/31/2001	Depreciation expense	$870	
	Accumulated depreciation: van		$870
To record May depreciation expense on the van			

Adjustment 5

Record the $100 monthly depreciation expense on the computer.

Date	Transaction	Debit	Credit
5/31/2001	Depreciation expense	$100	
	Accumulated depreciation: computer		$100
To record May depreciation expense on the computer			

Adjustment 6

Half of the shirts were delivered to the school. Reclassify half of the unearned revenue as earned and record the cost of goods sold.

Date	Transaction	Debit	Credit
5/31/2001	Unearned revenue	$4,950	
	Sales		$4,950
To record delivery of half of the shirts to the school			
5/31/2001	Cost of goods sold	$1,800	
	Inventory		$1,800
To record the expense cost of goods sold and reduce the inventory by 450 × $4			

Adjustment 7

Accrue Sam Cubbie's $1,000 salary for May, including the employer portion of payroll taxes (Social Security 6.2%; Medicare 1.45%) and withholding tax 20%.

Date	Transaction	Debit	Credit
5/31/2001	Salary expense	$1,000	
	Employer's payroll tax expense	77	
	Payroll taxes withheld		$277
	Other payables		77
	Salaries payable		723
To record the accrual of Sam Cubbie's salary, withholding, and payroll taxes			

Adjustment 8

Accrue interest expense on the van note.

Date	Transaction	Debit	Credit
5/31/2001	Interest expense	$250	
	Interest payable		$250
To record the interest expense on the van for May			

T-Accounts for Tom's Wear with May Journal Entries and Adjustments

Cash
Debit		Credit	
BB	$3,295	1	$300
2	7,900	3	4,000
5	9,900	4	4,400
		7	500
		9	3,090
	$8,805		

Accounts receivable
Debit		Credit	
BB	$8,000	2	$7,900
6a	8,800		
	8,900		

Inventory
Debit		Credit	
BB	$1,100	6b	$3,200
4	4,400	Adj-6	1,800
8	4,200		
	4,700		

Prepaid insurance
Debit		Credit	
BB	$25	Adj-1	$75
1	300		
	250		

Prepaid rent
Debit		Credit	
5	$1,800	Adj-2	$1,200
	600		

Prepaid web service
Debit		Credit	
7	$300	Adj-3	$50
	$250		

Equipment: computer
Debit		Credit	
BB	$4,000		
	4,000		

Accumulated Depreciation: computer
Debit		Credit	
		BB	$200
		Adj-5	100
			300

Equipment: van
Debit		Credit	
BB	$30,000		
	30,000		

Accumulated Depreciation: van
Debit		Credit	
		BB	$725
		Adj-4	870
			1,595

Accounts payable
Debit		Credit	
3	$4,000	BB	$4,000
		8	4,200
			4,200

Interest payable
Debit		Credit	
			$310
9	60		250
			500

Short-term notes payable
Debit		Credit	
9	$3,000	BB	$3,000
			0

Salaries payable
Debit		Credit	
		Adj-7	$723
			723

Payroll taxes withheld
Debit		Credit	
			$277
		Adj-7	277

Other payables
Debit		Credit	
			$77
		Adj-7	77

Unearned revenue
Debit		Credit	
5	$4,950	BB	$9,900
			4,950

Long-term notes payable
Debit		Credit	
		BB	$30,000
			30,000

Common stock
Debit		Credit	
		BB	$5,000
			5,000

Retained earnings
Debit		Credit	
		BB	$4,985
			4,985

Revenue
Debit		Credit	
		6a	$8,800
		Adj-6	4,950
			13,750

Cost of goods sold
Debit		Credit	
6b	$3,200		
Adj-6	1,800		
	5,000		

Depreciation expense
Debit		Credit	
Adj-4	$870		
Adj-5	100		
	970		

Miscellaneous expenses
Debit		Credit	
7	$200		
Adj-3	50		
	250		

Insurance expense
Debit		Credit	
Adj-1	$75		
	75		

Rent expense
Debit		Credit	
Adj-2	$1,200		
	1,200		

Salary expense
Debit		Credit	
Adj-7	$1,000		
	1,000		

Employer's payroll tax expense
Debit		Credit	
Adj-7	$77		
	77		

Interest expense
Debit		Credit	
9	$30		
Adj-8	250		
	280		

Tom's Wear, Inc.
Adjusted Trial Balance
May 31, 2001

Cash	$ 8,805	
Accounts receivable	8,900	
Inventory	4,700	
Prepaid insurance	250	
Prepaid rent	600	
Prepaid web service	250	
Equipment: computer	4,000	
Accumulated depreciation: computer		$ 300
Equipment: van	30,000	
Accumulated depreciation: van		1,595
Accounts payable		4,200
Interest payable		500
Unearned revenue		4,950
Payroll taxes withheld		277
Other payables		77
Salaries payable		723
Long-term notes payable		30,000
Common stock		5,000
Retained earnings		4,985
Sales		13,750
Cost of goods sold	5,000	
Depreciation expense	970	
Other operating expense	250	
Employer's payroll tax expense	77	
Insurance expense	75	
Rent expense	1,200	
Interest expense	280	
Salary expense	1,000	
Totals	$66,357	$66,357

Financial Statements

Tom's Wear, Inc.
Income Statement
For the Month Ended May 31, 2001

Sales revenue		$13,750
Expenses		
Cost of goods sold	$ 5,000	
Insurance expense	75	
Rent expense	1,200	
Depreciation expense	970	
Salary expense	1,000	
Other operating expenses	327	
Interest expense	280	(8,852)
Net income		$ 4,898

Tom's Wear, Inc.
Statement of Changes in Shareholders' Equity
For the Month Ended May 31, 2001

Beginning contributed capital	$ 5,000	
Contributions during the month	0	
Ending contributed capital		$ 5,000
Beginning retained earnings	4,985	
Net income for the month	4,898	
Dividends	0	
Ending retained earnings		9,883
Total shareholders' equity		*$14,883*

Tom's Wear, Inc.
Balance Sheet
At May 31, 2001

Assets		Liabilities and Shareholders' equity	
Cash	$ 8,805	Accounts payable	$ 4,200
Accounts receivable	8,900	Interest payable	500
Inventory	4,700	Unearned revenue	4,950
		Salaries payable	723
Prepaid insurance	250	Payroll taxes payable	277
Prepaid rent	600	Other payables	77
Prepaid Web service	250	Total current liabilities	10,727
Total current assets	*23,505*	Notes payable	30,000
		Total liabilities	*40,727*
Computer (net of $300 accumulated depreciation)	3,700	Common stock	5,000
		Retained earnings	9,883
Van (net of $1,595 accumulated depreciation)	28,405		
		Total liabilities and	
Total assets	*$55,610*	*shareholders' equity*	*$55,610*

Tom's Wear, Inc.
Statement of Cash Flows
For the Month Ended May 31, 2001

Cash from operating activities		
Cash collected from customers	$17,800	
Cash paid for operating expenses	(800)	
Cash paid to vendors	(8,400)	
Cash paid for interest	(90)	
Total cash from operations		$8,510
Cash from investing activities		0
Cash from financing activities		
Repaid loan principal		(3,000)
Net increase (decrease) in cash		$5,510

$8,805	Ending cash balance (May 31)	
3,295	Beginning cash balance (May 1)	
$5,510	Net increase in cash	

Questions

1. What are the common cost flow methods for accounting for inventory? Describe the differences.
2. If inventory costs are rising, which method results in the lowest net income?
3. Does LIFO or FIFO give the best balance sheet value for the ending inventory? Why?
4. How do taxes affect the choice between LIFO and FIFO?
5. What is the difference between a periodic and perpetual inventory system?
6. Does the periodic or perpetual choice affect the choice of a cost flow (LIFO versus FIFO) method? Explain.
7. Why would it be necessary to estimate, instead of count, the ending inventory?
8. Does the shipping cost related to inventory affect the recorded inventory cost? Explain.
9. Explain the terms *FOB shipping point* and *FOB destination*. What are the accounting and business implications of the shipping terms? Why is it important to know who owns goods during shipping?
10. Explain the terms of a purchase described as *2/15, n/30*. Would you take advantage of this offer? Why or why not?
11. What is the *lower-of-cost-or-market* rule and why is it necessary?
12. If there were an error in the ending inventory, where else would there be an error in the financial statements?
13. What is a contingent liability?
14. According to GAAP, how should probable contingent losses that can be reasonably estimated be treated? What about gains?

Short Exercises

L.O. 6-1

SE6-1 The Woods Company purchased 500 electric saws from the Jordan's Equipment Company, FOB shipping point. Each electric saw cost $300. The saws are to be sold for $650 each. Woods paid $1,550 for freight and $280 for insurance while the saws were in transit. Woods Company also hired two more salespeople for a cost of $4,000 per month.

Calculate the cost of the inventory of electric saws to be recorded in Woods' accounting records.

SE6-2 Tone Company acquired 4,000 transformers from the Ochoa Company, FOB shipping point. Each transformer cost $100. Tone will sell them for $125 each. Tone paid $950 for freight and $200 for insurance while the transformers were in transit. Tone Company paid $900 to advertise the transformers in a local real estate magazine.

L.O. 6-1

What is the cost of the inventory of transformers that Tone will record in the accounting records?

SE6-3 Given the following information, calculate the amount by which taxable income would differ between FIFO and LIFO.

L.O. 6-2

Beginning inventory	5,000 units @ $100
Purchases	7,000 units @ $130
Units sold	6,000

SE6-4 Calculate the cost of the ending inventory using the weighted-average cost flow assumption:

L.O. 6-2

Sales	100 units @ $30 per unit
Beginning inventory	60 units @ $12 per unit
Purchases	80 units @ $13 per unit

SE6-5 How would each of the following inventory errors affect net income for the year? Assume each is the only error during the year.

L.O. 6-4

a. Ending inventory is understated by $3,000.
b. Ending inventory is overstated by $2,500.
c. Beginning inventory is overstated by $2,000.
d. Beginning inventory is understated by $1,000.

SE6-6 The Long Company records showed the following at the end of the fiscal year:

L.O. 6-4

Beginning inventory	$ 26,000
Ending inventory	38,000
Cost of goods sold	128,000

A physical inventory was taken and showed that the inventory was actually $39,000. If the Long Company fails to correct the error, what effect will it have on the financial statements for the year?

SE6-7 The Hawking Company records reported the following at the end of the fiscal year:

L.O. 6-4

Beginning inventory	$ 40,000
Ending inventory	28,500
Cost of goods sold	280,000

A physical count showed that the ending inventory was actually $26,000. If the inventory amount is not corrected, what is the effect on each of the financial statements?

SE6-8 Guessing Games, Inc. wants to estimate its inventory balance for its quarterly financial statements for the first quarter of the year. Given the following, what is your best estimate?

L.O. 6-5

Beginning inventory	$75,800
Net sales	$92,500
Net purchases	$50,500
Gross margin rate	30%

L.O. 6-6

SE6-9 The following information pertains to item 006A of inventory of the James Company:

	Per Unit
Cost	$180
Replacement cost	150
Selling price	195
Disposal costs	5
Normal profit margin	20%

How much should the balance sheet reflect for this inventory item?

L.O. 6-6

SE6-10 In each case, select the correct amount for the inventory on the year-end balance sheet:

a. Ending inventory at cost $24,500
    Ending inventory at replacement cost $27,000
b. Ending inventory at cost $27,000
    Ending inventory at replacement cost $24,500

What information, in addition to the amounts for the financial statements, does the comparison between cost and market provide to a company's management?

L.O. 6-7

SE6-11 Dayco Company ended its fiscal year with inventory recorded at its cost of $15,679. Dayco believes it will be able to sell the inventory for approximately $20,000. Due to changes in the market, Dayco would be able to replace this inventory for $15,000. How much will the Dayco balance sheet show for inventory on the year-end balance sheet?

Exercises

L.O. 6-1

E6-1 The Ribbon Company began operations on May 1. The following transactions took place in the month of May:

a. Cash purchases of merchandise during May were $300,000.
b. Purchases of merchandise on account during May were $400,000.
c. The cost of freight to deliver the merchandise to Ribbon Company was $25,000, paid in cash by Ribbon during May.
d. Ribbon returned $22,000 of merchandise purchased in part a to the supplier for a full refund.
e. The store manager's salary was $3,000 for the month.

Calculate the amount that the Ribbon Company should record for purchases of merchandise inventory for May.

L.O. 6-1

E6-2 The following information is given related to the purchases of inventory during the month of February:

Invoice price	$5,000
Terms of sale	2/10, n/30
Shipping terms	FOB Shipping point
Shipping costs	$250
Salary for inventory stocker	$750
Electricity for storage area	$300

Calculate the amount that would be recorded as the total cost of inventory. All invoices are paid within 5 days of receipt.

E6-3 For each of the following situations, calculate the amount that the purchasing company would record as the cost of the inventory purchase:

a. Invoice price of goods is $5,000. Purchase terms are 2/10, n/30 and the invoice is paid in the week of receipt. The shipping terms are FOB shipping point, and the shipping costs amount to $200.

b. Invoice price of goods is $3,000. Purchase terms are 4/10, n/30 and the invoice is paid in the week of receipt. The shipping terms are FOB destination, and the shipping costs amount to $250.

c. Invoice price of goods is $2,500. Purchase terms are 2/10, n/30 and the invoice is paid 15 days after receipt. The shipping terms are FOB shipping point, and the shipping costs amount to $250.

d. Invoice price of goods is $9,000. Purchase terms are 3/10, n/30 and the invoice is paid in the week of receipt. The shipping terms are FOB destination, and the shipping costs amount to $200.

E6-4 Sonic Corp. uses a periodic inventory system. At December 31, 2002, the end of the company's fiscal year, a physical count of inventory revealed an ending inventory balance of $220,000. The following items were *not* included in the physical count:

Merchandise shipped to a customer on December 30, FOB destination (goods arrived at customer's location on January 5, 2003)	$10,000
Merchandise shipped to a customer on December 29, FOB shipping point (merchandise arrived at customer's location on January 3, 2003)	5,000
Merchandise purchased from a supplier, shipped FOB destination on December 29, in transit at year-end	4,000

What should Sonic correctly report as the amount of inventory on their December 31, 2002 balance sheet?

E6-5 Given the following information:

January 1	Beginning inventory	20 gallons @ $10 each
February 28	Purchase	50 gallons @ $12 each
April 30	Purchase	40 gallons @ $13 each
September 15	Purchase	60 gallons @ $14 each
December 31	Ending inventory	35 gallons

a. Calculate the cost of goods sold and the cost of the ending inventory using FIFO.
b. Calculate the cost of goods sold and the cost of the ending inventory using LIFO.
c. Are you using perpetual or periodic accounting? Why?

E6-6 Given the following information, calculate the gross margin under FIFO and under LIFO:

Sales	200 units @ $50 per unit
Beginning inventory	50 units @ $40 per unit
Purchases	175 units @ $45 per unit

E6-7 Given the following information for March 2001, calculate the cost of goods sold for the month using LIFO periodic.

Inventory, March 1, 2001	10 units @ $5 each
Purchase, March 10	30 units @ $6 each
Sale, March 15	12 units
Purchase, March 20	15 units @ $7

L.O. 6-2, 3

E6-8 Given the following information for March 2001, calculate the cost of goods sold for the month using (1) FIFO periodic, and then using (2) FIFO perpetual. Explain when the two methods will produce a different amount for cost of goods sold.

Inventory, March 1, 2001	10 units @ $5 each
Purchase, March 10	30 units @ $6 each
Sale, March 15	12 units
Purchase, March 20	15 units @ $7

L.O. 6-2, 3

E6-9 Starnes TV Sales and Service began the month of May with two identical TV sets in inventory. During May, six additional TV sets (identical to the two in beginning inventory) were purchased as follows:

two on May 10
one on May 16
three on May 24

The company sold two of the TV sets on May 13, another one on May 18, and two more on May 27.

   a. Assume Starnes uses a perpetual inventory system and the FIFO cost flow method:

   (1) Which two TV sets were booked as cost of goods sold on May 13?
   (2) Which one was booked as cost of goods sold on May 18?
   (3) Which two TV sets were booked as cost of goods sold on May 27?
   (4) The cost of which three TV sets will be included in Starnes' inventory cost calculation at the end of May?

   b. If Starnes uses a periodic inventory system and the LIFO cost flow method, the cost of which three TV sets will be included in the inventory at the end of May?

L.O. 6-4

E6-10 Sloppy Company uses a periodic inventory system. On December 31, 2002, at the end of the fiscal year, the clerks miscounted the inventory left on hand. They counted $130,000 worth of inventory, but they forgot to count a stack of goods in the corner with a cost of $20,000. If this error goes undetected, how will it affect the financial statements for the year ending December 31, 2002 and the financial statements for the year ending December 31, 2003? Give the effect on each of the financial statements.

L.O. 6-4

E6-11 The Rim Company records reported the following at the end of the fiscal year:

Beginning inventory	$ 90,000
Ending inventory	60,000
Cost of goods sold	395,000

A physical inventory count showed that the inventory was actually $64,000. If this error is not corrected, what effect will it have on the financial statements for this fiscal year and for the following fiscal year?

L.O. 6-5

E6-12 The following information is available for the Rocklin Office Supply Company:

Inventory, October 1, 2000	$240,000
Net purchases for the month of October	750,000
Net sales for the month of October	950,000
Gross profit ratio (historical)	30%

Estimate the cost of goods sold for October and the ending inventory at October 31.

L.O. 6-5

E6-13 The records of Seattle Ship Products, Inc. revealed the following information related to inventory destroyed in an earthquake:

Inventory, beginning of period	$300,000
Purchases to date of earthquake	160,000
Net sales to date of earthquake	450,000
Gross profit ratio	30%

The company needs to file a claim for lost inventory with its insurance company. What is the estimated value of the lost inventory?

E6-14 A company calculated its inventory turnover for the past 2 years. This year the inventory turnover is approximately five, and last year the inventory turnover was approximately four. Will the company view this as good news or bad news? Does it indicate that more or less capital has been tied up in inventory this year compared with last year?

L.O. 6-7

E6-15 For each item in the list that follows, tell whether it is a definitely determinable liability, an estimated liability, or a contingent liability?

a. Amount owed to vendor for purchase of inventory.
b. Potential loss from a pending lawsuit.
c. Amount of warranty obligations.
d. Amount of loan payment due next year.
e. Amount of vacation pay to accrue for employees for next year.

L.O. 6-8

E6-16 If a company has gross payroll of $20,000, federal income tax withheld of $4,000, and FICA (Social Security) taxes withheld of $1,600:

a. How much will the balance sheet show for salaries payable (to employees)?
b. How much will the income statement show for salary expense?
c. What type of liability is salaries payable?

L.O. 6-9

E6-17 What risks are associated with inventory, and what specific controls minimize those risks?

L.O. 6-10

Problems—Set A

P6-1A The Battier Company made the following purchases in March of the current year:

L.O. 6-1

March 2	Purchased $5,000 of merchandise, terms 1/10, n/30, FOB shipping point
March 5	Purchased $2,000 of merchandise, terms 2/15, n/45, FOB shipping point
March 10	Purchased $4,000 of merchandise, terms 3/05, n/15, FOB destination

Required:

a. For each of the listed purchases, how many days does the company have to take advantage of the purchase discount?
b. What is the amount of the cash discount allowed in each case?
c. Assume the freight charges are $350 on each purchase. What is the total amount of freight that Battier has to pay?
d. What is the total amount of inventory costs for Battier Company for the month of March assuming that all discounts were taken?

P6-2A The Williams Company made the following purchases in May of the current year:

L.O. 6-1

May 3	Purchased $3,000 of merchandise, terms 2/10, n/30, FOB destination
May 12	Purchased $2,800 of merchandise, terms 2/10, n/60, FOB shipping point
May 22	Purchased $6,000 of merchandise, terms 3/05, n/20, FOB destination

Required:

a. For each purchase, when is the payment due assuming the company takes advantage of the discount?

b. For each purchase, when is the payment due if the company does not take advantage of the discount?

c. In each case, what is the amount of the cash discount allowed?

d. Assume the freight charges are $400 on each purchase. For which purchases is Williams Company responsible for the freight charges?

e. What is the total amount of inventory costs for the month of May assuming that all discounts were taken?

L.O. 6-2

P6-3A Jefferson Company had the following sales and purchases during 2003, its first year of business:

January 5	Purchase	40 units @ $100 each
February 15	Sale	15 units @ $150 each
April 10	Sale	10 units @ $150 each
June 30	Purchase	30 units @ $105 each
August 15	Sale	25 units @ $150 each
November 28	Purchase	20 units @ $110 each

Required: Calculate the ending inventory, the cost of goods sold, and the gross margin for the December 31, 2003 financial statements under each of the following assumptions:

a. FIFO perpetual
b. FIFO periodic
c. LIFO periodic
d. Weighted-average periodic

L.O. 6-2, 3

P6-4A The following series of transactions occurred during 2002:

January 1	Beginning inventory	50 units @ $10
January 15	Purchase	100 units @ $11
February 4	Sale	60 units @ $20
March 10	Purchase	50 units @ $12
April 15	Sale	70 units @ $20
June 30	Purchase	100 units @ $13
August 4	Sale	110 units @ $20
October 1	Purchase	80 units @ $14
December 5	Sale	50 units @ $21

Required: Calculate the value of the ending inventory and cost of goods sold using the following methods (each case is independent):

a. FIFO perpetual
b. FIFO periodic
c. LIFO periodic
d. Weighted-average periodic

L.O. 6-2, 3

P6-5A The For Fish Company sells commercial fish tanks. The company began 2002 with 10,000 units of inventory on hand. These units cost $150 each. The following transactions related to the company's merchandise inventory occurred during the first quarter of 2002:

January 20	Purchase	5,000 units @ $160 each
February 18	Purchase	6,000 units @ $170 each
March 28	Purchase	4,000 units @ $180 each
Total purchases		15,000 Units

All unit costs include the purchase price and freight charges paid by For Fish. During the quarter ending March 31, 2002, sales in units totaled 17,000 units leaving 8,000 units in ending inventory. The company uses a periodic inventory system.

Required: Calculate ending inventory at March 31 and cost of goods sold for the quarter using:

a. FIFO
b. LIFO
c. Weighted average

P6-6A Given the following information for Grant's Print Shop, Inc. for the year ending December 31, 2003, at January 1, 2003:

L.O. 6-2, 3

- Cash amounted to $19,375.
- Beginning inventory was $16,000 (160 units @ $100 each).
- Contributed capital was $15,000.
- Retained earnings was $20,375.

Transactions during 2003 included:

- The company purchased 150 units @ $110 each for cash.
- The company purchased 190 more units @ $120 each for cash.
- Cash sales were $290 units @ $200 each.
- The company paid $11,500 cash for operating expenses.
- The company paid cash for income tax at a rate of 30% of net income.

Required:

a. Compute the cost of goods sold and ending inventory using (1) FIFO, (2) LIFO, and (3) weighted average. (Are you using perpetual or periodic record keeping?)
b. Compute the net income before taxes and after taxes under each of the three inventory cost flow assumptions.
c. Prepare the 2003 balance sheets, income statements, and statements of cash flows for Grant's Print Shop, Inc., using all three inventory methods.

P6-7A The following merchandise inventory transactions occurred during the month of June for the Furlong Corp.:

L.O. 6-2, 3

June 1	Inventory on hand totaling 3,000 units @ $3.00 each
7	Sold 2,000 units
18	Purchased 4,000 units @ $3.50 each
21	Sold 5,000 units
27	Purchased 4,000 units @ $4.00 each

Required:

a. Calculate ending inventory at June 30 and cost of goods sold for the month using a periodic inventory system under each of the following cost flow methods:

1. Weighted-average cost
2. First-in, First-out (FIFO)
3. Last-in, First-out (LIFO)

b. Assume that Furlong uses the perpetual inventory system. What would be the *cost of goods sold* for the June 21 sale applying the FIFO inventory system?

P6-8A Cheny Company buys and then resells a single product. The product is a commodity and is subject to rather severe cost fluctuations. Following is information concerning the inventory activity during the month of June 2003:

L.O. 6-2, 3

June 1	Had 430 units on hand, $3,010
June 4	Sold 200 units
June 6	Purchased 500 units @ $11 per unit
June 10	Purchased 200 units @ $9 per unit
June 15	Sold 300 units
June 20	Purchased 150 units @ $6 per unit
June 25	Sold 400 units
June 29	Purchased 50 units @ $8 per unit

Cheny uses a perpetual inventory system.

Required: Calculate cost of goods sold (units and cost) for the month of June 2003 and ending inventory (units and cost) at June 30, 2003 using FIFO.

L.O. 6-2, 3

P6-9A Stiles Company and Wycoff Company both began their operations on January 2, 2004. Both companies had exactly the same amount of business during 2004. They purchased exactly the same number of units of merchandise inventory during the year at exactly the same cost, and they sold exactly the same number of inventory units at exactly the same selling price during the year. They also purchased exactly the same type and amount of property, plant, and equipment, paying exactly the same amount for those items. At the end of 2004, the two companies prepared income statements for the year. Stiles reported net income of $92,000 and Wycoff reported net income of $65,000.

What could have caused the reported net income for the two companies to be different?

L.O. 6-2, 3, 4

P6-10A Brickey, Inc., had 800 units of inventory on hand on April 1, 2002, costing $20 each. Purchases and sales of inventory during the month of April were as follows:

Date	Purchases	Sales
Beginning inventory	800 units @ $20 each	
April 5		500 units
15	400 units @ $21 each	
20	400 units @ $22 each	
27		400 units

Brickey uses a periodic inventory system.

Required:

a. Calculate the ending inventory using FIFO.
b. Calculate the ending inventory using LIFO.
c. Suppose that 100 units were left out of the count of the ending inventory. What effect would that have on the *cost of goods sold* under each of the cost flow assumptions in parts a and b?

L.O. 6-4

P6-11A Beard Company uses a perpetual inventory system, so both the cost of goods sold is recorded and the inventory records are updated at the time of every sale. The company's accounting records showed the following related to June 2003 transactions:

	Units	Cost
Beginning inventory, June 1	200	$ 600
+ Purchases during June	1,700	5,100
= Goods available for sale	1,900	$5,700
− Cost of goods sold	1,500	4,500
= Ending inventory, June 30	400	$1,200

On June 30, 2003, Beard conducted a physical count of its inventory and discovered there were only 375 units of inventory actually on hand.

Required:

a. Correct Beard's records to reflect the results of the physical inventory count.
b. How would this correction change the financial statements for the year?
c. What are some possible causes of the difference between the inventory amounts in the Beard Company's accounting records and the inventory amount from the physical count?

L.O. 6-5

P6-12A Carter Company sells peanuts to tourists on Route 15 in Georgia. A hurricane destroyed the entire inventory in late August. To file an insurance claim, Jimmy, the owner of the company, must estimate the value of the lost inventory. Records from January 1 through the date of the hurricane in August indicated that Carter Company started the year with $4,000 worth of inventory on hand. Purchases for the year amounted to $9,000, and sales up to the date of the hurricane were $16,000. Gross margin percentage has traditionally been 30%.

Required:

a. How much should the Carter Company request from the insurance company?
b. Suppose that one case of peanuts was spared by the hurricane. The cost of that case was $700. How much was the inventory loss under these conditions?

P6-13A The following information is given from the financial statements of Music Stores Corp.

L.O. 6-7

Required: Calculate the gross margin ratios and the inventory turnover ratios for the 2 years shown. What information do these comparisons give?

For year ended (in thousands)	December 31, 2004	December 31, 2003	December 31, 2002
Sales	$1,891,828	$1,846,882	
Cost of goods sold	1,200,993	1,190,582	
Inventory	444,492	446,710	$ 440,890

Problems—Set B

P6-1B The Winning Lacrosse Company made the following purchases in April of the current year:

L.O. 6-1

April 4	Purchased $6,000 of merchandise, terms 2/15, n/15, FOB shipping point
April 9	Purchased $7,500 of merchandise, terms 3/5, n/30, FOB destination
April 13	Purchased $8,000 of merchandise, terms 1/10, n/45, FOB shipping point

Required:

a. For each of the listed purchases, how many days does the company have to take advantage of the purchase discount?
b. What is the amount of the cash discount allowed in each case?
c. Assume the freight charges are $425 on each purchase. What is the total amount of freight that Winning Lacrosse Company has to pay?
d. What is the total amount of inventory costs for Winning Lacrosse Company for the month of April assuming that all discounts were taken?

P6-2B Billy Bob's Baseball Barn made the following purchases in March of the current year:

L.O. 6-1

March 1	Purchased $4,500 of baseball gloves, terms 3/15, n/25, FOB shipping point
March 10	Purchased $7,200 of sportswear, terms 2/10, n/20, FOB destination
March 15	Purchased $4,900 of softballs and baseballs, terms 1/05, n/15, FOB shipping point

Required:

a. For each purchase, when is the payment due assuming the company takes advantage of the discount?
b. For each purchase, when is the payment due if the company does not take advantage of the discount?
c. In each case, what is the amount of the cash discount allowed?
d. Assume the freight charges are $275 on each purchase. For which purchases is Billy Bob's Baseball Barn responsible for the freight charges?

e. What is the total amount of inventory costs for the month of May assuming that all discounts were taken?

L.O. 6-2, 3

P6-3B Sandy's Clean Carpet Company sells commercial vacuums. The company began June 30, 2003 with 15,000 units of inventory on hand. These units cost $200 each. The following transactions related to the company's merchandise inventory occurred during the first quarter of the year ended June 30, 2004:

July 15	Purchased	4,500 units for $210 each
August 28	Purchased	5,750 units for $190 each
September 10	Purchased	6,000 units for $185 each
Total purchases		*16,250 Units*

All unit costs include the purchase price and freight charges paid by Sandy's Clean Carpet. During the quarter ending September 30, 2003, sales in units totaled 19,500 units leaving 11,750 units in ending inventory. The company uses the periodic inventory system.

Required: Calculate ending inventory and cost of goods sold for the quarter ending September 30 using:

a. FIFO
b. LIFO
c. Weighted average

L.O. 6-2, 3

P6-4B The following information is given for Nan's Toy Extravaganza, Inc. for the year ended June 30, 2004:

At July 1, 2003:

- Cash amounted to $25,000.
- Beginning inventory was $32,000 (800 units @ $40 each).
- Contributed capital was $12,000.
- Retained earnings was $45,000.

Transactions for the year ended June 30, 2004:

- Nan's purchased 700 units @ $41 each for cash.
- The company purchased 300 more units @ $43 each for cash.
- The company had cash sales of 1,000 units @ $56 each.
- Nan's paid $7,500 cash for operating expenses.
- The company paid cash for income taxes at a rate of 40% of net income.

The company uses periodic record keeping.

Required:

a. Compute the cost of goods sold and ending inventory using (1) FIFO, (2) LIFO, and (3) weighted average. (Round unit cost calculations to the nearest cent.)
b. Compute the net income before taxes and after taxes under each of the three inventory cost flow assumptions.
c. Prepare the balance sheets, income statements, and statements of cash flows for the year ended June 30, 2004, under each of the three inventory cost flow assumptions.

L.O. 6-2, 3

P6-5B The following merchandise inventory transactions occurred during the month of November for Party Heaven, Inc.:

November	5	Inventory on hand, 2,000 units @ $4.00 each
	12	Sold 1,500 units
	16	Purchased 4,000 units @ $4.40 each
	23	Sold 4,300 units
	29	Purchased 5,000 units @ $5.00 each

Required: Calculate ending inventory at November 30 and cost of goods sold for the month using a periodic inventory system and each of the following cost flow methods:

1. Weighted-average cost
2. First-in, first-out (FIFO)
3. Last-in, first-out (LIFO)

P6-6B Hillary's Diamonds' buys and then resells a single product. The product, a diamond, is a commodity and is subject to rather severe cost fluctuations. Some information concerning Hillary's Diamonds' inventory activity during the month of June 2004 follows:

L.O. 6-2, 3

June 2	Had 860 units on hand, @ $7 per unit
June 6	Sold 400 units
June 8	Purchased 1,000 units @ $11 per unit
June 12	Purchased 400 units @ $9 per unit
June 15	Sold 600 units
June 21	Purchased 300 units @ $6 per unit
June 24	Sold 800 units
June 31	Purchased 100 units @ $8 per unit

Required: Hillary's Diamonds uses a periodic inventory system. Calculate cost of goods sold (in both units and cost) for the month of June 2004 and ending inventory (units and cost) at June 30, 2004, using each of the following cost flow assumptions:

a. FIFO.
b. LIFO.
c. Which of the two methods resulted in the highest cost of goods sold for June?
d. Which one will provide the highest ending inventory value for Hillary's balance sheet?
e. How would the differences between the methods affect Hillary's income statement and balance sheet for June?

P6-7B Brutus Company and Gabrielle Company both began their operations on July 1, 2005. Both companies had exactly the same amount of business during the fiscal year ended June 30, 2006. They purchased exactly the same number of units of merchandise inventory during the year at exactly the same cost, and they sold exactly the same number of inventory units at exactly the same selling price during the year. They also purchased exactly the same type and amount of property, plant, and equipment, paying exactly the same amount for those items. At the end of the fiscal year, the two companies prepared income statements for the year. Brutus reported a gross margin of $84,250 and Gabrielle reported a gross margin of $75,680.

L.O. 6-2, 3

Required:

a. If both companies reported $120,000 for sales revenue, what was the cost of goods sold for each?
b. What could have caused the reported gross margin for the two companies to be different? Be specific, and use some numbers to illustrate.

P6-8B Joe's Medical Supply, Inc. had 750 units of inventory on hand on August 1, 2008, at a cost of $30 each. Purchases and sales of inventory during the month of August were as follows:

L.O. 6-2, 3, 4

Date	Purchases	Sales
Beginning inventory	750 units @ $30 each	
August 4		550 units
12	325 units @ $28 each	
23	275 units @ $26 each	
31		500 units

The company uses a periodic inventory system.

Required:

    a. Calculate the ending inventory using FIFO.

    b. Calculate the ending inventory using LIFO.

    c. Suppose that 50 units were left out of the count of the ending inventory. What effect would that omission have on the *cost of goods sold* under each of the cost flow assumptions in parts a and b?

L.O. 6-4

P6-9B   Barney's Flowerpot Company uses a perpetual inventory system, so the cost of goods sold is recorded and the inventory records are updated at the time of every sale. The company's accounting records showed the following related to June 2004 transactions:

	Units	Cost
Beginning inventory, June 1	200	$ 600
+ Purchases during June	1,700	5,100
= Goods available for sale	1,900	$5,700
− Cost of goods sold	1,500	4,500
= Ending inventory, June 30	400	$1,200

On June 30, 2004, Barney conducted a physical count of its inventory and discovered there were actually 425 units of inventory actually on hand.

Required:

    a. Give the adjustment that would correct Barney's Flowerpot Company's records to reflect the results of the physical inventory count.

    b. How would this correction change the financial statements for the year?

    c. What are some possible causes of the difference between the inventory amounts in Barney's Flowerpot Company accounting records and the inventory amount from the physical count?

L.O. 6-5

P6-10B   Cynthia's Cotton Candy Company sells cotton candy to visitors at a traveling county fair. During a drought a fire destroyed the entire inventory in late July. To file an insurance claim, Cynthia, the owner of the company, must estimate the value of the lost inventory. Records from January 1 through the date of the fire in August indicated that Cynthia's Cotton Candy Company started the year with $4,250 worth of inventory on hand. Purchases for the year amounted to $8,000, and sales up to the date of the fire were $17,500. Gross margin percentage has traditionally been 35%.

Required:

    a. How much should the company request from the insurance company?

    b. Suppose that one bag of cotton candy mix was spared by the fire. The cost of that bag was $50. How much was the inventory loss under these conditions?

L.O. 6-7

P6-11B   The following information is given in the financial statements of Bessy's Salsa, Inc. for 2003 and 2004. Also, the inventory on December 31, 2002 amounted to $528,850.

Required: Calculate the gross margin ratios and the inventory turnover ratios for the 2 years shown. What information do these comparisons give?

For year ended	December 31, 2004	December 31, 2003
Sales	$1,732,571	$1,642,352
Cost of goods sold	1,105,725	1,118,745
Inventory	337,781	526,820

Recording Transactions

R6-1 (SE6-1) The Woods Company purchased 500 electric saws from the Jordan's Equipment Company. Each electric saw cost $300. The saws are to be sold for $650 each. Woods paid $1,550 for freight and $280 for insurance while the saws were in transit. Woods Company also hired two more salespeople for a cost of $4,000 per month. Give the journal entry for the purchase of inventory. Assume the company uses perpetual record keeping for inventory.

Date	Account	Debit	Credit

R6-2 (SE6-2) Tone Company acquired 4,000 transformers from the Ochoa Company. Each transformer cost $100. Tone will sell them for $125 each. Tone paid $950 for freight and $200 for insurance while the transformers were in transit. Tone Company paid $900 to advertise the transformers in a local real estate magazine. Give the journal entry for the purchase of inventory. Assume the company uses perpetual record keeping for inventory.

Date	Account	Debit	Credit

R6-3 (SE6-7) The Hawking Company's records reported the following at the end of the fiscal year:

Beginning inventory	$ 40,000
Ending inventory	28,500
Cost of goods sold	280,000

A physical count showed that the ending inventory was actually $26,000. What is the journal entry needed to correct the accounting records?

Date	Account	Debit	Credit

R6-4 (E6-1) The Ribbon Company began operations on May 1. The following transactions took place in the month of May.

a. Cash purchases of merchandise during May were $300,000.
b. Purchases of merchandise on account during May were $400,000.
c. The cost of freight to deliver the merchandise to Ribbon Company was $25,000, paid in cash by Ribbon during May.
d. Ribbon returned $22,000 of merchandise purchased in part a to the supplier for a full refund.
e. The store manager's salary was $3,000 for the month.

Assume Ribbon Company uses periodic record keeping for inventory. Give the journal entry for each transaction described above.

Transaction	Account	Debit	Credit

R6-5 (E6-3) For each of the following situations, give the journal entry that the purchasing company would record for the inventory purchase (including the cost of the freight, where applicable). Assume any freight charges are paid in cash at the time of receipt. Then, record the payment to the vendor for each purchase. Assume the company uses periodic record keeping. Assume discounts are recorded only when the payment is actually made and the purchase discount is taken.

  a. Invoice price of goods is $5,000. Purchase terms are 2/10, n/30, and the invoice is paid in the week of receipt. The shipping terms are FOB shipping point, and the shipping costs amount to $200.

  b. Invoice price of goods is $3,000. Purchase terms are 4/10, n/30, and the invoice is paid in the week of receipt. The shipping terms are FOB destination, and the shipping costs amount to $250.

  c. Invoice price of goods is $2,500. Purchase terms are 2/10, n/30, and the invoice is paid in 15 days after receipt. The shipping terms are FOB shipping point, and the shipping costs amount to $250.

  d. Invoice price of goods is $9,000. Purchase terms are 3/10, n/30, and the invoice is paid in the week of receipt. The shipping terms are FOB destination, and the shipping costs amount to $200.

Transaction	Account	Debit	Credit

R6-6 (E6-16) For a specific accounting period, a company has gross payroll of $20,000, federal income tax withheld of $4,000, and FICA (Social Security) taxes withheld of $1,600. Give the journal entry(s) to record the salary expense for the period. Include any related employer expenses.

Date	Account	Debit	Credit

R6-7 (P6-1A) The Battier Company made the following purchases in March of the current year:

- March 2: Purchased $5,000 of merchandise, terms 1/10, n/30, FOB shipping point
- March 5: Purchased $2,000 of merchandise, terms 2/15, n/45, FOB shipping point
- March 10: Purchased $4,000 of merchandise, terms 3/5, n/15, FOB destination

Required: Record the journal entries for each purchase. In each case, the freight charges are $350 and are paid in cash. Assume Battier Company records purchases at the full invoice amount and records purchase discounts only when the payment to the vendor is made and the discount is taken. The company uses perpetual record keeping for inventory.

Date	Account	Debit	Credit

R6-8 (P6-5A) The For Fish Company sells commercial fish tanks. The company began 2002 with 10,000 units of inventory on hand. These units cost $150 each. The following transactions related to the company's merchandise inventory occurred during the first quarter of 2002:

January 20	Purchase	5,000 units for $160 each
February 18	Purchase	6,000 units for $170 each
March 28	Purchase	4,000 units for $180 each
Total Purchases		*15,000 units*

The costs shown include all related inventory costs. During the quarter ending March 31, 2002, sales in units totaled 17,000 units, leaving 8,000 units in ending inventory. The company uses a periodic record-keeping system.

Required: Give the journal entry required at March 31 to record the cost of goods sold for the quarter using:

a. FIFO
b. LIFO
c. Weighted-average

Date	Account	Debit	Credit

R6-9 (P6-8A) Cheny Company buys and then resells a single product. The product is a commodity and is subject to rather severe cost fluctuations. Following is information concerning Cheny's inventory activity during the month of June 2003:

June 1	430 units on hand, $3,010
June 4	Sold 200 units
June 6	Purchased 500 units @ $11 per unit
June 10	Purchased 200 units @ $9 per unit
June 15	Sold 300 units
June 20	Purchased 150 units @ $6 per unit
June 25	Sold 400 units
June 29	Purchased 50 units @ $8 per unit

Cheny uses a perpetual, FIFO inventory system.

Required: Assume Cheny sold each unit for $20 per unit. Give the journal entries to record the sales and reduction in inventory if appropriate:

Date	Account	Debit	Credit

R6-Comprehensive

Chapter 6: Comprehensive Financial Statement Preparation Problem

This is the post-closing trial balance for Tulsa Tire Company, prepared on December 31, 2004:

Account	DR	CR
Cash	$200,000	
Accounts receivable	130,000	
Merchandise inventory	100,000	
Accounts payable		$150,000
Salaries payable		4,000
Long-term notes payable		50,000
Common stock		126,000
Retained earnings		100,000
	$430,000	$430,000

The following events took place during January 2005. Tulsa Tire uses perpetual FIFO as its inventory method. The inventory on hand at 12/31/04 consisted of 10,000 tires that cost $10 each.

1. Purchased 1,000 tires for $12 each, on account.
2. Paid salaries owed to employees at 12/31/04.
3. Sold 500 tires to various tire stores for $20 each, on account.
4. Collected $100,000 from customers.
5. Paid entire accounts payable balance (including purchase in 1 above).
6. Purchased 1,000 tires for $13 each, on account.
7. Sold 5,000 tires to various tire stores for $20 each, on account.
8. To reduce inventory at the end of the month, sold 5,000 tires for $20 each, with terms 2/10, n/30, and FOB destination. Shipping costs, paid in cash, were $250. Sales discounts are recorded if and when the customers take them.
9. Made a payment on the long-term loan of $5,000. Of this amount, $4,500 was principal and $500 was interest for January.
10. Recorded accrued expense for January (to be paid in February): utilities $500, salaries $4,500, other expenses $3,000.

Required: Prepare the income statement, balance sheet, and statement of cash flows for January 2005.

Issues for Discussion

Financial statement analysis

1. Use the financial statements of Pier 1 Imports, Inc. to answer the following questions:
   a. What inventory methods does the company use?
   b. Compute the inventory turnover ratio for at least two consecutive years. (The company's inventory at year-end for fiscal 1999 was $258,773 thousand.) What information does this provide?
   c. Is cost of goods sold a significant expense for the company? How can you tell?

Business risk

2. A potential control for managing the risk of employee fraud is to require employees to take vacations. Relate that control to the payroll function. Why would it be a good idea to require the payroll clerk, who writes the checks, to go on vacation?

Ethics

3. Jim's Music Company uses LIFO for inventory, and the company's profits are quite high this year. The cost of the inventory has been steadily rising all year, and Jim is worried about his taxes. His accountant has suggested that the company make a large purchase of inventory to be received during the last week in December. The accountant has explained to Jim that this would reduce his income significantly.
   a. Jim doesn't understand the logic of the accountant's suggestion. Explain how the purchase would affect taxable income.
   b. Is this ethical? Jim is uncertain about the appropriateness of this from a legal and an ethical perspective. Give your opinion and explain the ethical implications of making the purchase.

Internet Exercise: Coca-Cola Company

Coca-Cola Company is the world's largest producer of soft drink concentrates, syrups, and juices. The firm does no actual bottling, but sells more than 230 brands of beverages in 200 nations. Coca-Cola products include Coca-Cola Classic, Diet Coke, Sprite, Fanta, Mr. Pibb, Mello Yello, and Minute Maid.

Please go to the www.prenhall.com/myphlip *Web site, register, and add this textbook to your myphilip page (if you haven't done so already). Go to Chapter 6 and use the Internet Exercise company link.*

IE6-1 Use the "search" scroll bar to select *Ticker* and then search for KO, the stock symbol for Coca-Cola Company. Click on the *Financials* tab. Under "Free Financial Information" click on *Annual Financials*.

  a. For the three most recent years, identify the amounts reported for revenue and total net income. Is revenue increasing or decreasing? Is total net income increasing or decreasing? Are these trends favorable or unfavorable? Explain why or why not.
  b. For the three most recent years, identify the amount reported for the gross profit margin (gross margin on sales ratio). Is the trend for this ratio increasing or decreasing? Is it considered favorable or unfavorable? What might this trend indicate?
  c. For the three most recent years, identify the amount reported for cost of goods sold and ending inventories. For the two most recent years, calculate the inventory turnover ratio. Is Coca-Cola selling inventory more quickly in the most recent year? How can you tell? Is this good for Coca-Cola? Explain why or why not.
  d. Review the information gathered in the preceding a through c and comment on the overall profitability of Coca-Cola Company.

IE6-2 Click on the *Company Capsule* tab and then on the URL for Coca-Cola Company (http://www.cocacola.com).

  a. Take the *Virtual Plant Tour* and explore "Ingredient Delivery." What are the ingredients of Coca-Cola? Which ingredient is rigorously filtered and cleansed? Explain why. Can you open the truck door and load the ingredients onto the loading dock? Close the *Virtual Plant Tour* window.
  b. Under "Business Today" select the *Investor Center* and then the most recent annual report. "Operations Review" reports worldwide unit case volume. Does Coca-Cola report greater domestic or international unit case volume? What percentage of the Coca-Cola worldwide case volume is from outside North America? Does the global economy impact the Coca-Cola sale of inventory? Explain why or why not.

Please note: Internet Web sites are constantly being updated. Therefore, if the information is not found where indicated, please explore the Web site further to find the information.

SALES AND COLLECTION CYCLE

**Inventory
and
Liabilities**

Here's where you've been...

In Chapter 6, you learned about how a company acquires and accounts for inventory and payables. You learned to value inventory with cost flow assumptions like LIFO and FIFO and how that information is shown on a company's financial statements.

Here's where you're going...

When you are finished with Chapter 7, you should understand how a company accounts for *sales, cash,* and *accounts receivable*. You'll learn how that information is presented on the financial statements.

Sales and Accounts Receivable

7

Financing

Property, Plant, and Equipment

Sales and Accounts Receivable

Financial Reporting and Business Events

Inventory and Liabilities

Learning Objectives

More specifically, when you are finished studying this chapter, you should be able to answer these questions:

1. How are sales for cash and sales on account made, recognized, and reported?
2. What is a bank (cash) reconciliation? How is it done? Why is it necessary?
3. How does a company estimate, report, and evaluate the effects of uncollectible accounts?
4. How are credit card sales recorded and reported?

5. How does a company estimate and report warranties and the related expenses?
6. What information about accounts receivable is disclosed on the financial statements? How can we use it to help us evaluate the business?
7. What risks are associated with sales, cash, and accounts receivable?

BUSINESS PROCESS

The two business activities discussed in Chapter 5—the purchase of property, plant, and equipment—and in Chapter 6—the acquisition of inventory—are done by a business in preparation for its revenue-generating activities. These activities in the acquisition/payment process set the stage for the sales and collection process. The business process of making a sale and accounting for the sale are closely related. When the managers of a company make decisions about what to sell and how much to charge for it, they use accounting information. Conversely, the accounting information reflects the underlying business process.

Sales, for example, are reported net of sales discounts given to customers. The business decision to give sales discounts will be reflected in the accounting related to those sales, and the accounting information about sales discounts will be an input into the subsequent decisions about sales discounts. A similar relationship exists between the business decision to offer a warranty and accounting for warranties. When a company makes a decision about offering a warranty on a product, it must consider the full cost of that warranty. The accounting treatment, which we will discuss in more detail later in this chapter, includes matching the full cost of a warranty with its related sale. The information needed for the decisions about warranties and the accounting treatment reflect the close link between the business process and accounting for the business transactions. As the transactions in the sales and collection process are discussed, you will see this close link between the underlying business process and the related accounting.

Sales Cycle

Understand how a business makes cash and credit sales.

We discussed the steps in the sales and collection process, shown in Exhibit 7-1, briefly back in Chapter 1. Technology has made it possible for computers to do some of those steps. Whether a firm performs the steps manually or with a computer, the objectives of those steps are the same:

Understanding Business

MANAGING ACCOUNTS RECEIVABLE

Accounts receivable is commonly one of a company's largest current assets. Because current assets support operations, managing the size of those assets and the timing of their use or conversion to cash is a crucial business activity.

How does a company control the size of its accounts receivable? The obvious way is to set credit policies that help achieve the desired level of credit sales and related collections. If the amount of a company's accounts receivable is larger than the company desires, it can tighten credit policies to reduce the amount of credit sales or it can increase collection efforts to speed up the collection of the related cash. If a company has a small amount of accounts receivable and is willing to increase that amount, the company may want to loosen its credit policies. Companies often do that when they want to increase sales.

There are other, less obvious ways for a company to manage its accounts receivable. If a company has a large amount of accounts receivable and it needs cash

for operations, the company may sell its accounts receivable to a bank or finance company. This is called *factoring* accounts receivable, and the buyer is called a *factor*. When a company sells accounts receivable to a factor, the factor will keep a percentage of the value of the accounts receivable, similar to a credit card provider. For example, if a company sold $100,000 worth of receivables, the factor would pay the company a percentage of the face value of the receivables—often between 97% and 98%. The company removes the total accounts receivable from its records and records the remaining 2% or 3% as factoring expense. The factor takes ownership of the receivables and collects the accounts receivable as they come due.

Managing accounts receivable is an important part of the sales and collection business process. Accounting information—the size and collection time for accounts receivable—provides crucial input for the decisions in this process.

- to assure that the firm sells its goods or services to customers who will pay
- to assure that the goods or services delivered are what the customers order
- to assure that the customers are billed correctly
- to make sure the money received in payment gets deposited into the firm's appropriate bank accounts

Many steps in the sales and collection process—planning, marketing, and production—must take place before a company can make a sale and fill its customers' orders. To prepare the financial statements, we are particularly interested in:

Exhibit 7-1   Sales and Collection Process

1. recording the sale to make sure the revenue is recognized in the appropriate accounting period
2. collecting the payment for the goods or services and making sure that the payment is properly recorded

Timing of Revenue Recognition

Explain when revenue should be recognized.

In Chapter 3, you learned that the timing of business transactions and the timing of their appearance on the financial statements are important in accounting. Revenue is *recognized*—in an accounting manner of speaking—when it is reported on the income statement. When to recognize revenue has been a high-profile issue in accounting for the past several years. *Fortune Magazine's* August 2, 1999 cover story addressed the problems with the attempts of management to "manage" earnings by varying the timing of revenue recognition.

Corporate executives are anxious to show that the business has earned revenue. Sometimes *managing* earnings becomes *manipulating* earnings. One of the most common ways to manipulate earnings is by cheating with respect to the timing of revenue recognition. The Securities and Exchange Commission (SEC) is very concerned with *when* a company recognizes revenue.

Consider an information technology company—like IBM or Hewlett Packard—that provides hardware, software, support, and training for the information systems it sells. Over a period of several years, the company will perform work to earn the revenue for this complicated sale. How should the revenue be recognized? Remember that accrual accounting is not concerned with when the cash is collected. The timing of cash collection does not dictate the timing of revenue recognition. If you don't have an answer to this question, you are not alone. The chief financial officer for IBM wrestles with this problem every day.

Recall from Chapter 2 that, according to the accounting standards, revenue is recognized when "the earnings process is virtually complete" and collection is reasonably assured. Whatever a company must do to earn the revenue must be substantially done before the revenue appears on the income statement. Generally accepted accounting principles (GAAP) says that the work must be substantially completed and the cash collection must be reasonably assured. *Virtually, substantially,* and *reasonably assured* are words that leave a lot of room for interpretation and judgment. This is a very complicated problem even for the most experienced accountant.

In practice, revenue for services is recognized when the work is completed. For sales, revenue is typically recognized when the goods are delivered. For example, when Intel sells computer chips to IBM, the time the shipment leaves Intel will most likely be the point at which Intel recognizes the revenue—not when the order is placed and not when IBM pays for the purchase. Notice that this step—delivery of the goods—is preceded by many crucial activities in the sales and collection process—planning, marketing, and securing orders, for example. Yet, no revenue is recognized until it is actually *earned*. It is easy to see that in many situations it may be difficult to identify exactly when the earnings process is virtually complete. Does payment have to be received before revenue is recognized? *No!* Remember, GAAP is accrual accounting.

Revenue Recognition: Some Examples

Let's look at some examples that illustrate the difficulty in judging the timing of revenue recognition. If you've ever traveled by airplane, you have probably purchased your ticket well in advance of your actual trip. Airlines usually require payment in advance. When should Delta Airlines recognize the revenue from your payment for a flight? Delta should recognize the revenue only after it has actually provided the service—transported you via the flight you purchased. As you might expect, Delta reports a significant liability each year on its balance sheet for *advanced ticket sales,* Delta's term for *unearned revenue.*

Do you buy season tickets to see your favorite sports team? During the winter months when the Atlanta Braves collect hundreds of thousands of dollars for season tickets, they do not recognize any revenue, because they have not earned it at that time. As the baseball season progresses and games are played, the revenue is earned and, therefore, recognized. If the financial statements of the Braves were publicly available, we would see a liability reflecting the unearned revenue at certain times of the year, whenever they have collected money for games not yet played. By the time a current year of revenue is earned, the Braves' ticket office is collecting money for season tickets for the next year.

If the Atlanta Braves collected $450,000 in advance ticket sales in March 2001 before the first game is played and 10% of the ticket sales related to games played in April, the journal entries to record the receipt of the cash in March to record collection for advance ticket sales would be:

Date	Transaction	Debit	Credit
3/2001	Cash	$450,000	
	Unearned ticket revenue		$450,000

The entry to recognize revenue earned from advance ticket sales would be:

Date	Transaction	Debit	Credit
4/2001	Unearned revenue	$45,000	
	Ticket revenue earned		$45,000

Both the airlines selling tickets for future flights and the baseball team selling tickets for games not yet played must make a judgment about when to recognize the revenue from their ticket sales. It is a question of timing. Many other businesses have difficult judgments to make concerning revenue recognition. We'll leave those problems to more advanced accounting classes where specific problems with revenue recognition like this will be discussed.

The FSU ticket office has sold $100,000 worth of tickets for the upcoming football season. There are six home games. Prepare the journal entry to record this sale, assuming the tickets were sold several months before the football season starts. Prepare the journal entries to record the revenue recognition in September (half the games played) and October (one-third of the games played).

STUDY BREAK 7-1
SEE HOW YOU'RE DOING

Sales Discounts

A company will frequently offer a cash discount as an incentive for customers to pay their bills promptly. This practice is common in wholesale markets. These discounts, called sales discounts, are just like purchase discounts, but now we are on the other side. A business decision to offer discounts must include the cost of offering such discounts. The accounting for sales discounts reflects the economic consequences of offering the discounts.

 L.O. 1

Understand how sales are made and reported.

BUSINESS PROCESS

Sales discounts are typically expressed as:

$$2/10, n/30$$

Recall that what the first part—2/10—means is this: If the bill is paid within 10 days of the invoice date, then the buyer will receive a 2% discount off the invoice price. So when you see 2/10, think about it as a 2% discount for paying the bill in full within 10 days of the invoice date. Recall that the second part—n/30—means: If the bill is not paid within 10 days, then the full amount—no discount—is due within 30 days. So when you see n/30, think of n as meaning *no discount* and the bill must be paid in 30 days. If the bill isn't paid within 30 days, it is considered past due. Just as with any bill you do not pay on time, the penalty varies. Often there is a late fee if a bill is not paid on time.

Sales discounts work like purchase discounts. The only difference is whether you are *offering* the discount to your customers—sales discounts—or whether you are *being offered* the discount by one of your vendors—purchase discounts. As a customer, taking advantage of such discounts can amount to significant savings. As a seller, you would offer the sales discounts as an incentive for customers to buy from you and to pay you early.

Sales discounts are deducted from sales on the income statement. Sales discounts are recorded in a separate account called a *contra-revenue* account. It's called *contra-revenue* because it is deducted from a revenue account. The word *contra* means *opposite*. Recall that a contra-asset, like accumulated depreciation, is deducted from an asset account.

Suppose you sold $1,000 worth of merchandise to a customer with the terms 2/10, n/30, and the customer paid within the discount period. The transactions would affect the accounting equation as shown:

Assets	=	Liabilities	+	Contributed capital	+	Retained earnings
The sale						
+1,000 Accounts receivable						+1,000 Sales
The collection						
+980 Cash						(20) Sales
(1,000) Accounts receivable						discounts

The journal entry to record the sale of inventory, terms 2/10, n/30 is:

Date	Transaction	Debit	Credit
	Accounts receivable	$1,000	
	Sales		$1,000

The journal entry to record accounts receivable collections is:

Date	Transaction	Debit	Credit
	Cash	$980	
	Sales discounts	20	
	Accounts receivable		$1,000

The sales discount is shown as a reduction in retained earnings because a sales discount reduces net income. The income statement would show sales of $1,000 minus sales discounts of $20, giving a net sales amount of $980.

In March, Good Buy Company sold merchandise for $3,500, terms 3/10, n/30. Customers always take advantage of cash discount offers. Prepare the journal entries to record Good Buy Company's March sales and accounts receivable collections.

Sales Returns

As you may know from standing in line on December 26 to return a Christmas gift you didn't like, customers often return merchandise. Most companies accept returns. When goods are returned, sometimes a full refund is issued—in cash or with a credit to the customer's account. Other times, the customer is given a partial refund or some credit toward a replacement purchase. A business typically keeps track of the amount of sales returns because it is useful information for evaluating the performance of its products. This, in turn, is important information for decisions, such as how much inventory to purchase and which suppliers provide high-quality goods. In the accounting records, the amount of returned goods is kept separate from sales. Sales returns is a contra-revenue account, contra to sales, just like sales discounts. For example, if you sold merchandise for $10,000 and $2,000 of it was returned, you would want to be able to see both numbers. If you simply reduced sales whenever there was a return, you would not be able to identify the amount that was sold and the amount that was returned. There is different information in the fact that sales were $10,000 but that $2,000 worth of merchandise was returned, compared with simply knowing that sales of $8,000 were made. Once again, it is clear that the accounting treatment of a business transaction is important to the underlying business process. The amount of sales returns is very important information for any merchandising firm. The amount of the returns—called sales returns—is deducted from sales to arrive at net sales on the income statement.

The journal entry for the merchandise sale is:

Date	Transaction	Debit	Credit
	Cash or accounts receivable	$10,000	
	Sales		$10,000

The entry for the return of merchandise is:

Date	Transaction	Debit	Credit
	Sales returns	$2,000	
	Cash or accounts receivable		$2,000

L.O. 1

Understand how sales are made and recorded.

BUSINESS PROCESS

Payment for Goods and Services

Customers usually have two choices when paying for goods and services: cash or credit. A company will analyze the risks associated with a method of payment and then put controls in place to minimize them. For example, if a company collects a lot of cash, it may keep large amounts in a locked safe. That is a control that helps protect the firm from robbery. If a company makes sales on credit, it is important that the company keep accurate records so that the customers can be billed for the sales. Millions of dollars of revenue are lost by busi-

L.O. 1

Understand how a company accounts for and collects for sales made.

nesses each year because either they miss capturing revenue they have earned or they miss collecting payment for goods and services they have delivered. By studying cash and the related controls, you will see how a company protects one of its most important assets.

Accounting for Cash

Understand the purpose of a cash reconciliation.

An important part of properly accounting for cash is comparing a firm's recorded cash balance with the firm's monthly bank statement. A key control, one used in many different business processes, is segregation of duties. For cash that means the person who has the physical custody of cash—anyone who has actual physical access to cash at any time—is not the same person who does the record keeping for cash. For example, the person who makes the daily bank deposit should not be the same person who does the record keeping for cash.

Making the comparison between the cash balance in the company's records and the cash balance shown on the bank statement is called a *cash* or *bank reconciliation*. This is more than simply part of the record keeping for cash. The cash reconciliation is a crucial part of the collection process, controlling cash. As we all know, the bottom line in our checkbook seldom agrees with the bottom line on our monthly bank statement. It's true for a business, too. The cash balance in a company's records seldom agrees with the cash balance shown on the monthly bank statement. These balances don't agree so they have to be reconciled.

Reconciling the bank statement with the company's books is an important element in internal control. It is the process of comparing the company's accounting records with the bank's records and resolving any differences between the two. Reconciliation requires two major steps:

1. Take the bank's balance—the balance on the periodic bank statement—and adjust that balance for all the transactions that have been recorded in the company's books but not recorded on the bank's balance because the bank did not get the transaction recorded as of the date of its last statement.
2. Take the company's cash balance, called the *balance per books*. Adjust that balance for all the transactions that the bank has reported but have not been recorded on the company's books.

When the two steps of the reconciliation are complete, both should show the same reconciled cash balance. That will be actual amount of cash the company had on the date of the bank statement. The actual amount is called the *true cash balance*.

Adjustments to a company's records will always be required for the transactions the bank reported that had not been included in the company's accounting records (from step 2 of the reconciliation). Adjustments will *never* be required for transactions that had already been recorded in the company's books (from step 1 of the reconciliation).

Doing a bank reconciliation enables the company to:

1. locate any errors, whether made by the bank or the company, and
2. make adjustments to the cash account in the company's books for information the bank has reported that the company has not yet recorded in its cash account.

The bank reconciliation begins with the *balance per bank statement* and the *balance per books* as of the bank statement date. Each of these balances is then adjusted to arrive at the true cash balance. Some examples of common adjustments include:

1. Outstanding checks are deducted from the balance per bank statement.
2. Deposits in transit are added to the balance per bank statement.
3. Service charges by the bank appear on the bank statement and are deducted from the balance per books.
4. A customer's nonsufficient funds (NSF) check is deducted from the balance per books.
5. Interest earned on a checking account is added to the balance per books.
6. Miscellaneous charges are deducted from the balance per books; miscellaneous credits are added to the balance per books.

The following two items are what the company's books "know"—that's the information already included in the calculation of the company's cash balance—but the bank hasn't included these transactions in *its* balance yet:

1. Outstanding checks are those the company has written but haven't cleared the bank: Deduct the total amount of the outstanding checks from the balance per bank statement.
2. Deposits in transit are those the company made too late to get them included on the bank statement: Add the total amount of these deposits to the balance per bank statement.

The following six items are what the bank knows—that's the information already included in the calculation of the bank's balance at the date of the bank statement—but unknown to the company until the bank statement is received:

1. Service charges are those amounts the bank charges for its services: Deduct them from the balance per books.
2. NSF checks are checks the bank received in the company's deposit that bounced: Deduct them from the balance per books.
3. Miscellaneous charges, including new checks, for example: Deduct them from the balance per books.
4. Miscellaneous credits include previous bank charges made by mistake, for example: Add them to the balance per books.
5. Interest earned may be on checking accounts, for example: Add this to the balance per books.
6. Notes collected by the bank: Add them to the balance per books.

The difficult part of reconciling the company's cash account with the company's bank statement is gathering all the relevant information. In a textbook where all the information is provided, you can only see and do the easy part—preparing the bank reconciliation—also known as a cash reconciliation.

Let's take the relevant information that follows and prepare the cash reconciliation. Make sure you can identify where each amount is included in the reconciliation.

Low Company	
Balance per bank statement, May 31, 2002	$4,890
Company's books cash balance, May 31, 2002	1,774
Note collected by bank for Low Company in May	1,030
Bank charges for May	10
Deposit made after bank hours by Low Company on May 31, 2002	1,750
Customer check marked NSF in May	100
Checks outstanding on May 31, 2002	
298	1,300
304	456
306	2,358

- The bank statement showed the bank had mistakenly charged Low Company for a $150 check that was written by the High Company.
- During May, the Low Company bookkeeper recorded payment of an account payable incorrectly as $346. The check was paid by the bank in the correct amount of $364.

Low Company Bank Reconciliation May 31, 2002	
Balance per bank statement, May 31, 2002	$4,890
Add: **Deposits in transit**	1,750
(Company has made the deposit but it wasn't recorded by the bank as of the date of the bank statement)	
Bank error	150
Deduct: **Outstanding checks** (298, 304, 306)	(4,114)
Correct (adjusted) balance, May 31, 2002	▸$2,676
Balance per books, May 31, 2002	$1,774
Add: **Note collected by bank**	1,030
Deduct: **Bank charges**	(10)
NSF check	(100)
Correct error	(18)
(+346 − 364 = −18)	
Correct (adjusted) balance, May 31, 2002	▸$2,676

A bank reconciliation is simply a work sheet—it is not a formal part of the company's accounting system. Nothing on it actually corrects the accounting records. For every item on the bottom half of the reconciliation, the part that started with the balance per books, the accounting records will need to be adjusted to account for the items. For example, the bank charges would be recorded as:

Assets	=	Liabilities	+	CC	+	Retained earnings
$(10) Cash						(10) Operating expenses

Every adjustment to the balance per books requires a journal entry to update the cash account, as well as adjust other accounts as needed. Based on the Low Company example, the following journal entries are required:

Date	Transaction	Debit	Credit
5/31/2002	Cash	$1,030	
	Notes receivable		$1,000
	Interest revenue		30

To record collection of a notes receivable by the bank (assuming $1,000 principal and $30 interest)

Date	Transaction	Debit	Credit
5/31/2001	Operating expense	$ 10	
	Accounts receivable	100	
	Accounts payable	18	
	Cash		$128

To record bank service charges and necessary account balance corrections

ABC Company's unadjusted book balance for cash amounted to $2,400. The company's bank statement included a debit memo for bank service charges of $100. There were two credit memos: one for $300, which represented a collection that the bank made for ABC, and the other for $100, which represented the amount of interest that ABC had earned on its bank accounts during the period. Outstanding checks amounted to $250, and there were no deposits in transit. Prepare the journal entries that would be required to adjust ABC Company's cash account.

STUDY BREAK 7-3
SEE HOW YOU'RE DOING

Accounts Receivable: Collecting Payment for Sales Made on Account

Accounts receivable, also called *receivables,* are current assets that arise from sales on credit to customers. Receivables are a current asset, usually listed just below cash on the firm's balance sheet. Unfortunately, a firm cannot expect to collect 100% of its accounts receivable—not all customers will pay what they owe. Some customers go bankrupt or run off to Acapulco without paying. If the amount of collected accounts receivable as a percentage of total accounts receivable is low, the uncollected receivables will be costly to the firm. However, if collected receivables as a percentage of total receivables is high, that could be costly to the firm, too. It could mean that the firm is making it difficult for customers to get credit, and this could mean eliminating potential sales and potential profits. Accounting information is crucial for decisions about credit policies.

When a firm reports accounts receivable on its balance sheet, the amount reported must reflect what the business expects to collect—that's the real asset. There are two methods of accounting for uncollectible accounts (Exhibit 7-2). The first is called the direct write-off method; the second is called the allowance method.

L.O. 3

Understand how accounts receivable are recorded and reported.

BUSINESS PROCESS

Direct Write-Off Method

The actual amount of accounts receivable may be reported on the balance sheet without any adjustment—to reflect expected collections—*only if* the amount of total estimated uncollectible receivables is very small—that is, only if it is not *material.* Only when a customer's account is determined to be uncollectible is the balance in Accounts Receivable reduced. The bad account is removed from the accounting records by subtracting it from accounts receivable. This is the **direct write-off method.** The accounting equation is balanced with an expense called **bad debt expense.**

The **direct write-off method** is used when bad debt expense is recorded only after the specific customer's account is identified as uncollectible.

Bad debt expense is the expense related to the cost of extending credit to customers who don't pay.

Direct Write-Off Method:		Allowance Method:
• Not GAAP • Write off accounts when they are identified as uncollectible and **record bad debt expense.**	Or	• Bad debt expense is estimated and matched to sales. • Bad debt expense is recorded during end-of-period adjustment. • GAAP

Exhibit 7-2
Accounting for Uncollectible Accounts

Use SALES to estimate the bad debt expense.	Or	Use ACCOUNTS RECEIVABLE to estimate the bad debt expense.

If you use the **direct write-off method,** no **bad debt expense** is recorded until a specific debt is determined to be uncollectible. For example, if you determine that a $150 account is uncollectible, to record the write-off, the journal entry is:

Date	Transaction	Debit	Credit
	Bad debt expense	$150	
	Accounts receivable		$150

The direct write-off method does *not* provide a particularly good match between the revenue—that is, the sale—and the expense—that is, the bad debt expense. A company may make a sale in one period and recognize the bad debt expense in a subsequent period. The direct write-off method can be used only if the amount of bad debt expense is insignificant compared with total sales, either because the company has very strict credit policies (almost everyone pays) or the company has very few credit sales. The direct write-off method is not GAAP.

STUDY BREAK 7-4
SEE HOW YOU'RE DOING

Gloria's Glassware uses the direct write-off method to account for bad debts. In 2005, Gloria sold $20,000 on account. She estimated that between $100 and $150 would eventually go uncollected. No specific accounts were identified as uncollectible during 2005. In 2006, a credit customer who owed Gloria $35 filed for bankruptcy. Gloria wants to remove that customer's account from her outstanding accounts receivable. Prepare the journal entries to account for Gloria's bad debt expense that are required in 2005 and 2006.

Allowance Method

Most companies have a considerable amount of credit sales, and, as a result, they have uncollectible accounts. If the amount of those uncollectible accounts is significant, the company can't use the direct write-off method. When preparing financial statements, the company must determine how much of its recorded accounts receivable it believes will be collected. In other words, the company must value its accounts receivable, where *value* means assigning a value, a dollar amount, to those accounts.

GAAP wants the financial statements to match the *expense* of having customers who don't pay with the *revenue* from sales made to those customers. To do this, a company will estimate the amount it believes it won't collect each period and then the company will expense that amount each period. By making this estimate, the company can go ahead and recognize the expense, and therefore, the company will be matching the expense with the related sales. This method is called the **allowance method.** It is the method required by GAAP.

Let's consider terminology.

The accounts that a company estimates it will not collect are called **uncollectible accounts.** Uncollectible accounts and the amount of their losses should be *matched* with the sales that generated them.

The **allowance for uncollectible accounts** appears on the balance sheet as a deduction from accounts receivable; it is subtracted from the total amount of accounts receivable. The amount of the allowance for uncollectible accounts reduces the amount of accounts receivable to the amount expected to be collected in cash.

The amount expected to be collected in cash from accounts receivable is called the **net realizable value** of accounts receivable, or simply *net* accounts

The **allowance method** is used when bad debt expense is estimated and recognized *before* the specific customers who won't pay are identified in order to match the expense with the sales in a given accounting period.

Because the accounts that won't be collected, called **uncollectible accounts,** are unidentified at year-end when the expense is estimated, the amount cannot be directly deducted from accounts receivable. When that amount appears on the balance sheet as a reduction in accounts receivable, it is called the **allowance for uncollectible accounts.** The balance in accounts receivable minus the allowance for uncollectible accounts gives the amount of receivables the company believes it will collect—that's the **net realizable value** of accounts receivable.

receivable. It is the amount the company expects to realize, or in other words, the amount the company expects to get from credit customers.

The amount remaining when the allowance for uncollectible accounts is deducted from the total amount of accounts receivable is called the *book value* or the *carrying value* of accounts receivable. This terminology is used consistently for many different amounts on the balance sheet. Do you recall the name of the remainder when accumulated depreciation is subtracted from the cost of equipment? It's called the book value or carrying value of equipment on the balance sheet.

The amount of expense due to uncollectible accounts that reduces net income is called *bad debt expense* or *uncollectible accounts expense*. By understanding the meaning of the terms, we can look at the procedures that are expressed in these terms.

Uncollectible accounts expense, also called bad debt expense, is estimated at the end of each accounting period and included on the income statement as an operating expense at the estimated amount.

There are two allowance methods of estimating uncollectible accounts expense. One method of calculating the allowance is the sales method; the sales method focuses on the income statement and the amount of the current period sales for which collection will not be made. For the purpose of putting the most meaningful amount on the income statement, the question is: How much of the sales will go uncollected? The bad debt expense is recorded as a percentage of sales. This method is sometimes called the income statement method.

The other method is the accounts receivable method; this method focuses on the balance sheet. You start by estimating how much of the year-end balance of accounts receivable you believe will not be collected. This estimate of what will not be collected reduces the amount of accounts receivable on the balance sheet to the amount you *think* you will collect. For the purpose of putting the most meaningful amount on the balance sheet, the question is: How much of the total amount of accounts receivable will not be collected? The bad debt expense equals the amount needed to get the balance in the Allowance for Uncollectible Accounts to the amount that needs to be subtracted from Accounts Receivable to make it equal to the net realizable value. This method is sometimes called the balance sheet method.

Suppose your company had sales of $100,000 during the year. At the end of the year, when you are ready to prepare the financial statements, you need to estimate the portion of those sales for which you will not collect payment. If you knew exactly which customers would not pay, you'd never extend credit to them in the first place—but you don't know that. That's why you have to *estimate* the amount of bad debt expense. You base the estimate on past experience.

Sales. Let's start with the sales method. The focus is on the income statement, and the company makes its estimate of uncollectible accounts based on credit sales (or on total sales, when credit and cash sales are not easily separated). Suppose you routinely lose about 5% of your sales due to nonpayment. Why do you want to show bad debt expense of $5,000 on your income statement in the same period as the $100,000 worth of sales on which that $5,000 is estimated? You do this to match the expenses with the related revenues. That's why you don't wait until the nonpayers—represented as bad debts—are actually identified to recognize the expense. The adjustment records the bad debt expense that will be reported on the income statement and reduces total accounts receivable in the same period as the sale, long before the specific bad debt customers have been identified. The amount of the adjustment is recorded in a contra-asset account called the Allowance for Uncollectible Accounts. The adjustment to recognize bad debt expense would affect the accounting equation as follows:

Assets	=	Liabilities	+	Contributed capital	+	Retained earnings
(5,000) Allowance for uncollectible accounts						(5,000) Bad debt expense

Under the sales method, the bad debt expense estimate is based on a percentage of sales. If sales for the year total $100,000 and you estimate 5% of that amount is uncollectible, to record the estimate for bad debts based on the sales method, the journal entry is:

Date	Transaction	Debit	Credit
	Bad debt expense	$5,000	
	Allowance for uncollectible accounts		$5,000

A **contra-asset** is the opposite of an asset. It is deducted from its asset partner on the balance sheet.

The allowance for uncollectible accounts is a **contra-asset** account. The contra-asset holds the decreases for accounts receivable that represent estimated uncollectible accounts. Those decreases cannot be recorded directly in accounts receivable because you don't know exactly which accounts will go unpaid.

Sometime later, when you eventually identify the specific uncollectible account, you will write it off—remove it from the books—by deducting the amount from accounts receivable (and the customer's outstanding balance from detailed records of the company) and also by removing the amount from the allowance for uncollectible accounts. Removing the amount from accounts receivable reduces assets, and removing the amount from the allowance increases assets by reducing the amount deducted from accounts receivable on the balance sheet. There is no bad debt expense recorded when you actually write off an account using the allowance method. That's because you already recognized the bad debt expense when you made your estimate of bad debts at the time you prepared the financial statements. When you actually write off a specific account, you are simply reclassifying an *unnamed* bad debt to a *named* bad debt. You are cleaning up your books.

Suppose your company uses the allowance method and an actual $150 account is determined to be uncollectible, the journal entry reduces the allowance account and accounts receivable. No bad debt expense is recorded at the time of an actual write-off. To record the write-off of an uncollectible account:

Date	Transaction	Debit	Credit
	Allowance for uncollectible accounts	$150	
	Accounts receivable		$150

Accounts Receivable. Now let's estimate bad debt expense—still using the allowance method—but this time with the balance in accounts receivable as the starting point—the accounts receivable method. Suppose the balance in accounts receivable for Good Guys Company at December 31, 2003, before any adjustments have been made, is $43,450. Notice that this method focuses on the balance sheet. (In this example, we haven't even been told the amount of sales.) To use the accounts receivable method, most companies prepare an aging schedule of accounts receivable. An aging schedule is an analysis of the amounts owed to a company by the length of time they have been outstanding. Exhibit 7-3 shows an aging schedule for the accounts receivable in this example.

Based on the aging of accounts receivable, management estimates the end-of-year uncollectible accounts receivable to be $2,078. So the net realizable value—the amount of Accounts Receivable the company thinks it will collect—

Customer	Total	Current	Number of days past due				
			1–30	31–60	61–90	Over 90	
J. Adams	$ 500	$ 300	$ 200				
K. Brown	200	200					
L. Cannon	650		300	$ 350			
M. Dibbs	600				$ 200	$ 400	
Others	41,500	25,000	10,000	3,000	2,500	1,000	
	$43,450	$25,500	$10,500	$3,350	$2,700	$1,400	
Estimated percentage uncollectible			1%	3%	8%	20%	50%
Total estimated bad debts	$ 2,078	$ 255	$ 315	$ 268	$ 540	$ 700	

Exhibit 7–3
Aging Schedule of Accounts Receivable

is $41,372. That amount is what Good Guys Company wants the balance sheet to show—the book value—at December 31, 2003 (Exhibit 7-4). GAAP requires the company to show the total accounts receivable and the net realizable value.

In the first year of using the allowance method, Good Guys Company estimated uncollectible accounts of $2,078. Recognizing the expense has the following effect on the accounting equation:

Assets	=	Liabilities	+	Contributed capital	+	Retained earnings
(2,078) Allowance for uncollectible accounts						(2,078) Bad debt expense

The journal entry relating to bad debt expense and the allowance for doubtful accounts for the first year is:

Date	Transaction	Debit	Credit
12/31/2003	Bad debt expense	$2,078	
	Allowance for uncollectible accounts		$2,078

Remember, instead of deducting the $2,078 directly from accounts receivable, we will keep it separately in a contra-asset account, show it on the balance sheet as a deduction from accounts receivable. The bad debt expense—also known as uncollectible accounts expense—will be shown on the income statement as an operating expense.

During the following year, specific accounts will be identified as uncollectible and removed from the books. That's when specific accounts are actually written off.

Balance sheet, December 31, 2003	
Current assets	
Accounts receivable	$43,450
Allowance for doubtful accounts	(2,078)
Net accounts receivable	$41,372

Exhibit 7–4
Balance Sheet Presentation of Accounts Receivable

One problem with the allowance method of accounting for bad debts is that the bad debt expense is estimated. Suppose the estimate is wrong. When you make an estimate of uncollectible accounts for the *next* year, you adjust it for the overestimate or underestimate for the current year. Writing off the specific accounts, when you know exactly who is not going to pay, involves taking the amount of the bad account out of the allowance and accounts receivable. Because accounts receivable is an asset and the allowance for uncollectible accounts is a contra-asset, both can be reduced while keeping the accounting equation in balance.

> Only when you use *the allowance method with accounts receivable as the basis for estimating bad debt expense* do you "correct" for any inaccuracy in your estimate the previous accounting period.

Suppose M. Dibbs, who owes the company $600, has been identified as an uncollectible account. That means Good Guys has received information that makes it believe this specific account will not be collected. The effect on the accounting equation is a reduction in the allowance and a reduction in accounts receivable. There is no effect on *net* accounts receivable. Writing off a specific account is a matter of cleaning up the company's books. Instead of having only unidentified bad accounts, the company can now associate a name with $600 worth of bad debts.

> With the allowance method, there is no effect on a company's net accounts receivable when a specific account is written off.

The expense was already recognized with the estimate made at the end of the prior year, so no bad debt expense is recognized when a specific name is associated with the uncollectible account. Here's how writing-off an account affects the accounting equation:

Assets	=	Liabilities	+	Contributed capital	+	Retained earnings
(600) Accounts receivable (Dibbs) +600 (Allowance for uncollectible accounts)						

The journal entry to record the write-off of M. Dibb's account is:

Date	Transaction	Debit	Credit
	Allowance for uncollectible accounts	$600	
	Accounts receivable (Dibbs)		$600

There is no net effect on a company's total assets of writing off a specific account.

Suppose that by the end of the year, Good Guys Company has identified and written off $2,000 worth of specific bad accounts. (This is done on an ongoing basis during the year as the bad accounts are identified.) That means last year's estimate of bad debts of $2,078 was $78 too high. For the moment, the company will ignore that and estimate next year's bad debt expense in the same way it did for the prior year. Good Guys Company would prepare an aging schedule and again make an estimate of uncollectible accounts. Suppose the balance in Accounts Receivable was $50,000 and the aging schedule gave an estimate of uncollectible accounts of $2,500. Good Guys Company wants the balance sheet to reflect this estimate, showing the book value or carrying value of Accounts Receivable as $47,500.

At this point we have to take into consideration that bad debts were over-estimated last year. Good Guys Company will record bad debt expense this year of only $2,422 (= $2,500 − $78). The overestimate carried over from last year, $78, is still in the allowance account, so only $2,422 needs to be added to the allowance for uncollectible accounts to get the total $2,500 needed for the balance sheet. Thus, the bad debt expense recognized in the second year would be $2,422; and the allowance for uncollectible accounts will be $2,500.

Date	Transaction	Debit	Credit
1/1–12/31 2004	Allowance for uncollectible accounts	$1,400	
	Accounts receivable (various)		$1,400

To record the write-off of specific uncollectible accounts during the year

Date	Transaction	Debit	Credit
12/31/2004	Bad debt expense	$2,422	
	Allowance for uncollectible accounts		$2,422

To record the estimate for bad debts based on the accounts receivable aging method ($2,500 estimated uncollectible amount − $78 overestimated amount from 2003)

When the accounts receivable method for estimating the allowance for uncollectible accounts is used, the balances in the allowance account and the bad debt expense are only guaranteed to be equal in the first year. After that, they would be equal only if the estimate of bad debts for the previous year had been perfect—and that rarely happens. Each year, the expense usually reflects a little adjustment for the misestimate in the previous year. Making the adjustment for the allowance for uncollectible accounts is done at the end of the accounting period and is an adjustment to the books.

Suppose at the end of the year, Pendleton Corp. records showed the following:

Allowance for uncollectible accounts (excess from prior year)	100
Bad debt expense[a]	0
Accounts receivable	10,000

[a]Bad debt expense has a zero balance because no adjustments have been made.

Based on an aging schedule of current accounts receivable, Pendleton estimated the end-of-year uncollectible accounts receivable to be $500. Prepare the journal entry to record bad debt expense for the year.

Credit Card Sales

One way to avoid the risk of extending credit to your customers is to accept payment with their credit cards. Banks or other financial institutions—also known as credit card companies—issue credit cards; and the users often have to pay the issuer a fee to use the card. The credit card companies take the responsibility for evaluating a person's creditworthiness, and they also handle billing the customers and collecting payments. If a company allows customers to use a credit card to pay for their purchases, the company will have to pay the credit card company for these services. This is an important business decision, especially for small companies. The cost of allowing customers to make purchases using credit cards must be compared with the benefits. The most significant cost is the credit

Be able to explain the difference between *credit* sales and *credit card* sales and the business implications of the difference.

BUSINESS PROCESS

card expense. Benefits may include increasing the number of customers and eliminating the risks associated with extending credit to customers. In addition, the company doesn't have to keep track of customers' credit, payments, and outstanding balances; and will not face any problems with late or uncollectible accounts.

This is how credit card sales are handled. The company will submit all the credit card sales receipts to the credit card company, and the credit card company will pay the company immediately. The amount the company receives will not be the gross amount of the sales. It will be a smaller amount because the credit card company will deduct a percentage of total sales as its fee for the services it provides. The company classifies the fees withheld by the credit card company as operating expenses.

Suppose that Wally's Tire Company accepts MasterCard, and total credit card sales for the day were $1,000. Suppose the MasterCard fee is 5% of sales. Wally's would record the sales for the day in its accounting records as follows:

Assets	=	Liabilities	+	Shareholders' equity	
Accounts receivable— MasterCard +$950				Sales revenue Credit card expense	+$1,000 (50)

The journal entry to record the day's credit card sales is:

Date	Transaction	Debit	Credit
	Accounts receivable (MasterCard)	$950	
	Credit card expense	50	
	Sales revenue		$1,000

When the company receives payment from MasterCard—typically daily or weekly, depending on the procedures for submitting credit card receipts to MasterCard—the company will record the increase in cash and the decrease in accounts receivable.

STUDY BREAK 7-6
SEE HOW YOU'RE DOING

During December, Magic Cow Company made a $5,000 MasterCard sale to a customer. MasterCard charges Magic Cow a fee of 3% of sales for its services. Prepare the journal entry to record this transaction.

Warranties

L.O. 5

Understand how a business uses warranties and how the accounting treatment and business implications are related.

A significant amount of a company's time and attention related to the sales and collection cycle is devoted to collections. As we have seen, there are crucial issues related to cash and the collection of accounts receivable for a business to handle. However, there is one more issue related to sales that is very important and has become increasingly important in our customer-service-oriented business world: warranties.

Why would a company provide a warranty on a product or service? It's a sales and marketing tool, and whether or not to provide a warranty is one of the strategic decisions a company must make. For financial statement pur-

BUSINESS PROCESS

poses, a company wants to recognize warranty expense at the time of the sale of the product. Why? The *matching principle* applies to this situation. Revenues and expenses that go together should be on the same income statement. The company does not know exactly how much it will cost to honor the warranty, so the cost must be estimated. Because the company is not actually disbursing the cash to fix or replace the item yet—at the time of the sale—a liability is recorded along with the warranty expense. It's an adjustment made either at the time of the sale or when it's time to prepare financial statements. Liabilities are increased by the same amount as warranty expense.

The accounting treatment that requires estimates of future warranty costs reflects the underlying business process. It is crucial for a company to consider and estimate such costs to make sound business decisions. These future costs may be significant, and the accounting rules force companies to record these costs when the sale is made instead of when the warranty is honored.

What happens when the cash is actually paid to fix a product with a warranty? No expense is recorded. Instead, the liability previously set up is reduced. So actual expenditures result in a reduction in cash or some other asset (used to fix the item) and an equal reduction in the amount of the liability.

Let's look at an example. Suppose Brooke's Bike Company sold 100 bicycles during June and provided a 1-year warranty. The accountant estimated that future repairs and replacement related to the June sales would be approximately $30 per bicycle. (No expenditures were made related to the warranties during the month of June.) What amount of warranty expense would appear on the income statement for the month ended June 30? Brooke's Bike Company would want to show the entire amount, $3,000, as an expense for the month. What is the amount of the June 30 liability (warranty payable or estimated warranty liability)? The total $3,000 would be shown as a liability on the balance sheet.

Assets	=	Liabilities	+	Contributed capital	+	Retained earnings
		+3000 Estimated warranty liability				(3,000) Warranty expense

The journal entry to record the estimated warranty expense and related liability for June sales is:

Date	Transaction	Debit	Credit
6/30	Warranty expense	$3,000	
	Estimated warranty liability		$3,000

July was a slow month, and Brooke's Bike Company didn't sell any bicycles. However, there were several bicycles, from sales in June, which were repaired in July. The repairs cost Brooke's Bike Company $250. What amount of warranty expense would appear on the income statement for the month ended July 31? None. Brooke's Bike Company recognized the expense when the sale was made, so no expense is recognized when the repairs are made. The cost of the repairs is deducted from the amount "owed" to the customers. So the amount of the July 31 liability (warranty payable or estimated warranty liability) is $3,000 − 250 = $2,750.

Assets	=	Liabilities	+	Contributed capital	+	Retained earnings
(250) Cash		(250) Estimated warranty liability				

The journal entry to record the warranty repair costs made in July is:

Date	Transaction	Debit	Credit
7/1–7/31	Estimated warranty liability	$250	
	Cash		$250

**STUDY BREAK 7-7
SEE HOW YOU'RE DOING**

August was another slow month for bicycle sales (none were made), but Brooke's Bike Company did some warranty repairs on previous sales. The total spent to make warranty repairs was $500. Prepare the journal entry to record the repairs.

Finding and Using Information About Sales and Accounts Receivable

L.O. 6

Understand the information disclosed on the financial statements about accounts receivable and how to use it.

Because a company's revenue is recognized when it is earned, which is often *before* it is collected, it is important for the financial statement users to have information about the collectibility of the receivables. The way this is done is by reporting accounts receivable at their net realizable value and disclosing the balance in the allowance for uncollectible accounts. Some balance sheets show only the net realizable value of accounts receivable, whereas others show both the gross and the net amounts. An example of the disclosure of this information is shown in Exhibit 7-5.

**Exhibit 7-5
Accounts Receivable and
Related Disclosures**

From the Balance Sheet of Sound Advice, Inc.
for the Fiscal Year Ended January 31, 2000

Current assets	
Cash	$ 564,898
Receivables	
Vendors	3,979,027
Trade	1,024,652
Employees	431,775
Total receivables	5,435,454
Less allowance for doubtful accounts	508,640
Net receivables	$4,926,814

The notes to the financial statements include this information about receivables:

Receivables from vendors consist of cooperative advertising and other amounts earned based on market development agreements along with various promotional and other incentive programs. The funds received under these programs are determined based upon specific agreements with the vendors and/or the inclusion of the vendors' products in the Company's advertising and promotional programs. Once earned, the funds are recorded as a reduction of advertising expense. Also included in receivables from vendors are amounts due for warranty repairs. Trade receivables consist primarily of amounts due from custom design accounts and credit card and finance companies resulting from customer purchases.

Using the Financial Statement Information for Analysis

The information about sales and accounts receivable can be used to help measure a company's ability to meet its short-term obligations. When the *current ratio* is computed—that is, *current assets divided by current liabilities*—the numerator includes accounts receivable, because it is a current asset. Another ratio similar to the current ratio is called the *quick ratio,* also known as the *acid test ratio.* Instead of using all of a company's current assets in the numerator, the quick ratio uses only cash, short-term investments, and net accounts receivable. These three assets are the most liquid—easiest to covert to cash— so they are the most readily available assets for paying off current liabilities. The quick ratio provides a stricter test of a company's ability to meet its short-term obligations.

BUSINESS PROCESS

Another important ratio that involves accounts receivable is the **accounts receivable turnover ratio.** This ratio—net sales divided by average net accounts receivable—measures a company's ability to collect the cash from its credit customers. Let's look at the information from 2 years of financial statement information for Home Depot. This particular ratio is useful for a company to track over time to make sure receivables are being collected promptly.

The **accounts receivable turnover ratio** helps a company figure out how well it is collecting for its credit sales.

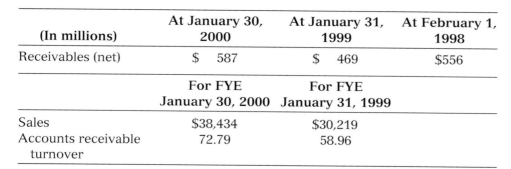

(In millions)	At January 30, 2000	At January 31, 1999	At February 1, 1998
Receivables (net)	$ 587	$ 469	$556

	For FYE January 30, 2000	For FYE January 31, 1999
Sales	$38,434	$30,219
Accounts receivable turnover	72.79	58.96

If the average turnover of accounts receivable is 72.79, we can calculate how long it takes for Home Depot, on average, to collect for a sale. If we divide 365—the number of days in a year—by the accounts receivable turnover ratio, we will get the number of days it takes, on average, to collect accounts receivable. For the fiscal year ended (FYE) January 30, 2000, we will divide 365 by 72.79 = 5 days. That's pretty good. One of the reasons it is so low is that Home Depot has a very significant amount of cash sales. Because we don't have credit sales alone to use in the numerator of the ratio, and we have to use total sales, the turnover in days is quite low. It is useful, however, to compare it with last year's turnover. Last year, the accounts receivable turnover ratio was 58.96. If we divide 365 by 58.96, we get 6.19 days. Home Depot has reduced its average time to collect its sales dollars.

If we were to calculate the accounts receivable turnover ratio for a manufacturing firm or a wholesale company, we would expect the turnover ratio to be lower and the average number of days to collect for a sale to be higher than our calculations for a retail company. That's because a wholesale company does not have as many cash sales in its total sales number. For example, look at the following information for Pepsi Bottling Group, Inc.

(Dollars in millions)	Accounts receivable at December 25, 1999	Accounts receivable at December 26, 1998	Sales for FYE December 25, 1999
	$827	$808	$7,505

The accounts receivable turnover ratio is:

$$\frac{\$7,505}{(827 + 808)/2} = 9.18$$

To get the average number of days to collect accounts receivable, we divide 365 by 9.18, which gives 39.76 days. That is quite a bit longer than the average number of days for Home Depot to collect its accounts receivable.

This ratio is quite useful for internal monitoring of receivables. Remember, every day that a dollar is owed to a company—often referred to as being *tied up* in accounts receivable—is a day that the company could have had the dollar to use in the business.

Business Risks

Identify the risks associated with sales, cash, and accounts receivable.

Preventive controls try to stop the problem before it starts—to prevent it.

Detective controls are designed to *find* errors.

Corrective controls are designed to *fix* errors.

BUSINESS PROCESS

The policies and procedures that management establishes to ensure its directions are followed are called the company's control activities. Control activities are designed to manage the risks a company identifies. There are three types of control activities, defined by their purpose:

■ **Preventive controls** are designed to prevent an error or irregularity. For example, the policy of handling one customer at a time is a control designed to prevent a customer from getting the wrong purchase. (An *error* is an unintended mistake on the part of an employee whereas an *irregularity* is an *intentional* mistake—often fraud.)

■ **Detective controls** are designed to identify when an error or irregularity has occurred. Balancing your checkbook with your monthly bank statement is a control designed to detect, that is to find, any errors in your records or the bank records.

■ **Corrective controls** are directed at recovering from, repairing the damage from, or minimizing the cost of, an error or irregularity. Weekly staff meetings to discuss customer complaints are a control designed to correct errors. A corrective control for past errors can become a preventive control for future errors.

Let's identify the specific risks associated with cash and accounts receivable and see how the three control activities discussed here are used to minimize those risks.

First, consider cash. Because cash is easy to conceal and it's difficult to prove who owns it, cash presents a significant risk to a business. Cash is an asset that must be safeguarded with physical controls, such as locked cash drawers and safes. Such controls are preventive. When the cash must be handled, separation of duties is a crucial preventive control. For example, two or more employees should handle cash—*checks* are considered *cash* in this context—received by mail. Also, the cash reconciliation, discussed earlier in the chapter, should be performed by a person who does not have physical control of the cash either by making deposits or by writing checks. The purpose of these separation-of-duties controls is to reduce the opportunity for a person to walk away with the company's cash. A cash reconciliation is also a detective control. It is done to detect any errors that may have been made with the cash account. The company may also have a policy of calling the bank if any errors are identified. This would be a corrective control, one in place to be sure any discovered errors are corrected.

Second, selling on credit creates a business risk for a company. The risk is that the customers will not pay for the purchases they have made on account. The most effective way for a company to minimize this risk is to have credit policies and procedures in place to identify which customers may be bad credit risks *before* allowing those customers to buy on account. This is a preventive control, designed to prevent the business from extending credit to customers who will not pay. The record keeping for accounts receivable should be frequent and thorough. The individual customers' accounts should be reconciled to the total amount of accounts receivable recorded in the company's records. This routine reconciliation is a detective control, designed to detect any errors in records. Finally, a company should have a policy in place to help identify customers who are slow in paying their accounts or who do not pay at all. Denying future credit to these customers may be viewed as a corrective control. This corrects a previous error in extending credit to someone who should not have been given credit, and at the same time prevents future risk associated with these customers.

Summary Problem: Tom's Wear Increases Sales in June

When Tom began his T-shirt business, his first customers were a few friends, so collection of accounts receivable was not a problem. Then he branched out to sporting goods stores and local schools. Again, bad debts did not represent a significant problem, so Tom's Wear did not use the allowance method of accounting for bad debts. However, since hiring Sam to manage the inventory flow, Tom has been able to devote his time to increasing sales. Tom's customer base has now grown to a size that makes it necessary for him to give serious attention to the collectibility of his accounts receivable. The June 1 balance sheet is shown in Exhibit 7-6, followed by the transactions for June (Exhibit 7-7). Study the transactions during June before you prepare the adjustments and the financial statements for June.

As part of the month-end adjustments, Tom has decided to set up an allowance for uncollectible accounts. He has decided to use the sales method and, after consulting with some local businesses and some accountants, he will set up an allowance equal to 3% of credit sales.

Tom has also decided to offer a warranty against defects in his T-shirts. He estimates that 2% of total sales will provide an adequate amount for his warranty obligations.

Both of these decisions are based on the matching principle. Tom wants to match the bad debt and warranty expenses with the sales to which they pertain, even though he doesn't know how many customers won't pay or how many customers will return a T-shirt.

At the end of the quarter (June 30), Tom's accountant suggests the company classify next year's loan payment as a current liability. So Tom's Wear will divide the $30,000 long-term note into current and long-term portions.

Required:
Make the needed journal entries and adjustments to the accounts, post to T-accounts, prepare an adjusted trial balance, and then prepare the four basic financial statements (solution is provided near the end of the chapter).

Exhibit 7-6

Tom's Wear, Inc.
Balance Sheet
June 1, 2001

Assets		Liabilities and shareholders' equity	
Cash	$ 8,805	Accounts payable	$ 4,200
Accounts receivable	8,900	Interest payable	500
Inventory	4,700	Unearned revenue	4,950
		Salaries payable	723
		Payroll taxes payable	277
		Other payables	77
Prepaid insurance	250	Total current liabilities	10,727
Prepaid rent	600		
Prepaid Web service	250	Notes payable	30,000
Total current assets	23,505	Total liabilities	40,727
Computer (net of $300 accumulated depreciation)	3,700	Common stock	5,000
Van (net of $1,595 accumulated depreciation)	28,405	Retained earnings	9,883
Total assets	$55,610	Total liabilities and shareholders' equity	$55,610

Exhibit 7-7
Transactions for June 2001 for Tom's Wear, Inc.

1	June 1	Pays cash of $2,400 for 2 months of rent on the warehouse, beginning June 15
2	June 5	Pays Sam Cubbys' salary for May; gross pay, $1,000; also, makes the payroll tax deposit, including the employer's matching payroll taxes
3	June 10	Delivers the second half of the shirts to the school system—450 shirts—and recognizes revenue of $4,950
4	June 12	Pays accounts payable of $4,200
5	June 14	Signs a contract with the school system to deliver 500 shirts per month for September through December, at a price of $10 per shirt; the shirts will be delivered on the last day of the month with the invoice attached to the delivery; Tom has serious competition for this deal, so he decides to offer the purchase terms, 2/10, n/30, to the school system to secure the contract
6	June 20	Purchases 5,000 T-shirts from a new vendor; the cost of the shirts is only $3.79 each, but the shipping terms are free on board (FOB) shipping point; the shipping costs for the month are $50; Tom's Wear pays cash for the shipping, but makes the purchase on account
7	June 20	Tom's sales efforts pay off with the addition of several sporting goods stores as customers; during June, the company sells 4,000 shirts to various stores for $11 each; all sales are on account
8	June 21	Collects $8,800 on accounts receivable
9	June 30	Pays miscellaneous operating expenses of $600 for the month
10	June 30	Pays a dividend of $1,000

Understanding Excel

In this exercise you create an accounts receivable aging schedule for Tom's Wear, Inc.

Requirements

1. Open a new Excel work sheet.
2. Beginning in cell B1, input the following chart. Resize columns and wrap text as needed. See *Hint* that follows for help with formatting.

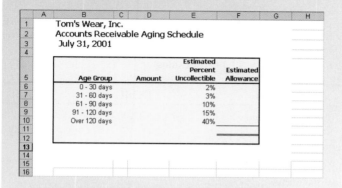

Hint: You can improve the appearance of a work sheet by changing the font type and sizes and by adding color.

Change the font type and size by using the pull-down menus on the toolbar. To change a large area, highlight the cells you want to change before selecting the font and size. Select Tahoma or any other font you prefer.

To change the color of selected areas of a spreadsheet, select Format, Cells, and Patterns. Highlight the areas to be changed and select the color of your choice. Colors can be layered. In other words, highlight A1 to G15 and choose white. Next, highlight B5 to F12 and choose light yellow.

3. At the end of June, the Tom's Wear, Inc. accounts receivable balance was as follows:

Accounts receivable	$44,100
Less: allowance	(1,320)
Net accounts receivable	$42,780

Tom's July sales totaled $99,000 (all on account), $37,000 of accounts receivable were collected, and $1,000 was written off as uncollectible. Based on this information, calculate the balance of accounts receivable and the allowance account at the end of July before the adjustment for bad debts.

4. Assume for this problem only that Tom has done an aging of his July 31 accounts receivable balance and determined the following:

Accounts Due in	% of Total Accounts Receivable
0–30 days	55
31–60 days	30
61–90 days	10
90–120 days	4
Over 120 days	1
	100

Based on your calculations from step 3, determine the dollar amount for each category in the aging schedule and complete the aging schedule. Remember to use formulas where appropriate.

5. Beginning in cell B17, input and complete the following information at July 31, 2001:

Accounts receivable	$
Less: allowance	( )
Net accounts receivable	$

Hint: All these numbers should be calculated using formulas. Use the information from your aging schedule to create a formula for accounts receivable.

6. Print your file and save it to disk. Name your file TomsWear7.

Answers to Study Break Questions

Study Break 7-1

Date	Transaction	Debit	Credit
	Cash	$100,000	
	Unearned ticket revenue		$100,000
	To record collection of advance ticket sales		
9/1–9/30	Unearned revenue	$ 50,000	
	Ticket revenue earned		$ 50,000
	To recognize revenue earned from advance ticket sales		
10/1–10/31	Unearned revenue	$ 33,333	
	Ticket revenue earned		$ 33,333
	To recognize revenue earned from advance ticket sales		

Study Break 7-2

1. The company will record sales as $3,500 and then deduct the sales discounts on the face of the income statement.
2. Cash collected will be: $3,500 × 0.97 = $3,395 (net sales)

Date	Transaction	Debit	Credit
3/1–3/31	Accounts receivable	$3,500	
	Sales		$3,500
	To record the sale of inventory, terms 3/10, n/30		
	Cash	$3,395	
	Sales discounts	105	
	Accounts receivable		$3,500
	To record accounts receivable collections		

Study Break 7-3

Book balance	$2,400
Interest	100
Collection	300
Service charge	(100)
True cash balance	$2,700

Date	Transaction	Debit	Credit
	Cash	$300	
	Miscellaneous operating expenses	100	
	Accounts receivable		$300
	Interest revenue		100
	To record bank statement adjustments		

Study Break 7-4

With use of the direct write-off method, only the accounts specifically identified and written off are counted as bad debt expense. (Contrast this with the allowance method where the *estimates* are the bad debt expense and the specific write offs have no effect.) In this case, there is no bad debt expense for 2005. Bad debt expense for 2006 is $35.

Date	Transaction	Debit	Credit
2005	No journal entries required		
2006	Bad debt expense	$35	
	Accounts receivable		$35
	To record the write-off of an uncollectible account		

1. $400 ($500 estimate less prior year overstatement)
2. $9,500 ($10,000 less allowance of $500)

Study Break 7-5

Date	Transaction	Debit	Credit
12/31	Bad debt expense	$400	
	Allowance for uncollectible accounts		$400
To record bad debt expense			

Sales is $5,000.
Accounts receivable = $5,000 × 0.97 = $4,850.
The remaining 3% will be classified as credit card expense.
At the time of the sale, Accounts Receivable increase by $4,850, Sales increase by $5,000, and Expenses (credit card expense) increase by $150. When the cash is received from MasterCard, Accounts Receivable will decrease by $4,850, and cash will increase by $4,850.

Study Break 7-6

Date	Transaction	Debit	Credit
Dec.	Accounts receivable (MasterCard)	$4,850	
	Credit card expense	150	
	Sales revenue		$5,000
To record bad debt expense			

- This problem is a continuation of the example started in the chapter text.
- There is *no* Warranty Expense. That was previously recorded when the sales were made.
- The Warranty Liability is the amount originally recorded minus any amounts that have been spent on warranty repairs to date, in this case, $2,250.

Study Break 7-7

Date	Transaction	Debit	Credit
8/1–8/31	Estimated warranty liability	$500	
	Cash		$500
To record August warranty repairs			

Solution to Summary Problem

Transaction 1

Pays cash of $2,400 for 2 months of rent on the warehouse beginning June 15.

Date	Transaction	Debit	Credit
6/1/2001	Prepaid rent	$2,400	
	Cash		$2,400
To record the prepayment of 2 months rent			

Transaction 2

Pays Sam Cubby's salary for May; gross pay $1,000; also makes the payroll tax deposit, including the employer's matching payroll taxes.

Date	Transaction	Debit	Credit
6/5/2001	Salaries payable	$723	
	Payroll taxes payable	277	
	Other payables	77	
	Cash		$1,077
To record payment of salary and taxes			

Transaction 3

Delivers the second half of the shirts to the school system (450 shirts) and recognizes revenue of $4,950.

Date	Transaction	Debit	Credit
6/10/2001	Unearned revenue	$4,950	
	Revenue		$4,950
To record delivery of the second half of the shirts to the school			
6/10/2001	Cost of goods sold	$1,865	
	Inventory		$1,865
To record cost of goods sold (125 @ $4.00 and 325 @ $4.20)			

Transaction 4

Pays accounts payable of $4,200.

Date	Transaction	Debit	Credit
6/12/2001	Accounts payable	$4,200	
	Cash		$4,200
To record payment on account			

Transaction 5

Signs a contract with the school system to deliver 500 shirts per month for September through December at a price of $10 per shirt. No journal entry is required.

Transaction 6

Purchases 5,000 T-shirts @ $3.79 each; shipping terms—FOB shipping point and shipping costs of $50. Tom's Wear pays cash for the shipping but makes the purchase on account.

Date	Transaction	Debit	Credit
6/20/2001	Inventory	$19,000	
	Cash		$ 50
	Accounts payable		18,950
To record the purchase of 5,000 T-shirts, FOB shipping point at $3.79 each + $50 shipping cost (cost: $3.80 per shirt)			

Transaction 7

Sells 4,000 shirts to various stores for $11 each. All sales are on account.

Date	Transaction	Debit	Credit
6/20/2001	Accounts receivable	$44,000	
	Revenue		$44,000
To record the sale of 4,000 T-shirts on account			
6/20/2001	Cost of goods sold	$15,470	
	Inventory		$15,470
To record cost of goods sold (675 @ $4.20 and 3,325 @ $3.80)			

Transaction 8

Collects $8,800 in accounts receivable.

Date	Transaction	Debit	Credit
6/21/2001	Cash	$8,800	
	Accounts receivable		$8,800
To record the collection of accounts receivable			

Transaction 9
Miscellaneous operating expenses for the month are $600.

Date	Transaction	Debit	Credit
6/30/2001	Other operating expenses	$600	
	Cash		$600

To record the payment of miscellaneous operating expenses

Transaction 10
Tom's Wear pays a dividend of $1,000.

Date	Transaction	Debit	Credit
6/30/2001	Retained earnings	$1,000	
	Cash		$1,000

To record the payment of a cash dividend

Adjustment 1
Record depreciation expense for June: $100 for the computer and $1,160 for the van (8,000 miles × $0.145).

Date	Transaction	Debit	Credit
6/30/2001	Depreciation expense	$1,260	
	Accumulated depreciation: computer		$ 100
	Accumulated depreciation: van		1,160

To record June depreciation expense

Adjustment 2
Record interest expense on the van note.

Date	Transaction	Debit	Credit
6/30/2001	Interest expense	$250	
	Interest payable		$250

To record interest expense for June

Adjustment 3
Record insurance expense of $100 for the month of June.

Date	Transaction	Debit	Credit
6/30/2001	Insurance expense	$100	
	Prepaid insurance		$100

To record insurance expense for June

Adjustment 4
Record rent expense of $1,200 for the month of June.

Date	Transaction	Debit	Credit
6/30/2001	Rent expense	$1,200	
	Prepaid rent		$1,200

To record rent expense for June

Adjustment 5
Record web costs of $50 for June.

Date	Transaction	Debit	Credit
6/30/2001	Other operating expenses	$50	
	Prepaid web service		$50

To record web maintenance services for June

Adjustment 6

Accrue Sam Cubbie's salary for June, including the employer portion of payroll taxes.

Date	Transaction	Debit	Credit
6/30/2001	Salary expense	$1,000	
	Employer's payroll tax expense	77	
	Payroll taxes payable		$277
	Other payables		77
	Salaries payable		723
	To record the accrual of Sam Cubbie's salary, withholding, and payroll taxes		

Adjustment 7

Bad debt estimate = 3% of credit sales.

Date	Transaction	Debit	Credit
6/30/2001	Bad debt expense	$1,320	
	Allowance for bad debts		$1,320
	To record the bad debt estimate for June		

Adjustment 8

Warranty liability estimate = 2% of total sales.

Date	Transaction	Debit	Credit
6/30/2001	Warranty expense	$979	
	Warranties payable		$979
	To record the estimated warranty liability for June		

T-Accounts for Tom's Wear with June journal entries and adjustments

Cash

BB	$8,805	$2,400	1
8	8,800	1,077	2
		4,200	4
		50	6
		600	9
		1,000	10
$8,278			

Accounts receivable

BB	$8,900	$8,800	8
7	44,000		
44,100			

Allowance for bad debts

	$1,320	Adj-7
	1,320	

Inventory

BB	$4,700	$1,865	3
6	19,000	15,470	7
6,365			

Prepaid insurance

BB	$250	$100	Adj-3
150			

Prepaid web service

BB	$250	$50	Adj-5
$200		

Prepaid rent

BB	$600	$1,200	Adj-4
1	2,400		
1,800			

Equipment: Computer

BB	$4,000
	4,000

Equipment: van

BB	$30,000
	30,000

Accumulated Depreciation: van

	$1,595	BB
	1,160	Adj-1
	2,755	

Accumulated Depreciation: Computer

	$300	BB
	100	Adj-1
	400	

Accounts payable

4	$4,200	$4,200	BB
		18,950	6
		18,950	

Interest payable

	$500	BB
	250	Adj-2
	750	

Unearned revenue

3	$4,950	$4,950	BB
		0	

Payroll taxes payable (withheld)

2	277	$277	BB
		277	Adj-6
		277	

Salaries payable

2	723	$723	BB
		723	Adj-6
		723	

Warranties payable

	$979	Adj-8
	979	

Notes payable

	$30,000	BB
	30,000

Common stock

	$5,000	BB
	5,000

Other payables

2	77	$77	BB
		77	Adj-6
		77	

(continued)

Retained earnings

		$9,883	BB
10	$1,000		
		8,883	

Revenue

	$4,950	3
	44,000	7
	48,950	

Cost of goods sold

3	$1,865	
7	15,470	
	17,335	

Depreciation expense

Adj-1	$1,260	
	1,260	

Employer's payroll tax

Adj-6	$77	
	77	

Other operating expenses

9	$600	
Adj-5	50	
	650	

Insurance expense

Adj-3	$100	
	100	

Rent expense

Adj-4	$1,200	
	1,200	

Interest expense

Adj-2	$250	
	250	

Salary expense

Adj-6	$1,000	
	1,000	

Bad debt expense

Adj-7	$1,320	
	1,320	

Warranty expense

Adj-8	$979	
	979	

tom's wear

Tom's Wear, Inc.
Adjusted Trial Balance
June 30, 2001

	Debits	Credits
Cash	$ 8,278	
Accounts receivable	44,100	
Allowance for bad debts		$ 1,320
Inventory	6,365	
Prepaid insurance	150	
Prepaid web service	200	
Prepaid rent	1,800	
Equipment: computer	4,000	
Accumulated depreciation: computer		400
Equipment: van	30,000	
Accumulated depreciation: van		2,755
Accounts payable		18,950
Interest payable		750
Payroll taxes payable		277
Other payables		77
Salaries payable		723
Warranties payable		979
Notes payable		30,000
Common stock		5,000
Retained earnings		8,883
Revenue		48,950
Cost of goods sold	17,335	
Depreciation expense	1,260	
Employer's payroll tax expense	77	
Other operating expense	650	
Insurance expense	100	
Rent expense	1,200	
Interest expense	250	
Salary expense	1,000	
Bad debt expense	1,320	
Warranty expense	979	
Totals	$119,064	$119,064

Tom's Wear, Inc.
Income Statement
For the Month Ended June 30, 2001

Sales revenue		$48,950
Expenses		
Cost of goods sold	$17,335	
Insurance expense	100	
Rent expense	1,200	
Depreciation expense	1,260	
Salary expense	1,000	
Other operating expenses	727	
Warranty expense	979	
Bad debt expense	1,320	
Interest expense	250	(24,171)
Net income		$24,779

Tom's Wear, Inc.
Statement of Changes in Shareholders' Equity
For the Month Ended June 30, 2001

Beginning contributed capital	$ 5,000	
Contributions during the month	0	
Ending contributed capital		$ 5,000
Beginning retained earnings	$ 9,883	
Net income for the month	24,779	
Dividends	(1,000)	
Ending retained earnings		33,662
Total shareholders' equity		$38,662

Tom's Wear, Inc.
Balance Sheet
At June 30, 2001

Assets		Liabilities and shareholders' equity	
Cash	$ 8,278	Accounts payable	$18,950
Accounts receivable (net	42,780	Interest payable	750
of allowance of $1,320)		Warranty liability	979
Inventory	6,365	Salaries payable	723
Prepaid insurance	150	Payroll taxes payable	277
Prepaid rent	1,800	Other payables	77
Prepaid Web service	200	Current portion of	6,000
Total current assets	59,573	long-term note	
		Total current liabilities	27,756
Computer (net of $400	3,600		
accumulated depreciation)		Notes payable	24,000
Van (net of $2,755	27,245	Total liabilities	51,756
accumulated depreciation)			
Total assets	$90,418	Common stock	5,000
		Retained earnings	33,662
		Total liabilities and	
		shareholders' equity	$90,418

tom's wear

Tom's Wear, Inc.
Statement of Cash Flows
For the Month Ended June 30, 2001

Cash from operating activities
    Cash collected from customers $ 8,800
    Cash paid for operating expenses   (4,127)
    Cash paid to vendors   (4,200)
Total cash from operations $ 473
Cash from investing activities   0
Cash from financing activities
    Dividends paid to owner   (1,000)
Net increase (decrease) in cash $ (527)

$ 8,278   Ending cash balance (June 30)
(8,805)   Beginning cash balance (June 30)
$ (527)   Net decrease in cash

Questions

1. When is revenue recognized?
2. What's the difference between recognizing revenue and realizing revenue?
3. Which asset is extremely easy to steal because there is no common or practical way to identify the owner?
4. What is a major control for safeguarding cash?
5. What are the two methods for accounting for bad debts?
6. What are the main issues in controlling and managing the collection of receivables?
7. How is the net realizable value for accounts receivable calculated? On which financial statement is net realizable value shown?
8. What is the reason for using the allowance method?
9. If a company uses the allowance method, what effect does writing off a specific account have on income?
10. When using the allowance method, what two ways are used to estimate the amount of bad debts?
11. Which method of calculating the allowance provides the best number for the income statement? Explain.
12. Which method of calculating the allowance provides the best number for the balance sheet? Explain.
13. What is the reason for estimating warranty expense? Why not record the expense as it is incurred to actually honor the warranties?

Short Exercises

SE7-1 Static Company had sales of $100,000 during January. Customers returned $5,000 worth of merchandise for a full refund. Static Company also reduced a customer's invoice balance by $150 due to a minor defect in the product shipped. Static anticipates that, in the future, it will spend $1,200 to honor warranties related to January sales. How much should Static report on the January income statement for net sales?

L.O. 7-1

SE7-2 For each of the following items, indicate whether or not the balance per books should be adjusted. For each item that affects the balance per books, indicate whether the item should be added to (+) or subtracted from (−) the balance per books.

L.O. 7-2

Item	Balance per books adjusted?	+/−
Outstanding checks	No	n/a
Service charge by bank		
NSF check from customer		
Deposits in transit		
Error made by the bank		
Note receivable collected by the bank		

L.O. 7-2

SE7-3 For each item listed next, indicate whether or not the balance per bank should be adjusted. For each item that affects the balance per bank, indicate whether the item should be added to (+) or subtracted from (−) the balance per bank.

Item	Balance per bank adjusted?	+/−
Outstanding checks	Yes	—
Service charge by bank		
NSF check from customer		
Deposits in transit		
Error made by the bank		
Note receivable collected by the bank		

L.O. 7-2

SE7-4 Datatech's accountant wrote a check to a supplier for $1,050, but erroneously recorded it on the company's books as $1,500. She discovered this when she saw the monthly bank statement and noticed that the check had cleared the bank for $1,050. How would this be handled in a bank reconciliation? Would Datatech need to make any adjustments to its accounting records?

L.O. 7-2

SE7-5 On the September bank statement, the ending balance as of September 30 was $9,550.48. The cash balance in the books was $10,053.57. Consider the following information:

Outstanding checks	$1,876.67
Interest earned on the account	32.18
NSF check from G. Murphy	391.55
Deposits in transit	2,020.39

What is the company's true cash balance on September 30?

L.O. 7-3

SE7-6 Beret and Sons Furniture has a liberal credit policy and has been experiencing a high rate of uncollectible accounts. The company estimates that 5% of credit sales become bad debts. Due to the significance of this amount, the company uses the *allowance* method for accounting for bad debts. During 2003, credit sales amounted to $430,000. The year-end accounts receivable balance was $192,000. What was the bad debt expense for the year?

L.O. 7-3

SE7-7 Quality Autoparts Company sells merchandise to auto repair shops and car dealerships. Quality has always used the direct *write-off method* of accounting for bad debts because of very tight credit policies and predominately cash sales. During 2003, credit sales were $520,450 and the year-end balance in accounts receivable is $173,500. Quality estimates that about half of 1% of the accounts receivable will not be collected. Unfortunately, just prior to the end of 2003, one of Quality's best customers filed for bankruptcy and has informed Quality that it will not be able to pay its outstanding balance of $23,000. That amount is included in the $173,500 accounts receivable balance. How should Quality record this in its accounting records? That is, what amount of bad debt expense will Quality recognize on the income statement for the year ended December 31, 2003?

L.O. 7-3

SE7-8 On January 1, 2002, a company's accounts receivable balance was $8,900 and the allowance for doubtful accounts normal balance was $600. This information came from the December 31, 2001 balance sheet. During 2002, the company reported $77,000 of credit sales. During 2002, $400 of specific receivables were written off as uncollectible. Cash collections of receivable were $69,000 for the year. The company estimates that 3% of the year-end accounts receivable will be uncollectible. What is bad debt expense for the year ending December 31, 2002?

SE7-9 At the end of the year, before any adjustments are made, the accounting records for Raley Company show a balance of $100,000 in accounts receivable. The allowance for uncollectible accounts has a normal balance of $2,000. (This means the estimate of bad debt expense last year was too large by $2,000.) The company uses accounts receivable to estimate bad debt expense. An analysis of accounts receivable accounts results in an estimate of $27,000 of uncollectible accounts. What is bad debt expense for the year? What is the net realizable value of accounts receivable on the year-end balance sheet?

L.O. 7-3

SE7-10 Bett, Inc. had the following balances at year-end prior to recording any adjustments:

L.O. 7-3, 6

Credit sales	$160,000
Accounts receivable	30,000
Allowance for uncollectible accounts	100 shortfall[a]

[a]Bett wrote off $100 more accounts during the year than estimated, i.e., allowance was too small this year.

Following completion of an aging analysis, the accountant for Bett estimated that $1,100 of the receivables would be uncollectible. What amount of bad debt expense would Bett show on the year's income statement? What information would be disclosed on the balance sheet?

SE7-11 The 2001 year-end accounts show the following normal balances: Accounts Receivable (AR), $50,000; Allowance for Uncollectibles, $1,000; and Net Sales, $200,000. By using the sales method, the company estimates 2% of sales will become uncollectible. What is the bad debt expense for 2001? What will be the net realizable value of AR on the year-end balance sheet?

L.O. 7-3

SE7-12 The 2003 year-end accounts show the following normal balances: Accounts Receivable (AR), $50,000; Allowance for Uncollectibles, $500; and Net Sales, $400,000. By using the accounts receivable method, the company estimates $4,000 of ending accounts receivable will be uncollectible. What is the bad debt expense for 2003? What will be the net realizable value of AR on the year-end balance sheet?

L.O. 7-3

SE7-13 Selby Company accepts MasterCard from its customers. MasterCard charges Selby Company 4% of sales for its services. During 2004, Selby's customers used MasterCard to purchase $43,560 worth of merchandise. How much did Selby show as sales on the income statement for the year ended December 31, 2004? How much cash did Selby actually receive from these sales?

L.O. 7-4

SE7-14 Harpo, Inc. accepts VISA from its customers. VISA charges Harpo a fixed fee of $100 per month plus 3% of VISA sales. If Harpo had VISA sales of $435,500 during 2001, how much did Harpo pay VISA for its services?

L.O. 7-4

SE7-15 Matt's Rug Company had sales of $100,000 in 2002. The company expects to incur future warranty expenses related to these sales that will amount to 6% of sales. There were $4,000 of warranty obligations paid in cash during 2002 related to the 2002 sales. How much warranty expense would Matt's Rug Company show on the income statement for the 2002 fiscal year? What is the amount of the warranty liability on the balance sheet at the end of 2002?

L.O. 7-5

SE7-16 When Handle's Pet Shop sells a puppy, it provides a health warranty for the little critter. If a puppy should become ill in the first 2 years after the sale, Handle's Pet Shop will pay the vet bill up to $200. Because this is normally a significant expense for the shop, the accountant insists that Handle's Pet Shop record an estimated warranty liability at the end of every year before the financial statements are prepared. On

L.O. 7-5

December 31, 2004, the accountant made the appropriate entry to record that liability. On March 30, 2005, the store received a $50 vet bill from one of its customers, who had bought a puppy in 2004. Handle's Pet Shop wrote a check for $50 to reimburse the puppy's owner. What effect did this payment have on the financial statements for the year ended December 31, 2005 of Handle's Pet Shop?

Exercises

L.O. 7-1

E7-1   Rachet's Tool Company sells tools to hardware and plumbing supply stores. Mr. Rachet, the owner, has asked you for some advice about the flow of documents in his business. Currently, he has instructed his accounting clerk to prepare an invoice for the customer by using the customer's original sales order. After it is prepared, the accounting clerk promptly mails it to the customer. The customer's sales order is copied and sent to the inventory control clerk, who passes the copy along to the shipping department with the goods. For some reason, Mr. Rachet's customers are continually complaining about inaccurate invoices. To help Mr. Rachet solve this problem, what information would you like to have? What suggestions would you make?

L.O. 7-2

E7-2   The bank statement for David's Landscaping as of February 28 had an ending balance of $38,334.96. Also listed on the statement was a service charge for $16. A check that David wrote to pay for equipment purchased February 25 had not cleared the bank yet—the amount was $7,250. Deposits in transit were $4,115.73. David's bank collected a $1,100 note for him in February. After reviewing the bank statement and cancelled checks, David discovered that the bank mistakenly deducted $297.15 from his account for a check that was written by David's Lighting.

Calculate the true cash balance as of February 28.

L.O. 7-2

E7-3   The advertising firm, Carolyn & Company, had the following information available concerning its cash account for the month of July:

Balance per Carolyn & Company books, July 31		$18,280.54
Outstanding checks		6,440.29
NSF check from customer		2,800.00
Note collected by bank		3,000.00
Deposits in transit		5,860.50
Miscellaneous bank fees		
Charge for collection of note	$25.00	
Order for checks	62.50	
Interest earned on bank account		$ 421.38

Calculate the true cash balance as of July 31.

L.O. 7-2

E7-4   Prepare a bank reconciliation for Jay Gordon's Brake Shop for the month of November using the following information:

Balance per First National Bank statement at November 30	$14,003.90
Outstanding checks	5,765.44
NSF checks from customer	366.71
Deposits in transit	3,542.26
Interest revenue earned on checking account	184.56
Service charge	30.00
Cash balance per Jay Gordon's Brake Shop's books at November 30	$11,992.87

After appropriate adjustments resulting from this reconciliation are recorded in the books, what will be the effect on net income (i.e., will net income be increased or decreased) and by what amount?

E7-5 Prepare a bank reconciliation for Cheri's Bakery using the following information:

L.O. 7-2

Company's cash account balance, March 31	$5,599.20
Bank statement ending balance, March 31	3,904.37
Deposits in transit	2,504.57
Outstanding checks	
3941	633.15
3956	194.59

Error found in Cheri's books—check 3928 for $142.60 was correctly deducted from the bank account, but was mistakenly recorded in the books as $124.60.

E7-6 Compute Right uses the allowance method to account for bad debts. Indicate the effect that each of the following transactions will have on gross accounts receivables, the allowance for uncollectible accounts, net accounts receivable, and bad debt expense. Use (+) for increase, (−) for decrease, and (0) for no effect.

L.O. 7-3

a. A customer pays his bill.
b. Of $500,000 in sales, 1% is estimated to be uncollectible.
c. Of $100,000 in accounts receivable, 5% is estimated to be uncollectible. Last year, an excess of $400 beyond what was expected was written off.
d. A specific account receivable previously written off is reinstated.

E7-7 A company started the year with Accounts Receivable of $20,000 and an Allowance for uncollectible accounts of $2,500. During the year, sales (all on account) were $80,000 and cash collections for sales amounted to $77,000. Also, $2,400 worth of uncollectible accounts were specifically identified and written off. Then at year-end, the company estimates that 5% of ending Accounts Receivable will be uncollectible. (The company tightened up its credit policy this year.) Answer the following questions:

L.O. 7-3

a. What amount will be shown on the year-end income statement for bad debt expense?
b. What is the balance in the allowance after all entries and adjustments have been made?

E7-8 The Beautiful Bow Company uses the allowance method to account for bad debts. During 2000, the company recorded $800,000 in credit sales. At the end of 2000, before adjustments, account balances were Accounts Receivable, $120,000; and Allowance for Uncollectible Accounts, $3,000 (normal balance). If bad debt expense is estimated to be 3% of credit sales, how much bad debt expense will be on the year-end income statement?

L.O. 7-3

E7-9 Havana Honda, Inc. uses the allowance method for bad debts and adjusts the allowance for uncollectible accounts to a desired amount based on an aging of accounts receivable. At the beginning of 2000, the allowance for uncollectible accounts had a balance of $18,000. During 2000, credit sales totaled $480,000 and receivables of $14,000 were written off. The year-end aging indicated that a $21,000 allowance for uncollectible accounts was required. What is the bad debt expense for 2000? What information will be disclosed on the balance sheet at year-end? What information does this provide someone who is evaluating Havana Honda's annual performance?

L.O. 7-3, 6

E7-10 Western Wear Corp. began 2003 with accounts receivable of $1,240,000 and a normal balance in the allowance for uncollectible accounts of $36,000. During 2003, credit sales totaled $5,190,000 and cash collected from customers totaled $5,380,000. Also, actual write offs of specific accounts receivable in 2003 were $33,000. At the end of the year, an accounts receivable aging schedule indicated a required allowance of $32,300. No accounts receivable previously written off were collected.

L.O. 7-3, 6

a. What is the net realizable value of accounts receivable at year-end?
b. What is the bad debt expense for the year 2003?
c. Why would Western Wear use the allowance method?

L.O. 7-3, 6

E7-11 Use the following information from the financial statements in the La-Z-Boy 2000 annual report to answer the following questions:

Current assets (amounts in thousands)	April 20, 2000	April 24, 1999
Cash and equivalents	$ 14,353	$ 33,550
Receivables, less allowance of $25,474 in 2000 and $19,550 in 1999	394,453	265,157

a. Does La-Z-Boy have significant credit sales? If so, what evidence supports your opinion?

b. Sales for the fiscal year ending on April 20, 2000 were $1,717,420,000. Compute the accounts receivable turnover ratio and comment on what it tells you about the La-Z-Boy credit and collection policies. What would make the ratio more useful for this assessment?

c. Can you tell what bad debt expense was for the fiscal year ending April 20, 2000? Explain.

L.O. 7-3, 6

E7-12 An examination of the balance sheet of Toys-Я-Us shows no allowance for bad debts.

a. Under what conditions would a company be allowed to omit this account from the balance sheet? Does this make sense for Toys-Я-Us?

b. Many of Toys-Я-Us customers pay with credit cards. How are those sales reflected on the financial statements?

L.O. 7-4

E7-13 Trane Air Company accepts cash or credit card payment from customers. During July, Trane sold merchandise with a sales price of $100,000 to customers who used VISA to pay for their purchases. VISA charges Trane 4% of sales for their services. How will this transaction be recorded in Trane's financial records? Why would Trane accept VISA?

L.O. 7-4

E7-14 The owner of Suzy's Dress Shop is trying to decide whether to extend credit to her customers, to accept MasterCard, or to do both. Suppose Suzy expects to sell approximately $50,000 worth of merchandise each quarter if she offers her customers one of these choices. What costs and benefits should Suzy consider in making her decision? Explain the difference between the alternatives.

L.O. 7-5

E7-15 In June, Hopps, Inc. had sales of $3,500 of its pogo sticks. The company gives a 6-month warranty with the purchase of a pogo stick. When Hopps recorded the sales in June, the company also estimated that it will spend $350 to honor those warranties. When the company prepared its June financial statements, no sticks had been brought in for repair. In July, however, five people brought in their broken pogo sticks, and Hopps spent a total of $50 repairing them (at no charge to the customers, because the sticks were under warranty). Assume no additional sales were made in July (i.e., no new warranties were given in July).

a. How much warranty expense would Hopps show on an income statement for the month of June?

b. Would Hopps have a warranty liability on the balance sheet at June 30, and if so, how much?

c. How much warranty expense would Hopps show on an income statement for the month of July?

d. Would Hopps have a warranty liability on the balance sheet at July 31, and if so, how much?

Problems—Set A

L.O. 7-2

P7-1A Consider the following concerning the Computer Tech cash account for the month of April.

■ Cash per the Computer Tech records was $85,834.99.

■ Customer payments of $16,008.13 were received April 30, but not deposited until May 1.

- Checks totaling $22,461.87 were issued in April, but had not cleared the bank as of the statement date (April 30).
- According to the bank statement, service charges for April were $54.50, and the bank collected a $4,900 note on April 19.

Required: Determine the April 30 cash balance that appears on the Computer Tech bank statement. (*Hint:* compute the true cash balance first.)

P7-2A The Central Copy Center (CCC) ending cash balance for October was $9,110.45. The owner deposited $773.14 on October 31 that did not appear on the bank statement. The bank collected a note of $500 for CCC and charged them $25 for the service. The ending balance on the bank statement for October was $9,022.39. After comparing the company's records with the bank statement, checks totaling $503.65 were found to be outstanding. Besides the collection fee, there was $30 in other service charges. Also, the statement showed that CCC earned $180 in interest revenue on the account and that checks amounting to $380.57 turned out to be NSF. Finally, a bank error was discovered: check number 4320 for $318.04 was paid to one of the CCC vendors. The bank incorrectly deducted $381.04 from the CCC account referencing check number 4320.

Required: Using the preceding information concerning the CCC cash account, prepare a bank reconciliation for the month of October.

L.O. 7-2

P7-3A Given the following errors:

a. The bank recorded a deposit of $200 as $2,000.
b. The company's bookkeeper mistakenly recorded a deposit of $530 as $350.
c. The company's bookkeeper mistakenly recorded a payment of $250 received from a customer as $25 on the bank deposit slip. The bank caught the error and made the deposit for the correct amount.
d. The bank statement shows a check written by the company for $255 was erroneously paid (cleared the account) as $225.
e. The bookkeeper wrote a check for $369 but erroneously wrote down $396 as the cash disbursement in the company's records.

Required: For each error, describe how it would be shown on a cash reconciliation.

L.O. 7-2

P7-4A Consider the following:

a. At year-end, Vio Company has accounts receivable of $14,000. The allowance for uncollectible accounts has a normal balance prior to adjustment of $300. (Last year, uncollectible accounts were overestimated by $300.) An aging schedule prepared on December 31 estimates that $1,100 of the Vio accounts receivable are uncollectible accounts.
b. At year-end, Demato Company has accounts receivable of $25,700. The allowance for uncollectible accounts has a negative balance prior to adjustment of $400. (Last year, uncollectible accounts were *underestimated* by $400.) An aging schedule prepared on December 31 indicates that $2,300 of the Demato accounts receivable are uncollectible accounts.

Required: For each of the previously described situations compute the bad debt expense for the year, the balance in the allowance for doubtful accounts, and the net realizable value of accounts receivable for the year-end financial statements. In both cases, the company uses the accounts receivable balance as the basis for estimating bad debts.

L.O. 7-3

P7-5A Consider the situations that follow:

a. At year-end, Nash Company has accounts receivable of $84,000. The allowance for uncollectible accounts has a normal balance prior to adjustment of $300. (Last year, uncollectible accounts were *overestimated* by $300.) Net credit sales for the year were $250,000 and 3% is estimated to be uncollectible.
b. At year-end, Bridges Company has accounts receivable of $83,000. The allowance for uncollectible accounts has a negative balance prior to adjustment of $400. (Last year, uncollectible accounts were *underestimated* by $400.) Net credit sales for the year were $250,000 and 3% is estimated to be uncollectible.

L.O. 7-3

Required: For each of the preceding situations, compute the bad debt expense for the year, the balance in the Allowance for Doubtful Accounts, and the net realizable value of Accounts Receivable for the year-end financial statements. In both cases, the company uses net credit sales as the basis for estimating bad debts.

L.O. 7-3, 6

P7-6A The following information has been adapted from the annual financial statements of the Pepsi Bottling Group, Inc.

From the balance sheet:

December 25, 1999 and December 26, 1998 In millions, except per share data	1999	1998
Assets		
Current assets		
Cash and cash equivalents	$ 190	$ 36
Trade accounts receivable, less allowance of $48 and $46, in 1999 and 1998, respectively	827	808
Inventories	293	296
Prepaid expenses, deferred income taxes and other current assets	183	178
Total current assets	*1,493*	*1,318*
Property, plant and equipment, net	**2,218**	2,055
Intangible assets, net	**3,819**	3,806
Other assets	89	143
Total assets	**$7,619**	*$7,322*

From the income statement:

Fiscal years ended December 25, 1999, December 26, 1998, and December 27, 1997 Dollars in millions, except per share data	1999	1998	1997
Net revenues	**$7,505**	$7,041	$6,592
Cost of sales	4,296	4,181	3,832
Gross profit	**3,209**	2,860	2,760

Required:

1. What are the total amounts of accounts receivable for the 2 years given *before* considering the possible uncollectible accounts? That is, what are gross accounts receivable?
2. Do you think the company has a significant amount of bad debts? Why or why not?
3. Shortly after the financial statements were released, the company was notified that a major customer, who owes the company over $10 million had filed for bankruptcy. If the company had received that information before the financial statements were released, what amounts would have been changed to reflect the write-off of the accounts receivable of the bankrupt customer? Explain.
4. Calculate the accounts receivable turnover ratio for 1998 and 1999. (Net accounts receivable at the end of 1997 was $800 million.) Also, calculate the number of days it takes, on average, to collect an accounts receivable. Explain this information to the company's management.

L.O. 7-4

P7-7A The following took place during the month of July at Holly's Hoops:

- The company sold $5,000 worth of hoops. Each is guaranteed for 12 months. Any defective hoop will be repaired or replaced free of charge during that period.
- Holly estimated that it will cost $600 during the next year to honor the warranties on the July sales.
- During August, Holly spent $250 dollars to honor warranties related to July sales.
- The company did not sell any hoops in August.

Holly's Hoops prepares monthly financial statements.

Required:

    a. What amount of warranty expense would be shown on the July income statement?

    b. What amount of warranty liability would be shown on the July balance sheet?

    c. What amount of warranty expense would be shown on the August income statement?

    d. What effect did recording the warranty expense have on owner's equity?

    e. What effect did spending the $250 in August have on owner's equity?

Problems—Set B

P7-1B Considering the following information concerning Martin Office Furniture for the month of June.

L.O. 7-2

- Deposits in transit as of June 30, were $3,785.15.
- Interest revenue earned was $1,300.
- Bank service charges amounted to $48.
- An error was discovered: The bank deducted from the Martin Office Furniture account a check for $161.03 that was written by Morton Office Supply.
- The following checks were still outstanding as of the bank statement date:

16012	$10,460.60
16006	200.58
16017	532.27

- The Martin Office Furniture accountant recorded a deposit of $332 as $223.
- The bank returned a check from a customer as NSF in the amount of $1,059.17.
- Balance per the bank June 30 was $45,020.59.

Required: Given this information, determine the ending cash balance that appears on the Martin Office Furniture books. (*Hint:* compute the true cash balance first.)

P7-2B Given the following errors:

L.O. 7-2

    a. The bank recorded a deposit of $300 as $30.

    b. The company's bookkeeper mistakenly recorded a deposit of $240 as $420.

    c. The company's bookkeeper mistakenly recorded a payment of $450 received from a customer as $45 on the bank deposit slip. The bank caught the error and made the deposit for the correct amount.

    d. The bank statement shows a check written by the company for $392 was erroneously paid (cleared the account) as $329.

    e. The bookkeeper wrote a check for $275 but erroneously wrote down $257 as the cash disbursement in the company's records.

Required: For each error, describe how the correction would be shown on the company cash reconciliation.

P7-3B Information about credit sales and collections for June Company for the fiscal year ending June 30, 2002 follows:

L.O. 7-3

    a. June Company had credit sales of $560,000 during the year.

    b. June began the year with accounts receivable of $23,500 and an allowance for uncollectible accounts of $(800). During the year, the company collected $555,000 cash for payments of accounts receivable. The company also wrote off the balances of two bankrupt customers, totaling $750.

    c. June uses the accounts receivable balance to estimate uncollectible accounts.

    d. June decides that 4% of accounts receivable will be uncollectible.

Required: Calculate the bad debt expense and the net realizable value of accounts receivable for June Company for the year ended June 30, 2002. How does the June estimate of uncollectible accounts for the year compare to the June estimate for the previous year? What factors may have caused this change?

L.O. 7-3, 6

P7-4B Gerard's Merchandising Mart has provided the following information about the company's sales and accounts receivable for the fiscal year ending December 31, 2003.

Accounts receivable at December 31, 2002	$ 42, 500
Allowance for uncollectible accounts at December 31, 2002 (after adjustments)	1,275
Credit sales for the year ended December 31, 2003	135,750
Cash collections on accounts receivable during 2003	142,600
Specific accounts written off during 2003	1,050

Required:

1. Suppose Gerard's used the accounts receivable balance to estimate the uncollectible accounts expense at the end of 2002. When 2003 is completed, can you tell if Gerard's over- or underestimated the uncollectible accounts expense at the end of 2002? Explain.
2. If Gerard's used the sales method for estimating the allowance, can you tell what percentage of the sales the company believes will not be collected? Why or why not?
3. Suppose Gerard's uses accounts receivable to estimate the allowance. The company estimates that 3% of ending accounts receivable will be uncollectible. Compute (1) the uncollectible accounts expense for the year ended December 31, 2003, and (2) the net realizable value of accounts receivable on the December 31, 2003 balance sheet.
4. Suppose Gerard's uses the sales method to estimate the allowance for uncollectible accounts, and the company believes 1% of credit sales will be uncollectible. Compute (1) the uncollectible accounts expense for the year ended December 31, 2003, and (2) the net realizable value of accounts receivable on the December 31, 2003 balance sheet.
5. Do you have a preference for a method of computing the allowance? Explain why or why not.

L.O. 7-5

P7-5B In July 2000, Jim started a business selling custom bicycle helmets on the Internet. Jim and his staff make the helmets based on measurements provided by the customer. The helmets are guaranteed to fit for 2 years. When one is returned, Jim and his staff completely rework the helmet to the customer's revised measurements, a very labor-intensive job. The data from Jim's first 2 years of business follow:

	Fiscal year ended June 30, 2001	Fiscal year ended June 30, 2002
Sales	$252,000	$375,000
Units sold	1,050	1,500
Units returned	100	285
Average cost to repair	$150/unit	$160/unit

Jim estimates that about 20% of the helmets will be returned to be reworked during the 2 years following the sale.

Required:

1. Suppose Jim follows GAAP and matches the warranty cost with the sales. Calculate the estimated warranty liability and the warranty expense for both years. Do you think Jim's estimate of 20% is a good one? Explain.
2. Suppose Jim does *not* follow GAAP, but instead records warranty expense whenever he incurs the repair cost. Calculate the warranty expense for both years.
3. Compare the two methods. If you were a financial statement user (bank loan officer or investor), which method would you prefer? That is, which method do you think gives a better picture of Jim's warranty situation and why?

P7-6B The following took place during the month of May at Mega TV Shop:

■ Mega sold $50,000 worth of its own brand of television. Each television is guaranteed for 12 months. Any defective television will be repaired or replaced free of charge during that period.
■ The company has estimated that it will cost $5,000 during the next year to honor the warranties on the May sales.
■ During June, Mega TV Shop spent $1,050 dollars to honor warranties related to May sales.
■ The company did not sell any televisions during June.

Mega TV Shop prepares monthly financial statements.

Required:

   a. What amount of warranty expense would be shown on the May income statement?
   b. What amount of warranty liability would be shown on the May 31 balance sheet?
   c. What amount of warranty expense would be shown on the June income statement?
   d. What effect does recording the warranty *expense* have on owner's equity?
   e. What effect did spending the $1,050 in June have on owner's equity?

P7-7B On June 1, Evan's Doughnuts, Inc., had a $290,000 balance in Accounts Receivable. During June, the company had credit sales revenue of $758,000. During June, Evan's collected $578,000 of accounts receivable and wrote off specific accounts of $7,200. On June 30, the unadjusted (normal) balance in Allowance for Uncollectible Accounts is $2,800 (i.e., after the write offs, there is still $2,800 in the Allowance). Uncollectible Account Expense is estimated to be 2% of credit sales.

Required:

   1. Show all increases and decreases to Accounts Receivable, Allowance for Uncollectible Accounts, and Bad Debt Expense for the month of June.
   2. What amount of bad debt expense will Evan's Doughnuts, Inc. report on the income statement for the month ended June 30?
   3. What amount of *net* accounts receivable will Evan's Doughnuts, Inc. report on its June 30 balance sheet?
   4. How would this information about uncollectible receivables help Evan make decisions about the credit policies of his company?

Recording Transactions

R7-1 (SE7-4) Datatech's accountant wrote a check to a supplier for $1,050 but erroneously recorded it on the company's books as $1,500. She discovered this when she saw the monthly bank statement and noticed that the check had cleared the bank for $1,050. Give the journal entry Datatech needs to make to its accounting records to correct this error.

Date	Account	Debit	Credit

R7-2 (SE7-8) On January 1, 2002, a company's accounts receivable balance was $8,900, and the allowance for doubtful accounts balance was $600. This information came from the December 31, 2001, balance sheet. During 2002, the company reported $77,000 of credit sales, and $400 of specific receivables were written off as uncollectible. Cash collections of receivables were $69,000 for the year. The company estimates that 3% of the year-end accounts receivable will be uncollectible. Use T-accounts to analyze the problem, and then make the journal entry to record the bad debt expense for the year ended December 31, 2002.

Accounts receivable	Allowance for uncollectible accounts	Bad debt expense
$8,900	$600 1/1	

Date	Account	Debit	Credit

R7-3 (E7-11) The 2001 year-end unadjusted trial balance shows: accounts receivable (AR) $50,000 debit; allowance for uncollectibles $1,000 credit; and net sales $200,000. Using the "percent of sales" method, the company estimates 2% of sales will become uncollectible. Give the journal entry to record the bad debt expense for 2001.

Date	Account	Debit	Credit

R7-4 (SE7-13) Selby Company accepts MasterCard from its customers. MasterCard charges Selby Company 4% of sales for its services. During 2004, Selby's customers used MasterCard for $43,560 worth of purchases. Record the journal entry for these sales.

Date	Account	Debit	Credit

R7-5 (SE7-16) When Handle's Pet Shop sells a puppy, it provides a health warranty for the little critter. If a puppy should become ill in the first 2 years after the sale, Handle's Pet Shop will pay the vet bill up to $200. Because this is normally a significant expense for the shop, the accountant insists that Handle's Pet Shop record an estimated warranty liability at the end of every year before the financial statements are prepared. On December 31, 2004, the accountant made the appropriate entry to record that liability. On March 30, 2005, the store received a $50 vet bill from one of its customers, who had bought a puppy in 2004. Handle's Pet Shop wrote a check for $50 to reimburse the puppy's owner. Give the journal entry for this payment.

Date	Account	Debit	Credit

R7-6 (E7-6) Compute Right uses the allowance method to account for bad debts. Show the journal entry for each item below.

a. A customer pays his bill of $50.
b. 1% of $500,000 in sales is estimated to be uncollectible.

c. 5% of $100,000 in accounts receivable is estimated to be uncollectible. Last year, an excess of $400 beyond what was expected was written off.

d. A specific account receivable in the amount of $65 is reinstated.

Transaction	Account	Debit	Credit

R7-7 (E7-10) Western Wear Corporation began 2003 with accounts receivable of $1,240,000 and a balance in the allowance for uncollectible accounts of $36,000. During 2003, credit sales totaled $5,190,000 and cash collected from customers totaled $5,380,000. Also, actual write-offs of specific accounts receivable in 2003 were $33,000. At end of the year, an accounts receivable aging schedule indicated a required allowance of $32,300. No accounts receivable previously written off were collected. Use T-accounts to show what happened in each of the accounts shown below. Then, give the journal entry to record the bad debt expense for the year ended December 31, 2003.

Accounts receivable

1/1 $1,240,000

Allowance for uncollectible accounts

1/1 $36,000

Bad debt expense

Date	Account	Debit	Credit

R7-8 (E7-13) Trane Air Company accepts cash or credit card payment from customers. During July, Trane sold $100,000 worth of merchandise to customers who used VISA to pay for their purchases. VISA charges Trane 4% of sales for their services. Give the journal entry to record this transaction in Trane's financial records.

Date	Account	Debit	Credit

R7-9 (P7-3A) Given the following errors:

a. The bank recorded a deposit of $200 as $2,000.

b. The company's bookkeeper mistakenly recorded a deposit of $530 as $350.

c. The company's bookkeeper mistakenly recorded a payment of $250 received from a customer as $25 on the bank deposit slip. The bank caught the error and made the deposit for the correct amount.

d. The bank statement shows that a check that was written by the company for $255 was erroneously paid (cleared the account) as $225. This was the bank's error.

e. The bookkeeper wrote a check for $369 but erroneously wrote down $396 as the cash disbursement in the company's records.

Required: Determine which of the errors would require the company to record a journal entry. Then, record the journal entry.

Transaction	Account	Debit	Credit

R7-10 (P7-4A) Consider the following:

a. At year-end, Vio Company has accounts receivable of $14,000. The allowance for uncollectible accounts has a credit balance prior to adjustment of $300. An aging schedule prepared on December 31 indicates that $1,100 of Vio's accounts receivable are uncollectible accounts.

b. At year-end, Demato Company has accounts receivable of $25,700. The allowance for uncollectible accounts has a debit balance prior to adjustment of $400. An aging schedule prepared on December 31 indicates that $2,300 of Demato's accounts receivable are uncollectible accounts.

Required: For each situation described above, give the journal entry to record bad debt expense. In both cases, the company uses the accounts receivable balance as the basis for estimating bad debts.

Transaction	Account	Debit	Credit

R7-11 (P7-5A) Consider the following situations:

a. At year-end, Nash Company has accounts receivable of $84,000. The allowance for uncollectible accounts has a credit balance prior to adjustment of $300. Net credit sales for the year were $250,000, and 3% is estimated to be uncollectible.

b. At year-end, Bridges Company has accounts receivable of $83,000. The allowance for uncollectible accounts has a debit balance prior to adjustment of $400. Net credit sales for the year were $250,000, and 3% is estimated to be uncollectible.

Required: For each situation described above, give the journal entry to record bad debt expense. In both cases, the company uses net credit sales as the basis for estimating bad debts.

Transaction	Account	Debit	Credit

R7-Comprehensive

Chapter 7: Comprehensive Financial Statement Preparation Problem

Tracy's Service Company started the year with the following trial balance.

Account	Debit	Credit
Cash	$161,000	
Accounts receivable	186,000	
Allowance for uncollectible accounts		$ 9,500
Office equipment	50,000	
Accumulated depreciation		10,000
Interest payable		7,000
Notes payable		70,000
Common stock		200,000
Retained earnings		100,500
	$397,000	$397,000

During 2004, the company:

1. Paid the $7,000 interest payable. The company pays interest on the note at a rate of 10% annually. Interest for the year ending December 31, 2003, was accrued at the end of last year and was remitted to the bank on the second day of January 2004. The principal of the note is due on December 31, 2010.
2. Performed services for customers amounting to $156,800 all on accounts. Tracy's Service Company decided this year to provide a 6-month warranty for its services. The company estimates that it will cost approximately 2% of the price of the service to fulfill these obligations.
3. Collected $145,700 cash on accounts receivable.
4. Found out two customers, M. Smith and J. Jones, had both filed for bankruptcy and wrote off their accounts receivable. The total amount the two customers owed was $7,500.
5. Paid cash of $50,000 for employee salaries.
6. Paid consultants $2,700 to provide the warranty service to customers.

Additional information:

1. Office equipment with a useful life of 10 years and no residual value needs to be depreciated. Tracy's Service Company uses straight-line depreciation.
2. Tracy's estimates that 5% of the ending balance of accounts receivable will be uncollectible.

Record the journal entries and adjustments for the year and post them to T-accounts. Prepare an adjusted trial balance, and then prepare the income statement, balance sheet (at December 31, 2004), statement of changes in shareholders' equity, and statement of cash flows for the year.

Issues for Discussion

Financial statement analysis

L.O. 7-6, 7

1. Use the Pier 1 Imports' financial statements to answer the following questions:

   a. Does Pier 1 have a significant amount of bad debts? How can you tell?
   b. Compute the accounts receivable turnover ratio for two consecutive years. What information does this provide?

Business risk

2. Consider the following:

   a. Suppose one person opens the cash receipts (checks received in the mail), makes the bank deposits, and keeps the accounts receivable records. What potential problems could arise from the lack of separation of duties?

   b. Why would a store offer a free purchase to a customer who does not receive a receipt?

Ethics

3. Bargain Books offers a customer discount card for an annual fee of $25. With this card, a customer receives a 10% discount on all purchases. One evening a customer was making a purchase of approximately $80, and the cashier asked the customer if she had a discount card. The customer thought she might have purchased one but did not have it with her. The cashier attempted to call the main office to obtain the number of the customer's discount card, but the cashier was put on hold for several minutes. Impatient to complete the transaction, the cashier told the customer that, because the main office was so slow, he would use his own discount card and give the customer the 10% discount on the purchase. The cashier reached into his own wallet, extracted his discount card, swiped it in the electronic cash register, and proceeded to ring up the customer's order.

   a. Why would a company offer a discount card?

   b. Do you think the cashier acted in an ethical manner? Explain why or why not?

Internet Exercise: Intel Corporation

Intel, by far the world's number one maker of semiconductor chips, commands more than 80% of the PC microprocessor market. Compaq and Dell are Intel's largest customers.

Please go to the www.prenhall.com/myphlip Web site, register, and add this textbook to your myphlip page (if you haven't done so already). Go to Chapter 7 and use the Internet Exercise company link.

IE7-1   Under "Quotes and Research" enter the company symbol INTC, the stock symbol of the Intel Corp., and then choose *Financials*. Find the *Annual Income Statement* to answer the following questions.

   a. Identify the amounts reported for total (net sales) revenue for the three most recent years.

   b. In general, who are Intel's customers? Who are Intel's two largest customers? Do you think Intel primarily has credit sales or cash sales? Why? Does Intel extend credit to its customers or do Intel's customers use credit cards to pay the amounts owed?

IE7-2   Find the Annual Balance Sheet to answer the following questions:

   a. Identify the amounts reported for trade accounts receivable, net for the three most recent year-ends. Does this represent amounts owed by customers or amounts that the company estimates it will actually collect from customers?

   b. Does Intel use the allowance method or the direct write-off method to record uncollectible accounts? How can you tell?

IE7-3

a. Compute the accounts receivable turnover ratio for the two most recent years. In which year did the company collect receivables the quickest? How can you tell?

b. For the most recent year, how long does it take on average for Intel to collect for a sale? Do you think the credit terms might be net/45 or net/60? Explain why.

Please note: Internet Web sites are constantly being updated. Therefore, if the information is not found where indicated, please explore the Web site further to find the information.

SPECIAL ACQUISITIONS: FINANCING A BUSINESS WITH DEBT

Sales and Accounts Receivable

Here's where you've been...

In Chapter 7, you learned about how a company accounts for *sales, cash,* and *accounts receivable*. You learned that the amount of accounts receivable shown on the balance sheet has been reduced by the amount the company believes it will not collect. You also learned the importance of collecting accounts receivable in a timely manner.

Here's where you're going...

When you are finished with Chapter 8, you should understand how a company obtains financing from creditors. You should be able to calculate both present and future values of cash flows. You'll study long-term notes and bonds, two ways a company borrows money, and interest payments associated with using someone else's money.

Financing

8

Financing

Sales and Accounts Receivable

Financial Reporting and Business Events

Property, Plant, and Equipment

Inventory and Liabilities

Learning Objectives

More specifically, when you are finished studying this chapter, you should be able to answer these questions:

1. What is a long-term note payable and how does a company account for this type of debt?
2. What is the time value of money, and how do you calculate the future value and the present value of a lump sum and a series of cash flows?
3. What are bonds payable, and how does a company record and report the transactions associated with bonds?
4. How is information about a company's debt used in financial statement analysis?
5. What risks are associated with long-term debt?

So far, you have seen how a business firm operates and how the firm's operations are reflected in its financial statements. Now, you are ready to see how a firm gets the money it needs to get started, to operate as a business, and to expand. That's what financing a firm is all about.

Financing is easier to understand after you're comfortable with how a business firm operates. That's why we've postponed the discussion of financing a business firm until this chapter, even though it is the *first* concern of someone starting a business firm. Tom couldn't have started his T-shirt company without financing—the loan from his mom and his own cash. Obtaining financing is always necessary to start a business firm, as well as later when the owners look for sources of money so the firm can better compete, improve, or expand.

Recall that there are two sources of financing—creditors and owners. Creditors lend a company money over a specified duration and for a specified rate of return. Owners invest money in the business for an unspecified duration and an *unspecified* return. **Debt financing** means obtaining capital—usually dollars but it could include other assets—from creditors. As we discuss financing as a business process and the accounting related to financing, you will see the close relationship between this business process and the accounting for it.

The most crucial part of obtaining debt financing is the *cost* of using someone else's money. You are already familiar with that cost—it's referred to as *interest*. This chapter will go into more detail about how to calculate the cost of borrowing money. Decisions about obtaining debt financing depend on accurate measurement of the related interest costs. In this chapter, you will see how to measure the cost of borrowing money, as well as how it is reported on a company's financial statements.

Tom's mom is a creditor—when she loaned money to Tom's Wear, she did so with the understanding that she would be repaid the amount of the loan plus a small amount of interest. No matter how much income Tom's Wear earns, Tom's mom receives only the principal of the loan plus interest, details generally specified as part of the loan agreement. Creditors do not share in the profits of a firm beyond what they have loaned plus some specified amount of interest. Owners take more risk when they invest money in a firm because they stand a greater

Debt financing means a company is borrowing money from creditors.

L.O. 1

Understand the cost of debt.

BUSINESS PROCESS

Understanding Business

FINANCING YOUR BUSINESS: USING A LINE OF CREDIT

Almost every company will need to borrow money during its life—sometimes to maintain a positive cash flow for regular operations and sometimes to expand or make other major changes to the business. Selecting the type of financing to obtain is a major business decision. In this chapter, the focus is on long-term financing. One common way to help a company manage its cash flow *without* long-term borrowing is called a *line of credit.* This is an excellent choice for financing the regular operations of a business.

What is a line of credit? It's an arrangement between a company and its bank in which the bank allows the company to borrow money for routine operating expenses up to the maximum amount of the credit line. The interest rate charged by the bank for this type of loan is usually much lower than the interest rate for credit card purchases, but it may be a bit higher than a typical bank loan for a specific amount and term. There is typically a very short repayment "window" for a line of credit—60 to 90 days.

What kind of business should use a line of credit? First, the business must be a profitable, established business. Second, the business should have predictable cash flows. A line of credit works best when there is a predictable, temporary, short-term shortage of cash. The amount used—that's the amount borrowed—needs to be repaid in a short time to make a line of credit a cost-effective financing

choice. Having a line of credit is also a good choice for a company that does not have a current cash flow problem but would like a backup in case of a cash flow problem.

When is a line of credit a poor financing choice? If your company needs to make large purchases of major long-term assets, then a loan with a longer term and a lower interest rate would be a better type of financing. If the cash shortage is more than temporary, the company should make a long-term plan for a solution. It is also not a good idea to use a line of credit to pay employees. Payroll is an expense that should be a priority for a company's regular cash inflow. In most cases, a company that must borrow money to meet its payroll needs to rethink its financial situation.

What does a business need to provide to get a line of credit? One of the most important items a company should have is a set of financial statements, particularly a balance sheet and an income statement. In addition to the basic financial statements, a company should have a detailed schedule of projected cash inflows and outflows. Other important items are several years of tax returns, a list of current bank accounts, a current business plan, and appraisals of any assets that might be used as collateral.

Check out the financial statements of some well-known companies. You'll find information about their lines of credit in the notes to the financial statements.

chance of losing their investment. Creditors' claims to the assets of a company always have priority over owners' claims. Thus, owners are the ones who are rewarded with the potential for a higher return. Owners have a chance to make a lot more money than they have invested in the company, more than they would have made if they had simply been creditors.

In this chapter, we'll look at ways a business firm *borrows* money. That is, we'll look at creditors, sources of funding outside the business, and how these transactions are reported on the financial statements. In the next chapter, we'll look at owners using their own money to finance their firms.

Long-Term Notes Payable and Mortgages

When a company borrows money for longer than 1 year, that obligation is called a *long-term note payable*. Long-term notes differ from short-term notes in several ways. Recall that short-term notes are debt obligations that will be

BUSINESS PROCESS

Interest is the cost of using someone else's money. Interest rates are typically given as *annual* rates.

repaid in 1 year or sooner. Long-term notes are typically repaid with a series of equal payments over the life of the note.

A car loan is an example of a long-term note payable. The monthly payments are a combination of interest and principal. With each monthly payment, you are paying that month's interest on the loan as well as a small part of the principal balance due. With each monthly payment, the principal of the note is reduced. Each month when the interest is calculated on the outstanding loan balance, the interest amount becomes a smaller portion of the payment. This is because the total amount of each payment stays the same, but over time the principal decreases and the interest on that declining principal goes down. That leaves a larger part of each monthly payment available to reduce the outstanding principal.

Exhibit 8-1 shows how this works for a loan of $100,000, with a 15-year term, and an **interest** rate of 10% per year. The annual payment is the same every year, but the portion of the payment that is interest expense decreases, whereas the portion of the payment that reduces the outstanding principal balance increases.

A mortgage is a special kind of note payable—it is a loan to a borrower for the specific purpose of purchasing property and gives the lender a claim against that property if the payments are not made. People often use this type of note payable—commonly referred to as a mortgage loan—to buy a house. Like most long-term notes, mortgage loans are debt obligations commonly repaid in periodic installments—each payment is part principal and part interest.

Suppose you sign, on January 1, a 3-year $100,000 mortgage with an 8% annual interest rate to buy a piece of land. Payments are to be made annually on December 31 of each year in the amount of $38,803.35. How did the bank figure out the annual payment for the $100,000 loan for 3 years at 8% interest? (Remember, the interest rate is given as an *annual* rate.)

The calculation of the annual payment is based on the time value of money. "Time value of money" means there is value in having money for a period of time. That value is the interest the money can earn. The bank gives you $100,000 today, so you must repay that amount plus interest for the time you have the borrowed amount or any part of it. The bank figures out what amount, received in three equal annual installments, would give it the same amount of money at the end of 3 years as it would have if it invested the $100,000 today and it grew at a rate of 8% per year. The equivalent value of the sum of those three payments—a $38,803.35 payment at the end of each of the next 3 years—is called the **present value** of those three payments. Each payment is discounted to an amount equivalent to having the money today. **Discounting** the cash flows strips them of the interest built in for the passage of time, bringing them back to equivalent dollars today. In this example, the dollars today amount to $100,000. The interest rate used in the calculation of present value amounts is also called the **discount rate**. In this example the discount rate is 8%.

To get a clearer sense of what is going on here, think about the following:

The **present value** is the amount a future amount of money is worth today.

Discounting means finding the present value.

Discount rate is another name for the interest rate in a present value problem.

- A dollar you have today is worth exactly a dollar.
- A dollar you received a year ago is worth more than a dollar today, because it has had a year to earn some interest (as long as you put it in the bank instead of spending it).
- A dollar to be received a year from now is worth less than a dollar today, because today's dollar can earn some interest during the year.

Thus, in our example, $100,000 is the present value. What annual payment for 3 years at 8% per year is equivalent to $100,000 today? In this example, this

Exhibit 8-1
Payments Composed of Interest and Principal

	Annual payment	Interest expense (principal balance × 0.10)	Reduction in principal	Principal balance
0				$100,000.00
1	$13,147.38	$10,000.00	$ 3,147.38	96,852.62
2	13,147.38	9,685.26	3,462.12	93,390.50
3	13,147.38	9,339.05	3,808.33	89,582.17
4	13,147.38	8,958.22	4,189.16	85,393.01
5	13,147.38	8,539.30	4,608.08	80,784.93
6	13,147.38	8,078.49	5,068.89	75,716.04
7	13,147.38	7,571.60	5,575.78	70,140.26
8	13,147.38	7,014.03	6,133.35	64,006.91
9	13,147.38	6,400.69	6,746.69	57,260.22
10	13,147.38	5,726.02	7,421.36	49,838.86
11	13,147.38	4,983.89	8,163.49	41,675.37
12	13,147.38	4,167.54	8,979.84	32,695.53
13	13,147.38	3,269.55	9,877.83	22,817.70
14	13,147.38	2,281.77	10,865.61	11,952.09
15	13,147.30	1,195.21	11,952.09	—

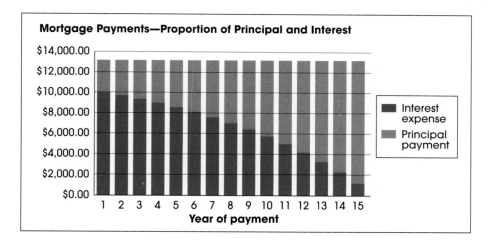

Note: This exhibit shows the payment schedule for a $100,000 loan for 15 years at 10% annual interest, with equal annual payments of $13,147.38. Each payment is made up of principal and interest. With each payment, the principal balance is reduced, so there is less interest expense each year. Because the payment stays the same, more of the payment goes toward reducing the principal each year. The graph shows how, over the term of the loan, the proportion of interest in each payment goes down, while the proportion of principal in each payment goes up.

calculation is done for you, but later in this chapter you will learn how to do it. The concept for you to understand here and now is the *concept* of present value. In this example, the bank has calculated the three payments to be $38,803.35. The present value of those three payments, discounted at the interest rate of 8%, equals $100,000. After the three payments are made, both the principal and the interest will be repaid.

When is the first payment due? In this example, the payments are annual, and the first payment will be made at the end of the first year of the loan. (Many loans are repaid monthly or quarterly, but the first payment is usually made after some time has passed.)

How much of the first payment is interest expense and how much goes toward paying back the principal? Remember, *interest* is the cost of borrowing money. The interest is based on the amount of the principal, the interest rate, and the amount of time for which the money is borrowed. (Interest = principal × rate × time.) The bank lends you $100,000 on day 1 of the note. On day 365, you make a $38,803.35 payment to the bank. The interest on the $100,000 for the year that has just passed is:

$$Interest = Principal \times Rate \times Time$$
$$\$100,000 \times 0.08/year \times 1\,Year = \$8,000$$

The entire $100,000 was borrowed for a full year, so you simply multiply principal × the annual rate × the 1-year duration to get the interest expense for the year. Of the $38,803.35 payment, $8,000 is interest, so the remaining portion of the payment—$30,803.35—is repayment of principal. The first payment affects the accounting equation, as shown next:

Assets	=	Liabilities	+	Contributed capital	+	Retained earnings
$(38,803.35) Cash		$(30,803.35) Mortgage payable				$(8,000) Interest expense

The journal entry to record the first principal and interest payment on the $100,000, 8%, 3-year note is:

Date	Transaction	Debit	Credit
12/31/2001	Mortgage payable	$30,803.35	
	Interest expense	8,000.00	
	Cash		$38,803.35

The principal of the mortgage has been reduced. Another way of saying that is, the outstanding balance of the mortgage is lower—meaning you have less of the bank's money at the end of the first year. Therefore, the interest owed the bank for the second year will be smaller than the interest paid for the first year. That's because the interest rate will be applied to a smaller principal, that is, a smaller outstanding balance. Use the interest formula to calculate the portion of the payment that is interest for the second year, and then subtract the interest from the total payment to calculate the amount of the payment that reduces the principal.

■ Interest = principal × rate × time.
■ Outstanding balance due at the start of the second year: $69,196.65 = $100,000 original principal − $30,803.35 reduction in principal from the first payment.
■ Principal of $69,196.65 for year 2 × 0.08 annual interest rate × 1 year = $5,535.73.
■ Principal of $69,196.65 × 0.08 per year × 1 year = $5,535.73.

The journal entry to record the second principal and interest payment on the $100,000, 8%, 3-year note is:

Date	Transaction	Debit	Credit
12/31/2002	Mortgage payable	$33,267.62	
	Interest expense	5,535.73	
	Cash		$38,803.35

Notice the amount of interest you owe the bank is smaller each year. The reason is because the outstanding balance of the mortgage is smaller each year. At the end of year 2, the bank receives the second payment of $38,803.35. As the preceding calculation shows, $5,535.73 of that payment is interest expense. The rest of the payment—$33,267.62 (= $38,803.35 − $5,535.73)—reduces the outstanding balance. After the second payment, the outstanding balance is $35,929.03. For the third payment of $38,803.35, the interest portion is:

- Interest = principal × rate × time.
- New principal = $35,929.03 = $100,000 original principal − $30,803.35 reduction in principal from the first payment − $33,267.62 reduction in principal from the second payment.
- Interest expense for year 3 = $35,929.03 principal for year 3 × 0.08 annual interest rate × 1 year = $2,874.32.
- Principal of $35,929.03 × 0.08 per year × 1 year = $2,874.32.

The journal entry to record the third principal and interest payment on the $100,000, 8%, 3-year note is:

Date	Transaction	Debit	Credit
12/31/2002	Mortgage payable	$35,929.03	
	Interest expense	2,874.32	
	Cash		$38,803.35

When you subtract the interest of $2,874.32 from the third payment of $38,803.35, the remaining $35,929.03 reduces the principal—in this case, it reduces it to exactly zero dollars.

Is it just luck that the remaining outstanding balance plus interest is exactly equal to the amount of the last payment? No, the bank did the present value calculations with the principal, interest rate, and length of the loan so that it would come out to exactly zero at the end of the third year. Look at Exhibit 8-2 to see the amortization schedule for this loan.

Tompkins Corp. purchased a building on January 1, signing a long-term, $600,000 mortgage, with monthly payments of $5,500. The interest rate is 9% per year. Prepare the journal entry to record the first payment.

STUDY BREAK 8-1
SEE HOW YOU'RE DOING

Exhibit 8-2
Amortization Schedule for a Mortgage

Mortgage balance		Annual payment	Interest portion of payment (8% × mortgage balance)	Amount of mortgage reduction (annual payment—interest portion)
Beginning balance	$100,000.00	$38,803.35	$8,000.00	$30,803.35
After first payment	69,196.65	38,803.35	5,535.73	33,267.62
After second payment	35,929.03	38,803.35	2,874.32	35,929.03
After third payment	0			

Time Value of Money

Understand the time value of money.

To understand what happens when a company borrows money, it is necessary to learn about the *time value of money*. This is a common expression in business, and it affects the financial life of every business and of every individual. If you have ever bought anything on credit or borrowed money for longer than 1 year, you have already had experience with the time value of money. The expression means just what it says: money has value over time. That's because invested money can earn interest. A person would prefer to receive a dollar today rather than a year from now because the dollar received today can earn interest during the year. Then it will be worth *more* than a dollar a year from now.

Simple versus Compound Interest

We've calculated the interest on the principal of a loan several times in previous chapters. When interest is computed on the principal only, it is called *simple interest*. Simple interest usually applies to short-term loans, those loans with terms of 1 year or less.

When interest is computed on the principal of a loan *plus* any interest that has been earned but not collected or paid, it is called *compound interest*. The interest earned during a year is added to the original principal, and that new larger amount is used to calculate the interest earned during the next year. Each year, the interest is calculated on a larger amount—the interest earned each successive year is added to the sum, which includes the initial principal and the interest earned in prior years.

Exhibit 8-3 shows what happens to $1,000 if we invest it today and watch it grow over 10 years. You can easily compare simple interest to compound interest. Compound interest makes your money grow much faster.

When you get familiar with compound interest, you can calculate:

1. the *future* value of an amount of money you deposit today; and
2. the amount of money you need to deposit today, the *present value* of an amount, to grow to a specific amount by some future date.

We'll discuss each in detail.

Future Value

If you deposit some money in your savings account today, the amount in your savings account will grow over time because your saved money is earning interest. The amount of money you will have in the future depends on the:

1. amount you have deposited today
2. annual interest rate
3. amount of time your money has to earn interest

To save money for your future, you could deposit a single amount today and watch it grow; or you could make a series of deposits, at regular intervals over time.

Single Amount. If you deposit $100 today in your savings account, how much will it be worth a year from today? Suppose the interest rate is 10%. You will earn 10% interest, or $10, on your $100 principal, 1 year from today when you'll have $110. If you leave it in the bank for another year at 10% interest, your $110 will grow to $121, as shown in Exhibit 8-4.

Exhibit 8-3 Simple versus Compound Interest

Deposit today at 10% annual interest	You'll have this much									
	At the end of year 1	At the end of year 2	At the end of year 3	At the end of year 4	At the end of year 5	At the end of year 6	At the end of year 7	At the end of year 8	At the end of year 9	At the end of year 10
Simple interest										
$1,000	$1,100	$1,200	$1,300	$1,400	$1,500	$1,600	$1,700	$1,800	$1,900	$2,000
Compound interest										
$1,000	$1,100	$1,210	$1,331	$1,464	$1,610	$1,771	$1,948	$2,143	$2,357	$2,593

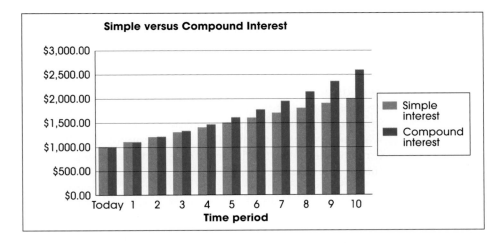

How much money will you have in 10 years if you deposit $1,000 today and it earns 10% interest per year?
If the money earns simple interest, you'll have $2,000 at the end of 10 years. Each year, the principal of $1,000 will earn $100.
If the money earns compound interest, you'll have $2,593 at the end of 10 years. Each year, the principal *plus the previously earned interest* will earn interest.

Future Value of $100 in 2 years at 10% per year =
$$[\$100(1.10)]\,1.10 = \$121$$

| This is the amount you'll have after one year. | So you increase this amount by 10% to get the amount you'll have at the end of the second year. |

If you extend this example to 3 years, you would multiply the amount at the end of 2 years, $121, by 1.10, which would give you $133.10. To generalize, you could use the following formula:

$$FV_n = PV(1 + i)^n$$

where

n = Number of periods during which the compounding occur
i = Interest rate for a single period
PV = Present Value or original amount invested at the beginning of the first period
FV_n = Future Value of the investment at the end of n periods

Exhibit 8-4
Future Value of a Lump Sum

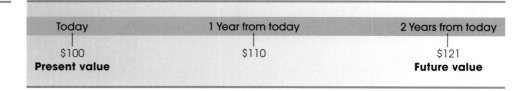

Today	1 Year from today	2 Years from today
$100	$110	$121
Present value		**Future value**

Try this formula with the $100 invested for 2 years at 10%.

$$\text{Future Value} = 100(1+0.10)^2$$
$$= \$100(1.10)(1.10)$$
$$= \$121$$

Instead of using a formula to calculate the future value of a single amount, you could do the calculation by using a future value table. Someone did all the multiplication work using various interest rates for many different periods of time, and put the factors in a table. The table is based on $1, so you simply find the number in the table that corresponds to the interest rate and the number of periods that apply to your situation. The interest rates and periods in the table are not labeled as annual, because they can be used for any length of time. The important point is that you use an interest rate based on the time period you want to use for compounding. An example will help you understand the relationship between the interest rate and the time period used and how to use future value tables.

Suppose you invested $100 at 10% per year with semiannual compounding, instead of the annual compounding we used in the previous example. We would then change the interest rate to a 6-month rate of 5% and use the number of 6-month periods in the problem. If you invested your $100 for 2 years at 10%, compounded semiannually, you would use an interest rate of 5% and 4 as the number of periods:

$$\text{Future Value} = \$100(1+0.05)^4$$
$$= \$121.55$$

By using the future value of $1 table (shown in Exhibit 8-5), you can find the column with the interest rate of 5% and the row with the number of periods equal to 4. That factor is 1.21551. Because you have $100, you multiply the factor by 100. That gives you $121.55.

Notice that the more frequently your principal is compounded the faster it will grow.

In addition to using a formula or a future value table, you could use a financial calculator to do the calculation. To use a financial calculator, put the calculator in financial mode.

Exhibit 8-5
Partial Future Value of $1 Table

(n) Periods	3%	4%	5%	6%
1	1.03000	1.04000	1.05000	1.06000
2	1.06090	1.08160	1.10250	1.12360
3	1.09273	1.12486	1.15763	1.19102
4	1.12551	1.16986	**1.21551**	1.26248

- Put in 100 and press the *PV* key. *PV* stands for present value, and $100 is the present value in this problem.
- Then, put in 4 and press the *N* key. *N* means the number of periods, which is 4 in this problem.
- Next, put in 5 and press the *i%* key, the interest rate for each period. It will change to 0.05 automatically on most calculators.
- Then, press the *CPT* key—that means compute—and then press the *FV* key. That is the future value key.
- You should see the answer in the display: 121.55.

Suppose you invested $500 at 12% interest per year for 10 years. How much would you have at the end of that time? Use three methods—formula, table (Appendix B), and calculator (if you have one) to determine the amount.

Future Value of an Annuity

Instead of saving a lump sum, you may prefer to make periodic deposits to your savings account. A stream of deposits or payments that are the same amount and made periodically over equally spaced intervals is called an **annuity**. Its name comes from the idea of annual payments, because most annuities are annual. There are two types of annuities:

An **annuity** is a series of equal payments over equally spaced intervals of time. With an **ordinary annuity** a series of payments are made at the end of each interval or period. With an **annuity due** a series of payments are made at the beginning of each period.

1. An **ordinary annuity,** also known as an *annuity in arrears,* is a series of payments in which the payments occur at the *end* of each period.
2. An **annuity due** is a series of payments in which the payments occur at the *beginning* of each period.

If you conclude that the difference between the two types of annuities is the length of time a payment has to earn interest, you are correct. Let's look at an example of an annuity with five deposits of $100 each.

Ordinary Annuity. Exhibit 8-6 shows the annuity as an ordinary annuity, with deposits at the end of each period.

Because the deposits are made at the end of the year, the first deposit would have 4 years to earn interest; the second deposit, 3 years to earn interest; the third, 2 years; the fourth, 1 year; and the last deposit would earn no interest. One way to calculate the total you would have at the end of 5 years is to take each single deposit and calculate the future value of that deposit, and then add all those amounts together. By using an annual interest rate of 10%, the calculations for the future value of each deposit follow:

$$\text{FV of }\$100\,(4\text{ Years}) = 100\,(1+0.10)^4$$
$$\text{FV of }\$100\,(3\text{ Years}) = 100\,(1+0.10)^3$$
$$\text{FV of }\$100\,(2\text{ Years}) = 100\,(1+0.10)^2$$
$$\text{FV of }\$100\,(1\text{ Year}) = 100\,(1+0.10)^1$$
$$\text{Last Deposit}\,(0\text{ Years}) = 100\,(1)$$

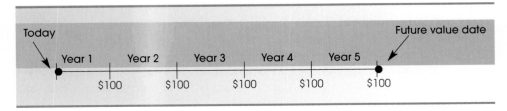

Exhibit 8–6

Future Value of an Ordinary Annuity

Exhibit 8-7
Partial Future Value of an
Ordinary Annuity Table

(*n*) Periods	8%	9%	10%	11%
4	4.50611	4.57313	4.64100	4.70973
5	5.86660	5.98471	**6.10510**	6.22780
6	7.33592	7.52334	7.71561	7.91286
7	8.92280	9.20044	9.48717	9.78327

Adding the equations gives:

FV (Annuity)
$= 100(1+0.10)^4 + 100(1+0.10)^3 + 100(1+0.10)^2 + 100(1+0.10)^1 + 100(1)$

If we factor out the deposit amount of 100, we get:

FV (Annuity) $= 100[(1+0.10)^4 + (1+0.10)^3 + (1+0.10)^2 + (1+0.10)^1 + 1]$
FV (Annuity) $= 100$ (Sum of the factors from the Future Value of a $1 Table)
FV (Annuity) $= 100(1.4641 + 1.331 + 1.21 + 1.1 + 1)$
FV (Annuity) $= 100(6.1051) = \$610.51$

Once again, just as you saw in problems with the future value of $1, you don't have to use the formulas to calculate the future value of an annuity. There are tables with the factors for the future value of an ordinary annuity. The table is based on a series of payments of $1, so you simply find the number in the table that corresponds to the interest rate and the number of periods that apply to your situation. Remember, with the future value of an ordinary annuity, the same payment is made at the end of each period.

Let's find the future value of the $100 annuity at 10% per year using the table in Exhibit 8-7: Find the row for 5 periods and the column for 10%. The factor from this table is 6.10510. Can you see how the table is just a compilation of the factors from the future value $1 table in Exhibit 8-5? Multiply the deposit amount, $100, by the future value factor from the table to get $610.51. That's just what we calculated with the formula.

Let's do the problem using a financial calculator. With your calculator in the FIN mode:

■ Enter 5 for the number of periods (*n*).
■ Enter 10 for the interest rate (*i*%).
■ Enter $100 and press *PMT* for payment.
■ Press *CPT* (for compute) and *FV* (for future value).

You should see $610.51. That's what the deposits would be worth at the end of 5 years. (Your calculator may give a negative number. This is because it is assuming *payments* instead of *deposits*.)

Annuity Due. Suppose you decided to put away some money for the future in a series of equal payments. Let's say the first deposit is made at the beginning of the year—today when you decided on this savings plan—and each subsequent deposit is made at the beginning of each following year. This annuity would be an annuity *due*. Look at the time line in Exhibit 8-8 and compare it with the ordinary annuity time line in Exhibit 8-6. For the annuity due, the first payment is made today, and the last payment will have a year to earn interest before reaching the future value date. This scenario is more typical when saving money for the future.

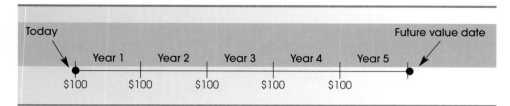

Exhibit 8-8
Future Value of an Annuity Due

Because the deposits are made at the beginning of the year, the first deposit would have 5 years to earn interest; the second deposit, 4 years; the third, 3 years; the fourth, 2 years; and the last payment, 1 year. As we have seen with an ordinary annuity, one way to calculate the total you would have at the end of 5 years is to take each single deposit and calculate the future value of that amount, and then add those amounts together.

By using an interest rate of 10% per year, the calculations for the future value of each deposit of this annuity due are as follows:

$$FV \text{ of } \$100\,(5\text{ Years}) = 100\,(1+0.10)^5$$
$$FV \text{ of } \$100\,(4\text{ Years}) = 100\,(1+0.10)^4$$
$$FV \text{ of } \$100\,(3\text{ Years}) = 100\,(1+0.10)^3$$
$$FV \text{ of } \$100\,(2\text{ Years}) = 100\,(1+0.10)^2$$
$$FV \text{ of } \$100\,(1\text{ Years}) = 100\,(1+0.10)^1$$

Adding the equations gives:

$$FV\,(\text{Annuity})$$
$$= 100\,(1+0.10)^5 + 100\,(1+0.10)^4 + 100\,(1+0.10)^3 + 100\,(1+0.10)^2 + 100\,(1+0.10)^1$$

If we factor out the deposit amount of 100, we get:

$$FV\,(\text{Annuity}) = 100[(1+0.10)^5 + (1+0.10)^4 + (1+0.10)^3 + (1+0.10)^2 + (1+0.10)^1]$$
$$FV\,(\text{Annuity}) = 100\,(\text{Sum of the factors from the future value of \$1 table}) \text{ (see Appendix B)}$$

$$FV\,(\text{Annuity}) = 100\,(1.6105 + 1.4641 + 1.331 + 1.21 + 1.1)$$
$$FV\,(\text{Annuity}) = 100\,(6.7156) = \$671.56$$

Just as with the future value of an ordinary annuity, there is a table to help you calculate the future value of an annuity due. Like all the future value tables, the future value of an annuity due table in Exhibit 8-9 is based on $1, so you simply find the number in the table that corresponds to the interest rate and the number of periods that apply to your situation. Remember, with the future value of an annuity due, the same payment is made at the beginning of each period.

Let's find the future value of the $100 annuity at 10% annual interest using the future value of an annuity due table in Exhibit 8-9. Find the row for 5 periods and the column for 10%. The factor from this table is 6.71561. Multiply the regular annual payment amount, $100, by the future value factor from the table to get $671.56. That's just what we calculated with the formula.

Exhibit 8-9
Future Value of an Annuity Due Table

(n) Periods	8%	9%	10%	11%
3	3.50611	3.57313	3.64100	3.70973
4	4.86660	4.98471	5.10510	5.22780
5	6.33592	6.52334	**6.71561**	6.91286
6	7.92280	8.20044	8.48717	8.78327

STUDY BREAK 8-3
SEE HOW YOU'RE DOING

Find the future value of a series of 4 deposits of $200 at the _end_ of each of the next 4 years at an annual interest rate of 11%. Try using the formula, the future value of an ordinary annuity table, and your financial calculator (if you have one).

Present Value

Sometimes we want to know how much a future amount is worth today. That is, we want to know the present value of a future amount. That's the opposite of the future value of a present amount. In addition to the future value of a single amount ($1) and the future value of an annuity, we will look at the present value of a single amount and the present value of an ordinary annuity.

Single Amount. The present value of a sum of money to be received in the future is the value in _today's dollars_. If you are promised a payment of $100 in 1 year from today, how much is it worth today? In other words, how much would you have to deposit today to have it grow to be $100 in a year? This is just the reverse of finding the future value of today's dollars. It involves inverse compounding. The difference between finding the present value of a future amount and finding the future value of a present amount comes about from the switch in the investor's point of view.

Earlier, to find the future value of a single amount, we took the present value of the amount and multiplied it by the interest factor. You'll recall that:

$$FV_n = PV(1+i)^n$$

where

$$n = \text{Number of periods}$$
$$i = \text{Interest rate for a single period}$$
$$PV = \text{Present Value of the future sum of money}$$
$$FV_n = \text{Future Value of the investment at the end of } n \text{ periods}$$

If we solve the equation for _PV_, we get:

$$PV = FV_n\left(\frac{1}{(1+i)^n}\right)$$

Let's figure out the present value of $100 1 year from now—1 year _hence_, in the jargon of the finance world—at an annual interest rate of 10%.

$$PV = \$100(1/(1+0.10)^1)$$
$$PV = \$100(0.90909)$$
$$PV = \$90.91$$

That means that having $90.91 today is equivalent to having $100 in 1 year, when the annual interest rate is 10%. We can check it out logically.

If we deposit $90.91 today and it earns 10% interest per year, at the end of the year we will have $100.

Let's figure out the present value of $100 for 2 years from now—2 years _hence_—at an annual interest rate of 10%.

$$PV = \$100(1/(1+0.10)^2)$$
$$PV = \$100(0.82645)$$
$$PV = \$82.65$$

Exhibit 8-10
Partial Present Value of $1 Table

(n) Periods	8%	9%	10%	11%
1	0.92593	0.91743	0.90909	0.90090
2	0.85734	0.84168	**0.82645**	0.81162
3	0.79383	0.77218	0.75131	0.73119
4	0.73503	0.70843	0.68301	0.65873

That means that having $82.65 today is equivalent to having $100 in 2 years, when the interest rate is 10%. We can check it out logically.

If we deposit $82.65 today and earn 10% interest, we will have $90.91 [= 82.64 (1 + 0.10)] after 1 year. Then our $90.91 has a year to earn 10% interest, so at the end of the second year we will have $99.99—which rounds to $100.

Once again, we do not have to use the formula to calculate the present value of a future amount. We can use a present value of $1 table or a financial calculator. Let's look at a present value table first.

The present value of $1 table is based on $1. Find the factor from the table in Exhibit 8-10 and multiply it by the dollars in our problem. Find the 10% column and the 2-year row. The factor from the table is 0.82645. Multiply that factor by $100, and the present value is $82.65.

Try it on your financial calculator:

- Enter $100 for the future value (*FV* key).
- Enter 10 for the interest rate (*i%* key).
- Enter 2 for the number of periods (*n* key).
- Press *CPT* and then *PV* to compute the present value.

You should see $82.65 in the display.

Finding the present value of a future amount is called discounting the cash flow, and when discounting a cash flow, the interest rate is called the discount rate.

STUDY BREAK 8-4
SEE HOW YOU'RE DOING

John wants to have $5,000 in 5 years. How much should he deposit today to have $5,000 in 5 years if the annual interest rate is 10%? In other words, what is the present value of $5,000 received 5 years from now? Try using the formula, the present value of $1 table, and your financial calculator (if you have one).

Annuity. In addition to discounting a single amount—often referred to as a lump sum—we may need to calculate the present value of a *series* of payments. The present value of an annuity has lots of practical applications. Most present value problems involving annuities have payments at the end of the period, and so they are *ordinary annuities*. First, let's look at a simple example to see how the formulas work. Then we'll look at some examples that should be familiar to you—buying a motorcycle or a car by borrowing money and making payments to repay the loan.

Suppose you are selling your old motorcycle and a friend offers you a series of four payments of $500 each at the end of each of the next 4 years. How much is the friend actually offering for your motorcycle? It's *not* simply 4 × $500, or $2,000, because of the time value of money. Getting $500 a year from now is *not* the same as getting $500 today. To find out how much a series of four payments of $500 over the next 4 years is worth today, you need to use an appropriate interest rate and discount the payments to get the present value of each payment. Suppose the interest rate is 8% per year.

The first payment, made at the end of 1 year, will be discounted back one year. The second payment, made at the end of 2 years, will be discounted back 2 years, and so on, for the third and fourth payments. The present value of the series of payments will be the sum of the present value of each payment. The formula is as follows:

$$PV = FV_n\left(\frac{1}{(1+i)^n}\right)$$

$$PV = \$500\,(1/(1+0.08)^1) = 500\,(0.92593) = \$\quad 462.97$$
$$PV = \$500\,(1/(1+0.08)^2) = 500\,(0.85734) = \$\quad 428.67$$
$$PV = \$500\,(1/(1+0.08)^3) = 500\,(0.79383) = \$\quad 396.92$$
$$PV = \$500\,(1/(1+0.08)^4) = 500\,(0.73503) = \$\quad 367.52$$
$$\textit{Total}\ PV \qquad\qquad = \$1,656.08$$

That means that, if you could deposit $1,656.08 today to earn 8%, you would be indifferent between receiving $1,656.08 today and receiving four payments of $500 each at the end of each of the next 4 years. Another way to express the same idea is that your friend is paying you $1,656.08 for your motorcycle by offering you the four $500 annual payments. The difference between the total payments of $2,000 and the $1,656.08 price of the motorcycle is interest.

Just as the future value of an ordinary annuity table in Exhibit 8-7 is a compilation of factors from the future value of $1 table, the present value of an ordinary annuity table, shown in Exhibit 8-11, has done the work of compiling the individual factors from the present value of $1 table. Use the present value of an annuity table to solve the same problem. Find the column for 8% and the row for four periods, and you'll see the factor of 3.31213. If you multiply the payment of $500 by the factor 3.31213, you'll get $1,656.07. (It's off a cent due to rounding the factors shown earlier.)

Try it on your financial calculator.

- Enter $500 as the payment (*PMT* key).
- Enter 4 as the number of periods (*n* key).
- Enter 8 as the interest rate (*i%* key).
- Press the *CPT* key, followed by the *PV* key.

You'll see $1,656.06 in the display. That's the present value of the series of payments.

Let's look at buying a car as an example. Suppose you have found a car that you want to buy for $23,000. You have $1,000 for a down payment, and you'll

Exhibit 8-11
Partial Present Value of an Ordinary Annuity Table

(n) Periods	8%	9%	10%	11%
3	2.57710	2.53129	2.48685	2.44371
4	**3.31213**	3.23972	3.16987	3.10245
5	3.99271	3.88965	3.79079	3.69590
6	4.62288	4.48592	4.35526	4.23054

Exhibit 8-12
Partial Present Value of an
Ordinary Annuity Table

(n) Periods	½%	1%	2%	3%
35	32.03537	29.40858	24.99862	21.48722
36	**32.87102**	30.10751	25.48884	21.83225
37	33.70250	30.79951	25.96945	22.16724
38	34.52985	31.48466	26.44064	22.49246

have to borrow $22,000. If you borrow the money for 3 years at an annual interest rate of 6%, how much will your monthly payments be? Pay special attention to the timing of the payments in this situation. Instead of making annual payments, you will make monthly payments. To accommodate this payment plan, you'll need to make sure your time periods, n, and your interest rate, $i\%$, are both expressed with the same time frame. If the period is a month, then the annual interest rate must be changed to a monthly interest rate. You are borrowing money for 36 periods (= 3 years × 12/months per year) at a rate of 1/2% (= 0.5% or 0.005) per month (that's an annual rate of 6%).

In this case, you have the present value of the loan—that's the amount you are borrowing for the car. We want to calculate the *series of payments*. Do it using the present value of an ordinary annuity table, shown in Exhibit 8-12, and then try it with a financial calculator.

$$PV(A) = PMT(\text{Factor for 36 Periods, } 0.5\%)$$

where

$$PV(A) = \text{Present Value of an ordinary annuity}$$
$$PMT = \text{Amount of each payment in the series of}$$
payments and the *factor for* 36 *periods,* 0.5% per period

where period means month, and the factor comes from the present value of an annuity table, like the one shown in Exhibit 8-10.

Instead of knowing the payment and calculating the present value of the payments, we know the present value of the payments and need to compute the amount of the payment.

$$\$22,000 = PMT(32.87102)$$

Solving for *PMT*, we get $669.28. Thus, your monthly car payment will be $669.28.

Try it on your financial calculator.

- Enter $22,000 as the present value (*PV* key).
- Enter 36 as the number of periods (*n* key).
- Enter 0.5 as the interest rate (*i%* key).
- Press the *CPT* key, followed by the *PMT* key.

You'll see $669.28 in the display.

Suppose you want to borrow $50,000 from your rich uncle, and he is willing to let you repay him over the next 10 years, with a payment every 6 months. He has determined that 10% is a fair (annual) interest rate. How much will your payments be? Use the present value of an ordinary annuity table, and then check your answer by using your financial calculator if you have one.

STUDY BREAK 8-5
SEE HOW YOU'RE DOING

Long-Term Liabilities: Raising Money by Issuing Bonds

BUSINESS PROCESS

L.O. 3

Understand how a company borrows money by issuing bonds and how the company repays the bondholders.

What Is a Bond?

When firms want to borrow large amounts of money, they usually go to the general public to raise the money. They do this by issuing, i.e. selling, bonds. Issuing bonds means they borrow money from investors—individuals, like you and me, and companies that want to invest their extra cash. Insurance companies, for example, invest a great deal of money in stocks and bonds. A bond is a written agreement that specifies the company's responsibility to pay interest and repay the principal to the bondholders at the end of the term of the bond.

Revisit the discussion of the stock market in Chapter 1. There is a bond market that serves a similar function—to bring together buyers and sellers of bonds. Just like there is a New York Stock Exchange, there is also a New York Bond Exchange. The company borrowing the money is sometimes called the seller, or more accurately, the issuer. What the company sells, or more accurately issues, is bonds, which are legally binding promises to repay the buyer. The buyer isn't really *buying* but, is instead *lending* the price paid for the bond.

Why would a company borror money by issuing bonds instead of going to a bank for a loan? There are two reasons.

First, bondholders are typically willing to lend money for a longer time period than banks. Many bonds are 20-, 30-, or 50-year bonds. Most banks won't lend money for such long periods of time. One reason for the willingness of the bondholders to lend money for a long time is that bondholders can convert bonds into cash at any time. The existence of a bond market provides a way for bondholders to sell their bonds to another investor—and get their cash back—without affecting the firm that issued the bond.

Second, the rate of interest on a bond—that's the rate the borrower has to pay the bondholder—is commonly lower than the rate on loans charged by banks. Banks pay one rate of interest to people who deposit their money in saving accounts—that's the savings rate of interest—but charge a higher interest rate to lend money—that's the borrowing rate of interest. This difference is used to pay the expenses of operating the bank and to pay a return to the owners of the bank. This is one reason why a firm's cost of borrowing money via bonds can be lower than borrowing via bank loans.

One disadvantage to borrowing money by issuing bonds is the restrictions placed on a firm that issues bonds. The company may be restricted, by the terms of the bond agreement, from borrowing any additional money from any sources, or the company may need to maintain a certain current ratio—the ratio of current assets to current liabilities. These restrictions, called bond covenants, are specified in the bond agreement to protect the interests of the bondholders. Recall that creditors, including bondholders, have priority over the claims of owners.

Exhibit 8-13 shows the information an actual bond will have.

> **From the *Wall Street Journal Primer on Bonds* from WSJ.com**
>
> A bond is something familiar—a loan—dressed up in unfamiliar terminology.
>
> Say you lend out $1,000 for 10 years in return for a yearly payment of 7% interest. That arrangement translates into bond-speak: You didn't make a loan, you *bought* a bond. The $1,000 of principal is the *face value* of the bond, the yearly interest payment is its *coupon*, and the length of the loan—10 years—is the bond's *maturity*.
>
> There's a good reason for the jargon. If you talk about lending money in these terms, it's easier to think of a loan as something that can be bought or sold like any other investment.

Company name, date of issue, par value, interest rate, payment terms

More About Bonds

Bondholders are creditors of the company; they are not owners of the company. Bonds require the issuer to make periodic interest payments. Most bonds issued (i.e., sold) in the United States pay the bondholders semiannual interest payments during the life of the bonds. Bondholders are entitled to receive periodic interest payments and, at a specific future date called the maturity date, a lump sum payment equal to the amount given on the face of the bond. Most bonds are issued with a face value in multiples of $1,000.

BUSINESS PROCESS

Bonds can be bought and sold in a secondary market. Just like stock, after the corporation completes the original issue, buyers and sellers get together via the bond market to trade bonds. The price of a bond on the secondary market will be different from the original bond price, depending on whether interest rates have increased or decreased since the date of the original bond issue. Bond prices have an inverse relationship with interest rates: when interest rates increase, bond prices decrease, and vice versa. Because interest payments on a bond are fixed, when the market rate of interest goes down, those fixed rates look better. For example, suppose a $1,000 bond pays 9% interest per year. If the market rate of interest is 9%, the bond would sell for $1,000. If the market rate of interest goes up to 10%, this 9% bond of $1,000 is not as attractive as other investments. Thus, the price of this bond will go down. That's the inverse relationship: Market interest rate goes up, and the bond price goes down. If the market rate of interest goes down to 8%, then the 9% bond of $1,000 is a very attractive investment; and the price of the bond will go up.

The price of a bond when it is issued is stated in terms of a percentage of its face value. If a bond is stated as selling for 98 3/8, that means it is selling for 98 3/8% of $1,000 ($1,000 × 0.98375), or $983.75.

A bond that is selling at 100 is selling at par—100% of its face value.
A bond selling below 100 is selling at a discount.
A bond selling above 100 is selling at a premium.

Bonds may be secured or unsecured.

- Secured bonds give the bondholders a claim to a specific asset of the company in case of default.
- Unsecured bonds, also known as debentures, are not linked to specific assets and are issued on the general credit of the company.

Bonds may be *term* or *serial*.

- Term bonds describe bonds that all mature on the same date.
- Serial bonds mature periodically over a period of several years.

If a $1,000 bond is selling for 95 1/2, how much cash does the bondholder pay for the bond? If a $1,000 bond is selling for 102, how much cash does the bondholder pay for the bond?

STUDY BREAK 8-6
SEE HOW YOU'RE DOING

Issuing Bonds Payable

Understand how a company borrows money by issuing bonds and how the company repays the bondholders.

Getting the Money

A company may issue bonds at par, at a premium, at a discount. A company's financial statements will show (1) the unamortized discount or premium on the bonds, (2) the periodic payment of interest on these bonds, and (3) the value of the bonds at maturity.

Suppose a company issues a single 10-year bond of $1,000 at 11.5% per year, on January 1, 2004. The market rate of interest at the time of issue is 11.5%. That means other investments with the same risk are paying an annual return of 11.5%. How does this transaction affect the accounting equation?

First, cash is increased by $1,000. Remember, when a company issues bonds, it is borrowing money. The cash receipt is recorded, and a liability is recorded. The $1,000 increase in *cash* is balanced with a $1,000 increase in *bonds payable.*

The journal entries to record the sale of a 10-year, 11.5%, $1,000 bond when the market rate of interest is also 11.5% is:

Date	Transaction	Debit	Credit
	Cash	$1,000	
	Bonds payable		$1,000

The company must pay the bondholder interest for the use of the $1,000 over the term of the bonds. At the time the bond is issued, the frequency and dates of the interest payments are specified in the contract between the company and the bondholders. Suppose the interest on this bond is paid annually. This means every year the bondholder receives interest from the company. At the end of the term of the bond, the principal—the face amount of the bond—is repaid.

Paying the Bondholders

On December 31, 2004, the company owes its bondholder the first annual interest payment. This payment is calculated with the interest formula:

$$\text{Interest} = \text{Principal} \times \text{Interest Rate} \times \text{Time}$$

In this case:

$$\text{Interest} = \$1,000 \, \text{Principal} \times 0.115 \, \text{Annual Interest rate} \times 1 \, \text{Year} = \$115$$

On December 31, the transaction of paying the interest has the following effect on the accounting equation:

Assets	=	Liabilities	+	Shareholders' equity
$(115) Cash				$(115) Interest expense

The journal entry to record the first interest payment of the 10-year, $1,000, 11.5% bond is:

Date	Transaction	Debit	Credit
12/31/2004	Interest expense	$115	
	Cash		$115

Bonds issued at	Interest rates	Bonds will sell for
Par	Stated rate of interest = market rate of interest	Face amount
Discount	Stated rate of interest < market rate of interest	Less than the face amount
Premium	Stated rate of interest > market rate of interest	More than the face amount

Exhibit 8-14
Bonds Issued at Par, Discount, Premium

Each interest payment will be identical. Remember, the company has to pay the bondholders according to the terms printed on the face of the bond. The cash to be paid at each interest date is determined before the company goes to the market to sell the bond. *Whether the bond is issued at par, at a discount, or at a premium, the cash paid to the bondholder is determined by the terms on the face of the bond.* The principal amount, to be repaid at the end of the term of the bond, is stated on the face of the bond and is used to calculate the interest payments.

It is not difficult to understand how a company reports and makes the payments for bonds issued at par. However, the real world is often not so simple. Bonds may be issued when the market interest rate is *not* the same as the rate stated on the bonds. Why? Even though the company issuing the bonds tries to pick the market interest rate to use as the stated rate on the face of the bonds, it may not work out as planned. That's because it's not possible to issue bonds on the exact day when the interest for the bond is specified. There is a time delay before the bonds are actually issued. The bond certificates have to be printed and the bond issue has to be filed along with prospective financial statements with state regulators and the Securities and Exchange Commission (SEC) *before* the issuance date of the bonds. Very often the market interest rates will change between the time a face interest rate is selected for the bonds and the time the bonds are issued. The market rate of interest is the interest rate that other investments with the same risk are paying on the issue date of the bonds. When the market rate of interest and the stated rate of interest on the bonds are different, the bonds are issued at a premium or a discount. Exhibit 8-14 shows the relationship between the market interest rate and stated interest rate of the bonds, and the selling price of the bonds.

BUSINESS PROCESS

Accounting for Bonds Payable

Issuing Bonds at a Discount or a Premium

 L.O. 3

Understand how a company borrows money by issuing bonds and how the company repays the bondholders.

Suppose a company is offering a $1,000 bond with a stated rate of 10% when the market rate of interest is 11%. That means that other opportunities exist— with the same risk—that would earn 11%. Would you be willing to buy a $1,000 bond of 10% if you could invest that same $1,000 in an equivalent investment that pays 11%? Of course you would not. The company issuing the bond will pay $100 in annual interest whereas other investments—similar to the bond in all respects—are willing to pay $110 in annual interest. Because the issuing company went to a lot of expense to print the bonds and prepare them for issue, it's not possible to simply change the rate of interest stated on the bonds. The company is stuck with what is stated on the bonds—10% annual interest payments, that's $100 annually, and the face of $1,000 to be paid out at maturity.

To make up for the difference between the stated interest rate of 10% and the market rate of 11%, the company issuing the bonds has to be willing to sell the bonds for *less* than $1,000, that is, sell them at a discount. There is an amount that an investor would pay for a bond that has a $1,000 face value and a stated interest rate of 10% when the market rate of interest is 11%. That amount is equal to the present value of the future cash flows the bondholder will receive. Bonds sold at less than the face value are sold at a *discount*. We'll do the calculations for a bond sold at a discount in the next section of this chapter.

On the other hand, if the company were offering a bond that has a face value of $1,000 and a stated interest rate of 10% when the market rate of interest is 8%, that bond would be a great investment for the investor. If the market rate of return for an investment of equivalent risk were less than the stated interest rate on the bonds, people would flock to buy the bonds, *if* the bonds were issued at the $1,000 face value. However, that won't happen because the market for bonds will respond by bidding up the price of that bond. The rules of supply and demand work well in the bond market. The demand for the bond causes the price of the bond to increase above face value.

Investors should be willing to pay more than $1,000 for that bond because the bond will pay $100 in annual interest when other similar investments only pay $80 for the same $1,000 invested. The extra amount the bondholder is willing to pay for that bond—because the bondholder will collect $100 in interest every year—is called a *premium*. In this case, the bondholder would be willing to pay more than $1,000 for the bond. The bondholder will pay an amount equal to the present value of the future cash flows. The bond still pays $100 interest annually and a lump sum amount for the principal at maturity of $1,000. Later in the chapter, we'll look at the calculations.

Remember, no matter how much the bondholder pays for the bond—whether the issue price is above or below the price stated on the bond—the series of payments is established by what is printed on the face of the bond. That series of cash flows is what the bondholder is buying. In this example, the cash flows are set at $100 interest annually and a lump sum of $1,000 at maturity.

STUDY BREAK 8-7
SEE HOW YOU'RE DOING

If Jon-med Company issues a $1,000 bond with a stated interest rate of 9% when the market interest rate is 8%, will the bond sell for a discount or a premium? How much interest will the bondholders receive each year from Jon-med Company?

Calculating the Proceeds from Bonds Issued at a Premium. Suppose the Biz Corp. issues a $1,000 face value, 10-year, 11.5% bond, with interest payable annually. At the time of issue, the market interest rate is 10%. How much money will Biz get for the bond?

- First, calculate the bond's annual interest payments of $115 (= $1,000 × 0.115 per year × 1 year). There will be 10 of these payments (one each year for 10 years).
- Next, calculate the present value of an ordinary annuity of $115 for 10 years at an annual interest rate of 10%—the market rate of interest. What we need to determine is the equivalent amount of all those interest payments in today's dollars. As you learned earlier in this chapter, tables have been devised and financial calculators have been programmed using interest-compounding formulas to help do this calculation. Recall, the process is called **discounting a series of cash flows.** By using the present value of an ordinary annuity table (Appendix B), the relevant factor is 6.14457, so the present value of the 10 annual interest payments over 10 years is:

$$\$115 \times 6.14457 = \underline{\underline{\$706.63}}$$

Discounting a series of future cash flows means to calculate the present value of those future cash flows.

Alternatively, you could use your financial calculator to discount the cash flows:

- PMT = 115.
- $i\%$ = 10%.
- n = 10 periods.
- Press CPT and then PV.
- The display will show $706.63 (rounded to the nearest cent).

This means $706.63 today is equivalent to getting 10 payments of $115 over the next 10 years, if the market interest rate is 10% per year.

- Determine the present value of the principal repayment. It will be a single $1,000 payment 10 years from now. At the current market rate of interest, how much would you have to invest today to have it grow to be $1,000 in 10 years? To calculate today's value of this $1,000 future payment, use the factor from the present value of $1 table (a single payment instead of a series of payments, in Appendix B)—for 10 years at 10%. The factor is 0.38554 so the present value of the $1,000 principal is

$$\$1,000 \times 0.38554 = \underline{\underline{\$385.54}}$$

- Alternatively, by using your financial calculator:

  - FV = $1,000.
  - $i\%$ = 10%.
  - n = 10 periods.
  - Press CPT, then PV.
  - The display will show $385.54.

- Today's value—the present value—of the total of the future cash flows is $1,092.17 (= 706.63 + 385.54), even though the face amount of the bond is only $1,000. This bond would be selling today for around 109 1/4, according to the convention of pricing bonds. The way this bond issue would affect the accounting equation is shown next:

Assets	=	Liabilities	+	Shareholders' equity
+$1,092.17 Cash		+$1,000 Bonds payable +$92.17 Premium on bonds payable		

The journal entry to record the issue of a 10-year, $1,000, 11.5% bond is:

Date	Transaction	Debit	Credit
	Cash	$1,092.17	
	Bonds payable		$1,000.00
	Premium on bonds payable		92.17

The amount of the face of the bond ($1,000) and the premium ($92.17) are both liabilities. They appear next to each other on the balance sheet. *Premium on* bonds payable is called an adjunct liability. Adjunct means an add-on and describes the relationship between the bonds payable and the premium on bonds payable. The premium is a partner of the bonds payable liability it is matched with, and they are added together on the balance sheet.

Calculating the Proceeds from Bonds Issued at a Discount. Now, suppose the Biz Corp. is issuing a $1,000, 10-year, 11.5% bond at a time when the market interest rate is 12%. Who would be interested in buying Biz's bond? No one would want to pay $1,000 for the series of payments at the stated 11.5% annual interest rate. Biz would have to offer the bond at a discount. What price for the bond will attract buyers?

- First calculate the annual interest payments of $115 (= 1,000 × 0.115 × 1). There will be 10 of these payments.
- Use the factor from the present value of an ordinary annuity table to calculate the present value of the interest payments over 10 years at 12% interest per year. The relevant factor is 5.65022, so the value of the interest payments is:

$$5.65022 \times \$115 = \$649.77$$

- Then find the value of the principal repayment. How much is needed today to grow to $1,000 in 10 years at 12% per year? The present value is calculated with a factor for 10 periods with 12% per period. The present value of $1 gives us a factor of 0.32197, so the present value is:

$$\$1,000 \times 0.32197 = \$321.97$$

- Biz will sell the bond for a total of $971.74 (= $649.77 + $321.97) even though its face value is $1,000. The bond market would quote a price of approximately 97 1/8, or 97.125, according to the usual way of expressing bond prices.

This bond is being sold at a discount. The transaction has the following effect on the accounting equation:

Assets	=	Liabilities	+	Shareholders' equity
+$971.74 Cash		+$1,000 Bonds payable $(28.26) Discount on bonds payable		

The journal entry to record the issue of the 10-year, $1,000, 11.5% bond when the market rate of interest is 12% is:

Date	Transaction	Debit	Credit
	Cash	$971.74	
	Discount on bonds payable	28.26	
	Bonds payable		$1,000.00

Discount on bonds payable is a contra-liability and it is deducted from bonds payable on the balance sheet. It works like the other contra-accounts—accumulated depreciation and allowance for uncollectible accounts—we have studied in prior chapters. It is shown on the balance sheet with its partner account, and it is deducted from the balance in its partner account. Contra-accounts are valuation accounts. They are used to value the associated asset or liability.

Amortizing Bond Discounts and Premiums: Effective Interest Method

Bond discounts and bond premiums are written off over the life of the bonds. That means the amount of the discount or premium is reduced until it reaches zero.

To show how a discount is written off, let's continue the example of a bond issued at a discount—a $1,000 bond issued for $971.74. The stated rate of interest on the bond is 11.5% and the market rate of interest is 12%. When the bonds are issued, the value of the net liability, bonds payable minus the discount, is $971.74 (= $1,000 − $28.26). Each time interest is paid to the bondholders, a portion of the discount is written off. The amount of the write off is the difference between the interest expense and the interest payment to the bondholders.

Suppose the bond is issued on January 1. The first interest payment to the bondholders, on December 31, will be in the amount of $115 (= $1,000 × 0.115 × 1 year). The **interest expense**—shown on the income statement—is *not equal* to the **interest payment** to the bondholders. The interest expense is calculated using the usual interest rate formula: $I = P \times R \times T$. In this case, the principal amount borrowed is $971.74. That's the amount the bondholders actually loaned the company on the date of the bond issue. The interest rate is 12%—that's the market rate at the date of issue, and the time period is 1 year.

$$\text{Interest Expense} = \$971.74 \times 0.12 \times 1 = \$116.61$$

The difference between the interest payment of $115 and the interest expense of $116.61 is the amount that reduces the discount. After the payment is made, the discount is reduced by $1.61 (= $115 − $116.61). The discount that began with $28.26 at issue is now reduced to $26.65. The same thing happens each time a payment is made. The amount of the discount is reduced. The accounting terminology for that process is called writing off or amortizing the discount, and this method is called the *effective interest method* of amortization.

The value of the bonds payable minus the *unamortized* discount is called the carrying value or book value of the bonds. Remember, that's the net amount added to the total liabilities on the balance sheet. Over the life of the bonds, the discount is amortized, so that the carrying value of the bonds at the date of maturity is exactly the face value. In other words, the amount of the discount is reduced—a portion at each interest payment date—to zero over the life of the bonds. Getting the discount to zero will make the face value of the bond equal to the carrying value. After all, the face value is exactly the amount that must be paid to the bondholders at the maturity date of the bonds.

- Amortizing a bond *discount* will *decrease* the unamortized bond discount and *increase* the carrying value of the bond.
- Amortizing a bond *premium* will *decrease* the unamortized bond premium and *decrease* the carrying value of the bond.

The amortization of bond premiums or discounts is a natural result of calculating the correct amount of interest expense for the period when the company makes an interest payment to the bondholder. Remember, the amount of the cash payments to the bondholders is established before the bond is issued. Consequently, the calculation of the payments to the bondholders is completely independent of the market interest rate at the date of the bond issue. However, the market rate of interest determines the amount of money the bondholders are willing to lend—which is really the amount they are willing to pay for the bonds—to get the fixed payments at specified times in the future.

The demand from the bond market will set the price of the bond so that it will earn exactly the market rate of return. To make the business decision to issue bonds, a company must understand this fact and estimate the cash proceeds when planning the bond issue.

Let's take a closer look at bonds issued at a discount to see how the interest payments to the bondholder and the interest expense to the issuer are different.

Interest expense is calculated by multiplying the carrying value of a bond by the market rate of interest at the date of the bond issue.

Interest payment is calculated by multiplying the face value of the bond and the interest rate stated on the bond.

BUSINESS PROCESS

Exhibit 8-15
Amortization Schedule for a Bond Issued at a Discount

Period	Annual Interest expense	Interest payment (cash)	Amortization of bond discount	Unamortized bond discount	Carrying value of bond
0				$28.26	$971.74
1		$115			
		115			
		115			
		115			
		Etc.			

Payment of Interest to Bondholders and Amortization of a Discount.
Organizing the information about a bond issue in a table like the one shown in Exhibit 8-15 emphasizes the pattern in the calculation of the interest expense related to a bond issued at a discount. The bond is a 10-year, annual interest bond. Notice how the details of the bond issue are shown in Exhibit 8-15: cash proceeds amount to $971.74, even though its face value is $1,000. Why wouldn't bondholders pay the full $1,000 for the bond? As stated earlier in the chapter, no one will pay $1,000 because the market rate of interest is 12% and this bond has a stated interest rate of only 11.5%.

How much interest does the firm that issued the bond owe the bondholder on the first interest date? The bondholder actually loaned the firm $971.74 at the market rate of 12% interest. For the first year of the life of the bond, the entire principal balance of $971.74 was outstanding. Thus, the calculation of the interest expense for the first year is:

$$\$971.74 \times 0.12 \times 1 = \$116.61$$

Although the interest expense is $116.61, the firm is going to pay the bondholder only $115—that's the amount predetermined by the stated rate of interest and face value of the bond. The firm actually owes the bondholder an additional $1.61. Because the payment to the bondholder is fixed, the extra $1.61 will be added to the outstanding principal balance of $971.74. After the first interest payment, the new principal balance is $973.35 (= $971.74 + 1.61). The $1.61—the difference between the interest expense and the interest payment—is amortization of the discount.

The payment to the bondholder of $115 and the discount amortization affects the accounting equation as follows:

Assets	=	Liabilities	+	Shareholders' equity
$(115) Cash		+$1.61 Discount on bonds payable[a]		$(116.61) Interest expense

[a]Remember that the discount is a contra-liability. That is, the discount is subtracted from the bonds payable. As it is amortized, less and less is subtracted, until zero is subtracted from bonds payable. Thus, a reduction in the discount is actually an increase (hence the +) in total liabilities.

The journal entry to record the first interest payment on the bond issued at a discount for the annual discount amortization and cash interest payment is as follows:

Date	Transaction	Debit	Credit
12/31/2004	Interest expense	$116.61	
	Cash		$115.00
	Discount on bonds payable		1.61

Period	Annual interest expense (0.12 × carrying value)	Interest payment (cash)	Amortization of discount (interest expense − cash paid)	Unamortized bond discount	Carrying value of bond ($1,000 − unamortized bond discount)
0				$28.26	$971.74
1	**$116.61**	$115	**$1.61**	26.65	973.35
2	**116.80**	115	**1.80**	24.85	975.15
3		115			
4		115			

Exhibit 8-16
Continuation of the Amortization Schedule for a Bond Issued at a Discount

Without getting too technical, let's try to reason out why issuing a bond at a discount results in interest expense that is *greater* than the actual cash payment to the bondholder. Because the interest rate in the market is higher than the interest rate the bond is paying, the difference between the $1,000 face amount to be repaid and the $971.74 issue price may be thought of as some extra interest—in addition to the periodic interest payments—that the bond issuer has to pay to borrow the $971.74.

Each time an interest payment is made to the bondholder, a small portion of the discount is written off as interest expense. At the maturity date of the bond, the discount will be zero.

See if you can fill in the table in Exhibit 8-16 for the first two interest dates. We just calculated the interest expense of $116.61 for the first year. Because the bond annually pays $115, the amount of $1.61 was added to the amount owed to the bondholder. Because a discount is used to reduce the face value of the bonds to the amount actually owed, the discount must get smaller. What's the goal? You want the discount to be zero at maturity. A discount of zero means the book value of the bonds equals the face value of the bonds. See if you can figure out how the numbers for the second interest payment have been calculated.

When you are sure you understand the calculations needed to get the figures for the second interest payment, fill in the numbers for the third and fourth interest payments. (The amortization of discount for the third and fourth years are $2.02 and $2.26, respectively.)

STUDY BREAK 8-8
SEE HOW YOU'RE DOING

Try this example with semiannual interest payments. Divide the annual interest rate by two and consider each period as a 6-month period, so the number of periods will be the number of 6-month periods. Knollwood Corp. issued $200,000 of 6% per year, 20-year bonds at 98 on January 1, 2003. Assume the market rate of interest was 6.5%. Interest is paid on June 30 and December 31. The company uses the effective interest method of amortization. Prepare the journal entries to record the bond issue and the first two interest payments.

Payment of Interest to Bondholders and Amortization of a Premium. Let's use the same bond but assume it was issued at a premium. Recall, the market rate of interest of 10% is lower than the stated rate on the bond of 11.5%, so the bondholder will pay a premium for the bond's series of payments. The format for the amortization schedule is shown in Exhibit 8-17.

Exhibit 8-17 Amortization Schedule for a Bond Issued at a Premium

Period	Annual interest expense	Interest payment (cash)	Amortization of bond premium	Unamortized bond premium	Carrying value of bond
0				$92.17	$1,092.17
1		$115			
		115			
		115			
		115			
		Etc.			

In this example, the amount the bondholder pays—which we should not forget is actually a loan to the firm—is $1,092.17 for the bond. The interest expense incurred is calculated using the market rate interest. For the first year, the interest expense is:

$$\$1,092.17 \times 0.10 \times 1 = \$109.22$$

When the bond issuer makes the cash payment of $115, that amount pays the bondholder the interest for the 6 months plus a small amount of the principal. The amount of principal paid off is the difference between the interest payment and the interest expense:

$$\$115 - 109.22 = \$5.78$$

This $5.78 is amortization of the premium on bonds payable. The premium of $92.17 will be reduced a little bit each time the bond issuer makes an interest payment to the bondholder, until the premium is zero at maturity. At maturity, the bond issuer pays the bondholder the $1,000 face amount.

The following shows how the interest payment to the bondholder affects the accounting equation:

Assets	=	Liabilities	+	Shareholders' equity
$(115) Cash		$(5.78) Premium on bonds payable		$(109.22) Interest expense

The entry to record the annual premium amortization and cash interest payment is:

Date	Transaction	Debit	Credit
12/31/2004	Interest expense	$109.22	
	Premium on bonds payable	5.78	
	Cash		$115.00

Issuing a bond at a premium results in interest expense (to the bond issuer) that is *less* than the actual cash payment of interest to the bondholder because the 10% interest rate in the market is lower than the 11.5% interest rate specified on the bond. With that in mind, we can think of the premium the bondholder paid as a payment in advance to the bond issuer to help meet the 11.5% payment due the bondholder.

Each time a cash payment for interest is made to the bondholder, a little of the premium is written off. How much? The difference between the interest payment and the interest expense will be the amount of the premium amortization. At maturity, the premium will be zero.

See if you can fill in the table in Exhibit 8-18 for the first two interest rate dates. As calculated previously, the interest expense for the first year is $109.22.

Exhibit 8-18 Continuation of the Amortization Schedule for a Bond Issued at a Premium

Period	Annual interest expense	Interest payment (cash)	Amortization of bond premium	Unamortized bond premium	Carrying value of bond
0				$ 92.17	$ 1,092.17
1	**109.22**	$115	**5.78**	**86.39**	**1,086.39**
2	**108.64**	115	**6.36**	**80.03**	**1,080.03**
3		115			
4		115			
		Etc.			

Because the cash paid as interest to the bondholder each time it is due is $115, there is a difference of $5.78 that will be deducted from the premium. Because the original premium increases the amount owed to the bondholder to an amount *larger* than the face of the bond, the premium must be made smaller over the life of the bond.

The goal is to reduce the premium to zero at maturity, so that the bond will have a book value equal to its face value. When you understand the calculations needed to get the figures for the second interest payment, fill in the numbers for the third and fourth interest payments.

Wood Corp. issued $200,000 of 20-year, 10% interest bonds at 102 on January 1, 2003. Assume the market rate of interest was 9%. Interest is paid annually on December 31. The company uses the effective interest method of amortization. Prepare the journal entries to record the bond issue and the first interest payment.

STUDY BREAK 8-9
SEE HOW YOU'RE DOING

Straight-Line Amortization of Bond Discounts and Premiums

In addition to the effective interest method of amortizing a bond discount or premium, there is another method sometimes used called the straight-line method. Straight-line amortization simply divides the premium or discount equally over the number of interest payment periods. The effective interest method makes logical sense with respect to interest expense being calculated on the outstanding principal, but there is no particular logic to the straight-line method. It is a simple calculation, much easier than the effective interest method, and this simplicity is its only attractive feature. Straight-line amortization often does a poor job of matching and is not a generally accepted accounting principle (GAAP). However, if the straight-line method and the effective interest method produce similar amounts for interest expense and for net bonds payable, the accounting standards allow the use of the straight-line method of amortization.

Let's look at the last example—10 year bonds, 11.5% stated rate, $1,000 face value, market rate at issue of 10%—and see how straight-line amortization works. Recall, the bond will be issued at a premium, and we calculated the issue price to be $1,092.17. The difference between the face of $1,000 and the issue price of $1,092.17 is a premium. As was shown in Exhibit 8-18, we have already seen how the premium of $92.17 would be amortized using the effective interest method.

To amortize the premium using the straight-line method, divide the premium by the number of interest payments to the bondholders. That means the same amount will be amortized each time an interest payment is made. In this example, in which the premium is $92.17, the amount of premium amortized

Exhibit 8-19 Straight-Line Amortization Schedule for a Bond Issued at a Premium

Period	Annual interest expense	Interest payment (cash)	Amortization of bond premium	Unamortized bond premium	Carrying value
0				$92.17	$1,092.17
1	**$105.78**	$115	**9.22**	**82.95**	**1,082.95**
2	**105.78**	115	**9.22**	**73.73**	**1,073.73**
3	**105.78**	115	**9.22**	**64.51**	**1,064.51**
4		115	Etc.		
		Etc.			

will be $9.22 per year. The amortization schedule for the first 3 years is shown in Exhibit 8-19.

The journal entry to record the annual premium amortization and cash interest payment using the *straight-line method* of amortization is:

Date	Transaction	Debit	Credit
12/31/2004	Interest expense	$105.78	
	Premium on bonds payable	9.22	
	Cash		$115.00

To use the straight-line method of amortization, you don't have to know the market interest rate to calculate the interest expense. Each period the interest expense is the same; the amortization of the discount or premium is the same; and, of course, the payment is the same. You can see how that makes the calculations easy. However, it is only permissible to use the straight-line method when the interest expense calculated with this method is not significantly different than the interest expense calculated using the effective interest method. The numbers in this example are small, and the difference doesn't seem to be very significant. When a company has hundreds of thousands or even millions of dollars of bonds outstanding, the two methods can produce very different amounts of interest expense.

Zero-Coupon Bonds

L.O. 3

Understand how a company borrows money by issuing bonds and how the company repays the bondholders.

We've seen that bonds result in two sets of payments to the purchaser. One is the periodic (usually annual or semiannual) payment of interest. The other is the repayment of the principal at maturity.

Certain bonds do *not* make periodic payments of interest. Instead, they make only one payment—the face value of the bond paid to the purchaser at the maturity date. These bonds are known as zero-coupon bonds. What's a coupon? It's a little part on a bond that the bondholder tears off and takes to the bank to collect the interest periodically. (The bank acts as an agent for the bond issuer.) A zero-coupon bond means the bond has no coupons—and thus no interest payments during the life of the bond.

The purchaser of a $1,000 zero-coupon bond is promised a $1,000 payment when the bond matures. However, the purchaser does not get any periodic interest payments. Because purchasers are only willing to pay for what they get, calculating the price of a zero-coupon bond is easy: it's simply the present value of the future $1,000 payment.

Let's consider the $1,000 bond issued by Biz Corp. Suppose Biz is issuing a 10-year, 10% interest (compounded annually) zero-coupon bond. Assume the market rate of interest is also 10%. What is the present value of the principal repayment?

From the present value of $1 table, the factor for the present value of a lump sum for 10 years at 10% is 0.38554. By using that factor to calculate the present value, the bond's issue price is $385.54 (= 0.38554 × $1,000). This is the *entire* price a purchaser pays for this particular zero-coupon bond. Over the life of the bond, the interest is added to the principal, and it grows to be $1,000 at maturity.

The entry to record the sale of the Biz Corporation 10% zero-coupon bond is:

Date	Transaction	Debit	Credit
	Cash	$385.54	
	Discount on bonds payable	614.46	
	Bonds payable		$1,000.00

At each interest payment date, the discount will be amortized based on the outstanding principal balance. For example, the interest due on the first annual payment date would be $38.55 [$385.54 × 0.10 (or 10%)], and the entry to record the annual interest expense on a zero-coupon bond would be:

Date	Transaction	Debit	Credit
	Interest expense	$38.55	
	Discount on bonds payable		$38.55

Callable and Convertible Bonds

Callable Bonds

Almost all bonds contain a *call* feature, which allows the issuer to buy back and retire the bonds—get rid of the debt—at a given price, usually at a price above face value, before maturity. This allows corporations to save money by refinancing their debt if interest rates drop.

Understand how a company borrows money by issuing bonds and how the company repays the bondholders.

Convertible bonds

Convertible bonds can be converted into common stock at the option of the investor. This feature can make bonds more attractive, because investors can receive interest on the bond, and then convert the bond into stock to benefit from future increases in the market price of the stock.

BUSINESS PROCESS

On January 1, 2003, Stanton Corp. issued $100,000 face value of 8% interest bonds to yield 10%. (That's another way of saying that the market rate of interest on the date of the bond issue was 10%.) The bonds are dated January 1, 2003, call for annual interest payments on December 31, and mature on December 31, 2006. Stanton uses the effective interest method for amortizing discounts and premiums.

STUDY BREAK 8-10
SUMMARY PROBLEM

1. Calculate the proceeds for the bond issue. (Then round the selling price to the nearest whole percentage point to answer the rest of the questions.)
2. Prepare the journal entry to record the bond issue.
3. Prepare the journal entry to record the first interest payment.
4. Prepare the journal entry to record the second interest payment.
5. What is the carrying value of the bonds on the December 31, 2003 balance sheet and on the December 31, 2004 balance sheet?

Financial Statement Analysis

BUSINESS PROCESS

Understand how information about a company's debt is used in financial statement analysis.

Financial leverage refers to using borrowed money to increase earnings.

We know that the two ways to finance a business are debt and equity. The combination of debt and equity that a company chooses is called its capital structure. That's because debt and equity are the two sources of capital, and every company can choose the proportion of each that makes up its total capital.

When should a company borrow money? A very simplistic cost and benefit analysis would suggest that when the benefit of borrowing the money—what it can earn for the business—exceeds the cost of borrowing the money—interest expense—then borrowing money is a good idea.

Financial leverage is the concept of using borrowed funds to increase earnings. If a company earns more with the money it borrows than it has to pay to borrow that money, it is called *positive financial leverage*. Suppose Anna Chase has invested $50,000 in her new business and has no debt. If the business earns $5,000 net income, then she has earned a return on her investment of 10%. Suppose Anna wants to expand her business. She could earn an additional $5,000 if she borrows an additional $50,000. If the after-tax cost of borrowing the money is 8%, then Anna would be taking advantage of financial leverage if she borrows the money. That's because earnings would increase by more than the cost of borrowing the money. The new total income—$5,000 + $5,000 − $4,000 interest—would be $6,000. Now Anna's return on equity is $6,000/$50,000 = 12%.

Two financial ratios measure a company's debt position and its ability to meet its interest payments. The first is the **debt-to-equity** ratio. This is often calculated as:

Debt-to-equity ratio is total liabilities divided by stockholders' equity. It compares the value of claims of creditors with the value of the claims of owners.

$$\frac{\text{Total Liabilities}}{\text{Shareholders' Equity}}$$

This ratio compares the amount of creditors' claims to the assets of the firm with owners' claim to the assets of the firm. A firm with a high debt-to-equity ratio is often referred to as a highly leveraged firm.

Another way to express the relationship between debt and equity is to calculate the total liabilities as a percentage of total liabilities plus shareholders' equity. That is just expressing total debt as a percentage of the total claims to the assets of the firm. When you are reading about debt-to-equity ratios, be sure you know how the ratio is defined.

The second ratio related to long-term debt is called the **times-interest-earned** ratio. This ratio measures a company's ability to meet its interest obligations. It is calculated as:

Times-interest-earned ratio describes a company's ability to make the interest payments on its debt.

$$\frac{\text{Net Income + interest expense + taxes}}{\text{Interest Expense}}$$

It is important to make sure you've added back the company's interest expense to the numerator. The ratio measures the number of times operating income can cover interest expense. The more interest expense a company has, the smaller the ratio will be. If a company has any trouble covering its interest expense, that company clearly has too much debt.

The details about a company's long-term debt are often found in the notes to the financial statements, instead of the face of the balance sheet. For example, the liabilities section of the Sherwin Williams balance sheet, shown in Exhibit

8-20, shows only the basic amounts of long-term obligations. The accompanying notes give the details. The more you learn about analyzing financial statements, the more you will come to appreciate the importance of the information in the notes to the financial statements.

Calculate the debt-to-equity ratio for Sherwin Williams for each of the years shown in Exhibit 8-20. What trend do you see, and how might an investor interpret it?

STUDY BREAK 8-11
SEE HOW YOU'RE DOING

Exhibit 8-20   Details of Long-Term Debt from the Financial Statements of Sherwin Williams

From Liabilities and Shareholders' Equity Section
(Thousands of Dollars)

	At December 31		
	1999	1998	1997
Total current liabilities	$1,189,862	$1,111,973	$1,115,663
Long-term debt	**624,365**	**730,283**	**843,919**
Postretirement benefits other than pensions	206,591	204,763	199,839
Other long-term liabilities	332,740	302,503	284,200
Shareholders' equity			
Total shareholders' equity	1,698,532	1,715,940	1,592,180
Total liabilities and shareholders' equity	$4,052,090	$4,065,462	$4,035,801

From the Notes to the Financial Statements
Note 7—Long-Term Debt

		Amount outstanding		
	Due date	1999	1998	1997
6.85% Notes	2007	$ 199,775	$ 199,742	$ 199,710
7.375% Debentures	2027	149,907	149,903	149,900
7.45% Debentures	2097	149,402	149,396	149,390
6.5% Notes	2002	99,978	99,966	99,955
6.25% Notes	2000		99,974	99,948
Floating rate notes				50,000
5.5% Notes	2027			49,922
9.875% Debentures	2007–2016	15,900	15,900	15,900
6% to 9% Promissory notes	Through 2004	5,752	10,623	23,791
8% to 12% Promissory notes partial secured by certain land and buildings and other	Through 2005	3,569	3,884	4,495
4.75% Promissory note	2000		800	800
Other obligations		82	95	108
		$624,365	**$730,283**	**$843,919**

Business Risk

Identify the risks associated with
long-term debt.

BUSINESS PROCESS

The risks associated with debt are different from the risks associated with
assets like cash or inventory. A company must put controls in place to minimize
the risk of losing cash and inventory.

The risk associated with debt is risk to both the company and to its creditors. The primary risk for a company associated with long-term debt is the
risk of not being able to make the debt payments. The more debt a business
has, the more risk there is that the company won't be able to pay the debt as it
becomes due. That would result in serious financial trouble, possibly even
bankruptcy. This is, of course, a significant risk for the creditors, too. If a
company has trouble making its debt payments, you would not like to be one
of its creditors.

There are two steps a company can take to minimize the risk associated
with long-term debt.

1. Be sure a thorough business analysis accompanies any decision to borrow money. This is where the concept of positive financial leverage
comes in. The company must make sure there is a high probability of
earning a higher return with the borrowed funds than the interest costs
associated with borrowing the funds. How high should the probability
be? That's an individual business decision. The point is that this should be
a consideration. The more money involved, the higher the probability
should be.
2. Study the characteristics of various types of debt—terms, interest rates,
and ease of obtaining the money—and evaluate their attractiveness in
your specific circumstances, given the purpose of the debt and the financial situation of the company. For example, bonds are more flexible—the
terms and cash flows can be varied, whereas a bank loan can be arranged
much more quickly.

Summary Problem: Tom's Wear Obtains Debt Financing in July

When Tom started his T-shirt business in January, he borrowed a small amount
of money from his mom. Now that he has the business up and running, Tom
decides he needs more space for inventory and for the actual business operations. This is crucial if he wants to take advantage of the demand for his shirts.
Tom finds an excellent deal on a small office complex with a large warehouse;
so he goes to his local bank and secures a mortgage loan for $75,000, the cost of
the office complex. The balance sheet from June 30 is shown in Exhibit 8-21,
and the transactions for July are shown in Exhibit 8-22.

Additional information needed to make the month-end adjustments:

1. The van was driven 10,000 miles this month.
2. Bad debt expense and warranty expense are calculated based on the same
percentages as Tom's Wear used in June: 3% of credit sales for bad debts
and 2% of sales for warranties.

Required:
Record the journal entries and the needed adjustments. Post the entries to
T-accounts, and prepare an adjusted trial balance. Then prepare the four basic
financial statements for Tom's Wear for the month of July. Ignore income taxes.
(Solution provided near the end of the chapter.)

Exhibit 8-21

Tom's Wear, Inc.
Balance Sheet
At June 30, 2001

Assets		Liabilities and shareholders' equity	
Cash	$ 8,278	Accounts payable	$18,950
Accounts receivable (net of allowance of $1,320)	42,780	Interest payable	750
Inventory	6,365	Warranty liability	979
Prepaid insurance	150	Salaries payable	723
Prepaid rent	1,800	Payroll taxes payable	277
Prepaid Web service	200	Other payables	77
		Current portion of long-term note	6,000
Total current assets	59,573		
		Total current liabilities	27,756
Equipment (net of $400 accumulated depreciation)	3,600		
Van (net of $2,755 accumulated depreciation)	27,245	Notes payable	24,000
Total assets	$90,418		
		Total liabilities	51,756
		Common stock	5,000
		Retained earnings	33,662
		Total liabilities and shareholders' equity	$90,418

1	July 1	For a new office complex, Tom borrows $75,000 at an annual interest rate of 8% for a term of 15 years. The terms of the loan call for quarterly payments of principal and interest. The first payment will be made on September 30. (The principal portion of the quarterly payments due in 2001 of $2,710 will be shown as the current portion of the mortgage payable.)
		As part of his decision to buy the office complex, Tom had an appraisal done on the land and building. Recall, we discussed "market basket" purchases in Chapter 5. Tom has to separate the cost of the land and building, so he can depreciate only the building. The land was appraised at 10% of the purchase price and the building at 90%. The building has an estimated useful life of 40 years and an estimated residual value of $5,100. The company will use straight-line depreciation.
2	July 5	Pays Sam's June salary and deposits the related payroll taxes.
3	July 10–30	Collects cash on accounts receivable of $37,000.
4	July 12	Pays accounts payable of $18,950.
5	July 14	Tom has been concentrating on increasing sales, so he must increase inventory purchases as well. Tom has found a supplier who will give him a significant discount with a large quantity purchase, so the company purchases 10,000 T-shirts. The cost is $3.60 each. The shipping terms are FOB destination. Tom's Wear makes the purchase on account.
6	July 20	Tom finds out that Big Bend Sports has closed and filed for bankruptcy. He writes off their account, which has a balance of $1,000.
7	July 15–30	Tom's sales efforts continue to pay off with the addition of several more sporting goods stores as customers. During July, Tom sells 500 shirts for $11 each to 18 different stores. All sales are on account.
8	July 15–30	During July, 200 shirts are returned with defects. Tom replaces all of them with new shirts.
9	July 15–30	Pays other operating expenses of $2,600 for the month.
10	July 30	Tom has hired a firm to handle his payroll because he has hired several new employees. He sends the payroll company a check for $3,500 by the 30th of each month to cover the monthly payroll and payroll tax expenses. The payroll company pays the employees, the payroll taxes, and charges a fee based on the number of employees. Tom's Wear records the total expense as salary expense for financial statement purposes.
11	July 30	Pays a dividend of $2,000.

Exhibit 8-22
Transactions for July 2001 for Tom's Wear, Inc.

Understanding Excel

In this exercise you create an amortization schedule for the building Tom's Wear, Inc. purchased.

Requirements

1. Open a new Excel work sheet.
2. Beginning in cell B1, input the following chart. Resize columns, wrap text, and add color and borders as required. You may also choose the font type and size as desired. (See Chapter 7 Excel Exercise for formatting hints.)

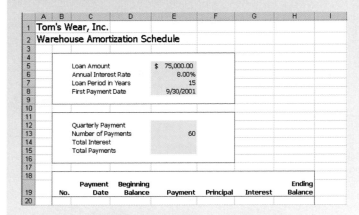

3. To calculate the quarterly payment amount click the Paste Function button fx and then select Financial and PMT.

4. Select cell E12 and input the information that follows to calculate the quarterly payment. Note that when entering formulas, the "=" sign is not required.

   Hint: To remove the negative sign, multiple your results by −1.

5. By using appropriate formulas, calculate the total interest and the total payments to be made on the loan.
6. Complete the amortization table as follows:

   ■ Input the number and date of each payment.

   Hint: Input the first three numbers (1 to 3) or the first four payment dates and Excel will complete the series if you use the fill handle and drag over the rest of the range.

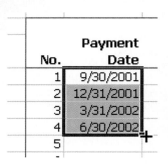

   ■ Input the beginning balance and payment amount using the appropriate cell reference.

   Hint: Input the payment amount as = E12. The dollar signs allow you to copy the payment without the cell reference changing.

   ■ Use appropriate formulas and cell references to calculate the interest, principal, and ending balance for payment 1. Copy the formulas and cell references to complete the schedule.

   Hint: To copy the beginning balance, you must enter the correct cell reference for payment 2: "= H20."

7. Print your file and save it to disk. Name your file TomsWear8.

Answers to Study Break Questions

Interest expense = $600,000 × 0.09 × 1/12 (1 month) = $4,500 interest per month.   **Study Break 8-1**
Total payment = $5,500, so $4,500 is interest and the remaining $1,000 is principal.

Date	Transaction	Debit	Credit
2/1	Mortgage payable	$1,000	
	Interest expense	4,500	
	Cash		$5,500

To record the first principal and interest payment on the $600,000, 9% note

Future value = $1,552.92   **Study Break 8-2**

FV ordinary annuity = PMT × (factor from FV of an ordinary annuity table)   **Study Break 8-3**
$$= 200 × (4.70973)$$
$$= \$941.95$$

PV = $5,000 × (factor from PV of $1 table)   **Study Break 8-4**
PV = $5,000 × 0.62092
PV = $3,104.60

PV = PMT (n, i%)   **Study Break 8-5**
50,000 = PMT (20, 5%)
50,000 = PMT (12.46221)
PMT = $4,012.13

$1,000 × 0.955 = $ 955   **Study Break 8-6**
$1,000 × 1.02 = $1,020

■ The bond will sell for a *premium*, because the bond's stated interest rate is higher than   **Study Break 8-7**
  the market rate of interest.
■ The interest payment is calculated by the information on the face of the bond: $1,000
  × 0.09 = $90 per year.

Interest *expense* (as opposed to interest *payment*) is calculated by multiplying the bond's   **Study Break 8-8**
carrying value (the loan) by the market rate of interest. The amount of proceeds (selling
price of the bonds) equals the carrying value of the bonds on the date of the first interest
payment. Thus, $196,000 × 0.065 × 1/2 = $6,370 is the interest expense for the first 6
months. Because the payment (fixed by the par value of the bond and the stated interest
rate) for the 6 months is $6,000 (= $200,000 × 6% × 1/2), the difference of $370 will be
subtracted from the discount on bonds payable. That will increase the carrying value of
the bonds to $196,370 after the first interest payment. Then, at December 31, 2003,
Knollwood will accrue interest expense for the last half of the year; the expense is
$196,370 × 0.065 × 1/2 year = $6,382. The payment is $6,000, so the difference of $382 will
be subtracted from the discount. The carrying value of the bonds on December 31, 2003,
will be $196,752. The total interest expense for the year is $6,370 + $6,382 = $12,752.

Date	Transaction	Debit	Credit
1/1/2003	Cash	$196,000	
	Discount on bonds payable	4,000	
	Bonds payable		$200,000
	To record the issue of $200,000, 6% bonds at 98		
6/30/2003	Interest expense	$6,370	
	Cash		$6,000
	Discount on bonds payable		370
	To record the first semi-annual interest payment on bonds		
	(expense = $196,000 × 0.0325)		
12/31/2003	Interest expense	$6,382	
	Cash		$6,000
	Discount on bonds payable		382
	To record the second semi-annual interest payment on bonds		
	(expense = $196,370 × 0.0325)		

Study Break 8-9 Interest *expense* (as opposed to interest *payment*) is calculated by multiplying the bond's carrying value (the loan) by the market rate of interest. The amount of proceeds (selling price of the bond) equals the carrying value of the bonds on the date of the first interest payment.

Thus, $204,000 × 0.09 = $18,360 is the first year's interest expense.

The interest payment (fixed by the par value of the bonds and the stated interest rate) for the first year is $20,000 (= $200,000 × 0.10), the difference of $1,640 will be deducted from the premium on bonds payable. That will decrease the carrying value of the bonds to $202,360 ($204,000 − $1,640) after the first interest payment. (Remember, the carrying value will decrease over the life of these bonds to go from $204,000 to the face amount of $200,000 by maturity.)

Date	Transaction	Debit	Credit
1/1/2003	Cash	$204,000	
	Bonds payable		$200,000
	Premium on bonds payable		4,000
	To record the issue of $200,000, 6% bonds at 102		
12/31/2003	Interest expense	$18,360	
	Premium on bonds payable	1,640	
	Cash		$20,000
	To record the first annual interest payment on bonds (expense = $204,000 × 0.09)		

Study Break 8-10 1. For computing bond price *PV* = present value.

Principal: $100,000 × *PV* of $1 for 4 periods at 10% = $100,000 × 0.68301[a] = $68,301

Interest: $8,000 × *PV* of an ordinary annuity of $1 for 4 periods at 10% =
$8,000 × 3.16987[b] = $25,359

Total price (PV) $93,660

This means that the bonds were issued for approximately 94, which means 94% of the face or par value. Use 94 to answer these questions:

[a]Where 0.68301 is from *PV* of $1 table.
[b]Where 3.16987 is from *PV* of an annuity table.

2. Show how the actual issue of these bonds affects the accounting equation:

Assets	=	Liabilities	+	Contributed capital	+	Retained earnings
+$94,000 Cash		+100,000 Bonds payable (6,000) Discount on bonds payable				

Date	Transaction	Debit	Credit
1/1/2003	Cash	$94,000	
	Discount on bonds payable	6,000	
	Bonds payable		$100,000
	To record the issue of $100,000, 10% bonds at 94		

3. Show how the payment of interest on December 31, 2003 affects the accounting equation:

Assets	=	Liabilities	+	Contributed capital	+	Retained earnings
$(8,000) Cash		+1,400 Discount on bonds payable				$(9,400) Interest expense

Date	Transaction	Debit	Credit
6/30/2003	Interest expense	$9,400	
	Cash		$8,000
	Discount on bonds payable		1,400

To record the first annual interest payment on bonds
(expense = $94,000 × 0.10)

Note: Interest expense: $94,000 × 0.10 = $9,400. Because the payment is fixed at $8,000, you amortize the discount (it becomes interest expense) by the difference, $1,400. Deducting $1,400 from the discount actually increases the carrying value of the bonds to $95,400. (You're working up to the face.)

4. Show how the payment of interest on December 31, 2004 affects the accounting equation:

Assets	=	Liabilities	+	Contributed capital	+	Retained earnings
$(8,000) Cash		+1,540 Discount on bonds payable				(9,540) Interest expense

Date	Transaction	Debit	Credit
12/31/2003	Interest expense	$9,540	
	Cash		$8,000
	Discount on bonds payable		1,540

To record the second annual interest payment on bonds
(expense = $95,400 × 0.10)

Note: $95,400 × 0.10 = $9,540 interest expense. Because the payment is $8,000, you amortize $1,540 as additional interest expense. So the new book value for B/P = $96,940.

5. The carrying value of the bonds on the December 31, 2003 balance sheet is $95,400; and on the December 31, 2004 balance sheet, $96,940.

Debt to equity:

Study Break 8-11

$$1999 \quad \frac{\$2,353,558}{\$1,698,532} = 1.386$$

$$1998 \quad \frac{\$2,349,522}{\$1,715,940} = 1.369$$

$$1997 \quad \frac{\$2,443,621}{\$1,592,180} = 1.535$$

The company has reduced its debt-to-equity ratio. An investor would likely see this as good news.

Solution to Summary Problem

Transaction 1
Tom borrows $75,000 for a new office complex (land and building).

Date	Transaction	Debit	Credit
7/1/2001	Buildings	$67,500	
	Land	7,500	
	Mortgage payable		$75,000

To record the purchase of a building and land

Transaction 2
Pays Sam Cubby's salary for June and deposits the related payroll taxes.

Date	Transaction	Debit	Credit
7/2/2001	Salaries payable	$723	
	Payroll taxes withheld	277	
	Other payables	77	
	Cash		$1,077
To record payment of salary and taxes			

Transaction 3
Collects cash on accounts receivable of $37,000.

Date	Transaction	Debit	Credit
7/10–7/30/2001	Cash	$37,000	
	Accounts receivable		$37,000
To record the collection of accounts receivable			

Transaction 4
Pays accounts payable of $18,950.

Date	Transaction	Debit	Credit
7/12/2001	Accounts payable	$18,950	
	Cash		$18,950
To record payment on account			

Transaction 5
Purchases 10,000 T-shirts @ $3.60 each, FOB destination.

Date	Transaction	Debit	Credit
7/14/2001	Inventory	$36,000	
	Accounts payable		$36,000
To record the purchase of 10,000 T-shirts at $3.60 each.			

Transaction 6
Writes off accounts receivable of Big Bend Sports, $1,000.

Date	Transaction	Debit	Credit
7/20/2001	Allowance for bad debts	$1,000	
	Accounts receivable (Big Bend)		$1,000
To record the write-off of Big Bend Sports' account			

Transaction 7
Sells 500 shirts to 18 stores for $11 each, for a total of 9,000 shirts. All sales are on account.

Date	Transaction	Debit	Credit
7/15–7/30/2001	Accounts receivable	$99,000	
	Sales revenue		$99,000
To record the sale of 500 T-shirts on account			
7/15–7/30/2001	Cost of goods sold	$32,735	
	Inventory		$32,735
To record cost of goods sold = [(1,675 × $3.80) + (7,325 × $3.60)]			

Transaction 8

During July, 200 shirts are returned with defects. Tom replaces them all with new shirts.

Date	Transaction	Debit	Credit
7/15–7/30/2001	Warranties payable	$720	
	Inventory		$720

To record the replacement of 200 defective shirts (200 × $3.60)

Transaction 9

Other operating expenses for the month are $2,600.

Date	Transaction	Debit	Credit
7/30/2001	Other operating expenses	$2,600	
	Cash		$2,600

To record the payment of miscellaneous operating expenses

Transaction 10

Records salary expense of $3,500.

Date	Transaction	Debit	Credit
7/30/2001	Salary expense	$3,500	
	Cash		$3,500

To record the payment of payroll, related taxes, and fees

Transaction 11

Tom's Wear pays a dividend of $2,000.

Date	Transaction	Debit	Credit
7/30/2001	Retained earnings	$2,000	
	Cash		$2,000

To record the payment of a cash dividend

Adjustment 1

Record operating expenses: $1,200 for rent, $100 for insurance, and $50 for web service.

Date	Transaction	Debit	Credit
7/31/2001	Rent expense	$1,200	
	Insurance expense	100	
	Other operating expenses	50	
	Prepaid rent		$1,200
	Prepaid insurance		100
	Prepaid web service		50

To record July's operating expenses

Adjustment 2

Record depreciation expense for June: $100 for the computer, $1,450 for the van (10,000 miles × $0.145) and $130 for the building ($62,400/40)/12.

Date	Transaction	Debit	Credit
7/31/2001	Depreciation expense	$1,680	
	Accumulated depreciation: computer		$ 100
	Accumulated depreciation: van		1,450
	Accumulated depreciation: building		130

To record July depreciation expense

Adjustment 3

Record interest expense on the notes: van—$250 ($30,000 × 10%)/12; mortgage—$500 ($75,000 × 8%)/12.

Date	Transaction	Debit	Credit
7/31/2001	Interest expense	$750	
	Interest payable		$750
To record interest expense for July			

Adjustment 4

Bad debt estimate = 3% of credit sales.

Date	Transaction	Debit	Credit
7/31/2001	Bad debt expense	$2,970	
	Allowance for bad debts		$2,970
To record the bad debt estimate for July (3% × $99,000)			

Adjustment 5

Warranty liability estimate = 2% of total sales.

Date	Transaction	Debit	Credit
7/31/2001	Warranty expense	$1,980	
	Warranties payable		$1,980
To record the estimated warranty liability for July			

T-Accounts for Tom's Wear with July journal entries and adjustments

Cash

BB	$8,278	1,077	2
3	37,000	18,950	4
		2,600	9
		3,500	10
		2,000	11
	17,151		

Accounts receivable

BB	$44,100	$37,000	3
7	99,000	1,000	6
	105,100		

Prepaid insurance

BB	$150	$100	Adj-1
	50		

Allowance for bad debts

6	$1,000	$1,320	BB
		2,970	
		3,290	

Inventory

BB	$6,365	$32,735	7
5	36,000	720	8
	8,910		

Accumulated depreciation: computer

	$400	BB
	100	Adj-2
	500	

Equipment: van

BB	$30,000	
	30,000	

Equipment: computer

BB	$4,000	
	4,000	

Accounts payable

4	$18,950	$18,950	BB
		36,000	5
		36,000	

Land

1	$7,500	
	7,500	

Accumulated depreciation: buildings

	$130	Adj-2

Warranties payable

8	$720	$979	BB
		1,980	Adj-5
		2,239	

Salaries payable

2	723	$723	BB
		0	

Other payables

2	77	$77	BB
		0	

Prepaid web service

BB	$200	$50	Adj-1
	$150		

Prepaid rent

BB	$1,800	$1,200	Adj-1
	600		

Buildings

1	$67,500	
	67,500	

Payroll taxes withheld

2	$277	$277	BB
		0	

Accumulated depreciation: van

	$2,755	BB
	1,450	Adj-2
	4,205	

Interest payable

	$750	BB
	750	Adj-3
	1,500	

(continued)

T-Accounts for Tom's Wear with July journal entries and adjustments

Common stock

	$5,000	BB
	5,000	

Miscellaneous operating expenses

9	$2,600	50	
Adj-1			
	2,650		

Bad debt expense

Adj-5	$2,970	
	2,970	

Retained earnings

11	$2,000	$33,662	BB
		31,662	

Salary expense

10	$3,500	
	3,500	

Warranty expense

Adj-5	$1,980	
	1,980	

Notes payable

	$30,000	BB
	30,000	

Sales revenue

	$99,000	7
	99,000	

Insurance expense

Adj-1	$100	
	100	

Mortgage payable

	$75,000	1
	75,000	

Cost of goods sold

7	$32,735	
	32,735	

Rent expense

Adj-1	$1,200	
	1,200	

Depreciation expense

Adj-2	$1,680	
	1,680	

Interest expense

Adj-3	$750	
	750	

tom's wear

Tom's Wear, Inc.
Adjusted Trial Balance
July 31, 2001

	Debits	Credits
Cash	$ 17,151	
Accounts receivable	105,100	
Allowance for bad debts		$ 3,290
Inventory	8,910	
Prepaid insurance	50	
Prepaid web service	150	
Prepaid rent	600	
Equipment: computer	4,000	
Accumulated depreciation: computer		500
Equipment: van	30,000	
Accumulated depreciation: van		4,205
Buildings	67,500	
Accumulated depreciation: buildings		130
Land	7,500	
Accounts payable		36,000
Interest payable		1,500
Warranties payable		2,239
Notes payable		30,000
Mortgage payable		75,000
Common stock		5,000
Retained earnings		31,662
Revenue		99,000
Cost of goods sold	32,735	
Depreciation expense	1,680	
Miscellaneous operating expense	2,650	
Salary expense	3,500	
Insurance expense	100	
Rent expense	1,200	
Interest expense	750	
Bad debt expense	2,970	
Warranty expense	1,980	
Totals	*$288,526*	*$288,526*

Tom's Wear, Inc.
Income Statement
For the Month Ended July 31, 2001

Sales revenue		$ 99,000
Less cost of goods sold		(32,735)
Gross margin on sale		$ 66,265
Expenses		
Salary expense	$3,500	
Rent expense	1,200	
Insurance expense	100	
Depreciation expense	1,680	
Interest expense	750	
Bad debt expense	2,970	
Warranty expense	1,980	
Miscellaneous operating expenses	2,650	
Total expenses		(14,830)
Net income		**$51,435**

Tom's Wear, Inc.
Statement of Changes in Shareholders' Equity
For the Month Ended July 31, 2001

Beginning contributed capital	$ 5,000	
Contributions during the month	0	
Ending contributed capital		$ 5,000
Beginning retained earnings	$33,662	
Net income for the month	51,435	
Dividends	(2,000)	
Ending retained earnings		83,097
Total shareholders' equity		**$88,097**

Tom's Wear, Inc.
Balance Sheet
At July 31, 2001

Assets		=	Liabilities and shareholders' equity	
Cash	$ 17,151		Accounts payable	$ 36,000
Accounts receivable (net	101,810		Interest payable	1,500
of allowance of $3,290)			Warranty liability	2,239
Inventory	8,910		Current portion of long-term note	6,000
Prepaid insurance	50		Current portion of mortgage	2,710
Prepaid rent	600		Total current liabilities	48,449
Prepaid Web service	150			
Total current assets	128,671		Notes payable	24,000
Computer (net of $500	3,500		Mortgage payable	72,290
accumulated depreciation)			Total liabilities	144,739
Van (net of $4,205	25,795			
accumulated depreciation)			Common stock	5,000
Land	7,500		Retained earnings	83,097
Building (net of $130	67,370			
accumulated depreciation)			Total liabilities and shareholders'	
Total assets	$232,836		equity	$232,836

tom's wear

Tom's Wear, Inc.
Statement of Cash Flows
For the Month Ended July 31, 2001

Cash from operating activities		
Cash from customers	$ 37,000	
Cash paid to vendor for T-shirts	(18,950)	
Cash paid for operating expenses	(7,177)	
Total cash from operations		$10,873
Cash from investing activities		0
Cash from financing activities		
Dividends	$ (2,000)	(2,000)
Net increase in cash		**$ 8,873**

Note: Building and land purchased with a mortgage payable of $75,000.

Cash on July 31	$17,151
Cash on July 1	8,278
Net increase	**$ 8,873**

Questions

1. What are the two main sources of financing for a business?
2. What is a mortgage?
3. What does the expression *time value of money* mean?
4. What is an annuity?
5. What are bonds?
6. How are the interest payments associated with a bond calculated?
7. What is the difference between the stated rate of interest and the effective rate (market rate) of interest on a bond?
8. What is another name for the face value of a bond?
9. When is a bond issued at a discount?
10. When is a bond issued at a premium?
11. What does it mean to amortize a discount or premium?
12. What is a convertible bond?
13. What does it mean to "call" a bond?
14. How is the carrying value of a bond computed?
15. At maturity, what is the carrying value of a bond that was issued at a premium?
16. What is the difference between the straight-line method and the effective-interest method of amortizing a bond discount or premium?
17. What advantage is there to obtaining financing using bonds as opposed to getting a loan from a bank?
18. What is the difference between term bonds and serial bonds?
19. What is a debenture?
20. When installment loan payments (on a mortgage) are made, the amount paid reduces cash. What other two items (financial statement amounts) are affected?

Short Exercises

SE8-1 Nunez Company has arranged to borrow $25,000 for 5 years at an annual interest rate of 8%. The annual payments will be $6,261.41. When Nunez makes its first payment at the end of the first year of the loan, how much of the payment will be interest?

L.O. 8-1

L.O. 8-1

SE8-2 Feathers and Furs borrowed $75,000 to buy a new fur storage facility. The company borrowed the money for 10 years at 12% per year, and the monthly payment is $1,076.03. When the company makes the first monthly payment, how much will that payment reduce the principal of the loan?

L.O. 8-1

SE8-3 Curtain Company borrowed $10,000 at 9% for 7 years. The loan requires annual payments of $1,986.91. When Curtain Company makes the first annual payment, how much of the payment will be interest and how much will reduce the principal of the loan?

L.O. 8-1

SE8-4 On July 1, 2004, Maxine's Equipment Company signed a long-term note with the local bank for $50,000. The term of the note was 10 years, with an annual interest rate of 8%. If Maxine's makes annual payments of $7,451.47, beginning on June 30, 2005, how much of the first payment will be interest?

L.O. 8-2

SE8-5 GuGa's Shirt Company wants to borrow $35,000, and the bank has quoted an interest rate of 8% for 5 years. If GuGa's makes equal annual payments at the end of each year, how much will each payment be?

L.O. 8-2

SE8-6 Suppose you want to have $100,000 in 5 years and you know the interest rate is approximately 10%. If you are willing to make a deposit of the same amount at the beginning of every month, what will your deposit be?

L.O. 8-3

SE8-7 If a $1,000 bond is selling at 95, how much cash will the issuing company receive? If a $1,000 bond is selling at par, how much cash will the issuing company receive? If a $1,000 bond is selling at 101, how much cash will the issuing company receive?

L.O. 8-3

SE8-8 If $100,000 of 8% bonds are issued (sold) for $95,000, to result in an effective yield of 9%, how much interest will be paid in cash during the first year? How much interest expense will be incurred for the first year?

L.O. 8-3

SE8-9 For each of the following situations, tell whether the bond described will be issued at a premium, at a discount, or at par.

a. Colson Company issued $200,000 worth of bonds with a stated interest rate of 10%. At the time of issue, the market rate of interest for similar investments was 9%.
b. Dean Company issued $100,000 worth of callable bonds with a stated rate of 12%. At the time of issue, the market rate of interest for similar investments was 9%.
c. Liddy Company issued $200,000 worth of bonds with a stated rate of 8%. At the time of issue, the market rate of interest for similar investments was 9%.

L.O. 8-3

SE8-10 For each of the following, compute the proceeds from the bond issue.

- Haldeman Hair Systems issued $20,000 worth of bonds at 106.
- Erlichman Egg Company issued $100,000 worth of bonds at 99.
- Carl's Cutlery Company issued $500,000 worth of bonds at 96 1/2.

L.O. 8-3

SE8-11 Altoona Company was able to issue (sell) $200,000 of 9% bonds for $220,000, because their credit rating is excellent and market interest rates have fallen. The resulting effective yield on these bonds is 8%.

a. How much interest will be paid in cash during the first year?
b. What will interest expense be for the first year, using effective interest amortization?

Exercises

L.O. 8-1

E8-1 Stephen's Storage Company needed some long-term financing and arranged for a 20-year, $100,000 mortgage loan on December 31, 2000. The stated interest rate is 9% per year, with $11,000 payments made at the end of each year.

a. What is the amount of interest expense related to this loan for the year ended December 31, 2001?
b. What amount of liability should appear on the December 31, 2001 balance sheet?
c. What is the amount of interest expense related to this loan for the year ended December 31, 2002?
d. What amount of liability should appear on the December 31 2002 balance sheet?

E8-2 Grace's Gems purchased some property on December 31, 2000, for $100,000, paying $20,000 in cash and obtaining a mortgage loan for the other $80,000. The interest rate is 8% per year, with $2,925 payments made at the end of March, June, September, and December.

a. What amounts should appear as interest expense on the quarterly income statements and as a liability on the quarterly balance sheets during 2001?
b. What amount of interest expense should appear on the income statement for the year ended December 31, 2001?

L.O. 8-1

E8-3 For each of the following, calculate the payment each loan would require. Assume the payments are made at the end of the period in each case. Interest rates are annual rates.

a. Principal = $30,000; interest rate = 5%; term = 5 years; payments = annual.
b. Principal = $30,000; interest rate = 8%; term = 5 years; payments = annual.
c. Principal = $30,000; interest rate = 8%; term = 10 years; payments = annual.
d. Principal = $30,000; interest rate = 8%; term = 10 years; payments = semiannual.
e. Principal = $30,000; interest rate = 12%; term = 5 years; payments = monthly. [Note: Financial calculator required.]

L.O. 8-2

E8-4 For each of the following, how much would you need to save today (a single amount) to have the amount needed in the future?

a. In 5 years $40,000, interest rate = 8%.
b. In 10 years $25,000, interest rate = 8%.
c. In 2 years $25,000, interest rate = 10%.
d. In 8 years $100,000, interest rate = 5%.
e. In 20 years $500,000, interest rate = 6%.

L.O. 8-2

E8-5 On December 31, 2000, Bert's Batteries, Inc. issued $10,000 worth of 10% bonds at 94. The market rate of interest at the time of issue was approximately 11%. These are 10-year bonds with interest paid annually on December 31. By using the effective interest method to amortize the discount, calculate the following:

a. interest payments for the first 2 years
b. interest expense for the years ending December 31, 2001 and December 31, 2002
c. carrying value of the bonds on the balance sheet at December 31, 2001 and December 31, 2002.

L.O. 8-3

E8-6 On December 31, 2000, Carl's Cartons, Inc. issued $100,000 worth of 9% bonds at 104 because the market rate of interest at the time of issue had fallen to 8%. The interest on these bonds is paid annually on December 31. By using the effective interest method to amortize the premium, calculate the following:

a. interest payments for the first two interest payment dates
b. interest expense for the years ended December 31, 2001 and December 31, 2002
c. carrying values of the bonds on the balance sheets at December 31, 2001 and December 31, 2002

L.O. 8-3

E8-7 On December 31, 2003, Dave's Delivery Service issued $10,000 worth of 10% bonds at approximately 89. The market rate of interest at the time of issue had risen to 12%. These are 10-year bonds with interest paid semiannually on June 30 and December 31. By using the effective interest method to amortize the discount, calculate:

a. interest payments for the first four interest payment dates
b. total interest expense for the years ending December 31, 2004 and December 31, 2005
c. carrying values of the bonds on the balance sheets at December 31, 2004 and December 31, 2005

L.O. 8-3

L.O. 8-3

E8-8 On June 30, 2003, Ellie's Electronics issued $20,000 face value of 10% bonds at 105. The market rate of interest at the time of issue was approximately 9%. They were 10-year bonds with interest paid semiannually, on December 31 and June 30. By using the effective interest method to amortize the premium, calculate:

a. interest payments for the first three payments
b. total interest expense for the years ended December 31, 2003 and December 31, 2004
c. carrying values of the bonds on the balance sheets at December 31, 2003 and December 31, 2004

L.O. 8-3

E8-9 On June 30, 2001, Fred's Fudge Company issued $50,000 worth of 10% bonds for $50,000. The interest is paid annually on June 30. Calculate:

a. interest payments for the first two interest payment dates
b. total interest expense for the fiscal years ending December 31, 2001 and December 31, 2002
c. long-term liability reported on the December 31, 2001 and December 31, 2002 balance sheets
d. interest payable on December 31, 2001 and December 31, 2002

L.O. 8-3

E8-10 On September 30, 2001, Gene's Garden Shop, Inc. issued $100,000 worth of 9% bonds at 100. The interest is paid semiannually on March 31 and September 30. Calculate:

a. interest payments for the first four interest payment dates
b. total interest expense for the fiscal years ending December 31, 2001 and December 31, 2002
c. long-term liabilities reported on the December 31, 2001 and December 31, 2002 balance sheets
d. interest payable on December 31, 2001 and December 31, 2002

L.O. 8-3

E8-11 On January 1, 2004, John's Electronics issued $10,000 worth of 10% bonds at 96. The market rate of interest at the time of issue was approximately 10.66%. They were 10-year bonds with interest paid semiannually. John's uses the effective interest method for amortizing any bond discounts or premiums. Calculate:

a. interest payments for the first four interest dates
b. total interest expense for the fiscal years ending December 31, 2004 and December 31, 2005
c. carrying value of the bonds on the balance sheet at December 31, 2004 and December 31, 2005

Problems—Set A

L.O. 8-1

P8-1A The SD Company engaged in the following transactions related to long-term liabilities during 2003.

a. On March 1, the firm borrowed $25,000 for a machine. The loan is to be repaid in equal annual payments at the end of each of the next 5 years (beginning February 28, 2004); and the interest rate SD is paying for this loan is 8.5%.
b. On October 1, the company borrowed $120,000 from Suwannee Local Bank at an interest rate of 7.25%. The loan is for 10 years, and SD Company will make annual payments on September 30 of each year.

Required: [Note: Financial calculator required.]

a. For each loan described, prepare an amortization schedule for the first four payments. Be sure to show the reduction in principal and the interest expense for each payment.
b. What total interest expense related to these two loans would SD Company show on its income statement for the year ended 2003?
c. How much interest payable would be shown on the SD balance sheet at December 31, 2003?

P8-2A Joe Brinks is making plans to finance a series of projects. Several projects he is considering are described next.

L.O. 8-2

a. He will purchase a truck for $30,000 to be repaid in equal monthly payments over the next 5 years. The bank has quoted an interest rate of 7.5%. [Note: Financial calculator required.]

b. He will purchase a piece of land, whose owner is offering to sell it to Joe for $25,000. The seller would accept five annual payments at 10%.

c. He will sell old equipment for $4,000. Joe is willing to accept quarterly payments for the next 2 years at an interest rate of 8%.

d. He will purchase land and building for $50,000, with a down payment of $5,000, and a semi-annual payment for the next 10 years at an interest rate of 6.5%. [Note: Financial calculator required.]

Required: For each situation, calculate the amount of the payment involved. Assume all payments are made at the end of the period.

P8-3A Given the following situations, what annual interest rate is implied in the transaction?

L.O. 8-2

a. Sam borrowed $10,000, and the annual payments are approximately $2,571 at the end of each of the next 5 years.

b. Don purchased a piece of land for $120,000. He made a down payment of $20,000, and he is making semiannual payments of $7,358.18 at the end of each 6-month period for the next 10 years.

c. Abbie borrowed $30,000 from the local bank. She will repay the money in a lump sum at the end of 2 years. The banker told her that the payment would be $36,300.

d. Tommy bought a new stereo system and the store will provide financing. The total purchase came to $8,634. Tommy will make semiannual payments for the next 3 years of $1,647.04 each.

Required: For each situation, calculate the annual interest rate implied by the principal amount and the payment schedule

P8-4A Hewitt's Paints issued $1,000,000 worth of 5-year bonds with a stated interest rate of 8% and interest payable annually on December 31. The bonds were issued when the market interest rate was 10%. Hewitt's issued the bonds on January 1, 2005. The fiscal year-end for Hewitt's Paints is December 31.

L.O. 8-3

Required: Calculate the proceeds from the bond issue. Then by using the effective interest method of amortization, calculate the interest payments, interest expense, and year-end carrying value for each of the 5 years.

P8-5A Julie's Jewels issued $20,000 worth of 10-year bonds at 102 1/2. The bonds have a stated rate of 8%.

L.O. 8-3

Required:

a. Was the market interest rate at the time of issue higher or lower than 8%? How do you know?

b. What were the proceeds from the bond issue?

c. If the bonds were issued on January 1 and the interest is paid annually on December 31, what is the carrying value of the bonds at the end of the first year? Julie's uses the effective interest method of amortization. (Assume the interest rate at the time of issue was 7.63%.)

d. If the bonds were issued on July 1 and the interest is paid semiannually on December 31 and June 30, what is the amount of interest expense at the date of each interest payment in the first year? Julie's uses the effective interest method of amortization.

e. Calculate the interest expense each period if Julie's Jewels used the straight-line method of amortizing discount or premiums. Assume interest is paid semi-annually.

P8-6A Matrix Construction issued $1 million of its 10% bonds on July 1, 2002, at 98. The bonds mature on June 30, 2007. Interest is payable semiannually on June 30 and December 31.

L.O. 8-3

Required:

a. What were the proceeds from the bond issue?
b. Was the market interest rate at the time of issue higher or lower than 10%?
c. The Matrix Construction Company fiscal year-end is December 31. The company uses the straight-line method for amortizing discounts and premiums. Calculate the interest expense for each year, 2002 through 2007.

L.O. 8-3

P8-7A Newman Corp. issued $100,000 of bonds on January 1, 2002. The bonds mature on January 1, 2012. Interest is payable annually on December 31. The stated rate of interest is 8%, and the market rate of interest was 10% at the time of issue.

Required:

a. Calculate the proceeds for the bond issue. How would issuing the bonds affect the financial statements for Newman (on the date of issue)?
b. Prepare an amortization schedule for the first 3 years of the life of the bonds, showing the interest expense and the carrying value at the end of each interest period. Newman uses the effective interest method for amortizing discounts and premiums.
c. How much interest expense related to these bonds would Newman show on its income statement for the year ended December 31, 2003? (Assume effective interest method.)
d. Calculate the interest expense for the year ended December 31, 2003, using the straight-line method of amortization. Then compare that amount to the amount calculated using the effective interest method. Which method do you think Newman should use and why?

L.O. 8-4, 5

P8-8A The following information comes from annual report of La-Z-Boy Company.

Consolidated Balance Sheet (Amounts in thousands, except par value)

	As of April 29, 2000	As of April 24, 1999
Assets (not shown)	$1,218,297	$629,792
Liabilities and shareholders' equity		
Current liabilities		
Current portion of long-term debt	$ 13,119	$ 2,001
Current portion of capital leases	457	784
Accounts payable	90,392	45,419
Payroll/other compensation	74,724	53,697
Income taxes	5,002	4,103
Other current liabilities	53,312	26,424
Total current liabilities	*237,006*	*132,428*
Long-term debt	233,938	62,469
Capital leases	2,156	219
Deferred income taxes	50,280	5,697
Other long-term liabilities	31,825	14,064
Commitments and contingencies		
Shareholders' equity		
Preferred shares—5,000 authorized; none issued	—	—
Common shares, $1 par value— 150,000 authorized; 61,328 issued in 2000 and 52,340 issued in 1999	61,328	52,340
Capital in excess of par value	211,450	31,582
Retained earnings	392,458	332,934
Currency translation adjustments	(2,144)	(1,941)
Total shareholders' equity	*663,092*	*414,915*
Total liabilities and shareholders' equity	*$1,218,297*	*$629,792*

Required:

a. Calculate the debt-to-equity ratio for the years ended April 29, 2000 and April 24, 1999.
b. Who would be interested in this information and why?
c. Suppose you were considering investing in some La-Z-Boy stock. What do you think of the change in this ratio from 1999 to 2000?
d. If La-Z-Boy has bonds payable, where do you think they might be included on the balance sheet?
e. What risks are associated with the long-term debt on La-Z-Boy's balance sheet?

Problems—Set B

P8-1B The McIntyre Company engaged in the following transactions related to long-term liabilities during 2002:

L.O. 8-1

a. On July 1, the firm borrowed $50,000 for a new piece of office equipment. The loan is to be repaid in equal annual payments at the end of each of the next 8 years (beginning June 30, 2003); and the interest rate McIntyre is paying for this loan is 8%.
b. On October 1, McIntyre borrowed $200,000 from Shell Point Local Bank at an interest rate of 9.5%. The loan is for 10 years, and the company will make annual payments on September 30 of each year. [Note: Financial calculator required.]

Required:

a. For each loan described, prepare an amortization schedule for the first four payments. Be sure to show the reduction in principal and the interest expense for each payment.
b. What total interest expense related to these two loans would McIntyre Company show on its income statement for the year ended 2002?
c. How much interest payable would be shown on the McIntyre balance sheet at December 31, 2002?

P8-2B Don Black is making plans to finance a series of projects. Several projects he is considering are described next:

L.O. 8-2

a. He will purchase a boat for $50,000 to be repaid in equal *monthly* payments over the next 6 years. The bank has quoted an interest rate of 12%. [Note: Financial calculator required.]
b. He will purchase property for $125,000. The seller would accept 10 semiannual payments at 8%.
c. He will sell old equipment for $8,000. Don is willing to accept quarterly payments for the next 2 years at an interest rate of 8%.
d. He will purchase land and building for $250,000, with a down payment of $50,000, and semiannual payments for the next 10 years at an interest rate of 10%

Required: For each situation, calculate the amount of the payment. Assume all payments are made at the end of the period.

P8-3B Given the following situations, what annual interest rate is implied in the transaction?

L.O. 8-2

a. Robert borrowed $10,000, and the annual payments are approximately $2,439 at the end of each of the next 5 years.
b. Marc purchased a piece of land for $240,000. He made a down payment of $40,000, and he is making semiannual payments of $13,443.14 at the end of each 6-month period for the next 10 years.
c. Carol borrowed $25,000 from the local bank. She will repay the money in a lump sum at the end of 3 years. The banker told her that the payment would be $30,198.74.
d. Joan bought a new big screen television; the store will provide financing. The total purchase came to $5,450. Joan will make quarterly payments for the next 2 years of $760.10 each.

Required: For each situation, calculate the annual interest rate implied by the principal amount and the payment schedule.

L.O. 8-3

P8-4B   Glassworks, Inc. issued $150,000 worth of 6-year bonds with a stated interest rate of 7.5% and interest payable annually on December 31. The bonds were issued when the market interest rate was 8%. The bonds were issued on January 1, 2003. The fiscal year-end for Glassworks, Inc. is December 31.

Required: Calculate the proceeds from the bond issue. Then by using the effective interest method of amortization, calculate the interest payments, interest expense, and year-end carrying value for each of the 6 years.

L.O. 8-3

P8-5B   Venus Rug Company issued $80,000 worth of 10-year bonds when the market rate of interest was 8.5%. The bonds have a stated interest rate of 9%.

Required: [Note: Financial calculator required.]

a. What were the proceeds from the bond issue?
b. If the bonds were issued on January 1 and the interest is paid annually on December 31, what is the carrying value of the bonds at the end of the first year? Venus Rug uses the effective interest method of amortization.
c. If the bonds were issued on July 1 and the interest is paid semiannually on December 31 and June 30, what is the amount of interest expense at the date of each of the first two interest payments? Venus Rug uses the effective interest method of amortization.
d. Calculate the interest expense each period if Venus Rugs used the straight-line method of amortizing discount or premiums. Assume semi-annual interest payments.

L.O. 8-3

P8-6B   Slam Racquet Company issued $1 million of its 6% bonds on July 1, 2003, at 98. The bonds mature on June 30, 2007. Interest is payable annually on June 30. Slam uses the straight-line method of amortizing discounts and premiums.

Required:

a. What were the proceeds from the bond issue?
b. Was the market interest rate at the time of issue higher or lower than 6%?
c. The Slam Racquet Company fiscal year-end is December 31. Calculate the interest expense for each year, 2003 through 2007.

L.O. 8-3

P8-7B   Morgan Corp. issued $1,000,000 of bonds on January 1, 2004. The bonds mature on January 1, 2012. Interest is payable annually each December 31. The stated rate of interest is 11%, and the market rate of interest was 10% at the time of issue.

Required:

a. Calculate the proceeds for the bond issue. How would issuing the bonds affect the accounting equation for Morgan (on the date of issue)?
b. Prepare an amortization schedule for the first 4 years of the life of the bonds, showing the interest expense and the carrying value at the end of each interest period. Morgan uses the effective interest method for amortizing discounts and premiums.
c. How much interest expense related to these bonds would Morgan show on its income statement for the year ended December 31, 2005. (Assume effective interest method.)
d. Calculate the interest expense for the year ended December 31, 2005, using the straight-line method of amortization. Then compare that amount to the amount calculated using the effective interest method. Which method do you think Morgan should use and why?

P8-8B The following information comes from annual report of The Limited.

L.O. 8-4, 5

From the Consolidated Balance Sheet (In Thousands)

	At January 29, 2000	At January 20, 1999
Liabilities and shareholders' equity		
Current liabilities		
Accounts payable	$ 256,306	$ 289,947
Current portion of long-term debt	250,000	100,000
Accrued expenses	579,442	661,784
Income taxes	152,458	128,273
Total current liabilities	*1,238,206*	*1,180,004*
Long-term debt	400,000	550,000
Other long-term liabilities	183,398	195,641
Minority interest	119,008	105,504
Contingent stock redemption agreement	—	351,600
Shareholders' equity		
Common stock	189,727	180,352
Paid-in capital	178,374	157,214
Retained earnings	6,109,371	5,470,689
	6,477,472	5,808,255
Less: treasury stock, at average cost	(4,330,395)	(3,641,296)
Total shareholders' equity	*2,147,077*	*2,166,959*
Total liabilities and shareholders' equity	$ 4,087,689	$ 4,549,708

Required:

a. Calculate the debt-to-equity ratio for the years ending January 29, 2000 and January 20, 1999.

b. Who would be interested in this information and why?

c. Suppose you were considering investing in The Limited stock. What do you think of the change in the debt-to-equity ratio from 1999 to 2000?

d. If The Limited has bonds payable, where might they be included on the balance sheet?

e. What risks are associated with the long-term debt on The Limited balance sheet?

Recording Transactions

R8-1 (SE8-3) Curtain Company borrowed $10,000 at 9% for 7 years. The loan requires annual payments of $1,986.91. Give the journal entry to record the first annual payment.

Date	Account	Debit	Credit

R8-2 (SE8-8) $100,000 of 8% bonds are issued (sold) for $95,000, to result in an effective yield of 9%. Give the journal entry to record the first annual interest payment.

Date	Account	Debit	Credit

R8-3 (SE8-10) For each of the following, give the journal entry to record the bond issue.

- Haldeman Hair Systems issued $20,000 worth of bonds at 106.
- Erlichman Egg Company issued $100,000 worth of bonds at 99.
- Carl's Cutlery Company issued $500,000 worth of bonds at $96\frac{1}{2}$.

Transaction	Account	Debit	Credit

R8-4 (SE8-11) Altoona Company was able to issue (sell) $200,000 of 9% bonds for $220,000 because their credit rating is excellent and market interest rates have fallen. The resulting effective yield on these bonds is 8%. Give the journal entry to record the first annual interest payment.

Date	Account	Debit	Credit

R8-5 (E8-5) On December 31, 2000, Bert's Batteries, Inc. issued $10,000 worth of 10% bonds at 94. The market rate of interest at the time of issue was approximately 11%. These are 10-year bonds with interest paid annually on December 31. The company uses the effective interest method to amortize bond premiums and discounts. Give the journal entries to record the first two interest payments.

Date	Account	Debit	Credit

R8-6 (E8-8) On June 30, 2003, Ellie's Electronics issued $20,000 face value of 10% bonds at 105. The market rate of interest at the time of issue was approximately 9%. They were 10-year bonds with interest paid semi-annually on December 31 and June 30. The company uses the effective interest method to amortize bond premiums and discounts. Give the journal entries for the first three interest payments.

Date	Account	Debit	Credit

R8-7 (E8-11) On January 1, 2004, John's Electronics issued $10,000 worth of 10% bonds at 96. The market rate of interest at the time of issue was approximately 10.66%. They were 10-year bonds with interest paid semi-annually. Give the journal entries for the interest payments for the first four interest dates. John's Electronics uses the effective interest method for amortizing any bond discounts or premiums.

Date	Account	Debit	Credit

R8-8 (P8-1A) The SD Company engaged in the following transactions related to long-term liabilities during 2003: [Note: Financial calculator required.]

1. On March 1, borrowed $25,000 for a machine. The loan is to be repaid in equal annual payments at the end of each of the next 5 years (beginning February 28, 2004), and the interest rate SD is paying for this loan is 8.5%.
2. On October 1, borrowed $120,000 from Suwannee Local Bank at an interest rate of 7.25%. The loan is for 10 years, and SD Company will make annual payments on September 30 of each year.

Required: For each loan described, give the journal entries for the first two interest payments.

Transaction	Account	Debit	Credit

R8-9 (P8-7A) Newman Corporation issued $100,000 of bonds on January 1, 2002. The bonds mature on January 1, 2012. Interest is payable annually on December 31. The stated rate of interest is 8%, and the market rate of interest was 10% at the time of issue.

Required:

a. Calculate the proceeds for the bond issue. Give the journal entry to record the issue of the bonds.
b. Give the journal entries to record the first two interest payments. Newman uses the effective interest method for amortizing discounts and premiums.
c. Assume, instead, that Newman uses the straight-line method for amortizing discounts and premiums. Give the journal entries to record the first two interest payments.

Transaction	Account	Debit	Credit

R8-Comprehensive

Chapter 8: Comprehensive Financial Statement Preparation Problem

Ultra Corporation began operations on January 1, 2005, when it issued bonds with a face value of $100,000, a term of 10 years, and a stated interest rate of 9%. At the time of issue, the market rate of interest was 10%. Interest will be paid annually on December 31. Jeff Ultra, the founder of the corporation, also contributed $100,000 to start the company and received ownership in the form of common stock. After receiving the proceeds from these transactions, Ultra Corporation completed the following transactions during 2005 and 2006.

In 2005, Ultra Corporation:

1. Purchased land and building for $60,000. An independent appraisal valued the land at 10% of the total purchase price. The building will be depreciated using straight-line depreciation, and Ultra estimates it will be useful for 20 years and have a residual value of $1,600 at the end of that time. Ultra will take a full year's depreciation in 2005.

2. Purchased office and store equipment for $20,000, with a useful life of 10 years and an estimated residual value of $2,000. Ultra will take a full year's depreciation in 2005.
3. Purchased inventory of $70,000 for cash and sold all of it for $140,000 on account. Ultra Corporation estimates that 3% of the ending balance in accounts receivable will be uncollectible.
4. Paid cash expenses of $20,000.
5. Paid interest on the bonds (on December 31).

In 2006, Ultra Corporation:

1. Purchased inventory of $100,000 for cash and sold 90% of it for $180,000, all on account.
2. Collected $200,000 from customers on accounts receivable.
3. Paid cash expenses of $25,000.
4. Paid interest on bonds (on December 31).
5. Wrote off L. James's account in the amount of $3,000 after finding out that this customer had filed for bankruptcy.

Prepare the four basic financial statements for Ultra Corporation for both years (ended December 31, 2005, and December 31, 2006). Don't forget to make the appropriate adjustments each year for depreciation and the allowance for uncollectible accounts

Issues for Discussion

L.O. 8-4, 5

Financial statement analysis

1. Use the Pier 1 Imports, Inc. financial statements to answer the following questions:

   a. What types of debt does Pier 1 Company have? Where did you find this information?
   b. Compute the times-to-interest earned ratio and the debt-to-equity ratio for the last 2 years. What information do these ratios provide?

Business risk

2. Consider the following:

   a. By using the level of long-term debt and the ratios calculated in 1, how would you describe the level of risk for the creditors of Pier 1?
   b. Are there any indications that the level of the Pier 1's long-term debt presents a serious risk to the company?

Ethics

3. Lucy Shafer wants to borrow $100,000 to expand her dog-breeding business. She is preparing a set of financial statements to take to the local bank with her loan application. She currently has an outstanding loan from her uncle for $50,000. Lucy's uncle is allowing her to borrow the money at a very low interest rate, and she does not have to make any principal payments for 5 years. Due to the favorable terms of the loan from her uncle, Lucy has decided that it is not significant enough to disclose on her financial statements. Instead, Lucy has classified the $50,000 as contributed capital (ownership), and the interest payments are included in miscellaneous expenses on Lucy's income statement.

   a. What are the effects of Lucy's classifications on the financial statements?
   b. Are there any ratios that might be of concern to the local bank that will be misstated by Lucy's actions?
   c. Do you think Lucy's actions are unethical? Suppose Lucy's uncle agrees to be a partner in the company until Lucy can afford to buy his share by repaying the $50,000 with interest. Does that change your opinion?

Internet Exercise: General Motors and Starbucks

General Motors Corp. remains the world's number one maker of cars and trucks, including brands such as Buick, Cadillac, Chevrolet, GMC, Pontiac, Saab, and Saturn.

Please go to the www.prenhall.com/myphlip *Web site, register, and add this textbook to your myphilp page (if you haven't done so already). Go to Chapter 8 and use the Internet Exercise company link.*

IE8-1   Under "Quotes and Research" enter the company symbol GM, the stock symbol of General Motors Corp., and then choose *Financials*. Find the *Annual Balance Sheet*.

  a. Identify amounts reported for total long-term debt at the three most recent year-ends. For the most recent year-end how much of the debt does GM have to pay back? Do these amounts reflect the future value of the debt? Explain why or why not.
  b. Identify amounts reported for interest expense for the three most recent years. Did interest expense increase or decrease? What might cause this change? Is this the amount of interest paid during the year? Which financial statement reports this information?
  c. Identify amounts reported for total liabilities and total equity at the three most recent year-ends. Calculate the debt-to-equity ratio (total liabilities to total equity) for each year-end. Is General Motors primarily financing assets with liabilities or equities? How can you tell? Is the ratio increasing or decreasing? Is this trend favorable or unfavorable? Explain why.

IE8-2   Starbucks Corp. is the number one specialty coffee retailer, operating more than 4,600 shops. The company also sells coffee beans to restaurants, businesses, airlines, and hotels, and offers mail order and online shopping.

  a. Under "Quotes & Research" enter the company symbol SBUX, the stock symbol of the Starbucks Corp., and then choose *Financials*. Find the *Annual Balance Sheet*. Identify amounts reported for total liabilities and total equity at the three most recent year-ends.
  b. Calculate the debt-to-equity ratio (total liabilities to total equity) for each year-end.
  c. Do owners or creditors have more claims on the Starbucks' assets? How can you tell?

IE8-3   Review the information recorded earlier. Which corporation has a higher level of financial risk? Explain why.

Please note: Internet Web sites are constantly being updated. Therefore, if the information is not found where indicated, please explore the Web site further to find the information.

SPECIAL ACQUISITIONS: FINANCING A BUSINESS WITH EQUITY

Financing

Here's where you've been...

In Chapter 8, you learned how a company obtains financing from creditors. Two common ways are long-term notes and bonds. You learned how the debt is repaid and how interest on debt is calculated and paid to the creditors.

Here's where you're going...

Financing

When you are finished with Chapter 9, you should understand how a company obtains financing from owners. You'll learn how the money that a corporation receives from its owners—stockholders—and how the money the corporation earns are shown on the financial statements. You will also learn about how the corporation pays a return to its owners with dividends.

9

Financing

Financial Reporting and Business Events

Sales and Accounts Receivable

Property, Plant, and Equipment

Inventory and Liabilities

Learning Objectives

More specifically, when you are finished studying this chapter, you should be able to answer these questions:

1. How does a corporation account for owners' contributions to a company? What are the major types of paid-in capital?
2. What are dividends—for common and preferred shareholders? How are they computed, recorded, and reported?
3. What is treasury stock, and how is it recorded and reported?
4. What are stock dividends and stock splits?
5. What is retained earnings? How is it valued, recorded, and reported?
6. How is information about a company's equity used in financial statement analysis?
7. What risks are associated with equity financing?

Owners of a Business

L.O. 1

Understand how a company finances its business with equity.

BUSINESS PROCESS

Every business firm has owners. As you know from Chapter 1, there are three common forms of business organization:

- sole proprietorships
- partnerships
- corporations

No matter which form a firm takes, the firm always needs contributions from owners. We refer to them as contributions because we are looking at them from the point of view of the firm. As you know from earlier chapters, owners' contributions are called contributed capital and shown on the firm's balance sheet.

For sole proprietorships and partnerships, acquiring money is a personal matter. The individual owners may use their own money or they may borrow money from family, friends, or banks.

For a corporation, there are more options. There are more opportunities to acquire funds—that's one of the advantages of the corporate form of business organization.

You learned about financing a company with debt in Chapter 8. In this chapter, you will learn about acquiring funds from owners of the corporation.

Components of Shareholders' Equity in a Corporation: Contributed Capital

The owners' claims to the assets of the firm are called shareholders' equity or stockholders' equity. Recall, there are two parts to stockholders' equity in a corporation—contributed capital and retained earnings. Each part is recorded and reported on the balance sheet as a separate amount. We'll spend most of the chapter discussing contributed capital.

Contributed capital is the amount owners have invested in the corporation. From an individual owner's point of view, a share of ownership in a corporation is an investment. From the firm's point of view, the amount paid for a share of ownership is a contribution to the firm. Another name for these contributions is **paid-in capital** because these contributions are literally paid into the firm by the owners. Paid-in capital is subdivided into two parts: **capital stock** and **additional paid-in capital**. These two classifications are determined by the legal requirements of the state in which the corporation is formed and reflect the legal requirements of the amount of capital that must be retained in the business. You'll learn more about this later in the chapter.

The form of capital contributions is usually cash, but contributions of other assets are possible. For example, an owner may contribute an asset in the form of land or a machine in return for ownership in the corporation. Whether the capital contribution is cash or another asset, the owner who makes the contribution receives shares of stock equal to the value of the contribution. As you learned at the beginning of this textbook, a share of stock represents ownership in a corporation.

> **Contributed capital** and **paid-in capital** are both names for the same thing—owners' contributions to the firm. Owners' contributions are divided into **capital stock** and **additional paid-in capital**.

Stock: Authorized, Issued, and Outstanding

In return for their contributions, the owners receive shares of stock, representing ownership equal to the value of those contributions. When a corporation is initially organized—with legal articles of incorporation issued by the state where the business is located—a certain number of shares of stock are *authorized* in the corporate charter. This number of shares is the maximum number of shares of stock a corporation is allowed to issue. The number of shares actually *issued* will be less than the total number of shares authorized. It's common that shares of stock are offered—made available for sale to potential owners—in batches, during times when a company needs capital.

After a share of stock has been issued, it can never be *un*issued. However, an issued share of stock does not have to remain outstanding. Outstanding shares are ones that are currently owned by investors. Often, the managers of the company will buy back—not as individuals but for the company itself—the company's own stock from other investors who own shares through prior purchase in the stock market. There are several reasons why a firm would buy its own stock. For example, a firm would purchase its own shares to bolster the market price or to have shares available for bonuses to employees.

When a company buys back its own stock, that stock is called **treasury stock**. That's because it is kept in the company's "treasury," the place where stock certificates for shares of repurchased stock are kept. Any stock that has been issued by a company may be either outstanding, which is owned by investors, or treasury stock, which is held in the company's treasury (Exhibit 9-1).

Common Stock. As the name suggests, **common stock** is the most common type of stock representing ownership of a corporation. All corporations have common stock. The owners of common stock have specific rights:

1. To vote for members of the board of directors.
2. To share in the corporation's profits.
3. To share in any assets left if the corporation has to dissolve (e.g., if the company has to go out of business due to bankruptcy).
4. To acquire more shares when the corporation issues new stock.

BUSINESS PROCESS

> **Treasury stock** is a company's own stock that the company has purchased via the stock market.

BUSINESS PROCESS

> **Common stock** represents the most common form of ownership in a corporation. Common stockholders have a vote in running the company.

Exhibit 9-1
Authorized, Issued, and
Outstanding Stock

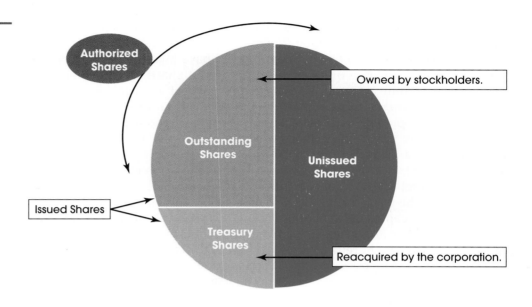

Common stock is what most people mean when they refer to a corporation's stock or shares of stock.

Preferred stock represents a special type of ownership in a corporation. Preferred stockholders don't get to vote in running the company, but they do get their dividends first.

Preferred Stock. Corporations may also have **preferred stock**. It is called *preferred* because the owners of this type of stock have a preference over common shareholders when the corporation pays dividends. The preferred shareholders must receive their dividends before any of the common shareholders are paid. They also have a preferred claim on assets. That means if a firm goes out of business, the preferred shareholders will receive leftover company assets—left after the creditors have been paid—before the common shareholders. However, the owners of preferred stock do not have many of the rights common shareholders have. Preferred shareholders usually do not have voting rights or the right to maintain their proportionate share of stock.

Par value of stock is a monetary value assigned to, and printed on, each share of stock. For common stock, par value has little relevance to the company or the shareholders. For preferred stock, par value is commonly the basis for calculating the dividend payment.

Par Value of Common and Preferred Stock. Printed on the stock certificates of most stock is a fixed per-share amount called the **par value** of the stock. The par value of common stock does not have any relationship to the market value of the stock. It has a single function: The par value defines the maximum responsibility of a stockholder if a company goes out of business. Generally, the corporation must maintain a specific amount of capital in the business, determined by the state and contained in the legal documents of the corporation, and that amount is often the total par value of the outstanding stock.

When stock is issued—that is, ownership in the corporation is sold—it is usually sold for more than the par value of the stock. Suppose the par value of a company's stock is $2, and the market price of the stock on the date the stock is originally issued is $10. If the company issues 100 shares of stock, the par value multiplied by the number of shares issued—$2 par × 100 shares = $200—will be shown on the balance sheet in an account separate from any contributions in excess of the par value ($8 excess over par × 100 shares = $800). The total par value amount—$200—is called capital stock, or common stock, and the excess contributions amount—$800—is called *paid-in capital in excess of par* or *additional paid-in capital*. Both amounts are reported on the balance sheet. The terminology may sound a bit technical, but after you see some examples, you'll get the idea behind the terminology. Remember that paid-in capital designates both capital stock and additional paid-in capital. All amounts of contributed capital are called paid-in capital.

Suppose the corporate charter of Mrs. Callahan's Cookies authorizes 100,000 shares of common stock at par value $1. The company's first stock issue is 30,000 shares at $6 per share. The transaction of issuing the stock affects the accounting equation, as shown next:

Assets	=	Liabilities	+	Contributed capital	+	Retained earnings
$180,000				$ 30,000 Common stock		
Cash				150,000 Paid-in capital in excess of par		

The journal entry to record Mrs. Callahan's Cookies first stock issue of 30,000 shares of $1 par stock at $6 per share is:

Date	Transaction	Debit	Credit
	Cash	$180,000	
	Common stock		$ 30,000
	Paid-in-capital in excess of par		150,000

The amount the stock sells for above the par value is shown on the balance sheet as a separate amount—paid-in capital in excess of par. Only the par value times the number of shares issued will be recorded as common stock.

How would this be shown on Mrs. Callahan's Cookies financial statements? The owner's equity section of the balance sheet would show this information in the section representing contributed capital.

Contributed capital	
Common stock (par value $1; 100,000 shares authorized; 30,000 shares issued and outstanding)	$ 30,000
Paid-in capital in excess of par	150,000

The par value of preferred stock has an additional function—it is the basis for calculating the dividends that preferred shareholders receive. You'll learn about that in the next section of this chapter.

Exhibit 9-2 shows the shareholders' equity section of the Pepsi Bottling Group balance sheet at December 25, 1999. For now, focus on the information given for the common stock category. The par value is given, as well as the number of shares authorized and issued. Even though the number of shares outstanding is not explicitly stated, it can be computed by subtracting the num-

December 25, 1999
(In millions, except per share data)

Shareholders' equity	
Common stock, par value $0.01 per share	
Authorized 300 shares, issued 155 shares	$ 2
Treasury stock: 5 shares	(90)
Additional paid-in capital	1,736
Retained earnings	138
Accumulated other comprehensive loss	(223)
Total shareholders' equity (deficit)	1,563
Total liabilities and shareholders' equity	$7,619

Exhibit 9-2
Shareholders' Equity from the Pepsi Bottling Group, Inc.

ber of treasury shares from the number of shares issued—thus, 150 million shares are outstanding. Another item you should recognize on the statement is additional paid-in capital. That's the amount over the par value that the initial shareholders paid for their shares of stock when it was first issued. Retained earnings is also an item you should recognize. You'll read more about retained earnings later in the chapter.

STUDY BREAK 9-1 SEE HOW YOU'RE DOING

Use the following information from the equity section of these comparative balance sheets to answer the questions that follow.

Shareholders' equity	At December 31, 2005	At December 31, 2004
Common stock ($10 par)	$210,000	$200,000
Additional paid-in capital	163,000	153,000
Retained earnings	55,000	51,000
Total shareholders' equity	*$428,000*	*$404,000*

1. **How many shares of common stock were issued during the period from January 1, 2005 through December 31, 2005?**
2. **What was the average issue price of the stock?**

L.O. 2

Define cash dividends and know who decides whether dividends will be paid. Understand the allocation of dividends between common and preferred shareholders.

Dividends are distributions of a corporation's earnings to the shareholders—usually in the form of cash.

Cash Dividends. People buy stock in a corporation—that is, they buy partial ownership in the corporation—because they hope the value of the corporation—and therefore, their part of the ownership—will increase in value. Selling stock for more than its cost is one way the shareholder can make money on the investment.

Shareholders also receive distributions from the earnings of the corporation called **dividends**. Dividends are distributions of a corporation's assets—usually cash—to its stockholders. The board of directors decides the amount of dividends to be paid and when they will be paid to the shareholders. The directors are also free *not* to pay dividends at any time they believe it is in the best interests of the corporation. For example, the board of directors may want to reinvest the available cash in the business by buying more equipment or inventory.

When the board of directors decides that a cash dividend will be paid, there are three important dates relating to that dividend: the declaration date, the date of record, and the payment date.

Declaration Date. The dividend declaration date is the date on which the board of directors decides a dividend will be paid. On this date, a legal liability is created. This particular liability is called *dividends payable*. The amount of this liability is balanced in the accounting equation by a reduction in retained earnings.

Remember, dividends are not included as an expense on the income statement because they are not related to generating revenue. Instead of a *deduction* from a company's earnings, dividends are considered a *distribution* of a company's earnings to owners in proportion to their share of ownership. Dividends are not deducted from contributed capital because they are a distribution of earnings, not a distribution of an owner's original paid-in capital.

Assets	=	Liabilities	+	Contributed capital	+	Retained earnings
		+Dividends payable				−Dividends

Date of Record. The date of record is used to determine exactly who will receive the dividends. Anyone owning the stock on this date is entitled to the dividend. After a corporation originally sells stock to its investors, who become owners of the company, these owners are free to trade—sell and buy—shares of stock with other people. Whoever owns the stock on the *date of record* will receive the dividend. A stockholder may own the stock for only one day and receive the full dividend amount. After this date, stock is said to be ex-dividend. That is, if it is traded after the date of record, the new owner will not get the dividend.

Payment Date. The third date of importance for a dividend is the payment date. This is when the cash is actually paid to the shareholders. This payment has the same effect on the accounting equation as the payment of any liability: assets (cash) are reduced and liabilities (dividends payable) are reduced.

Preferred Stock Dividends. Preferred stock has preference over common stock for dividends. The holders of preferred stock must receive, from the corporation, a certain amount of dividends before common stockholders can receive any dividends. Dividends on preferred stock are usually fixed at

Understanding Business

WHY DO COMPANIES HAVE PREFERRED STOCK?

One way a firm can obtain needed funds is to issue preferred stock. Just like issuing common stock, issuing preferred stock is a source of financing. Preferred stock is a special class of stock that has certain features that common stock does not have. These features can include shareholders' rights: to receive dividends before the common shareholders receive any dividends, to receive a share of the assets in the event of bankruptcy before common shareholders get any, and to exchange their preferred stock for common stock under certain conditions. Preferred stock may be bought back by the issuing corporation directly from the shareholders (this means it is "callable" preferred stock), and preferred shareholders to not get a vote in running the company. Because of the features of the stock, preferred shareholders may seem more like creditors than owners.

Because the holders of preferred stock are more like creditors, preferred stock may be used as a weapon in a hostile takeover attempt—that's when someone tries to buy enough of the target company's stock to get the majority of shares so that the person (or a company), the new buyer, will be able to take over and run the target company. This could happen when a corporation is

formed initially, and the corporate charter authorizes a certain number of shares of stock to be issued over the company's life. At the same time, the corporate charter may also give the board of directors (BOD) complete discretion about when and how to offer preferred stock. If necessary, the BOD can issue a very large number of shares of preferred stock to make a takeover more difficult. The newly issued preferred stock will be issued to the current shareholders at a reduced rate, and the shareholders will convert it to common stock. This way to defend against a hostile takeover has been called a *poison pill.*

Of the total amount of all stock issued, the BOD will set a maximum amount that a single outside party may acquire. If an outsider acquires a number of shares of the firm's stock exceeding that amount, the BOD will activate the poison pill. Poison pills became a great defense in the 1980s when they were devised to prevent hostile takeovers that were prevalent at that time. The poison pill is a trigger point that, once activated, means the BOD uses the blank check proviso to issue preferred stock at a reduced rate to current stockholders. This, in turn, increases the price of taking over to an outside party and in most cases kills the takeover efforts by the outside party.

a percentage of the par value of the stock. For example, preferred stock characterized as *$100 par, 10%* will pay a dividend of $10 in any year the corporation's board of directors declares a dividend. The preferred shareholders must get their $10 per preferred share before the common shareholders receive any dividends. The board of directors has discretion about whether to pay dividends to the preferred shareholders, but the board doesn't decide on the amount of the dividend for the preferred shareholders. The dividend for preferred shareholders is typically shown on the face of the preferred stock certificate.

There are two types of preferred stock—cumulative and noncumulative—identified by a characteristic of their dividends.

Cumulative preferred stockholders must receive any past, unpaid dividends before a company can pay any current dividends.

Noncumulative preferred stockholders do *not* receive past, unpaid dividends. Past dividends do not accumulate.

Dividends owed to holders of cumulative preferred stock but not yet declared are called **dividends in arrears.**

- **Cumulative preferred stock** means the fixed dividend amount accumulates from year to year, and the entire amount of all past unpaid dividends must be paid to the preferred shareholders before any dividends can be paid to the common shareholders.
- If the stock is **noncumulative preferred stock,** it is up to the board to determine whether it will make up any missed dividends to the preferred shareholders.

Any dividends on cumulative preferred stock from past years but undeclared and unpaid are called **dividends in arrears.** Such dividends are not considered liabilities. Only after a dividend is actually declared is it considered a liability.

Example of Dividend Payment. Suppose JG Company has outstanding 1,000 shares of $100 par at 9% cumulative preferred stock and 50,000 shares of $0.50 par common stock. The company last paid dividends in December 2001.

With the 2001 payment, JG paid all dividends through December 31, 2001. There were no dividends in arrears. No dividends were declared in 2002.

On October 1, 2003, the board of directors declares a total of $30,000 in dividends for its shareholders to be paid on December 15 to all shareholders of record on November 1.

How much will go to the preferred shareholders and how much to the common shareholders?

First, calculate the annual dividend for the preferred shareholders—1,000 shares × $100 par value × 0.09 dividend rate = $9,000. Because the preferred stock is cumulative and no dividends were paid to the preferred shareholders in 2002, JG must first pay the 2002 dividend of $9,000 to the preferred shareholders. Then JG has to pay the current year dividend of $9,000 to the preferred shareholders. Thus, a total of $18,000 must be paid to the preferred shareholders, and the remaining $12,000 will be paid to the common shareholders.

On the date of declaration, October 1, the legal liability for the dividend payment is incurred. The company must record the transaction, which has the following effect on the accounting equation:

Assets	=	Liabilities	+	Shareholders' equity	
				CC	**RE**
		+$18,000 Dividends payable to preferred shareholders +12,000 Dividends payable to common shareholders			$(30,000) Retained earnings

The journal entry to record the declaration of dividends to stockholders is:

Date	Transaction	Debit	Credit
	Retained earnings	$30,000	
	Dividends payable to preferred shareholders		$18,000
	Dividends payable to common shareholders		12,000

On the declaration date, the company records the liability. If JG were to prepare financial statements between October 1 and the payment of the dividends on December 15, the balance sheet would show a current liability called *dividends payable*. This liability is a debt owed to the shareholders for dividends. A corporation may list the liability to common shareholders separately from the liability to preferred shareholders, as shown in the preceding example; or the corporation may combine the preferred and common dividends into one amount for total dividends payable.

The date of record, November 1, has no significance in the accounting records. It is simply the date that indicates who will get the dividend. The shareholders as of November 1 will receive this dividend.

On December 15, when JG actually pays the cash to the shareholders to fulfill the obligation, cash is reduced and the liability—dividends payable—is removed from the records. How that looks is shown in the following accounting equation:

Assets	=	Liabilities	+	Shareholders' equity	
				Contributed capital	Retained earnings
$(30,000) Cash		$(18,000) Dividends payable to preferred shareholders (12,000) Dividends payable to common shareholders			

The journal entry to record the payment of the dividends is:

Date	Transaction	Debit	Credit
	Dividends payable to preferred shareholders	$18,000	
	Dividends payable to common shareholders	12,000	
	Cash		$30,000

Suppose the preferred stock was noncumulative. Then JG would only have to pay the current year dividend of $9,000 to the preferred shareholders, and the remaining $21,000 would go to the common shareholders.

A corporation has 10,000 shares of 8% cumulative preferred stock and 20,000 shares of common stock outstanding. Par value for each share of either stock is $100. No dividends were paid last year, but this year $200,000 of dividends will be paid to stockholders. Prepare the journal entry required on the date of the dividend declaration.

STUDY BREAK 9-2
SEE HOW YOU'RE DOING

Treasury Stock

Define treasury stock and explain why a company would purchase treasury stock.

Treasury stock is a company's own stock that the company has purchased via the stock market. It is shown on the balance sheet as a **contra-equity** account—a reduction in total shareholders' equity.

Company Buys Its Own Stock

Companies are allowed to trade—buy and sell—their own stock on the open market like anyone else. **Treasury stock** is the term given to common stock that has been issued and later reacquired by the company that issued it. Once it is purchased by the company, until it is resold, it is considered treasury stock. Companies purchase shares of their own stock for several reasons:

1. To have stock to distribute to employees through stock option plans
2. To increase the company's earnings per share
3. To reduce chances of a hostile takeover

Some important facts about treasury stock include:

Why Do Companies Buy Their Own Stock?
October 3, 2001
From the *Wall Street Journal: Inside Track*
"Slump in Energy Stocks Has Triggered Buying"
By Cassell Bryan-Low
Betting that oil and natural gas prices should go up eventually, some energy company insiders have been buying their own shares.

Energy stock prices tumbled following the terrorist attacks on fears that an accelerated economic slowdown would reduce demand for oil and gas.

- The purchase of treasury stock reduces a company's assets (cash) and stockholders' equity.
- Treasury stock holdings for the company are shown as a reduction in the total of shareholders' equity on the balance sheet. Therefore, treasury stock is a type of shareholders' equity; but the value of treasury stock reduces owner's equity. Due to its presence in the shareholders' equity section of the balance sheet and its negative effect on total equity, it is called a **contra-equity** account. It is subtracted from total shareholders' equity.
- No gains or losses are ever recorded in the company's financial records when a company purchases treasury stock or later resells it.

Accounting for treasury stock can take several forms, but the most common is to account for it at cost. That means when the stock is repurchased, the company records the treasury stock—a contra-shareholders' equity account—at the amount the company paid for it. The par value doesn't matter, and how much the stock was previously issued for doesn't matter. Treasury stock is simply recorded at cost. Suppose a company repurchased 100 shares of its own stock at $30 per share. Cash would decrease by $3,000, and treasury stock—a contra-equity account that decreases equity—is increased by $3,000. When the financial statements are prepared, treasury stock is listed at the end of the owner's equity section of the balance sheet and is subtracted from total equity. The purchase of the treasury stock affects the accounting equation as follows:

Assets	=	Liabilities	+	Shareholders' equity	
				Contributed capital	Retained earnings
$(3,000) Cash				$(3,000) Treasury stock	

Exhibit 9-3
Treasury Stock on The Limited
Balance Sheet

From The Limited Balance Sheets (Amounts in Thousands)		
Shareholders' equity	January 29, 2000	January 30, 1999
Common stock	$ 189,727	$ 180,352
Paid-in capital	178,374	157,214
Retained earnings	6,109,371	5,470,689
	6,477,472	5,808,255
Less: treasury stock, at average cost	(4,330,395)	(3,641,296)
Total shareholders' equity	$ 2,147,077	$ 2,166,959

The journal entry to record the purchase of 100 shares of $1 par value treasury stock when it has a market value of $30 per share is:

Date	Transaction	Debit	Credit
	Treasury stock	$3,000	
	Cash		$3,000

Exhibit 9-3 shows how treasury stock is reported on the balance sheet. It is deducted from total shareholders' equity.

Suppose a company originally issued 100,000 shares of $1 par common stock for $15 per share. Several years later, the company decides to buy back 1,000 shares of common stock. The stock is selling for $50 per share at the time of the stock repurchase. What effect would this have on the accounting equation?

Assets	=	Liabilities	+	Contributed capital	+	Retained earnings
$(50,000) Cash				$(50,000) Treasury stock (contra-equity)		

The journal entry to record the purchase of 1,000 shares of $1 par value treasury stock when it has a market value of $50 per share is:

Date	Transaction	Debit	Credit
	Treasury stock	$50,000	
	Cash		$50,000

The reduction in shareholders' equity is accomplished by increasing an amount that is subtracted from equity—treasury stock. Treasury stock is not an asset. It is recorded at cost—what the company paid to repurchase the stock.

Selling Treasury Stock

If treasury stock is resold at a later date, the shares sold will be removed from treasury stock at the price paid for the stock when it was repurchased. If the treasury stock is sold at a price higher than its cost, the excess will be classified as paid-in capital from treasury stock transactions.

Suppose the company sold half of the shares (500 of the 1,000 treasury shares) for $60 each. Removing 500 shares of treasury stock (at $50 cost) will increase total shareholders' equity (by reducing a contra-equity account.) Selling 500 shares of stock (that cost $50 per share) for $60 per share would affect the accounting equation as follows:

Assets	=	Liabilities	+	Contributed capital	+	Retained earnings
+$30,000 Cash				+$25,000 Treasury stock (contra-equity) +5,000 Paid-in capital, treasury stock transactions		

The journal entry to record the resale of 500 shares of the treasury stock for $60 per share is:

Date	Transaction	Debit	Credit
	Cash	$30,000	
	Treasury stock		$25,000
	Paid-in-capital, treasury stock transactions		5,000

There would be 500 shares remaining in the treasury, each at a cost of $50.

Suppose we sold those shares for $48 per share. As in the previous example, the cost of the treasury stock must be removed from the total amount of treasury stock. In this example, instead of having additional paid-in capital, we must reduce a paid-in-capital account to balance the accounting equation. The difference between the cost and the reissue price—$2 per share × 500 shares = $1,000—will be deducted from paid-in capital, treasury stock transactions. This is how selling 500 treasury shares—that originally cost the company $50 per share—for a reissue cost of $48 per share would affect the accounting equation:

Assets	=	Liabilities	+	Contributed capital	+	Retained earnings
+24,000 Cash				+25,000 Treasury stock (contra-equity) (1,000) Paid-in capital, treasury stock transactions		

The journal entry to record the resale of 500 shares of the treasury stock for $48 per share is:

Date	Transaction	Debit	Credit
	Cash	$24,000	
	Paid-in-capital, treasury stock transactions	1,000	
	Treasury stock		$25,000

If the amount of the paid-in capital from treasury stock transactions were insufficient to cover the deficit, then retained earnings would be reduced by the amount needed to balance the accounting equation.

Always remember, there are never any gains or losses from treasury stock transactions. Exchanges between a company and its owners—issue of stock, payment of dividends, purchase or sale of treasury stock—do not affect the income statement. Recall, the separate entity assumption requires a company and its owners *not* to mix their financial records. A company and its owners are separate entities, *not* the same entity—so there may be transactions between the owners and the company. However, these transactions are never shown on the income statement.

Surety Corp. started the year 2002 with 125,000 shares of common stock with par value of $1 issued and outstanding. The issue price of these shares averaged $6 per share. During 2002, Surety purchased 1,000 shares of its own stock at an average price of $7 per share. Prepare the journal entry to record the purchase of the treasury stock.

Stock Dividends

A corporation may want to pay a dividend to its shareholders but not have suf-ficient cash on hand to do so. Instead of a cash dividend, the corporation may issue a **stock dividend**. When this happens, the corporation seems to be giving a shareholder something of value, but is it really? Stock dividends are not a dis-tribution of assets such as cash. Instead of giving the shareholders cash, the cor-poration gives the shareholders additional shares of stock in the company. The accounting equation is affected only by the way in which the amounts in the dif-ferent equity accounts are distributed. The corporation that pays a stock divi-dend converts retained earnings to contributed capital, thereby giving the stockholders a more direct claim to that portion of equity. Suppose a company issued $150,000 worth of new common stock (market value) by distributing it to its current shareholders as a stock dividend. That transaction would affect the accounting equation as shown next:

L.O. 4

Be able to define stock dividends and stock splits.

A **stock dividend** is a company's distribution of new shares of stock to the company's current stockholders.

Assets =	Liabilities +	Contributed capital +	Retained earnings
		+$150,000 Common stock and additional paid-in capital	$(150,000) Retained earnings

The journal entry to record the stock dividend of $150,000 would be:

Date	Transaction	Debit	Credit
	Retained earnings	$150,000	
	Common stock (par value)		$ 10,000
	Additional paid-in-capital (excess of market value over par)		140,000

When considering stock dividends, remember

1. There are no income tax effects for the corporation.
2. *Stock dividends do not increase any shareholder's percentage of ownership in the company.* If you owned 5% of the company before the stock dividend, you own 5% of the company after the stock dividend. After the dividend, your 5% includes more shares—but every shareholder's share increases proportionally.
3. As with cash dividends, three dates are important

   ■ date of declaration
   ■ date of record (specifically, who is going to receive the shares of stock)
   ■ date of distribution

Stock Splits

A **stock split** is the division of the current shares of stock by some multiple, to increase the number of shares. For example, a 2-for-1 stock split means every share becomes two shares, with the par value divided in half for each new share.

BUSINESS PROCESS

Stock splits occur when a corporation increases the number of shares authorized, issued, and outstanding and proportionately decreases the par value. It's different than a stock dividend. There are no *new* shares issued, but instead the outstanding shares are "split" into two or more shares with a corresponding division of the par value. Suppose you own 100 shares of Micromoney, Inc. It has a par value of $10 per share and a market value of $80 per share. Micromoney's board of directors votes to split the stock 2 for 1. After the split, instead of having 100 shares with a par value of $10 per share, you have 200 shares with a par value of $5 per share. Of course, the stock market doesn't get fooled by the split. It seems logical that your 200 shares would now have a market value of $40 per share, so your total Micromoney stock after the split would continue to be worth $8,000.

Why does a corporation split its stock? Financial analysts have different opinions.

One reason a corporation splits its stock is to lower the price of a share of stock. If a single share of stock has a high price—over $100, for example—it may be a barrier to the stock's trading. An investor may believe the price is too much to pay for one share, that too much money is at risk for a single share.

Another reason is that a stock split may be a signal to the stock market concerning some future "good news." The rationale for stock splits comes from many observations that when a stock is split, a split share trades for proportionately more than the share was trading for before the stock was split. For example, let's say your stock that is trading for $80 per share is split 2 for 1. After the split, the stock is likely to trade at some price *higher* than $40—even though it is theoretically only worth half of the presplit price. No formal recording is necessary for stock splits. Instead, the details of the stock split are shown parenthetically in the owners' equity part of the financial statements.

STUDY BREAK 9-4
SEE HOW YOU'RE DOING

1. Compare a stock split and a stock dividend.
2. Suppose you own 1,500 shares of $2 par common stock, which is 3% of the ABC Company outstanding stock. If ABC declares a 2-for-1 stock split, how many shares will you own? What percentage ownership will your shares now represent?

Components of Shareholders' Equity in a Corporation: Retained Earnings

Shareholders' equity includes contributed capital (which itself is made up of common stock and additional paid-in capital) and **retained earnings.** Retained earnings is the amount of all the earnings of the firm—since its beginning—that have not been distributed to the stockholders. Retained earnings may also be called **earned capital.**

Retained earnings equals:

1. Profits since the day the company began, minus
2. Losses since the day the company began, minus
3. Dividends paid to stockholders since the company began, minus
4. Stock dividends distributed to shareholders since the company began.

A complete set of financial statements includes a statement of changes in shareholders' equity. Because retained earnings is a part of shareholders' equity, the change in retained earnings during the period is contained in the statement of changes in shareholders' equity. Sometimes the part of the statement that provides the details of the changes in retained earnings is shown separately and called a statement of retained earnings.

L.O. 5

Understand the meaning of **retained earnings** and how it is recorded and reported.

Retained earnings, also known as **earned capital,** is the total amount of net income minus all dividends paid since the company began.

Suppose B&B Company started the year with retained earnings of $84,500. During the year, B&B had net income of $25,600 and paid dividends of $12,200. What was the ending balance in retained earnings?

STUDY BREAK 9-5
SEE HOW YOU'RE DOING

Analysis of Shareholders' Equity

The shareholders' equity of a firm, expressed in several different ratios, can provide information useful for the financial statement analysis of that firm. We will discuss three ratios using shareholders' equity:

1. Return on equity
2. Earnings per share
3. Book value per share

Return on equity (ROE) is a measure of how well a company produces income with the amount of investment the common shareholders have made in the company. It is calculated exactly as it sounds: return (net income) divided by average shareholders' equity. To calculate this ratio, we need the amount of common shareholders' equity at the beginning and at the end of the period. We'll get those amounts from two comparative balance sheets and use the average of those amounts in the denominator. Common shareholders' equity will be all the equity *except* the preferred shareholders' equity. The ratio uses common shareholders' equity because common shareholders are considered the *true* owners of the firm. Then we use the net income, reduced by the amount of preferred dividends paid, for the numerator. The reason for deducting preferred

Return on equity is net income divided by average shareholders' equity.

BUSINESS PROCESS

dividends from net income is that we are calculating the return to the *common* shareholder. The ratio takes the claims of preferred shareholders' out of both the numerator and denominator. You may recall from our discussion earlier in the chapter that common shareholders are entitled to the earnings of the firm only after preferred dividends are paid. Return on equity provides information about how well the company is using the owners' contributions and earnings retained in the business.

Exhibit 9-4 shows the information needed to calculate the ROE for Safeway, Inc., for two consecutive years. The ratio should be compared with other similar companies or with industry standards for a meaningful analysis. We'll discuss in Chapter 11 how to make the most of the information provided by financial statement ratios. For now, notice that Safeway's ROE has decreased which is unfavorable, and that changes in either net income or total equity will affect the ratio. Potential investors are interested in this information.

Earnings per share (EPS) is the most well-known and most used ratio derived from the information on the basic financial statements. The earnings in the numerator of this ratio begins with net income. Because EPS is designated as the earnings for the common shareholders, preferred dividends must be deducted from net income, just as in the calculation of the numerator of return on (common) shareholders' equity. The denominator is the average number of common shares outstanding during the year. To calculate this average, you need to know if and when any new shares were issued during the year and if and when any shares were purchased for the treasury. Then you calculate a weighted average for the denominator of the EPS ratio.

Fortunately, all financial statements provide EPS. Often, two different EPS ratios are shown. One is called basic EPS and is calculated as just described: net income for the common shareholders divided by the weighted average number of common shares outstanding. The other is called diluted EPS and is calculated as if all outstanding securities that could be converted into common stock and would reduce the basic ratio actually *were* converted. This would make the denominator—the weighted average number of shares outstanding—larger. Calculations for diluted EPS can be complicated and are done often by a company's accountant when the annual financial statements are prepared.

EPS is the most common indicator of a company's overall performance. Earnings are forecast by financial analysts, anticipated by investors, managed by business executives, and announced with great anticipation by major corporations. The Limited's income statements, in Exhibit 9-5, show that this company uses the name *income per share* instead of the more common name, *earnings per share*, for this ratio.

Book value per (common) share is another ratio whose name says what it means. We've referred to the accounting records as "books," even though these records may not actually be kept in a book in modern businesses. The ratio, book

---

Earnings per share (EPS) is the most well-known accounting number because financial analysts use it to evaluate a company's performance. It's a company's net income on a per share basis.

Book value per (common) share is total shareholders' equity (minus any equity represented by preferred stock) divided by the average number of outstanding shares.

Exhibit 9–4
Return on Equity for Safeway, Inc.

(In millions)	For the 52 weeks of 2000[a]	For the 52 weeks of 1999
Net income	$1,091.9	$ 970.9
Average equity	$4,737.8	$3,584.0
Return on equity	23.0%	27.1%

[a]The Safeway fiscal year ends on the Saturday nearest December 31.

Limited 1999 Annual Report Consolidated Statements of Income (Thousands Except per Share Amounts)	1999[a]	1998[b]	1997[c]
Net sales	$9,723,334	$9,346,911	$9,188,804
Cost of goods sold, occupancy, and buying expenses	(6,365,857)	(6,375,651)	(6,393,322)
Gross income	3,357,477	2,971,260	2,795,482
General, administrative, and store operating expenses	(2,460,338)	(2,286,917)	(2,112,768)
Special and nonrecurring items, net	23,501	1,740,030	(213,215)
Operating income	920,640	2,424,373	469,499
Interest expense	(78,297)	(68,528)	(68,728)
Other income, net	51,037	59,265	36,886
Minority interest	(72,623)	(63,616)	(55,610)
Gain on sale of subsidiary stock	11,002	—	8,606
Income before income taxes	831,759	2,351,494	390,653
Provision for income taxes	371,000	305,000	179,000
Net income	$ 460,759	$2,046,494	$ 211,653
Net income per share			
Basic	$ 2.10	$ 8.50	$ 0.78
Diluted	$ 2.00	$ 8.29	$ 0.77

Note: The accompanying notes are an integral part of these consolidated financial statements.
[a]Year ended January 20, 2000.
[b]Year ended January 20, 1999.
[c]Year ended January 31, 1998.

Exhibit 9-5
Earnings per Share Reported After Net Income

value per common share, simply tells us how much of the shareholders' equity is associated with each share. The numerator is common shareholders' equity and the denominator is average number of common shares outstanding.

The financial information from Johnson & Johnson provided in Exhibit 9-6 is used to compute the book value per share for two consecutive years. The usefulness of this ratio, like all others, depends on how it compares with the same ratio for similar companies or how it changes over time. The increase in the book value per share is positive information.

If you were considering making an investment in a firm, would you be more interested in the firm's earnings per share ratios for the past few years or in its book value per share for the past few years? What factors would influence your opinion? Explain the information provided by each ratio.

STUDY BREAK 9-6
SEE HOW YOU'RE DOING

(In millions)	For the year 2000[a]	For the year 1999
Total equity	$18,808	$16,213
Average common shares outstanding	1,390.3	1,390.1
Book value per share	$ 13.53	$ 11.66

[a]Johnson & Johnson's fiscal year ends on the Sunday nearest December 31.

Exhibit 9-6
Book Value per Share for Johnson & Johnson, Inc.

Business Risks

As discussed in Chapter 1, owners of a company take a risk that the company will not be successful. Owners invest their money in hopes of making more money, and there is always the risk it won't actually happen. In the history of the stock market, there have been many shareholders who have risked their money and lost it. The risk associated with a share of ownership in a company and the potential return on that investment are the two most important characteristics of stock ownership. Investors are often willing to take significant risks for the potential of earning a corresponding significant return. The evaluation of personal financial investments in the stock of corporations is the topic of many finance texts and courses. There are also many Web sites that address personal finance and investing.

> **Risk Associated with Ownership of Corporations**
> From *Barron's Online* September 24, 2001
>
> *The Price of Risk*
>
> *Americans faced the judgment of the marketplace last week: Our lives and property are about 10% less secure than we thought they were two weeks ago, before terrorists hijacked four planes and crashed three of them into the World Trade Center and the Pentagon. The initial calculation was tallied at 7% Monday on the New York Stock Exchange and Nasdaq, two institutions that along the way proved equal to the task of redistributing wealth by the exchange of securities.*
>
> *A loss of only 7% seemed a victory, and trading was more orderly than expected. Stock markets had not been closed by government order since 1933, and no one really knew in advance how many investors would run to get their money out.*

Summary Problem: Tom's Wear Goes Public

When a privately owned company decides it wants to offer ownership to the public—to raise a significant amount of capital, the form of the business organization must be a corporation. (A sole proprietorship or a partnership wanting to offer ownership to the public must first change its form to a corporation.) The first public offering of stock on one of the stock exchanges is called an initial public offering (IPO). Much like the work done before a company issues bonds, a company must do a great deal of work to prepare for an IPO. The Securities and Exchange Commission (SEC) requires the company to provide many reports, including a set of financial statements contained in a report called a prospectus. Remember, the job of the SEC is to protect the public.

In August, Tom decides his company could raise a great deal of capital by "going public." The company has a substantial amount of debt, and Tom decides it would be a good long-term strategy to increase the company's equity. As you know, a company's creditors and owners have claim to the company's assets, and the relationship between the amount of debt and the amount of equity in a company is called the company's *capital structure*. Tom decides that his company's capital structure is weighted too heavily toward debt, and he wants to increase the cash available to pay off some of that debt. To increase his company's equity, Tom will offer the opportunity to the general public to become part owners in Tom's Wear.

Exhibit 9-7 shows the balance sheet for Tom's Wear at the beginning of August. This is the July 31 balance sheet you prepared at the end of Chapter 8.

The first transaction for August is the Tom's Wear IPO. Although the form of the company has been a corporation, Tom's Wear has a lot of work to do to prepare to go public. The SEC requirements for this initial public offering are extensive, and we'll let the investment bankers do the work behind the scenes.

Exhibit 9-7
Balance sheet for Tom's Wear, Inc.
at August 1, 2001

Tom's Wear, Inc.
Balance Sheet
At August 1, 2001

Assets		Liabilities and Shareholders' equity	
Cash	$ 17,151	Accounts payable	$ 36,000
Accounts receivable (net	101,810	Interest payable	1,500
of allowance of $3,290		Warranty liability	2,239
Inventory	8,910	Current portion of long-	6,000
Prepaid insurance	50	term note	
Prepaid rent	600	Current portion of mortgage	2,710
Prepaid Web service	150	Total current liabilities	48,449
Total current assets	128,671	Notes payable	24,000
Computer (net of $500	3,500	Mortgage payable	72,290
accumulated depreciation)		Total liabilities	144,739
Van (net of $4,205	25,795	Common stock	5,000
accumulated depreciation)		Retained earnings	83,097
Land	7,500		
Building (net of $130	67,370		
accumulated depreciation)			
Total assets	$232,836	Total liabilities and	$232,836
		shareholders' equity	

These are finance, accounting, and legal experts in the area of IPOs. The accounting changes in the balance sheet depend on the characteristics of the debt and equity of the company and the agreements the creditors and owners make. We'll make it very simple for Tom's Wear, but in a real-world IPO, transactions could be much more complicated.

Tom works with an investment banking firm and an accounting firm to prepare the stock offering—the IPO. The investment bankers do the legal work and essentially buy the stock and then offer it to the public. The accountants prepare extensive financial information, required by the SEC, in a document called a prospectus. Tom's Wear's corporate charter has 50,000,000 shares of common stock authorized with a par value of $0.01. Tom's personal ownership, which we have simply referred to as common stock without any details of the number of shares, is actually 500,000 shares. (Recall, his contribution was $5,000.) Tom wants to retain a majority of the stock so that he can retain control of the company, so Tom's Wear decides to issue 250,000 additional common shares in this initial offering. The shares are issued at $5 per share.

Assets	=	Liabilities	+	Contributed capital	+	Retained earnings
$1,250,000 Cash				+$2,500 Common stock		
				+$1,247,500 Additional paid-in capital		

The rest of the transactions for Tom's Wear follow. Record the transactions in the accounting equation work sheet and then check your work with the work sheet provided in the solution before you continue.

Transactions for August 2001 for Tom's Wear, Inc.

1	August 1	Tom's Wear issues stock for $1,250,000
2	August 10	Collects cash on accounts receivable of $96,000
3	August 12	Pays accounts payable of $30,000
4	August 14	Tom has been concentrating on increasing sales, so he must increase inventory purchases as well. With the new inflow of cash from the stock offering, Tom decides to buy 25,000 shirts. He gets a quantity discount from the vendor, paying $3.50 for each shirt. He pays cash for the purchase.
5	August 20	Tom finds out that Play Ball Sports Shop has closed and filed bankruptcy. He writes off the account, which has a balance of $3,000.
6	August 15–30	Tom's sales efforts continue to pay off with the addition of several more customers. He lowers the price slightly, and he is able to dramatically increase sales. During August, Tom's Wear sells 20,151 shirts at $10 each. All sales are on account.
7	August 15–30	During August, 300 shirts are returned with defects, and Tom replaces them with new shirts.
8	August 15–30	Miscellaneous operating expenses amount to $42,500 for the month.
9	August 30	The payroll has grown considerably because Tom has hired several new employees, including an on-site manager to run the warehouse. He has also put himself on the management payroll. He sends the payroll company a check for $22,000 by the 30th of the month to cover the payroll and payroll tax expenses for the month.
10	August 30	Tom's Wear pays for insurance to cover the business from August 15 to December 31, for a total of $675.
11	August 31	By the end of the month, Tom sees that he needs to increase the number of delivery vans and purchase some new office equipment. Tom buys two vans for a total cost of $100,000 and new office equipment for $100,000.

Additional information for August includes the following: Tom's Wear drove the van 20,000 miles in August; Tom also decided to reduce the warranty liability from 2% to 1% of sales, because he noticed that the liability appeared to be larger than needed. Due to the huge increase in sales, Tom decided to keep the allowance for uncollectible accounts at 3% of credit sales.

Required:
Prepare the journal entries and adjustments, and post them to T-accounts. Prepare an adjusted trial balance. Then, prepare the four basic financial statements.

Understanding Excel

The following is a copy of the Tom's Wear, Inc. stockholders' equity section of the balance sheet at August 31, 2001:

Common stock (50,000,000 shares authorized, 750,000 shares issued and outstanding)	$ 7,500
Additional paid-in capital	1,247,500
Retained earnings	136,616
Total stockholders' equity	$1,391,616

For purposes of this problem only, assume that in the month of September:

■ Tom was authorized to sell 10,000 shares of $100 par, 6% preferred stock.

■ Tom sold 1,000 shares of the preferred stock at its par value.

■ A cash dividend of $1.00 per share was paid to the preferred stockholders.

■ Tom declared and issued a 5% stock dividend on the common stock when the market value of the stock was $2.25.

■ Net income for the month was $54,345.

Requirements

1. Open a new Excel work sheet.

2. Beginning in cell A1, input the stockholders' equity section of the Tom's Wear, Inc. balance sheet. Use appropriate formatting. Complete requirement 3 before inputting any numerical data.

3. Calculate the appropriate balances of the stockholders' equity accounts as of September 30, 2001, based on the preceding information. Show all work and use formulas as appropriate. Place your calculations under the stockholders' equity section. Use appropriate labels, formatting, and formulas.

4. Input the numbers into the equity section using formulas as appropriate.

5. Print your file and save it to disk. Name your file TomsWear9.

Answers to Study Break Questions

Study Break 9-1

1. $210,000 − $200,000 = $10,000 (increase in common stock account)
   $10,000/$10 par value per share = **1,000 shares**
2. Issue price is par ($10) plus the per share increase in additional paid-in capital (A-PIC): ($163,000 − $153,000)/1,000 shares = $10 per share. So total issue price is $10 par + $10 A-PIC = **$20 per share.**

Study Break 9-2

Because the preferred stock is cumulative, the preferred shareholders must receive from the corporation all the dividends in arrears (those from the past that weren't paid to preferred shareholders) plus the current year dividends, before any dividends can be paid to the common shareholders.

10,000 shares × $100 par value per share × 0.08 = $80,000 (annual dividend to preferred stockholders). The company owes preferred shareholders for last year and the current year, for a total of **$160,000**; that will leave $40,000 for the common shareholders.

Date	Transaction	Debit	Credit
	Retained earnings	$200,000	
	Dividends payable to preferred shareholders		$160,000
	Dividends payable to common shareholders		40,000
	To record the declaration of a dividend		

Study Break 9-3   Assets are decreased by $7,000 (cash outflow). Owner's equity is also reduced by $7,000 with a contra-equity account called treasury stock.

Date	Transaction	Debit	Credit
2002	Treasury stock	$7,000	
	Cash		$7,000
To record the purchase of treasury stock			

Study Break 9-4   1. A company would issue a stock dividend to give its shareholders *something*, even though the company may be short of cash. Distributing shares of stock as dividends involves recording a transfer of retained earnings to contributed capital. A stock split involves increasing the number of shares by turning a single share into two or more shares and reducing the par value proportionately. For example, a 2-for-1 split would make the new par value half of the par value prior to the split. There is no formal recording of a stock split in the accounting records. A stock split is most often done to lower the trading price of a company's shares of stock.

     2. You will now own 3,000 shares with a par value of $1, but you will still own 3%, just as you did before the split.

Study Break 9-5

Beginning retained earnings	$84,500
+ Net income	25,600
− Dividends paid	(12,200)
Ending retained earnings	$97,900

Study Break 9-6   Earnings per share (EPS) is the more relevant of the two numbers; EPS is extremely important to investors. It is very current because it is based on the current year's income. Book value per share, on the other hand, may have a numerator that is less current. Its relevance is influenced by the age of the company's assets, and by any differences between the market value of the assets and the historical cost of those assets.

Solution to Summary Problem

Transaction 1

Tom's Wear issues stock for $1,250,000.

Date	Transaction	Debit	Credit
7/1/2001	Cash	$1,250,000	
	Common stock		$ 2,500
	Additional paid-in capital		1,247,500
To record the issue of 250,000 shares of $0.01 par common stock at $5.00 per share			

Transaction 2

Collects cash on accounts receivable of $96,000.

Date	Transaction	Debit	Credit
8/10/2001	Cash	$96,000	
	Accounts receivable		$96,000
To record the collection of accounts receivable			

Transaction 3

Pays accounts payable of $30,000.

Date	Transaction	Debit	Credit
8/12/2001	Accounts payable	$30,000	
	Cash		$30,000
To record payment on account			

Transaction 4
Purchases 25,000 T-shirts @ $3.50 each for cash.

Date	Transaction	Debit	Credit
8/14/2001	Inventory	$87,500	
	Cash		$87,500

To record the purchase of 25,000 T-shirts
@ $3.50 each

Transaction 5
Writes off the $3,000 accounts receivable for Play Ball Sports.

Date	Transaction	Debit	Credit
8/20/2001	Allowance for bad debts	$3,000	
	Accounts receivable		$3,000

To record the write-off of Play Ball Sports' account

Transaction 6
Sells 20,151 shirts for $10 each. All sales are on account.

Date	Transaction	Debit	Credit
8/15–8/31/2001	Accounts receivable	$201,510	
	Sales revenue		$201,510

To record the sale of 20,151 T-shirts on account

Date	Transaction	Debit	Credit
8/15–8/31/2001	Cost of goods sold	$70,776	
	Inventory		$70,776

To record cost of goods sold [(2,475 @ $3.60) + (17,676 @ $3.50)]

Transaction 7
During August, 300 shirts are returned with defects. Tom replaces them all with new shirts.

Date	Transaction	Debit	Credit
8/15–8/31/2001	Warranties payable	$1,050	
	Inventory		$1,050

To record the replacement of 300 defective shirts
(300 × $3.50)

Transaction 8
Miscellaneous operating expenses for the month are $42,500.

Date	Transaction	Debit	Credit
8/15–8/31/2001	Miscellaneous operating expenses	$42,500	
	Cash		$42,500

To record the payment of miscellaneous operating expenses

Transaction 9
Records salary expense of $22,000.

Date	Transaction	Debit	Credit
8/30/2001	Salary expense	$22,000	
	Cash		$22,000

To record the payment of payroll, related taxes, and fees

Transaction 10

Pays $675 for insurance coverage for the period August 15 to December 31.

Date	Transaction	Debit	Credit
8/30/2001	Prepaid insurance	$675	
	Cash		$675
To record insurance payment			

Transaction 11

Purchases two new vans and some new office equipment.

Date	Transaction	Debit	Credit
8/31/2001	Office furniture and fixtures	$100,000	
	Equipment: van	100,000	
	Cash		$200,000
To record the purchase of equipment and two vans			

Adjustment 1

Records rent expense of $600 for the month of August.

Date	Transaction	Debit	Credit
8/31/2001	Rent expense	$600	
	Prepaid rent		$600
To record rent expense for August			

Adjustment 2

Records insurance expense of $125 for the month of August.

Date	Transaction	Debit	Credit
8/31/2001	Insurance expense	$125	
	Prepaid insurance		$125
To record insurance expense for August			

Adjustment 3

Records web costs of $50 for August.

Date	Transaction	Debit	Credit
8/31/2001	Miscellaneous operating expenses	$50	
	Prepaid web service		$50
To record web maintenance services for August.			

Adjustment 4

Records depreciation expense of $2,900 on the van (20,000 miles $\times$ $0.145).

Date	Transaction	Debit	Credit
8/31/2001	Depreciation expense	$2,900	
	Accumulated depreciation: van		$2,900
To record August depreciation expense on the van			

Adjustment 5
Record depreciation expense of $100 on the computer.

Date	Transaction	Debit	Credit
8/31/2001	Depreciation expense	$100	
	Accumulated depreciation: computer		$100
To record August depreciation expense on the computer			

Adjustment 6
Records depreciation expense of $130 on the building.

Date	Transaction	Debit	Credit
8/31/2001	Depreciation expense	$130	
	Accumulated depreciation: building		$130
To record August depreciation expense on the building			

Adjustment 7
Records interest expense on the van note.

Date	Transaction	Debit	Credit
8/31/2001	Interest expense	$250	
	Interest payable		$250
To record interest expense on the van for August			

Adjustment 8
Records interest expense on the mortgage.

Date	Transaction	Debit	Credit
8/31/2001	Interest expense	$500	
	Interest payable		$500
To record interest expense on the mortgage for August			

Adjustment 9
Bad debt estimate = 3% of credit sales.

Date	Transaction	Debit	Credit
8/31/2001	Bad debt expense	$6,045	
	Allowance for bad debts		$6,045
To record the bad debt estimate for August			

Adjustment 10
Warranty liability estimate = 1% of total sales.

Date	Transaction	Debit	Credit
8/31/2001	Warranty expense	$2,015	
	Warranties payable		$2,015
To record the estimated warranty liability for August			

Cash

BB	$17,151	$30,000	3
1	1,250,000	87,500	4
2	96,000	42,500	8
		22,000	9
		675	10
		200,000	11
	980,476		

Accounts receivable

BB	$105,100	$96,000	2
6	201,510	3,000	5
	207,610		

Allowance for bad debts

		$3,000	BB
5	$3,290	6,045	Adj-9
		6,335	

Inventory

BB	$8,910	$70,776	6
4	87,500	1,050	7
	24,584		

Prepaid insurance

BB	$50	$125	Adj-2
10	675		
	600		

Prepaid web service

BB	$150	$100	Adj-3
	$100		

Prepaid rent

BB	$600	$600	Adj-1
	0		

Equipment: computer

BB	$4,000
	4,000

Equipment: van

BB	$30,000		
11	100,000		
	130,000		

Accumulated depreciation: computer

	$500	BB
	100	Adj-5
	600	

Accumulated depreciation: van

	$4,205	BB	
	2,900	Adj-4	
	7,105		

Buildings

BB	$67,500
	67,500

Accumulated depreciation: buildings

	$130	BB
	130	Adj-6
	260	

Land

BB	$7,500
	7,500

Office furniture and fixtures

11	$100,000
	100,000

Accounts payable

3	$30,000	$36,000 BB
		6,000

Interest payable

		$1,500 BB
		250 Adj-7
		500 Adj-8
		2,250

Warranties payable

7	$1,050	$2,239 BB
		2,015 Adj-10
		3,204

Notes payable

	$30,000 BB
	30,000

Mortgage payable

	$75,000 BB
	75,000

Common stock

	$5,000 BB
	2,500 1
	7,500

Additional paid-in capital

	$1,247,500 1
	1,247,500

Retained earnings

	$83,097 BB

Sales revenue

	6 $201,510
	201,510

Cost of goods sold

6 $70,776	
70,776	

Miscellaneous operating expenses

8 $42,500	
Adj-3 50	
42,550	

Salary expense

9 $22,000	
22,000	

Insurance expense

Adj-2 $125	
125	

Rent expense

Adj-1 $600	
600	

Depreciation expense

Adj-4 $2,900	
Adj-5 100	
Adj-6 130	
3,130	

Interest expense

Adj-7 $250	
Adj-8 500	
750	

Bad debt expense

Adj-9 $6,045	
6,045	

Warranty expense

Adj-10 $2,015	
2,015	

Tom's Wear, Inc.
Adjusted Trial Balance
August 31, 2001

	Debits	Credits
Cash	$ 980,476	
Accounts receivable	207,610	
Allowance for bad debts		$ 6,335
Inventory	24,584	
Prepaid insurance	600	
Prepaid web service	100	
Equipment: computer	4,000	
Accumulated depreciation: computer		600
Equipment: van	130,000	
Accumulated depreciation: van		7,105
Buildings	67,500	
Accumulated depreciation: buildings		260
Land	7,500	
Office furniture and fixtures	100,000	
Accounts payable		6,000
Interest payable		2,250
Warranties payable		3,204
Notes payable		30,000
Mortgage payable		75,000
Common stock		7,500
Additional paid-in capital		1,247,500
Retained earnings		83,097
Sales revenue		201,510
Cost of goods sold	70,776	
Depreciation expense	3,130	
Miscellaneous operating expense	42,550	
Salary expense	22,000	
Insurance expense	125	
Rent expense	600	
Interest expense	750	
Bad debt expense	6,045	
Warranty expense	2,015	
Totals	*$1,670,361*	*$1,670,361*

Financial Statements

Tom's Wear, Inc.
Income Statement
For the Month Ended
August 31, 2001

Sales revenue		$201,510
Less: cost of goods sold		70,776
Gross margin		130,734
Expenses[a]		
Salary expense	$22,000	
Rent expense	600	
Insurance expense	125	
Depreciation expense	3,130	
Bad debt expense	6,045	
Warranty expense	2,015	
Interest expense	750	
Miscellaneous operating expenses	42,550	
Total expenses		*77,215*
Net income		$ 53,519

[a]It is unlikely that a company would itemize the expenses at this level of detail. However, they are detailed here to make it easy for you to follow the numbers.

Tom's Wear, Inc.
Statement of Changes in Shareholders' Equity
For the Month Ended
August 31, 2001

Beginning balances		
Common stock	$ 5,000	
Additional paid-in capital	0	
Contributions made during the year		
Common stock	2,500	
Additional paid-in capital	1,247,500	
Total common stock		$ 7,500
Total additional paid-in capital		1,247,500
Total contributed capital		1,255,000
Beginning retained earnings	83,097	
Net income	53,519	
Dividends paid to shareholders	0	
Ending retained earnings		136,616
Ending shareholders' equity		$1,391,616

Tom's Wear, Inc.
Balance Sheet
At August 31, 2001

Assets		Liabilities and shareholders' equity	
Cash	$ 980,476	Accounts payable	$ 6,000
Accounts receivable (net	201,275	Interest payable	2,250
of allowance of $6,335)		Warranty liability	3,204
Inventory	24,584	Current portion of	6,000
Prepaids	700	long-term note	
Total current assets	1,207,035	Current portion of	2,710
Land	7,500	mortgage	
Equipment (net of	103,400	Total current liabilities	20,164
accumulated			
depreciation of $600)		Notes payable	24,000
Van (net of accumulated	122,895	Mortgage payable	72,290
depreciation of $7,105)		Total liabilities	116,454
Building (net of	67,240	Common stock	7,500
accumulated depreciation		(50,000,000 shares	
of $260)		authorized, 750,000	
		shares issued and	
		outstanding)	
		Additional paid-in	1,247,500
		capital	
		Retained earnings	136,616
Total assets	$1,508,070	Total liabilities and shareholders' equity	$1,508,070

Tom's Wear, Inc.
Statement of Cash Flows
For the Month Ended August 31, 2001

Cash from operating activities

Cash collected from customers	$ 96,000	
Cash paid for salaries	(22,000)	
Cash paid to vendors	(117,500)	
Cash paid for other expenses	(43,175)	
Total cash from operating activities		$ (86,675)
Cash from investing activities		0
Purchase of fixed assets		(200,000)
Cash from financing activities		
Proceeds from common stock issue		1,250,000
Net increase in cash		**$963,325**

Questions

1. What is contributed capital?
2. What are retained earnings?
3. What is the difference between common stock and preferred stock?
4. What is the relationship between the par value of common stock and its market price?
5. What is the difference between *paid-in capital* and *additional paid-in capital*?
6. Are dividends expenses of a corporation? Explain why or why not.
7. Who gets their dividends first: common or preferred shareholders?
8. What is the difference between cumulative and noncumulative preferred stock?
9. What is treasury stock?
10. Would treasury stock be considered authorized, issued, or outstanding?
11. Who decides the amount and timing of dividend payments?
12. What are stock dividends?
13. What are dividends payable?

Short Exercises

SE9-1 The Delta Corp. corporate charter authorizes the company to sell 1 million shares of $2 par common stock. As of December 31, 2002, the company had issued 575,000 shares for $5 each. Delta has no treasury stock. How many shares of common stock will be disclosed as authorized, issued, and outstanding on the December 31, 2002 balance sheet?

L.O. 9-1

SE9-2 Sunshine Corp. began operations on July 1, 2003. When the first fiscal year of Sunshine ended on June 30, 2004, the balance sheet showed 300,000 shares of common stock issued and 300,000 shares of common stock outstanding. During the second year, Sunshine repurchased 10,000 shares for the treasury. After the purchase, how many shares would be classified as issued? How many shares are outstanding?

L.O. 9-1

SE9-3 If Vest Corp. sells 100 shares of its $10 par value common stock at $11 per share, how will the transaction be reflected in the accounting equation?

L.O. 9-1

SE9-4 Ice Video Corp. issued 5,000 shares of its $0.05 par value common stock for $6.55 per share. How much cash did Ice Corp. receive from the stock issue? How will the proceeds be shown in the equity section of the balance sheet?

L.O. 9-1

SE9-5 If 10,000 shares of $1 par common stock are issued for $10 per share, what is the effect on total paid-in capital? What is the effect on additional paid-in capital (also known as paid-in capital in excess of par)?

L.O. 9-1

SE9-6 Stockton Company reported total stockholders' equity of $58,000 on its December 31, 2006 balance sheet. During 2006, it reported a net income of $4,000, declared and paid a cash dividend of $2,000, and issued additional capital stock of $20,000. What was total stockholders' equity at the beginning of the year, on January 1, 2006?

L.O. 9-1

SE9-7 On December 15, 2001, the board of directors of Seat Corp. declared a cash dividend, of $2 per share on the 100,000 common shares outstanding, payable January 8, 2002. The accounting period ends December 31. How will this be reflected on the balance sheet at December 31, 2001?

L.O. 9-2

SE9-8 In 2004, the board of directors of Best Bakery Corp. declared total dividends of $50,000. The company has 2,000 shares of 8% preferred stock at $100 par. No dividends are in arrears. How much of the $50,000 will be paid to the preferred shareholders? How much will be paid to the common shareholders?

L.O. 9-2

L.O. 9-2

SE9-9 Cab Company paid $30,000 to its preferred shareholders in 2002. The preferred stock has a par value of $100 and a dividend rate of 6%. If there were no dividends in arrears, how many shares of preferred stock were outstanding (on the date of record)?

L.O. 9-2

SE9-10 Bates Corp. has 7,000 shares of $100 par, 5% cumulative, preferred stock outstanding and 50,000 shares of $1 par common stock outstanding. If the board of directors declares $100,000 of total dividends and the company did not pay dividends the previous year, how much will the preferred shareholders receive (in total)?

L.O. 9-3

SE9-11 Fitness and Fashion Corp. decided to buy back some of its own stock to have on hand for end-of-year bonuses. If there were 30,000 shares issued and outstanding before the stock repurchase and the company bought 250 shares, how many shares were issued and outstanding after the treasury stock purchase?

L.O. 9-3

SE9-12 If Fitness and Fashion Corp. paid $10 per share for 250 shares of its own stock, how would the transaction affect the accounting equation? How would the transaction be reflected in the shareholders' equity section of the balance sheet?

L.O. 9-3

SE9-13 Suppose Fitness and Fashion Corp. paid $10 per share for 250 shares of its own stock on August 30, 2004, and then resold these treasury shares for $12 per share on September 25, 2004. How would the transaction of September 25, 2004 affect the accounting equation?

L.O. 9-4

SE9-14 Borax Company declared and paid a 10% stock dividend on June 1, 2004. Before this dividend was declared and distributed, there were 120,000 shares of $1 par common stock outstanding. After the stock dividend, how many shares are outstanding? What is the par value of each share?

L.O. 9-4

SE9-15 Romax Company announced a 2-for-1 stock split on its common stock. Before the announcement, there were 120,000 shares of $1 par common stock outstanding. After the stock split, how many shares will be outstanding? What will be the par value of each share?

L.O. 9-5

SE9-16 On January 1, 2003, Netto Inc. started the year with a $22,000 balance in retained earnings. During 2003, the company earned net income of $40,000 and declared and paid dividends of $10,000. Also, the company received cash of $15,000 from a new issue of common stock. What is the balance in retained earnings on December 31, 2003?

L.O. 9-5, 6

SE9-17 Details Corp. had a return on shareholders' equity of 12% in 2004. If average shareholders' equity for Details Corp. was $500,000 and the company has no preferred stock, what was net income for 2004?

L.O. 9-5, 6

SE9-18 Home Depot reported the following information on the financial statements for 2000. Were any new shares of common stock issued between February 1, 1999 and January 30, 2000? Did the company report net income for the year ended January 30, 2000?

(Dollars are in millions.)

	January 30, 2000	January 31, 1999
Common stock, par value $0.05		
Authorized: 5,000,000,000 shares		
Issued and outstanding		
2,304,317,000 shares at January 30, 2000		
2,213,178,000 shares at January 31, 1999	$ 115	$ 111
Additional paid-in capital	4,319	2,817
Retained earnings	7,941	5,876

L.O. 9-6

SE9-19 Spikes, Inc. started and ended the year with 400,000 shares of common stock issued and outstanding. Net income was $35,000. Calculate earnings per share for the year.

Exercises

E9-1 The ABC Company corporate charter allows it to sell 200,000 shares of $1 par value common stock. To date, the company has issued 50,000 shares for a total of $125,000. Last month, ABC repurchased 1,000 shares for $3 per share.

L.O. 9-1

a. If ABC were to prepare a balance sheet, how many shares would it show as (1) authorized, (2) issued, and (3) outstanding?
b. In addition to the owner's equity previously described, ABC Company also has $350,000 in retained earnings. Using this information, prepare the owner's equity section of the ABC Company balance sheet.

E9-2 DEF Company had a net income of $250,000 for the year ended December 31, 2003. On January 15, the board of directors met and declared a dividend of $0.50 per share for each of the 300,000 outstanding shares of common stock. The board voted to distribute the dividend on March 1 to all shareholders of record as of February 1.

L.O. 9-2

What is (1) the date of declaration, (2) the date of record, and (3) the date of payment? If DEF Company were to prepare a balance sheet on January 30, how would the dividends be shown (if at all)?

E9-3 G-Hi Company has 4,000 shares of $100 par, 9% cumulative preferred stock outstanding and 10,000 shares of $1 par value common stock outstanding. The company began operations on January 1, 2003. The cash dividends declared and paid during each of the first 3 years of G-Hi's operations are shown next. Calculate the amounts that went to the preferred and the common shareholders each year.

L.O. 9-2

Year	Total dividends paid	Dividends to preferred stockholders	Dividends to common stockholders
2003	$60,000		
2004	20,000		
2005	60,000		

E9-4 JKL Company had the following stockholders' equity section on the December 31, 2004 balance sheet:

L.O. 9-1, 2, 3

Preferred stock, $100 par, 8% cumulative	$1,250,000
Common stock, $2 par value	800,000
Paid-in capital in excess of par, common stock	3,500,000
Retained earnings	3,467,000
Total	$9,017,000

a. How many shares of common stock are issued?
b. How many shares of common stock are outstanding?
c. How many shares of preferred stock are outstanding?
d. What was the average selling price of a share of common stock?
e. If $150,000 of dividends were declared and no dividends were in arrears, how much of that amount would go to the common shareholders?

E9-5 The following balances were shown on the year-end balance sheets for 2003 and 2004 for MNO Company. For each item, give the most likely reason for the change from one year to the next.

L.O. 9-1, 2, 3, 5

	12/31/03	12/31/04	Explanation?
Common stock	$ 45,000	$ 50,000	
Paid-in capital in excess of par	200,000	230,000	
Retained earnings	182,500	200,000[a]	
Treasury stock	(3,450)	(5,450)	

[a]Net income for the year was $20,000.

Problems—Set A

L.O. 9-1, 2, 3

P9-1A The following information pertains to the shareholders' equity section of the December 31, 2005 balance sheet of Sammie's Soap Company, Inc:

a. Contributed capital on January 1, 2005 was made up of (1) 70,000 issued and outstanding shares of common stock with par value of $0.50, (2) additional paid-in capital in excess of par of $350,000, and (3) retained earnings of $500,000.

b. During January 2005, Sammie's issued an additional 10,000 shares of common stock for $7 per share.

c. On the December 31, 2004 balance sheet, Sammie's noted that there were 150,000 shares of common stock authorized.

d. Net income for 2005 was $49,500.

e. Sammie's paid shareholders a dividend of $0.25 per share on October 1.

f. During November, Sammie's CEO decided the company should buy 1,000 shares of its own stock to have on hand for end-of-year bonuses. At that time, the stock was trading for $6 per share in the stock market.

Required: Prepare the equity section of the balance sheet at December 31, 2005.

L.O. 9-4

P9-2A As of December 31, 2004, Ginger's Snap Company had 100,000 shares of $10 par value common stock issued and outstanding. The retained earnings balance was $125,000. On January 15, 2005, Ginger's issued a 5% stock dividend to its common shareholders. At the time of the dividend, the market value of the stock was $15 per share, so the dollar amount of the stock dividend was $75,000 (100,000 shares × 5% = 5,000 shares; 5,000 shares × $15 per share = $75,000).

Required:

a. What effect did the stock dividend have on the accounting equation?

b. How many shares of stock are outstanding after the stock dividend?

c. If you owned 3% of the outstanding common stock of Ginger's Snap Company before the stock dividend, what is your percentage of ownership after the stock dividend?

L.O. 9-1, 2, 3

P9-3A The following information is from the shareholders' equity sections from comparative balance sheets for Wildwood Company:

	At December 31,	
	2005	**2004**
Common stock ($10 par)	$420,000	$400,000
Additional paid-in capital	326,000	306,000
Retained earnings	55,000	51,000
Total shareholders' equity	*$801,000*	*$757,000*

Note: Net income for the year ended December 31, 2005 was $70,000.

Required:

a. How many shares of common stock were issued to new shareholders during 2005?

b. What was the average issue price of the stock issued during 2005?

c. What was the amount of dividends declared during 2005?

d. Did the company have any treasury shares at the end of 2005?

L.O. 9-1, 5

P9-4A The Coca-Cola Company reported the following information on its comparative balance sheet at December 31 (amounts in millions):

	December 31	
	2000	**1999**
Common stock		
Authorized: 5,600 shares		
Issued		
3,482 shares in 2000	$ 870	
3,466 shares in 1999		$ 867
Additional paid-in capital	3,196	2,584
Retained earnings	21,265	20,773

Required:

a. What is the approximate par value of the Coca-Cola common stock?

b. How many new shares of common stock did the company issue during the fiscal year ended December 31, 2000?

c. What was the approximate (average) issue price of the stock issued during the year?

d. Did Coca-Cola earn net income during the year?

e. If Coca-Cola paid dividends of $0.60 per share, what would you estimate net income for the year to be?

P9-5A The following information is from the comparative balance sheets of Linens 'n Things:

L.O. 9-1, 3, 5

Adapted from Linens 'n Things, Inc. & Subsidiaries
Consolidated Balance Sheets
(In Thousands, Except Share Amounts)

Shareholders' equity	December 31, 1999	December 31, 1998
Preferred stock, $0.01 par value,	—	—
1,000,000 shares authorized; none issued		
and outstanding		
Common stock, $0.01 par value;	$ 396	$ 391
135,000,000 shares authorized at		
December 31, 1999 and 60,000,000 shares		
authorized at December 31, 1998; 39,600,000		
shares issued and _____ shares		
outstanding at December 31, 1999;		
and 39,100,000 shares issued and		
_____ shares outstanding at		
December 31, 1998.		
Additional paid-in capital	220,751	211,378
Retained earnings	165,249	113,197
Treasury stock, at cost, 76,477 shares		
at December 31, 1999 and 53,333 shares at		
December 31, 1998	(2,434)	(1,390)
Total shareholders' equity	$383,962	$323,576

Required:

a. How many shares of common stock were outstanding at December 31, 1999?

b. How many shares of common stock were outstanding at December 31, 1998?

c. What was the average issue price per share of the 39,600,000 shares classified as "issued" at December 31, 1999? (Round the answer to the nearest cent.)

d. How many shares of treasury stock did the company purchase during 1999?

e. What was the average price per share paid for the treasury shares purchased during the fiscal year ended December 31, 1999?

f. What was the average issue price of the 500,000 shares of common stock issued during the fiscal year ended December 31, 1999?

Problems—Set B

L.O. 9-1, 2, 3

P9-1B The following information pertains to All Batteries Company, Inc:

   a. Contributed capital on October 1, 2004 was composed of (1) 50,000 issued and outstanding shares of common stock with par value of $1, (2) additional paid-in capital in excess of par of $250,000, and (3) retained earnings of $400,000.

   b. During October 2004, All Batteries Company issued an additional 20,000 shares of common stock for $8 per share.

   c. On the September 30, 2005 balance sheet, the company showed 500,000 shares of common stock authorized.

   d. Net income for the year ended September 30, 2005 was $87,500.

   e. All Batteries Company paid its shareholders a dividend of $0.50 per share on August 1.

   f. During November, the All Batteries Company CEO decided the company should buy 600 shares of its own stock to have on hand for end-of-year bonuses. At that time, the stock was trading for $7 per share.

Required: Prepare the equity section of the September 30, 2005 balance sheet.

L.O. 9-4

P9-2B At December 31, 2003, Robby's Shoe Company had 200,000 shares of $5 par common stock issued and outstanding. The retained earnings balance was $165,000. On January 15, 2004, Robby's issued a 3% stock dividend to its common shareholders. At the time of the dividend, the market value of the stock was $20 per share, so the dollar amount of the stock dividend was $75,000 (200,000 shares × 0.03 = 6,000 shares; 6,000 shares × $20 per share = $120,000).

Required:

   a. What effect did the stock dividend have on the accounting equation?

   b. How many shares of stock are outstanding after the stock dividend?

   c. If you owned 5% of the outstanding common stock of Robby's Shoe Company before the stock dividend, what is your percentage of ownership after the stock dividend?

L.O. 9-1, 2, 3

P9-3B The following information was shown on the recent comparative balance sheets for Paul's Dot-Com Company:

	At December 31, 2006	At December 31, 2005
Common stock ($1 par)	$520,000	$400,000
Additional paid-in capital	326,000	296,000
Retained earnings	65,000	50,000
Total shareholders' equity	$911,000	$746,000

Note: Net income for the year ended December 31, 2006 was $75,000.

Required:

   a. How many shares of common stock were issued to new shareholders during 2006?

   b. What was the average issue price of the stock issued during 2006?

   c. What was the amount of dividends declared during 2006?

   d. Did the company have any treasury shares at the end of 2006?

L.O. 9-1, 5

P9-4B At June 30, 2007, High Quality Mining Company reported the following on its comparative balance sheets (amounts in millions):

	June 30	
	2007	2006
Common stock		
Authorized: 2,500 shares		
Issued		
1,450 shares in 2007	$14,500	
1,400 shares in 2006		$14,000
Paid-in capital in excess of par	4,350	2,890
Retained earning	15,500	14,300

Required:

a. What is the par value of the company's common stock?
b. Did the company issue any new shares during the fiscal year ended June 30, 2007?
c. What was the approximate (average) issue price of the stock issued during the year?
d. Did High Quality Mining Company earn net income during the year?
e. Assume no dividends were paid this year. What would you estimate net income for the year to be?

P9-5B This information is from the equity section of the comparative balance sheets of Tick Tock, Inc.

L.O. 9-1, 3, 5

Consolidated Balance Sheets
(In Thousands, Except Share Data)

Shareholders' equity	September 30, 2000	September 30, 1999
Common stock, $0.10 par value; 450,000 shares issued and _____ shares outstanding at September 30, 2000; and 425,000 shares issued and _____ shares outstanding at September 30, 1999	$ 45.0	$ 42.5
Additional paid-in capital	9,475	8,925
Retained earnings	25,237	21,450
Treasury stock, at cost, 21,340 shares at September 30, 2000 and 17,148 shares at September 30, 1999	448	343

Required:

a. What was the average issue price per share of the 450,000 shares classified as "issued" at September 30, 2000? (Round the answer to the nearest cent.)
b. What was the average issue price of the 25,000 shares of common stock issued during the fiscal year ending September 30, 2000?
c. How many shares were outstanding at September 30, 2000? How many shares were outstanding at September 30, 1999?
d. How many shares did the company buy back during the year? What was the average cost of a share of the treasury shares purchased during the year?
e. If no dividends were paid, what was net income for the year ending September 30, 2000?

Recording Transactions

R9-1 (SE9-3) If Vest Corporation sells and issues 100 shares of its $10 par value common stock at $11 per share, what is the journal entry needed to record the transaction?

Date	Account	Debit	Credit

R9-2 (SE9-7) On December 15, 2001, the board of directors of Seat Corporation declared a cash dividend, payable January 8, 2002, of $2 per share on the 100,000 common shares outstanding. The accounting period ends December 31. Give the journal entry to record the December 15 transaction.

Date	Account	Debit	Credit

R9-3 (SE9-10) Bates Corporation has 7,000 shares of $100 par, 5%, cumulative preferred stock outstanding and 50,000 shares of $1 par common stock outstanding. If the board of directors declares $100,000 of total dividends and the company did not pay dividends the previous year, what is the journal entry that Bates should record?

Date	Account	Debit	Credit

R9-4 (SE9-13) Suppose Fitness and Fashion Corporation paid $10 per share for 250 shares of its own stock on August 30, 2004, and then resold these treasury shares for $12 per share on September 25, 2004. Give the journal entries for each of these transactions.

Date	Account	Debit	Credit

R9-5 (SE9-15) Romax Company announced a 2-for-1 stock split on its common stock. Before the announcement, there were 120,000 shares of $1 par common stock outstanding. After the stock split, how many shares will be outstanding? What is the journal entry needed to record this transaction?

Date	Account	Debit	Credit

R9-6 (E9-2) DEF Company had a net income of $250,000 for the year ended 12/31/03. On January 15, the board of directors met and declared a dividend of $0.50 per share for each of the 300,000 outstanding shares of common stock. The board voted to distribute the dividend on March 1 to all shareholders of record as of February 1. Give the journal entry for the declaration of the dividend.

Date	Account	Debit	Credit

R9-7 (E9-3) G-Hi Company has 4,000 shares of $100 par, 9%, cumulative preferred stock outstanding and 10,000 shares of $1 par value common stock outstanding. The company began operations on January 1, 2003. The cash dividends declared and paid during each of the first 3 years of G-Hi's operations were: $60,000 in 2003, $20,000 in 2004, and $60,000 in 2005. Give the journal entry for the dividend declaration for each of the 3 years.

Date	Account	Debit	Credit

R9-8 (P9-1A) The following information pertains to the equity section of the December 31, 2005, balance sheet of Sammie's Soap Company, Inc.

a. Contributed capital on January 1, 2005, consisted of (1) 70,000 issued and outstanding shares of common stock with par value of $0.50, (2) additional paid-in capital in excess of par of $350,000, and (3) retained earnings of $500,000.
b. During January 2005, Sammie's issued an additional 10,000 shares of common stock for $7 per share.
c. Sammie's paid shareholders a dividend of $0.25 per share on October 1.
d. During November, Sammie's CEO decided the company should buy 1,000 shares of its own stock to have on hand for end-of-year bonuses. At that time, the stock was trading for $6 per share in the stock market.
e. Net income for 2005 was $49,500.

Required: Use the following T-accounts to record the beginning balances in the equity accounts and to record the transactions described in parts b–e.

Common stock	Additional paid-in capital	Retained earnings	Treasury stock

R9-9 (P9-2A) As of December 31, 2004, Ginger's Snap Company had 100,000 shares of $10 par value common stock issued and outstanding. The retained earnings balance was $125,000. On January 15, 2005, Ginger's issued a 5% stock dividend to its common shareholders. At the time of the dividend, the market value of the stock was $15 per share, so the dollar amount of the stock dividend was $75,000 [100,000 shares × 5% = 5,000 shares; 5,000 shares × $15 per share = $75,000]. Give the journal entry for the stock dividend.

Date	Account	Debit	Credit

R9-Comprehensive

Chapter 9: Comprehensive Financial Statement Preparation Problem

Shelby's Pet Mart, Inc. began operations in January 2003. The company's corporate charter authorizes the company to issue up to 500,000 shares of $2 common stock and 100,000 shares of $100 par, 10%, cumulative preferred stock. The company completed the following transactions during its first 2 years of operations.
   In 2003, Shelby's Pet Mart, Inc.:

1. Issued 50,000 shares of common stock for $3 per share on January 1.
2. Issued 10,000 shares of preferred stock for $120 per share on January 20.
3. Issued 20,000 shares of common stock for $5 per share on March 30.

4. Earned and collected $320,000 revenue during the year.
5. Paid cash expenses of $121,000 during the year.
6. Declared dividends of $50,000 on December 31. The dividend will be paid on February 1, 2004, to stockholders of record at January 15, 2004.

In 2004, the company completed these transactions:

1. On February 1, paid the cash dividend declared on December 31, 2003.
2. On March 30, issued 10,000 shares of preferred stock for $130 per share.
3. On July 1, purchased 1,000 shares of its own common stock at $6 per share for the treasury.
4. On November 1, resold half of the shares of treasury stock for $7 per share.
5. Earned $400,000 of revenue; collected $300,000 of it in cash, during the year.
6. Paid cash expenses of $150,000 during the year.
7. Declared dividends of $15,000 on December 31. The dividend will be paid on February 1, 2005, to stockholders of record at January 15, 2005.

Record the transactions in T-accounts. Then, prepare the four basic financial statements for both fiscal years.

Issues for Discussion

L.O. 9-6, 7

Financial statement analysis

1. Use the annual report of Pier 1 Imports to answer the following:

    a. In addition to selling treasury stock, a company may use treasury stock when stock options are exercised or when debt is converted to stock. Pier 1 used some of its treasury shares to do this during 2000 and 2001. Where is this disclosed in the financial statements? Describe how the dollar amount of treasury shares on the comparative balance sheets decreased while, at the same time, the statement of cash flows shows cash outflow for the purchase of treasury shares.

    b. Compute the return-on-equity for the two consecutive years ending in 2000 and 2001. What information do these ratios provide?

Business risk

2. a. What kinds of risks do the owners of Pier 1 face?

    b. Would you prefer to be a creditor or an owner of Pier 1? Explain why.

Ethics

3. AVX Electronics is very close to bringing a revolutionary new computer chip to the market. The company fears that it could soon be the target of a takeover by a giant telecommunications company if this news were to leak before the product is introduced. The current AVX management intends to redistribute the company's stock holdings so its managers will have a larger share of ownership. Thus, management has decided to buy back 20% of the company's common stock while the price is still quite low and distribute it to the managers—including themselves—as part of the company's bonus plan. Are the actions of AVX management ethical? Explain why this strategy would reduce the risk of a hostile takeover. Was any group hurt by this strategy?

Internet Exercise: Hershey Foods Corporation

Hershey is the market leader, ahead of Mars, in the U.S. candy. The company makes such well-known chocolate and candy brands as Hershey's Kisses, Reese's peanut butter cups, Twizzlers licorice, Jolly Rancher, Mounds, Super Bubble gum, and Kit Kat (licensed from Nestlé). Its products are sold throughout North America and exported to over 90 countries.

Please go to the www.prenhall.com/myphlip *Web site, register, and add this text-book to your myphilp page (if you haven't done so already). Go to Chapter 9 and use the Internet Exercise company link. Click on* Investor Relations.

IE9-1 Explore "Investor's Overview." In what city is the Hershey factory located? The current stock quote (market price) of Hershey's stock is how much per share? Is this market price reflected on the Hershey balance sheet? If it is, where?

Access the most recent annual report and find the consolidated balance sheets to answer the following questions. (*Note:* These financial statements are read with an Acrobat Reader, which may be downloaded free by clicking on *Get Acrobat Reader.*)

IE9-2 How many types of stock have been authorized and issued? For the most recent year, how many shares are issued and are outstanding?

IE9-3 For the most recent year-end identify total stockholders' equity. Of this total, how much was contributed by shareholders for issued shares? On average, how much did shareholders pay per issued share? Is the average issue price more or less than the current market price? Give an explanation for this difference.

IE9-4 For the most recent year-end, what amount of stockholders' equity is earned capital? What is the name of the earned capital account? Did earned capital increase or decrease compared with the previous year? What might cause this change?

IE9-5 Has the company reacquired any of its common stock? How you can tell? What is reacquired stock called? When a company reacquires stock does total stockholders' equity increase or decrease? Why might a company want to reacquire issued shares?

IE9-6 (*Optional*) For a study break visit Hershey's Kidztown at *www.kidztown.com* and go to "Fun and Games" to play. (Hope you have fun.)

Please note: Internet Web sites are constantly being updated. Therefore, if the information is not found where indicated, please explore the Web site further to find the information.

PREPARING THE STATEMENT OF CASH FLOWS

Here's where you've been...

Financing

In Chapter 9, you learned about how a company obtains financing from its owners. You learned that stockholders' equity is made up of *contributed capital* and *retained earnings*. You studied how the financial statements reflect that information and how the company pays a return—dividends—to its owners.

Here's where you're going...

Chapter 10 will give you a better understanding of the statement of cash flows that we've been discussing throughout this book. You'll learn two ways to prepare and present the statement of cash flows. You will get a clearer understanding of the difference between cash basis accounting and accrual basis accounting.

Financial Reporting

10

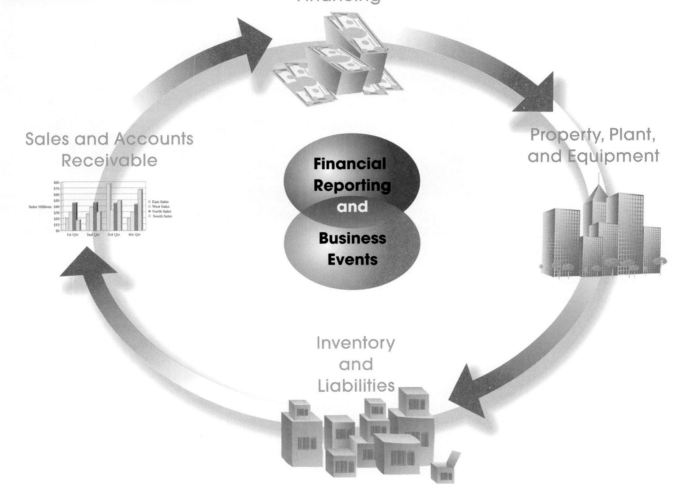

Financing

Sales and Accounts
Receivable

**Financial
Reporting
and
Business
Events**

Property, Plant,
and Equipment

Inventory
and
Liabilities

Learning Objectives

**More specifically, when you are finished studying this chapter, you
should be able to answer these questions:**

1. Why is the statement of cash flows so important to a business?
2. What are the three types of cash flows shown on the statement
   of cash flows and what transactions are included in each?
3. How is the statement of cash flows prepared using the direct
   method?
4. How is the statement of cash flows prepared using the indirect
   method?
5. What are the important elements of the statement of cash flows
   for financial statement analysis?

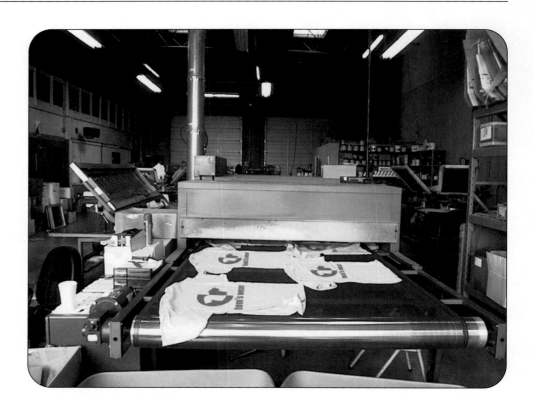

Importance of the Statement of Cash Flows

L.O. 1

Explain the importance of the statement of cash flows.

BUSINESS PROCESS

The statement of cash flows—one of the four financial statements a company must prepare as part of generally accepted accounting principles (GAAP)—shows all the cash the company has received and all the cash the company has disbursed during the accounting period. Each cash flow relates to one of three business activities—operating, investing, or financing activities. The statement explains the details of the change in the cash balance—that's the net increase or decrease in cash—during the accounting period.

Thousands of companies go bankrupt each year because they fail to plan their cash flows effectively. When the time comes to pay their bills, they do not have enough cash on hand. They do not manage their cash very well. Preparing a cash budget is a crucial activity for all companies. It's more complicated than just estimating cash inflows and outflows for the accounting period. The sources of cash and the uses of cash must be estimated in detail—both the amounts of cash and when cash is needed. Each month, projected cash inflows and outflows must be budgeted by source. With this level of detail, a company can plan ahead for any cash shortage by (1) securing a line of credit from a local bank, (2) borrowing the money, or (3) altering the timing of its receipts (tightening up credit policies) or disbursements (postponing purchases).

A cash budget is a detailed plan of a company's estimated cash receipts and estimated cash disbursements, with very specific forecasts of the sources, uses, and the timing of the cash flows. The budgeted cash flows in the cash budget can then be compared with actual cash flows, and the comparison is the basis for planning and evaluating performance. In that sense, a budget is a tool for planning and evaluating performance.

To compare the actual cash flows for an accounting period with the period's cash budget, a company has to produce details about the actual sources of cash and actual uses of cash from the company's records. Comparing actual cash flows with budgeted cash flows gets a company ready to prepare the next

Understanding Business

IT'S ALL ABOUT CASH FLOW

A business firm must have cash when it needs it. This is true for all kinds of firms in all kinds of businesses. When the tragic terrorist attack on the World Trade Towers in New York City occurred, the repercussions were felt beyond the primary loss—human lives—to the distant secondary losses—business loss. The consequences of the tragedy in terms of business losses emphasized the crucial role of sufficient cash in every business.

Airlines need cash

Taken from *Flying Pork Barrels*... The airline bailout enriches stockholders at the expense of taxpayers; MSNBC.com, September 27, 2001, by Steven E. Landsburg.

In the past few weeks, politicians have been transformed into statesmen, and George W. Bush has perhaps had greatness thrust upon him. But you can't escape your origins. Congress and the president have pulled off the neat trick of rising to the occasion while simultaneously stooping to pork-barrel politics as usual.

I refer to the airline bailout—$5 billion in cash and an additional $10 billion in loan guarantees. You might think that in times like these our leaders would be too busy for everyday pursuits like handing out giant dollops of corporate welfare. You'd be wrong.

Some companies are short of cash to pay dividends

Goodyear Slashes Quarterly Dividend
October 2, 2001 1:11:00 P.M. ET

AKRON, Ohio (Reuters)—Goodyear Tire & Rubber Co. *(GT)*, the world's largest tire producer, on Tuesday said it would cut its quarterly dividend by more than half, due to current economic and business conditions.

The company, which last week lowered its third-quarter earnings outlook because of weak demand, said it will now pay out 12 cents a share, down from 30 cents. The dividend is payable Dec. 17 to shareholders of record Nov. 15, Goodyear said.

Evaluating a company's cash flow is more important than ever

Taken from the *Wall Street Journal*, "Heard on the Street October 3, 2001 with Forecasts in Disarray, Analysts Turn to New, Old" by Steve Liesman

To be sure, earnings decline every time the economy sours, and so the most popular corporate gauge, a price-to-earnings ratio, loses its value for many companies and industries. But the shock of the terrorist attacks has forced analysts to rethink how they value companies. For example, where once they followed growth rates, analysts are now focused more keenly than ever on whether a company has enough cash for its interest payments.

---

period's budgeted cash flows. Even though the focus of financial reporting is financial statements for shareholders and investors, the information about cash flows is equally useful to managers of a company.

Since Tom started his T-shirt business in January 2001, we have prepared the four basic financial statements for his business every month, including the statement of cash flows. The way we've prepared the statement of cash flows has been to:

1. identify every cash transaction from the asset column on our accounting equation work sheet, and then
2. classify each cash amount into one of three categories: operating, investing, or financing.

Exhibit 10-1
Sources and Uses of Cash

CASH
Where did we get it? Examples:

From customers	From selling fixed assets	From a bank loan
Operating Activities	Investing Activities	Financing Activities

How did we spend it? Examples:

To pay vendors	To purchase fixed assets	To repay loan principal

When we use a separate column in the accounting equation work sheet for cash transactions, we simply take each addition of cash and each subtraction of cash; then we classify each cash flow as cash from operations, cash from investing, or cash from financing activities. Because a real company has a much more complex accounting system, needed to handle thousands or millions of transactions, examining each transaction is not a feasible way for a company to prepare the statement of cash flows.

Exhibit 10-1 shows a summary of the information presented on the statement of cash flows—the sections of a statement of cash flows and the questions the statement is designed to answer. Next, we'll discuss how the statement is actually prepared.

Two Methods of Preparing and Presenting the Statement of Cash Flows

L.O.2

Know the different classification of various types of cash flows on the statement of cash flows.

The **direct method** shows every cash inflow and every cash outflow.

The **indirect method** starts with net income and makes adjustments for all the items that are not cash.

Cash from operations includes all cash receipts and cash disbursements for routine sales and purchases made in the course of doing business.

GAAP describes two ways of preparing the statement of cash flows: the **direct method** and the **indirect method**. These two methods are named for the way in which the operating section of the statement of cash flows—**cash from operations**—is prepared, either directly—by converting every number on the income statement to its cash amount—or indirectly—by starting with net income and adjusting it until you have the cash from operations. For the other two sections, investing and financing, there is only one way to compute the cash flows: The transactions are directly identified. Thus, in any discussion about different methods of preparing a statement of cash flows, the difference between the direct method and the indirect method applies only to cash from operations.

Before we discuss the two different methods in detail, let's look at a simple example of the difference between these methods of preparing the statement of cash flows.

We'll start with the first month of business for a simple company, with the following transactions:

1. purchase of inventory for $250—paid cash of $200 to vendor with the remaining $50 on account (accounts payable);
2. sales of all inventory for $600—$500 for cash and $100 on account (accounts receivable);
3. paid $30 for supplies and used $20 worth of them, with $10 worth of supplies remaining for next month.

Direct method		Indirect method	
Cash from operations		Cash from operations	
Cash collected from customers	$500	Net income	$330
		+ Or – change in accounts receivable	(100)
Cash paid for supplies	(30)		
		+ Or – change in supplies	(10)
Cash paid to vendors for inventory	(200)	+ Or – change in accounts payable	50
Net cash from operations	$270	Net cash from operations	$270

Exhibit 10-2
Example of Direct Versus Indirect Methods for the Statement of Cash Flows

Net income is calculated as follows:

Sales $600 – Cost of goods sold ($250) – supplies expense ($20) = $330 Net Income

You can easily calculate the amount of cash the company collected and disbursed:

$(200) Inventory + $500 Cash Sales – $(30) Supplies = $270 Net Cash Inflow

Exhibit 10-2 shows how the statement of cash flows would be presented using the direct and indirect methods. Notice the only cash flows in this example are cash flows from operations; and both methods produce the same amount of cash from operations.

Both methods of preparing the operating section of the statement of cash flows require information about the underlying transactions so the cash can be separated from the accrual accounting numbers. For example, the amount of sales has to be examined to get the actual cash collected from making those sales. Supplies expense has to be examined to get the actual cash paid for supplies.

This change from accrual basis numbers to cash basis numbers can be done in the two ways shown in Exhibit 10-2—direct or indirect. The direct method examines each item on the income statement, one by one. The indirect method is more mechanical: Net income is adjusted for all the changes in the current assets and current liabilities, excluding cash, that relate to the items on the income statement.

Before we discuss each in detail, let's quickly review the three sections of the statement of cash flows and the items contained in each section.

Review of the Three Sections of the Statement of Cash Flows

The three sections of the statement of cash flows are operating, investing, and financing.

■ The first section of the statement of cash flows is the *operating* section, also known as cash from operations, where the cash inflows and cash outflows from the firm's normal, day-to-day operations of the business are included; cash flows such as:

Cash inflows	*Cash outflows*
Cash collected from customers	Cash paid to employees
Cash collected for interest	Cash paid for inventory
	Cash paid for expenses
	Cash paid for interest
	Cash paid for taxes

Cash from investing activities includes all cash receipts and all cash disbursements for long-term business assets.

■ The second section of the statement of cash flows is the *investing* section, also known as **cash from investing activities,** where the cash flows related to investments are shown. GAAP defines investing activities as activities that involve buying and selling assets that the company plans to keep for at least a year, such as:

Cash inflows	*Cash outflows*
Cash proceeds from the sale of property, plant, & equipment	Cash paid to buy property, plant, & equipment
Cash from the sale of certain securities	Cash paid for long-term investments
	Cash loaned to others

Cash from financing activities includes all cash receipts and all cash disbursements for loans (principal only), contributions from owners, and distributions to owners.

■ The third section is the *financing* section, also known as **cash from financing activities,** where the cash flows related to all financing activities are included, such as:

Cash inflows	*Cash outflows*
Cash proceeds from the sale of the company's stock	Cash paid for treasury stock
Cash received from borrowing	Cash paid to retire debt principal
	Cash payment of dividends

STUDY BREAK 10-1
SEE HOW YOU'RE DOING

What are the three classifications of cash flows? Give an example of a cash inflow and a cash outflow in each category.

Accrual Accounting Versus Cash

L.O. 3

Know how to convert accrual numbers to cash.

Companies that follow GAAP maintain their accounting records using the accrual basis. Preparing the statement of cash flows is actually converting the records of the business to cash basis. That's what we did in Exhibit 10-2. There are many reasons why accrual basis accounting and cash basis accounting are not generally the same.

For example, a company will record a sale and recognize the revenue on the income statement when the merchandise is shipped or delivered. Does the company always receive the cash at that time? No. Thus, the amount of revenue earned from sales for an accounting period may not be the same as the amount of cash collected during the period. At the end of the accounting period, when the company is preparing its financial statements, customers may still owe the company some money—there may be outstanding accounts receivable. That is one reason the cash collected from sales might not equal the amount of the sales for a specific accounting period.

Also, the company may have collected cash during the current period from sales made during the prior accounting period—accounts receivable from the prior year may have been collected. Thus, to calculate the cash collected from customers for the statement of cash flows, we have to consider and make an adjustment for the change in accounts receivable.

Suppose a company began 2003 with accounts receivable of $500. These accounts receivable were recorded during 2002, when the revenue from the sales was recognized. All sales are made on credit; and during 2003, the company had sales of $3,000. At the end of 2003, the balance in accounts receivable was $600. How much cash was collected from customers during 2003? Because accounts receivable started with a balance of $500 and ended with a balance of $600, the increase represents sales that have not been collected from the customers. Therefore, while sales amounted to $3,000, only $2,900 worth of those sales must have been collected in cash. Another way to think about it is first to suppose that customers paid off their old accounts of $500. If total sales were $3,000 and if an ending accounts receivable balance were $600, then $2,400 of the current sales must have been collected. The beginning balance of $500 was collected plus current sales of $2,400 have been collected—making the total cash collected from customers during the period of $2,900. This is the sort of reasoning that must be applied to each item on the income statement to prepare the statement of cash flows using the direct method.

The number for every item on the income statement is potentially different from the cash related to it. For example, sales is potentially different from cash collected from customers. Cost of goods sold is potentially different from cash paid for inventory. Insurance expense is potentially different from the cash paid to the insurance company—and so on, for all items on the income statement.

The change in a current asset or a current liability will reflect the difference between the accrual-based income statement amount and the cash amount. Consider an expense on the income statement. Suppose salary expense is shown on the year's income statement as $75,000. For the statement of cash flows, we want to have cash paid to employees as an operating cash outflow. What could make salary expense different from cash paid to employees? First, we could have paid some employees cash that we owed them from last year. The cash payment would reduce the liability salaries payable. If we did pay some salaries we owed at the beginning of the year, that cash paid would be in addition to any current year's salary paid to employees. What else could make cash paid to employees different from salary expense? We could have incurred salary expense that will not be paid until next year. In other words, we recognized some salary expense that did not get paid to the employees. We must have recorded it as salaries payable. In both cases, the difference between salary expense and cash paid to employees is reflected in the change in salaries payable from the beginning of the year to the end of the year. This is the sort of reasoning that must be applied to each current asset and each current liability on the balance sheet to prepare the statement of cash flows using the indirect method.

Suppose we started the year with salaries payable of $690. Our salary expense for the year, as shown on the income statement, is $75,000. If the balance in salaries payable is $500 at year-end, how much cash was actually paid to employees? First, we must have paid off the amount we owed at the beginning of the year, $690. Then, because the ending balance in salaries payable is $500, we must have paid only $74,500 (= $75,000 − $500) of the current year's salary expense. Thus, the total cash paid to employees is $75,190 (= $690 + $74,500). Another way to interpret what happened is to say that we paid the full $75,000 of this year's expense in cash and we paid down our salaries payable by $190 ($690 down to $500). That total is $75,190.

Using the T-account approach, we can trace the transactions through the salaries payable account:

	Salaries payable	
	$ 690	BB
Cash payments 75,190	75,000	Salaries expense
	500	EB

With those simple examples in mind, let's prepare an entire statement of cash flows.

Robo Company began the year with $25,000 in accounts receivable. During the year, sales totaled $50,000. The year-end accounts receivable balance was $15,000. Using a T-account, determine the amount of cash collected from customers during the year.

Preparing the Statement of Cash Flows

First, the cash from operations section of the statement of cash flows is prepared using one of the following two methods we've already discussed:

1. Direct method: Each item on the accrual-based income statement is converted to cash; or
2. Indirect method: Net income is the starting point, and adjustments are made by adding and subtracting amounts necessary to convert net income into cash.

After you have determined the cash flows from operations, you determine the cash flows from investing activities and cash flows from financing activities. These two sections of the statement of cash flows are prepared by examining the noncurrent assets and noncurrent liabilities in the company's balance sheets at the beginning and the end of the year, and by examining the company's financial records to identify any investing and financing related transactions.

L.O. 3

Know how to prepare a statement of cash flows using the direct method.

Direct Method of Computing Cash from Operations

The direct method of computing cash flows from operations begins with the income statement. Item by item, every amount on the statement is analyzed to determine how much cash was actually collected or disbursed related to that item.

The first item on the income statement is usually revenue. What makes revenue on the income statement different from cash collected from customers? Any cash collected for sales in previous periods—that is, accounts receivable—must be counted as cash collected even though it is not included as revenue. Conversely, any sales for the period for which cash has *not* been collected must be excluded from cash collections. Both cash collected but not counted as revenue and cash not collected but included in revenue can be identified by looking at the change in accounts receivable during the period.

Let's use Tom's Wear's third month of business—March—to see how this works. We start at the beginning of the income statement, shown in Exhibit 10-3, for the month and analyze each amount to change it from accrual to cash.

Exhibit 10-3
Income Statement for Tom's Wear, Inc. for the Month Ended March 31

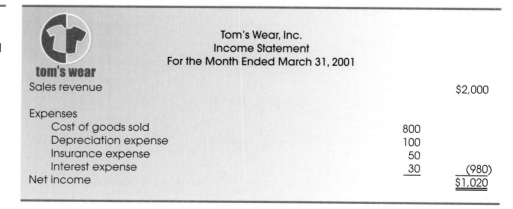

Tom's Wear, Inc.
Income Statement
For the Month Ended March 31, 2001

Sales revenue		$2,000
Expenses		
Cost of goods sold	800	
Depreciation expense	100	
Insurance expense	50	
Interest expense	30	(980)
Net income		$1,020

Exhibit 10-4   Comparative Balance Sheets for Tom's Wear, Inc.

Tom's Wear, Inc.
Balance Sheet
At March 1 and March 31, 2001

tom's wear

	March 31	March 1		March 31	March 1
Cash	$ 3,995	$ 6,695	Accounts payable	$ 0	$ 800
Accounts receivable	2,000	150	Other payables	0	50
Inventory	300	100	Interest payable	30	0
Prepaid insurance	75	125	Notes payable	3,000	0
Prepaid rent	0	0	Total liabilities	$ 3,030	$ 850
Equipment (net of $100	3,900	0			
accumulated			Common stock	5,000	5,000
depreciation)			Retained earnings	2,240	1,220
Total assets	$10,270	$7,070	Total liabilities and shareholders' equity	$10,270	$7,070

Sales on the income statement for March amounted to $2,000. What we need to know for the statement of cash flows is how much cash was collected from customers during March. We need to see how accounts receivable changed during the month. On March 1, 2001, the beginning of the month, Tom's Wear had $150 worth of accounts receivable, and ended the month with $2,000 worth of accounts receivable. By comparing the balance sheet at the beginning of the month with the balance sheet at the end of the month, both shown in Exhibit 10-4 , we can see accounts receivable increased by $1,850. The amount of the change in accounts receivable came from the current period's sales not collected.

One way to compute cash collected from customers is to analyze what happened to accounts receivable. It started with $150. Then during the month, credit sales of $2,000 were made. (That's *sales* on the income statement.) The ending balance in accounts receivable is $2,000. Thus, the cash collected from customers must have been $150 (= $2,000 − $1,850). If you go back and look at the transactions for Tom's Wear during March (in Chapter 3), you'll find *$150 was exactly the amount of cash the company collected from customers.*

Using the T-account approach, start with accounts receivable, where the beginning balance is $150 and the ending balance is $2,000. During the month, $2,000 of credit sales were made. That means total cash collected must have been $150:

Accounts receivable

BB	$ 150		
Credit sales	2,000	150	Cash collections
EB	2,000		

Continuing down the March income statement, the next item is cost of goods sold of $800. This is the cost of the merchandise sold during the month. How does that compare with the amount of cash paid to vendors during the month? Did Tom's Wear sell anything it bought the previous month from the beginning inventory; or did the company buy more goods in March than it actually sold in March? We need to look at what happened to the amount of inventory during the month. The beginning inventory balance was $100. The ending inventory balance was $300. That means Tom's Wear bought enough inventory to sell $800 worth and to build up the inventory by an additional $200. Thus, purchases of inventory must have been $1,000.

Here is the analysis using T-accounts:

Inventory

BB	$ 100	$800		Cost of goods sold
Purchases	1,000			
EB	300			

Did Tom's Wear pay cash for these purchases of inventory?

To see how the purchase of $1,000 worth of inventory compares with the cash paid to vendors, we have to look at the change in accounts payable (to vendors). The beginning balance in accounts payable was $800, and the ending balance was zero. That means Tom's Wear must have paid $1,000 to vendors for the month's purchases *and* the $800 owed from February. Thus, the total paid to vendors was $1,800.

Here is the analysis using the accounts payable T-account:

Accounts payable

		$ 800		**BB**
Cash paid	1,800	1,000		Purchases
		0		**EB**

The next expense on the March 31 income statement is depreciation expense. Depreciation expense is a noncash expense. That means we don't have any cash outflow when we record depreciation expense. The cash we spend to buy equipment is considered an investing cash flow, and our periodic depreciation does not involve cash. Depreciation is one expense we can skip when we are preparing the cash flow from operations using the direct method.

Insurance expense of $50 is shown on the March 31 income statement. How much cash was actually paid for insurance? When a company pays for insurance, the payment is generally recorded as prepaid insurance. Examining the change in prepaid insurance will help us figure out how much cash was paid for insurance during the month. Prepaid insurance started with a balance of $125 and ended with a balance of $75. Because the decrease in prepaid insurance is exactly the same as the insurance expense, Tom's Wear must not have paid for any insurance this month. All the expense came from insurance that was paid for in a previous period.

The T-account analysis confirms that no cash was paid this period.

Prepaid insurance

BB	$125	$50		Insurance expense
Insurance purchased	0			
EB	75			

The last expense we need to consider is interest expense. On the income statement for March, we see interest expense of $30. Did Tom's Wear pay that in cash? On the balance sheet, the company began the month with no interest payable, and ended the month with $30 interest payable. If it started the month without owing any interest and ended the month owing $30, how much of the $30 expense did the company pay for with cash? None. Tom's Wear must not have paid any cash for interest because it owes the entire amount of the expense at year end.

Again, the T-account analysis confirms that no cash was paid for interest.

Interest payable

		$ 0	**BB**
Cash paid	0	30	Interest expense
		30	**EB**

Tom's Wear paid out one more amount of cash related to operations during the month. Can you find it? On the March 1 balance sheet, there is $50 that Tom's Wear owed; it's called *other payables*. By the end of March, that payable has been reduced to zero. Only one thing could have caused that reduction: a cash payment to settle the obligation related to advertising. Thus, we'll also have to put that on the statement of cash flows.

Here is the T-account analysis. The beginning balance was $50, and the ending balance was $0. No expense was recorded for the month. That means cash paid must have been $50.

Other payables

		$50	**BB**
Cash paid	50		
		0	**EB**

To summarize, we have "translated" the accrual amounts found on the income statement to cash amounts for the statement of cash flows. The cash collected from customers was $150. Tom's Wear paid its vendors cash of $1,800. It also paid $50 of other payables. Net cash flow from operations was $(1,700). The operating section of the statement of cash flows is shown in Exhibit 10-5.

Remember, Exhibit 10-5 shows only the cash flow from operations. To explain the entire change in cash from March 1 to March 31, the investing and financing cash flows must be included.

Flex Company began the year 2003 with $350 in prepaid insurance. For 2003, the company's income statement showed insurance expense was $400. Flex Company ended the year with $250 of prepaid insurance. Using a T-account, determine the amount of cash paid for insurance during the year.

STUDY BREAK 10-3
SEE HOW YOU'RE DOING

---

tom's wear

Tom's Wear, Inc.
Partial Statement of Cash Flows
For the Month Ended March 31, 2001

Cash from operations

Cash collected from customers	$ 150
Cash paid to vendors	(1,800)
Cash paid for other expenses	(50)
Net increase (decrease) in cash from operations	**$(1,700)**

Exhibit 10-5
Cash from Operations—
Direct Method

Know how to prepare a statement of cash flows using the indirect method.

If a company uses the direct method, GAAP requires that the company also provide a **reconciliation of net income and cash from operating activities.**This means that the company has to present the indirect method, too. How do you think this requirement affects a company's choice of which method to use?

Indirect Method of Computing Cash from Operations

Even though the Financial Accounting Standards Board (FASB) suggested that companies use the direct method of preparing the statement of cash flows, more than 90% of companies use the indirect method. That's because most accountants think it is easier to prepare the statement of cash flows using the indirect method. Also, the requirement that a company using the direct method provide a **reconciliation of net income and cash from operating activities** means more work for the company using the direct method.

Preparing the statement of cash flows using the indirect method—applied just to the operating section of the statement of cash flows—starts with net income. Following net income, any amounts on the statement that are noncash must be removed to leave only cash amounts. The logic and reasoning we use to prepare the statement of cash flows using the indirect method are not too different from the reasoning we use with the direct method.

Let's start with net income for Tom's Wear for March. Exhibits 10-3 and 10-4 show the numbers we need to prepare the statement of cash flows using the indirect method.

The net income for March was $1,020.

The first adjustment we make is to add back any noncash expenses like depreciation. For Tom's Wear, we add back to net income the $100 depreciation expense. When we calculated the net income of $1,020, we subtracted $100 that was not a cash outflow. Thus, we have to add it back to net income to change net income to a cash number.

Then, just as we do when we prepare the statement of cash flows using the direct method, every amount on the income statement has to be evaluated for its relationship to cash flows. Recall that in the direct method, we use changes in accounts receivable to convert sales revenue into cash collected from customers, and we use changes in inventory and accounts payable to convert cost of goods sold to cash paid to vendors. For the indirect method, if we adjust net income for every change in each current asset—with the exception of cash—and every change in each current liability, we will make every adjustment we need to convert net income into net cash from operations. Let's continue preparing the statement of cash flows using the indirect method with Tom's Wear for March.

We start with net income of $1,020 and add back any noncash expenses. Depreciation of $100 is added back. Then using Exhibit 10-4, we examine each current asset account and each current liability account for changes during the month.

Accounts receivable increased by $1,850. That increase represents sales for which we did not collect any cash yet. Thus, we need to subtract this increase in accounts receivable from net income to convert net income into a cash number.

The next change in a current asset is the increase in inventory of $200. This $200 represents purchases made that have not yet been reported as part of cost of goods sold on the income statement because the items have not been sold. Still, we did pay cash for them (or we'll assume cash was paid and make any adjustment when we examine accounts payable), so the amount needs to be deducted from net income because it was a cash outflow.

Prepaid insurance decreased from $125 to $75. This decrease of $50 was deducted as insurance expense on the income statement, but it was not a cash outflow this period. This amount will have to be added back to net income because it was not a cash outflow.

The last changes in current assets and current liabilities are the changes in payables. Tom's Wear started the month with $800 of accounts payable and $50 of other payables. Tom's Wear ended the month with a zero amount of each of these. The other current liability is interest payable. It started the month with no interest payable but ended the month with $30 of interest payable. The total change in current liabilities is a net decrease of $820. This $820 amount was not included on the income statement—*not* deducted in the calculation of net income. Because the amount was a cash outflow, we need to deduct an additional $820 from net income to finish converting net income into cash from operations.

Following the example in the text, you can use the indirect method of preparing a statement of cash flows with a spreadsheet as follows:

A Spreadsheet Approach to Computing Cash from Operations with the Indirect Method

	A	B	C	D	E	F	G	H
1			Tom's Wear, Inc.					
2			Spreadsheet for Operating Activities Statement of Cash Flow					
3			(Indirect Method) For the month ended March 31, 2001					
4								
5			March 1,		Analysis of Changes			March
6			2001		Debit		Credit	31, 2001
7	**Balance Sheet: Debits**							
8	Cash		$6,695				$2,700	$3,995
9	Accounts receivable		150	(b)	$1,850			2,000
10	Inventory		100	(c)	200			300
11	Prepaid insurance		125			(d)	50	75
12	Plant assets		0		4,000			4,000
13			$7,070					$10,370
14	**Balance Sheet: Credits**							
15	Accumulated depreciation		$0			(e)	$100	$100
16	Accounts payable		800	(f)	$800			0
17	Other payables		50	(g)	50			0
18	Interest payable		0			(h)	30	30
19	Notes payable		0				3,000	3,000
20	Common stock		5,000					5,000
21	Retained earnings		1,220			(a)	1,020	2,240
22			$7,070					$10,370
23								
24	**Operating Activities**							
25	Net income			(a)	$1,020			
26	Increase in accounts receivable					(b)	$1,850	
27	Increase in inventory					(c)	200	
28	Decrease in prepaid insurance			(d)	50			
29	Depreciation expense			(e)	100			
30	Decrease in accounts payable					(f)	800	
31	Decrease in other payables					(g)	50	
32	Increase in interest payable			(h)	30			
33					$8,100		$9,800	
34	Net increase (decrease in cash from operations)						(1,700)	
35					$8,100		$8,100	
36								

Exhibit 10-6
Cash from Operations—Indirect
Method

tom's wear

Tom's Wear, Inc.
Partial Statement of Cash Flows
For the Month Ended March 31, 2001

Net income	$ 1,020
+ Depreciation expense	100
− Increase in accounts receivable	(1,850)
− Increase in inventory	(200)
+ Decrease in prepaid insurance	50
− Decrease in payables	(820)
Net cash from operations	**$(1,700)**

Look at the operating section of the statement of cash flows for Tom's Wear for March in Exhibit 10-6. The statement starts with net income and makes all the adjustments we discussed. Compare the operating section of this statement of cash flows prepared using the indirect method with the operating section we prepared using the direct method shown in Exhibit 10-5. The net cash flow from operations is the same no matter how we prepare it—when we prepare the statement by examining every cash transaction, as we did in Chapter 3, when we prepare it using the direct method; as we did earlier in this chapter; and when we prepare it using the indirect method, as we just did in this chapter. Which way is easier to understand? The presentation produced by the direct method—the presentation shown in Exhibit 10-5—gives details about cash that are easier to understand than the details provided by the indirect method. Still, over 90% of companies today use the indirect method. A change in this practice could be a real benefit to users of financial statements.

**STUDY BREAK 10-4
SEE HOW YOU'RE DOING**

What's the major difference between the direct and indirect methods of presenting the statement of cash flows? What are the similarities?

Cash from Investing and Financing Activities

In addition to cash from operations, there are two other sections of the statement of cash flows: cash from investing activities and cash from financing activities. No matter which method you use to prepare the statement of cash flows, direct or indirect, the cash from investing activities and cash from financing activities sections are prepared the same way—by reviewing noncurrent balance sheet accounts. The primary amounts on the balance sheet to review are property, plant, and equipment; notes payable; bonds payable; common stock; and retained earnings.

For Tom's Wear during March, start in the noncurrent assets section of the balance sheet. The balance sheet at March 31 shows equipment with a cost of $4,000. The carrying value is $3,900 and the accumulated depreciation is $100, for a total cost of $4,000. The asset representing this equipment *was not* on the March 1 balance sheet, so Tom must have purchased $4,000 worth of equipment during March. The purchase of equipment is an investing cash flow. When we see that a company purchased a noncurrent asset, we must investigate how the company paid for the asset. In this case, we find that Tom paid cash of $1,000 and signed a note for $3,000. We include only the $1,000 cash outflow in the statement of cash flows, but we must add a footnote disclosing the amount of the loan and its purpose. All investing and financing activities must be disclosed, even if there was no cash involved.

Next we review the liability section of the balance sheet for changes in non-current liabilities. Notice that on the balance sheet at March 1, Tom's Wear shows no notes payable. On the balance sheet at March 31, notes payable shows a balance of $3,000. That means Tom borrowed $3,000 during March. Again, when we discover such a change, we must find out the details of the transaction before we can decide how the transaction affects the statement of cash flows. Generally, borrowing money using a long-term note would result in a financing cash inflow. However, in this case, the note was given in exchange for equipment.

Notice that the loan is disclosed, even though the amount is not included on the statement of cash flows. Whenever a company engages in a financing or investing activity, it must be disclosed on the statement of cash flows, even though the company never actually received or paid out any cash. The cash is considered *implicit* in the transaction. It's *as if* Tom's Wear received the cash from the loan and immediately turned around and purchased the equipment with it.

Other transactions we should look for when preparing the financing section of the statement of cash flows include any principal payments on loans, any new capital contributions—such as stock issued or dividends paid to the stockholders. For Tom's Wear for March 2001, none of these transactions took place.

When we put the information about investing activities and financing activities with the cash from operations we have already prepared, we have all the information we need to complete the statement of cash flows. Look at the two statements in Exhibits 10-7 and 10-8. Then look back to Chapter 3 and find the statement of cash flows in the solution to the summary problem. We used different methods to prepare the statements, but they are similar in form and amounts.

Check it out. The balance sheets in Exhibit 10-4 show that cash went from $6,695 on March 1 to $3,995 on March 31. The difference is a $2,700 decrease in cash. Explaining that change in the cash balance is the purpose of the statement of cash flows.

---

tom's wear

Tom's Wear, Inc.
Statement of Cash Flows
For the Month Ended
March 31, 2001

Exhibit 10-7
Statement of Cash Flows (Direct)

Cash from operations		
Cash collected from customers	$ 150	
Cash paid to vendors	(1,800)	
Cash paid for other expenses	(50)	
Net cash from operations		$(1,700)
Cash from investing activities		
Purchase of equipment	$(1,000)ᵃ	
Net cash from investing activities		(1,000)
Cash from financing activities		0
Net increase (decrease) in cash		$(2,700)

ᵃEquipment was purchased for $4,000. A note was signed for $3,000 and cash paid was $1,000.

Exhibit 10-8
Statement of Cash Flows (Indirect)

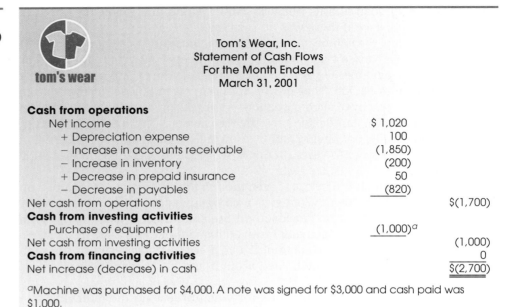

Tom's Wear, Inc.
Statement of Cash Flows
For the Month Ended
March 31, 2001

Cash from operations		
Net income	$ 1,020	
+ Depreciation expense	100	
− Increase in accounts receivable	(1,850)	
− Increase in inventory	(200)	
+ Decrease in prepaid insurance	50	
− Decrease in payables	(820)	
Net cash from operations		$(1,700)
Cash from investing activities		
Purchase of equipment	(1,000)[a]	
Net cash from investing activities		(1,000)
Cash from financing activities		0
Net increase (decrease) in cash		$(2,700)

[a]Machine was purchased for $4,000. A note was signed for $3,000 and cash paid was $1,000.

Summary of Direct and Indirect Methods

There are two ways, both ways acceptable using GAAP, to prepare and present the statement of cash flows: the direct method and the indirect method. The direct method provides more detail about cash from operating activities. It shows the individual operating cash flows. When a company uses the direct method, GAAP requires that the company also show a reconciliation of operating cash flows to net income in a supplemental schedule. That reconciliation looks exactly like the operating section of the statement of cash flows using the indirect method.

The indirect presentation of the statement of cash flow is easier to prepare from the income statement and the beginning and ending balance sheets for the period, but the presentation of the information is not easily understood. A company that uses the indirect method must make separate disclosures for cash paid for interest and cash paid for taxes somewhere in the financial statements. This is required by GAAP.

Keep in mind that the investing activities and the financing activities sections for the two methods are identical; and the total net cash flow is the same for both methods.

Financial Statement Analysis

Know how to do a simple analysis of the statement of cash flows.

Look at the statement of cash flows for Home Depot, Inc., shown in Exhibit 10-9. First, notice the organization of the statement. The statement has the three required parts: (1) cash provided by operations, (2) cash flows from investing activities, and (3) cash flows from financing activities. Second, notice the first section—cash provided by operations—is prepared using the indirect method. The statement starts with the amount for *net earnings*—another name for *net income*—and makes several adjustments to that amount. Look at the adjustments and see if you understand what information they provide. For example,

Exhibit 10-9

Consolidated Statements of Cash Flows

The Home Depot, Inc. and Subsidiaries

(Amounts in millions)	Fiscal Year Ended		
	January 30, 2000	January 31, 1999	February 1, 1998
Cash provided from operations			
Net earnings	$2,320	$1,614	$1,160
Reconciliation of net earnings to net cash provided by operations			
Depreciation and amortization	463	373	283
(Increase) decrease in receivables, net	(85)	85	(166)
Increase in merchandise inventories	(1,142)	(698)	(885)
Increase in accounts payable and accrued expenses	820	423	577
Increase in income taxes payable	93	59	83
Other	(23)	61	(23)
Net cash provided by operations	2,446	1,917	1,029
Cash flows from investing activities			
Capital expenditures, net of $37, $41, and $44 of noncash capital expenditures in fiscal 1999, 1998, and 1997, respectively	(2,581)	(2,053)	(1,420)
Purchase of remaining interest in The Home Depot Canada	—	(261)	—
Payments for businesses acquired, net	(101)	(6)	(61)
Proceeds from sales of property and equipment	87	45	85
Purchases of investments	(32)	(2)	(194)
Proceeds from maturities of investments	30	4	599
Advances secured by real estate, net	(25)	2	20
Net cash used in investing activities	(2,622)	(2,271)	(971)
Cash flows from financing activities			
(Repayments) issuance of commercial paper obligations, net	(246)	246	—
Proceeds from long-term borrowings, net	522	—	15
Repayments of long-term debt	(14)	(8)	(40)
Proceeds from sale of common stock, net	267	167	122
Cash dividends paid to stockholders	(255)	(168)	(139)
Minority interest contributions to partnership	7	11	10
Net cash provided by (used in) financing activities	281	248	(32)
Effect of exchange rate changes on cash and cash equivalents	1	(4)	—
Increase (decrease) in cash and cash equivalents	$ 106	$(110)	$ 26
Cash and cash equivalents at beginning of year	62	172	146
Cash and cash equivalents at end of year	168	62	172
Supplemental disclosure of cash payments made for			
Interest, net of interest capitalized	26	36	42
Income taxes	$1,396	$ 940	$ 685

depreciation and amortization are added back to net income to work toward cash from operations because the amounts for depreciation and amortization were *subtracted* in the original computation of net income but they were not cash expenditures. That subtraction is *undone* by adding the amounts back to net income. Investors are looking for a positive cash flow from operations. In the long run, this is crucial for the continuing success of any business.

The cash flows from investing activities section of the statement shows capital expenditures as the first entry. Those are items like property, plant, and equipment. Recall the discussion in Chapter 5 about capital versus revenue expenditures—capitalizing a cost versus expensing a cost. These are costs that have been capitalized by Home Depot. Other entries in the cash flows from investing activities section include cash inflows and outflows related to the purchase and sale of assets *not* related to the normal operations of Home Depot. (When Home Depot buys the items that it resells in the normal course of business, the cash flows are included in the first section—cash provided from operations.) The cash flow from investing activities section of the statement of cash flows gives information about the company's plans for the future. Investments in property, plant, and equipment may indicate an expansion or, at the very least, a concern about keeping the company's infrastructure up to date. Over time, a company's failure to invest in the infrastructure may indicate a problem.

The cash flows from financing activities section of the statement of cash flows shows the cash flows related to the way the company is financed. Some of the items should be recognizable—proceeds from sale of stock, long-term borrowings, and dividends paid. Other items are beyond the scope of an introductory course. However, all of them relate to the Home Depot financing. This information, when combined with the information on the balance sheet, gives the financial statement user a complete picture of the way the company is financing the business.

We should consider two more characteristics of the statement. First, following the calculation of the net cash flow for the year, the reconciliation from the year's beginning cash balance to the year's ending cash balance is shown. Second, there is supplementary information disclosed concerning the cash paid for interest and the cash paid for taxes during the year. This is required by GAAP.

Free cash flow is net cash from operations minus dividends and minus capital expenditures.

When analyzing the statement of cash flows, managers and analysts often calculate one more amount called **free cash flow**. Free cash flow is defined as *cash flows from operations minus dividends and capital expenditures*. This gives a measure of a firm's ability to engage in long-term investment opportunities. It is sometimes seen as a measure of a company's financial flexibility.

The net change in cash, $106 million, can be traced back to the comparative balance sheets for Home Depot. At the beginning of the year, the cash balance was $62 million. At the end of the year, the cash balance was $168 million. The purpose of the statement of cash flows is to describe in detail this change in the cash balance.

The statement of cash flows is a crucial part of the financial reporting for any company. Often creditors and investors will look at this statement first when they are analyzing the financial condition of a firm. For the firm, however, the importance of the statement of cash flows is tied to the cash budget and how the actual sources and uses of cash compare to the budgeted amounts. This analysis is an important function of **managerial accounting.**

Managerial accounting is the study of how managers use accounting information that is internal to the firm—that information is generally not shown on the financial statements.

The statement of cash flows provides important information for managers, creditors, and investors. In corporate annual reports, the statement of cash flows is presented with the other three basic financial statements—the income statement, the balance sheet, and the statement of changes in shareholders' equity—to provide information needed to evaluate a company's performance and to provide a basis for predicting a company's future potential.

Summary Problem: Tom's Wear for April 2001 Revisited

The income statement for Tom's Wear for April is shown in Exhibit 10-10 (and is also given in the solution to the summary problem for Chapter 5). The comparative balance sheets at March 31 and April 30 are shown in Exhibit 10-11.

Required
Use this information to prepare the statement of cash flows for April, first using the direct method and then the indirect method.

Exhibit 10-10 Income Statement

tom's wear

Tom's Wear, Inc.
For the Month Ended
April 30, 2001

Sales revenue		$ 8,000
Expenses		
Cost of goods sold	$3,200	
Insurance expense	50	
Rent expense	600	
Depreciation expense	825	
Other operating expenses	300	
Interest expense	280	(5,255)
Net income		$ 2,745

Exhibit 10-11 Comparative Balance Sheets

tom's wear

Tom's Wear, Inc.
Balance Sheet
At April 30 and
March 31

	April 30	March 31		April 30	March 31
Cash	$3,295	$ 3,995	Accounts payable	$ 4,000	$ 0
Accounts receivable	8,000	2,000	Other payables	0	0
Inventory	1,100	300	Interest payable	310	30
Prepaid insurance	25	75	Currrent portion of Notes payable	3,000	3,000
			Total current liabilities	7,310	3,030
Prepaid rent	1,800	0	Notes payable	30,000	0
Total current assets	14,220	6,370	Total liabilities	37,310	3,030
Equipment (net of $200 and $100 accumulated depreciation)	3,800	3,900	Common stock	5,000	5,000
			Retained earnings	4,985	2,240
Van (net of $725 accumulated depreciation)	29,275	0			
Total assets	$47,295	$10,270	Total liabilities and shareholders' equity	$47,295	$10,270

Understanding Excel

In this exercise you prepare a statement of cash flow for Tom's Wear, Inc. for the month of August, 2001 (indirect method).

Requirements:

1. Open a new Excel work sheet.
2. Beginning in cell A1, input the following chart. Resize columns and wrap text as required. You may also choose the font type and size as desired. Use appropriate formulas to calculate the change in the balances.

3. Beginning in cell F1, prepare a statement of cash flows for Tom's Wear, Inc. for the month ended August 31. Use appropriate headings, formats, and formulas.

   Hint: To change a negative number to a positive, multiple your formula or input cell by "−1."

4. Print your file and save it to disk. Name your file TomsWear10.

	July 31, 2001	August 31, 2001	Change
Assets			
Cash	$ 17,151	$ 980,476	
Accounts receivable	105,100	207,610	
Allowance for doubtful accounts	(3,290)	(6,335)	
Inventory	8,910	24,584	
Prepaids	800	700	
Land	7,500	7,500	
Equipment	4,000	104,000	
Accumulated depreciation, equipment	(500)	(600)	
Van	30,000	130,000	
Accumulated depreciation, van	(4,205)	(7,105)	
Building	67,500	67,500	
Accumulated depreciation, building	(130)	(260)	
Total assets	$232,836	$1,508,070	
Liabilities and Equity			
Accounts payable	$ 36,000	$ 6,000	
Interest payable	1,500	2,250	
Warranty liability	2,239	3,204	
Notes payable*	105,000	105,000	
Common stock	5,000	7,500	
Additional paid-in capital	0	1,247,500	
Retained earnings	83,097	136,616	
Total liabilities and shareholders' equity	$232,836	$1,508,070	

Note: Current and long-term notes and mortgages did not change and are combined here to simplify the presentation.

Answers to Study Break Questions

The three classifications are (1) operating cash flows (e.g., payment from customers is an inflow and payment to employees is an outflow); (2) financing (e.g., owners contributing cash to a business is an inflow, and the company paying dividends is an outflow); and (3) investing cash flows (e.g., the sale of a long-term asset is an inflow, and the purchase of equipment that will be used for more than 1 year is an outflow).

Robo probably collected the beginning accounts receivable first during the year, for a cash collection of $25,000. Then sales of $50,000 were made. Because the accounts receivable balance at year-end was $15,000, then $35,000 worth of the sales has been collected. Thus, total cash inflow from customers = $25,000 + 35,000 = **$60,000.** Another way to look at the problem is to take sales of $50,000 and adjust that for the change in accounts receivable. Because the change is a $10,000 decrease in accounts receivable, that would be $10,000 of collections, making the cash inflow from customers $50,000 + 10,000 = **$60,000.** Cash collected from customers should be reported in the cash from operations section of the statement of cash flows.

	Accounts receivable		
BB	$25,000		
Sales	50,000	60,000	Cash collected
EB	$15,000		

Start by thinking about the expense as a cash outflow and then adjusting it for why it is not all cash. Insurance expense is $400. Then look at the change in prepaid insurance. It started at $350 and ended at $250. That means $100 of prepaid insurance was used. That reduction in prepaid insurance must be part of the $400 expense shown on the income statement. Thus, the cash paid for insurance must have been **$300** (= $400 − $100).

	Prepaid insurance		
BB	$350		
Cash paid	300	400	Insurance expense
EB	$250		

The major difference between the two is the way the cash from operations section is presented. Even though the amount of cash from operations is the same, the method used to calculate the number is different. The other parts—cash from investing activities and cash from financing activities—are exactly the same.

Solution to Summary Problem

tom's wear

Tom's Wear, Inc.
Statement of Cash Flows
For the Month Ended April 30, 2001

Cash from operating activities (direct)		
Cash collected from customers	$ 2,000	
Cash paid for rent	(2,400)	
Cash paid for other operating expenses	(300)	
Total cash from operations		$(700)
Cash from investing activities		0
Cash from financing activities		0
Net increase (decrease) in cash		$(700)

Note: A long-term note for $30,000 was issued to purchase a van.

(If the company had received the cash and then purchased the van, there would be a $30,000 outflow from investing activities for the purchase of the van, and a $30,000 inflow from financing activities from the note payable.)

Solution details for the direct method follow.

Cash collected from customers	
Sales	$ 8,000
– Increase in accounts receivable	(6,000)
	$2,000
Cash paid to vendors	
Cost of goods sold	$ 3,200
+ Increase in inventory	800
– Increase in accounts payable	(4,000)
	0
Cash paid for insurance	
Insurance expense	$ 50
– Decrease in prepaid insurance	(50)
	0
Cash paid for rent	
Rent expense	$ 600
+ Increase in prepaid rent	1,800
	$2,400
Cash paid for other operating expenses	
Other operating expenses	$ 300
No balance sheet items	
related to this expense	0
	$ 300
Cash paid for interest expense	
Interest expense	$ 280
– Increase in interest payable	(280)
	0

Solution for indirect method follows.

Tom's Wear, Inc.
Statement of Cash Flows
For the Month Ended April 30, 2001

Cash from operating activities (indirect)		
Net income	$ 2,745	
+ Depreciation expense	825	
– Increase in accounts receivable	(6,000)	
– Increase in inventory	(800)	
+ Decrease in prepaid insurance	50	
– Increase in prepaid rent	(1,800)	
+ Increase in accounts payable	4,000	
+ Increase in interest payable	280	
Net cash from operations		$(700)
Cash from investing activities		0
Cash from financing activities		0
Net increase (decrease) in cash		$(700)

Note: A long-term note for $30,000 was issued to purchase a van.

Solution details for indirect method follow.

	A	B	C	D	E	F	G	H
1					Tom's Wear, Inc.			
2				Spreadsheet for Statement of Cash Flow (Indirect Method)				
3				For the month ended April 30, 2001				
4								
5			March 31,		Analysis of Changes			April 30,
6			2001		Debit		Credit	2001
7	**Balance Sheet: Debits**							
8	Cash		$3,995			©	$700	$3,295
9	Accounts receivable		2,000	(b)	$6,000			8,000
10	Inventory		300	(c)	800			1,100
11	Prepaid insurance		75			(d)	50	25
12	Prepaid rent		0	(e)	1,800			1,800
13	Equipment		4,000					4,000
14	Van		0	(i-1)	30,000			30,000
15			$10,370					$48,220
16	**Balance Sheet: Credits**							
17	Accumulated depreciation		$100			(f)	$825	$925
18	Accounts payable		0			(g)	4,000	4,000
19	Other payables		0					0
20	Interest payable		30			(h)	280	310
21	Current portion of notes payable		3,000					3,000
22	Notes payable		0			(i-2)	30,000	30,000
23	Common stock		5,000					5,000
24	Retained earnings		2,240			(a)	2,745	4,985
25			$10,370					$48,220
26								
27	**Statement of Cash Flows**							
28	Operating activities							
29	Net income			(a)	$2,745			
30	Increase in accounts receivable					(b)	$6,000	
31	Increase in inventory					(c)	800	
32	Decrease in prepaid insurance			(d)	50			
33	Increase in prepaid rent					(e)	1,800	
34	Depreciation expense			(f)	825			
35	Increase in accounts payable			(g)	4,000			
36	Increase in interest payable			(h)	280			
37	**Non-cash investing and financing activities**							
38	Purchase of a van with a note			(i-2)	30,000	(i-1)	30,000	
39					$46,500		$47,200	
40	Net increase (decrease) in cash					(j)	(700)	
41					$46,500		$46,500	
42								

Questions

1. What is the purpose of the statement of cash flows?
2. Define the three types of cash flows shown on the statement of cash flows.
3. Why is the statement of cash flows so important to a company?
4. Explain how modern technology could enable a company to prepare the statement of cash flows using a *very* direct method—identifying each cash flow, as we have done with Tom's Wear.
5. What are the two traditional ways of preparing and presenting the statement of cash flows? Which is easier for a reader to interpret?
6. Give three examples of transactions that would be classified as cash flows from operations.
7. Give three examples of transactions that would be classified as cash flows from investing activities.
8. Give three examples of transactions that would be classified as cash flows from financing activities.
9. How is depreciation expense treated when using the direct method of preparing the statement of cash flows? How is this expense treated when using the indirect method?
10. How is interest, collected or paid, classified on the statement of cash flows?

Short Exercises

L.O. 10-1

SE10-1 One common reason for small business failure is the lack of planning concerning cash flows. Explain this problem and why cash planning is so important to the successful operation of a business.

L.O. 10-2

SE10-2 Given the following cash transactions, classify each as a cash flow from (1) operating activities, (2) investing activities, or (3) financing activities:

a. payment to employees for work done
b. dividends paid to shareholders
c. payment for new equipment
d. payment to vendor for inventory
e. interest payment to the bank related to a loan

L.O. 10-2

SE10-3 Given the following cash transactions, classify each as a cash flow from: (1) operating activities, (2) investing activities, or (3) financing activities:

a. principal payment to the bank for a loan
b. collection from customers to whom sales were previously made on account
c. collection from customers for cash sales
d. collection for sale of land that had been purchased as a possible factory site
e. cash used to pay for doughnuts for staff

L.O. 10-3

SE10-4 College Television Company had Supplies worth $20,000 on its balance sheet at December 31, 2003. The income statement for 2004 showed a supplies expense of $50,000. The balance sheet at December 31, 2004 showed supplies of $25,000. If no supplies were purchased on account (all were cash purchases), how much cash did College Television Company spend on supplies during 2004? How would that cash outflow be classified on the statement of cash flows?

L.O. 10-3

SE10-5 Jill Corp. reported sales of $950,000 for 2001. Jill's accounts receivable from sales were $40,000 at the beginning of 2001 and $50,000 at the end of 2001. What was the amount of cash collected from customers in 2001?

L.O. 10-3

SE10-6 A building cost $55,000 and had accumulated depreciation of $15,000 when it was sold for a gain of $5,000. It was a cash sale. Where would the cash from this transaction appear on the statement of cash flows?

SE10-7 Sales for 2005 were $50,000; cost of goods sold was $35,000. If accounts receivable increased by $2,000, inventory decreased by $1,300, accounts payable decreased by $2,000, and other accrued liabilities decreased by $1,000, how much cash was paid to vendors and suppliers during the year?

L.O. 10-3

SE10-8 During 2004, Cameron Company had $300,000 in cash sales and $3,500,000 in credit sales. The accounts receivable balances were $450,000 and $530,000 at December 31, 2003 and 2004, respectively. What was the total cash collected from all customers during 2004?

L.O. 10-3

SE10-9 The income statement for Lilly's Company for the year ended June 30, 2004 showed sales of $50,000. During the year, the balance in accounts receivable increased by $7,500. What adjustment to net income would be shown in the operating section of the statement of cash flows prepared using the indirect method related to this information? How much cash was collected from customers during the fiscal year ended June 30, 2004?

L.O. 10-3, 4

SE10-10 The income statement for Sharp Inc. for the month of May showed insurance expense of $250. The beginning and ending balance sheets for the month showed an increase of $50 in prepaid insurance. There were no payables related to insurance on the balance sheet. What adjustment to net income would be shown in the operating section of the statement of cash flows prepared using the indirect method related to this information? How much cash was paid for insurance during the month?

L.O. 10-3, 4

SE10-11 During 2003, Cable Direct Inc. incurred salary expense of $37,500, as shown on the income statement. The January 1, 2003 balance sheet showed salaries payable of $10,450; and the December 31, 2003 balance sheet showed salaries payable of $15,200. What adjustment to net income would be shown in the operating section of the statement of cash flows prepared using the indirect method related to this information? How much cash was paid to employees (for salary) during 2003?

L.O. 10-3, 4

SE10-12 Havelen's Road Paving Company had a depreciation expense of $43,000 on the income statement for the year. How would this be shown on the statement of cash flows prepared using the indirect method? Why?

L.O. 10-4

SE10-13 Beta Company spent $40,000 for a new delivery truck during the year. Depreciation expense of $2,000 related to the truck was shown on the income statement. How are the purchase of the truck and the related depreciation reflected on the statement of cash flows prepared using the indirect method?

L.O. 10-4

SE10-14 If you were interested in investing in a company, what item or items on the statement of cash flows would be of most interest to you? Why?

L.O. 10-4

Exercises

E10-1 For each of the following items, tell whether it is a cash inflow or a cash outflow and the section of the statement of cash flows in which the item would appear.

L.O. 10-2

Item	Inflow or outflow	Section of the statement
(a) Cash collected from customers		
(b) Proceeds from issuing stock		
(c) Interest payment on loan		
(d) Principal repayment of loan		
(e) Cash paid for advertising		
(f) Proceeds from sale of treasury stock		
(g) Money borrowed from the local bank		
(h) Cash paid to employees (salaries)		
(i) Purchase of equipment		
(j) Cash paid to vendors for inventory		
(k) Taxes paid		

L.O. 10-2

E10-2 For each of the following transactions, give the section of the statement of cash flows prepared using the direct method in which the item would be found:

a. issued 100 shares of $2 par common stock for $12 per share
b. borrowed $5,000 from a local bank to expand the business
c. purchased supplies for $400 cash
d. paid a carpenter $500 cash to build some bookcases for the office
e. earned revenue of $9,000 cash
f. hired a student to do some typing and paid him $300 cash
g. repaid $1,000 of the bank loan along with $150 interest
h. paid dividends of $400

L.O. 10-3

E10-3 Use the income statement for Clark Corp. and the information from the comparative balance sheets shown for the beginning and the end of the year to prepare the operating section of the statement of cash flows using the direct method.

Sales	$100,000	
Cost of goods sold	35,000	
Gross margin		$65,000
Operating expenses		
Wages	$ 2,500	
Rent	1,200	
Utilities	980	
Insurance	320	5,000
Net income		$60,000

Account	Beginning of the year	End of the year
Accounts receivable	$10,000	$12,000
Inventory	21,000	18,500
Prepaid insurance	575	400
Accounts payable	9,000	10,400
Wages payable	850	600
Utilities payable	150	0

L.O. 10-4

E10-4 Use the information from E10-3 to prepare the operating section of the statement of cash flows using the indirect method. Then compare it with the statement you prepared for E10-3. What are the similarities? What are the differences? Which do you find more informative?

L.O. 10-3

E10-5 Given the following information, calculate the change in cash for the year:

Cash received from sale of equipment	$ 20,000
Cash paid for salaries	8,250
Depreciation expense for the year	12,450
Cash received from issuing stock	150,000
Cash collected from customers	87,900
Cash received from sale of land	14,500
Cash paid for operating expenses	2,000
Cash paid to vendor for inventory	32,480

L.O. 10-3

E10-6 Use the information for Sharp Company to calculate:

a. cash paid for salaries
b. cash paid for income taxes
c. cash paid for inventory
d. cash collected from customers

From the financial statements for Sharp Company	Income statement amount for the year	Balance sheet Beginning of the year	Balance sheet End of the year
Sales revenue	$95,600		
Accounts receivable		$8,700	$10,000
Salary expense	31,400		
Salaries payable		2,300	2,100
Cost of goods sold	24,300		
Inventory		4,800	9,000
Accounts payable		2,500	3,000
Income tax expense	28,500		
Income taxes payable		7,400	8,200

E10-7 The following events occurred at Gadgets, Inc., during 2004:

L.O. 10-3, 4

January	Issued bonds for $250,000
February	Purchased new machinery for $80,000
March	Sold old machinery for $30,000, resulting in a $10,000 loss
April	Paid interest of $20,000 on bonds issued in prior years
May	Borrowed $5,000 from a local bank
June	Purchased a new computer for $3,000
July	Paid cash dividends of $4,600

Compute Gadgets' net cash flow from (1) investing activities and from (2) financing activities for the year ended December 31, 2004.

E10-8 The following information applies to Computer Company:

L.O. 10-3

Income Statement for the Year Ended 2002

Sales	20,000
Cost of goods sold	(15,200)
Gross margin	4,800
Rent expense	(1,000)
Net income	$ 3,800

- Accounts receivable started the year with a balance of $1,000 and ended the year with a balance of $3,300.
- The beginning balance in accounts payable (to vendors) was $2,000, and the ending balance was zero. Inventory at the end of the year was the same as it was at the beginning of the year (i.e., there was no change in inventory).
- The company started the year with $5,000 of prepaid rent, and ended the year with $4,000 of prepaid rent.

For 2002, give the amount of cash that was

a. collected from customers for sales   c. paid for rent
b. paid to vendors for inventory

E10-9 The following information has been taken from the most recent statement of cash flows of Expansion Company:

L.O. 10-5

Net cash used by operating activities	$ (932,000)
Net cash provided by investing activities	1,180,500
Net cash provided by financing activities	2,107,000

a. What information do these subtotals from the statement of cash flows tell you about Expansion Company?
b. What additional information would you want to see before you analyze the ability of Expansion Company to generate positive operating cash flows in the future?
c. Can you tell if Expansion had a positive net income for the period? What information would you like to see to help you predict next year's net income?

Problems — Set A

L.O. 10-1, 2, 3, 4, 5

P10-1A   The Samsula Service income statement for the year ended December 31, 2005 and the balance sheets at December 31, 2004 and December 31, 2005 follow.

Samsula Service Company
Income Statement
For the Year Ended December 31, 2005
(In Thousands, Except Earnings per Share)

Service revenue		$92,000
Expenses		
Wages and salaries	$60,000	
Advertising	10,000	
Rent	4,800	
Depreciation	3,600	
Miscellaneous	5,200	
Total expenses		83,600
Income before taxes		8,400
Income taxes		2,940
Net income		5,460
Earnings per share		0.55

Samsula Service Company
Comparative Balance Sheets
($ in Thousands)

	December 31, 2005		December 31, 2004	
Assets				
Current assets:				
Cash		$ 6,910		$ 3,500
Accounts receivable		12,000		14,000
Supplies		200		370
Prepaid advertising		800		660
Total current assets		$19,910		$18,530
Property, plant, and equipment				
Equipment	$ 44,000		$ 40,000	
Less: Accumulated depreciation	(21,600)		(18,000)	
Total property, plant, and equipment		22,400		22,000
Total assets		$42,310		$40,530
Liabilities and stockholders' equity				
Current liabilities				
Wages and salaries payable		$ 2,700		$ 3,300
Taxes payable		1,900		1,780
Total current liabilities		4,600		5,080
Stockholders' equity				
Common stock	$30,000		$ 30,000	
Retained earnings	7,710		5,450	
		37,710		35,450
Total liabilities and stockholders' equity		$42,310		$40,530

Required:

a. Prepare a statement of cash flows for the year ended December 31, 2005 using (1) the direct method and (2) the indirect method.

b. Why is this information important to the company and to parties outside the company?

c. As a user, which format would you prefer and why?

P10-2A The following information is from the comparative balance sheets of Reba's Record Company at December 31, 2003 and 2002:

L.O. 10-4

	At December 31	
(In thousands)	**2003**	**2002**
Current assets		
Cash	$3,500	$2,990
Accounts receivable	1,825	2,200
Inventory	2,150	1,380
Prepaid rent	320	270
Total current assets	$7,795	$6,840
Current liabilities		
Accounts payable	$1,890	$1,050
Salaries payable	2,500	3,800
Total current liabilities	$4,390	$4,850

Net income for 2003 was $356,000. Depreciation expense of $135,000 was included in the operating expenses for the year.

Required: Prepare the cash from operations section of the statement of cash flows using the indirect method for Reba's Record Company for the year ended December 31, 2003.

P10-3A The following information comes from the balance sheets of TCB Company at June 30, 2004 and 2003:

L.O. 10-4

TCB Company
Information from Balance Sheets
June 30, 2004, and June 30, 2003
Current Assets and Current Liabilities Only

(In thousands)	**2004**	**2003**
Current assets		
Cash	$2,110	$2,650
Accounts receivable	1,254	977
Inventory	730	856
Prepaid insurance	127	114
Total current assets	$4,221	$4,597
Current liabilities		
Accounts payable	$1,054	$1,330
Wages payable	2,100	1,750
Total current liabilities	$3,154	$3,080

Net income for the year ended June 30, 2004 was $86,900. Included in the operating expenses for the year was depreciation expense of $102,000.

Required: Prepare the cash from operating activities section of the TCB Company statement of cash flows for the year ended June 30, 2004. Use the indirect method.

L.O. 10-4

P10-4A Ridge Oak Land Corp. had the following information available for 2005:

	January 1	December 31
Accounts receivable	$78,000	$71,000
Prepaid insurance	48,000	36,000
Inventory	56,000	75,000

Ridge Oak Land Corp. reported net income of $270,000 for the year. Depreciation expense, included on the income statement, was $24,200.

Required: Assume this is all the information relevant to the statement of cash flows. Prepare the cash flow from operating activities section of the Powers Corp. statement of cash flows.

L.O. 10-3, 4

P10-5A To prepare its statement of cash flows for the year ended December 31, 2003, Myers Company gathered the following information:

Loss on sale of machinery	$ 8,000
Proceeds from sale of machinery	50,000
Proceeds from bond issue (face value $100,000)	80,000
Amortization of bond discount	1,000
Dividends declared	25,000
Dividends paid	15,000
Purchase of treasury stock	30,000

Required: Prepare the cash from investing section of the statement of cash flows for Myers Company for the year ended December 31, 2003.

L.O. 10-3, 4

P10-6A To prepare its statement of cash flows for the year ended December 31, 2005, Martin Company gathered the following information:

Gain on sale of equipment	$ 4,000
Proceeds from sale of equipment	10,000
Purchase of equipment	80,000
Dividends declared	5,000
Dividends paid	2,000
Proceeds from sale of treasury stock	90,000
Repayment of loan principal	21,000
Payment of interest on loan	210

Required:

a. Prepare the cash from investing section of the statement of cash flows.
b. Prepare the cash from financing section of the statement of cash flows.

L.O. 10-3, 4

P10-7A To prepare its statement of cash flows for the year ended December 31, 2006, Repass Company gathered the following information:

Dividends paid	$ 18,500
Purchase of treasury stock	50,000
Proceeds from bank loan	150,000
Gain on sale of equipment	7,000
Proceeds from sale of equipment	20,000
Proceeds from sale of common stock	260,000

Required: Prepare the cash from financing section of the statement of cash flows for Repass Company for the year ended December 31, 2006.

P10-8A Use the statement of cash flows for the Matlock Company to answer the following questions:

L.O. 10-1, 2, 5

Matlock Company
Statement of Cash Flows
For the Year Ended December 31, 2002

		(In thousands)
Cash flows from operating activities		
Net income		$1,500
Depreciation expense	$ 210	
Decrease in accounts receivable	320	
Increase in inventory	(70)	
Increase in prepaid rent	(10)	
Increase in accounts payable	150	600
Net cash provided by operating activities		2,100
Cash flows from investing activities		
Purchase of equipment	(1,000)	
Proceeds from sale of old equipment	200	
Net cash used by investing activities		(800)
Cash flows from financing activities		
Repayment of long-term mortgage	(1,350)	
Proceeds from sale of common stock	500	
Payment of cash dividends	(200)	
Net cash used by financing activities		(1,050)
Net increase in cash during 2002		250
Cash balance, January 1, 2002		346
Cash balance, December 31, 2002		$ 596

Required:

a. How did Matlock Company use the majority of its cash during 2002?
b. What information does this give you about Matlock Company?
c. How did Matlock Company obtain the majority of its cash during 2002?
d. Is this an appropriate source of cash for the long run? Explain.

Problems—Set B

P10-1B The following income statement for the year ending December 31, 2005 and the balance sheets at December 31, 2004 and December 31, 2005 are given for Oviedo Oil:

L.O. 10-1, 2, 3, 4, 5

Oviedo Oil Company
Income Statement
For the Year Ended December 31, 2002

		(In thousands)
Sales revenue		$150,000
Cost of goods sold		63,000
Gross margin		87,000
Other expenses		
Wages and salaries	$ 32,000	
Depreciation	4,500	
Miscellaneous	12,400	
Total other expenses		48,900
Income before taxes		$ 38,100
Income taxes		8,200
Net income		$ 29,900

Oviedo Oil Company
Comparative Balance Sheets

($ In thousands)	December 31,			
	2005		2004	
Assets				
Current assets				
Cash		$ 0		$ 6,400
Accounts receivable		2,900		2,700
Inventory		60,000		42,000
Total current assets		$ 62,900		$51,100
Property, plant, and equipment				
Equipment	$82,300		$39,000	
Less: accumulated depreciation	(20,100)		(15,600)	
Total property, plant, and equipment		62,200		23,400
Total assets		$125,100		$74,500
Liabilities and stockholders' equity				
Current liabilities				
Accounts payable	$ 6,400		$ 5,700	
Salaries payable	1,500		1,300	
Taxes payable	1,900		2,100	
Total current liabilities	9,800		9,100	
Notes payable	30,000		10,000	
Total liabilities		39,800		19,100
Stockholders' equity				
Common stock	$40,000		$40,000	
Retained earnings	45,300		15,400	
		85,300		55,400
Total liabilities and stockholders' equity		$125,100		$74,500

Required:

a. Prepare a statement of cash flows for the year ending December 31, 2005 using (1) the direct method and (2) the indirect method.

b. Why is this information important to the company and to parties outside the company?

c. As a user, which format would you prefer and why?

d. Evaluate the way the company spent its cash during the year. Do you think the company is in a sound cash position?

L.O. 10-4

P10-2B The following information shown below is from the comparative balance sheets of Faith's Music Company at December 31, 2005 and 2004:

(In thousands)	At December 31	
	2005	2004
Current assets		
Cash	$2,500	$2,990
Accounts receivable	3,725	2,080
Inventory	1,050	1,300
Prepaid insurance	520	470
Total current assets	$7,795	$6,840
Current liabilities		
Accounts payable	$2,890	$1,650
Salaries payable	1,500	3,200
Total current liabilities	$4,390	$4,850

Net income for the year ended December 31, 2005 was $206,000. Depreciation expense of $85,000 was included in the operating expenses for the year.

Required: Prepare the cash from operations section of the statement of cash flows for Faith's Music Company for the year ended December 31, 2005. Use the indirect method.

P10-3B Information that follows comes from the balance sheets of Walker Corp. at September 30, 2004 and 2003:

L.O. 10-4

From the Balance Sheets of Walker Corp. September 30, 2004, and September 30, 2003		
(In thousands)	2004	2003
Current assets		
Cash	$2,110	$1,650
Accounts receivable	1,254	1,977
Inventory	700	656
Prepaid insurance	157	314
Total current assets	$4,221	$4,597
Current liabilities		
Accounts payable	$2,000	$2,330
Wages payable	1,154	750
Total current liabilities	$3,154	$3,080

Net income for the year ended September 30, 2004 was $146,000. Included in the operating expenses for the year was a depreciation expense of $112,000.

Required: Prepare the cash from the operating activities section of the Walker Corp. statement of cash flows for the year ended September 30, 2004.

P10-4B Treasures Corp. had the following information available for 2001:

L.O. 10-4

	January 1	December 31
Accounts receivable	$70,000	$76,000
Prepaid insurance	58,000	36,000
Inventory	86,000	65,000

Treasurers Corp. reported net income of $130,000 for the year. Depreciation expense, included on the income statement, was $20,800.

Required: Assume this is all the information relevant to the statement of cash flows. Prepare the cash flow from operations section of the Treasures Corp. statement of cash flows.

P10-5B To prepare its statement of cash flows for the year ended December 31, 2002, Wright's Company gathered the following information:

L.O. 10-2, 3, 4

Proceeds from bond issue (face value $100,000)	$120,000
Amortization of bond premium	1,000
Dividends declared	15,000
Dividends paid	12,000
Purchase of treasury stock	50,000
Loss on sale of machinery	18,000
Proceeds from sale of machinery	30,000

Required: Prepare the cash from investing section of the statement of cash flows for Wright's Company for the year ended December 31, 2002.

L.O. 10-2, 3, 4

P10-6B To prepare its statement of cash flows for the year ended December 31, 2005, Bowden Company gathered the following information:

Dividends declared	$15,000
Dividends paid	12,000
Proceeds from sale of treasury stock	70,000
Repayment of loan principal	32,000
Payment of interest on loan	320
Gain on sale of equipment	3,500
Proceeds from sale of equipment	11,000
Purchase of equipment	75,000

Required:

a. Prepare the cash from investing section of the statement of cash flows.
b. Prepare the cash from financing section of the statement of cash flows.

L.O. 10-2, 3, 4

P10-7B   To prepare its statement of cash flows for the year ended December 31, 2004, Mango Company gathered the following information:

Proceeds from bank loan	$257,000
Gain on sale of equipment	17,500
Proceeds from sale of equipment	45,000
Proceeds from sale of common stock	160,000
Dividends paid	15,400
Purchase of treasury stock	75,000

Required: Prepare the cash from the financing section of the statement of cash flows for Mango Company for the year ended December 31, 2004.

L.O. 10-1, 2, 5

P10-8B   Use the statement of cash flows for the SS&P Company to answer the following questions:

SS&P Company
Statement of Cash Flows
For the Year Ended December 31, 2002

	(In thousands)	
Cash flows from operating activities		
Net income		$ 2,500
Depreciation expense	$ 510	
Decrease in accounts receivable	720	
Increase in inventory	(90)	
Increase in prepaid rent	(20)	
Decrease in accounts payable	(150)	970
Net cash provided by operating activities		3,470
Cash flows from investing activities		
Purchase of equipment	$(3,000)	
Proceeds from sale of old equipment	900	
Net cash used by investing activities		(2,100)
Cash flows from financing activities		
Repayment of long-term mortgage	$(7,500)	
Proceeds from sale of common stock	2,100	
Payment of cash dividends	(1,200)	
Net cash used by financing activities		(6,600)
Net increase in cash during 2002		(5,230)
Cash balance, January 1, 2002		10,580
Cash balance, December 31, 2002		$ 5,350

Required:

   a. How did SS&P Company use the majority of its cash during 2002?
   b. What information does this give you about SS&P Company?
   c. How did SS&P Company obtain the majority of its cash during 2002?
   d. Is this an appropriate source of cash in for the long run? Explain.

Recording Transactions

R10-1 (SE10-5) Jill Corporation reported credit sales of $950,000 for 2001. Jill's accounts receivable from sales were $40,000 at the beginning of 2001 and $50,000 at the end of 2001. Use the T-account approach to determine the amount of cash from customers collected in 2001.

Accounts receivable

R10-2 (SE10-11) During 2003, Cable Direct, Inc. incurred salary expense of $37,500. The January 1 balance in salaries payable was $10,450, and the December 31 balance was $15,200. Use the T-account approach to determine the amount of cash paid to employees during 2003.

Salaries payable

R10-3 (SE10-13) Beta Company spent $40,000 for a new delivery truck during the year. Depreciation expense of $2,000 related to the truck was shown on the income statement. Give the journal entries to record the purchase of the asset and the depreciation expense. What effect do these transactions have on the statement of cash flows?

Date	Account	Debit	Credit

R10-4 (E10-2) Suppose Kianna's Company completed the following cash transactions during the year ended June 30, 2004. For each transaction, give the appropriate journal entry. Then, prepare a statement of cash flows for the year ended June 30, 2004.

   a. Issued 100 shares of $2 par common stock for $12 per share.
   b. Borrowed $5,000 from a local bank to expand the business.
   c. Purchased supplies for $400 cash.
   d. Hired a carpenter to build some bookcases for the office for $500 cash.
   e. Earned revenue of $9,000 cash.
   f. Hired a student to do some typing and paid him $300 cash.
   g. Repaid $1,000 of the bank loan along with $150 interest.
   h. Paid dividends of $400.

Date	Account	Debit	Credit

R10-5 (E10-3) Given the income statement for Clark Corporation for last year and selected information from the comparative balance sheets shown for the beginning and the end of the year, give a journal entry that would explain the change in each balance sheet account balance. The first one is done as an example.

Sales	$100,000	
Cost of goods sold	35,000	
Gross margin		$65,000
Operating expenses		
Wages	2,500	
Rent	1,200	
Utilities	980	
Insurance	320	5,000
Net Income		$60,000

Account	Beginning of the year	End of the Year
Accounts receivable	$10,000	$12,000
Inventory	21,000	18,500
Prepaid insurance	575	400
Accounts payable	9,000	10,400
Wages payable	850	600
Utilities payable	150	0

Item	Accounts	Debit	Credit
Change in AR	Accounts receivable	$2,000	
	Sales revenue		$2,000
Change in inventory			
Change in prepaid insurance			
Change in accounts payable			
Change in wages payable			
Change in utilities payable			

R10-6 (E10-7) The following events occurred at Gadgets Inc. during 2004:

January	Issued bonds for $250,000
February	Purchased new machinery for $80,000
March	Sold old machinery for $30,000, resulting in a $10,000 loss
April	Paid interest of $20,000 on the bonds
May	Borrowed $5,000 from a local bank
June	Purchased a new computer for $3,000
July	Paid cash dividends of $4,600

Required: Give the journal entry for each transaction. Suppose Gadgets began the year with $10,000 cash. Determine the ending cash balance, and prepare the statement of cash flows for 2004.

Date	Account	Debit	Credit
January			
February			
March			
April			
May			
June			
July			

R10-7 (P10-1A) Use the information about Samsula Service Company from Problem 10-1A.

Required: Prepare a statement of cash flows for the year ending December 31, 2005, using the indirect method with spreadsheet analysis.

Issues for Discussion

L.O. 10-1, 5

Financial statement analysis

1. Use the annual report of Pier 1 Imports to answer the following:

   a. What were the major sources and uses of cash during the fiscal year ended March 3, 2001? What do these indicate about the company's cash position?
   b. Is there any evidence on the statement of cash flows that Pier 1 is expanding its business?

Business risk

2. To be successful, a company must anticipate its cash flows. What evidence can you find in the Pier 1 annual report that this company does adequate cash planning? Is there any information not available in the annual report that would help you make this evaluation?

Ethics

3. After two years of business, the Lucky Ladder Company decided to apply for a bank loan to finance a new store. Although the company had been very successful, it had never prepared a cash budget. The owner of Lucky Ladder used the information from the first two years of business to reconstruct cash forecasts, and presented them with his financial statements as though they had been prepared as part of the company's planning. Do you think this behavior was ethical? What would you do in similar circumstances? Why?

Internet Exercise: Carnival Corp.

Carnival Corp. prides itself on being "The Most Popular Cruise Line in the World®"—a distinction achieved by offering a wide array of quality cruise vacations.

Please go to the www.prenhall.com/myphlip *Web site, register, and add this textbook to your myphlip page (if you haven't done so already). Go to Chapter 10 and use the Internet Exercise company link.*

IE10-1 Select *About Carnival.*

a. Select *World's Leading Cruise Lines* and watch the introduction. List three of the six cruise lines operated by the Carnival Corp. Close *the World's Leading Cruise Lines* window.
b. Select *Virtual Press Kit* and then *Carnival Cruise Lines' Fleet Information.* Within the past 5 years, how many new ships has Carnival put into service?
c. Are the payments for ships considered capital expenditures or revenue expenditures? On the statement of cash flows, which business activity category will report these payments?

IE10-2 Go to *http://www.forbes.com,* under "Quotes and Research" enter the company symbol CCL (the stock symbol of the Carnival Corp.), and then choose *Financials.* Find the *annual cash flow* statement to answer the following questions.

a. Does Carnival use the direct or the indirect method to prepare the statement of cash flows? How can you tell? Which activity section is affected by this choice of method?
b. For the most recent year list the amount of net cash inflow or outflow from each of the three major types of activities reported on the statement of cash flows. Which type of activity is providing the most cash? Is this considered favorable or unfavorable?
c. For the most recent year, what amount is reported for *net income* and *total cash from operating activities*? Are these amounts the same? Explain why or why not?

d. For the most recent year did Carnival report cash inflows or outflows for capital expenditures? Is this considered favorable or unfavorable? Explain why. What do you think these capital expenditures are primarily for? What was the net amount of the capital expenditure? Which activity section reports this information?

e. For the most recent year what amount of cash dividends did Carnival pay out? For the most recent year did Carnival issue or retire more common stock? What was the net amount issued or retired? For the most recent year did Carnival issue or retire more debt? What was the net amount issued or retired? Which activity section reports this information?

f. Does this statement of cash flows indicate a strong or weak cash position? Explain why.

Please note: Internet Web sites are constantly being updated. Therefore, if the information is not found where indicated, please explore the Web site further to find the information.

FINANCIAL STATEMENT ANALYSIS

Financial Reporting

Here's where you've been...

In Chapter 10, you learned the details involved in preparing the statement of cash flows. You learned that there are two ways to prepare and present the statement: the direct method and the indirect method. You learned the importance of planning cash flows and what can be learned from an analysis of the statement of cash flows.

Here's where you're going...

When you are finished with Chapter 11, you will be able to recognize several new items on the financial statements—discontinued operations, extraordinary items, cumulative effect of a change in accounting priniciple, comprehensive income, and investments in securities. You should be able to do horizontal analysis, vertical analysis, and ratio analysis of a set of financial statements.

Financial Reporting and Business Events

11

Financing

Property, Plant, and Equipment

Sales and Accounts Receivable

Financial Reporting and Business Events

Inventory and Liabilities

Learning Objectives

More specifically, when you are finished studying this chapter, you should be able to answer these questions:

1. What items are shown separately from *income from operations* on the income statement and why?
2. What is comprehensive income and where is it shown on the financial statements?
3. How are investments in securities classified and reported on the financial statements?
4. What are vertical and horizontal analyses?
5. How are ratios used to analyze financial statements?

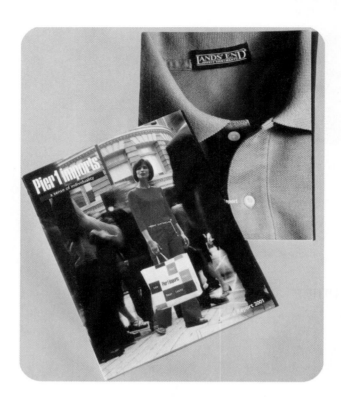

Financial Information: Looking Beneath the Surface

L.O. 1

Know the components of net income that are disclosed separately, after net income from operations: discontinued operations, extraordinary items, and cumulative effect of a change in accounting principle.

You can easily see some information from the data in the financial statements. There's still more information in that same data but you have to look harder to see it. To use all the information contained in the financial statements, you have to get beneath the surface, to look beyond the size and source of the numbers to what the numbers mean. As we've worked our way through the business cycle, examining the major business processes, we've been examining individual parts of the financial statements. Now we'll take a look at the statements in a comprehensive way, examining parts of the four financial statements together to find more of the information available within the numbers in those statements. To put it as simply as possible: What information do financial statements provide? What does the information mean? How can we use it?

A Closer Look at the Income Statement

Before beginning the detailed analysis of the financial statements, we need to take a closer look at some of the characteristics of the income statement. Because earnings—that is, net income—is the focus of financial reporting, companies worry about the effect their earnings will have when announced. It's not uncommon for companies to be accused of manipulating their earnings to make them appear better than they actually are. In an effort to make the components of earnings clear and to communicate exactly what they should mean to financial statement users, the Financial Accounting Standards Board (FASB) has defined three items that need to be separated from the regular earnings of a business:

1. Discontinued operations
2. Extraordinary items
3. Changes in accounting principles

These three items, along with net income from operations, shown in Exhibit 11-1, are reported net of taxes, that is, with the related taxes already subtracted.

Discontinued Operations

If you pay attention to the financial news, you're bound to hear about a company selling off a division or disposing of one of its business segments. Firms are always evaluating the contribution that a firm's various business segments make to the profits of the firm. A part of a company's operations that is eliminated is referred to as **discontinued operations.**

When a segment's operation is discontinued, the financial implications related to that segment are separated from the regular operations of the firm. Why would this separation be useful? Earnings, or income, is an important number because it is used to evaluate the performance of a firm and to predict its future performance. To make those evaluations and predictions more meaningful, it is important for one-time occurrences to be separated out. In this way investors see them as exceptions to the normal operations of the firm. The financial implications of discontinuing a business segment—the gain or loss on the disposal—are nonrecurring, so those items are reported separately. The income or loss for the accounting period for the discontinued operations must also be shown separately.

Let's look at an example of a firm with discontinued operations. Containers, Inc. sold off a major business segment, the package mailing division, during 2003. Whenever a business segment is discontinued, the income or loss from that segment for the year of disposal must be shown separately. Doing this will make the firm's income from continuing operations more useful for predicting the firm's future performance. Both the current year's income or loss from the discontinued operations and the gain or loss from the sale of those operations are shown separately. Suppose:

1. The Containers income from continuing operations before taxes was $400,000.
2. Taxes related to income from continuing operations were $160,000.
3. The discontinued segment contributed income of $12,400 during the year.
4. Taxes related to that income were $2,300.
5. The discontinued segment was sold for a profit of $60,000.
6. The taxes related to the profit from that sale were $25,000.

Discontinued operations are those that a company has gotten rid of, usually by selling a segment or division. The related gain or loss is shown net of taxes after income from continuing operations.

Exhibit 11–1
Components of Net Income

Exhibit 11-2
Discontinued Operations

Containers, Inc.
Partial Income Statement
For the Year Ended December 31, 2003

Income before taxes		$400,000
Income tax expense		160,000
Income from continuing operations		240,000
Discontinued operations		
Income from discontinued operations,		
net of taxes of $2,300	$10,100	
Gain on disposal of segment,	35,000	
net of taxes of $25,000		45,100
Net income		$285,100

Exhibit 11-2 shows how this information would be presented on the income statement for Containers, Inc.

Extraordinary Items

Extraordinary items are events that are both unusual and infrequent. The gain or loss related to them is shown separately on the income statement after income from continuing operations and after any discontinued operations.

Events that are *unusual* in nature and *infrequent* in occurrence are considered **extraordinary items.** To qualify as extraordinary, the events must be abnormal and must not be reasonably expected to occur again in the foreseeable future. Obviously, there is a great deal of judgment required to decide whether an event should be considered extraordinary. Examples of occurrences that have been considered extraordinary include eruptions of a volcano, takeover of foreign operations by a foreign government, and effects of new laws or regulations that result in a one-time cost for compliance. Each situation is unique and must be considered in the environment in which the business operates.

Suppose Containers, Inc. lost a factory in a foreign country, when the government of that country expropriated (took possession of) all American businesses in the country. The book value of the lost factory was $105,000. Because a loss like this is tax deductible, there is a tax saving that must be deducted, so the extraordinary loss is reported net of tax. Suppose the applicable tax saving is $35,000. Exhibit 11-3 shows how the information would be shown on the Containers, Inc. income statement for the year.

Exhibit 11-3
Extraordinary Items

Containers, Inc.
Partial Income Statement
For the Year Ended December 31, 2003

Income before taxes		$400,000
Income tax expense		160,000
Income from continuing operations		240,000
Discontinued operations		
Income net of taxes of $2,300	$10,100	
Gain on disposal net of taxes of $25,000	35,000	
		45,100
Income before extraordinary item		285,100
Extraordinary item		
Loss from expropriation of foreign operation,		
net of tax savings of $35,000		70,000
Net income		$215,100

Understanding Business

ORDINARY EXTRAORDINARY ITEMS?

You have seen that managers separate the income statement into sections such as gross profit, operating income, income before income taxes, and net income. Occasionally, something unusual and infrequent happens in a company, and the company must report it separately as an extraordinary item. Generally, each company will use its own criteria to determine whether an item should be classified as extraordinary. Different companies could experience the same or similar events but choose to classify them differently. For example, hurricanes are common in the Florida peninsula, where they would probably not be classified as extraordinary items. However, if a hurricane struck a company in Newport, Rhode Island, and damaged its assets, that company would probably classify the loss as an extraordinary item.

On September 18, 2001, eight airlines wrote a letter to the Financial Accounting Standards Board (FASB) requesting that a number of costs associated with the September 11, 2001 terrorist attack be classified as extraordinary items. Such costs would include costs associated with increased airport security, costs associated with laying off workers due to the decreased demand for air travel, and cost of employee benefits (such as long-term disability and workers' compensation related to the attacks).

Initially, in a news release on September 28, 2001, the FASB indicated it tentatively agreed that many of the incremental losses attributable to the events of September 11 should be classified as extraordinary and agreed on guidance as to what kinds of losses should be included. However, after considerable debate, the FASB decided to reject its original tentative position. The Chairman of the Emerging Issues Task Force of the FASB, Tim Lucas, said, "The task force understood that this was an extraordinary event in the English language sense of the word, but in the final analysis, we decided it wasn't going to improve the financial-reporting system to show it" (as an extraordinary item). The FASB believed it would be impossible to come up with clear, objective guidelines for all companies in all affected industries. The main problem was how to value the losses of assets not physically damaged in the attack. The airline industry was in the midst of economic problems before the terrorist attack, and the FASB determined that it would be impossible to disentangle those economic problems and the effect of the terrorist attack.

Company managers will still be allowed to deduct losses from operating income, and still be able to give their opinions about how the attack affected their firms. However, this extraordinary event, in any sense of the word, will be given an ordinary treatment in the financial statements. It will be up to the financial statement users to determine how earnings were affected by the terrorist attacks of September 11, 2001.

Changes in Accounting Principle

Generally accepted accounting principles (GAAP) are constantly evolving. Some of the changes are additions of new disclosures and new ways of valuing financial statement items. There are instances in which a company may change accounting methods simply to benefit from the resulting financial statement changes—something the Security and Exchange Commission (SEC) refers to as "cooking the books." When the accounting profession changes one of its principles or when a company chooses a different principle from the available choices (e.g., change in depreciation method), the effect of such a change on net income must be segregated from the effects of other items on income. That amount is called the **cumulative effect** of a change in accounting principle. As you can see, this separate disclosure is meant to discourage companies from trying to manipulate income by changing accounting principles they use for financial reporting. Because the change has to be

The **cumulative effect** of a change in accounting principle is the amount of gain or loss from changing accounting methods. It must be shown separately on the income statement, after income from continuing operations, discontinued operations, and any extraordinary items.

Exhibit 11-4
Straight-line Versus Double-Declining Balance Depreciation

Method	Straight-line	Double-declining balance
Year ended		
December 31, 2001	$1,000	$2,000
December 31, 2002	1,000	1,600
Total for 2 years	$2,000	$3,600

singled out and identified, the company can't "hide" the change from financial statement users.

Let's continue with Containers, Inc. Suppose the company changed from depreciating equipment using the straight-line method to depreciating the equipment using the double-declining-balance method. The equipment was purchased on January 1, 2001, at a cost of $10,000, and has a useful life of 10 years, with no salvage value. The depreciation schedules for the two methods are shown in Exhibit 11-4.

The income for Containers, Inc. would have been lower by $1,600 if double-declining balance had been used from the beginning. A switch now means the company will have to subtract $1,600, net of any tax effect, as a cumulative effect of a change in accounting principle.

How about the depreciation expense for 2003? It will be included in the regular part of the income statement and will be calculated using the new method, double-declining balance.

Assume that the tax savings would have been $400 if we had used the larger depreciation amounts in the two previous years. Exhibit 11-5 shows how the change would appear on the income statement for 2003.

STUDY BREAK 11-1
SEE HOW YOU'RE DOING

Why are discontinued operations, extraordinary items, and cumulative effect of a change in accounting principle shown *net of tax*? What's the alternative?

Exhibit 11-5
Cumulative Effect of a Change in Accounting Principle

Containers, Inc.
Partial Income Statement
For the Year Ended December 31, 2003

Income before taxes		$400,000
Income tax expense		160,000
Income from continuing operations		240,000
Discontinued operations		
Income net of taxes of $2,300	$10,100	
Gain on disposal net of taxes of $25,000	35,000	
		45,100
Income before extraordinary item and cumulative effect of change in accounting principle		285,100
Extraordinary item		
Loss from expropriation of foreign operation net of tax savings of $35,000		70,000
Cumulative effect of a change in accounting principle		
Effect on prior years of change in depreciation method, net of $400 tax savings		1,200
Net income		$213,900

Other Financial Statement Items

Before we discuss the overall analysis of the financial statements, there are two more items commonly found on a set of financial statements. Although we will not discuss the details here, you should be able to recognize the items—comprehensive income and investments in securities—and what they mean when you see them.

Define *comprehensive income* and *other comprehensive income* and understand what these two items represent.

Comprehensive Income

Even though most revenues and expenses are included on the income statement, there are a small number of transactions that affect owner's equity but are *excluded* from the calculation of net income. We already know about two of them:

1. owners making contributions (paid-in capital)
2. owners receiving dividends

There are several other transactions that affect equity without going through the income statement. The most common examples of these transaction are (1) unrealized gains and losses from foreign currency translations, and (2) unrealized gains and losses on certain investments. Instead of including either of these gains and losses on the income statement, they are reported as a direct adjustment to equity.

Because these special items are not included in the calculation of net income, the FASB was concerned that they may not be getting the attention they deserve by the users of financial statements. To keep these transactions that directly affect equity from getting lost among all the financial statement numbers, the FASB decided to require the reporting of net income *plus* these other transactions that affect shareholders' equity in an amount called **comprehensive income.** Comprehensive income includes all changes in shareholders' equity during a period *except* those changes in equity resulting from contributions by shareholders and distributions to shareholders. There are two parts of comprehensive income: *net income* and *other comprehensive income.* We know what types of transactions are included in net income—revenues, expenses, extraordinary items, etc. Items included in other comprehensive income include unrealized gains and losses from foreign currency translation and unrealized gains and losses on certain types of investments. Exhibit 11-6 shows all the items that affect shareholders' equity.

Comprehensive income is the total of all items that affect shareholders' equity *except* transactions with the owners (paid-in capital and dividends). Comprehensive income has two parts: *net income* and *other comprehensive income.*

Investments in Securities

Know the three categories of investments in debt and equity securities and how they are reported on the financial statements.

Another item found on many financial statements is the investment in securities. When a company has extra cash, the owners want that cash to be earning money. When interest rates are low, a company's extra cash may earn more in the stock or bond market than it would earn by sitting in the bank in a savings account or a certificate of deposit. That's when a company buys stocks and bonds of other companies with its extra cash. For firms such as banks and insurance companies, investing cash in other companies is a crucial part of managing their assets. As you learned in previous chapters, stocks are equity securities and bonds are debt securities. Both may be purchased with a company's extra cash. The accounting rules require firms to classify their investments in securities into one of three categories: *held-to-maturity, trading,* and *available-for-sale.*

Exhibit 11-6
Items that Affect Shareholders' Equity

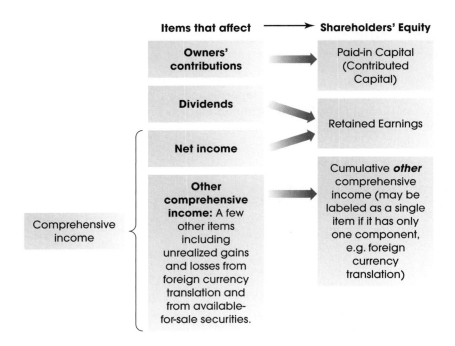

Held-to-maturity securities are investments in debt securities that the company plans to hold until the securities mature.

Held-to-Maturity Securities. Sometimes a company purchases debt securities and intends to keep them until they mature. Recall that all bonds have a maturity date. (There is no maturity date with equity securities.) If a company plans to keep the securities until maturity and its financial condition indicates that it should be able to do this, the investments will be classified as **held-to-maturity securities.** Such investments are recorded at cost, and are reported at that same amount (plus or minus any discount or premium amortization) on the balance sheet. No matter how much they are actually worth on the market, when the balance sheet is prepared, these held-to-maturity investments will always be reported at cost.

Trading securities are investments in debt and equity securities that the company has purchased to make a short-term profit.

Trading Securities. If a company buys the securities solely to trade them and make a short-term profit, they are classified as **trading securities.** Trading securities are shown at their market (i.e., current) value on the balance sheet. When a company gets ready to prepare the financial statements, the current values of the investments are obtained from the *Wall Street Journal* or a similar source of market prices. Those values are then shown on the balance sheet. Recording the securities at their market value is called *marking to market.* If the cost of the securities is lower than current market value, then the difference is recorded as an unrealized gain. If the cost of the securities is higher than their market value, then the difference is recorded as an unrealized loss. *Realizing* means actually getting something. Because any gain or loss on an investment the company is holding (holding means *not* selling) is something the company doesn't get (a gain) or give up (a loss) until the securities are actually sold, it is called an **unrealized gain or loss.** Such a gain or loss may also be called a *holding* gain or loss.

An increase or decrease in the market value of a company's investments in securities is an **unrealized gain or loss,** recognized either on the income statement—for trading securities—or in other comprehensive income in the equity section of the balance sheet—for available-for-sale securities—when the financial statements are prepared, even though the securities have *not* been sold.

For example, suppose Avia Company has invested $130,000 of its extra cash in securities, stocks and bonds traded on the stock market. At the end of the year, the securities that cost Avia $130,000 have a market value of $125,000. On the income statement for the year, Avia will show an unrealized loss of $5,000. It is recorded in an adjustment made before the financial statements are prepared. How the adjustment affects the accounting equation follows:

Assets	= Liabilities +	Contributed + capital	Retained earnings
$(5,000) Investments in trading securities[a]			$(5,000) Unrealized loss on trading securities

[a]Investments in trading securities are shown as current assets on the balance sheet.

The $125,000 current value of the securities has replaced their original cost. Remember, the company purchased these trading securities as investments to trade in the short run, so the firm's investment portfolio is likely to look very different at the next balance sheet date.

Available-for-Sale Securities. Sometimes a company is not sure how long it will keep the debt or equity securities it has purchased. If the company does not definitely intend to sell the securities in the short term to try to make a quick profit and does not intend to hold them until maturity, the securities would be classified as **available-for-sale.** Every year, when it is time to prepare the annual balance sheet, the cost of this group of securities is compared with the market value at the balance sheet date. The book value of the securities is then adjusted to market value, and the corresponding gain or loss is recorded directly to owner's equity. Such a gain or loss is called an *unrealized,* or *holding,* gain or loss, just as it is called for trading securities. However, these gains and losses don't go on the income statement. Instead, they are included as part of other comprehensive income in the equity section of the balance sheet.

Suppose Avia Company classified its portfolio of securities that cost $130,000 as available-for-sale. If the market value of the securities is $125,000 at the date of the balance sheet, the securities must be shown on the balance sheet at the lower market value. In this case, the unrealized loss will *not* be shown on the income statement. Instead of going through net income to retained earnings, the loss of $5,000 will go directly to the owner's equity section of the balance sheet. It will be shown after retained earnings, either alone—and labeled as an unrealized loss from investments in securities—or combined with other non-income statement gains and losses—and labeled as other comprehensive income loss.

Available-for-sale securities are investments the company may hold or sell; the company's intention is not clear enough to use one of the other categories—held-to-maturity or trading.

A corporation has invested $50,000 in the securities of other companies. At the end of the year, that corporation's portfolio has a market value of $52,000. Describe where these securities would be shown on the annual financial statements and give the amount, under each of the following conditions:

1. The investment is classified as *trading.*
2. The investment is classified as *available-for-sale.*
3. The investment is classified as *held-to-maturity.*

STUDY BREAK 11-2
SEE HOW YOU'RE DOING

Analysis of Financial Information

Now that you are prepared to recognize some new items—extraordinary items, cumulative effect of a change in accounting principle, investments in securities, for example—that may appear on financial statements, you are ready to analyze an entire statement or set of statements. We'll discuss three ways to approach the analysis of financial information: horizontal analysis, vertical analysis, and ratio analysis.

Horizontal Analysis

Perform and interpret a horizontal analysis of financial statement information.

Horizontal analysis is a technique for evaluating a series of financial statement data over a period of time. The purpose of a horizontal analysis is to express the changes in an item in percentages, based on a specific past year chosen as the base year. Suppose we wanted to analyze the change in the capital expenditures of Lands' End over the past 6 years.

		Lands' End, Inc.			
		Capital Expenditures—Base Year 1995			
		(In Thousands)			
2000	1999	1998	1997	1996	1995
$28,013	$46,750	$48,228	$17,992	$14,780	$27,005

The difference between each year and the base year is expressed as a percentage of the base year. In this example, 1995 has been chosen as the base year and is assigned 100%. Then 1995 capital expenditures are subtracted from 1996 expenditures. That difference is then expressed as a percentage of the base year.

$$\frac{14,780 - 27,005}{27,005} = \frac{-12,225}{27,005} = -45.3\% \quad \text{(The negative sign means decrease.)}$$

During 1996, the company reduced capital expenditures by over 45% of the base year expenditures.

See if you can figure out the calculations for the other percentages for Lands' End.

		Lands' End, Inc.			
		Capital Expenditures—Base Year 1995			
		(In Thousands)			
2000	1999	1998	1997	1996	1995
28,013	46,750	48,228	17,992	14,780	27,005
3.7%	73.1%	78.6%	−33.4%	−45.3%	100%

It is often difficult to understand the significance of a single number or to interpret a trend when looking at the absolute amounts in dollars. It may be useful to express the change in percentage form, to make the magnitude of the change more apparent.

Vertical Analysis

Perform and interpret a vertical analysis of financial statement information.

Vertical analysis is a technique similar to horizontal analysis, but it involves items on a single year of a financial statement. Each item in a financial statement is expressed as a percentage of a selected item on the statement. For example, a common income statement analysis uses *sales* as the base amount and then expresses the other income statement items as a percentage of sales. This type of analysis can point out areas in which the costs might be too large or growing without an obvious cause. This analysis is shown in Exhibit 11-7 for

Statement of Operations Lands' End, Inc. For the Period Ended				
In millions	January 28, 2000		January 29, 1999	
Net sales	$1,319.82	100.0%	$1,371.38	100.0%
Cost of sales	727.29	55.1%	754.66	55.0%
Gross profit	592.53	44.9%	616.72	45.0%
S&A expenses	515.37	39.0%	544.45	39.7%
Nonrecurring charge (credit)	(1.77)	(0.1)%	12.60	0.9%
Income from operations	78.93	5.8%	59.67	4.4%
Other income				
Interest expense	(1.89)	(0.1)%	(7.74)	(0.6%)
Interest income	0.88	0.1%	0.02	0.0%
Other	(1.68)	(0.1)%	(2.45)	(0.2%)
Total other income (expense)	(2.69)	(0.1)%	(10.17)	(0.8%)
Income before taxes	76.24	5.7%	49.50	3.6%
Income tax provision	28.21	2.1%	18.32	1.3%
Net income	$ 48.03	3.6%	$ 31.18	2.3%

Exhibit 11-7
Vertical Analysis

Lands' End's income statements for the years ended January 28, 2000 and January 29, 1999.

The analysis for a single year provides some information, but the comparison of 2 years reveals more about what's going on with Lands' End. What item stands out in the analysis? The nonrecurring charge in the year ended in 1999 is worth further investigation. The notes to the financial statements would be the first place to look for additional information whenever an analysis reveals something interesting or suspicious.

Ratio Analysis

Throughout the previous chapters, you have seen financial statement ratios that apply to the various topics we've discussed. You have learned that ratio analysis uses information in the financial statements to calculate specific values that give some measure of a company's financial performance. Most ratios can be classified as one of four types. You have already been introduced to the first three types in the previous chapters; we will briefly recap each here. The fourth type is new and will be described in detail following the review of the first three.

The basic ratio classifications and the questions each ratio helps answer are:

Understand the information provided by ratio analysis, and perform a basic ratio analysis of a set of financial statements.

1. *Liquidity:* Can a company pay the bills as they come due?
2. *Solvency:* Can the company survive over a long period of time?
3. *Profitability:* Can a company earn a satisfactory rate of return?
4. *Market indicators:* Is the company a good investment?

A summary of the ratios is shown in Exhibit 11-8; we will discuss each ratio next.

Liquidity Ratios. Liquidity ratios measure the ability of the company to pay its maturing obligations and to meet unexpected needs for cash in the short run. These are of special interest to bankers and suppliers who want to assess a company's ability to meet its short-term obligations.

Exhibit 11-8 Common Ratios

Ratio	Definition	Uses	Chapter
Liquidity			
Current Ratio	$$\frac{\text{current assets}}{\text{current liabilities}}$$	This ratio measures a company's ability to pay current liabilities with current assets. Creditors want to know if a company can meet its short-term obligations.	2
Acid-test Ratio (also known as the quick ratio)	$$\frac{\text{cash + trading securities + net accounts receivable}}{\text{current liabilities}}$$	This ratio is similar to the current ratio. However, by limiting the numerator to very liquid current assets, it is a stricter test of a company's ability to meet its short-term obligations.	11
Working Capital	current assets – current liabilities	Although technically not a ratio, working capital is often measured as part of financial statement analysis. It is another measure of a firm's ability to meet its short-term obligations.	3
Inventory Turnover Ratio	$$\frac{\text{cost of goods sold}}{\text{average inventory}}$$	This ratio measures how quickly a company is turning over its inventory.	6
Accounts Receivable Turnover Ratio	$$\frac{\text{net sales}}{\text{average net accounts receivable}}$$	This ratio measure's a company's ability to collect the cash from its credit customers.	7
Solvency			
Debt to Equity	$$\frac{\text{total liabilities}}{\text{total shareholders' equity}}$$	This ratio compares the amount of debt a company has with the amount the owners have invested in the company.	8
Times Interest Earned	$$\frac{\text{net income + interest expense + taxes}}{\text{interest expense}}$$	This ratio compares the amount of income that has been earned with the interest obligation for the same period.	8
Profitability			
Return on Assets	$$\frac{\text{net income + interest expense}}{\text{average total assets}}$$	This ratio measures a company's success in using its assets to earn income for the persons who are financing the business. Because interest is the return to creditors, not the owners, it is often added back to net income. Average total assets are the average of beginning assets and ending assets for the year.	5
Return on Equity	$$\frac{\text{net income – preferred dividends}}{\text{average common stockholders' equity}}$$	This ratio measures how much income is earned with the common shareholders' investment in the company.	9
Gross Margin on Sales	$$\frac{\text{gross margin}}{\text{sales}}$$	This ratio is used to measure a company's profitability. It is one of the most carefully watched ratios by management. It describes the percentage of sales price that is gross profit. A small shift usually indicates a big change in the profitability of the company's sales.	6

Exhibit 11-8 (continued)

Earnings per Share	$$\dfrac{\text{net income} - \text{preferred dividends}}{\text{average number of outstanding common shares}}$$	This gives the amount of net income per share of common stock.	9
Market Indicators			
Price-Earnings (PE) Ratio	$$\dfrac{\text{market price per share}}{\text{earnings per share}}$$	This ratio indicates the market price for $1 of earnings.	11
Dividend Yield	$$\dfrac{\text{dividend per share}}{\text{market price per share}}$$	This ratio gives the percentage return on the investment in a share of stock via dividends.	11

The following are several common liquidity measures:

1. Current ratio:

$$\frac{\text{current assets}}{\text{current liabilities}}$$

2. Acid-test ratio (sometimes called the quick ratio):

$$\frac{\text{cash} + \text{trading securities} + \text{net accounts receivable}}{\text{current liabilities}}$$

3. Working capital:

$$\text{current assets} - \text{current liabilities}$$

4. Inventory turnover ratio:

$$\frac{\text{cost of goods sold}}{\text{average inventory}}$$

5. Accounts receivable turnover ratio:

$$\frac{\text{net sales}}{\text{average (net) accounts receivable}}$$

Although working capital is not a ratio, it is often included in the analysis of financial statements as a measure of liquidity.

A corporation pays off a current liability with cash. What effect would this have on the company's current ratio and on the company's working capital?

STUDY BREAK 11-3
SEE HOW YOU'RE DOING

Solvency Ratios. Solvency ratios measure the ability of the company to survive over a long period of time. Long-term creditors and shareholders are interested in these ratios as a measure of long-term expectations. They want to be sure that a company can meet its interest obligations and repay any debts at maturity. Two common ratios that measure solvency are:

1. Debt to equity:

$$\frac{\text{total liabilities}}{\text{total shareholders' equity}}$$

2. Times interest earned:

$$\frac{\text{net income} + \text{interest expense} + \text{taxes}}{\text{interest expense}}$$

Profitability Ratios. Profitability ratios measure the operating success of a company for a given period of time. Some financial statement users see these ratios as a measure of management's performance. These ratios are important for a company's ability to obtain debt and equity financing. These ratios also provide information to management about specific areas of the business that need attention. There are many different profitability ratios that measure different aspects of profitability. Following are four of the most common:

1. Return on Assets:

$$\frac{\text{net income} + \text{interest expense}}{\text{average total assets}}$$

2. Return on equity (sometimes called return on investment):

$$\frac{\text{net income} - \text{preferred dividends}}{\text{average stockholders' equity}}$$

3. Gross margin ratio:

$$\frac{\text{gross margin}}{\text{sales}}$$

4. Earnings per share (EPS):

$$\frac{\text{net income} - \text{preferred dividends}}{\text{average number of common shares outstanding}}$$

**STUDY BREAK 11-4
SEE HOW YOU'RE DOING**

Company A has a gross margin ratio of 30%, and Company B has a gross margin ratio of 60%. Can you tell which company is more profitable? Explain why or why not.

Market Indicator Ratios. There are two ratios that use the current market price of a share of stock to indicate the return an investor might earn by purchasing that stock. Because the share price is what an investor would pay for the stock, the market price is the investment on which the shareholder earns a return.

Price earnings (PE) ratio equals the market price of a share of stock divided by that stock's earnings per share.

One ratio is the **price-earnings (PE) ratio.** This ratio is defined by its name: It's the price of a share of stock divided by the current EPS. Investors and financial analysts believe this ratio gives an indication of the future earnings. A high PE ratio means investors believe that the company has the potential for significant growth. If the PE ratio is extremely large (50 or greater), some analysts believe the stock is overpriced. A stock with a very low PE ratio may be underpriced.

1. Price-earnings ratio (PE ratio):

$$\frac{\text{market price per share}}{\text{earnings per share}}$$

The other ratio is the **dividend-yield ratio.** It is the dividend per share divided by the market price per share. You may find that the values for the dividend-yield ratio are quite low, compared with the return an investor would expect. Investors are willing to accept a low-dividend yield when they anticipate an increase in the price of the stock. On the other hand, stocks with low-growth potential may offer a higher dividend yield to attract investors.

Dividend-yield ratio equals dividend per share divided by the current market price per share.

2. Dividend-yield ratio:

$$\frac{\text{dividend per share}}{\text{market price per share}}$$

Exhibit 11-9 shows the EPS, the dividends per share, and the market price per share for Lucent Technology and for Sherwin Williams for their fiscal years ending in 1999. Which stock would be a better buy for long run growth? Which would be better if you needed regular dividend income?

The types of stock that will appeal to an investor depend on the investor's preferences for income and growth. If an investor does not need dividend income (e.g., a young investor may have a retirement fund invested in stocks) and has plenty of time to realize growth, the investor would prefer to invest in companies with high-growth potential, no matter what the dividend yield. Lucent Technology may be more attractive, with its high PE ratio, than Sherwin Williams. (The extremely high PE ratio could, on the other hand, indicate that the stock is overpriced. Check out what happened to Lucent's stock price and earnings in 2001. It indicates the caution needed regarding stock with enormous PE ratios.) Investors who need dividend income for living expenses (e.g., a retiree may be using dividend income for food and rent), will be more concerned with the size of the dividend yield of an investment and less concerned with the investment's long-term growth. Sherwin Williams would be better than Lucent Technology for dividends.

These market-related ratios are very important to management and to investors. If you examine a company's annual report, you are likely to see these ratios reported, usually for the most recent 2 or 3 years.

Understanding Ratios. A ratio by itself does not give much information. To be useful, a ratio must be compared with other ratios from previous periods, ratios of other companies in the same industry, or industry averages. Keep in mind that, with the exception of EPS, the calculations to arrive at a specific ratio may vary from company to company. There are no "standard" or required formulas to calculate a ratio. One company may calculate a debt ratio as *debt* to *equity,* whereas another company may calculate a debt ratio as *debt* to *debt plus equity.* When regarding and using any company's ratios, be sure you know how those ratios have been computed. When you are computing ratios, be sure to be consistent in your calculations so you can make meaningful comparisons among them.

For fiscal years ending in 1999	Lucent Technology	Sherwin Williams
Earnings per share	$ 0.35	$ 1.81
Dividends per share	0.0775	0.48
Ending market price per share	64.88	21.00
Price-earnings ratio	185.37	11.6
Dividend-yield ratio	0.001	0.023

Exhibit 11-9
Price-Earnings and Dividend-Yield Ratios

Exhibit 11-10
Income Statements for La-Z-Boy

La-Z-Boy
Consolidated Statement of Income

(Amounts in thousands, except per share data)	Fiscal Year Ended		
	April 29, 2000 (53 weeks)	April 24, 1999 (52 weeks)	April 25, 1998 (52 weeks)
Sales	$1,717,420	$1,287,645	$1,108,038
Cost of sales	1,284,158	946,731	825,312
Gross profit	433,262	340,914	282,726
Selling, general and administrative	288,962	234,075	205,523
Operating profit	144,300	106,839	77,203
Interest expense	(9,655)	(4,440)	(4,157)
Interest income	1,976	2,181	2,021
Other income	3,692	2,658	4,207
Pretax income	140,313	107,238	79,274
Income tax expense			
Federal current	49,491	41,286	28,467
deferred	(3,288)	(4,727)	(2,046)
State current	7,048	5,114	3,287
deferred	(552)	(577)	(354)
Total tax expense	52,699	41,096	29,354
Net income	$ 87,614	$ 66,142	$ 49,920
Basic average shares[a]	54,488	52,890	53,654
Basic net income per share[a]	$1.61	$1.25	$0.93
Diluted weighted average shares[a]	54,860	53,148	53,821
Diluted net income per share[a]	$1.60	$1.24	$0.93

Note: The accompanying notes to consolidated financial statements are an integral part of these statements.
[a]Restated to reflect the September 1998 three-for-one stock split, in the form of a 200% stock dividend.

Even though the only ratio that must be calculated and presented as part of the financial statements is EPS, managers typically include in their company's annual report many of the ratios we've discussed in this chapter. If these ratios are not shown as part of the financial statements, they may be included in other parts of the annual report, often in graphs depicting trends of the ratios over several years.

Any financial statement analysis requires more than a cursory review of ratios. The analyst must look at trends, components of the values that make up the ratios, and other information about the company that may not even be contained in the financial statements. Financial statements are only one source of information for investors, and ratio analysis is only one tool for analyzing financial statements.

Using Ratio Analysis. Let's compute the ratios shown in Exhibit 11-8 for La-Z-Boy, using its 2000 Annual Report. The income statements for 3 years are shown in Exhibit 11-10, and the balance sheets for two years are shown in Exhibit 11-11.

Other information needed for the analysis: include market price per share at the close of business on April 29, 2000 = $15.69 and dividends paid during the 12 months of the year ended April 29, 2000 = $0.32 per share.

All the ratios shown in Exhibit 11-8 are calculated for La-Z-Boy for the fiscal year ending April 29, 2000. Even though one set of ratios does not give us much information, use this as an opportunity to become familiar with how the ratios are calculated. The computations for each ratio are shown in Exhibit 11-12.

Exhibit 11–11
Balance Sheets of La-Z-Boy

La-Z-Boy
Consolidated Balance Sheet

(Amounts in thousands, except par value)	As of April 29, 2000	As of April 24, 1999
Assets		
Current assets		
Cash and equivalents	$ 14,353	$ 33,550
Receivables, less allowance of $25,474 in 2000 and $19,550 in 1999	394,453	265,157
Inventories	245,803	96,511
Deferred income taxes	22,374	20,028
Other current assets	15,386	10,342
Total current assets	692,369	425,588
Property, plant, and equipment	451,371	322,667
Less: accumulated depreciation	223,488	196,678
Property, plant, and equipment, net	227,883	125,989
Goodwill, less accumulated amortization of $17,360 in 2000 and $13,583 in 1999	116,668	46,985
Trade names, less accumulated amortization of $1,052 in 2000	135,340	—
Other long-term assets, less allowance of $6,747 in 2000 and $6,077 in 1999	46,037	31,230
Total assets	$1,218,297	$629,792
Liabilities and shareholders' equity		
Total current liabilities	237,006	132,428
Long-term debt	318,199	82,449
Shareholders' equity		
Preferred shares—5,000 authorized; none issued	—	—
Common shares, $1 par value—150,000 authorized; 61,328 issued in 2000 and 52,340 issued in 1999[a]	61,328	52,340
Capital in excess of par value	211,450	31,582
Retained earnings	392,458	332,934
Currency translation adjustments	(2,144)	(1,941)
Total shareholders' equity	663,092	414,915
Total liabilities and shareholders' equity	$1,218,297	$629,792

Note: The accompanying notes to consolidated financial statements are an integral part of these statements.
[a]Weighted-average number of shares outstanding during the year = 54,488 (in thousands), given the notes to consolidated financial statements.

Exhibit 11–12   Ratio Analysis of La-Z-Boy

Ratio	Definition	Computation	Interpretation
Liquidity Current Ratio	$\dfrac{current\ assets}{current\ liabilities}$	$\dfrac{\$692,369}{\$237,006} = 2.92$	This is an excellent current ratio. A value over two is considered good.
Acid-Test Ratio (also known as the quick ratio)	$\dfrac{cash + trading\ securities + net\ accounts\ receivable}{total\ current\ liabilities}$	$\dfrac{\$14,353 + 394,453}{\$237,006} = 1.72$	This is a good acid-test ratio. This ratio should be at least 1; if not, a company could have problems meeting current obligations.
Working Capital (technically not a ratio, but still a measure of liquidity)	current assets – current liabilities	$\$692,369 - 237,006 = \$455,363$	The dollar amount of working capital doesn't give much information alone. It certainly should be positive!
Inventory Turnover Ratio	$\dfrac{cost\ of\ goods\ sold}{average\ inventory}$	$\dfrac{\$1,284,158}{\$(245,803 + 96,511)/2} = 7.50$	The company is turning over its inventory more than 7 times each year. It would be useful to compare this with previous years and with other companies in the industry.
Accounts Receivable Turnover Ratio	$\dfrac{net\ credit\ sales}{average\ net\ accounts\ receivable}$	$\dfrac{\$1,717,420}{\$(394,453 + 265,157)/2} = 5.21$	The company is turning over its receivables about 5 times each year. If you divide 365 days by 5, you'll see that it takes the company about 73 days to collect its receivables. For some companies, that would be too long. To evaluate the ratio for La-Z-Boy, you would need more information.
Solvency Debt to Equity	$\dfrac{total\ liabilities}{total\ equity}$	$\dfrac{\$237,006 + 318,199}{\$663,092} = 0.84$	The company has quite a lot of debt. But to evaluate the ratio, you would need ratios from other periods or other companies for comparison.
Times Interest Earned	$\dfrac{net\ income + interest\ expense + taxes}{interest\ expense}$	$\dfrac{\$87,614 + 9,655 + 52,699}{\$9,655^{a}} = 15.53$	The larger this number, the better. Its value should be compared with previous year ratios and with ratios of other companies in the industry.

Exhibit 11-12 (continued)

Ratio	Definition	Computation	Interpretation
Profitability			
Return on Assets	$\dfrac{\text{net income} + \text{interest}}{\text{average total assets}}$	$\dfrac{\$87,614 + 9,655}{\$(1,218,297 + 629,792)/2} = 0.11 = 11\%$	This is a good return on assets, but it should be compared with previous period ratios and to the ratios of other companies in the industry.
Return on Equity	$\dfrac{\text{net income} - \text{preferred dividends}}{\text{average common stockholders' equity}}$	$\dfrac{\$87,614 - 0}{\$(663,092 + 414,915)/2} = 0.16 = 16\%$	Most investors would be happy to earn a 16% return on their investment. Again, a comparison with previous periods or other companies would be informative.
Gross Margin Percentage	$\dfrac{\text{gross margin}}{\text{sales}}$	$\dfrac{\$433,262}{\$1,717,420} = 0.252 = 25.2\%$	The gross margin percentage is interesting (for every dollar of furniture the company sells, $0.75 was the cost of the item to La-Z-Boy), but it doesn't mean much by itself. For this ratio, a comparison to others in the same industry would be very useful.
Earnings per Share	$\dfrac{\text{net income} - \text{preferred dividends}}{\text{average number of common shares outstanding}}$	$\dfrac{\$87,614}{\$54,488^b} = \$1.61$	By itself, this ratio is not very informative, (at least we know that a positive number is good) the *trend* in EPS that gives the most information about the company.
Market Indicators			
Price-Earnings Ratio	$\dfrac{\text{market price per share}}{\text{earnings per share}}$	$\dfrac{\$15.69}{\$1.61} = 9.75$	This PE ratio is not very high, indicating a company that is established and stable (as opposed to being a potentially high-growth firm).
Dividend-Yield Ratio	$\dfrac{\text{dividend per share}}{\text{market price per share}}$	$\dfrac{\$0.32}{\$15.69} = 0.02 = 2\%$	The dividend yield also indicates an established firm. Some high-growth firms, like Cisco Systems, for example, don't pay any dividends.

Note: As you evaluate the ratios, keep in mind that a single ratio is not very useful. You should use the information from the previous year for La-Z-Boy, given in Exhibits 11-10 and 11-11, to compute another set of ratios. See what you can learn with two years worth of ratios.

[a] Technically, the interest expense should be net of tax.

[b] Weighted average, disclosed in the notes to the consolidated financial statements.

Conclusion

You've probably noticed at the end of every financial statement, "The accompanying notes to the financial statements are an integral part of these financial statements." Some analysts believe there is more real information about the financial health of a company in the notes than in the statements themselves. Look at the notes that accompany the statements of Pier 1 Imports in Appendix A. The notes are extensive and detailed. The more you learn about analyzing and evaluating a company's performance, whether in subsequent courses or in actual business experience, the better you will understand the information in the notes to the financial statements.

We've seen what a business firm does and why it does it. To be successful in adding value and making a profit, a firm must be able to record the details of its transactions in a way that makes the information available to the people inside and outside the firm when they need it. To better appreciate the importance of the role of accounting information, look at a business plan. A business plan is a detailed analysis of what it would take to start and maintain the operation of a successful business firm. Financial information is a large and crucial component of a business plan. Sales must be forecast, and expenses must be estimated. A full set of financial statements called **pro-forma financial statements** must be prepared. These are "what if" financial statements, forecasts that fit the business plan.

Pro-forma financial statements are forecasted financial statements.

Because accounting is such an integral part of business, accounting principles will continue to change as business changes. Each year, the FASB and the SEC add to and change the rules for including, excluding, and valuing items on the financial statements. Further, because accountants are concerned with the continued usefulness and reliability of the accounting data, the accounting profession will be increasingly concerned with new developments such as electronic transactions, e-business, and real-time access to financial data. As competition takes on new dimensions, particularly due to new technology, and the strength of the economy is uncertain, the financial information needed for good decision making will be more important than ever.

Summary Problem: Analysis of the Financial Statements of Tom's Wear

Even though we don't have several years of Tom's Wear financial statements needed to perform a typical analysis, we do have several months of financial statements to examine. Publicly held corporations—those that trade on the stock exchanges—provide quarterly statements to their shareholders, and investors and financial analysts often analyze those quarterly statements. First, we'll put the January, February, and March financial statements together to give us the first quarter financial statements; and then we'll combine the April, May, and June statements together for the second quarter. Exhibit 11-13 shows the financial statements for the first two quarters.

Income statements for the	First quarter	Second quarter
Sales revenue	$ 4,750	$ 70,700
Cost of goods sold	(1,900)	(25,535)
Gross margin	2,850	45,165
Interest expense	(35)	(810)
Other expenses	(375)	(11,933)
Net income	$ 2,440	$ 32,422

Balance sheets at	March 31, 2001	June 30, 2001
Assets		
Cash	$ 3,995	$ 8,278
Accounts receivable	2,000	42,780
Inventory	300	6,365
Prepaid insurance	75	150
Prepaid Web service		200
Prepaid rent		1,800
Total current assets	6,370	59,573
Equipment (net)	3,900	3,600
Van (net)		27,245
Total assets	$10,270	$ 90,418
Liabilities		
Accounts payable	$ 0	$ 18,950
Other payables	30	2,806
Notes payable (current)	3,000	6,000
Total current liabilities	$ 3,030	27,756
Notes payable (long-term)	0	24,000
Total liabilities	3,030	51,756
Equity		
Common stock	$ 5,000	$ 5,000
Additional paid-in capital		
Retained earnings	2,240	33,662
Total shareholders' equity	7,240	38,662
Total liabilities and shareholders' equity	$10,270	$ 90,418

Exhibit 11-13

Financial Statements for Tom's Wear for First and Second Quarters of 2001

tom's wear

Required

Calculate the following ratios using the financial statements for Tom's Wear for the first two quarters of 2001.

1. Current ratio
2. Acid-test ratio
3. Working capital
4. Debt-to-equity ratio
5. Times interest earned
6. Return on assets
7. Return on equity
8. Gross margin percentage

Comment on the meaning and interpretation of each ratio.

Solution

These are the ratios for Tom's Wear for the first two quarters of 2001.

Selected Ratios for	First Quarter	Second Quarter	Comments
Current ratio	2.10	2.15	The current ratio is in line with many businesses. (Current ratio of 2 or higher is considered good.) We'd need an industry average or another couple of quarters to interpret this ratio.
Acid test	1.98	1.84	The closer the acid test to the current ratio, the more liquid Tom's current assets are.
Working capital	$3,340.00	$31,817.00	This doesn't give us much information yet. We need many more quarters to get a feeling for the amount of working capital that Tom needs.
Debt to equity	0.42	1.34	The change in this ratio indicates Tom's Wear's increasing amount of debt. The second quarter value is quite high.
Times interest earned	70.71	41.03	Even with a large amount of debt, Tom's Wear is having no trouble covering its interest payments.
Return on assets	48%	66%	This ratio is a good sign, indicating that Tom's Wear is earning an excellent return on its assets.
Return on equity	67%	141%	This return on equity is very, very good. Only a small number of companies have a return on equity over 100%. Check it out on the Internet. See if you can find any companies that earned a return on equity over 100% last year.
Gross margin %	60%	64%	This ratio doesn't tell us very much because we have little basis for evaluation. The ratio has increased slightly, a positive change. Tom's Wear is earning more money on every sale in the second quarter than it did the first quarter. Can you recall anything in the transactions that would account for this?

Understanding Excel

In this exercise you perform ratio analyses for Tom's Wear, Inc. for the third quarter of the year.

Requirements

1. Open a new Excel work sheet.
2. Beginning in cell A1, input the following chart that details Tom's Wear, Inc.'s financial statement information at the end of the second quarter, as given in the chapter. For this problem only, assume the numbers given in the chart are Tom's results at the end of the third quarter. Use formulas as appropriate to calculate totals. You may also choose the font type and size as desired.

Income statements for the	Second quarter	Third quarter
Sales revenue	$70,700	$ 522,171
Cost of goods sold	(25,535)	(177,826)
Gross margin	45,165	344,345
Interest expense	(810)	(2,250)
Other expenses	(11,933)	(185,603)
Net income	$32,422	$ 156,492

Balance sheets at	June 30, 2001	September 30, 2001
Assets		
Cash	$ 8,278	$ 921,249
Accounts receivable	42,780	331,611
Inventory	6,365	30,269
Prepaid insurance	150	450
Prepaid Web service	200	50
Prepaid rent	1,800	1,800
Total current assets	59,573	1,285,429
Land	0	7,500
Building, net	0	67,110
Equipment, net	3,600	101,715
Van, net	27,245	110,970
Total assets	$90,418	$1,572,724
Liabilities		
Accounts payable	$18,950	$ 18,711
Other payables	2,806	4,359
Current portion of long-term debt	6,000	8,710
Total current liabilities	27,756	31,780
Notes payable	24,000	96,290
Total liabilities	51,756	128,070

Equity		
Common stock	$ 5,000	$ 7,500
Additional paid-in capital		1,247,500
Retained earnings	33,662	189,654
Total shareholders' equity	38,662	1,444,654
Total liabilities and shareholders' equity	$90,418	$1,572,724

3. Beginning in column F, calculate the following ratios for Tom's Wear, Inc. for the third quarter of 2001:
   a. Current
   b. Acid test
   c. Working capital
   d. Debt to equity
   e. Times interest earned
   f. Return on assets
   g. Return on equity
   h. Gross margin percentage
   i. Inventory turnover
   j. Accounts receivable turnover

   Hint: All the ratios can be calculated using your table input and formulas. Use parentheses as needed to ensure the correct calculation.

4. Beginning in column H, comment on each ratio. (Use the comments for the first and second quarters as your guide, and don't forget to consider the change from the earlier quarters.)

   Hint: Widen column H to 50 and then wrap text as needed for your comments.

5. Print your file and save it to disk. Name your file TomsWear11.

Answers to Study Break Questions

Study Break 11-1   These items are shown net of tax; thus, the tax effect is shown along with the accounting effect. If they were not shown net of tax, the tax effect would have to be included in the taxes for the period. Including the tax effects of these three items in the current tax expense would distort the tax expense of the period.

Study Break 11-2
1. Trading securities are shown as a current asset on the balance sheet at market value of $52,000 (unrealized gain of $2,000 will be shown on the income statement).
2. Available-for-sale securities are shown as either a current asset or a noncurrent asset on the balance sheet at market value of $52,000. (Unrealized gain is shown as a direct addition to *owner's equity*—either shown separately as unrealized gain or shown with other items in *other comprehensive income.*
3. Held-to-maturity securities are shown as a long-term asset on the balance sheet at a cost of $50,000.

Study Break 11-3   If a company pays off a current liability with cash, the current ratio would go up. Equal numbers would be subtracted from the numerator and from the denominator. Try it — see what happens. Suppose the current ratio equals $5/$4 or 1.25. Then if current assets and current liabilities were each reduced by 1, the new current ratio would be $4/$3 or 1.33.

Working capital would not change. In the example it is $5 − 4 = $1 before the debt is paid off, and it is $4 − 3 = $1 after the debt is paid off.

Study Break 11-4   No, you cannot tell how profitable a company is from a gross margin percentage. For the comparison to be useful, you would have to know whether the companies are in the very same business. Otherwise, you can tell nothing about the profitability of one company relative to the profitability of the other. If a company has a very low gross margin percentage, it could still make a significant profit by turning over the inventory rapidly. Grocery stores are a good example of an industry with low margins but very high turnover. Furthermore, gross profit is not net income. Two companies may have very different selling and administrative expenses, which will have an impact on net income.

Questions

1. What items are required to be shown separately on the income statement, after income from operations, and why?
2. Why would a company want to change an accounting principle? Do the accounting requirements encourage or discourage such changes? Why?
3. What does it mean to show an item *net of tax?*
4. What is comprehensive income, and where is it shown on the financial statements?
5. Give an example of an item that would be part of *other comprehensive income.*
6. How are investments in securities classified, and how are they reported on the financial statements?
7. What is the difference in the accounting treatment of unrealized gains and losses on trading securities and the accounting treatment of unrealized gains and losses on available-for-sale securities?
8. What is horizontal analysis?
9. What is vertical analysis?
10. What ratios are useful for measuring liquidity?
11. What ratios are useful for measuring solvency?
12. What ratios are useful for measuring profitability?

Short Exercises

L.O. 11-1

SE11-1   In 2003, Earthscope Company decided to sell its satellite sales division, even though the division had been profitable during the year. During 2003, the satellite division earned $54,000 and the taxes on that income were $12,500. The division was sold for a gain of $750,000, and the taxes on the gain amounted to $36,700. How would these amounts be reported on the income statement for the year ended December 31, 2003?

SE11-2 In 2004, Office Products, Inc., decided to sell its furniture division because it had been losing money for several years. During 2004, the furniture division lost $140,000. The tax savings related to the loss amounted to $25,000. The division was sold for a loss of $350,000; and the tax savings related to the loss on the sale amounted to $50,000. How would these amounts be reported on the income statement for the year ended December 31, 2004?

L.O. 11-1

SE11-3 After the disaster at the World Trade Center in 2001, Congress passed a law requiring new security devices in airports. One airport security firm had to get rid of several scanning devices and suffered a significant loss on the disposal of the devices. The loss amounted to $320,000, with a related tax benefit of 10% of the loss. How would this be reported on the firm's income statement?

L.O. 11-1

SE11-4 Sew and Save Company suffered an extraordinary loss of $30,000 last year. The related tax savings amounted to $5,600. How would this be reported on the income statement?

L.O. 11-1

SE11-5 LaFluentes Electronics, Inc., purchased an asset for $30,000 at the beginning of 2004. The asset was expected to last for 4 years with no residual value. The company used double-declining balance depreciation for the first 2 years; but for 2006, the company decided to switch to straight-line depreciation. How would this change in accounting principle be reflected in the financial statements? Give both financial statement line items and amounts. Assume a 30% tax rate.

L.O. 11-1

SE11-6 Often a change in accounting principle is the result of a change in GAAP. Suppose Hasty Company had been correctly capitalizing the costs associated with a certain type of software development. At December 31, 2003, costs worth $50,000 had been capitalized as a long-term asset. Suppose that during 2004, the Financial Accounting Standards Board decided the costs of this particular type of development should be expensed as incurred. What effect would this have on the income statement for Hasty Company for the year ended December 31, 2004? Assume a 30% tax rate.

L.O. 11-1

SE11-7 Give an example of a gain or loss that would be excluded from the income statement and shown directly on the balance sheet as part of other comprehensive income.

L.O. 11-2

SE11-8 Convey Company had some extra cash, so the company purchased some stocks in various companies, with the objective of making a profit in the short run. The cost of Convey's portfolio was $79,450. At December 31, 2006, the market value of the portfolio was $85,200. How would this increase in value be reflected in Convey's financial statements for the year ended December 31, 2006?

L.O. 11-3

SE11-9 Olin Copy Corp. reported the following amounts on its 2004 comparative income statement:

L.O. 11-4

(In thousands)	2004	2003	2002
Revenues	$6,400	$4,575	$3,850
Cost of sales	3,900	2,650	2,050

Perform a horizontal analysis of revenues and gross profit in both dollar amounts and in percentages for 2004 and 2003, using 2002 as the base year.

L.O. 11-4

SE11-10 Use the following information about the capital expenditures of Andes Company to perform a horizontal analysis, with 2001 as the base year. What information does this provide about Andes Company?

(In millions)	2004	2003	2002	2001
Capital expenditures	$41,400	$45,575	$43,850	$50,600

L.O. 11-4

SE11-11 Bessie's Quilting Company reported the following amounts on its balance sheet at December 31, 2004:

Cash	$ 5,000
Accounts receivable, net	40,000
Inventory	35,000
Equipment, net	120,000
Total assets	$200,000

Perform a vertical analysis of the assets of Bessie's Company. Use *total assets* as the base. What information does the analysis provide?

L.O. 11-4

SE11-12 Perform a vertical analysis on the following income statement, with sales as the base amount. What other information would you need to make this analysis meaningful?

Sales	$35,000
Cost of goods sold	14,000
Gross margin	21,000
Other expenses	7,000
Net income	$14,000

L.O. 11-5

SE11-13 Fireworks, Inc., reported current assets of $720,000 and a current ratio of 1.2. What were current liabilities? What was its working capital?

L.O. 11-5

SE11-14 A 5-year comparative analysis of the Low Light Company current ratio and quick ratio follows:

	2001	2002	2003	2004	2005
Current ratio	1.19	1.85	2.50	3.40	4.02
Acid-test ratio	1.15	1.02	0.98	0.72	0.50

a. What has been happening to the liquidity of Low Light Company over the 5 years from 2001 through 2005?
b. Does the trend in the two ratios give any information about what has happened to the makeup of the Low Light current assets over the 5-year period?

L.O. 11-5

SE11-15 A company's debt-to-equity ratio has been increasing for the past 4 years. Give at least two steps the company might have taken during this time that would have resulted in this increase.

L.O. 11-5

SE11-16 The following is a 5-year comparative analysis of the Accent Company return on assets and return on equity:

	2001	2002	2003	2004	2005
Return on assets	8%	7.5%	7.12%	6.54%	6%
Return on equity	20%	21%	21.8%	22.2%	23%

a. What does this analysis tell you about the overall profitability of Accent Company over the 5-year period?

b. What does this analysis tell you about what has happened to Accent's amount of debt over the past 5 years?

SE11-17 Earnings for Archibold Company have been fairly constant over the past 6 months, but the price-earnings ratio has been climbing steadily. How do you account for this? What does it tell you about the market's view of the future of the company?

L.O. 11-5

Exercises

E11-1 Use the following information to construct the part of an income statement beginning with income from continuing operations:

L.O. 11-1

Income from continuing operations	$230,000
Loss during the year from discontinued operations	50,000
Tax benefit of loss	8,500
Loss from sale of discontinued operations	138,500
Tax savings from loss on the sale	1,900

E11-2 Devon's Central Processing Agency suffered a $560,000 loss due to a disaster that qualifies as an extraordinary item for financial statement purposes. The tax benefit of the loss amounts to $123,000. Devon's also changed accounting principles and must record a cumulative effect of a change in accounting principle amounting to an addition to income of $24,500 with related taxes of $3,750. If income from continuing operations (net of tax) amounted to $1,300,500, what is net income?

L.O. 11-1

E11-3 CFI, Inc., began operations in 2001 and selected FIFO periodic as its inventory method. In 2004, before preparing the financial statements, CFI decided to change to average cost. Use the following information—net income under each of the inventory methods for the years from 2001 to 2004—to calculate the cumulative effect of the change in accounting principle, as it would appear on the income statement for the year ended December 31, 2004. Ignore tax considerations.

L.O. 11-1

	FIFO	Average cost
2001	$26,000	$24,000
2002	30,000	25,000
2003	28,000	27,000
2004	34,000	30,000

E11-4 Omicron Corp. invested $125,000 of its extra cash in securities. Under each of the following scenarios, calculate the (1) amount at which the investments would be valued for the year-end balance sheet, and (2) any other financial statement effects.

L.O. 11-3

a. All the securities were debt securities, with a maturity date of 2 years. Omicron will hold the securities until they mature. The market value of the securities at year-end was $123,000.

b. Omicron purchased the securities for trading, hoping to make a quick profit. At year-end the market value of the securities was $120,000.

c. Omicron is uncertain about how long it will hold the securities. At year-end the market value of the securities is $126,000.

E11-5 Jones Furniture, Inc., reported the following amounts for its sales during the past 5 years. By using 2000 as the base year, perform a horizontal analysis. What information does the analysis provide that was not apparent from the raw numbers?

L.O. 11-4

2004	2003	2002	2001	2000
$30,000	$28,400	$26,300	$23,200	$25,400

L.O. 11-4

E11-6 Use the income statement from Color Copy, Inc., to perform a vertical analysis with sales as the base.

Color Copy, Inc.
Income Statement
For the Year Ended September 30, 2004

Sales revenue		$10,228
Cost of goods sold		5,751
Gross profit on sales		4,477
Operating expenses		
Depreciation—buildings and equipment	$ 100	
Other selling and administrative	2,500	
Total expenses		*2,600*
Income before interest and taxes		1,877
Interest expense		350
Income before taxes		1,527
Income taxes		150
Net income		1,377

L.O. 11-5

E11-7 Calculate the current ratio and the amount of working capital for Albert's Hotels, Inc., for the years given in the following comparative balance sheets. Although a period of 2 years is not much of a trend, what is your opinion of the direction of these ratios?

Albert's Hotels, Inc.
Balance Sheet
At December 31, 2003 and 2002

	2003	2002
Current assets		
Cash	$ 98,000	$ 90,000
Accounts receivable, net	110,000	116,000
Inventory	170,000	160,000
Prepaid expenses	18,000	16,000
Total current assets	396,000	382,000
Equipment, net	184,000	160,000
Total assets	$580,000	$542,000
Total current liabilities	$206,000	$223,000
Long-term liabilities	119,000	117,000
Total liabilities	325,000	340,000
Common stockholders' equity	90,000	90,000
Retained Earnings	165,000	112,000
Total liabilities and stockholders' equity	$580,000	$542,000

E11-8 Use the balance sheets from Albert's Hotels, Inc., given in E11-7 to compute the debt-to-equity ratio at December 31, 2003 and 2002. Suppose you calculated a debt ratio using debt plus equity as the denominator. Which ratio—*debt-to-equity* or *debt-to-debt plus equity*—seems easier to interpret? As an investor, do you view the "trend" in the debt-to-equity ratio as favorable or unfavorable? Why?

L.O. 11-5

Problems—Set A

P11-1A Each of the following items was found on the financial statements for Hartsfield Company for the year ended December 31, 2004:

L.O. 11-1, 2, 3

Cumulative effect of a change in accounting principle, net of taxes of $10,000	$ 49,500
Net income from operations	136,500
Other comprehensive income	(24,000)
Investments in securities, held for short-term trading	75,000
Gain on the sale of a discontinued segment	140,000
Taxes due on the gain on the sale of discontinued segment	14,000
Investments held to maturity	40,000

Required: For each item, give the financial statement and section, where applicable, where the item would appear. Describe the item and give as many details of each item's financial statement presentation as possible.

P11-2A The following income statements are from the annual report of Sherwin Williams:

L.O. 11-4

	Year ended December 31		
(Thousands of dollars)	**1999**	**1998**	**1997**
Net sales	$5,003,837	$4,934,430	$4,881,103
Cost of goods sold	2,755,323	2,804,459	2,784,392
Gross profit	2,248,514	2,129,971	2,096,711
Selling, general, and administrative expenses	1,673,449	1,598,333	1,573,510
Operating income	575,065	531,638	523,201
Interest expense	61,168	71,971	80,837
Interest and net investment income	(5,761)	(6,482)	(8,278)
Other expense — net	29,540	26,046	23,365
Income before income taxes	490,118	440,103	427,277
Income taxes	186,258	167,239	166,663
Net income	$ 303,860	$ 272,864	$ 260,614

Required:

a. For each of the years shown, prepare a vertical analysis, using sales as the base. Write a paragraph explaining what the analysis shows.

b. By using 1997 as the base year, prepare a horizontal analysis for sales and cost of goods sold. What information does this analysis give you?

L.O. 11-5

P11-3A Selected data from the financial statements of Sherwin Williams follow:

(Thousands of dollars)	1999	1998
Net sales	$5,003,837	$4,934,430
Cost of goods sold	2,755,323	2,804,459
Gross profit	2,248,514	2,129,971
Interest expense	61,168	71,971
Income taxes	186,258	167,239
Net income	$ 303,860	$ 272,864
Cash and cash equivalents	$ 18,623	$ 19,133
Accounts receivable, less allowance	606,046	604,516
Total current assets	1,597,377	1,547,290
Total assets	$4,052,090	$4,065,462
Total current liabilities	$1,189,862	$1,111,973
Long-term liabilities	1,163,696	1,237,549
Shareholders' equity		
Common stock—$1.00 par value	206,309	205,701
Additional paid-in capital	150,887	143,686
Retained earnings	2,020,851	1,797,945
Treasury stock, at cost	(553,891)	(386,465)
Cumulative other comprehensive loss	(145,624)	(44,927)
Total shareholders' equity	$1,698,532	$1,715,940
Total liabilities and shareholders' equity	$4,052,090	$4,065,462

Required:

1. Calculate the following ratios for Sherwin Williams for 1999 and 1998:
   (Total shareholders' equity at December 31, 1997 was $1,592,180 thousand.)
   a. current ratio
   b. acid-test ratio
   c. working capital
   d. accounts receivable turnover ratio
   e. debt-to-equity ratio
   f. times interest earned
   g. return on equity
   h. gross margin percentage

2. Suppose the changes from 1998 to 1999 in each of these ratios were consistent with the direction and size of the changes for the past several years. For each ratio, explain what the trend in the ratio would indicate about Sherwin Williams.

L.O. 11-5

P11-4A The following information was taken from annual report of Presentations, Inc.:

	At December 31	
(In thousands)	2002	2001
Assets		
Current assets		
Cash	$ 1,617	1,220
Accounts receivable	1,925	3,112
Merchandise inventory	2,070	966
Prepaid expenses	188	149
Total current assets	$ 5,800	$5,447
Plant and equipment		
Buildings, net	4,457	2,992
Equipment, net	1,293	1,045
Total plant and equipment	5,750	4,037
Total assets	$11,550	$9,484

(In thousands)	At December 31	
	2002	2001
Liabilities		
Current liabilities		
Accounts payable	$ 1,817	$1,685
Notes payable	900	1,100
Total current liabilities	2,717	2,785
Long-term liabilities	3,500	2,000
Total liabilities	$ 6,217	$4,785
Stockholders' equity		
Common stock, no par value	3,390	3,042
Retained earnings	1,943	1,657
Total stockholders' equity	$ 5,333	$4,699
Total liabilities and stockholders' equity	$11,550	$9,484

Presentations, Inc.
Income Statement
For the Year Ended December 31, 2002
(In Thousands)

Sales revenue		$12,228
Cost of goods sold		8,751
Gross profit on sales		3,477
Operating expenses		
Depreciation—Buildings and equipment	$ 102	
Other selling and administrative	2,667	
Total Expenses		2,769
Income before interest and taxes		$ 708
Interest expense		168
Income before taxes		$ 540
Income taxes		114
Net income		$ 426

Required: Calculate the following ratios for 2002:

1. Return on equity
2. Debt to equity
3. Gross profit percentage (of sales)
4. Current ratio
5. Acid-test ratio
6. Times interest earned

What interpretation can you give this set of ratios for 2002 for Presentations, Inc.? What additional information would be useful to you?

P11-5A   The financial statements of For the Kitchen, Inc., include the following items:

	At June 30, 2004	At June 30, 2003
Balance sheet		
Cash	$ 17,000	$ 12,000
Investments (in trading securities)	10,000	16,000
Accounts receivable (net)	54,000	50,000
Inventory	75,000	70,000
Prepaid expenses	16,000	12,000
Total current assets	$172,000	$160,000
Total current liabilities	$140,000	$ 90,000
Income statement for the year ended June 30, 2004		
Credit sales	420,000	
Cost of goods sold	250,000	

Required:

1. Compute the following ratios for the year ended June 30, 2004.

   a. current ratio
   b. accounts receivable turnover
   c. inventory turnover ratio
   d. gross margin percentage

2. Which financial statement users would be most interested in these ratios?
3. Suppose the industry average for similar retail stores for the current ratio is 1.7. Does this information help you evaluate For the Kitchen's liquidity?

P11-6A   You are interested in investing in Reese Company, and you have obtained the balance sheets for the company for the past 2 years.

Reese Company
Balance Sheet
At June 30, 2004 and 2003

	2004	2003
Current assets		
Cash	$198,000	$ 90,000
Accounts receivable, net	210,000	116,000
Inventory	270,000	160,000
Prepaid rent	15,000	16,000
Total current assets	693,000	382,000
Equipment, net	280,000	260,000
Total assets	$973,000	$642,000
Total current liabilities	$306,000	$223,000
Long-term liabilities	219,000	117,000
Total liabilities	525,000	340,000
Common shareholders' equity	150,000	90,000
Retained earnings	298,000	212,000
Total liabilities and shareholders' equity	$973,000	$642,000

Net income for the year ended June 30, 2004 was $80,000.

Required: Compute as many of the financial statement ratios you've studied as possible with the information from Reese Company. Do you want to invest in Reese Company? What else do you want to know to help you evaluate the company?

Problems—Set B

P11-1B Each of the following items was found on the financial statements for Logan Company for the year ended December 31, 2004:

L.O. 11-1, 2, 3

Loss from operation of discontinued segment, net of taxes of $2,500	$ (32,500)
Loss from sale of discontinued segment	(136,500)
Taxes saved from the loss on the sale of discontinued segment	14,000
Investments in securities, held to maturity	75,000
Extraordinary loss from earthquake	(140,000)
Investments held for short-term trading	40,000

Required: For each item, give the financial statement and section, and where the item would appear. Explain what the item is, and give as many details of each item's financial statement presentation as you can.

P11-2B The following income statements are from the annual report of Sherwin Williams:

L.O. 11-4, 5

	Year ended December 31		
(Thousands of dollars)	1999	1998	1997
Net sales	$5,003,837	$4,934,430	$4,881,103
Cost of goods sold	2,755,323	2,804,459	2,784,392
Gross profit	$2,248,514	$2,129,971	$2,096,711
Selling, general, and administrative expenses	1,673,449	1,598,333	1,573,510
Operating income	$ 575,065	$ 531,638	$ 523,201
Interest expense	61,168	71,971	80,837
Interest and net investment income	(5,761)	(6,482)	(8,278)
Other expense—net	29,540	26,046	23,365
Income before income taxes	$ 490,118	$ 440,103	$ 427,277
Income taxes	186,258	167,239	166,663
Net income	$ 303,860	$ 272,864	$ 260,614

Required:

a. Calculate the gross margin percentage and the times interest earned ratio for each of the years given. Explain what the ratios tell you about the company's performance.
b. By using 1997 as the base year, prepare a horizontal analysis for operating income, income before taxes, and net income. What information does this analysis give you?

P11-3B The financial statements of Compass Company contained the following:

L.O. 11-5

	At December 31		
(Thousands of dollars)	2001	2000	1999
Cash and cash equivalents	$ 19,380	$ 21,866	
Accounts receivable, less allowance	35,640	32,232	
Total current assets	187,899	194,731	
Total assets	433,123	427,784	$395,981
Total current liabilities	73,612	63,310	
Total liabilities	118,803	162,350	175,688
Common stock—$0.01 par value	296	294	
Additional paid-in capital	262,462	257,684	
Retained earnings	85,312	17,896	
Net sales for the year	679,321	571,838	
Cost of goods sold	363,746	323,600	

Required:

1. Calculate the following ratios for Compass Company for 2001 and 2000:

    a. current ratio
    b. Acid-test ratio
    c. working capital
    d. inventory turnover ratio
    e. accounts receivable turnover ratio

2. Suppose the changes from 2000 to 2001 in each of these ratios were consistent with the direction and size of the change for the past several years. For each ratio, explain what the trend in the ratio would indicate about Compass Company.

L.O. 11-5

P11-4B The following information was taken from the annual report of ROM, Inc.:

| | At December 31 | |
(In thousands)	2005	2004
Assets		
Current assets		
Cash	$ 1,220	
Accounts receivable	3,112	
Merchandise inventory	966	
Prepaid expenses	149	
Total current assets	$ 5,447	
Plant and equipment		
Buildings, net	$ 2,992	
Equipment, net	1,045	
Total plant and equipment	$ 4,037	
Total assets	$ 9,484	$8,980
Liabilities		
Current liabilities		
Accounts payable	$ 1,685	
Notes payable	1,100	
Total current liabilities	$ 2,785	
Long-term liabilities	2,000	
Total liabilities	$ 4,785	$4,535
Stockholders' equity		
Common stock, no par value	$ 3,042	
Retained earnings	1,657	
Total stockholders' equity	$ 4,699	$4,445
Total liabilities and stockholders' equity	$ 9,484	$8,980
Sales for the year	$10,200	
Cost of goods sold	6,750	

Required: Calculate the following ratios for the year ended December 31, 2005:

1. Return on equity
2. Debt to equity
3. Gross profit percentage
4. Current ratio
5. Acid-test ratio

What interpretation can you give this set of ratios for ROM, Inc.? What additional information would help you?

P11-5B The financial statements of Builder Bob's, Inc., include the following items:

L.O. 11-5

	At September 30, 2004	At September 30, 2003
Balance sheet		
Cash	$ 27,000	$ 22,000
Investments (in trading securities)	15,000	12,000
Accounts receivable (net)	44,000	40,000
Inventory	85,000	75,000
Prepaid rent	6,000	2,000
Total current assets	177,000	151,000
Total current liabilities	120,000	80,000
Income statement for the year ended September 30, 2004		
Credit sales	$320,000	
Cost of goods sold	150,000	

Required:

1. Compute the following ratios for the year ended September 30, 2004 and September 30, 2003. For each, indicate whether the direction is favorable or unfavorable for the company.

   a. current ratio
   b. quick ratio
   c. accounts receivable turnover (for 2004 only)
   d. inventory turnover ratio (for 2004 only)
   e. gross margin percentage (of sales)

2. Which financial statement users would be most interested in these ratios?
3. Suppose the industry average for similar retail stores for the current ratio is 1.2. Does this information help you evaluate Builder Bob's liquidity?

P11-6B You are interested in investing in Apples and Nuts Company, and you have obtained the balance sheets for the company for the past 2 years.

L.O. 11-5

Apples and Nuts Company
Balance Sheet
At December 31, 2004 and 2003

	2004	2003
Current assets		
Cash	$ 98,000	$ 90,000
Accounts receivable, net	310,000	216,000
Inventory	275,000	170,000
Prepaid rent	10,000	6,000
Total current assets	693,000	482,000
Equipment, net	180,000	258,000
Total assets	$873,000	$740,000
Total current liabilities	$206,000	$223,000
Long-term liabilities	219,000	217,000
Total liabilities	425,000	440,000
Stockholders' equity	250,000	190,000
Retained earnings	198,000	110,000
Total liabilities and stockholders' equity	$873,000	$740,000

Note: Net income for the year ended December 31, 2004 was $100,000.

Required: Compute as many of the financial statement ratios you've studied as possible with the information from Apples and Nuts Company. Do you want to invest in this company? What else do you want to know to help you evaluate the company?

Issues for Discussion

L.O. 11-5

Financial statement analysis

1. Use the Pier 1 financial statements to compute for the two most recent years all the ratios given in Exhibit 11-8. Comment on what your analysis reveals.

Business risk

2. Which financial ratios give you information about the riskiness of investing in a company? Comment on those ratios from Pier 1, which you computed in 1 that precedes.

Ethics

3. Atlantis Company sells computer components and plans on borrowing some money to expand. After reading a lot about earnings management, Andy, the owner of Atlantis, has decided he should try to accelerate some sales to improve his financial statement ratios. He has called his best customers and asked them to make their usual January purchases by December 31. He told them he would allow them until the end of February to pay for the purchases, just as if they had made their purchases in January.

    a. What do you think are the ethical implications of Andy's actions?
    b. Which ratios will be improved by accelerating these sales?

Internet Exercise: Papa John's International, INC.

Papa John's has surpassed Little Caesar to become the number three pizza chain, behind only number one Pizza Hut and number two Domino's. Papa John's 2,800 restaurants (about 75% are franchised) are scattered across the United States and 10 other countries. Let's examine how Papa John's compares with its competition.

Please go to the www.prenhall.com/myphlip *Web site, register, and add this textbook to your myphlip page (if you haven't done so already). Go to Chapter 11 and use the Internet Exercise company link.*

IE11-1 Go to *About Papa John's* and explore *"Papa John's Story"* and *"Our Pizza Story."* What differentiates Papa John's from its competition?

IE11-2 Go to *http://moneycentral.msn.com* and get the stock "Quote" for PZZA, the stock symbol of Papa John's International. Identify the current price-to-earnings ratio and dividend yield. What do these market indicators mean for Papa John's?

IE11-3 Select *Financial Results* and then *Key Ratios*.

    a. Select *Financial Condition*. Identify the current ratio and quick (acid-test) ratio for Papa John's and the industry. Who would find these ratios of primary interest? Identify the debt-to-equity ratio and interest coverage (another name for the times interest earned ratio) for Papa John's and the industry. Is Papa John's primarily financed by debt or equity? How can you tell? Does Papa John's have the ability to pay its interest obligations? Explain why or why not.
    b. Select *Investment Returns*. Identify return on equity and return on assets for Papa John's and the industry. What do these ratios measure?

c. Select *Ten-Year Summary*. Review the information provided for return on equity and return on assets. What additional information is revealed about Papa John's financial position? Is this information helpful?

IE11-4 Review the information recorded earlier. Does Papa John's compare favorably with industry averages? Support your judgment with at least two observations.

Please note: Internet Web sites are constantly being updated. Therefore, if the information is not found where indicated, please explore the Web site further to find the information.

Often the only difference between one store and the next is the sign on the door.

But shopping at Pier 1 is different – it's a journey to a place where customers lose

themselves in products that blend styles and thoughts from around the world.

It's no small wonder, then, that they also find themselves at Pier 1 – the one place

where they can explore their sense of individuality.

to our shareholders

Pier 1 Imports had an outstanding year of financial and strategic accomplishments. As I reflect on fiscal 2001, I am reassured that the initiatives we began almost two years ago have been realized in our results this past year. When I became Chairman and Chief Executive Officer in 1998, I committed our Company to refocusing on the basics and returning Pier 1's selling proposition to value. We worked on ways to improve, without reinventing all aspects of our business. Now, looking back on those changes, I believe that we successfully revitalized the brand. Customers have returned to our stores and they are buying more frequently than they did two years ago. The positive repositioning and returning to value has continued to gain us market share in the home furnishings industry, an achievement that makes me very proud.

We will continue to consider new formats and strategies to meet the challenges to grow Pier 1 stores. Last year, we promised to focus on long-term growth strategies for the Company. We delivered on our promise with the acquisition of Cargo, a 21-store retail chain, serving primarily the $8 billion children's furniture market. This is a new opportunity for our Company with an established brand that is synonymous with quality and value – like our Pier 1 brand. We envision Cargo to grow to a 200- to 300-store concept over the next ten years.

Pier 1 achieved record sales and earnings during fiscal 2001. Sales were $1.4 billion, an increase of 14.7% over last year's $1.2 billion. All-important same-store sales grew by 7.8%. Income before taxes was $150.2 million and net income was $94.7 million, with diluted earnings per share of $.97, up 29% from a year ago. But fiscal 2001 was not unusual; the Company's compounded growth rates over the past five years resulted in sales growth of 12% and income before tax growth of 20%. We believe continued growth in sales and profits are the result of the solid **execution** of our plans.

We have spent a considerable amount of effort over the last few years strengthening our balance sheet and preserving cash flow for projects that result in a solid return on investment. Cash from operations generated $110 million after working capital investments. We repurchased 3.3 million shares of our Company's stock during the year. Additionally, we funded $45 million of capital projects to strengthen the **infrastructure** for future growth. That pursuit continues this year as we approach the next phase of our growth cycle – with needs in systems technology, distribution facilities and outstanding people to support that growth.

During fiscal 2001, we opened 65 new Pier 1 stores in important markets and closed 24 stores primarily due to relocations to better trading areas. Beginning this year, fiscal 2002, we plan to accelerate Pier 1's new store growth plans. We see **opportunities** to have 1,200 to 1,400 Pier 1 stores in North America. Our plans include opening 85 new stores in fiscal 2002 and possibly 90 new stores in fiscal 2003. This will increase our new store square footage growth rate to 7% in fiscal 2002. Including Cargo's growth plans, our goal will be even higher next fiscal year. We ended fiscal 2001 with 826 stores in North America, 23 stores in the United Kingdom, 13 stores in Mexico, 7 stores in Puerto Rico, 9 stores in Japan and 21 new Cargo stores, for a total of 899 stores worldwide.

We launched a new national marketing campaign this past year with the tagline "Get in touch with your _senses_.℠" With the resolution of the Screen Actors' Guild strike last fall, we introduced our celebrity spokesperson, Kirstie Alley, on television this spring. Kirstie is passionate about Pier 1, and in the commercials she drives home the "sense of **individuality**" our customers enjoy when they shop in our stores. We have had many positive comments on the new TV ads this spring; they are fun and entertaining to watch.

When we think of our very best customers, the Pier 1 Credit Card comes to mind. Compared to a typical Pier 1 shopper, this group spends an average of three times more, or $152 per visit, compared to $43 on all other tender types. Pier 1's proprietary credit card was influential in our sales growth for the year. Sales on the credit card were up an impressive 25.5% for the year, or 28.9% of U.S. sales.

As a convenience to our customers, we began accepting proprietary credit card payments in the stores. Our customers like the convenience, and we like seeing our customers on a regular basis to pay down their card balances.

Last year, we launched our new online store at pier1.com. Customers can choose from over 2,000 items, or they can purchase a Pier 1 Gift Card. In particular, the Bridal & Gift Registry and the gift card purchases have been successful components of our e-commerce business. We expect the site to drive sales to our stores and to serve as a marketing tool that will allow new customers to discover our distinct merchandise brand from the convenience of their homes or offices. Customers are more willing to purchase online if they have confidence in the brand and have experience shopping in person at a Pier 1 store.

I have always believed that the fortunate should **support** the less fortunate. Pier 1 and our more than 14,000 enthusiastic associates join together to support the Susan G. Komen Breast Cancer Foundation, the United Way and other local causes. Pier 1 stores in North America are the largest retailers of UNICEF greeting cards in the world. We give back 100% of the proceeds received from the card sales to that organization for the health and well-being of children around the world.

We are extremely proud of our accomplishments this past year. I believe that we continue to have a distinct competitive advantage. The Pier 1 stores offer **unique** and proprietary hand-crafted merchandise presented in a one-of-a-kind shopping experience. Our customers are engaged by our stores because they can express their individual sense of style in a way that truly delights their senses. The Pier 1 Imports brand is a promise of value to our customers, associates and shareholders.

I want to thank those customers, suppliers, associates, the Board of Directors and shareholders who passionately join with me in the commitment to better things to come in the future of our Company.

Marvin J. Girouard
Chairman and Chief Executive Officer

You can copy someone else's recipe or have a taste all your own. Guess what we chose to do.

A sense of individuality

There is a sense of individuality to the Pier 1 brand. We stand apart from many retailers, because we deliver distinct merchandise, fun stores, outstanding customer service and consistent profitability to ensure growth for years to come.

Our strategy is simple: Leverage what we have learned over 39 years in merchandising, marketing, operations, real estate, human resources and international logistics. Then deliver to our associates, customers and shareholders what they expect from Pier 1: a fun and great place to work and shop.

A sense of value

Pier 1 is a place where customers can express their own sense of style and delight all their senses. It's a hands-on experience: the feel of a hand-crafted wicker chair…the scent of our exclusively fragranced candles…the sight of all the colors to choose from to make a personal decorating palette.

Fresh ideas don't just stand out in product design. They set our employees apart, too.

Pier 1 delights our customers' sense of savings. From furniture to dinnerware to decorative accessories, our merchandise is surprisingly affordable. Value means a product and a price that make sense for our customers, and that philosophy guides us as we import from over 50 countries worldwide.

As our buyers and product designers consider merchandise overseas, they ask many questions before committing to a product. The two most important: "Is it unique?" and "Is it affordable, offering great value to our customers?"

A sense of service

Whoever defined a store as a plain "box" has not visited Pier 1. Our stores are filled with eclectic merchandise and caring, helpful associates who bring the environment to life.

Outstanding customer service is essential to growing our successful retail concept to more than 1,200 stores. So we encourage each of our 14,000 associates who wear the blue apron to "Be a Retailer," to make the individual, on-the-spot decisions it takes to help the customer when she needs it.

Retailers that provide great service have the right values. We trust our associates, encourage them in their work and give them responsibility, authority and opportunity.

Something happens when you capture the spirit of your customer. You find a friend forever.

A sense of positioning

Customers have individual tastes, and that is the focus of our national advertising campaign "Get in touch with your *senses*.ᴿᴹ" It colorfully captures the Pier 1 shopping experience on TV, in magazines and newspapers, through direct mail and at pier1.com.

Our research tells us that our customers enjoy adventure, trying new things, being active, creating their own world. They do not go for stale ideas. Our campaign captures the casual culture of Pier 1's merchandise and store environment. It is more fun finding the perfect new chair for your home, discovering the price and realizing you can take it home tonight.

The advertising campaign features actress and avid Pier 1 shopper Kirstie Alley, who describes the store best in one of the lines she scripted herself for one of three new TV commercials: Pier 1 is "sexy *and* sensible."

A sense of giving

Pier 1 gives back to individuals in need around the world. In the past decade, Pier 1 has contributed nearly $20 million to local, national and global communities for those in need.

As a national partner of the Susan G. Komen Breast Cancer Foundation, we continue to support Race for the Cure® events across the country, including our sponsorship of the Washington, D.C., race, the largest 5K in the world.

Finding a unique gift feels great. But when you give to someone deserving, it feels even better.

We are the largest retailer of UNICEF greeting cards and the organization's longest-running corporate partner. Pier 1 donates 100% of the proceeds from card sales – $1.6 million in year 2000 – to improve the health and nutritional needs of children around the world. In the past 16 years, we have raised a total of more than $14 million. In 2001, we will be the national box distributor for "Trick-or-Treat for UNICEF," a program that raises nearly $5 million each year to help children.

A sense of growth

Pier 1 Imports will continue making sound strategic decisions that increase shareholder value.

We will expand the Pier 1 concept with 85 store openings planned this year and 90 next year. By leveraging special programs, we will increase our services for interior designers, couples registering for weddings and shoppers who like the convenience of our online store at pier1.com.

In the next few years, we expect Cargo to emerge as a national, value-oriented retailer of home furnishings for children and families. We foresee several opportunities to serve the 78 million children under 19 years of age and their families in the $8 billion youth furniture market.

Pier 1 continues to pursue growth opportunities by evaluating new retail formats, acquisitions or strategic alliances.

Key Financial Statistics
For the five years ended March 3, 2001

Total Sales
(Dollars in Millions)

Fiscal	1997	1998	1999	2000	2001
	$947.1	$1,075.4	$1,138.6	$1,231.1	$1,411.5

Net Income
(Dollars in Millions)

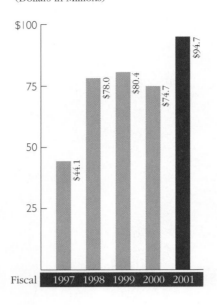

Fiscal	1997	1998	1999	2000	2001
	$44.1	$78.0	$80.4	$74.7	$94.7

Preferred Credit Card Sales
(Dollars in Millions)

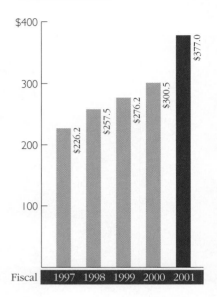

Fiscal	1997	1998	1999	2000	2001
	$226.2	$257.5	$276.2	$300.5	$377.0

Diluted Earnings Per Share
(Dollars)

Fiscal	1997	1998	1999	2000	2001
	$0.44	$0.72	$0.77	$0.75	$0.97

Stores Worldwide

Fiscal	1997	1998	1999	2000	2001
	720	763	805	834	899

Shareholders' Equity Per Share
(Dollars)

Fiscal	1997	1998	1999	2000	2001
	$3.34	$3.89	$4.12	$4.60	$5.52

Pier 1 imports®

Merchandise Sales Mix
For fiscal year 2001

Seasonal 9%
Housewares 12%
Bed & Bath 17%
Furniture 40%
Decorative Accessories 22%

Pier 1 Imports, Inc.

FINANCIAL SUMMARY
($ in millions except per share amounts)

	4-Year Compound Annual Growth Rate	Year Ended				
		2001(1)	2000	1999	1998	1997
SUMMARY OF OPERATIONS:						
Net sales	10.5%	$ 1,411.5	1,231.1	1,138.6	1,075.4	947.1
Gross profit	11.5%	$ 594.5	512.5	500.4	461.5	384.5
Selling, general and administrative expenses . .	9.9%	$ 399.8	349.4	334.6	315.8	274.5
Depreciation and amortization	21.5%	$ 43.2	40.0	31.1	23.9	19.8
Operating income.	13.8%	$ 151.5	123.2	134.7	121.7	90.2
Nonoperating (income) and expenses, net (2) . .	(39.8%)	$ 1.3	4.6	5.0	(2.3)	9.9
Income before income taxes and extraordinary charges	16.9%	$ 150.2	118.6	129.6	124.0	80.3
Income before extraordinary charges	18.4%	$ 94.7	74.7	80.4	78.0	48.2
Extraordinary charges from early retirement of debt, net of income tax benefit		$ –	–	–	–	4.1
Net income	21.1%	$ 94.7	74.7	80.4	78.0	44.1
PER SHARE AMOUNTS (ADJUSTED FOR STOCK SPLITS AND DIVIDENDS):						
Basic earnings before extraordinary charges . .	18.3%	$ .98	.78	.82	.77	.50
Basic earnings	20.8%	$ .98	.78	.82	.77	.46
Diluted earnings before extraordinary charges	19.9%	$ .97	.75	.77	.72	.47
Diluted earnings.	21.9%	$ .97	.75	.77	.72	.44
Cash dividends declared	21.0%	$ .15	.12	.12	.09	.07
Shareholders' equity	13.4%	$ 5.52	4.60	4.12	3.89	3.34
OTHER FINANCIAL DATA:						
Working capital (3).	11.5%	$ 333.0	239.3	252.1	280.8	215.3
Current ratio (3)	2.4%	3.3	2.4	2.9	3.3	3.0
Total assets	6.6%	$ 735.7	670.7	654.0	653.4	570.3
Long-term debt.	(31.6%)	$ 25.0	25.0	96.0	114.9	114.5
Shareholders' equity	13.3%	$ 531.9	440.7	403.9	392.7	323.0
Weighted average diluted shares outstanding (millions)		96.3	95.8	98.1	101.1	96.8
Effective tax rate (4)		37.0%	37.0	38.0	37.1	40.0
Return on average shareholders' equity.	5.1%	19.5%	17.7	20.2	21.8	16.0
Return on average total assets	14.0%	13.5%	11.3	12.3	12.8	8.0
Pre-tax return on sales (5).	5.7%	10.6%	9.6	11.4	11.5	8.5

(1) Fiscal 2001 consisted of a 53-week year. All other fiscal years presented reflect 52-week years.
(2) Nonoperating (income) and expenses, net, were comprised of interest expense and interest and investment income in each fiscal year presented, and in addition, included net recoveries associated with trading activities in fiscal 1998.
(3) The reduction in fiscal 2000 working capital and current ratio was the result of the Company's call of its outstanding 5¼% convertible subordinated notes. The notes were primarily converted into shares of the Company's common stock in March 2000. Excluding the reclassification of the 5¼% notes from long-term to short-term, working capital would have been $278.5 million with a current ratio of 3.0 to 1 at fiscal 2000 year-end.
(4) No income tax expense was provided on the net recoveries associated with trading activities, which resulted in a lower effective tax rate in fiscal 1998.
(5) Calculated before fiscal 1997 extraordinary charges from the early retirement of debt, net of income tax benefit.

Pier 1 Imports, Inc.

MANAGEMENT'S DISCUSSION AND ANALYSIS OF FINANCIAL CONDITION AND RESULTS OF OPERATIONS

Pier 1 Imports, Inc. (the "Company") is one of North America's largest specialty retailers of unique decorative home furnishings, gifts and related items, with nearly 900 stores in 48 states, Canada, Puerto Rico, the United Kingdom, Mexico and Japan as of fiscal 2001 year-end. The Company directly imports merchandise from over 50 countries around the world and designs proprietary offerings that become exclusive Pier 1 Imports offerings. In February 2001, the Company acquired certain assets and assumed certain liabilities of Cargo Furniture, Inc. ("Cargo"). Cargo, a 21-store retailer and wholesaler of casual lifestyle furniture, gifts and home décor, had no impact on the Company's fiscal 2001 operations due to the timing of the acquisition, but is reflected in the Company's fiscal 2001 year-end balance sheet. During fiscal 2001, the Company reported record sales of $1,411.5 million and net income of $94.7 million, or $.97 per diluted share.

FISCAL YEARS ENDED MARCH 3, 2001 AND FEBRUARY 26, 2000

During fiscal 2001, the Company recorded net sales of $1,411.5 million, an increase of $180.4 million, or 14.7%, over net sales of $1,231.1 million for the prior fiscal year. Due to the Company's fiscal calendar, fiscal 2001 consisted of a 53-week year, while fiscal 2000 and 1999 were 52-week years. Same-store sales for fiscal 2001 improved 7.8% excluding the 53rd week of sales activity. The Company's new advertising campaign, proprietary credit card and other promotions and continued focus on a value pricing initiative, which began in fiscal 2000, resulted in higher customer traffic, average purchases per customer and conversion ratios during fiscal 2001.

The Company's continued efforts to expand by opening new stores also contributed to sales growth during fiscal 2001. The Company opened 65 new stores and closed 24 stores in North America during fiscal 2001, bringing the Pier 1 North American store count up to 826 at year-end. With the addition of Cargo, the store count worldwide, including North America, Puerto Rico, the United Kingdom, Mexico

and Japan, totaled 899 at the end of fiscal 2001 compared to 834 at the end of fiscal 2000.

Increased use of the Company's proprietary credit card added to the Company's sales growth during fiscal 2001. Sales on the proprietary credit card were $377.0 million and accounted for 28.9% of U.S. store sales during fiscal 2001, an increase of $76.5 million over proprietary credit card sales in the prior year of $300.5 million, which represented 26.3% of U.S. store sales during that year. Proprietary credit card customers spent an average of $152 per transaction in fiscal 2001 compared to $142 per transaction in fiscal 2000. The Company attributes the growth in sales on the card to continued efforts to open new accounts, deferred payment options offered with furniture promotions and enhanced customer loyalty through targeted promotions.

Gross profit, after related buying and store occupancy costs, expressed as a percentage of sales, increased 50 basis points in fiscal 2001 to 42.1% from 41.6% in fiscal 2000. Merchandise margins, as a percentage of sales, declined from 54.6% in fiscal 2000 to 54.2% in fiscal 2001, a decrease of 40 basis points. The decrease was a result of management's concerted decision to continue to give value back to customers by offering unique merchandise at affordable prices. In addition, the effect of a full year of price reductions taken as a result of the value pricing initiative started in May 1999 and continuing throughout fiscal 2000 created downward pressure on fiscal 2001 merchandise margins. This decline was also due in part to higher freight rates during the first half of fiscal 2001 as compared to the same period in fiscal 2000. The decreases in merchandise margins were more than offset by the leveraging of relatively fixed rental costs over a higher sales base. Store occupancy costs improved 90 basis points as a percentage of sales from 13.0% in fiscal 2000 to 12.1% in fiscal 2001.

As a percentage of sales, selling, general and administrative expenses, including marketing, improved 10 basis points to 28.3% in fiscal 2001 from 28.4% in fiscal 2000. In total dollars, selling, general and

Pier 1 Imports, Inc.

MANAGEMENT'S DISCUSSION AND ANALYSIS OF FINANCIAL CONDITION AND RESULTS OF OPERATIONS
(continued)

administrative expenses for fiscal 2001 increased $50.4 million over the prior fiscal year. Expenses that normally increase proportionately with sales and number of stores, such as marketing, store payroll, supplies and equipment rental, increased by $34.3 million, but as a percentage of sales declined nearly 20 basis points to 20.2% this fiscal year. Marketing as a percentage of sales decreased 20 basis points as a result of reduced spending on newspaper and magazine advertisements, along with leveraging marketing expenditures over a higher sales base. As a percentage of sales, the decrease in marketing expenses was offset by a 10 basis point increase in store payroll when comparing the two fiscal years. This increase was largely attributable to store bonuses awarded based on sales gains. All other selling, general and administrative expenses increased by $16.0 million, and increased 10 basis points as a percentage of sales. This increase was primarily due to an increase in information technology and other non-store salaries, partially offset by effective management of other administrative expenses and a reduction in net credit card costs.

Depreciation and amortization increased by $3.2 million to $43.2 million in fiscal 2001 primarily because of the Company's increased capital expenditures throughout fiscal 2001 and 2000, especially expenditures on technology-related assets which tend to have relatively short useful lives.

In fiscal 2001, operating income for the year improved to $151.5 million, or 10.7% of sales, from $123.2 million, or 10.0% of sales, in fiscal 2000, an increase of 23.0% or $28.3 million.

Interest income decreased slightly to $1.9 million in fiscal 2001 from $2.3 million in fiscal 2000 due to lower average cash balances during the current fiscal year. Interest expense was $3.1 million in fiscal 2001 compared to $6.9 million in fiscal 2000, a decline of $3.8 million. The decrease in interest expense was primarily due to the repurchase of $28.6 million of the Company's 5¾% convertible subordinated notes during fiscal 2000 and the retirement

of the remaining $39.2 million of these notes during the first quarter of fiscal 2001. *See Note 5 of the Notes to Consolidated Financial Statements.*

The Company's effective tax rate remained constant at 37% of income before income taxes for both fiscal 2001 and 2000.

Net income in fiscal 2001 was $94.7 million, or $.97 per share on a diluted basis, an increase of $20.0 million, or 26.7%, as compared to fiscal 2000's net income of $74.7 million, or $.75 per share on a diluted basis. Net income, as a percentage of sales, improved from 6.1% in fiscal 2000 to 6.7% in fiscal 2001.

FISCAL YEARS ENDED FEBRUARY 26, 2000 AND FEBRUARY 27, 1999

During fiscal 2000, net sales increased $92.5 million to $1,231.1 million, or 8.1% above the sales level achieved in fiscal 1999. Same-store sales for fiscal 2000 grew 2.7%. The growth in sales was largely attributable to a net increase of 33 new North American stores in fiscal 2000. In fiscal 1999, the Company began to experience a slowdown in same-store sales growth, with same-store sales growth of 3.2%, a trend that continued into the first and second quarters of fiscal 2000. The lower same-store sales gains were believed to be the result of an overly aggressive pricing strategy that was not well-received by customers. As a result, the Company initiated a new value pricing strategy in the first quarter of fiscal 2000. This strategy was geared toward reducing prices to a more competitive level in certain merchandise categories, especially in decorative accessories and housewares. Throughout fiscal year 2000, the Company reduced prices on approximately 15% of its merchandise. In addition, the Company began focusing its buying strategy to include more basic merchandise at competitive price points, without sacrificing quality, style or gross margin rates. The results of the Company-initiated value pricing strategy were very positive for the latter half of fiscal 2000, a trend that continued into fiscal 2001. Net sales increases in fiscal 2000 were driven by sales of furniture, which delivered a 16.2% increase over the previous fiscal year. Additionally, the Company experienced increases for fiscal 2000 in housewares of 9.6%, bed and bath of 5.0% and decorative accessories of 3.9% over the results of fiscal 1999.

Net new store openings in fiscal 2000 were the primary contributor to sales growth in fiscal 2000 over fiscal 1999. The Company opened 63 new stores and closed 30 stores in North America during fiscal 2000, bringing the North American store count to 785 at the end of the 2000 fiscal year. Stores worldwide, including North America, Puerto Rico, the United Kingdom, Mexico and Japan, totaled 834 at the end of the 2000 fiscal year compared to 805 at the end of the 1999 fiscal year.

The Company's proprietary credit card was another important contributor to sales growth, with sales totaling $300.5 million for fiscal 2000. This represented an increase of $24.3 million, or 8.8%, over proprietary credit card sales of $276.2 million for fiscal 1999. During fiscal 2000, proprietary credit card sales accounted for 26.3% of total U.S. store sales compared to 26.0% for the prior fiscal year. Proprietary credit card customers spent an average of $142 per transaction in fiscal 2000 compared to $134 per transaction in fiscal 1999. The Company continued to grow sales on the proprietary credit card by opening new accounts and enhancing customer loyalty with marketing promotions targeted to cardholders.

Gross profit in fiscal 2000 totaled $512.5 million, an increase of $12.1 million, or 2.4%, over fiscal 1999. Expressed as a percentage of sales, the Company's gross profit, after related buying and store occupancy costs, decreased 240 basis points to 41.6% in fiscal 2000 from 44.0% in fiscal 1999. Merchandise margins, as a percentage of sales, decreased 160 basis points to 54.6% in fiscal 2000 from 56.2% in fiscal 1999. The decline in merchandise margins was principally the result of higher ocean freight rates coupled with the

value pricing of selected merchandise categories. The Company negotiated new carrier contracts during fiscal 2000 that should stabilize ocean freight rates until fiscal 2002. The Company's new value pricing strategy introduced at the beginning of fiscal 2000 also created downward pressure on margins for a majority of the year. Store occupancy costs, as a percentage of sales, increased to 13.0% during fiscal 2000 from 12.2% in fiscal 1999. This increase was primarily caused by two separate sale-leaseback transactions. In June 1998, the Company sold and leased back 25 store properties that it previously owned, which generated rental expense for those stores during the first half of fiscal 2000 compared to the first half of fiscal 1999. The Company also sold and leased back an additional 12 store properties in September 1999. As a result of these sale-leaseback transactions, the Company experienced a reduction in depreciation expense, which is not classified as a component of store occupancy costs.

Selling, general and administrative expenses, including marketing, as a percentage of sales, were 28.4% for fiscal 2000, a 100 basis point decrease from the 29.4% for fiscal 1999. In total dollars, selling, general and administrative expenses for fiscal 2000 increased $14.8 million over the prior fiscal period. Expenses that normally increase proportionately with sales and number of stores, such as store payroll, equipment rental, supplies and marketing expenses, increased $13.6 million, but declined 50 basis points as a percentage of sales from 20.9% last fiscal year to 20.4% this fiscal year. The slight increase in marketing expenditures was moderated by well-controlled store salaries and other store expenses. In fiscal 1999, the Company replaced leased point of sale equipment with purchased equipment, resulting in a decrease in equipment rental expense and an increase in depreciation expense for fiscal 2000. All other selling, general and administrative expenses increased $1.2 million, but also declined 50 basis points as a percentage of sales to 8.0% for fiscal 2000. The dollar increase was largely the result of a

Pier 1 Imports, Inc.

MANAGEMENT'S DISCUSSION AND ANALYSIS OF FINANCIAL CONDITION AND RESULTS OF OPERATIONS
(continued)

nonrecurring credit of $1.8 million received in fiscal 1999 as a settlement on a receivable previously deemed uncollectible. Excluding the effect of the nonrecurring item from fiscal 1999, other expenses declined for fiscal 2000, primarily as a result of lower non-store payroll costs, as a percentage of sales, coupled with a reduction in net credit card costs.

Depreciation and amortization expense for fiscal 2000 was $40.0 million, or 3.2% of sales, compared to $31.1 million, or 2.7% of sales, for fiscal 1999. Increased depreciation expense for fiscal 2000 was primarily the result of increased investments in capital expenditures throughout fiscal 2000 and 1999, the largest of which was the replacement of leased store point of sale equipment with purchased equipment during fiscal 1999. As a result, in fiscal 2000 the Company recorded a full year of depreciation expense on the fiscal 1999 capital expenditures compared to only a partial year of depreciation expense in fiscal 1999. Partially offsetting the increased expense was a reduction of depreciation expense on the stores which the Company opted to sell and lease back in the third quarter of fiscal 2000 and the second quarter of fiscal 1999.

Operating income declined $11.5 million to $123.2 million, or 10.0% of sales, in fiscal 2000 from $134.7 million, or 11.8% of sales, in fiscal 1999.

During fiscal 2000, net interest expense was $4.6 million compared to $5.0 million for the prior year. The decline in net interest expense was primarily the result of the repurchases of the Company's 5¾% convertible subordinated notes of $28.6 million in fiscal 2000 and $18.3 million in fiscal 1999.

The Company's effective income tax rate for fiscal 2000 was 37% compared to 38% for fiscal 1999. The decline in the estimated effective income tax rate was attributable to a reduction in state income taxes.

Fiscal 2000 net income totaled $74.7 million, representing 6.1% of sales, or $.75 per share on a diluted basis. In fiscal 1999, net income was 7.1% of sales and totaled $80.4 million, or $.77 per share on a diluted basis.

LIQUIDITY AND CAPITAL RESOURCES

As of the end of fiscal 2001, the Company's cash and temporary investments totaled $46.8 million compared to $50.4 million in fiscal 2000. Operating activities generated $110.1 million of cash versus $119.6 million last year. Increased inventory levels were the primary reason for the reduction in operating cash flow. Inventory levels were anticipated to be higher when compared to last year as a result of furniture promotions planned in the first quarter of fiscal 2002 along with an increase in store count for fiscal 2001. The Company opened 41 net North American stores during fiscal 2001 compared to 33 net new stores in fiscal 2000. Additionally, the Company plans to open 31 stores during the first half of fiscal 2002 compared to 19 stores opened during the first half of fiscal 2001.

Net cash used in investing activities totaled $70.4 million during fiscal 2001 versus last year's $39.8 million. Of that amount, capital expenditures were $45.3 million and were used primarily for new and existing store development. The Company opened 65 new stores in North America and three international retail locations, requiring $20.1 million of the total amounts expended for capital purchases. The Company remodeled 22 stores in fiscal 2001 at a cost of $6.4 million. Continuing with its commitment to invest in current store locations, the Company spent $5.1 million to improve floor plans and upgrade fixtures on existing stores. The Company also spent $7.6 million for technical resources and other system enhancements. During fiscal 2001, the Company continued to experience favorable sales trends on its proprietary credit card resulting in a net increase of $21.6 million in its beneficial interest in securitized receivables. This increase was primarily the result of the Company's recent "no payment, no finance charge" promotion in February 2001. The Company offered similar promotions on three separate occasions throughout fiscal 2001 versus one promotion offered in October of fiscal 2000. Additionally, the Company invested $3.9 million in the acquisition of Cargo.

Pier 1 Imports, Inc.

MANAGEMENT'S DISCUSSION AND ANALYSIS OF FINANCIAL CONDITION AND RESULTS OF OPERATIONS

(continued)

During fiscal 2001, the Company paid $34.3 million to repurchase 3,269,500 common shares under the Board of Directors-approved stock buyback program. In December 2000, the Board of Directors approved the repurchase of an additional five million shares of the Company's common stock. As of the end of the fiscal year, slightly less than 6.8 million shares remain authorized for repurchase. The Company expects that future repurchases of common stock will be made through open market or private transactions from time to time depending on prevailing market conditions, the Company's available cash, loan covenant restrictions and consideration of its corporate credit ratings. Cash used for dividends increased $3.0 million to $14.5 million in total as a result of the Company's 33% increase of its quarterly cash dividend in June 2000 to $.04 per share paid in fiscal 2001 from $.03 per share paid in fiscal 2000. Subsequent to fiscal 2001, the Company declared a cash dividend of $.04 per share payable on May 16, 2001 to shareholders of record on May 2, 2001. The Company expects to continue to pay cash dividends, in fiscal 2002, but to retain most of its future earnings for expansion of the Company's business. Other financing activities, primarily the exercise of stock options, provided cash of $5.6 million during fiscal 2001.

In March 2000, the Company redeemed its $39.2 million outstanding principal amount of 5¾% convertible subordinated notes originally due October 1, 2003. The notes were redeemable at 103% of par on March 23, 2000 or convertible into the Company's common stock at a price of $8.22 per share. Prior to redemption, the Company converted $39,164,000 of the notes into 4,764,450 shares of the Company's common stock and redeemed $15,000 of the notes for cash.

At fiscal 2001 year-end, the Company's sources of working capital were cash flow from operations, sales of proprietary credit card receivables and bank lines of credit. The bank facilities include a $125 million credit facility which expires in 2003, all of which

was available at fiscal 2001 year-end. Borrowings and repayments on this facility totaled $82.5 million for fiscal year 2001. Additionally, the Company has other long-term and short-term bank facilities used principally for the issuance of letters of credit totaling $148.9 million, of which $73.5 million was available at fiscal 2001 year-end. Most of the Company's loan agreements require the Company to maintain certain financial ratios and limit certain investments and distributions to shareholders, including cash dividends and repurchases of common stock. The Company's current ratio was 3.3 to 1 at fiscal 2001 year-end compared to 2.4 to 1 at fiscal 2000 year-end. Excluding the effect of the call of the Company's 5¾% convertible subordinated notes, which resulted in a reclassification of these notes from long-term to short-term, the current ratio would have been 3.0 to 1 at fiscal 2000 year-end. The Company's minimum operating lease commitments expected for fiscal 2002 total $139.6 million. The present value of total existing minimum operating lease commitments discounted at 10% is $625.0 million. The Company plans to continue to fund these commitments from operating cash flow.

The Company's inventory purchases are made almost entirely in U.S. dollars. When purchase commitments are denominated in foreign currencies, the Company may enter into forward foreign exchange contracts, when they are available, in order to manage its exposure to foreign currency fluctuations.

During fiscal 2002, the Company plans to open approximately 85 new stores and remodel or expand approximately ten existing stores. The Company also plans to close approximately 25 stores during fiscal 2002 as their leases expire or otherwise end, the majority of which will be relocated to more favorable locations within the same markets. The new store buildings and land will be financed primarily through operating leases. Total capital expenditures for fiscal 2002 are expected to be $55 to $60 million, with $36 million projected for store development and $18 million planned for information systems that will provide infrastructure and support for growth. The

Pier 1 Imports, Inc.

MANAGEMENT'S DISCUSSION AND ANALYSIS OF FINANCIAL CONDITION AND RESULTS OF OPERATIONS
(continued)

Company's working capital requirements for fiscal 2002 are not expected to increase significantly versus fiscal 2001 working capital.

In summary, the Company's primary uses of cash in fiscal 2001 were to fund operating expenses, satisfy inventory requirements, provide for new and existing store development and repurchase common stock of the Company. Historically, the Company has financed its operations primarily from internally generated funds and borrowings under the Company's credit facilities. The Company believes that the funds provided from operations, available lines of credit and sales of its proprietary credit card receivables will be sufficient to finance working capital and capital expenditure requirements through the end of fiscal year 2002.

MARKET RISK DISCLOSURES

Market risks relating to the Company's operations result primarily from changes in foreign exchange rates and interest rates. The Company has only limited involvement with derivative financial instruments, does not use them for trading purposes and is not a party to any leveraged derivatives.

The Company periodically enters into forward foreign exchange contracts to hedge some of its foreign currency exposure. The Company uses such contracts to hedge exposures to changes in foreign currency exchange rates, primarily Italian Lira, Canadian Dollars and British Pounds, associated with purchases denominated in foreign currencies. Gains and losses on these contracts have been deferred and recognized as an adjustment of the transaction price when it occurs. Forward contracts generally have maturities not exceeding six months. At March 3, 2001, the notional amount of the Company's foreign currency derivative instruments totaled approximately $2.4 million with a negligible fair market value.

The Company manages its exposure to changes in interest rates by optimizing the use of variable and fixed rate debt. The Company had $25.0 million of variable rate borrowings at March 3, 2001. A hypothetical 10% adverse change in interest rates would have a negligible impact on the Company's earnings and cash flows.

Collectively, the Company's exposure to these market risk factors was not significant and did not materially change from February 26, 2000.

IMPACT OF INFLATION AND CHANGING PRICES

Inflation has not had a significant impact on the operations of the Company during the preceding three years.

IMPACT OF NEW ACCOUNTING STANDARDS

In June 1998, the Financial Accounting Standards Board ("FASB") issued Statement of Financial Accounting Standard ("SFAS") No. 133, "Accounting for Derivative Instruments and Hedging Activities," which was amended by SFAS No. 137 and SFAS No. 138. This statement establishes accounting and reporting guidelines for derivatives and requires the Company to record all derivatives as assets or liabilities on the balance sheet at fair value. This statement is effective for the Company beginning in fiscal 2002. The Company has only limited involvement with derivative financial instruments, does not use them for trading purposes and is not a party to any leveraged derivatives. However, the Company periodically enters into forward foreign exchange contracts to hedge some of its foreign currency exposure. The Company uses such contracts to hedge exposures to changes in foreign currency exchange rates associated with purchases denominated in foreign currencies. The Company has analyzed the implementation requirements and does not anticipate that the adoption of SFAS No. 133 will have a material impact on the Company's consolidated balance sheets or statements of operations, shareholders' equity and cash flows.

In September 2000, the FASB issued SFAS No. 140, "Accounting for Transfers and Servicing of Financial Assets and Extinguishments of Liabilities." This statement replaces, in its entirety, SFAS No. 125 issued in June 1996. The new statement is effective for transfers and servicing of financial assets and extinguishments of liabilities occurring after March 31, 2001, and is not to be applied retroactively to financial statements for prior periods. SFAS No. 140 establishes new conditions for a securitization to be accounted for as a sale of receivables, changes the requirements for an entity to be a qualifying special-purpose entity and modifies under what conditions a transferor has retained effective control over transferred assets. The new statement also requires additional disclosures for fiscal years ending after December 15, 2000 relating to securitized financial assets and retained interests in securitized financial assets. These disclosures are included in Note 2 of the Notes of Consolidated Financial Statements. The Company has analyzed the new requirements of SFAS No. 140, made the necessary amendments to its securitization agreements and believes that it will continue to receive sale treatment for its securitized proprietary credit card receivables. Therefore, the Company does not anticipate that the implementation of SFAS No. 140 will have a material impact on the Company's consolidated balance sheets or statements of operations, shareholders' equity and cash flows.

FORWARD-LOOKING STATEMENTS

Certain matters discussed in this annual report, other than historical information, may constitute "forward-looking statements" that are subject to certain risks and uncertainties that could cause actual results to differ materially from those described in the forward-looking statements. The Company may also make forward-looking statements in other reports filed with the Securities and Exchange Commission and in material delivered to the Company's shareholders.

Forward-looking statements provide current expectations of future events based on certain assumptions. These statements encompass information that does not directly relate to any historical or current fact and often may be identified with words such as "anticipates," "believes," "expects," "estimates," "intends," "plans," "projects" and other similar expressions. Management's expectations and assumptions regarding planned store openings, financing of Company obligations from operations and other future results are subject to risks, uncertainties and other factors that could cause actual results to differ materially from the anticipated results or other expectations expressed in the forward-looking statements. Risks and uncertainties that may affect Company operations and performance include, among others, weather conditions that may affect sales, the general strength of the economy and levels of consumer spending, the availability of new sites for expansion along with sufficient labor to facilitate growth, the strength of new home construction and sales of existing homes, the ability of the Company to import merchandise from foreign countries without significantly restrictive tariffs, duties or quotas and the ability of the Company to ship items from foreign countries at reasonable rates in timely fashion. The foregoing risks and uncertainties are in addition to others discussed elsewhere in this annual report. The Company assumes no obligation to update or otherwise revise its forward-looking statements even if experience or future changes make it clear that any projected results expressed or implied will not be realized.

Pier 1 Imports, Inc.

REPORT OF INDEPENDENT AUDITORS

To the Board of Directors of Pier 1 Imports, Inc.

We have audited the accompanying consolidated balance sheets of Pier 1 Imports, Inc. as of March 3, 2001 and February 26, 2000, and the related consolidated statements of operations, shareholders' equity and cash flows for each of the three years in the period ended March 3, 2001. These financial statements are the responsibility of the Company's management. Our responsibility is to express an opinion on these financial statements based on our audits.

We conducted our audits in accordance with auditing standards generally accepted in the United States. Those standards require that we plan and perform the audit to obtain reasonable assurance about whether the financial statements are free of material misstatement. An audit includes examining, on a test basis, evidence supporting the amounts and disclosures in the financial statements. An audit also includes assessing the accounting principles used and significant estimates made by management, as well as evaluating the overall financial statement presentation. We believe that our audits provide a reasonable basis for our opinion.

In our opinion, the financial statements referred to above present fairly, in all material respects, the consolidated financial position of Pier 1 Imports, Inc. at March 3, 2001 and February 26, 2000, and the consolidated results of its operations and its cash flows for each of the three years in the period ended March 3, 2001, in conformity with accounting principles generally accepted in the United States.

Ernst & Young LLP

Fort Worth, Texas
April 10, 2001

Pier 1 Imports, Inc.

CONSOLIDATED STATEMENTS OF OPERATIONS
(in thousands except per share amounts)

	Year Ended		
	2001	**2000**	**1999**
Net sales	$ 1,411,498	$ 1,231,095	$ 1,138,590
Operating costs and expenses:			
Cost of sales (including buying and store occupancy)	817,043	718,547	638,173
Selling, general and administrative expenses	399,755	349,394	334,629
Depreciation and amortization	43,184	39,973	31,130
	1,259,982	1,107,914	1,003,932
Operating income	151,516	123,181	134,658
Nonoperating (income) and expenses:			
Interest and investment income	(1,854)	(2,349)	(2,868)
Interest expense	3,130	6,918	7,916
	1,276	4,569	5,048
Income before income taxes	150,240	118,612	129,610
Provision for income taxes	55,590	43,887	49,253
Net income	$ 94,650	$ 74,725	$ 80,357
Basic earnings per share	$ .98	$ .78	$ .82
Diluted earnings per share	$ .97	$ .75	$ .77

The accompanying notes are an integral part of these financial statements.

Pier 1 Imports, Inc.
CONSOLIDATED BALANCE SHEETS
(in thousands except share amounts)

	2001	2000
ASSETS		
Current assets:		
Cash, including temporary investments of $31,142 and $39,898, respectively	$ 46,841	$ 50,376
Beneficial interest in securitized receivables	75,403	53,820
Other accounts receivable, net of allowance for doubtful accounts		
of $295 and $44, respectively	8,370	5,637
Inventories	310,704	268,906
Prepaid expenses and other current assets	35,748	36,541
Total current assets	477,066	415,280
Properties, net	211,751	213,032
Other assets	46,893	42,398
	$ 735,710	$ 670,710
LIABILITIES AND SHAREHOLDERS' EQUITY		
Current liabilities:		
Notes payable and current portion of long-term debt	$ —	$ 39,179
Accounts payable and accrued liabilities	144,110	136,787
Total current liabilities	144,110	175,966
Long-term debt	25,000	25,000
Other noncurrent liabilities	34,721	29,081
Shareholders' equity:		
Common stock, $1.00 par, 500,000,000 shares authorized, 100,779,000 issued	100,779	100,779
Paid-in capital	139,424	155,711
Retained earnings	344,809	264,678
Cumulative other comprehensive income	(3,115)	(1,536)
Less – 4,619,000 and 6,949,000 common shares in treasury, at cost, respectively	(49,933)	(78,668)
Less – unearned compensation	(85)	(301)
	531,879	440,663
Commitments and contingencies		
	$ 735,710	$ 670,710

The accompanying notes are an integral part of these financial statements.

Pier 1 Imports, Inc.

CONSOLIDATED STATEMENTS OF CASH FLOWS

(in thousands except share amounts)

	Year Ended		
	2001	**2000**	**1999**
CASH FLOW FROM OPERATING ACTIVITIES:			
Net income	$ 94,650	$ 74,725	$ 80,357
Adjustments to reconcile to net cash provided by operating activities:			
Depreciation and amortization	43,184	39,973	31,130
Deferred taxes and other	9,137	11,033	(2,575)
Change in cash from:			
Inventories	(39,127)	(10,133)	(24,103)
Accounts receivable and other current assets	(5,847)	586	2,500
Accounts payable and accrued expenses	6,280	8,962	12,826
Other assets, liabilities and other, net	1,738	(5,528)	(4,409)
Net cash provided by operating activities	110,015	119,618	95,726
CASH FLOW FROM INVESTING ACTIVITIES:			
Capital expenditures	(45,251)	(45,984)	(78,055)
Proceeds from disposition of properties	353	19,425	36,408
Net cost from disposition of			
Sunbelt Nursery Group, Inc. properties	–	(439)	(597)
Acquisitions, net of cash acquired	(3,917)	–	(4,235)
Beneficial interest in securitized receivables	(21,583)	(12,820)	3,145
Net cash used in investing activities	(70,398)	(39,818)	(43,334)
CASH FLOW FROM FINANCING ACTIVITIES:			
Cash dividends	(14,494)	(11,504)	(11,522)
Purchases of treasury stock	(34,270)	(31,806)	(65,777)
Proceeds from issuance of long-term debt	82,500	4,035	–
Repayments of long-term debt	(82,515)	(36,242)	(20,325)
Proceeds from stock options exercised, stock purchase			
plan and other, net	5,627	4,148	6,448
Net cash used in financing activities	(43,152)	(71,369)	(91,176)
Change in cash and cash equivalents	(3,535)	8,431	(38,784)
Cash and cash equivalents at beginning of year	50,376	41,945	80,729
Cash and cash equivalents at end of year	$ 46,841	$ 50,376	$ 41,945
Supplemental cash flow information:			
Interest paid	$ 3,171	$ 7,137	$ 7,929
Income taxes paid	$ 58,302	$ 40,883	$ 43,084

During fiscal 2001, the Company issued 4,764,450 shares of its common stock upon the conversion of $39,164,000

principal amount of 5¾% convertible subordinated notes.

The accompanying notes are an integral part of these financial statements.

Pier 1 Imports, Inc.

CONSOLIDATED STATEMENTS OF SHAREHOLDERS' EQUITY

(in thousands except per share amounts)

	Common Stock	Paid-in Capital	Retained Earnings	Cumulative Other Comprehensive Income	Treasury Stock	Unearned Compensation	Total Shareholders' Equity
Balance February 28, 1998	$ 67,903	$ 166,824	$ 165,345	$ (1,108)	$ (3,149)	$ (3,084)	$ 392,731
Comprehensive income:							
Net income	–	–	80,357	–	–	–	80,357
Other comprehensive income, net of tax:							
Currency translation adjustments . . .	–	–	–	(742)	–	–	(742)
Comprehensive income							79,615
Purchases of treasury stock	–	–	–	–	(65,777)	–	(65,777)
Restricted stock forfeits and amortization	–	–	–	–	–	1,758	1,758
Exercise of stock options, stock purchase							
plan and other	–	(7,308)	–	–	14,272	–	6,964
Cash dividends ($.12 per share)	–	–	(11,522)	–	–	–	(11,522)
Three for two stock split	32,866	–	(32,723)	–	–	(143)	–
Conversion of 5¾% convertible debt	10	115	–	–	–	–	125
Balance February 27, 1999	100,779	159,631	201,457	(1,850)	(54,654)	(1,469)	403,894
Comprehensive income:							
Net income	–	–	74,725	–	–	–	74,725
Other comprehensive income, net of tax:							
Currency translation adjustments . . .	–	–	–	314	–	–	314
Comprehensive income							75,039
Purchases of treasury stock	–	–	–	–	(31,806)	–	(31,806)
Restricted stock forfeits and amortization	–	709	–	–	(1,392)	1,168	485
Exercise of stock options, stock purchase							
plan and other	–	(4,629)	–	–	9,184	–	4,555
Cash dividends ($.12 per share)	–	–	(11,504)	–	–	–	(11,504)
Balance February 26, 2000	100,779	155,711	264,678	(1,536)	(78,668)	(301)	440,663
Comprehensive income:							
Net income	–	–	94,650	–	–	–	94,650
Other comprehensive income, net of tax:							
Currency translation adjustments . . .	–	–	–	(1,579)	–	–	(1,579)
Comprehensive income							93,071
Purchases of treasury stock	–	–	–	–	(34,270)	–	(34,270)
Restricted stock forfeits and amortization	–	–	–	–	–	216	216
Exercise of stock options, stock purchase							
plan and other	–	(1,774)	(25)	–	9,119	–	7,320
Cash dividends ($.15 per share)	–	–	(14,494)	–	–	–	(14,494)
Conversion of 5¾% convertible debt	–	(14,513)	–	–	53,886	–	39,373
Balance March 3, 2001	$ 100,779	$ 139,424	$ 344,809	$ (3,115)	$ (49,933)	$ (85)	$ 531,879

The accompanying notes are an integral part of these financial statements.

Pier 1 Imports, Inc.
NOTES TO CONSOLIDATED FINANCIAL STATEMENTS

NOTE 1 - SUMMARY OF SIGNIFICANT ACCOUNTING POLICIES

Organization - Pier 1 Imports, Inc. is one of North America's largest specialty retailers of imported decorative home furnishings, gifts and related items, with retail stores located in the United States, Canada, Puerto Rico, the United Kingdom, Mexico and Japan. Concentrations of risk with respect to sourcing the Company's inventory purchases are limited due to the large number of vendors or suppliers and their geographic dispersion around the world. The Company sources its largest amount of imported inventory from China. Management believes that alternative merchandise could be obtained from manufacturers in other countries over time.

Basis of consolidation - The consolidated financial statements of Pier 1 Imports, Inc. and its consolidated subsidiaries (the "Company") include the accounts of all subsidiary companies except Pier 1 Funding, LLC, which is a non-consolidated, bankruptcy remote, securitization subsidiary. *See Note 2 of the Notes to Consolidated Financial Statements.* Material intercompany transactions and balances have been eliminated.

Acquisitions - The Company completed its acquisition of certain assets and assumption of certain liabilities of Cargo Furniture, Inc. ("Cargo") for $3,931,000, including cash acquired, on February 21, 2001. These assets and liabilities were included in the Company's consolidated balance sheet as of March 3, 2001; however, this acquisition had no effect on the Company's fiscal 2001 operations. Cargo is a 21-store retailer and wholesaler of casual lifestyle furniture, gifts and home décor with a focus on children's furniture. This acquisition was accounted for under the purchase method of accounting, and resulted in goodwill of $2,843,000 which will be amortized using the straight-line method over 20 years. The pro forma effect on the Company's results of operations, as if the acquisition had been completed at the beginning of fiscal 2001, was not significant.

Use of estimates - Preparation of the financial statements in conformity with generally accepted accounting principles requires management to make estimates and assumptions that affect the amounts reported in the financial statements and accompanying notes. Actual results could differ from those estimates.

Fiscal periods - The Company utilizes 5-4-4 (week) quarterly accounting periods with the fiscal year ending on the Saturday nearest the last day of February. Fiscal 2001 consisted of a 53-week year and fiscal 2000 and 1999 were 52-week years. Fiscal 2001 ended March 3, 2001, fiscal 2000 ended February 26, 2000 and fiscal 1999 ended February 27, 1999.

Cash and cash equivalents - The Company considers all highly liquid investments with an original maturity date of three months or less to be cash equivalents. The effect of foreign currency exchange rate fluctuations on cash is not material.

Translation of foreign currencies - Assets and liabilities of foreign operations are translated into U.S. dollars at fiscal year-end exchange rates. Income and expense items are translated at average exchange rates prevailing during the year. Translation adjustments arising from differences in exchange rates from period to period are included as a separate component of shareholders' equity and are included in comprehensive income.

Financial instruments - The fair value of financial instruments is determined by reference to various market data and other valuation techniques as appropriate. Unless otherwise disclosed, the fair values of financial instruments approximate their recorded values.

Risk management instruments: The Company may utilize various financial instruments to manage interest rate and market risk associated with its on- and off-balance sheet commitments.

The Company hedges certain commitments denominated in foreign currencies through the purchase of forward contracts. The forward contracts are purchased only to cover specific commitments to buy merchandise for resale; any gains or losses on such contracts are included in the cost of the merchandise purchased.

Pier 1 Imports, Inc.

NOTES TO CONSOLIDATED FINANCIAL STATEMENTS
(continued)

The Company enters into forward foreign exchange contracts with major financial institutions and continually monitors its positions with, and the credit quality of, these counterparties to its off-balance sheet financial instruments. The Company does not expect non-performance by any of the counterparties, and any losses incurred in the event of non-performance would not be material.

Beneficial interest in securitized receivables - In February 1997, the Company sold all of its proprietary credit card receivables to a special purpose wholly-owned subsidiary, Pier 1 Funding, Inc., predecessor to Pier 1 Funding, LLC ("Funding"), which transferred the receivables to the Pier 1 Imports Credit Card Master Trust (the "Master Trust"). The Master Trust issues beneficial interests in the Master Trust that represent undivided interests in the assets of the Master Trust consisting of the transferred receivables and all proceeds of such receivables. The beneficial interests in the Master Trust include the interests retained by Funding which are represented by the Class B Certificates ($14.1 million) and the residual interest in the Master Trust (the excess of the principal amount of receivables held in the Master Trust over the portion represented by the certificates sold to investors and the Class B Certificates). The Company estimates fair value of its beneficial interest in the Master Trust based on the present value of future expected cash flows estimated using management's best estimates of the key assumptions including credit losses and timeliness of payments.

Inventories - Inventories are comprised primarily of finished merchandise and are stated at the lower of average cost or market; cost is determined principally on a weighted average method.

Properties, maintenance and repairs - Buildings, equipment, furniture and fixtures, and leasehold interests and improvements are carried at cost less accumulated depreciation. Depreciation is computed using the straight-line method over estimated remaining useful lives of the assets ranging from three to thirty years. Depreciation costs were $41,882,000, $38,672,000 and $30,014,000 in fiscal 2001, 2000 and 1999, respectively. Amortization of improvements

to leased properties is based upon the shorter of the remaining lease term or the estimated useful lives of such assets.

Expenditures for maintenance, repairs and renewals which do not materially prolong the useful lives of the assets are charged to expense as incurred. In the case of disposals, assets and the related depreciation are removed from the accounts and the net amount, less proceeds from disposal, is credited or charged to income.

Revenue recognition - The Company recognizes revenue at the point of sale or at the time the merchandise is shipped to the customer. Revenue from gift cards, gift certificates and merchandise credits is deferred until redemption.

Advertising costs - All advertising costs are expensed the first time the advertising takes place. Advertising costs were $59,721,000, $54,970,000 and $47,491,000 in fiscal 2001, 2000 and 1999, respectively. The amounts of prepaid advertising at the end of fiscal years 2001 and 2000 were $2,086,000 and $727,000, respectively.

Income taxes - Income tax expense is based on the liability method. Under this method, deferred tax assets and liabilities are recognized based on differences between financial statement and tax bases of assets and liabilities using presently enacted tax rates. Deferred federal income taxes, net of applicable foreign tax credits, are not provided on the undistributed earnings of foreign subsidiaries to the extent the Company intends to permanently reinvest such earnings abroad.

Stock-based compensation - The Company grants stock options and restricted stock for a fixed number of shares to employees with stock option exercise prices equal to the fair market value of the shares on the date of grant. The Company continues to account for stock option grants and restricted stock grants in accordance with Accounting Principles Board ("APB") Opinion No. 25, "Accounting for Stock Issued to Employees," and, accordingly, recognizes no compensation expense for the stock option grants.

Pier 1 Imports, Inc.

NOTES TO CONSOLIDATED FINANCIAL STATEMENTS
(continued)

Earnings per share - Basic earnings per share amounts were determined by dividing net income by the weighted average number of common shares outstanding for the period. Diluted earnings per share amounts were similarly computed, but included the effect, when dilutive, of the Company's weighted average number of stock options outstanding and the average number of common shares that would be issuable upon conversion of the Company's convertible securities. To determine diluted earnings per share, interest and amortization of debt issue costs related to the subordinated notes, net of any applicable taxes, have been added back to net income to reflect assumed conversions.

The following earnings per share calculations reflect the effect of the Company's conversion of its 5¾% convertible subordinated notes, which were primarily converted, without interest, on or before March 23, 2000. Earnings per share amounts are calculated as follows (in thousands except per share amounts):

	2001	2000	1999
Net income.	$ 94,650	$ 74,725	$ 80,357
Plus interest and debt issue costs, net of tax, on the assumed conversion of the 5¾% subordinated notes	–	2,237	3,083
Diluted net income	$ 94,650	$ 76,962	$ 83,440
Average shares outstanding:			
Basic	96,306	95,766	98,120
Plus assumed exercise of stock options	1,325	644	1,101
Plus assumed conversion of the 5¾% subordinated notes . .	321	6,887	9,643
Diluted.	97,952	103,297	108,864
Earnings per share:			
Basic	$ .98	$ .78	$ .82
Diluted.	$ .97	$ .75	$ .77

Stock options for which the exercise price was greater than the average market price of common shares were not included in the computation of diluted earnings per share as the effect would be antidilutive. At the end of fiscal years 2001, 2000 and 1999, there were 1,078,200, 1,157,025 and 1,543,500, respectively, stock options outstanding with exercise prices greater than the average market price of the Company's common shares.

Impact of recently issued accounting standards - In June 1998, the Financial Accounting Standards Board ("FASB") issued Statement of Financial Accounting Standard ("SFAS") No. 133, "Accounting for Derivative Instruments and Hedging Activities," which was amended by SFAS No. 137 and SFAS No. 138. This statement establishes accounting and reporting guidelines for derivatives and requires the Company to record all derivatives as assets or liabilities on the balance sheet at fair value. This statement is effective for the Company beginning in fiscal 2002. The Company has only limited involvement with derivative financial instruments, does not use them for trading purposes and is not a party to any leveraged derivatives. However, the Company periodically enters into forward foreign exchange contracts to hedge some of its foreign currency exposure. The Company uses such contracts to hedge exposures to changes in foreign currency exchange rates associated with purchases denominated in foreign currencies. The Company has analyzed the implementation requirements and does not anticipate that the adoption of SFAS No. 133 will have a material impact on the Company's consolidated balance sheets or statements of operations, shareholders' equity and cash flows.

In September 2000, the FASB issued SFAS No. 140, "Accounting for Transfers and Servicing of Financial Assets and Extinguishments of Liabilities." This statement replaces, in its entirety, SFAS No. 125 issued in June 1996. The new statement is effective for transfers and servicing of financial assets and extinguishments of liabilities occurring after

Pier 1 Imports, Inc.

NOTES TO CONSOLIDATED FINANCIAL STATEMENTS
(continued)

March 31, 2001 and is not to be applied retroactively to financial statements for prior periods. SFAS No. 140 establishes new conditions for a securitization to be accounted for as a sale of receivables, changes the requirements for an entity to be a qualifying special-purpose entity and modifies under what conditions a transferor has retained effective control over transferred assets. The new statement also requires additional disclosures for fiscal years ending after December 15, 2000 relating to securitized financial assets and retained interests in securitized financial assets. These disclosures are included in Note 2 of the Notes to Consolidated Financial Statements. The Company has analyzed the new requirements of SFAS No. 140, made the necessary amendments to its securitization agreements and believes that it will continue to receive sale treatment for its securitized proprietary credit card receivables. Therefore, the Company does not anticipate that the implementation of SFAS No. 140 will have a material impact on the Company's consolidated balance sheets or statements of operations, shareholders' equity and cash flows.

NOTE 2 - PROPRIETARY CREDIT CARD INFORMATION

The proprietary credit card receivables, securitized as discussed below, arise primarily under open-end revolving credit accounts issued by the Company's subsidiary, Pier 1 National Bank, to finance purchases of merchandise and services offered by the Company. These accounts have various billing and payment structures, including varying minimum payment levels. The Company has an agreement with a third party to provide certain credit card processing and related credit services, while the Company maintains control over credit policy decisions and customer service standards.

As of fiscal 2001 year-end, the Company had approximately 4,583,000 proprietary cardholders and approximately 1,131,000 customer credit accounts considered active (accounts with a purchase within the previous 12 months). The Company's proprietary credit card sales accounted for 28.9% of total U.S. store sales in fiscal 2001. A summary of the

Company's proprietary credit card results for each of the last three fiscal years follows (in thousands):

	2001	2000	1999
Income:			
Finance charge income, net of debt service costs	$ 21,759	$ 16,780	$ 15,117
Insurance and other income	253	287	314
	22,012	17,067	15,431
Costs:			
Processing fees	13,608	10,763	9,456
Bad debts	5,285	4,664	6,356
	18,893	15,427	15,812
Net proprietary credit card income (expense) . . .	$ 3,119	$ 1,640	$ (381)
Proprietary credit card sales	$ 377,045	$ 300,462	$ 276,184
Costs as a percent of proprietary credit card sales	5.01%	5.13%	5.73%
Gross proprietary credit card receivables at year-end	$ 122,876	$ 100,095	$ 87,601
Proprietary credit card sales as a percent of total U.S. store sales . . .	28.9%	26.3%	26.0%

In February 1997, the Company securitized its entire portfolio of proprietary credit card receivables (the "Receivables"). The Company sold all existing Receivables to a special-purpose wholly-owned subsidiary, Pier 1 Funding, Inc., predecessor to Pier 1 Funding, LLC ("Funding"), which transferred the Receivables to the Pier 1 Imports Credit Card Master Trust (the "Master Trust"). The Master Trust issues beneficial interests in the Master Trust that represent undivided interests in the assets of the Master Trust consisting of the Receivables and all proceeds of the Receivables. On a daily basis, the Company sells to Funding for transfer to the Master

Trust all newly generated Receivables, except those failing certain eligibility criteria, and receives as the purchase price payments of cash (funded from the amount of undistributed principal collections from the Receivables in the Master Trust) and residual interests in the Master Trust. Proceeds received from sales of such Receivables approximated $347 million, $303 million and $290 million during fiscal 2001, 2000 and 1999, respectively. Gains/losses resulting from such sales were not material in any of the periods presented above. The Company has no obligation to reimburse Funding, the Master Trust or purchasers of any certificates issued by the Master Trust for credit losses from the Receivables.

Funding was capitalized by the Company as a special-purpose wholly-owned subsidiary that is subject to certain covenants and restrictions, including a restriction from engaging in any business or activity unrelated to acquiring and selling interests in receivables. The Master Trust is not consolidated with the Company.

In the initial sale of the Receivables, the Company sold $84.1 million of the Receivables and received $49.6 million in cash and $34.1 million in beneficial interests in the Master Trust. The Master Trust sold to third parties $50.0 million of Series 1997-1 Class A Certificates, which bear interest at 6.74% and mature in May 2002. Funding retained $14.1 million of Series 1997-1 Class B Certificates, which are currently non-interest bearing and subordinated to the Class A Certificates. Funding also retained the residual interest in the Master Trust. As of March 3, 2001 and February 26, 2000, the Company had $75.4 million and $53.8 million, respectively, in beneficial interests (comprised primarily of principal and interest related

to the underlying Receivables) in the Master Trust. Based on estimated future cash flow projections, the fair value of the Company's retained interest approximates historical cost.

Beginning in October 2001, unless prefunded through a new series of certificates, principal collections of Receivables allocable to Series 1997-1 Certificates will be used to amortize the outstanding balances of the Series 1997-1 Certificates and will not be available to fund the purchase of new receivables being transferred from the Company. Under generally accepted accounting principles, if the structure of the securitization meets certain requirements, these transactions are accounted for as sales of receivables. The Company's securitization, as discussed above, was accounted for as a sale. The Company expects no material impact on net income in future years as a result of the sale, although the precise amounts will be dependent on a number of factors such as interest rates and levels of securitization.

NOTE 3 - PROPERTIES

Properties are summarized as follows at March 3, 2001 and February 26, 2000 (in thousands):

	2001	2000
Land	$ 22,353	$ 22,384
Buildings	59,716	59,761
Equipment, furniture and fixtures	207,956	183,313
Leasehold interests and improvements	170,706	157,801
	460,731	423,259
Less accumulated depreciation and amortization	248,980	210,227
Properties, net	$211,751	$ 213,032

Pier 1 Imports, Inc.

NOTES TO CONSOLIDATED FINANCIAL STATEMENTS
(continued)

NOTE 4 - ACCOUNTS PAYABLE AND ACCRUED LIABILITIES/OTHER NONCURRENT LIABILITIES

The following is a summary of accounts payable and accrued liabilities and other noncurrent liabilities at March 3, 2001 and February 26, 2000 (in thousands):

	2001	2000
Trade accounts payable.	$ 52,637	$ 57,203
Accrued payroll and other		
employee-related liabilities.	33,685	23,515
Accrued taxes, other than income	15,576	13,073
Gift cards, gift certificates and		
merchandise credits outstanding	18,989	15,494
Accrued income taxes payable	7,786	12,152
Other	15,437	15,350
Accounts payable and		
accrued liabilities.	$144,110	$136,787
Accrued average rent	$ 17,590	$ 16,260
Other	17,131	12,821
Other noncurrent liabilities	$ 34,721	$ 29,081

NOTE 5 - LONG-TERM DEBT AND AVAILABLE CREDIT

Long-term debt is summarized as follows at March 3, 2001 and February 26, 2000 (in thousands):

	2001	2000
Industrial revenue bonds.	$ 25,000	$ 25,000
5¾% convertible		
subordinated notes	–	39,179
	25,000	64,179
Less – portion due within one year	–	39,179
Long-term debt.	$ 25,000	$ 25,000

In fiscal 1987, the Company entered into industrial revenue development bond loan agreements aggregating $25 million. Proceeds were used to construct three warehouse distribution facilities. The loan agreements and related tax-exempt bonds mature in the year 2026. The Company's interest rates on the loans are based on the bond interest rates, which are market driven, reset weekly and are similar to other tax-exempt municipal debt issues. The Company's

weighted average interest rates were 5.7% and 4.8% for fiscal 2001 and 2000, respectively.

In September 1996, the Company issued $86.3 million principal amount of 5¾% convertible subordinated notes due October 1, 2003. The notes were convertible at any time prior to maturity, unless previously redeemed or repurchased, into shares of common stock of the Company at a conversion price of $8.22 per share, adjusted for stock splits. The Company had the option to redeem the notes, in whole or in part, on or after October 2, 1999, at a redemption price (expressed as a percentage of principal amount) of 103% of par value which was scheduled to decline annually to 100% of par value at the maturity date. During fiscal 2000, the Company purchased and retired $28.6 million principal amount of these notes at an average price of 98.8% of par. Interest on the notes was payable semiannually on April 1 and October 1 of each year. In February 2000, the Company announced its intention to call the remaining $39.2 million outstanding principal amount of these notes for redemption on March 23, 2000. The notes were convertible into common stock of the Company at any time prior to the close of business on March 22, 2000, at a conversion price of $8.22 per share. During March 2000, the Company converted $39,164,000 of the notes into 4,764,450 shares of the Company's common stock and redeemed $15,000 of the notes for cash at a redemption price of 103% of par value. The conversion and redemption of these notes during fiscal 2001 reduced the Company's debt by $39.2 million and increased its capitalization by $39.4 million.

Long-term debt matures as follows (in thousands):

Fiscal Year	Long-term Debt
2002	$ –
2003	–
2004	–
2005	–
2006	–
Thereafter	25,000
Total long-term debt	$ 25,000

Pier 1 Imports, Inc.

NOTES TO CONSOLIDATED FINANCIAL STATEMENTS
(continued)

The Company has a $125 million unsecured credit facility available, which expires in November 2003. The interest rate on these borrowings is determined based upon a spread to LIBOR that varies depending upon either the Company's senior debt rating or leverage ratio. All of the $125 million revolving credit facility was available at fiscal 2001 year-end. The weighted average interest rate on borrowings outstanding was 7.2% for fiscal 2001. The Company had no borrowings under this facility during fiscal 2000.

The Company has a $120 million short-term line of credit, which may be used to issue merchandise letters of credit. At fiscal 2001 year-end, approximately $46.5 million had been utilized, leaving $73.5 million available. The Company also has $28.9 million of other special-purpose credit lines, all of which were fully utilized at fiscal 2001 year-end.

Most of the Company's loan agreements require that the Company maintain certain financial ratios and limit specific payments and equity distributions including cash dividends, loans to shareholders and repurchases of common stock.

NOTE 6 - FAIR VALUE OF FINANCIAL INSTRUMENTS

At March 3, 2001, the Company had approximately $2.4 million of forward foreign exchange contracts outstanding with negligible fair values and with maturities ranging from one to six months.

As of February 26, 2000, the fair value of the 5¾% convertible notes was $40.4 million compared to the recorded value of $39.2 million. The fair value of these debentures was estimated based on the quoted market value as of February 26, 2000 for the debentures. There were no other significant assets or liabilities with a fair value different from the recorded value as of March 3, 2001 and February 26, 2000.

NOTE 7 - EMPLOYEE BENEFIT PLANS

The Company offers a qualified, defined contribution employee retirement plan to all its full- and part-time personnel who are at least 18 years old and have been employed for a minimum of six months. Employees contributing 1% to 5% of their compensation receive a matching Company contribution of up to 3%. Company contributions to the plan were $1,790,000, $1,753,000 and $1,653,000 in fiscal 2001, 2000 and 1999, respectively.

In addition, a non-qualified retirement savings plan is available for the purpose of providing deferred compensation for certain employees whose benefits under the qualified plan are limited under Section 401(k) of the Internal Revenue Code. The Company's expense for this non-qualified plan was not significant for fiscal 2001, 2000 and 1999.

The Company maintains supplemental retirement plans (the "Plans") for certain of its executive officers. The Plans provide that upon death, disability or reaching retirement age, a participant will receive benefits based on highest compensation and years of service. The Company recorded expenses related to the Plans of $1,850,000, $1,409,000 and $1,633,000 in fiscal 2001, 2000 and 1999, respectively.

NOTE 8 - MATTERS CONCERNING SHAREHOLDERS' EQUITY

Stock split - On July 29, 1998, the Company distributed 32,866,000 common shares pursuant to a three for two stock split, effected in the form of a 50% common stock dividend, to shareholders of record on July 15, 1998.

Stock purchase plan - Substantially all employees and directors are eligible to participate in the Pier 1 Imports, Inc. Stock Purchase Plan under which the Company's common stock is purchased on behalf of employees at market prices through regular payroll deductions. Each employee participant may contribute up to 10% of the eligible portions of compensation and directors may contribute part or all of their directors' fees. The Company contributes from 10% to 100% of the participants' contributions, depending upon length of participation and date of

Pier 1 Imports, Inc.

NOTES TO CONSOLIDATED FINANCIAL STATEMENTS
(continued)

entry into the plan. Company contributions to the plan were $921,000, $954,000 and $1,032,000 in fiscal years 2001, 2000 and 1999, respectively.

Restricted stock grant plans - In fiscal 1998, the Company issued 238,500 shares of its common stock to key officers pursuant to a Management Restricted Stock Plan which provides for the issuance of up to 415,600 shares. The fiscal 1998 restricted stock grant vests over a four-year period of continued employment. The fair value at the date of grant of these restricted stock shares is being expensed over the aforementioned vesting period. The fair value at the date of grant of the restricted shares granted in fiscal 1998 was $3,000,000. Shares not vested are returned to the plan if employment is terminated for any reason. To date, 107,184 shares have been returned to the plan.

In fiscal 1991, the Company issued 726,804 shares of its common stock to key officers pursuant to a Restricted Stock Grant Plan which provided for the issuance of up to 1,037,214 shares. These shares vest, and the fair value at the date of grant is expensed, over a ten-year period of continued employment. Unvested shares are returned to the plan upon employment termination. As of March 3, 2001, 407,742 shares have been returned to the plan. In fiscal 2000, the Restricted Stock Grant Plan was terminated by the Board of Directors and is no longer available for issuance of common stock to key officers. The final vesting period was March 2000.

Total compensation expense for both of the restricted stock grant plans was $216,000, $485,000 and $1,759,000 for fiscal 2001, 2000 and 1999, respectively.

Stock option plans - In June 1999, the Company adopted the Pier 1 Imports, Inc. 1999 Stock Plan (the "Plan"). The Plan will ultimately replace the Company's two previous stock option plans, which were the 1989 Employee Stock Option Plan (the "Employee Plan") and the 1989 Non-Employee Director Stock Option Plan (the "Director Plan").

The Plan provides for the granting of options to directors and employees with an exercise price not less than the fair market value of the common stock on the date of the grant. Options may be either Incentive Stock Options authorized under Section 422 of the Internal Revenue Code or non-qualified options, which do not qualify as Incentive Stock Options. Current director compensation provides for non-qualified options covering 6,000 shares to be granted once each year to each non-employee director. Additionally, the Plan authorizes a Director Deferred Stock Program. As the program is currently implemented by the Board of Directors, each director must defer a minimum of 50% and may defer up to 100% of the director's cash fees into a deferred stock account. The amount deferred receives a 50% matching contribution from the Company. The Plan provides that a maximum of 7,000,000 shares of common stock may be issued under the Plan, of which not more than 250,000 may be issued in exchange for deferred stock units. Options issued to non-director employees vest equally over a period of four years while directors' options are fully vested at the date of issuance. Additionally, employee options will fully vest upon retirement or, under certain conditions, a change in control of the Company. As of March 3, 2001 and February 26, 2000, respectively, there were 3,525,887 and 4,913,638 shares available for grant under the Plan, of which 200,381 and 227,638 may be used for deferred stock issuance. Additionally, outstanding options covering 429,600 and 45,000 shares were exercisable and 49,619 and 22,362 shares were issuable in exchange for deferred stock units at fiscal years ended 2001 and 2000, respectively. The Plan will expire in June 2009, and the Board of Directors may at any time suspend or terminate the Plan or amend the Plan, subject to certain limitations.

Under the Employee Plan, options may be granted to qualify as Incentive Stock Options under Section 422 of the Internal Revenue Code or as non-qualified options. Most options issued under the Employee

Pier 1 Imports, Inc.

NOTES TO CONSOLIDATED FINANCIAL STATEMENTS
(continued)

Plan vest over a period of four to five years. As of March 3, 2001 and February 26, 2000, outstanding options covering 2,318,042 and 2,107,953 shares were exercisable and 878,059 and 747,409 shares were available for grant, respectively. The Employee Plan expires in June 2004. The Director Plan expired in fiscal 2000. As of March 3, 2001 and February 26, 2000, outstanding options covering 61,764 shares were exercisable under the Director Plan. Due to the expiration of the Director Plan during fiscal 2000, no

shares are available for future grants. Both plans were subject to adjustments for stock dividends and certain other changes to the Company's capitalization.

A summary of stock option transactions related to the stock option plans during the three fiscal years ended March 3, 2001 is as follows (the summary reflects the effect of the three for two stock split, effected in the form of a stock dividend, distributed July 29, 1998):

	Shares	Weighted Average Exercise Price	Weighted Average Fair Value at Date of Grant	Exercisable Shares Number of Shares	Weighted Average Exercise Price
Outstanding at February 28, 1998	3,988,949	$ 7.21		1,350,332	$ 5.16
Options granted	1,550,500	13.27	$ 5.38		
Options exercised	(662,889)	6.11			
Options cancelled or expired	(278,730)	10.72			
Outstanding at February 27, 1999	4,597,830	9.20		1,810,819	6.66
Options granted	2,379,500	6.20	3.18		
Options exercised	(134,936)	4.63			
Options cancelled or expired	(793,187)	10.63			
Outstanding at February 26, 2000	6,049,207	7.94		2,214,717	7.28
Options granted	1,584,000	10.49	5.31		
Options exercised	(569,326)	5.38			
Options cancelled or expired	(351,900)	8.47			
Outstanding at March 3, 2001	6,711,981	8.73		2,809,406	8.07

For shares outstanding at March 3, 2001:

Ranges of Exercise Prices	Total Shares	Weighted Average Exercise Price	Weighted Average Remaining Contractual Life	Shares Currently Exercisable	Weighted Average Exercise Price – Exercisable Shares
$ 2.85 - $ 4.61	747,408	$ 3.91	3.59	747,408	$ 3.91
$ 5.81 - $ 5.81	1,688,350	5.81	8.53	353,350	5.81
$ 6.25 - $10.44	3,129,098	9.09	8.10	1,035,673	7.72
$10.88 - $18.50	1,147,125	15.16	7.11	672,975	14.40

Pier 1 Imports, Inc.

NOTES TO CONSOLIDATED FINANCIAL STATEMENTS

(continued)

The Company accounts for its stock options using the intrinsic value-based method of accounting prescribed by APB Opinion No. 25, but is required to disclose the pro forma effect on net income and earnings per share as if the options were accounted for using a fair value-based method of accounting. The fair values for options issued in fiscal 2001, 2000 and 1999 have been estimated as of the date of grant using the Black-Scholes or a similar option pricing model with the following weighted average assumptions for 2001, 2000 and 1999, respectively: risk-free interest rates of 5.68%, 5.79% and 5.14%, expected volatility factors of .5586, .5150 and .3655, expected dividend yields of 1.0% and weighted average expected lives of six years from date of grant to date of exercise for all options. For purposes of computing pro forma net income and earnings per share, the fair value of the stock options is amortized on a straight-line basis as compensation expense over the vesting periods of the options. The pro forma effects on net income and earnings per share are as follows (in thousands except per share amounts):

	2001	2000	1999
Pro forma net income	$ 91,573	$ 72,317	$ 77,891
Pro forma basic earnings per share	$ .95	$ .76	$ .79
Pro forma diluted earnings per share	$ .93	$ .72	$ .74

Option valuation models are used in estimating the fair value of traded options that have no vesting restrictions and are fully transferable. In addition, option valuation models require the input of highly subjective assumptions, including the expected stock price volatility and the average life of options. Because the Company's stock options have characteristics significantly different from those of traded options, and because changes in the subjective input assumptions can materially affect the fair value estimate, in management's opinion, the existing models do not necessarily provide a reliable single measure of the fair value of its stock options. In addition, the pro forma net income and earnings

per share amounts shown above for fiscal 2001, 2000 and 1999 do not include the effect of any grants made prior to fiscal 1996.

Share purchase rights plan - On December 9, 1994, the Board of Directors adopted a Share Purchase Rights Plan and declared a dividend of one common stock purchase right (a "Right") payable on each outstanding share of the Company's common stock on December 21, 1994, and authorized the issuance of Rights for subsequently issued shares of common stock. The Rights, which will expire on December 21, 2004, are initially not exercisable, and until becoming exercisable will trade only with the associated common stock. After the Rights become exercisable, each Right entitles the holder to purchase at a specified exercise price one share of common stock. The Rights will become exercisable after the earlier to occur of (i) ten days following a public announcement that a person or group of affiliated or associated persons have acquired beneficial ownership of 15% or more of the outstanding common stock or (ii) ten business days (or such later date as determined by the Board of Directors) following the commencement of, or announcement of an intention to make, a tender or exchange offer the consummation of which would result in beneficial ownership by a person or group of 15% or more of the outstanding common stock. If the Company were acquired in a merger or other business combination transaction or 50% or more of its consolidated assets or earning power were sold, proper provision would be made so that each Right would entitle its holder to purchase, upon the exercise of the Right at the then current exercise price (currently the exercise price is $14.81), that number of shares of common stock of the acquiring company having a market value of twice the exercise price of the Right. If any person or group were to acquire beneficial ownership of 15% or more of the Company's outstanding common stock, each Right would entitle its holder (other than such acquiring person whose Rights would become void) to purchase, upon the exercise of the Right at the then current exercise price, that

Pier 1 Imports, Inc.

NOTES TO CONSOLIDATED FINANCIAL STATEMENTS
(continued)

number of shares of the Company's common stock having a market value on the date of such 15% acquisition of twice the exercise price of the Right. The Board of Directors may at its option, at any time after such 15% acquisition but prior to the acquisition of more than 50% of the Company's outstanding common stock, exchange all or part of the then outstanding and exercisable Rights (other than those held by such acquiring person whose Rights would become void) for common stock at an exchange rate per Right of one-half the number of shares of common stock receivable upon exercise of a Right. The Board of Directors may, at any time prior to such 15% acquisition, redeem all the Rights at a redemption price of $.01 per Right.

Shares reserved for future issuances - As of March 3, 2001, the Company had approximately 119,028,000 shares reserved for future issuances under the stock plans and the share purchase rights plan.

NOTE 9 - INCOME TAXES

The provision for income taxes for each of the last three fiscal years consists of (in thousands):

	2001	2000	1999
Federal:			
Current	$ 50,455	$ 39,463	$ 47,007
Deferred	583	355	(2,948)
State:			
Current	3,368	1,890	5,112
Deferred	152	1,370	(378)
Foreign:			
Current	1,032	809	460
	$ 55,590	$ 43,887	$ 49,253

Deferred tax assets at March 3, 2001 and February 26, 2000 are comprised of the following (in thousands):

	2001	2000
Deferred tax assets:		
Inventory.	$ 1,727	$ 4,339
Deferred compensation	7,292	5,268
Accrued average rent.	7,784	7,254
Losses on a foreign subsidiary.	3,301	2,497
Self insurance reserves.	910	2,049
Fixed assets, net	795	441
Other	2,326	1,637
	24,135	23,485
Valuation allowance.	(3,301)	(1,916)
Net deferred tax assets.	$ 20,834	$ 21,569

The Company has settled and closed all Internal Revenue Service ("IRS") examinations of the Company's tax returns for all years through fiscal 1999. Subsequent years are not yet under IRS audit.

At February 26, 2000, the net capital loss carryforward for income tax purposes of approximately $3.2 million expired. For financial reporting purposes, a valuation allowance remains at March 3, 2001 to partially offset the deferred tax asset relating to the losses of a foreign subsidiary.

Undistributed earnings of the Company's non-U.S. subsidiaries amounted to approximately $19.4 million at March 3, 2001. These earnings are considered to be indefinitely reinvested and, accordingly, no additional U.S. income taxes or non-U.S. withholding taxes have been provided. Determination of the amount of additional taxes that would be payable if such earnings were not considered indefinitely reinvested is not practical.

Pier 1 Imports, Inc.

NOTES TO CONSOLIDATED FINANCIAL STATEMENTS
(continued)

The difference between income taxes at the statutory federal income tax rate of 35% in fiscal 2001, 2000 and 1999, and income tax reported in the consolidated statements of operations is as follows (in thousands):

	2001	2000	1999
Tax at statutory federal tax rate	$ 52,584	$ 41,514	$ 45,364
State income taxes, net of federal benefit. . .	3,200	2,526	5,832
Work opportunity tax credit, foreign tax credit and R&E credit. . .	(207)	(283)	(327)
Net foreign income taxed at lower rates	(1,048)	(960)	(517)
Other, net	1,061	1,090	(1,099)
	$ 55,590	$ 43,887	$ 49,253

NOTE 10 - COMMITMENTS AND CONTINGENCIES

Leases - The Company leases certain property consisting principally of retail stores, warehouses and material handling and office equipment under leases expiring through the year 2015. Most retail store locations are leased for initial terms of 10 to 15 years with varying renewal options and rent escalation clauses. Certain leases provide for additional rental payments based on a percentage of sales in excess of a specified base. The Company's lease obligations are considered operating leases, and all payments are reflected in the accompanying consolidated statements of operations.

During fiscal 2000, the Company sold certain store properties for $19.3 million. These stores were leased back from unaffiliated third parties for periods of ten years. The resulting leases are being accounted for as operating leases. The Company deferred gains of $3.3 million in fiscal 2000 on these sale-leaseback transactions; the gains are being amortized over the initial lives of the leases. Future minimum lease commitments of these operating leases are included in the summary below of the Company's operating leases. The Company had no sale-leaseback transactions in fiscal 2001.

At March 3, 2001, the Company had the following minimum lease commitments in the years indicated (in thousands):

Fiscal Year	Operating Leases
2002	$ 139,589
2003	132,924
2004	124,574
2005	111,225
2006	99,131
Thereafter	333,485
Total lease commitments	$ 940,928
Present value of total operating lease commitments at 10%	$ 624,987

Rental expense incurred was $144,035,000, $131,835,000 and $114,966,000, including contingent rentals of $979,000, $794,000 and $884,000, based upon a percentage of sales, and net of sublease incomes totaling $2,650,000, $2,141,000 and $1,511,000 in fiscal 2001, 2000 and 1999, respectively.

Legal matters - There are various claims, lawsuits, investigations and pending actions against the Company and its subsidiaries incident to the operations of its business. Liability, if any, associated with these matters is not determinable at March 3, 2001; however, the Company considers them to be ordinary and routine in nature. The Company maintains liability insurance against most of these claims. While certain of the lawsuits involve substantial amounts, it is the opinion of management, after consultation with counsel, that the ultimate resolution of such litigation will not have a material adverse effect on the Company's financial position, results of operations or liquidity.

Pier 1 Imports, Inc.

NOTES TO CONSOLIDATED FINANCIAL STATEMENTS
(continued)

NOTE 11 - SELECTED QUARTERLY FINANCIAL DATA (UNAUDITED)

Summarized quarterly financial data for the years ended March 3, 2001 and February 26, 2000 are set forth below (in thousands except per share amounts):

	Three Months Ended			
Fiscal 2001	5/27/00	8/26/00	11/25/00	3/3/01
Net sales	$ 299,528	337,991	343,493	430,486
Gross profit	$ 126,646	135,616	147,160	185,033
Net income	$ 16,877	17,715	23,569	36,489
Basic earnings per share	$ .17	.18	.25	.38
Diluted earnings per share	$ .17	.18	.24	.38

	Three Months Ended			
Fiscal 2000	5/29/99	8/28/99	11/27/99	2/26/00
Net sales	$ 261,002	291,787	298,223	380,083
Gross profit	$ 110,083	113,212	126,029	163,224
Net income	$ 12,645	11,886	16,151	34,043
Basic earnings per share	$ .13	.12	.17	.36
Diluted earnings per share	$ .13	.12	.16	.34

Pier 1 Imports, Inc.
SHAREHOLDER INFORMATION

EXECUTIVE OFFICES

Suite 600
301 Commerce Street
Fort Worth, Texas 76102
(817) 252-8000
www.pier1.com

COMMON STOCK

Approximately 35,000 shareholders of record
Traded on the New York Stock Exchange
Symbol: PIR

INVESTOR RELATIONS AND FORM 10-K REPORT

A copy of the Pier 1 Imports, Inc. Form 10-K
report filed with the Securities and Exchange
Commission is available by writing the
Investor Relations Department at:

Pier 1 Imports, Inc.
P.O. Box 961020
Fort Worth, Texas 76161-0020
or by calling (817) 252-7835
Toll Free (888) 80-PIER1
        (888) 807-4371

Investor inquiries also may be directed to
that department.

INDEPENDENT AUDITORS

Ernst & Young LLP
Fort Worth, Texas

TRANSFER AGENT

Mellon Investor Services
85 Challenger Road
Ridgefield Park, New Jersey 07660
Shareholder Line Toll Free (888) 884-8086

ANNUAL MEETING

The annual meeting of shareholders will
be held at 10 a.m. Central Daylight Time,
Thursday, June 28, 2001, in the
Trinity Ballroom at the Renaissance
Worthington Hotel, Fort Worth, Texas.

MARKET PRICE AND DIVIDEND INFORMATION

The Company's common stock is traded on the New York Stock Exchange. The following tables show the high and low closing sale prices on such Exchange, as reported in the consolidated transaction reporting system, and the dividends paid per share, for each quarter of fiscal 2001 and 2000.

Fiscal 2001	Market Price High	Market Price Low	Cash Dividends Per Share (1)	Fiscal 2000	Market Price High	Market Price Low	Cash Dividends Per Share (1)
First quarter	$11.8750	$ 7.8750	$ .03	First quarter	$11.6875	$ 7.0625	$ .03
Second quarter	12.7500	8.5000	.04	Second quarter	12.2500	5.6875	.03
Third quarter	14.0000	10.4375	.04	Third quarter	7.2500	5.3750	.03
Fourth quarter	13.8750	8.1875	.04	Fourth quarter	9.1875	5.9375	.03

(1) For restrictions on the payments of dividends, see Management's Discussion and Analysis of Financial Condition and Results of Operations – Liquidity and Capital Resources.

Pier 1 Imports, Inc.
DIRECTORS AND OFFICERS

BOARD OF DIRECTORS

Marvin J. Girouard
Chairman and
Chief Executive Officer

John H. Burgoyne
Principal
Burgoyne and Associates

Dr. Michael R. Ferrari
Chancellor
Texas Christian University

James M. Hoak, Jr.
Chairman
Hoak Capital Corporation

Sally F. McKenzie
Civic Leader
Local, Regional and National

Tom M. Thomas
Senior Partner
Thomas & Culp, LLP

EXECUTIVE OFFICERS

Marvin J. Girouard
Chairman and
Chief Executive Officer

Charles H. Turner
Senior Vice President, Chief
Financial Officer and Treasurer

Robert A. Arlauskas
Senior Vice President,
Stores

Jay R. Jacobs
Senior Vice President,
Merchandising

J. Rodney Lawrence
Senior Vice President, Legal
Affairs and Corporate Secretary

Phil E. Schneider
Senior Vice President,
Marketing

David A. Walker
Senior Vice President,
Logistics and Allocations

E. Mitchell Weatherly
Senior Vice President,
Human Resources

ADDITIONAL MATERIAL FROM THE 2000 ANNUAL REPORT

Pier 1 Imports, Inc.

CONSOLIDATED BALANCE SHEETS
(in thousands except share data)

	2000	1999
ASSETS		
Current assets:		
Cash, including temporary investments of $39,898 and $32,434, respectively	$ 50,376	$ 41,945
Beneficial interest in securitized receivables	53,820	41,000
Accounts receivable, net of allowance for doubtful accounts		
of $44 and $230, respectively	5,637	9,060
Inventories	268,906	258,773
Prepaid expenses and other current assets	36,541	31,165
Total current assets	415,280	381,943
Properties, net	213,032	226,262
Other assets	42,398	45,786
	$ 670,710	$ 653,991
LIABILITIES AND SHAREHOLDERS' EQUITY		
Current liabilities:		
Notes payable and current portion of long-term debt	$ 39,179	$ 350
Accounts payable and accrued liabilities	136,787	129,482
Total current liabilities	175,966	129,832
Long-term debt	25,000	96,008
Other non-current liabilities	29,081	24,257
Shareholders' equity:		
Common stock, $1.00 par, 500,000,000 shares authorized, 100,779,000 issued	100,779	100,779
Paid-in capital	155,711	159,631
Retained earnings	264,678	201,457
Cumulative other comprehensive income	(1,536)	(1,850)
Less – 6,949,000 and 3,107,000 common shares in treasury, at cost, respectively	(78,668)	(54,654)
Less – unearned compensation	(301)	(1,469)
	440,663	403,894
Commitments and contingencies		
	$ 670,710	$ 653,991

The accompanying notes are an integral part of these financial statements.

APPENDIX B PRESENT AND FUTURE VALUE TABLES

Table 1   The Future Value of a Single Amount ($1)

$FV = P(1 + r)^n$. In this table $P = \$1.00$

Periods	0.50%	1%	2%	3%	4%	5%	6%	7%	8%	9%	10%	11%	12%	13%	14%	15%
1	1.00500	1.01000	1.02000	1.03000	1.04000	1.05000	1.06000	1.07000	1.08000	1.09000	1.10000	1.11000	1.12000	1.13000	1.14000	1.15000
2	1.01003	1.02010	1.04040	1.06090	1.08160	1.10250	1.12360	1.14490	1.16640	1.18810	1.21000	1.23210	1.25440	1.27690	1.29960	1.32250
3	1.01508	1.03030	1.06121	1.09273	1.12486	1.15763	1.19102	1.22504	1.25971	1.29503	1.33100	1.36763	1.40493	1.44290	1.48154	1.52088
4	1.02015	1.04060	1.08243	1.12551	1.16986	1.21551	1.26248	1.31080	1.36049	1.41158	1.46410	1.51807	1.57352	1.63047	1.68896	1.74901
5	1.02525	1.05101	1.10408	1.15927	1.21665	1.27628	1.33823	1.40255	1.46933	1.53862	1.61051	1.68506	1.76234	1.84244	1.92541	2.01136
6	1.03038	1.06152	1.12616	1.19405	1.26532	1.34010	1.41852	1.50073	1.58687	1.67710	1.77156	1.87041	1.97382	2.08195	2.19497	2.31306
7	1.03553	1.07214	1.14869	1.22987	1.31593	1.40710	1.50363	1.60578	1.71382	1.82804	1.94872	2.07616	2.21068	2.35261	2.50227	2.66002
8	1.04071	1.08286	1.17166	1.26677	1.36857	1.47746	1.59385	1.71819	1.85093	1.99256	2.14359	2.30454	2.47596	2.65844	2.85259	3.05902
9	1.04591	1.09369	1.19509	1.30477	1.42331	1.55133	1.68948	1.83846	1.99900	2.17189	2.35795	2.55804	2.77308	3.00404	3.25195	3.51788
10	1.05114	1.10462	1.21899	1.34392	1.48024	1.62889	1.79085	1.96715	2.15892	2.36736	2.59374	2.83942	3.10585	3.39457	3.70722	4.04556
11	1.05640	1.11567	1.24337	1.38423	1.53945	1.71034	1.89830	2.10485	2.33164	2.58043	2.85312	3.15176	3.47855	3.83586	4.22623	4.65239
12	1.06168	1.12683	1.26824	1.42576	1.60103	1.79586	2.01220	2.25219	2.51817	2.81266	3.13843	3.49845	3.89598	4.33452	4.81790	5.35025
13	1.06699	1.13809	1.29361	1.46853	1.66507	1.88565	2.13293	2.40985	2.71962	3.06580	3.45227	3.88328	4.36349	4.89801	5.49241	6.15279
14	1.07232	1.14947	1.31948	1.51259	1.73168	1.97993	2.26090	2.57853	2.93719	3.34173	3.79750	4.31044	4.88711	5.53475	6.26135	7.07571
15	1.07768	1.16097	1.34587	1.55797	1.80094	2.07893	2.39656	2.75903	3.17217	3.64248	4.17725	4.78459	5.47357	6.25427	7.13794	8.13706
16	1.08307	1.17258	1.37279	1.60471	1.87298	2.18287	2.54035	2.95216	3.42594	3.97031	4.59497	5.31089	6.13039	7.06733	8.13725	9.35762
17	1.08849	1.18430	1.40024	1.65285	1.94790	2.29202	2.69277	3.15882	3.70002	4.32763	5.05447	5.89509	6.86604	7.98608	9.27646	10.76126
18	1.09393	1.19615	1.42825	1.70243	2.02582	2.40662	2.85434	3.37993	3.99602	4.71712	5.55992	6.54355	7.68997	9.02427	10.57517	12.37545
19	1.09940	1.20811	1.45681	1.75351	2.10685	2.52695	3.02560	3.61653	4.31570	5.14166	6.11591	7.26334	8.61276	10.19742	12.05569	14.23177
20	1.10490	1.22019	1.48595	1.80611	2.19112	2.65330	3.20714	3.86968	4.66096	5.60441	6.72750	8.06231	9.64629	11.52309	13.74349	16.36654
21	1.11042	1.23239	1.51567	1.86029	2.27877	2.78596	3.39956	4.14056	5.03383	6.10881	7.40025	8.94917	10.80385	13.02109	15.66758	18.82152
22	1.11597	1.24472	1.54598	1.91610	2.36992	2.92526	3.60354	4.43040	5.43654	6.65860	8.14027	9.93357	12.10031	14.71383	17.86104	21.64475
23	1.12155	1.25716	1.57690	1.97359	2.46472	3.07152	3.81975	4.74053	5.87146	7.25787	8.95430	11.02627	13.55235	16.62663	20.36158	24.89146
24	1.12716	1.26973	1.60844	2.03279	2.56330	3.22510	4.04893	5.07237	6.34118	7.91108	9.84973	12.23916	15.17863	18.78809	23.21221	28.62518
25	1.13280	1.28243	1.64061	2.09378	2.66584	3.38635	4.29187	5.42743	6.84848	8.62308	10.83471	13.58546	17.00006	21.23054	26.46192	32.91895
30	1.16140	1.34785	1.81136	2.42726	3.24340	4.32194	5.74349	7.61226	10.06266	13.26768	17.44940	22.89230	29.95992	39.11590	50.95016	66.21177
35	1.19073	1.41660	1.99989	2.81386	3.94609	5.51602	7.68609	10.67658	14.78534	20.41397	28.10244	38.57485	52.79962	72.06851	98.10018	133.17552
40	1.22079	1.48886	2.20804	3.26204	4.80102	7.03999	10.28572	14.97446	21.72452	31.40942	45.25926	65.00087	93.05097	132.78155	188.88351	267.86355

(FV = future value, P = payment, r = interest rate per period in decimal form, n = number of periods)

Table 2 The Future Value of an Annuity of $1 in Arrears*

$$FV_a = \frac{(1+r)^n - 1}{r}$$

Periods	0.50%	1%	2%	3%	4%	5%	6%	7%	8%	9%	10%	11%	12%	13%	14%	15%
1	1.00000	1.00000	1.00000	1.00000	1.00000	1.00000	1.00000	1.00000	1.00000	1.00000	1.00000	1.00000	1.00000	1.00000	1.00000	1.00000
2	2.00500	2.01000	2.02000	2.03000	2.04000	2.05000	2.06000	2.07000	2.08000	2.09000	2.10000	2.11000	2.12000	2.13000	2.14000	2.15000
3	3.01502	3.03010	3.06040	3.09090	3.12160	3.15250	3.18360	3.21490	3.24640	3.27810	3.31000	3.34210	3.37440	3.40690	3.43960	3.47250
4	4.03010	4.06040	4.12161	4.18363	4.24646	4.31013	4.37462	4.43994	4.50611	4.57313	4.64100	4.70973	4.77933	4.84980	4.92114	4.99338
5	5.05025	5.10101	5.20404	5.30914	5.41632	5.52563	5.63709	5.75074	5.86660	5.98471	6.10510	6.22780	6.35285	6.48027	6.61010	6.74238
6	6.07550	6.15202	6.30812	6.46841	6.63298	6.80191	6.97532	7.15329	7.33593	7.52333	7.71561	7.91286	8.11519	8.32271	8.53552	8.75374
7	7.10588	7.21354	7.43428	7.66246	7.89829	8.14201	8.39384	8.65402	8.92280	9.20043	9.48717	9.78327	10.08901	10.40466	10.73049	11.06680
8	8.14141	8.28567	8.58297	8.89234	9.21423	9.54911	9.89747	10.25980	10.63663	11.02847	11.43589	11.85943	12.29969	12.75726	13.23276	13.72682
9	9.18212	9.36853	9.75463	10.15911	10.58280	11.02656	11.49132	11.97799	12.48756	13.02104	13.57948	14.16397	14.77566	15.41571	16.08535	16.78584
10	10.22803	10.46221	10.94972	11.46388	12.00611	12.57789	13.18079	13.81645	14.48656	15.19293	15.93742	16.72201	17.54874	18.41975	19.33730	20.30372
11	11.27917	11.56683	12.16872	12.80780	13.48635	14.20679	14.97164	15.78360	16.64549	17.56029	18.53117	19.56143	20.65458	21.81432	23.04452	24.34928
12	12.33556	12.68250	13.41209	14.19203	15.02581	15.91713	16.86994	17.88845	18.97713	20.14072	21.38428	22.71319	24.13313	25.65018	27.27075	29.00167
13	13.39724	13.80933	14.68033	15.61779	16.62684	17.71298	18.88214	20.14064	21.49530	22.95338	24.52271	26.21164	28.02911	29.98470	32.08865	34.35192
14	14.46423	14.94742	15.97394	17.08632	18.29191	19.59863	21.01507	22.55049	24.21492	26.01919	27.97498	30.09492	32.39260	34.88271	37.58107	40.50471
15	15.53655	16.09690	17.29342	18.59891	20.02359	21.57856	23.27597	25.12902	27.15211	29.36092	31.77248	34.40536	37.27971	40.41746	43.84241	47.58041
16	16.61423	17.25786	18.63929	20.15688	21.82453	23.65749	25.67253	27.88805	30.32428	33.00340	35.94973	39.18995	42.75328	46.67173	50.98035	55.71747
17	17.69730	18.43044	20.01207	21.76159	23.69751	25.84037	28.21288	30.84022	33.75023	36.97370	40.54470	44.50084	48.88367	53.73906	59.11760	65.07509
18	18.78579	19.61475	21.41231	23.41444	25.64541	28.13238	30.90565	33.99903	37.45024	41.30134	45.59917	50.39594	55.74971	61.72514	68.39407	75.83636
19	19.87972	20.81090	22.84056	25.11687	27.67123	30.53900	33.75999	37.37896	41.44626	46.01846	51.15909	56.93949	63.43968	70.74941	78.96923	88.21181
20	20.97912	22.01900	24.29737	26.87037	29.77808	33.06595	36.78559	40.99549	45.76196	51.16012	57.27500	64.20283	72.05244	80.94683	91.02493	102.44358
21	22.08401	23.23919	25.78332	28.67649	31.96920	35.71925	39.99273	44.86518	50.42292	56.76453	64.00250	72.26514	81.69874	92.46992	104.76842	118.81012
22	23.19443	24.47159	27.29898	30.53678	34.24797	38.50521	43.39229	49.00574	55.45676	62.87334	71.40275	81.21431	92.50258	105.49101	120.43600	137.63164
23	24.31040	25.71630	28.84496	32.45288	36.61789	41.43048	46.99583	53.43614	60.89330	69.53194	79.54302	91.14788	104.60289	120.20484	138.29704	159.27638
24	25.43196	26.97346	30.42186	34.42647	39.08260	44.50200	50.81558	58.17667	66.76476	76.78981	88.49733	102.17415	118.15524	136.83147	158.65862	184.16784
25	26.55912	28.24320	32.03030	36.45926	41.64591	47.72710	54.86451	63.24904	73.10594	84.70090	98.34706	114.41331	133.33387	155.61956	181.87083	212.79302
30	32.28002	34.78489	40.56808	47.57542	56.08494	66.43885	79.05819	94.46079	113.28321	136.30754	164.49402	199.02088	241.33268	293.19922	356.78685	434.74515
35	38.14538	41.66028	49.99448	60.46208	73.65222	90.32031	111.43478	138.23688	172.31680	215.71075	271.02437	341.58955	431.66350	546.68082	693.57270	881.17016
40	44.15885	48.88637	60.40198	75.40126	95.02552	120.79977	154.76197	199.63511	259.05652	337.88245	442.59256	581.82607	767.09142	1013.70424	1342.02510	1779.09031

* Payments (or receipts) at the end of each period.

(FV_a = future value of an annuity, r = interest rate per period in decimal form, n = number of periods in which a payment is made or received)

Table 3   The Present Value of a Single Amount ($1)

$$PV = \frac{\text{future value}}{(1 + r)^n}$$

Periods	0.50%	1%	2%	3%	4%	5%	6%	7%	8%	9%	10%	11%	12%	13%	14%	15%
1	0.99502	0.99010	0.98039	0.97087	0.96154	0.95238	0.94340	0.93458	0.92593	0.91743	0.90909	0.90090	0.89286	0.88496	0.87719	0.86957
2	0.99007	0.98030	0.96117	0.94260	0.92456	0.90703	0.89000	0.87344	0.85734	0.84168	0.82645	0.81162	0.79719	0.78315	0.76947	0.75614
3	0.98515	0.97059	0.94232	0.91514	0.88900	0.86384	0.83962	0.81630	0.79383	0.77218	0.75131	0.73119	0.71178	0.69305	0.67497	0.65752
4	0.98025	0.96098	0.92385	0.88849	0.85480	0.82270	0.79209	0.76290	0.73503	0.70843	0.68301	0.65873	0.63552	0.61332	0.59208	0.57175
5	0.97537	0.95147	0.90573	0.86261	0.82193	0.78353	0.74726	0.71299	0.68058	0.64993	0.62092	0.59345	0.56743	0.54276	0.51937	0.49718
6	0.97052	0.94205	0.88797	0.83748	0.79031	0.74622	0.70496	0.66634	0.63017	0.59627	0.56447	0.53464	0.50663	0.48032	0.45559	0.43233
7	0.96569	0.93272	0.87056	0.81309	0.75992	0.71068	0.66506	0.62275	0.58349	0.54703	0.51316	0.48166	0.45235	0.42506	0.39964	0.37594
8	0.96089	0.92348	0.85349	0.78941	0.73069	0.67684	0.62741	0.58201	0.54027	0.50187	0.46651	0.43393	0.40388	0.37616	0.35056	0.32690
9	0.95610	0.91434	0.83676	0.76642	0.70259	0.64461	0.59190	0.54393	0.50025	0.46043	0.42410	0.39092	0.36061	0.33288	0.30751	0.28426
10	0.95135	0.90529	0.82035	0.74409	0.67556	0.61391	0.55839	0.50835	0.46319	0.42241	0.38554	0.35218	0.32197	0.29459	0.26974	0.24718
11	0.94661	0.89632	0.80426	0.72242	0.64958	0.58468	0.52679	0.47509	0.42888	0.38753	0.35049	0.31728	0.28748	0.26070	0.23662	0.21494
12	0.94191	0.88745	0.78849	0.70138	0.62460	0.55684	0.49697	0.44401	0.39711	0.35553	0.31863	0.28584	0.25668	0.23071	0.20756	0.18691
13	0.93722	0.87866	0.77303	0.68095	0.60057	0.53032	0.46884	0.41496	0.36770	0.32618	0.28966	0.25751	0.22917	0.20416	0.18207	0.16253
14	0.93256	0.86996	0.75788	0.66112	0.57748	0.50507	0.44230	0.38782	0.34046	0.29925	0.26333	0.23199	0.20462	0.18068	0.15971	0.14133
15	0.92792	0.86135	0.74301	0.64186	0.55526	0.48102	0.41727	0.36245	0.31524	0.27454	0.23939	0.20900	0.18270	0.15989	0.14010	0.12289
16	0.92330	0.85282	0.72845	0.62317	0.53391	0.45811	0.39365	0.33873	0.29189	0.25187	0.21763	0.18829	0.16312	0.14150	0.12289	0.10686
17	0.91871	0.84438	0.71416	0.60502	0.51337	0.43630	0.37136	0.31657	0.27027	0.23107	0.19784	0.16963	0.14564	0.12522	0.10780	0.09293
18	0.91414	0.83602	0.70016	0.58739	0.49363	0.41552	0.35034	0.29586	0.25025	0.21199	0.17986	0.15282	0.13004	0.11081	0.09456	0.08081
19	0.90959	0.82774	0.68643	0.57029	0.47464	0.39573	0.33051	0.27651	0.23171	0.19449	0.16351	0.13768	0.11611	0.09806	0.08295	0.07027
20	0.90506	0.81954	0.67297	0.55368	0.45639	0.37689	0.31180	0.25842	0.21455	0.17843	0.14864	0.12403	0.10367	0.08678	0.07276	0.06110
21	0.90056	0.81143	0.65978	0.53755	0.43883	0.35894	0.29416	0.24151	0.19866	0.16370	0.13513	0.11174	0.09256	0.07680	0.06383	0.05313
22	0.89608	0.80340	0.64684	0.52189	0.42196	0.34185	0.27751	0.22571	0.18394	0.15018	0.12285	0.10067	0.08264	0.06796	0.05599	0.04620
23	0.89162	0.79544	0.63416	0.50669	0.40573	0.32557	0.26180	0.21095	0.17032	0.13778	0.11168	0.09069	0.07379	0.06014	0.04911	0.04017
24	0.88719	0.78757	0.62172	0.49193	0.39012	0.31007	0.24698	0.19715	0.15770	0.12640	0.10153	0.08170	0.06588	0.05323	0.04308	0.03493
25	0.88277	0.77977	0.60953	0.47761	0.37512	0.29530	0.23300	0.18425	0.14602	0.11597	0.09230	0.07361	0.05882	0.04710	0.03779	0.03038
30	0.86103	0.74192	0.55207	0.41199	0.30832	0.23138	0.17411	0.13137	0.09938	0.07537	0.05731	0.04368	0.03338	0.02557	0.01963	0.01510
35	0.83982	0.70591	0.50003	0.35538	0.25342	0.18129	0.13011	0.09366	0.06763	0.04899	0.03558	0.02592	0.01894	0.01388	0.01019	0.00751
40	0.81914	0.67165	0.45289	0.30656	0.20829	0.14205	0.09722	0.06678	0.04603	0.03184	0.02209	0.01538	0.01075	0.00753	0.00529	0.00373

(PV = present value, r = interest rate per period in decimal form, n = number of periods)

Table 4 The Present Value of Annuity $1.00 in Arrears*

$$PV_a = \frac{1}{r}\left[1 - \frac{1}{(1+r)^n}\right]$$

Periods	0.50%	1%	2%	3%	4%	5%	6%	7%	8%	9%	10%	11%	12%	13%	14%	15%
1	0.99502	0.99010	0.98039	0.97087	0.96154	0.95238	0.94340	0.93458	0.92593	0.91743	0.90909	0.90090	0.89286	0.88496	0.87719	0.86957
2	1.98510	1.97040	1.94156	1.91347	1.88609	1.85941	1.83339	1.80802	1.78326	1.75911	1.73554	1.71252	1.69005	1.66810	1.64666	1.62571
3	2.97025	2.94099	2.88388	2.82861	2.77509	2.72325	2.67301	2.62432	2.57710	2.53129	2.48685	2.44371	2.40183	2.36115	2.32163	2.28323
4	3.95050	3.90197	3.80773	3.71710	3.62990	3.54595	3.46511	3.38721	3.31213	3.23972	3.16987	3.10245	3.03735	2.97447	2.91371	2.85498
5	4.92587	4.85343	4.71346	4.57971	4.45182	4.32948	4.21236	4.10020	3.99271	3.88965	3.79079	3.69590	3.60478	3.51723	3.43308	3.35216
6	5.89638	5.79548	5.60143	5.41719	5.24214	5.07569	4.91732	4.76654	4.62288	4.48592	4.35526	4.23054	4.11141	3.99755	3.88867	3.78448
7	6.86207	6.72819	6.47199	6.23028	6.00205	5.78637	5.58238	5.38929	5.20637	5.03295	4.86842	4.71220	4.56376	4.42261	4.28830	4.16042
8	7.82296	7.65168	7.32548	7.01969	6.73274	6.46321	6.20979	5.97130	5.74664	5.53482	5.33493	5.14612	4.96764	4.79877	4.63886	4.48732
9	8.77906	8.56602	8.16224	7.78611	7.43533	7.10782	6.80169	6.51523	6.24689	5.99525	5.75902	5.53705	5.32825	5.13166	4.94637	4.77158
10	9.73041	9.47130	8.98259	8.53020	8.11090	7.72173	7.36009	7.02358	6.71008	6.41766	6.14457	5.88923	5.65022	5.42624	5.21612	5.01877
11	10.67703	10.36763	9.78685	9.25262	8.76048	8.30641	7.88687	7.49867	7.13896	6.80519	6.49506	6.20652	5.93770	5.68694	5.45273	5.23371
12	11.61893	11.25508	10.57534	9.95400	9.38507	8.86325	8.38384	7.94269	7.53608	7.16073	6.81369	6.49236	6.19437	5.91765	5.66029	5.42062
13	12.55615	12.13374	11.34837	10.63496	9.98565	9.39357	8.85268	8.35765	7.90378	7.48690	7.10336	6.74987	6.42355	6.12181	5.84236	5.58315
14	13.48871	13.00370	12.10625	11.29607	10.56312	9.89864	9.29498	8.74547	8.24424	7.78615	7.36669	6.98187	6.62817	6.30249	6.00207	5.72448
15	14.41662	13.86505	12.84926	11.93794	11.11839	10.37966	9.71225	9.10791	8.55948	8.06069	7.60608	7.19087	6.81086	6.46238	6.14217	5.84737
16	15.33993	14.71787	13.57771	12.56110	11.65230	10.83777	10.10590	9.44665	8.85137	8.31256	7.82371	7.37916	6.97399	6.60388	6.26506	5.95423
17	16.25863	15.56225	14.29187	13.16612	12.16567	11.27407	10.47726	9.76322	9.12164	8.54363	8.02155	7.54879	7.11963	6.72909	6.37286	6.04716
18	17.17277	16.39827	14.99203	13.75351	12.65930	11.68959	10.82760	10.05909	9.37189	8.75563	8.20141	7.70162	7.24967	6.83991	6.46742	6.12797
19	18.08236	17.22601	15.67846	14.32380	13.13394	12.08532	11.15812	10.33560	9.60360	8.95011	8.36492	7.83929	7.36578	6.93797	6.55037	6.19823
20	18.98742	18.04555	16.35143	14.87747	13.59033	12.46221	11.46992	10.59401	9.81815	9.12855	8.51356	7.96333	7.46944	7.02475	6.62313	6.25933
21	19.88798	18.85698	17.01121	15.41502	14.02916	12.82115	11.76408	10.83553	10.01680	9.29224	8.64869	8.07507	7.56200	7.10155	6.68696	6.31246
22	20.78406	19.66038	17.65805	15.93692	14.45112	13.16300	12.04158	11.06124	10.20074	9.44243	8.77154	8.17574	7.64465	7.16951	6.74294	6.35866
23	21.67568	20.45582	18.29220	16.44361	14.85684	13.48857	12.30338	11.27219	10.37106	9.58021	8.88322	8.26643	7.71843	7.22966	6.79206	6.39884
24	22.56287	21.24339	18.91393	16.93554	15.24696	13.79864	12.55036	11.46933	10.52876	9.70661	8.98474	8.34814	7.78432	7.28288	6.83514	6.43377
25	23.44564	22.02316	19.52346	17.41315	15.62208	14.09394	12.78336	11.65358	10.67478	9.82258	9.07704	8.42174	7.84314	7.32998	6.87293	6.46415
30	27.79405	25.80771	22.39646	19.60044	17.29203	15.37245	13.76483	12.40904	11.25778	10.27365	9.42691	8.69379	8.05518	7.49565	7.00266	6.56598
35	32.03537	29.40858	24.99862	21.48722	18.66461	16.37419	14.49825	12.94767	11.65457	10.56682	9.64416	8.85524	8.17550	7.58557	7.07005	6.61661
40	36.17223	32.83469	27.35548	23.11477	19.79277	17.15909	15.04630	13.33171	11.92461	10.75736	9.77905	8.95105	8.24378	7.63438	7.10504	6.64178

* Payments (or receipts) at the end of each period.
(PV_a = present value of an annuity, r = interest rate per period in decimal form, n = number of periods in which a payment is made or received)

CHAPTER 1

Problems

P1-2A	Net income = $220,500
P1-3A	Net increase in cash = $5,700
P1-4A	Total assets = $36,000
P1-6A	Net income = $4,700
P1-7A	Ending retained earnings = $127,000
P1-8A	Net increase in cash = $164,600
P1-2B	Total assets = $1,231,000
P1-3B	Net increase in cash = $8,100
P1-4B	Net income = $28,000
P1-6B	Ending shareholders' equity = $23,550
P1-7B	Ending retained earnings = $155,500
P1-8B	Net income = $194,700

CHAPTER 2

Problems

P2-1A	Ending capital = $6,205
P2-2A	Total assets = $1,500
P2-3A	Prepaid insurance at 12/31/05 = $1,000
P2-4A	Contributed capital at December 31, 2004 = $350
P2-1B	Total assets = $15,165
P2-2B	Assets increased by $3,400
P2-3B	Cash from financing activities = $5,700
P2-4B	Expenses = $480

CHAPTER 3

Problems

P3-2A	Net income = $12,750
P3-3A	Depreciation expense = $2,000 per year
P3-4A	Prepaid insurance = $3,750
P3-5A	Insurance expense = $2,400
P3-6A	Unearned rental income = $2,200

P3-7A	Retained earnings = $33,700
P3-8A	Net income = $10,425
P3-2B	Net income = $29,320
P3-3B	Depreciation expense = $6,000 per year
P3-4B	Prepaid insurance = $5,000
P3-5B	Insurance expense = $600
P3-6B	Unearned rental income = $3,200
P3-7B	Retained earnings = $46,083.33
P3-8B	Net income = $20,970

CHAPTER 4

Problems

P4-1A	Net income = $17,000
P4-2A	Total assets at 12/31/03 = $122,000
P4-3A	Net effect of closing entries on retained earnings = $15,471 debit
P4-4A	Ending capital = $4,200
P4-6A	Total assets at June 30 = $27,069
P4-7A	Total assets at December 31, 2002 = $135,900
P4-1B	Total assets at 12/31/03 = $37,000
P4-2B	Retained earnings at 12/31/03 = $39,000
P4-3B	Net effect of closing entries on retained earnings = $15,167 credit
P4-4B	Ending capital = $31,100
P4-5B	Net income = $23,150
P4-6B	Ending capital = $33,475

CHAPTER 5

Problems

P5-1A	Total cost = $164,945
P5-2A	Part (b), year 1, depreciation expense = $65,000
P5-3A	Double-declining balance, 2008 depreciation expense = $2,500
P5-4A	Depreciation expense 2002, activity method = $1,680
P5-5A	(a) $3,000 gain

P5-8A	(a) book value after 2002 = $500
P5-9A	(c) gain of $9,200
P5-1B	Total cost = $1,876,450
P5-2B	Part (b), 2003, depreciation expense = $4,000
P5-3B	Straight-line, 2008 depreciation expense = $6,000
P5-4B	Depreciation expense 2011, activity method = $23,520
P5-5B	(a) $2,000 gain
P5-8B	(b) 2004 depreciation expense = $1,000
P5-9B	(a) loss of $3,000
R5-C*	Net income = $23,870

CHAPTER 6

Problems

P6-1A	(d) $11,490
P6-2A	(e) $11,904
P6-3A	(a) gross margin = $2,450
P6-4A	(d) cost of goods sold = $3,526
P6-5A	(a) cost of goods sold = $2,640,000
P6-6A	(c) Net income using FIFO = $11,340
P6-7A	(a) 1. cost of goods sold = $24,818
P6-8A	FIFO cost of goods sold = $8,180
P6-10A	(a) $15,100
P6-11A	(b) net income would decrease by $75
P6-12A	(b) inventory loss = $1,100
P6-13A	Gross margin ratio for 1999 = 0.365
P6-1B	(d) $21,925
P6-2B	(e) $16,822
P6-3B	(b) LIFO cost of good sold = $3,797,500
P6-4B	(c) Net income using weighted average = $4,567
P6-5B	2. FIFO ending inventory = $25,880

*C = comprehensive problem

P6-6B	a. FIFO ending inventory = $6,860	**P8-7A**	(c) interest expense for 2003 = $8,848.16	**P10-3A**	Cash from operations = $98,900
P6-7B	a. cost of goods sold = $35,750			**P10-4A**	Cash from operations = $294,200

P6-6B   a. FIFO ending inventory = $6,860

P6-7B   a. cost of goods sold = $35,750

P6-8B   (a) $7,850

P6-10B   (b) inventory loss = $875

P6-11B   Gross margin ratio for 2004 = 0.3618

R6-C*   Net income = $95,250

CHAPTER 7

Problems

P7-1A   Balance per bank = $97,134.23

P7-2A   Correct balance = $9,354.88

P7-4A   (a) net realizable value = $12,900

P7-5A   (a) allowance after expense = $7,800

P7-7A   (a) $600

P7-1B   Correct balance = $37,773.32

P7-2B   (e) deduct $18 from balance per books (ledger)

P7-4B   3. bad debt expense = $813

P7-5B   1. Warranty expense , 6/30/01 = $31,500

P7-6B   (a) $5,000

P7-7B   3. net realizable value = $444,840

R7-C*   Net income = $84,184

CHAPTER 8

Problems

P8-1A   (a) payment = $6,344.14

P8-2A   (1) payment = $601.14

P8-3A   (1) interest rate = 9%

P8-4A   Proceeds = $924,183.20

P8-5A   (c) $20,464.15

P8-6A   (a) $980,000

P8-7A   (c) interest expense for 2003 = $8,848.16

P8-1B   (a) payment = $8,700.74

P8-2B   (1) payment = $977.51

P8-3B   (a) interest rate = 7%

P8-4B   Proceeds = $146,532.90

P8-5B   (a) proceeds = $82,624.54

P8-6B   (a) $980,000

P8-7B   (c) interest expense for 2005 = $104,869

R8-C*   Net income 2005 = $31,995
Net income 2006 = $48,846

CHAPTER 9

Problems

P9-1A   Total shareholders' equity = $978,500

P9-2A   Retained earnings = $75,000

P9-3A   (a) 2,000 shares

P9-4A   (c) $38.50 per share

P9-5A   (c) $5.58

P9-1B   Common stock = $70,000

P9-2B   Common stock = $30,000

P9-3B   (a) 120,000 shares

P9-4B   (c) $39.20 per share

P9-5B   (b) 22

R9-C*   Total assets at 12/31/03 = $1,649,000
Total assets at 12/31/04 = $3,146,500

CHAPTER 10

Problems

P10-1A   Cash from operations = $10,610

P10-2A   Cash from operations = $(414)

P10-3A   Cash from operations = $98,900

P10-4A   Cash from operations = $294,200

P10-5A   Cash from investing = $50,000

P10-6A   (b) cash from financing = $67,000

P10-7A   Cash from financing = $341,500

P10-8A   (c) operating activities

P10-1B   Cash from operations = $16,900

P10-2B   Cash from operations = $(1,614)

P10-3B   Cash from operations = $1,168

P10-4B   Cash from operations = $187,800

P10-5B   Cash from investing = $30,000

P10-6B   (b) cash from financing = $26,000

P10-7B   Cash from financing = $326,600

P10-8B   (a) financing activities

CHAPTER 11

Problems

P11-1A   Gain on sale of discontinued segment (net) = $126,000

P11-2A   Gross margin increased slightly, from 43% in 1997 to 44.9% in 1999.

P11-3A   Current ratio for 1999 = 1.3

P11-4A   Return on equity = 8.5%

P11-5A   Inventory turnover ratio = 3.4

P11-6A   Acid test ratio = 1.3 for 2004

P11-1B   Loss on disposal (net) = $122,500

P11-2B   Times interest earned ratio of 1999 = 9.0

P11-3B   Inventory turnover ratio for 2001 = 2.7

P11-4B   Debt to equity ratio = 1.02

P11-5B   Current ratio = 1.5

P11-6B   Working capital for 2004 = $487,000

GLOSSARY

accelerated methods. Depreciation methods that recognize more depreciation expense in the early years of an asset's life and less in later years.

access controls. Controls related to all business risks associated with protecting the system from unauthorized access.

accounting cycle. The set of steps used to analyze, record, classify, and summarize accounting information for the preparation of financial statements.

accounting period. A length of time, normally 1 year, used for preparing financial statements. An accounting period also can be a month or quarter.

accounts payable. A written record of all vendors (suppliers) to whom the business firm owes money.

accounts receivable. A written record of all customers who owe a business firm money for items or services they purchased on credit from the firm.

accounts receivable method. A method of estimating bad debt expense by focusing on the balance sheet and the amount of accounts receivable expected to go uncollected. It is one way to estimate uncollectible expense using the allowance method.

accrual. An accounting event in which the action of a transaction is completed before the cash value of that transaction is exchanged.

accrual basis accounting. The method of accounting in which revenues are recognized when earned and expenses are recognized when incurred, not necessarily when cash is exchanged.

accruing salary expense. Recording and recognizing salary expense that will be paid to employees at a later date.

accumulated depreciation. The total depreciation that has been reported as depreciation expense for the entire life of a long-term tangible asset. It is a contra-asset account.

acquisition/payment process. The group of business activities associated with acquiring and paying for goods and services.

additional paid-in capital. The contributed capital from the sale of stock that is above the par value of the stock. It is the issue price of the stock minus its par value times the number of shares issued.

adjunct liability. A liability that is added to another liability, such as *premium on bonds payable,* added to bonds payable.

adjusted trial balance. A list of all accounts and their balances after adjusting entries have been posted to the general ledger. It shows the debit and credit balances; its purpose is to confirm that the sum of debits = the sum of credits.

adjusting entries. Entries necessary at the end of the accounting period to adjust accounts for accrued revenues and expenses and deferred revenues and expenses.

adjusting the books. A crucial step in preparing the financial statements when the amounts recorded for assets and liabilities are reviewed to verify that every amount accurately reflects the financial situation of the business firm on the date of the balance sheet.

agents. The people involved in a transaction, representing the business firm in roles such as cashier, inventory clerk, and salesperson.

allowance for uncollectible accounts. The amount of accounts receivable that is expected to go uncollected. It is called a contra-asset because it is deducted from the asset, accounts receivable.

allowance method. A method of estimating bad debts and expensing them in the period the sales corresponding to those debts are recognized. Two ways to estimate the bad debt expense are the **accounts receivable method** and the **sales method.** Accounts receivable is reported at net realizable value in the financial statements. The allowance method is required by **generally accepted accounting principles (GAAP).**

amortization. The periodic allocation of the cost of intangible assets, such as bonds, over their useful lives, to the income statement as an expense.

annuity. A series of equal payments at regular intervals over a period of time.

asset exchange. A transaction in which one asset increases and another asset decreases.

assets. The economic resources of a business firm, resulting from past transactions; items of value to a business firm, used to generate the firm's revenue.

authorized stock. The maximum number of shares of stock that a corporation is allowed by its articles of incorporation to issue.

audit. An examination of a company's financial statements by a professional accountant, CPA, who then gives an opinion on the fairness with which the financial statements have been presented.

available-for-sale securities. One of three classifications of securities a company has purchased as an investment. These are debt and equity securities a company holds in a kind of investment limbo—the company does not intend to hold these debts and equity securities until maturity (or can't, because the securities are equity securities), and does not intend to sell to make a quick profit.

average cost method. An inventory cost flow method that allocates the average cost of all items between inventory and cost of goods sold. A weighted-average cost is calculated in a periodic inventory system and a moving weighted average cost is calculated in a perpetual inventory system.

---

bad debt expense. The expense associated with uncollectible accounts, also known as *uncollectible accounts expense.* When it is a significant amount, the bad debt expense is estimated with the **allowance method.** If it is not significant, bad debt expense represents the actual losses under the direct write-off method.

balance sheet. Describes the financial situation of a company at a specific point in time. One of the four basic financial statements, it gives the amount of assets, liabilities, and owner's equity that a company has at a specific point in time.

balance per bank statement. The company's cash account balance reported by the bank as of the bank statement date.

balance per books. The cash account balance on the company's books, used to begin the cash reconciliation.

bank. An institution that provides financial services to customers, such as lending money.

bank reconciliation. Compares the cash balance on the company's books and the company's cash balance on the bank statement, and identifies any differences between the two amounts. It also is called a *cash reconciliation.*

beginning inventory. Goods on hand (for sale) at the beginning of the accounting period.

blind purchase order. A copy of the purchase order that notifies the receiving department of an expected shipment but does not indicate the quantity of goods ordered.

bond. A form of long-term financing in which a company describes in a written agreement its responsibility to pay interest and repay the principle on money it has borrowed from investors.

bond covenants. Restrictions placed on the bond issuer and stated in the bond agreement, protecting the interests of the bondholders. For example, bondholders have priority with respect to assets of the firm over the owners' claims on the assets in the event the company goes bankrupt.

bondholder. The individual (or institution) who purchases the bond, thus loaning money to the company that issued the bond.

bond market. Facilitates the initial selling and buying, and subsequent trading of bonds.

book value of an asset. The cost of an asset minus its accumulated depreciation; also called the *net book value,* or the *carrying value.*

book value of a bond. Bonds payable plus the unamortized premium or the bonds payable minus the unamortized discount; also known as the *carrying value* of a bond.

book value per share. Total shareholders' equity (minus any equity represented in preferred stock) divided by the number of outstanding common shares.

bottom line. Refers to net income on the income statement.

business event risk. The risk associated with a business event being conducted according to specific company policies and procedures.

---

callable bond. A bond containing a call feature giving the bond issuer the right to buy back and retire the bonds before maturity.

capital. A business firm's financial resources, commonly meaning money .

capital contributions. The owners' investments in a company; also called *paid-in capital.*

capital expenditure. A substantial expenditure that will benefit several accounting periods, including those which improve the quality and life of an asset.

capital markets. Made up of investors who buy, trade, and sell financial instruments, including debt instruments such as bonds.

capitalizing. Accumulates the cost of an asset in a balance sheet account until that asset is used to generate revenue , at which time the cost is expensed.

carrying value. The cost of an asset minus its accumulated depreciation; book value.

carrying value of a bond. Bonds payable plus the unamortized premium of those bonds; or bonds payable minus their unamortized discount.

cash-basis accounting. The method of accounting that recognizes revenues when received and expenses when paid—that is, recognizes when the cash is exchanged.

cash disbursement. A payment of cash made by a company.

cash from financing activities. Cash receipts and disbursements related to a company's financing—cash transactions related to debt and equity, shown together on the statement of cash flows.

cash from investing activities. Cash receipts and disbursements related to a company's purchase and sale of long-term assets and investments, shown together on the statement of cash flows.

cash from operating activities. Cash receipts and disbursements related to a company's operations, shown together on the statement of cash flows. This section of the statement of cash flows may be prepared and presented using either the direct method or the indirect method.

cash receipt. Acquisition of cash by a company; cash collection.

certified public accountant (CPA). An accountant who has met certain professional requirements and has been licensed by a state government to provide accounting services to the public.

chart of accounts. An organized listing of company accounts, which serves as the basis for a general ledger accounting system.

claim. The legal right to a company's assets.

classified balance sheet. A balance sheet that has a subtotal for current assets and a subtotal for current liabilities.

closely held corporation. A corporation whose shares of stock are owned by a small number of people.

closing entries. Entries made to reduce temporary account balances to zero and to transfer the balances to permanent accounts at the end of an accounting period.

common stock. Issued by a corporation, is a basic class of stock that represents general ownership in the corporation. Common stockholders have the right to vote in running the business (usually by a vote in the election of the board of directors) and the right to receive declared dividends, although the common stockholders' right to declared dividends is secondary to preferred stockholders' right to dividends.

comparability. A quality of information based on the idea that it is more useful when related to the same type of information in another period, such as comparing financial statements across companies and financial statements.

comparative balance sheets. Two or more balance sheets from the same company for consecutive accounting periods, shown together to reflect the company's financial situation over two or more periods.

comprehensive income. The total of all items, except transactions with the owners (contributions and dividends), that affect shareholders' equity. Comprehensive income has two parts: **net income** and other comprehensive income (everything else).

conservatism principle. An accounting principle explaining that when doubt exists between two reporting alternatives, the user of the information should select the alternative with the least favorable impact on owner's equity.

consistency. A quality of useful information requiring accounting methods to be followed in the same manner from period to period, making the information comparable.

contingent liabilities. Liabilities that do not currently exist but are probable and reasonably estimable, such as lawsuits and tax disputes.

contra-asset. An amount deducted from its related asset account. A contra-account is used to offset (i.e., to reduce) its related account. For example, the contra-asset **accumulated depreciation** is deducted from the fixed **asset** to which the depreciation relates.

contra-liability. An amount deducted from its related liability. The contra-account is used to offset its related account. For example, the contra-liability **discount on bonds payable** is deducted from the liability bonds payable when the balance sheet is presented.

contra-revenue account. An account used to record reductions in its related revenue account. The contra-account is used to offset its related account. For example, sales discounts is the contra-revenue account to sales.

contributed capital. The total amount of economic resources the owners have invested in a business firm; also known as *paid-in capital.*

contribution. The resources invested in a business firm by the owners of the firm.

control. An activity performed by a business firm to minimize or eliminate risk; also known as *internal control.*

control activities. Are the activities intended to prevent, detect, and correct errors and irregularities relating to business risks.

control environment. Comprises the integrity and ethical values of the entire business organization, management's philosophy, and how the organization treats its employees.

convertible bond. A bond that can be converted into stock at the discretion of the bond holder.

corporation. A business firm that is a separate legal entity from its owners. Ownership is acquired through the purchase of shares in the corporation.

corrective controls. Control activities directed at recovering from, repairing the damage from, or minimizing the cost of an error or irregularity.

cost. The amount a company pays or agrees to pay for an item on the acquisition date; sometimes also called *historical cost*. For fixed assets, cost includes all expenditures to get the asset up and running.

cost of goods available for sale. The cost of all inventory a company has on hand, available to be sold during the accounting period; includes the cost of beginning inventory and the cost of the purchases made during the period.

cost of goods sold. The company's cost of goods purchased and then sold to its customers, also known as *cost of sales*.

cost-benefit analysis. The reasoning used to determine what financial information should be included in the financial statements of a business firm. This is a general type of analysis that weighs the cost of something against the benefit from it.

cost of sales. The total costs of goods made or purchased and sold; also known as *cost of goods sold*.

cost principle. An accounting rule that requires assets to be recorded on the date of acquisition at the amount paid for them (i.e., their cost); also called the *historical cost principle*.

credit. An entry made on the right side of an account; also means *to make* an entry on the right side of an account.

creditors. Individuals, or institutions, who lend companies money with a specified rate of return.

credit sale. Occurs when a customer does not pay cash at the time of the sale but instead agrees to pay later. The sale occurs now, with payment from the customer to follow at a later time.

creditworthiness. Indicates whether a borrower has in the past made loan payments when due.

cumulative effect. A change in accounting principle: gain or loss from changing accounting methods, shown on the income statement net of tax, after income from continuing operations, after discontinued operations, and after any discontinued operations.

cumulative preferred dividends. Dividend amounts owed to a person or company owning the related preferred stock.

current assets. Assets, such as cash and receivables, that will be converted into cash within 1 year or within an operating cycle, whichever is greater. Almost all businesses use a year to classify current assets.

current liabilities. Obligations that will be met with current assets, usually within 1 year.

current ratio. Current assets divided by current liabilities; measures a firm's ability to meet it short-term obligations.

cycle. A recurring sequence of business activities.

debit. An entry made on the left side of an account; also means *to make* an entry on the left side of an account.

debt financing. Obtaining financing by borrowing money.

debt-to-equity ratio. Total debt divided by total equity. This ratio measures the ability of a firm to meets its long-term obligations.

declaration date. The date on which the board of directors makes the official decision to pay a dividend.

deferral. An accounting event in which the exchange of the cash related to the transaction is completed before the activity related to the transaction is completed.

definitely determinable liabilities. Liabilities that can be exactly measured, such as bank loans and notes payable.

depletion. The periodic allocation of the cost of natural resources over their useful lives.

depreciable base. Cost minus residual value.

depreciation. The periodic allocation of the cost of long-term tangible assets—property, plant, and equipment—to expense on the income statement, over the useful lives of those assets.

depreciation expense. The amount recognized as an expense in one period resulting from the periodic recognition of the used portion of the cost of a long-term tangible asset over its life.

detective controls. Activities intended to identify when an error or irregularity has occurred.

direct method of preparing a statement of cash flows. Examining the income statement and converting each revenue and expense into its related cash inflow and cash outflow, comprising cash from operations.

direct write-off method. A method of recognizing actual uncollectible accounts as expenses in the period in which they become uncollectible, subtracting them from accounts receivable, and expensing them through bad debt expense. The direct write-off method is not approved by **generally accepted accounting principles (GAAP)**.

discount on bonds payable. The difference between the selling price and face amount of a bond when the face amount is greater than the selling price. This difference is recorded in a contra-liability account.

discount rate. Another name for the interest rate.

discounting a series of cash flows. Refers to calculating the value of a series of payments over a specified number of periods at a specified rate of return to today's dollars.

discontinued operations. Part of a business firm that has been disposed of, often by selling a segment or division. The related gain or loss from disposal is shown net of taxes after income from continuing operations.

distributions. Cash or other assets given by a company to its owners.

dividends. After-tax earnings of a business firm distributed to its owners. Dividends is the specific name for the distributions of a corporation to its owners.

dividends in arrears. Dividends due to the holders of cumulative preferred stock that a company has not declared.

dividend-yield ratio. A stock's dividend per share divided by the stocks's current market price per share.

double-declining balance method. An accelerated method of depreciation that uses 200% as the percentage of the straight-line rate.

double-entry system. An accounting system that uses debits and credits to record transactions to balance the accounting equation, assets = liabilities + owner's equity.

---

earned capital. A company's accumulation of earnings since it began, reduced by any distributions to stockholders or owners; commonly called *retained earnings*.

earnings before interest and taxes (EBIT). Income from operations before subtracting interest expense and income taxes.

earnings per share (EPS). Net income for the period divided by the average number of common shares outstanding. It is used by investors and analysts to evaluate a company's performance for a period.

economic substance. Refers to part of a transaction that involves an activity other than the exchange of cash. Providing a service or delivering goods would be considered the economic substance of a transaction. The exchange of cash may take place before or after the exchange of goods and services.

effective interest method. A method of amortizing bond premiums and discounts that calculates the amount of interest on the outstanding liability, which changes every time a payment is made.

encryption. A process of encoding data entered into an information system, storing or transmitting the data in coded form, and then decoding the data on its use or arrival at its destination.

ending inventory. Inventory on hand at the end of the accounting period, shown on the balance sheet in the current assets section.

enterprise. Another name for a business organization. Other similar terms are *business firm*, sometimes simply *business*, sometimes simply *firm*, as well as *company*, and *entity*.

enterprise resource planning systems (ERPs). Integrated information systems that capture all a company's information in a single database.

entrepreneur. A person who starts a business firm and takes the economic risks inherent in starting it.

equity. The owners' claims to the assets of their company.

estimated liabilities. Liabilities in amounts that are not certain, such as warranty liability.

estimated useful life. The length of time a company plans to, or can be expected to, use an asset.

events. The actual transactions of a business firm.

exchanges. Events in the business process that involve getting something and giving something in return.

expense. The cost a business firm incurs in selling its goods or providing its services.

expensing. To put on the income statement as an expense; produces an immediate reduction in net income.

external risks. Risks associated with a company's external environment, such as the economy and product demand.

extraordinary items. Events that are unusual and infrequent; and the gain or loss related to such events is shown separately, net of taxes, on the income statement after income from continuing operations and after any discontinued operations.

---

face value. The amount stated on bond or note; the principal; the amount of the bond that the issuer will pay back at the maturity date.

Financial Accounting Standards Board (FASB). An independent private organization responsible for establishing accounting rules concerning financial reporting, a responsibility delegated to them by the **Securities and Exchange Commission.**

financial leverage. Borrowed money used to increase return on assets.

financial services company. A business firm that provides services related to money, such as a bank or a mortgage company.

financial statements. Reports used by a business firm to communicate information to external users. There are four basic statements: the income statement, the balance sheet, the statement of changes in owner's equity, and the statement of cash flows.

financing cash flows. One of the three sections in the statement of cash flows, showing cash inflows and cash outflows related to the firm's sources of capital, such as contributions from, and distributions to, the owners.

first-in, first-out method (FIFO). An inventory cost flow method that assigns the cost of the first items purchased to the first items sold to calculate inventory and cost of goods sold.

fiscal year. Describes the business year, which may or may not coincide with the calendar year.

fixed assets. Long-term assets, assets that will last longer than a year.

for-profit organization. An entity that provides products or services with the primary objective of making a profit.

FOB destination. A condition of purchase requiring the supplier to pay for all transportation costs up to the destination point, which is when title to the purchased goods passes to the buyer. *FOB* means *free on board*.

FOB shipping point. A condition of purchase in which the buyer has title to the goods when they leave the supplier and is responsible for the cost of transportation from the supplier's shipping point to the buyer's destination.

free cash flow. Cash from operations minus dividends and capital expenditures.

freight-in. A part of the cost of inventory. It is the transportation cost of the goods purchased.

freight-out. Considered an operating expense. It is the transportation cost of goods delivered to customers.

gain. The increase in net assets resulting from certain kinds of transactions, usually transactions not part of the normal operations of the firm.

general ledger. A record of all accounts a company uses with the additions, deductions, and balances of each account.

general ledger system. The name for a traditional accounting system, based on the recording of transactions using debits and credits.

generally accepted accounting principles (GAAP). Accounting guidelines, issued by the Financial Accounting Standards Board (FASB), which a company must follow when preparing its financial statements for external users.

going-concern assumption. An accounting assumption that allows the preparation of financial statements as if a company will continue to exist in the future unless there is contrary evidence.

goods available for sale. Beginning inventory plus purchases for an accounting period. (*See cost of goods available for sale.*)

gross margin. Another term for *gross profit on sales.*

gross pay. The full amount an employee is paid before taxes are deducted.

gross profit on sales. Sales revenue minus *cost of goods sold;* also known as *gross margin* on sales.

gross profit percentage. Gross profit as a percentage of sales; also known as *gross margin ratio.*

held-to-maturity investments. One of three classifications of securities a company has purchased as an investment. These are debt securities that a company is able to, and intends to, hold until maturity.

historical cost. The original amount a company paid for an item.

historical cost principle. An accounting concept that requires companies to record assets at the their original cost.

income before interest and taxes. The income from business operations before interest expense and income taxes are subtracted.

income from operations. Income from normal business operations before any non-operating items, including interest and income taxes, have been deducted.

income statement. A statement that reports a company's net income for a period. It is a summary of all the revenues, expenses associated with those revenues, gains, and losses for the company. The income statement is also called the *statement of earnings* and the *profit and loss statement.*

indirect method of preparing a statement of cash flows. Starting with net income and adjusting for all changes in current assets and current liabilities, resulting in the amount of cash from operations.

information-processing risk. The risk associated with recording, maintaining, or reporting data or information.

information systems. Computerized systems that enable companies to record, organize, and maintain information.

input controls. Controls that help manage risk associated with the possibility that information will be fictitious, erroneous, or incomplete.

insurance company. A business firm that provides some financial protection in the case of loss of life or property.

intangible assets. Assets with value that cannot be seen or touched, such as copyrights, patents, trademarks, and franchises.

interest. Payment for the use of someone else's money; the excess amount paid or received over the principal of the loan.

interest expense. The cost a business incurs to borrow money. With respect to bonds payable, the interest expense is calculated by multiplying the market rate of interest by the carrying value of the bonds on the date of the payment.

interest payment. The payment to holders of bonds payable, calculated by multiplying the stated rate on the face of the bond by the par, or face, value of the bond. If bonds are issued at a discount or premium, the interest payment does not equal the interest expense.

interest rate. The rate applied to the principle of a loan to determine the amount of interest charged, traditionally given in terms of a year.

internal controls. The policies and procedures a company uses to provide reasonable assurance as to the accuracy and reliability of its accounting records.

internal control system. The framework of internal controls and security measures employed by a company.

Internal Revenue Service (IRS). A government agency that requires business firms to report information concerning their income and expenses, and monitors the payment and collection of income taxes.

inventory. Goods purchased for sale, or for making into goods for sale.

inventory cost flow. The flow of inventory costs from the balance sheet to the income statement (inventory to cost of goods sold).

inventory flow. The physical movement of goods through a business.

inventory turnover ratio. Sales divided by average inventory. This ratio measures how fast the company is selling its inventory.

investment. Sometimes used to describe an owner's capital contribution to the company, also, used to refer to the purchase of assets to make a profit (e.g., buying stocks or bonds of other companies).

investing cash flows. Cash inflows and outflows of activities related to the purchase and sale of assets in a firm not related to the firm's day-to-day operating activities. This is one of the three sections in the statement of cash flows. The purchases of any assets that need to be depreciated or amortized belong in this category.

invoice. A bill sent to a company (the buyer) by a vendor (the supplier).

issued stock. The actual number of shares of stock currently classified as *issued*—comprises all the shares given in return for ownership in the corporation less any shares that have been retired.

issuer. The company that borrows money from investors by issuing bonds.

journal. Book of original entry, in which transactions are recorded in a general ledger system.

last-in, first-out method (LIFO). An inventory cost flow method that assigns the cost of the most recent goods purchased to the first goods sold to calculate inventory and cost of goods sold.

liabilities. The claims creditors have against the resources of a business firm and the obligations of a business firm to perform services in the future.

limited liability. The idea that the owners of a corporation cannot be held personally liable for the actions of the corporation. Only the amounts of the owners' contributions and earnings are at risk of loss.

liquidity. How quickly and easily assets can be converted to cash and short-term obligations can be met.

long-term assets. Assets used in the normal course of business that will *not* be converted into cash within 1 year.

long-term liabilities. Obligations that will *not* be paid within 1 year.

long-term note payable. An obligation that occurs when a company borrows money from a financial institution, such as a bank, for longer than 1 year and is usually repaid with a series of payments of principle and interest over the life of the note.

loss. The decrease in net assets resulting from transactions that generally do *not* occur in the normal course of business.

lower-of-cost-or-market. The method for reporting inventory on the financial statements that requires valuing inventory at the lower of the cost of inventory or its market value.

MACRS. *See* **modified accelerated cost recovery system.**

managerial accounting. The study of how managers use accounting information that is internal to the firm. Information internal to the firm is generally not shown on the firm's financial statements.

manufacturing business. A business firm that makes the products it sells.

market interest rate. The interest rate in the market for investments with similar risk. It is usually a reference to the interest rate on the date bonds are sold.

market price. The price an asset could demand if it is sold on the open market.

market value. The price of an asset agreed on between a willing buyer and a willing seller; the price an asset could demand if it is sold on the open market.

matching. An accounting concept that establishes when expenses are recognized. Expenses are matched with the revenues they helped to generate and are recognized when those revenues are recognized. Matching means putting the related revenues and expenses on the same income statement.

materiality. Determines whether an item or transaction is significant enough to be reported in a specific way in the financial statements.

merchandise inventory. All goods owned, even those in transit, and held for sale by a company, often referred to as *inventory*.

merchandising business. A business firm that buys goods, adds value, and sells the goods to other companies or consumers. There are two types of merchandising business firms: a wholesale company and a retail company.

modified accelerated cost recovery system (MACRS). The method of depreciation used for tax purposes that allows the largest depreciation expense deduction in the early years of an asset's life.

monitoring. Examining controls to ensure they are operating properly.

mortgage. A note payable issued for property, such as a house, usually repaid in equal installments consisting of part principle and part interest, over a specified period.

mortgage company. A financial institution that lends money to borrowers to purchase property.

multi-step income statement. An income statement that shows *sales − cost of goods sold = gross margin,* and then shows all other revenues and expenses.

net earnings. Another name for *net income.*

net income. The difference between the revenues and the expenses during an accounting period; also called *net earnings.*

net loss. Occurs when expenses are greater than revenues.

net profit. Another term for *net income.*

net realizable value. Referring to *accounts receivable,* it is the amount of accounts receivable less any allowances for uncollectible accounts. It is the actual amount of accounts receivable expected to be collected.

net sales. All sales a company has made after returns and allowances (discounts) have been deducted.

noncumulative preferred stock. Preferred stock for which dividends not paid in any given year are *not* carried forward to the next year.

noncurrent assets. Assets that are not used up within 1 year.

noncurrent liabilities. Obligations that are not paid within 1 year.

nonsufficient funds (NSF) check. A customer's check that has been returned by the bank because the customer did not have enough funds in his or her account to cover the amount of the check.

notes to the financial statements. Information provided along with the four basic financial statements, considered to be an integral part of the statements. The notes describe the accounting methods used to prepare the statements and explain various aspects of the financial condition of the company.

not-for-profit organization. An entity that provides goods and services whose motivation is other than making a profit, usually providing social services.

on-account. Refers to selling or purchasing goods or services on credit.

open purchase order. A copy of the purchase order sent to the accounts payable department and reviewed prior to payment for the goods ordered.

operating cash flows. Shows the cash inflows and cash outflows from the general operating activities of the business; one of the three sections in the statement of cash flows.

operating cycle. A business period beginning with cash, converting cash to inventory, selling inventory, and turning inventory sales back into cash.

operating expenses. All expenses incurred in the normal operations of a business except interest and taxes.

operating income. Income from operations before interest expense and income taxes are deducted.

operational assets. Assets with useful lives of more than 1 year, purchased to generate revenue for the business firm.

other receivables. Amounts owed to a company by people and companies other than customers.

output controls. Controls related to the accuracy and completeness of a system's output.

outstanding stock. The amount of stock issued minus treasury stock.

owners. Individuals or institutions that invest money in a business for an unspecified return.

owner's equity. The amount left over after liabilities are netted out of assets; sometimes referred to as *net assets*. It is the total amount of owner's claims to the assets of the company.

packing slip. A document sent from the inventory department to the shipping department signaling the goods are on the way for shipping to the customer.

paid-in capital. The capital owners or shareholders have invested in a corporation; also called *contributed capital*.

paid-in capital in excess of par. The capital above the par value of stock that is sold. It is the issue price of the stock minus its par value times the number of shares issued; it also is called *additional paid-in capital*.

par value. The face value of a security; the fixed per-share amount printed on the stock certificate.

partnership. A business firm owned by two or more people in a legal form similar to a sole proprietorship. An LLP is a special case of a partnership, with some of the benefits of a corporation.

partnership agreement. A document that defines the specific terms of a partnership or business relationship, such as how much work each partner will do and how the profits are divided.

payment date. The date the assets are to be distributed to the stockholders as dividends.

periodic inventory system. Recordkeeping for inventory in which records are updated once, at the end of the accounting period when ending inventory is physically counted. The system can be used for FIFO, LIFO, or average cost inventory cost flow assumptions.

permanent accounts. Accounts whose balances carry over from period to period. These accounts include assets, liabilities, and owner's equity accounts.

perpetual inventory system. A system that updates inventory records after every purchase or sale, providing a current record of inventory and cost of goods sold; can be used for FIFO, LIFO, or average cost inventory cost flow assumptions.

physical access controls. Controls placed in a computerized environment to prevent unauthorized access to the enviroment.

picking slip. A document sent from the sales department to the warehouse requesting the goods ordered by the customer; also called a *stock request*.

positively correlated. Describes values or amounts of two items that move in the same direction. In accounting and finance, the amount of risk and the amount of return on an investment move in the same direction—when risk is high, the potential return will be high, when risk is low, the potential return will be low.

postclosing trial balance. A list of all a company's accounts, each with its debit or credit balance—prepared after closing entries are posted. Only real accounts will be found on the postclosing trial balance.

posting. Transferring transactions from the journal to the general ledger.

preferred stock. A class of stock that gives priority for dividends and for the company's assets in the event the company must default. This class of stock is usually nonvoting (i.e., preferred shareholders do not get to vote in the election of the board of directors).

premium. The difference between the selling price and face value of a bond when the selling price is greater than the face value.

premium on bonds payable. An adjunct liability account that records the difference between selling price and the face value of the bond when the selling price is higher than the face value.

prepaid insurance. An asset that exists when a company pays for insurance in advance, before receiving the protective services of that insurance.

prepaid rent. An asset that is recorded when a company makes its rent payments in advance.

present value. The current value of a future cash flow.

preventive controls. Control activities whose purpose is to prevent an error or irregularity.

price-earnings ratio. The market value of a share of a company's stock divided by that stock's earnings per share.

principal. The actual amount of cash borrowed or loaned; sometimes used to describe the face value of the bond.

proceeds. Cash collected from the sale of an asset, from issuing stock, or from selling bonds. It is a general term that indicates a cash inflow.

processing controls. Controls related to the storage and manipulation of data, such as segregation of duties, documentation controls, reconciliation, and cross-checking.

profit. The difference between the revenues and expenses from selling goods or providing services.

profit and loss statement (P&L). Another term for the income statement.

***pro forma* financial statements.** Financial statements prepared under a given set of potential circumstances; referred to as "what if" financial statements.

prospectus. A report detailing a future stock offering containing a set of financial statements; required by the SEC from a company that wishes to make an initial public offering of its stock.

purchase. A part of the acquisition and payment cycle in which the business gives up cash in return for inventory or another economic resource.

purchase discount. A cash discount a company is offered by its vendors to make prompt payments.

purchase order. A form on which items or services needed by a business firm are specified and then communicated to the vendor.

purchase requisition. A form, completed by an employee of the business firm, indicating what is to be purchased.

purchase returns and allowances. The cost of the inventory items a company has returned or the amount of credit given for a defective or substandard items purchased.

publicly traded corporation. A corporation whose stock is traded on the stock exchanges.

REA diagram. A diagram showing the relationships among the resources, events, and agents in a business exchange.

real accounts. Permanent accounts, which are the accounts on the balance sheet—assets, liabilities, and equity accounts. These accounts are never closed.

receiving report. A record of the actual goods received from a purchase.

recognition. Is considered to occur when an item is formally recorded in the accounting records and reported in the financial statements. For example, when revenue is earned, it is recognized and reported on the income statement. This term is most often applied to revenue and expenses, indicating that they are recorded on the income statement for a period.

recognize. To formally record a transaction in the accounting records and report it in the financial statements. For example, when revenue is earned, it is recognized and reported on the income statement.

record date. The date used to determine which stockholders are to receive declared dividends. Anyone owning the stock on this date will receive the dividend.

relative fair market value method. A method of assigning cost to separate assets obtained in a basket purchase. A percentage of the total purchase price is assigned to each asset.

relevant. Refers to information a business can use to evaluate past performance and predict future consequences.

reliable. Refers to information that can be verified for the truthfulness and the faithfulness of the economic events it represents.

replacement cost. The cost that would be incurred if a company had to replace an existing asset.

residual. Another term for owner's equity. It is the amount left over after the claims of creditors are deducted from the company's assets.

residual value. An asset's estimated value that can be realized at its disposal date; also called *salvage value.*

resources. Things of value, both tangible and intangible, that are exchanged in a transaction.

retail company. A merchandising company that buys goods, adds value, and sells the goods to consumers.

retained earnings. Equity belonging to the owners of a company as a result of earning income from business operations; also called *earned capital.* The amount of retained earnings on the balance sheet will be equal to all the net incomes minus all the net losses and distributions paid to the owners of the company since its inception to the date of the balance sheet.

return on equity. Net income divided by average shareholders' equity. This ratio is a measure of a company's profitability.

revenue. The amount a business earns for the goods sold or the services provided.

revenue expenditure. Any expenditure that benefits only the current accounting period. A simpler and clearer name is *expense.*

revenue recognition principle. Determines when revenue should be recognized. This principle allows recognition of revenue when the earnings process is substantially complete. This occurs when the economic substance of the transaction has been completed.

risk. The uncertainty associated with the amount and timing of future returns; the possibility of an unfavorable outcome relating to all aspects of business.

---

sale method. A method of estimating bad debt expense by focusing on the income statement and the amount of the sales of the current period expected to be uncollectible.

sales/collection process. The business process of selling goods or providing services to consumers and, in return, receiving payment for those goods and services.

sales discount. A cash discount provided by companies to encourage their customers to pay bills promptly. The difference between the selling price of the goods and the cash collected is the sales discount amount.

sales order. A record of a customer's order.

sales returns and allowances. The account that records the amount for returned goods and allowances for defective goods; a contra-sales account. This amount is deducted from sales on the income statement.

salvage value. An asset's estimated value that can be realized at its disposal date, also called *residual value.*

secured bond. A bond that gives the bondholder claim to a specific asset of the company in case the company fails to pay the bondholder the interest and principal payments promised.

Securities and Exchange Commission (SEC). A government entity set up to monitor the activities and financial reporting of corporations that sell shares of ownership on the stock exchanges.

separate-entity assumption. An assumption in accounting that requires the financial activities and records of the business enterprise to be separate and distinct from the personal financial activities and records of its owners.

separation of duties. A control used by a company to ensure the functions of authorization, recording, and physical custody are not all performed by the same individual.

serial bonds. Bonds in an issue that mature periodically over several years.

service business. A business firm that provides services to consumers, such as accounting and legal services.

shareholder. An owner of a share or shares in a corporation, also called a *stockholder.*

shares of stock. Units of ownership in a corporation.

short-term note payable. An obligation that occurs when a company borrows from a financial institution money to be repaid within 1 year, usually with a single payment of interest and principal at the end of the note.

single-step income statement. An income statement that shows all revenues and then deducts all expenses. There is no subtotal for gross margin (as there is a multistep income statement).

sole proprietorship. A business owned by a single person.

specific identification method. An inventory cost flow method that identifies exact items sold to calculate cost of goods sold.

statement of cash flows. A statement listing all the cash inflows and cash outflows of a business firm for a period of time; the statement of cash flows is divided into three sections: operating, investing, and financing cash flows.

statement of changes in shareholders' equity. A statement that reports the total changes in the amount of owners' equity over a period of time.

statement of earnings. Another name for the *income statement.*

statement of owner's capital. Another term for the statement of changes in owner's equity. This title is used by a sole proprietorship and reports the total changes in the amount of owner's equity over a period of time.

Statements of Financial Accounting Concepts (SFAC). Statements issued by the FASB explaining and describing the type of information required from financial reporting.

stockbrokers. A business person who represents people who want to buy shares and people who want to sell shares of a corporation on the stock exchange.

stock dividend. The payment of a dividend in the form of additional shares of the company's stock.

stock exchange. Marketplace for buying and selling shares of a publicly traded corporation.

stock request. A document sent to the warehouse requesting the goods ordered by the customer, also called a *picking slip.*

stock split. Occurs when the corporation increases the number of shares outstanding, reducing the **par value** of a share of its stock.

straight-line depreciation. A method that expenses an equal amount of depreciation for each year of the asset's useful life.

straight-line method of amortization. A method of amortization that writes off periodic, equal amounts of bond premium and discount over the life of the bond.

subsidiary ledger. A record that contains detailed information in support of a general ledger account. For example, an accounts receivable subsidiary ledger contains detailed accounts of all the customers who owe money to the business firm.

supplies. Items purchased in advance, used in a firm's business activities, and recognized as an expense when used.

T-account. A representation of a page in the general ledger with debits on the left side and credits on the right side.

tangible assets. Refers to assets, such as equipment and vehicles, that can be physically observed and used in the firm's operating activities.

temporary accounts. Account balances closed to owner's equity at the end of an accounting period. These accounts include revenues, expenses, and dividends.

term bonds. Bonds that mature on a specified date.

tickler file. A file that contains invoices filed in the order of the date they are due.

time cards. A card used by a firm to record the amount of time worked by an employee during each day.

times interest earned. Net income before interest and taxes, divided by interest expense; describes a company's ability to make interest payments on its debt.

timing differences. The difference between the time a transaction occurs and the time the cash related to the transaction is exchanged.

trading. Buying and selling shares of stock.

trading securities. Debt and equity securities that a company intends to trade in the short-run in an effort to make a quick profit; one of three classifications of securities purchased by a company as an investment.

transactions. An exchange or event between entities that has an economic impact on the business firm.

treasury stock. Stock that has been issued and later bought back by the issuing corporation.

trial balance. A list of all accounts and their balances; used to ensure debits = credits.

two-ten, net-thirty, or (2/10, n/30). Terms of a sales discount. Specifically, if the bill is paid within 10 days, the buyer will receive a 2% discount; if not, the balance is due within 30 days.

---

uncollectible accounts. The accounts company estimates it will not collect.

uncollectible accounts expense. An expense that recognizes the losses from uncollectible accounts, and therefore reduces net income; also called *bad debt expense.*

unearned revenue. A liability created when a business receives payment for goods or services before the goods are delivered or the services are rendered.

unit-of-measure assumption. Assumes assets, liabilities, and equity will be measured in monetary units.

units of production depreciation. A depreciation method based on the number of units to be produced by an asset as opposed to the years of useful life; also known as *activity depreciation.*

unsecured bond. A bond that does not give the bondholder a specific claim to a company asset, but instead issued on the general credit of the company; also known as a debenture.

usefulness. The most important quality of accounting information. How useful information is depends on how well it does what it is supposed to do. To be useful, information must be both relevant and reliable.

---

vendor. A business firm that supplies goods and services to other business firms.

---

warranty. An obligation of a company to replace defective goods or correct any deficiencies in performance or quality of a product.

wholesale company. A merchandising company that sells goods to other companies.

withdrawals. Distributions of a sole proprietorship's assets to its owner or distributions of a partnership's assets to the partners.

writing off. The allocation of the cost of an asset over several accounting periods. Also, to *expense* a cost, that is, put it on the income statement as an expense.

working capital. Current assets minus current liabilities; a measure of a company's ability to meet its short-term obligations.

---

zero-coupon bond. A bond that does not make periodic payments of interest. The full face value of the bond is due at its maturity date.

SUBJECT INDEX